IN SEARCH OF JYOTISH

30
THE KALACHAKRA DASA

SARAJIT PODDAR
AN EARNEST JYOTIṢA SEEKER

KINDLE DIRECT PUBLISHING
APRIL 2024

FIRST EDITION
April 2024

ISBN: 979-8323151592

Published by
Kindle Direct Publishing

https://www.facebook.com/sarajit.poddar
https://www.facebook.com/srivarahamihira
https://www.facebook.com/insearchofjyotish
https://twitter.com/srivarahamihira

फलानि ग्रह चारेण सूचयन्ति मनीषिणः।
को वक्ता तारतम्यस्य तमेकं वेधसं विना॥
phalāni graha cāreṇa sūcayanti manīṣiṇaḥ।
ko vaktā tāratamyasya tamekaṃ vedhasaṃ vinā॥
For human beings, the fruits of their actions are indicated by the movement of Grahas. Except for the creator Brahmā, who can certainly tell what will happen!

17 APRIL 2024

...Dedicated to *Ādiguru Śaṅkarācārya*...

मनोबुद्ध्यहङ्कारचित्तानि नाहं
न च श्रोत्रजिह्वे न च घ्राणनेत्रे ।
न च व्योमभूमिर्न तेजो न वायुः
चिदानन्दरूपः शिवोऽहं शिवोऽहम् ॥ १॥

manobuddhyahaṅkāracittāni nāhaṃ
na ca śrotrajihve na ca ghrāṇanetre ।
na ca vyomabhūmirna tejo na vāyuḥ
cidānandarūpaḥ śivo'haṃ śivo'ham ॥ 1॥

निर्वाणषट्कम्

मनोबुद्ध्यहङ्कारचित्तानि नाहं न च श्रोत्रजिह्वे न च घ्राणनेत्रे ।
न च व्योमभूमिर्न तेजो न वायुश्चिदानन्दरूपः शिवोऽहं शिवोऽहम् ॥ १॥
न च प्राणसंज्ञो न वै पञ्चवायुर्न वा सप्तधातुर्न वा पञ्चकोशः ।
न वाक्पाणिपादौ न चोपस्थपायुश्चिदानन्दरूपः शिवोऽहं शिवोऽहम् ॥ २॥
न मे द्वेषरागौ न मे लोभमोहौ मदो नैव मे नैव मात्सर्यभावः ।
न धर्मो न चार्थो न कामो न मोक्षश्चिदानन्दरूपः शिवोऽहं शिवोऽहम् ॥ ३॥
न पुण्यं न पापं न सौख्यं न दुःखं न मन्त्रो न तीर्थं न वेदा न यज्ञाः ।
अहं भोजनं नैव भोज्यं न भोक्ता चिदानन्दरूपः शिवोऽहं शिवोऽहम् ॥ ४॥
न मृत्युर्न शङ्का न मे जातिभेदः पिता नैव मे नैव माता न जन्म ।
न बन्धुर्न मित्रं गुरुर्नैव शिष्यश्चिदानन्दरूपः शिवोऽहं शिवोऽहम् ॥ ५॥
अहं निर्विकल्पो निराकाररूपो विभुर्व्याप्य सर्वत्र सर्वेन्द्रियाणाम् ।
सदा मे समत्वं न मुक्तिर्न बन्धश्चिदानन्दरूपः शिवोऽहं शिवोऽहम् ॥ ६॥

nirvāṇaṣaṭkam

I am not intellect, ego, mind. Neither am I hearing, taste, smell, sight. Nor am I space, earth, light, air, field of consciousness. I am the pure consciousness of bliss - I am Śiva. Śiva am I. ..1..

I am not prana, nor the five vital forces. I am not the seven elements of the body or the five sheaths forming the body. I am not the organ of speech, hand, foot, the organ of procreation or excretion. I am the pure consciousness of bliss - I am Śiva, I am Śiva. ..2..

I have nor attachment or aversion; No greed or delusion, not envy or vain; duty, acquisition, desire nor liberation do I aspire - since I am the embodiment of knowledge and bliss - I am Śiva, I am Śiva ..3..

I am neither virtue nor vice, Pleasure or pain that is experienced, no, no; A chant, a holy place, a scripture nor the sacrificial fire; I am neither the enjoyment, enjoyable nor the enjoyer; I am the embodiment of knowledge and bliss - I am Śiva, I am Śiva. ..4..

There is no death or fear, No one to distinguished by class or caste; No father, no mother, no birth at all; No friend, no kith or kin, Guru or Śiṣya - I am the embodiment of knowledge and bliss - I am Śiva, I am Śiva. ..5..

I am Changeless, formless, enveloping all, Untouched by senses, I am omnipresent, Unfathomable, I am beyond freedom - I am the embodiment of knowledge and bliss - I am Śiva, I am Śiva. ..6..

ॐ गणानां त्वा गणपतिं हवामहे
कविं कवीनामुपमश्रवस्तमम् ।
ज्येष्ठराजं ब्रह्मणाम् ब्रह्मणस्पत
आ नः शृण्वन्नूतिभिःसीदसादनम् ॥
ॐ महागणाधिपतये नमः ॥

ॐ सह नाववतु । सह नौ भुनक्तु ।
सह वीर्यं करवावहै ।
तेजस्वि नावधीतमस्तु मा विद्विषावहै ।
ॐ शान्तिः शान्तिः शान्तिः॥

om saha nāvavatu I saha nau bhunaktu I
saha vīryaṁ karavāvahai I
tejasvi nāvadhītamastu mā vidviṣāvahai I
om śāntiḥ śāntiḥ śāntiḥ II

OM! May He protect us!
May He nourish us!
May we work together with great energy!
May our intellect be sharp and study effective!
Let there be no animosity between us!
OM! Let there be Peace in me!
Let there be Peace in the world!
Let there be Peace in the forces that act on me!

PREFACE

Today is Caitra Śukla Navamī of Kālī 5126, a special day as Lord Śrī Rāma was born on this day in Treta Yuga. On this auspicious day of Śrī Ramanavami, I am excited to complete this work on the most important Daśā of Jyotiṣa, the Kālacakra Daśā system. It is the crown jewel of Daśā systems, one of the most complex Daśā that Lord Śiva shared with the world in a discourse with Devī Pārvati.

Regarding Kālacakra Daśā Maharṣi Parāśara states, अथा कालदशा चक्रदशा प्रोक्ता मुनीश्वरैः । कालचक्रदशा चाऽया मान्यासर्वदशासु या ॥ ६॥ It means, O Brāhmaṇa! Some Maharṣis have made a mention of Kāla and Cakra Daśā, but they have recognized the Kālacakra Daśā, as supreme *"kālacakradaśā cā'yā mānyāsarva daśāsu yā"*.

While introducing the subject of Daśās, Maharṣi Parāśara states:

कथयामि तवाग्रेऽहं दशभेदाननेकशः ॥२॥ दशाबहुविधास्तासु मुख्या विंशोत्तरी मता । कैश्चिदष्टोत्तरी कैश्चित् कथिता षोडशोत्तरी ॥३॥ द्वादशाब्दोत्तरी विप्र दशा पञ्चोत्तरी तथा । दशा शतसमा तद्वत् चतुराशीतिवत्सरा ॥४॥ द्विसप्ततिसमा षष्टिसमा षड्त्रिंशवत्सरा । नक्षत्राधारिकाश्चेताः कथिताः पूर्वसूरिभिः ॥५॥ अथा कालदशा चक्रदशा प्रोक्ता मुनीश्वरैः । कालचक्रदशा चाऽया मान्यासर्वदशासु या ॥६॥ दशाऽथ चरपर्याया स्थिराख्या च दशा द्विज । केन्द्राद्य च दशा ज्ञेया कारकादिग्रहोद्भवा ॥७॥ ब्रह्मग्रहाश्रितर्क्षाद्या दशा प्रोक्ता तु केनचित् । माण्डूकी च दशा नाम तथा शूलदशा स्मृता ॥८॥ योगार्धजदशा विप्र दृग्दशा च ततः परम् । त्रिकोणाख्या दशा नाम तथा राशिदशा स्मृता ॥९॥ पञ्चस्वरदशा विप्र विज्ञेया योगिनीदशा । दशा पैण्डी तथांशी च नैसर्गिकदशा तथा ॥१०॥ अष्टवर्गदश सन्ध्यादसा पाचकसंज्ञिका । अन्यास्तारादशाद्याश्च न स्वर्गाः सर्वसम्मताः ॥११॥

This means Daśās are of several kinds. Amongst them, Viñśottarī is the most appropriate (*mukhya, primary*) for most people. But the other Daśās, followed in special cases, are Aṣṭottarī, Ṣoḍaśottarī, Dvādaśottarī, Pañcottarī, Śatasamā, Caturāśītivatsarā, Dvisaptatisamā, Ṣaṣṭisamā, Ṣaḍtriṃśavatsarā. Our ancients have described these different kinds of Daśās, based on Nakṣatras *"nakṣatrādhārikāścetāḥ"*.

He continues that some Maharṣis have made a mention of Kāladaśā and Cakradaśā, but they have recognized the Kālacakradaśā as supreme. The other kinds of Daśās, propagated by the sages, are Caraparyāyā, Sthirākhyā, Kendrādya, Kārakādigrahodbhavā, Brahmagrahāśritarkṣādyā, Māṇḍūkī, Shūladaśā, Yogārdh-ajadaśā, Dṛgdaśā, Trikoṇākhyā, Rāśidaśā, Pañcasvaradaśā, Yoginīdaśā, Paiṇḍī, Aṃśī, Naisargikadaśā, Aṣṭavargadaśa, Sandhyādasā, Pācakasaṃjñikā, Tārādaśā etc. But in our view, not all are equally applicable (in Kaliyuga).

Maharṣi Parāśara could have meant that among Kāla, Cakra and Kālacakra Daśā, Kālacakra is the best. But it is also possible that he meant it is the supreme Daśā among all the Daśā systems. His emphasis on Kālacakra is known from the number of ślokas he dedicated to this Daśā. He explained the results in detail, including the effects of the Rāśis in several Kālacakra Navāñśas. Several Jyotiṣa savants believe that this is the most accurate timing system in Jyotiṣa, even better than Viñśottarī, the most used Daśā.

Despite its glory, it is not much used in the Jyotiṣa community. The main reason behind that is its complexity and differences in opinions. Unlike the other Daśās, where the rules are straightforward, for Kālacakra Daśā, it is not. It also requires an understanding of a few concepts, which are:

(1) Savya and Apasavya Nakṣatras

(2) Kālacakra Navāñśa

(3) Navanavāñśa

There are twenty-seven Nakṣatra in a zodiac, and they are grouped in threes, called the Triads (Tritārā) in sequence. Therefore, Aśvinī-Bharaṇī-Kṛttikā are a triad, followed by Rohiṇī-Mṛgaśirā-Ārdrā. The Triads represent a foot of the Kālapuruṣa, where the right foot is called Dakṣiṇa Pāda, and the left foot is called Vāma Pāda. As per Svaraśāstra, the right side of the human body is masculine, and the lefty side is feminine. Therefore, the right foot is masculine, and the left foot is feminine. This is very much like the Ojapada and Yugmapada classification of Rāśis, used in Caradaśā.

The right foot is called Savya (in regular order), while the left foot is called Apasavya (in reverse order). The twenty-seven Nakṣatras are grouped into nine Triads, of which the odd-numbered Triads are Savya, and the even number ones are Apasavya.

Therefore, the Savya Nakṣatra are (1) Aśvinī-Bharaṇī-Kṛttikā, (3) Punarvasu-Puṣya-Aśleṣā, (5) Hastā-Citrā-Svāti, (7) Mūla-Pūrvāṣāṛhā-Uttarāṣāṛhā and (9) Pūrvābhādra-Uttarābhādra-Revatī.

On the other hand, the Apasavya Nakṣatras are (2) Rohiṇī-Mṛgaśirā-Ārdrā, (4) Maghā-Pūrvāphālgunī-Uttarāphālgunī, (6) Viśākhā-Anurādhā-Jyeṣṭhā, and (8) Śravaṇa-Dhaniṣṭhā-Śatabhiṣā.

The first Nakṣatra of the Savya Triad is odd-numbered, whereas the first Nakṣatra of a Savya Triad is an even-numbered one. For instance, the first Nakṣatras of the Savya Triads are 1st, 7th, 13th, 19th and 25th. On the other hand, the first Nakṣatras of the Apasavya Triads are 4th, 10th, 16th and 22nd. There are odd numbers of Savya Triads (i.e., five) and even number of Apasavya Triads (i.e., four). In Jyotiṣa, odd numbers are considered masculine and even numbers are feminine. In the zodiac, the fifth Rāśi is Siṅha, ruled by Sūrya (Śiva, father), and the fourth Rāśi is Karka, ruled by Candra (Śakti, mother).

Now that we know the right-footed "Savya" and left-footed "Apasavya" Nakṣatras, what is their use? They are related to two different kinds of Navāñśas called the Savya and Apasavya Navāñśa. We know that the Nakṣatra Pādas are mapped to the Navāñśas. Therefore, the Nakṣatra Pādas of the Savya Nakṣatras are mapped to Savya Navāñśa, and the Apasavya Nakṣatras are mapped to Apasavya Navāñśa.

What are these Savya and Apasavya Navāñśas? They are special Navāñśas called the Kālacakra Navāñśas, dedicated to Puruṣa (Śiva) and Strī

(Śakti). The Savya Navāñśa is the same as the regular Navāñśa, but the Apasavya Navāñśa is the reverse of it. How? Unlike the Savya Navāñśa, the Apasavya Navāñśa starts with Vṛścika and ends with Dhanu. You may be thinking, counting the Navāñśas from Vṛścika in reverse order, ending with Dhanu. No, this is not the case. The Apasavya Navāñśa is constructed differently. The following diagram should explain that.

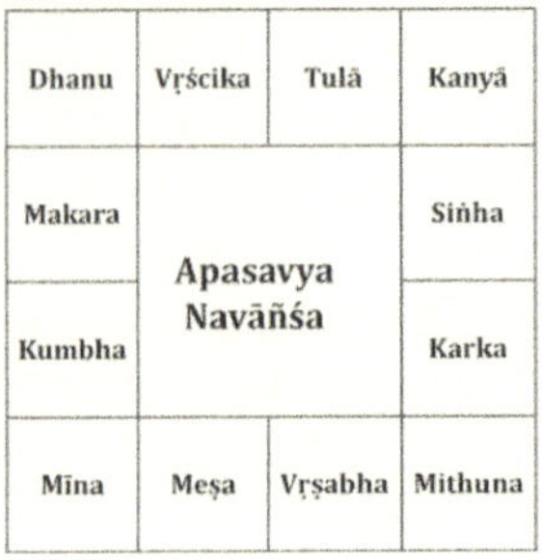

The Nakṣatra Pādas of Apasavya Nakṣatras map from Vṛścika to Dhanu in the order. This is different from the Savya Nakṣatras, whose Pādas map from Meṣa to Mīna in the order. This is the fundamental difference between the two Nakṣatra Triads and the Kālacakra Navāñśas. Once you understand this, things become clearer.

The next step is to understand the Navanavāñśa concept. Each Navāñśa is further broken down into nine parts called the Navanavāñśa. Imagine a Navāñśa embedded into a Nakṣatra Pāda.

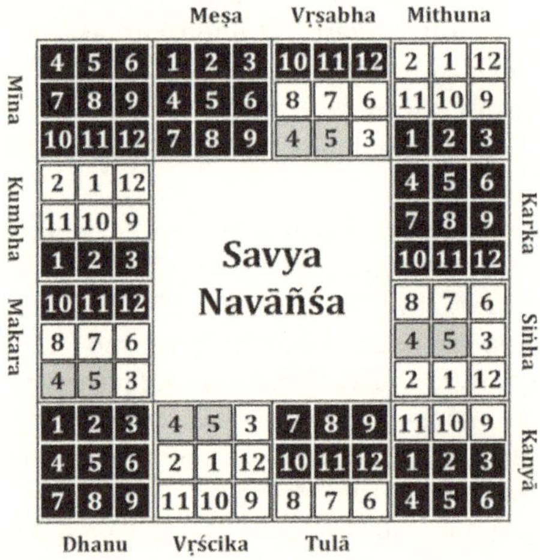

Look at this diagram carefully. Each Navāñśa has nine boxes, each representing a Navanavāñśa. For Meṣa Navāñśa, the Navanavāñśas are as follows. Here 1 = Meṣa, 2 = Vṛṣabha, ... 12 = Mīna. From the diagram, it is clear that Meṣa

Navāñśa is allotted nine Navanavāñśas, Meṣa-Vṛṣabha-Mithuna-Karka-Siṅha-Kanyā-Tulā-Vṛścika-Dhanu.

1	2	3
4	5	6
7	8	9

Let us go to the next Navāñśa, i.e., Vṛṣabha. The diagram requires an explanation. In Meṣa Navāñśa (the previous one), we ended with Dhanu. In this Navāñśa (Vṛṣabha), we started with the next Rāśi, Makara. After Makara-Kumbha-Mīna, we start with Vṛścika. Why so? Because after the completion of Savya Kālacakra, we move to Apasavya. The Apasavya Kālacakra is marked with a light background, while the Savya ones are marked with a dark background.

10	11	12
8	7	6
4	5	3

In the Apasavya order, the Navāñśas move from Vṛścika-Tulā-Kanyā. Ater that, we should expect Siṅha followed by Karka. But we notice that Karka follows Kanyā and Siṅha follows Karka. Why so?

This is called Karka-Siṅha flipping. In this order, the fourth position in the Apasavya Kālacakra is reserved for Karka and the fifth position for Siṅha. This causes the order of Apasavya Kālacakra to be Vṛścika-Tulā-Kanyā-Karka-Siṅha-Mithuna-Vṛṣabha-Meṣa-Mīna-Kumbha-Makara-Dhanu. This is explained using the following diagram.

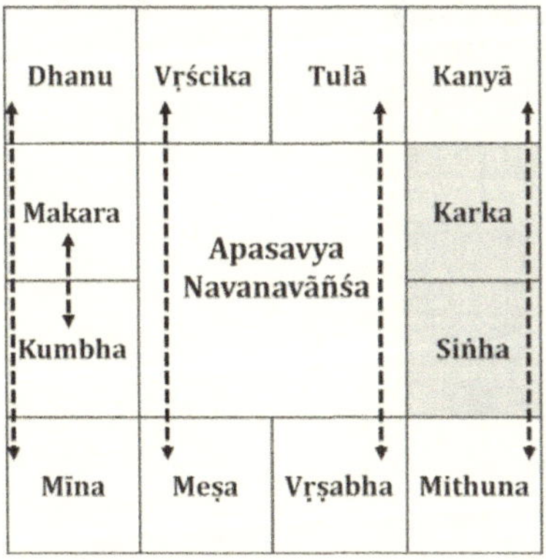

In this diagram, you can notice that the Rāśis of the same Graha is flipped. Meṣa is flipped with Vṛścika, Vṛṣabha with Tulā and so on. But there is no flipping between Karka and Siṅha, which reserves their spot in the fourth and fifth place as in the case of Savya Navanavāñśa. We must note that this is applicable only in the case of Apasavya Navanavāñśa and "not" in the case of Apasavya Navāñśa. The reason for that is explained later in the book. You may check the discourse section, where this question is answered. The reasoning behind that is this śloka of Maharṣi Parāśara.

46.89. मेषे शतं वृषेऽक्षाष्टौ मिथुने त्रिगजाः समाः । कर्कटेऽङ्गगजाः प्रोक्तास्तावन्तस्तत्त्रि-कोणयोः ॥८९॥ The number of years (Pūrṇāyu) allotted to the Añśas are: Meṣa 100 years, Vṛṣabha 85 years, Mithuna 83 years and Karka 86 years. The number of years will be the same for Rāśis, situated the 5th and 9th to them.

The above śloka maps the Āyuṣa to different Mahābhūtas, whereby Agni = 100, Pṛthvī = 85, Vāyu = 83 and Jala = 86.

If we keep the Karka-Siṅha unflipped in Apasavya "Navāñśa" while we flip the other Rāśis, then the above condition will not apply. That is because Karka will come to Trikoṇa of Meṣa (Agni Trikoṇa) and will be allotted 100 years. Similarly, Siṅha will fall into Jala Trikoṇa and will be allotted 86 years. This is not permissible. Therefore, the *Karka-Siṅha "fixity" rule* is applicable only to Apasavya Navanavāñśa and "not" to Apasavya Navāñśa.

Let us examine the Navanavāñśas assigned to Apasavya Navāñśas. The following diagram gives the Navanavāñśas of Apasavya Navāñśa. Closely look at the pattern, which is Utkramāpasavya–Utkramasavya–Utkramāpasavya. Here, Utkrama means revered. It is also called Apradakṣiṇa by the classical authors. In contrast, Krama is regular and is called Pradakṣiṇa. The Kramāpasavya (regular Apasavya) is Vṛścika to Dhanu. But Utkramāpasavya is from Dhanu to Vṛścika.

Also, notice that by accepting Siṅha after Kanyā and Karka after Siṅha in Apasavya "Navāñśa", we can explain the Navanavāñśa order allotted to Siṅha and Karka. Else, it will be misaligned.

The Navanavāñśas of Apasavya Kālacakra is a mirror image of Savya Kālacakra. Let me explain what is means. In the below table, the Navanavāñśas of Meṣa and Vṛṣabha are given for Savya and Apasavya Navāñśas. You can see that they are the mirror image of each other. Savya Meṣa is from Meṣa to Dhanu, but Apasavya Meṣa is Dhanu to Meṣa.

Table 1

Navāñśa	Savya Navāñśa	Apasavya Navāñśa
Meṣa	1 2 3 4 5 6 7 8 9	9 8 7 6 5 4 3 2 1
Vṛṣabha	10 11 12 8 7 6 4 5 3	3 5 4 6 7 8 12 11 10

The mirror image concept of Savya and Apasavya is a crucial foundation of Kālacakra Daśā.

Now that we understand the concept, how to apply them in a Kuṇḍalī? To understand that, we need to ascertain the Navāñśa elapsed by Candra. Suppose Candra's sphuṭa is Vṛṣabha 3°. This is equivalent to (2-1) * 30 + 3 = 33°. We can determine Candra's Navāñśa sphuṭa from this, which is mod (Candra * 9, 30) = mod (33 * 9, 30) = 27°. This means Candra has elapsed 27 out of 30° of its Navāñśa.

Before we step further, we must know whether Candra is in Savya or Apasavya Nakṣatra. Candra's Nakṣatra = roundup (Candra * 3/40, 0) = roundup (33 * 3/40, 0) = 3, which is Kṛttikā Nakṣatra. To find Candra's Nakṣatra Pāda, we use the formula roundup(mod(Candra*3/10,4),0) = 2. So, Candra is Kṛttikā "2". Kṛttikā is a Savya Nakṣatra, the third Nakṣatra of the first Triad. This maps to Savya Navāñśa.

Kṛttikā 2 is mapped to the first Navāñśa of Vṛṣabha, which is Dhanu. Therefore, Candra is in Dhanu Savya Navāñśa. Suppose Candra was in an Apasavya Nakṣatra, then we would have considered the Apasavya Navāñśa. In Apasavya Navāñśa, I would have placed Candra in Mīna Navāñśa (mirror image of Dhanu).

The native with Candra in Vṛṣabha 3° will undergo the Daśās of the following Navanavāñśas of Dhanu Navāñśa. This is Meṣa-Vṛṣabha-Mithuna-Karka-Siṅha-Kanyā-Tulā-Vṛścika-Dhanu.

1	2	3
4	5	6
7	8	9

Each contributes certain years. Maharṣi Parāśara states that the Daśāvarṣa of the Rāśis are based on their lord, i.e., 5, 21, 7, 9, 10, 16 and 4 years are the Daśāvarṣa of Sūrya, Candra, Maṅgala, Budha, Guru, Śukra and Śani. This also tells us the total Āyuṣa assigned to Dhanu Navāñśa, which is 100. We have seen before that Agni Navāñśas are allotted 100 years of longevity.

If the person is born at the beginning of Dhanu, he will be allotted 100 years of longevity. In this case, the person is born in the 27th degree of Dhanu Navāñśa, so the balance remaining is (30-27)/30 * 100 = 10 years. The last Daśā is of Dhanu, which is of 10 years (Guru). Therefore, the person is born in the beginning of Guru Daśā.

There are several such nuances of Kālacakra Daśā, which one must study diligently. Another crucial aspect of this Daśā is the special Gati. To explain this, let me take the Navanavāñśas of Savya Vṛṣabha.

10	11	12
8	7	6
4	5	3

Here, you notice that after Mīna, we arrive at Vṛścika. In this case, the Daśā jumped from Mīna to Vṛścika, nine houses jump. This is called Siṅhavalokana Gati. Similarly, the jump from Kanyā to Karka is an alternate Rāśi jump called the Maṇḍūka Gati. The sudden reversal of direction between Karka and Siṅha is called Marakaṭa Gati. These jumps are significant in one's life and must be carefully examined.

One of the important aspects of this Daśā is its sensitivity to Candra's sphuṭa. Candra's one Nakṣatra Pāda (3°20') is mapped to about 100 years. So, a mere change of Candra's sphuṭa by 2.2' can offset the Daśā by about a year. So, one must be precise with the birth time and the Ayanāñśa used. In my Kuṇḍalī, when I use Sṛṣṭi Ayanāñśa (approx. traditional Lahiri + 0:6:50), my Janma Daśā is Meṣa-Meṣa that spans between 25-Aug-74 and 28-Feb-79. If I use Traditional Lahiri, then the Meṣa-Meṣa Daśā spans between 25-Aug-74 and 29-Sep-75. A small change in Ayanāñśa offsets the Daśā by almost four years.

However, this is a good thing. Since this can be used for ascertaining the correct Ayanāñśa and the birth time. I suggest using Sṛṣṭi Ayanāñśa, which I found to be accurate. The rationale behind that Ayanāñśa is explained in my Siddhānta book.

Another crucial but debatable topic in this Daśā is how to determine the Antardaśās of a Daśā. I have explained that in detail in the forthcoming chapters. To get correct results from this Daśā, one must also identify the length of a year used in this Daśā. I have tested with both Sāvana (360) and Solar (360.2563) years and found reasonable results with the Solar years. Over the years, I realized that the Sāvana year is more applicable for Nakṣatra Daśās, such as Viñśottarī.

Still, the Solar or Saura year is applicable for Rāśi Daśās such as Cara, Sthira, Sudarśana and Kālacakra Daśā.

Kālacakra is a Rāśi based Daśā, and therefore, the year length is based on Sauravarṣa. In this book, I have examined both 360 days Sāvana year as well as Solar year based Daśās, and I let the seekers form their opinions after experimentations.

This is an outstanding Daśā, indeed a crown jewel of Jyotiṣa, and I hope that I did justice to this. With a sincere prayer to almighty Mahādeva, I hope that the seeker will benefit from this. I do not vouch to be perfect. But I hope that with time when I get more experienced using this Daśā, I will fine-tune it. I also hope that the seekers will continue their experiments with this Daśā and take it forward from here.

Wishing you all Śubha Rāmanavami, Kālī 5126 and Gregorian 2024.

Sarajit Poddar
(Varāhamihira)

ABOUT ME

I am an earnest seeker of Jyotiṣa, having an unquenching thirst for learning this discipline. I was born in Dhanu Lagna, Vṛścika Rāśi and Anurādhā Nakṣatra, on a Navamī Tithi, when Guru was in Kumbha, Śani, in Mithuna, and Surya, in Siṅha. In my thirteenth year, I stepped into the world of Jyotiṣa in 1988, and after that, guided by divine providence, to study it seriously. My paternal uncle and my first Jyotiṣa Guru, Śrī Manoj Kānti Poddar, an accomplished Jyotiṣaśastri and a Śakti Sādhaka guided me. My father was also a Śakti Sādhaka and an accomplished Palmist. Therefore, I was born into a family of Jyotiṣīs and Śakti Sādhakas, and Jyotiṣa runs down my family lineage.

I studied palmistry from 1988 to 1993, and eventually, in 1993, I got introduced to Jyotiṣa through Dr BV Raman's astrological magazine. I commenced my learning through the astrological magazine for months. After that, it continued through a Bengali edition of Bṛhatparāśara and Sarvārtha Cintāmaṇi that my uncle gave me. During my initial years, I learned immensely from Dr Raman's books, Hindu Predictive Astrology and How to Judge a Kuṇḍalī Vol I and II. In 1999, Pt Sanjay Rath accepted me as his student, an event I will always cherish. It was the beginning of learning advanced Jyotiṣa. From him, I learned several advanced topics, including Āruṛhas, Argalās, Vargas, Tithi Praveśa Cakra, etc. His books, Crux of Vaidika Astrology: Timing of Events and Jaimini Maharṣi's Upadeśa Sūtras, remained my constant companion for several years.

In my studies over thirty - three years, I always endeavoured to uncover the hidden meaning behind the ślokas and sūtras and reconcile the principles across several classical texts. My search slowly took the shape of this book, so I named it "In Search of Jyotiṣa". I started penning down my thoughts and experiences in a blog, "http://varahamihira.blogspot.com/" in 2004 and later continued to write in other mediums such as Facebook.com, Medium.com, and LinkedIn.com. I kept my pen name as Varāhamihira in honour of the great Jyotiṣaśastri, who adorned the court of King Vikramāditya as one of his Navaratnas (nine jewels).

Who am I? It is difficult to say who I am. Different people see me in so many ways. From my viewpoint, I am a Jīvātmā trapped inside the world of illusion! I am not a Paṇḍita, Ācārya, or Guru who claims to be a master of this discipline. I am a seeker who wishes to share his observations and experiences with like-minded seekers. I encountered numerous challenges navigating the arduous path of Jyotiṣa. In this book, I am narrating my reflections with a sincere prayer so it could be of some help to others in their journey.

Sarajit Poddar
(Varāhamihira)

Contents

30 THE KALACHAKRA DASA 1

30.1 KĀLACAKRA DAŚĀ 17

30.1.1 Kāla Daśā 20

30.1.2 Cakra Daśā 24

30.1.3 Kālacakra Daśā 27

30.1.3.1 Construction 38

30.1.3.2 Nakṣatra Caraṇa Navāñśa Mapping 43

30.1.3.3 The Mahādaśā 45

30.1.3.3.1 Savya Aśvinī Group 45

30.1.3.3.2 Savya Bharaṇī Group 46

30.1.3.3.3 Apasavya Rohiṇī Group 47

30.1.3.3.4 Apasavya Mṛgaśirā Group 47

30.1.3.3.5 Daśā Spans and Āyuṣa 60

30.1.3.3.6 Daśā Progression 62

30.1.3.4 The Daśā Balance 63

30.1.3.5 The Antardaśā 65

30.1.3.6 Deha and Jīva 70

30.1.3.7 Gati of Rāśis in Kālacakra 73

30.1.3.8 Effects of Daśās 77

30.1.3.8.1 Kālacakra and Travel 77

30.1.3.8.2 Effects of Specific Añśas 78

30.1.3.8.3 Effects of Deha and Jīva 78

30.1.3.8.4 Effects of Kālacakra Daśā of Bhāvas 79

30.1.3.8.5 Effects of the Kālacakra 82

30.1.3.9 Case Studies 90

30.1.3.9.1 Subhash Chandra Bose 90

30.1.3.9.2 Mahatma Gandhi 94

30.1.3.9.3 Sarajit Poddar 97

30.1.3.10 Advance Topics 102

30.1.3.10.1 Application to Vargas 102

30.1.3.10.2 Application to Relatives 105

30.1.3.10.3 Antardaśā Jumps 107

30.1.4 References 110

30.1.4.1 Bṛhatparāśara 110

30.1.4.2 Jātakapārijāta 120

30.1.4.3 Phaladīpikā 130

30.1.4.4 Praśnamārga 135

30.2 THE DISCOURSE 137

30.3 THE PRELIMINARIES 345

30.4 ABOUT "IN SEARCH OF JYOTISH" 387

30.1 KĀLACAKRA DAŚĀ

Kālacakra Daśā is a significant Daśā and is extensively covered in several classical texts such as Bṛhatparāśara, Phaladīpikā and Jātakapārijāta. It is mainly used as an Ayurdaya Daśā but can also be used for general delineation of one's lifeline. The computation of this Daśā is complex as the order of the Daśā changes based on the classes of Nakṣatras and their Caraṇas. In the heart of this Daśā, there are two Cakras, the Savya Cakra and Apasavya Cakra.

In this system, the Nakṣatras are classified into 15 Savya Tārās and 12 Apasavya Tārās. According to Jātakapārijāta 18.40, whichever Nakṣatra's Navāñśa Candra is in if the lord of that Navāñśa is having yutidṛṣṭi on Candra, Kālacakra Daśā is especially effective for such people. For instance, let us say in a Kuṇḍalī, Candra is in Vṛścika Rāśi and Anurādhā4 Nakṣatra and Maṅgala is in Siṅha Rāśi.

The Nakṣatra Caraṇa is mapped to Meṣa Navāñśa. The lord of Meṣa is Maṅgala and is aspecting Candra by his Caturtha Dṛṣṭi (4th sight). This implies that this Daśā is specifically effective for the native. You might have noticed that I have mapped Anurādhā-4 to Meṣa Navāñśa instead of Vṛścika Navāñśa.

This is because, as per Kālacakra Daśā, Anurādhā is an Apasavya Nakṣatra, and for such a Nakṣatra, the Rāśi is flipped from Vṛścika to Meṣa. The flipping of the Rāśis gives rise to the Apasavya Cakra, which is at the core of this Daśā system, along with the Savya Cakra. The Savya Cakra is the regular Bhācakra, whereas the Apasavya Cakra is derived by flipping the Rāśis based on their lords.

For instance, in the Apasavya Cakra, Meṣa and Vṛścika are exchanged, and likewise, there is an exchange of Vṛṣabha-Tulā, Mithuna-Kanyā, Karka-Siṅha, Dhanu-Mīna and Makara-Mīna. Jātakapārijāta continues that if the Deharāśi is afflicted, the body is afflicted by serious ailments. On the other hand, if the Jīvarāśi is afflicted, the native suffers from severe mental anxiety and psychological ailments. If the Deharāśi and the Jīvarāśi have weak Krūras (i.e., in the Nīca or Śatru Rāśis), then in the Daśā of that Rāśi, the native meets his death.

Maharṣi Parāśara narrates this Daśā immediately after narrating two other Daśās, called the Kāla Daśā and Cakra Daśā. These Daśās are not in vogue; however, since they are narrated in the same place as the Kālacakra Daśā, I believe it is important to understand these two Daśās before advancing to the Kālacakra Daśā.

Both the Kāladaśā and the Cakradaśā are based on the classification of a day into four segments, viz., the two twilights (Sandhyās), Day and Night. In the Kāla Daśā, the portion expired in the segment of the day in which the native is born used to compute the Daśās of the Navagrahas. Whereas, in the Cakradaśā, the segment in which the native is born is used for determining the Daśā commencing Rāśi, which can be one occupied by the Lagna, Lagneśa or the Dhanasphuṭa.

The computations are unique, but we notice that in both the Daśās, the basis is the same, i.e., the segmentation of a day into four parts, whereas the differences are in the reckoning of the Daśā. While Kāladaśā is a Graha Daśā, Cakra Daśā is a Rāśi Daśā. Kālacakra Daśā, on the other hand, is a hybrid Daśā, which takes into consideration the Candra's Nakṣatra Sphuṭa, but the Daśā sequence is based on the Rāśis (Navanavāñśas).

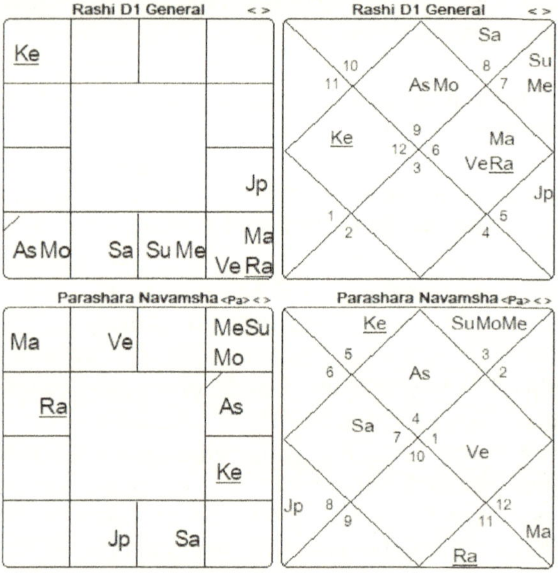

This Kālacakra Daśā is special to me *because I believe it was lord Śiva who taught this to me.* Many scholars wrote on this Daśā, but I did not find at least some portion of the writing satisfactory.

I studied the works of my Jyotiṣa Guru Pt. Sanjay Rath and Śrī Narasimha Rao, and also a detailed book on this subject by "Phalita Jyotiṣa Mein Kālacakra" by *Dīvān Rāmacandra Kapūr.* The book of Śrī Ramachandra is detailed and gives good foundational knowledge on this subject, and therefore highly recommended. The only challenge is that it is in Hindi!

There are two other books on this subject which are worth studying which are "Kalachakra Daśā System: The Ultimate Predictive Tool in Vedic

Astrology by Śrī Shakti Mohan Singh" and "Yogini and Kālacakra Daśā by Śrī Sumeet Chugh", which I have not reviewed yet, but looking forward to reading it.

After having studied the available materials and the original texts from Bṛhatparāśara, Jātakapārijāta, Phaladīpikā and Jātaka Deśa Mārga, I found some gaps in my understanding. It was in 2015 when I was intently trying to decode this Daśā, which I left untouched for several years due to the complexity, lack of clarity and differences in opinions.

When I was reflecting on this intently and simultaneously praying to lord Śiva for guidance, it was at *09:55 am on 15 Nov 2015, in Singapore*, suddenly there was a mental revelation, and everything started making sense. The chart of the moment is given here for those who are interested. At that time, 8L Candra was in Dhanu Lagna, and Lagneśa Bṛhaspati was in Siṅha Rāśi in the 9th house aspecting the Lagna, indicating Guru's blessings.

What I realized was that the Savya and Apasavya Cakras are dynamically flipped, which is why after the 12 Navāñśas of Savya Nakṣatras, the following 12 Navāñśas follow in regular order, i.e., from the 12th Rāśi to the 1st Rāśi, but the 1st Rāśi is now Vṛścika instead of Meṣa. This dynamical flipping of the Rāśis, along the line of Karka-Siṅha, is the backbone of the Kālacakra system. This flipping is seen even in the mapping of the Navanavāñśas to the Navāñśa.

According to Maharṣi Parāśara, the Apasavya Kālacakra is the mirror image of the Savya Cakra, in which the frame of the Cakra does not change. Still, the Rāśis change their position within the frame. This is different from reckoning Vṛścika in the 8th box, Tulā in the 7th box and so on. In the new configuration, Vṛścika is repositioned to the 1st box, Tulā in the 2nd box and so on. Therefore, instead of jumping a box from 12th to 8th, the transition is from the 12th box to the 1st box, but the Rāśi transition appears to be Mīna to Vṛścika.

So, from a cycle standpoint, it moves in a clockwise fashion (Krama order), but due to the flipping of the Rāśis, the jumps manifest! I believe if one understands this, one can clearly decipher the basis of both the Navāñśa mapping to the Nakṣatra Caraṇa, as well as the Antardaśā mapping to the Navāñśa.

Once we are able to derive the 9 Daśās assigned to the Navāñśas based on the Kālacakra Navanavāñśas, we can recursively apply them to the subperiods. For instance, whenever the Meṣa Navāñśa appears, whether in the Candra Navāñśa, Daśā, or Antardaśā, regardless, the sequence of the nine Navanavāñśas invariably remains the same. The only difference is that depending on whether Meṣa appears in the Savya or Apasavya Cakra, the direction is reversed. For instance, in Savya Meṣa Navāñśa, the Daśā is from Meṣa to Dhanu in regular order. This is reversed to Dhanu to Meṣa in the reverse order.

30.1.1 KĀLA DAŚĀ

Maharṣi Parāśara narrates the Kāla Daśā in śloka 44-49 of the 46th chapter of Bṛhatparāśara. The Daśā is defined based on the Sandhyās, or the twilights, dawn, and dusk. A Sandhyā is a period that is defined as 5 Ghaṭis before and after the Sūryodaya or Sūryāsta Kāla. 1 Ghaṭi is 24 min, and 10 Ghaṭi is 4 hours. 2 hrs before and 2 hrs after Sūryodaya Kāla is called the Prātaḥsandhyā and the same duration before and after the Sūryāsta Kāla is called the Sāyaṃsandhyā.

Maharṣi Parāśara calls the Prātaḥsandhyā as Khaṇḍa and Sāyaṃsandhyā as Sudhā. Khaṇḍa means broken or without blemish, whereas Sudhā means Pure or without blemish. In a day, there are 60 Ghaṭis, of which the two Sandhyās take 20 Ghaṭis. What remains is 40 Ghaṭis, which are divided into two equal segments, the day segment and the night segment, each of 20 Ghaṭis.

The night segment is called Purṇa, whereas the day segment is called Mugdha. Purṇa means complete. For a standard day, the Sūryodaya is at 6 am and Sūryāsta at 6 pm. The four different entities, Khaṇḍasandhyā, Mugdha segment, Sudhāsandhyā and Purṇa segment, are as follows. This must be adjusted based on the Sunrise and Sūryāsta time in a day, which varies depending on the Latitude and the Season.

Table 2

#	Segment	Meaning	Time	Duration
1	**Khaṇḍasandhyā**	Morning twilight, dawn, Prātaḥsandhyā	04:00 to 08:00	4 hours
2	**Mugdha segment**	Day, Dina	08:00 to 16:00	8 hours
3	**Sudhāsandhyā**	Evening twilight, dusk, Sāyaṃsandhyā	16:00 to 20:00	4 hours
4	**Purṇa segment**	Night, Rātri	20:00 to 04:00	8 hours

Bṛhatparāśara 46.44-49.

5 Ghaṭis before the sight of the semi-disk of the setting Sūrya 5 Ghaṭis after that and 5 Ghaṭis before and after the rising of Sūrya that is 10 Ghaṭis in the evening, and 10 Ghaṭis in the morning, respectively. The total period of both these Sandhyās (twilight) is said to be 20 Ghaṭis. The 20 Ghaṭis of the night have been given the name Purṇa, and the 20 Ghaṭis of the day have been given the name Mugdha. The Sandhyā at the time of Sunrise is called Khaṇḍa, and the Sandhyā at the time of Sūryāsta is said to be Sudhā. Both of these Sandhyās are of 10 Ghaṭis each. If the birth is in Purṇa or Mugdha, its past Ghaṭis should be multiplied by two, and the product should be divided by 15. The figure so arrived at should be converted into years, months etc. By multiplying it by the serial number of Sūrya and other Grahas in their normal order, we shall get the Kāla Daśā of these Grahas. If the birth is during Sandhyā, then its past Ghaṭis should be multiplied by four and the product divided by 15. The figure so arrived at in terms of years, months, etc., should

be multiplied by the serial number of Sūrya and the other Grahas to get the Kāla Daśā of all the nine Grahas.

The computation of this Daśā depends on whether the birth occurred during the twilights or the day-night segments. To find the Daśā for the day and night segments, i.e., Mugdha or Purṇa, respectively, we must multiply the expired Ghaṭis by two and divide the product by 15. The result should be converted to year, months, and days.

By multiplying this with the serial number of the Grahas, 1-Sūrya, 2-Candra, 3-Maṅgala, 4-Budha, 5-Bṛhaspati, 6-Śukra, 7-Śani, 8-Rāhu and 9-Ketu, we derive the Daśā periods of a native. Suppose the birth occurred during one of the two Sandhyās. In that case, the expired Ghaṭi should be multiplied by four and the product divided by 15 to arrive at the Daśā multiplier, which must be multiplied by the Serial number of the Grahas to arrive at the Daśās.

Table 3

#	Segment	Duration	Ghaṭi	Processing
1	**Sandhyā**	4 hours	10 Ghaṭi	Expired Ghaṭi * 4 / 15
2	**Mugdha segment**	8 hours	20 Ghaṭi	Expired Ghaṭi * 2 / 15

The Sandhyākāla is of 10 Ghaṭi duration, which is divided by 3.75 (=15/4), whereas the segments are of twice the duration of the Sandhyākāla, and are divided by twice the duration, i.e., 7.5 (15/2). Each of them gives us the result of 2.667, which is equivalent to 2 years and 8 months, which is the maximum multiplier possible.

The total of the planetary indices 1 to 9, which stand for Sūrya to Rāhu, is 45. This means that the maximum Āyuṣa Granted is 2.67 * 45 = 120 years. Seeing it from another perspective, the total Āyuṣa granted to a human being is 120 years, which is when divided into Ratios of 1: 2: 3: 4: 5: 6: 7: 8: 9, the maximum Āyuṣa granted to someone is as follows:

Table 4

	Sūr	Can	Maṅ	Bud	Bṛh	Śuk	Śan	Rāh	Ket
Index	1.00	2.00	3.00	4.00	5.00	6.00	7.00	8.00	9.00
Āyuṣa Granted	2.67	5.33	8.00	10.67	13.33	16.00	18.67	21.33	24.00
Total Āyuṣa	2.67	8.00	16.00	26.67	40.00	56.00	74.67	96.00	120.00

Let us now understand the expired Ghaṭi concept. Suppose one is born at 7:00 pm on a standard day. The Sūryāsta happened at 06:00 pm, which means that the person is born 1 hour after the Sūryāsta. This implies that the person is born during the Sāyaṃsandhyā. 1 hr is 2.5 Ghaṭis, while the total duration of a Sandhyā is 10 Ghaṭis.

The Sāyaṃsandhyā starts after 04:00 pm, i.e., 2 hours (10 Ghaṭis) before Sūryāsta. Therefore, the expired Ghaṭi for this native is 5 Ghaṭis (before Sūryāsta)

+ 2.5 Ghaṭis (after Sūryāsta) = 7.5 Ghaṭis. Out of 10 Ghaṭis, 7.5 Ghaṭis is elapsed. As per the calculation, the multiplier is 7.5 * 4 / 15 = 2.00.

Therefore, we can say that the total Daśā period for this native is 2 * 45 = 90 years, which is divided in the ratio of 2: 4: 6: 8: 10: 12: 14: 16: 18 for Sūrya to Rāhu, respectively. We can also do it this way – 7.5 Ghaṭis out of 10 Ghaṭis = 75%. 75% of the total multiplier 2.667 is 75 / 100 * 2.667 = 2.0 years.

The definition of the Sūryodaya and Sūryāsta Kāla is crucial here. There are several definitions for this, but among them, I think the most appropriate are the Civil Sunrise and Sunset. The civil Sunrise occurs when the first ray of Sūrya is seen on the eastern horizon. This happens even before the Sūrya's upper edge is actually on the horizon. The atmosphere causes the rays to be bent, causing the Sun to appear on the horizon before it actually does astronomically.

According to timeanddate.com, "Civil twilight occurs when the Sun is less than 6 degrees below the horizon. In the morning, civil twilight begins when the Sun is 6 degrees below the horizon and ends at sunrise. In the evening, it begins at Sūryāsta and ends when the Sun reaches 6 degrees below the horizon. Nautical twilight occurs when the geometrical centre of the Sun is between 6 degrees and 12 degrees below the horizon. This twilight period is less bright than civil twilight, and artificial light is generally required for outdoor activities. Astronomical twilight occurs when the Sun is between 12 degrees and 18 degrees below the horizon.

Several countries use this definition of civil twilight to make laws related to aviation, hunting, and the usage of headlights and streetlamps." Therefore, the twilight used for regulating the activities on earth is the Civil twilight. In Jagannath Horā software, this can be set by choosing the option "The tip of Sun's disk appears to be on the eastern horizon".

Let us compute this Daśā for my Kuṇḍalī. I am born at 14:34:28 (14.574 hrs), while the Sūryodaya is at 5:28:6 (5.468) and Sūryāsta 18:13:47 (18.230). The day duration is 18.230 - 5.468 (12.762), and the night duration is 24 - 12.762 = 11.238. The day duration should be divided into 5:20:5 for the morning twilight, day, and evening twilight, which gives us 5/30 * 12.762: 20/30 * 12.762: 5/30 * 12.762 = 2.127: 8.508: 2.127. Likewise, the night duration must also be divided into 5: 20: 5, which gives us 1.873: 7.492: 1.873. The four segments of the day are as follows.

Table 5

#	Segment	Start	End	Time	Duration
1	**Khaṇḍa sandhyā**	5.468 - 1.873 = 3.595	5.468 + 2.127 = 7.595		4 hours
2	**Mugdha segment**	7.595	7.595 + 8.508 = 16.103		8.508 hours
3	**Sudhā sandhyā**	16.103	18.230 + 1.873 = 20.103		4 hours

#	Segment	Start	End	Time	Duration
4	Purṇa segment	20.103	20.103 + 7.492 = 3.595		7.492 hours

The birth occurred at 14.574, which is in the Mugdha segment. The hours expired in the segment is 14.574 - 7.595 = 6.979, whereas the duration of the segment is 8.508 hours. Therefore, the % age of the segment expired is 6.979 / 8.508 = 82.03%. The duration of the multiplier is 82.03% of 8 / 3 = 2.187 = 2 years 2 months 7 days 28 Ghaṭi 31.14 Vighaṭi. The total Daśā duration for the native is 2.187 * 45 = 98.415 years. This is the Daśā longevity granted by this Daśā. The Daśā periods are as follows.

Table 6

#	Graha	Ratio	Duration	Ending Date & Time
1	Sūrya	1	2.187	20-10-1976 22:19
2	Candra	2	4.374	11-02-1981 13:40
3	Maṅgala	3	6.561	01-08-1987 12:43
4	Budha	4	8.748	15-03-1996 19:26
5	Bṛhaspati	5	10.935	25-12-2006 09:50
6	Śukra	6	13.122	01-12-2019 07:55
7	Śani	7	15.309	02-01-2035 13:40
8	Rāhu	8	17.496	01-04-2052 03:07
9	Ketu	9	19.683	26-08-2071 00:14

From 25-12-2006, I am running Śukra Kāladaśā, which shall continue till 01-12-2019. After that, I shall have Śani Daśā till 02-01-2035. If I were to find the subperiods in Śukra Daśā, I would need to break down Śukra's 13.122 years into nine parts with Ratio 1: 2: 3 and so on.

Since the sequence of the Antar is not narrated by the Maharṣi, I propose to take it in the same format as Viñśottarī, i.e., starting from the Daśānātha Śukra and ending with the previous Graha Bṛhaspati. Therefore, in Śukra Daśā the Antardaśā shall be of the sequence Śukra → Śani → Rāhu → Ketu → Sūrya → Candra → Maṅgala → Budha → Bṛhaspati. Based on this, the Antardaśā table is as follows:

Table 7

#	Graha	Ratio	Duration	Ending Date & Time
1	Śukra	6	1.7496	15-09-2008 06:23
2	Śani	7	2.0412	20-09-2010 02:21
3	Rāhu	8	2.3328	06-01-2013 21:44
4	Ketu	9	2.6244	09-08-2015 16:33
5	Sūrya	1	0.2916	22-11-2015 15:59
6	Candra	2	0.5832	19-06-2016 14:49
7	Maṅgala	3	0.8748	30-04-2017 13:06
8	Budha	4	1.1664	24-06-2018 10:48
9	Bṛhaspati	5	1.458	01-12-2019 07:55

This shows that from 24-06-2018, I am running Bṛhaspati Antardaśā in Śukra Daśā. What can we expect in Śukra Daśā - Bṛhaspati Antardaśā? Maharṣi Parāśara did not narrate the result for this Daśā. But I believe that this Daśā can be used for timing extreme events in one's life which are out of the ordinary. This is because Kāla means time, and the house of Kāla is the 11th house, governed by Bṛhaspati.

The lord of Kāla is Śani, the presider Devatā of time, and the Devatā is Mahākāla, the Jyotirliṅga of Ujjain. In this case, this period is marked by Śukra and Bṛhaspati. For Dhanu Lagna, Śukra is an Akāraka (unfavourable Graha), and Bṛhaspati is the Lagneśa/Sukheśa and the Kāraka for children.

During this period, my Daughter did exceedingly well in her Primary School Leaving exam. She earned a place in a prestigious Secondary School in Singapore, where she competed with several hundred students for a place among 27 selected. Such events are rare and perhaps can be indicated by the Kāla Daśā. Of course, the promise should also be there in the Janmakuṇḍalī, else, Daśā cannot give such results.

In my Janmakuṇḍalī, the 5th lord Maṅgala is in the 9th house, conjunct with the 9th lord Sūrya and aspected by Bṛhaspati, indicating prominence to children. This occurred in Śukra-Bṛhaspati. Again, I cannot be more certain than this, as this is a hidden Daśā, and Maharṣi Parāśara chose not to narrate its results.

In the calculation of the Daśā and Antardaśā, I have considered the Daśā duration as 360 Sāvana days, 12 months in a year having 30 days in a month. If one wishes, one might experiment with other year durations such as True Saura Varṣa or Mean Saura Varṣa of 365.2563 days. My recommendation is to use 360 days a year for Daśā calculations since it is a Graha Daśā.

—III—

30.1.2 CAKRA DAŚĀ

There is yet another Daśā, which is based on the classification of the day into the four segments that we discussed in Kāladaśā. This is called the Cakra Daśā because the reckoning of this Daśā is similar to the Sudarshana Cakra Daśā, which is progressing through the Rāśis.

Bṛhatparāśara 46.50-51.

If the birth is at night, the Daśā shall commence from Lagna Rāśi. If the birth is during the day, the Daśā shall start from the Rāśi, in which the Lagneśa is placed. If the birth is during Sandhyā, the Daśā is in from the Rāśi of the 2nd Bhāva. The Daśā of each Rāśi is 10 years. As it is the Daśā system of the 12 Rāśis in the Zodiac, it has been named as Cakra Daśā.

The commencement of the Daśā depends on whether the birth occurred during the day, night or one of the two twilights. Depending on the time of birth, the Daśā commences from either (1) the Lagna, (2) the Rāśi occupied by the Lagneśa, or (3) the 2nd house. We shall use the classification we used for the Kāladaśā, as shown below.

Table 8

#	Segment	Meaning	Time	Duration	Daśā commencement
1	**Khaṇḍa Sandhyā**	**Morning twilight, dawn, Prātaḥsandhyā**	04:00 to 08:00	4 hours	2nd house
2	**Mugdha Segment**	**Day, Dina**	08:00 to 16:00	8 hours	Lagneśa's Rāśi
3	**Sudhā Sandhyā**	**Evening twilight, dusk, Sāyaṃsandhyā**	16:00 to 20:00	4 hours	2nd house
4	**Purṇa Segment**	**Night, Rātri**	20:00 to 04:00	8 hours	Lagna's Rāśi

In the lifetime of the native, which is 120 years, the Daśā passes through the 12 Rāśis of the Jātaka's Kuṇḍalī. This implies that the duration of each Rāśi is 10 years. Now, how do we find the balance of Daśā at birth? For that, we must use the Sphuṭa of the Lagna, Lagneśa and the Dhana. While the Lagnasphuṭa and the Lagneśa's Sphuṭa are intuitive, one might be confused regarding the Dhanasphuṭa.

Although there are various notations regarding the Bhāvasphuṭas, I recommend the usage of Śrīpati's Bhāva computations, as Maharṣi Parāśara sanctions that alone. Once the Sphuṭa of the commencing entity is known, we can use the formula to find the Daśā balance - (30 - Sphuṭa)/ 30 * 10. In the absence of the narration on the Antardaśā, I propose that it should be reckoned from the Daśā Rāśi to the 12th from the Daśā Rāśi.

In the case used above, the native is born during the day, which means that the Daśā must commence from the Lagneśa. The Lagneśa is Bṛhaspati and his Sphuṭa is Kumbha 20:45:3.61 (Kumbha 20.751). The Daśā commences from Kumbha, and the balance of Daśā at birth is (30 - 20.751) / 30 * 10 = 3.083. After that, the Daśā moves in a Krama (zodiacal) fashion through Mīna, Meṣa and Makara eventually.

Table 9

#	Rāśi	Duration	Ending Date & Time
1	**Kumbha**	3.083	08-09-1977 11:45
2	**Mīna**	10	18-07-1987 11:45
3	**Meṣa**	10	26-05-1997 11:45
4	**Vṛṣabha**	10	04-04-2007 11:45
5	**Mithuna**	10	10-02-2017 11:45
6	**Karka**	**10**	**20-12-2026 11:45**
7	**Siṅha**	10	28-10-2036 11:45
8	**Kanyā**	10	06-09-2046 11:45

#	Rāśi	Duration	Ending Date & Time
9	Tulā	10	15-07-2056 11:45
10	Vṛścika	10	24-05-2066 11:45
11	Dhanu	10	01-04-2076 11:45
12	Makara	10	08-02-2086 11:45

The Karka Daśā runs from 10-12-2017 to 20-12-2026. What should be the Antardaśā? The Antardaśā should commence from Karka and end in Siṅha. The below table gives the Antardaśā, which is of 0.833 years or 10 months. In the calculation for the Daśā and Antardaśā, I have considered the Daśā duration as 360 Sāvana days, 12 months in a year having 30 days in a month. If one wishes, one might experiment with other year durations. My recommendation is always to use 360 days a year for the Daśā calculation.

Table 10

#	Rāśi	Duration	Ending Date & Time
1	Karka	0.833	07-12-2017 11:45
2	Siṅha	0.833	03-10-2018 11:45
3	Kanyā	0.833	30-07-2019 11:45
4	**Tulā**	**0.833**	**25-05-2020 11:45**
5	Vṛścika	0.833	21-03-2021 11:45
6	Dhanu	0.833	15-01-2022 11:45
7	Makara	0.833	11-11-2022 11:45
8	Kumbha	0.833	07-09-2023 11:45
9	Mīna	0.833	03-07-2024 11:45
10	Meṣa	0.833	29-04-2025 11:45
11	Vṛṣabha	0.833	23-02-2026 11:45
12	Mithuna	0.833	20-12-2026 11:45

How about the Antardaśās of the 1st Daśā? The Daśā ends at 08-09-1977 11:45, which means that it must have started 10 years earlier, i.e., 31-10-1967 11:45. The Antardaśā calculation can commence from 31-10-1967 11:45; however, since the birth occurred on 25th August 1974, the Antardaśās ending prior to the birth date/ time are inactive. The birth occurred in Kumbha Mahādaśā – Mīna Antardaśā.

Table 11

#	Rāśi	Duration	Ending Date & Time	Active?
1	Karka	0.833	26-08-1968 11:45	Inactive
2	Siṅha	0.833	22-06-1969 11:45	Inactive
3	Kanyā	0.833	18-04-1970 11:45	Inactive
4	Tulā	0.833	12-02-1971 11:45	Inactive
5	Vṛścika	0.833	09-12-1971 11:45	Inactive
6	Dhanu	0.833	04-10-1972 11:45	Inactive

#	Rāśi	Duration	Ending Date & Time	Active?
7	Makara	0.833	31-07-1973 11:45	Inactive
8	Kumbha	0.833	27-05-1974 11:45	Inactive
9	Mīna	0.833	23-03-1975 11:45	Active
10	Meṣa	0.833	17-01-1976 11:45	Active
11	Vṛṣabha	0.833	12-11-1976 11:45	Active
12	Mithuna	0.833	08-09-1977 11:45	Active

Today's date of 21-09-2019, which means that the native is right now undergoing Karka Daśā - Tulā Antardaśā. Karka is the 8H, housing Śukra, and Tulā is the 11H and lorded by Śukra. This means that Śukra is active right now, according to this Daśā. Śukra is the 6th and 11th lord in the Kuṇḍalī and is subjected to Pāpakartari Yoga, indicating that Śukra's Kārakatva shall suffer.

—III—

30.1.3
KĀLACAKRA DAŚĀ

Kāla means time, and Cakra means cycle. Therefore, Kālacakra means the "cycle of time". Given its complexity, Kālacakra Daśā is presumably a secretive and an often-misunderstood Daśā. The key characteristics of this Daśā are that it is highly precise in timing events, mainly misfortune, danger to life and death. The Daśā is precise because a slight change in the Candrasphuṭa causes a big change in the Daśā balance. Therefore, this Daśā is also best suited for birthtime rectification or things such as validation of Ayanāñśa.

One of the major challenges of this Daśā is the lack of a clear explanation of its computations by modern-day authors. They have, in fact, caused more confusion instead of clarifying them. There are several versions of interpretations, but they fail to present a consistent approach. My objective here is to present these principles in a structured manner and to dispel the darkness that surrounds this beautiful Daśā.

I shall also demonstrate the application of this Daśā with examples so that one can completely grasp it. I leave it to the judgement of the erudite readers to judge my method vis-à-vis those of others and decide which one is more logical and consistent. Furthermore, I also encourage the readers to experiment with the method given here and then draw their own conclusions. Let us see what Maharṣi Parāśara says about this Daśā.

BṚHATPARĀŚARA 46.52-53.
MAHARṢI PARĀŚARA SAID. O BRĀHMAṆA! NOW, AFTER MAKING OBEDIENCE TO LORD ŚIVA, I SHALL DESCRIBE THE KĀLACAKRA DAŚĀ. WHATEVER WAS RELATED BY LORD ŚIVA TO DEVĪ PĀRVATI IS BEING EXPLAINED BY ME FOR THE USE OF SAGES TO BE UTILIZED FOR THE WELFARE OF THE PEOPLE.

In the narration of the principles of Jyotiṣaśāstra, Maharṣi Parāśara also clarifies, in several places, whether the principles originated from Lord Brahmā or Lord Śiva. Lord Brahmā is certainly an important originator of this discipline, and this knowledge is carried forward by his sons, who are great Maharṣis. Bṛhat Parāśarī Horāśāstra is jutted with several such references.

For instance, in the context of the Ṣoḍaśavarga, Maharṣi Parāśara attributes the origin of the principles to Lord Brahmā. In fact, in this magnum opus, it is relatively easy to find the mention of Lord Brahmā, who is the main originator of this Śāstra. But, in some hidden and esoteric portions, mainly subjects that deal with the Tantra or Agama aspect of this subject, Lord Śiva is found to be narrating these principles to Mātā Pārvati. Kālacakra is one such subject, which is profound, hidden and highly secretive. This Cakra represents the flow of time and denotes the play of Puruṣa and Prakṛti, masculine and feminine, potential, and kinetic states.

Maharṣi Parāśara initiates his narration of this Daśā in Bṛhatparāśara 46.52-53, stating, "whatever was narrated by Lord Śiva to Devī Pārvati, is being explained by me for the use of sages to be utilized for the welfare of the people." Jātakapārijāta 17.1-2 also states, "bowing to lord Śiva, the supreme soul, the prime cause of all things, standing in the centre of the planetary systems and comprehending in his omniscience, the 64 branches of knowledge, the all-benign Devī Pārvati asked the supreme ruler of all Gods, as follows: "Tell me o lord, in detail the entire course of the wheel of time, the Kālacakra. To this, lord Īśvara replies, "I am of the nature of Sūrya and Candra. The whole universe, consisting of mobile and immobile things, is brought about by the conjunction and opposition of Sūrya and Candra."

Invariably, lord Śiva is referring to the 30 Tithis as the creator of everything that we see, which boils down to 16 Kalās of Candra, indicating gods 16 potencies. Among the Dasāvatāra, lord Kṛṣṇa is the Avatāra, who is born with all the 16 Kalās (solahakalāpurṇa), indicating full potencies of the divinity. One should study several classical texts on this subject, including the venerable Jātakapārijāta. But the narration of Jātakapārijāta is almost like Maharṣi Parāśara's; therefore, in my view, the study of Bṛhatparāśara should be adequate for understanding this Daśā.

The fundamental principle of Kālacakra is that time flows in two directions in Kālacakra, viz., Savya and Apasavya, forward and reverse. The normal interpretation of Savya and Apasavya is forward and reverse, whereas I have a slightly different interpretation. In a zodiac, which starts from Meṣa and ends with Mīna, we notice that the initiation is from a Puruṣa Rāśi (Masculine sign) and the ending is in a Strī Rāśi (feminine sign).

This is the Savya Cakra, which is masculine. When the cycle is reversed, i.e., the initiation is from a Strī Rāśi and ends in a Puruṣa Rāśi, it is called Apasavya. We can say that Masculinity dominates in the Savya Cakra and Femininity in the Apasavya Cakra. There are five sets of Savya Nakṣatras, each containing 3 Nakṣatras, whereas there are four sets of Apasavya Nakṣatras. The number 5 is odd and of Puruṣaprakṛti, whereas the number 4 is even and of Strīprakṛti. The Naisārgika 5th Rāśi is lorded by Masculine Sūrya, and the 4th Rāśi by Feminine Candra. This is the basis of the Savya and Apasavya classification - masculine and feminine.

We see the parallel of this concept in the Śrīcakra, which is the source of profound knowledge. In this Cakra, four Triangles are pointing upward - denoting the Śakti (Mātṛ rupa), whereas five Triangles pointing downward - denoting the Puruṣa (Pitṛ rupa). We can see nine Triangles that form the Śrīcakra, which is also the basis of the Kālacakra, which contains nine groups, comprised of five Savya and four Apasavya.

There is a Bindu in the middle, which is the centre of creation, from which the manifestation starts. It can be seen as the "singularity" from which the entire Brahmāṇḍa (universe) has manifested. I highly recommend one to study Śrī Śaṅkarācārya's Soundarya Lahiri, which narrates the philosophical aspect of Śrīcakra and several other hidden Cakras.

Praśnamārga calls Savya as Dakṣiṇa and Apasavya Vāma. Dakṣiṇa means right, and Vāma left, and they refer to the two major paths of Tantra, Dakṣiṇamārga and Vāmamārga. In this regard, the Brahmayamala talks about three currents of Tantric tradition, viz., Dakṣiṇa, Madhyama and Vāma, characterized respectively by the predominance of the three Guṇas, Sattva, Rajas, and Tamas. This is a profound subject and is beyond the scope of this chapter.

Those interested may study these paths from books dedicated to this subject. Equating them to the motion of the Grahas, Savya implies Mārgī Graha (direct motion), whereas Apasavya implies Vakrī Graha (retrogression). The terms are reversed in Phaladīpikā, which is called Savya Apasavya and Apasavya Savya. *In this delineation, I have followed the convention of Maharṣi Parāśara of Savya and Apasavya.*

In either of the Savya and Apasavya Cakra, there are two Kramas or directions of flow of time, Krama and Utkrama. Let us first focus on the Krama Savya and Apasavya Cakra. We have seen before that in the Savya Cakra, the flow of time from Meṣa to Mīna, which is reversed, from Vṛścika to Dhanu. *In the table below, we notice that the sequence of the Grahas ruling the Rāśis do not change; only the masculinity-femininity of the Rāśis is reversed.*

Table 12

#	Graha	Savya	Apasavya
1	**Maṅgala**	Meṣa	Vṛścika
2	**Śukra**	Vṛṣabha	Tulā
3	**Budha**	Mithuna	Kanyā
4	**Candra**	*Karka*	*Siṅha*
5	**Sūrya**	*Siṅha*	*Karka*
6	**Budha**	Kanyā	Mithuna
7	**Śukra**	Tulā	Vṛṣabha
8	**Maṅgala**	Vṛścika	Meṣa

#	Graha	Savya	Apasavya
9	**Bṛhaspati**	Dhanu	Mīna
10	**Śani**	Makara	Kumbha
11	**Śani**	Kumbha	Makara
12	**Bṛhaspati**	Mīna	Dhanu

The Krama direction is from Maṅgala to Bṛhaspati in the order Maṅgala → Śukra → Budha → Candra → Sūrya → Budha → Śukra → Maṅgala → Bṛhaspati → Śani → Śani → Bṛhaspati. When this direction is reversed, i.e., from Bṛhaspati → → → Maṅgala, it is called Utkrama. While Savya-Apasavya denotes the reversal of Masculinity-Femininity, the Krama-Utkrama denotes the reversal of direction.

In Krama, the flow of time is from Meṣa → Mīna in Savyacakra and Vṛścika → Dhanu in Apasavyacakra. Whereas in Utkrama. The flow of time is from Mīna → Meṣa in Savyacakra and Dhanu → Vṛścika in Apasavyacakra. Henceforth, we shall call the movement from (1) Meṣa → Mīna as Krama Savya, (2) Vṛścika → Dhanu as Krama Apasavya, (3) Mīna → Meṣa as Utkrama Savya, and (4) Dhanu → Vṛścika as Utkrama Apasavya. This is also shown in the table below:

Table 13

	Krama			Utkrama		
#	**Graha**	Savya	Apasavya	**Graha**	Savya	Apasavya
1	**Maṅgala**	Meṣa	Vṛścika	**Bṛhaspati**	Mīna	Dhanu
2	**Śukra**	Vṛṣabha	Tulā	**Śani**	Kumbha	Makara
3	**Budha**	Mithuna	Kanyā	**Śani**	Makara	Kumbha
4	**Candra**	Karka	Siṅha	**Bṛhaspati**	Dhanu	Mīna
5	**Sūrya**	Siṅha	Karka	**Maṅgala**	Vṛścika	Meṣa
6	**Budha**	Kanyā	Mithuna	**Śukra**	Tulā	Vṛṣabha
7	**Śukra**	Tulā	Vṛṣabha	**Budha**	Kanyā	Mithuna
8	**Maṅgala**	Vṛścika	Meṣa	**Sūrya**	Siṅha	Karka
9	**Bṛhaspati**	Dhanu	Mīna	**Candra**	Karka	Siṅha
10	**Śani**	Makara	Kumbha	**Budha**	Mithuna	Kanyā
11	**Śani**	Kumbha	Makara	**Śukra**	Vṛṣabha	Tulā
12	**Bṛhaspati**	Mīna	Dhanu	**Maṅgala**	Meṣa	Vṛścika

This Daśā is complex because the Daśā order is not fixed and changes based on certain conditions. Before delving into the details, let us understand at a high level what this Daśā entails. In the heart of this Daśā, there are two Kālacakras, the Savya Kālacakras and the Apasavya Kālacakra.

The Savya Kālacakra is the normal zodiac that is in vogue. In contrast, the Apasavya Kālacakra is the mirror image of the Savya Kālacakra, which is arrived at by dividing the zodiac by an imaginary line passing through the beginning of Kumbha and Siṅha and then flipping the two halves. This is better understood when the Kuṇḍalī is drawn in the South-Indian format, which is what Maharṣi Parāśara recommends.

In both the Savya and Apasavya Kālacakras, 12 Rāśis are mapped to the 12 Caraṇas of 3 consecutive Nakṣatras. For instance, Aśvinī-Bharaṇī-Kṛttikā is three consecutive Savya Nakṣatras that are mapped to Meṣa to Mīna in the Savya Kālacakra. The groups of 3 Nakṣatras are called the Triads. The Triad is followed by 3 Apasavya Nakṣatras Rohiṇī-Mṛgaśirā-Ārdrā, which are mapped to Vṛścika to Dhanu, in the Apasavya Kālacakra.

The Nakṣatras alternate between the Savya and Apasavya Triads. Let us now have a critical look at the Savya and Apasavya Kālacakras and their assignments to the Nakṣatra Caraṇas. Here, a question arises, which is whether these Savya and Apasavya Kālacakras are Rāśi Cakras or Navāñśa Cakras. Maharṣi Parāśara nowhere explicitly states that they are Rāśi Cakras.

However, from our understanding of the mapping of the Nakṣatra Caraṇas and the Navāñśas, we know that each Nakṣatra Caraṇa is precisely mapped to a Navāñśa. If we disregard this crucial point, I believe we miss the core concept of Kālacakra. Because of the Nakṣatra Caraṇa mapping, we must use the Savya and Apasavya Cakras as Navāñśa Kuṇḍalī and not Rāśi Kuṇḍalī.

Each Nakṣatra has 4 Caraṇas, which means the 3 Nakṣatras in the Aśvinī-Bharaṇī-Kṛttikā Triad, having 12 Caraṇas are precisely mapped to the 12 Navāñśas of the Savyacakra. On the other hand, the 12 Caraṇas of the 3 Nakṣatras, Rohiṇī-Mṛgaśirā-Ārdrā Triad are mapped to the 12 Navāñśas of the Apasavyacakra. Therefore, the mapping is Aśvinī1 - Meṣa, Ashvini2 - Vṛṣabha, Aśvinī3 - Mithuna, Aśvinī4 - Karka and so on.

Likewise, in the Apasavya Cakra, the mapping is Rohiṇī1 - Vṛścika, Rohiṇī2 - Tulā, Rohiṇī3 - Kanyā, Rohiṇī4 - Siṅha and so on. This is the fundamental design of the Kālacakra. Suppose one is born in Aśvinī4; we should say that the person is born in Savya Karka Navāñśa. Likewise, one born in Anuradha4 is said to be born in Apasavya Meṣa Navāñśa, which is the 8th Navāñśa in the Apasavya Cakra.

When we do the mapping of the Nakṣatra Caraṇas to either the Savya or Apasavya Navāñśas, we arrive at six distinct groups having the same mapping. For instance, for five Nakṣatras Aśvinī-Punarvasu-Hastā-Mūla-Pūrvābhādra, the Caraṇa 1 to 4 are respectively mapped to Meṣa, Vṛṣabha, Mithuna and Karka Navāñśas.

We can say that the five Nakṣatras, Aśvinī-Punarvasu-Hastā-Mūla-and Pūrvābhādra, belong to the Aśvinī group. Likewise, we have *Bharaṇī, Kṛttikā, Rohiṇī, Mṛgaśirā,* and *Ārdrā* group. The Nakṣatras belonging to Aśvinī, Bharaṇī and Kṛttikā are the Savya Nakṣatras, and each group contains five Nakṣatras, totalling fifteen Nakṣatras. On the other hand, Rohiṇī, Mṛgaśirā and Ārdrā are Apasavya Nakṣatras, and in each group, there are four Nakṣatras, totalling twelve Nakṣatras.

In this manner, the 27 Nakṣatras are classified under three Savya and three Apasavya groups. The six Groups are further reduced to four groups, led by Aśvinī, Bharaṇī, Rohiṇī and Mṛgaśirā Nakṣatras. Aśvinī and Kṛttikā groups are grouped into the "Savya-Aśvinī" group. Likewise, Mṛgaśirā and Ārdrā groups are grouped into the "Savya-Mṛgaśirā" group. Bharaṇī and Rohiṇī groups stay unchanged.

Immediately after mapping the 27 Nakṣatras to the Savya and Apasavya Cakras, Maharṣi Parāśara narrates two entities named Deha and Jīva that are determined based on the four Caraṇas of the Nakṣatras. However, he does not explain the basis for determining them, which causes confusion among scholars. Before advancing further, let us understand the concept of Navanavāñśas.

Each Navāñśa in the Savya or Apasavya Cakra contains nine Daśās, which represent nine Navanavāñśas. The Navanavāñśas are the Navāñśas within Navāñśas. The understanding of the Deha and Jīva requires the understanding of the Navanavāñśas assigned to a Navāñśa. The concept of Navanavāñśa is the 2nd crucial structural design of the Kālacakra. The sequence of Kālacakra Daśā and two important entities, the Deha and Jīva, are based on this Navanavāñśa sequence. Maharṣi Parāśara narrates the sequence of nine Navanavāñśas for each Navāñśa or Nakṣatra Caraṇa.

For instance, Bṛhatparāśara 46.60 states that Aśvinī-1 is mapped to Meṣa Navāñśa, having Meṣa as Deha and Dhanu as Jīva. The Navanavāñśas of Meṣa Navāṃśa are (1) Meṣa, (2) Vṛṣabha, (3) Mithuna, (4) Karka, (5) Siṅha, (6) Kanyā, (7) Tulā, (8) Vṛścika and (9) Dhanu and these denote the 9 Daśās of Aśvinī-1 or Meṣa Navāñśa. Although the Navanavāñśas is stated for all the Nakṣatra Caraṇas, the rationale for deriving them is not clarified by Maharṣi Parāśara. I have tried to provide the rational basis for the derivation of the Navanavāñśas.

Through god's grace and my reflections, I found that the assignment of Navanavāñśas is based on alternating Savya and Apasavya Cakras. Let us take the example of Aśvinī Nakṣatras. Four Caraṇas of Aśvinī Nakṣatra are mapped to four Navāñśas, and each of these Caraṇas (Navāñśas) has nine Navanavāñśas. Four Caraṇas * nine Navanavāñśas = thirty-six Navanavāñśas that are mapped to three cycles of twelve Rāśis.

We notice that in cycle one, Savya, the sequence of Navanavāñśas is from Meṣa to Mīna, which is the Savya order. Cycle 2 is Apasavya, and the sequence of Navanavāñśas is Vṛścika to Dhanu, which is the Apasavya order. This is then followed by the Savya order, i.e., Meṣa to Mīna. This sequence applies to the 9 Nakṣatras of Aśvinī group that are Aśvinī, Punarvasu, Hastā, Mūla, Pūrvābhādra, Kṛttikā, Aśleṣā, Svāti, Uttarāṣāṛhā, Revatī. In the Savya-Bharaṇī group, which consists of six Nakṣatras, Bharaṇī-Puṣya-Citrā-Pūrvāṣāṛhā-Uttarābhādra, the sequence of the three cycles is Krama + (Apasavya → Savya → Apasavya) [KASA].

The cycles of Navanavāñśas mentioned above are for Savya Nakṣatras, namely the Savya-Aśvinī group and the Savya-Bharaṇī group. This is different for the 12 Apasavya Nakṣatras - in which case we notice a reversal (Utkrama). The Krama Savya sequence is Meṣa → Mīna, and the Krama Apasavya sequence is Vṛścika → Dhanu.

In the Utkrama sequence that applies to the Apasavya Nakṣatras, the sequence is reversed. Thus, the Utkrama Savya sequence becomes from Meṣa →

Mīna to Mīna → Meṣa, and the Utkrama Apasavya Sequence becomes from Vṛścika → Dhanu to Dhanu → Vṛścika. For the Apasavya Rohiṇī group, which consists of four Nakṣatras, Rohiṇī-Maghā-Viśākhā-Śravaṇa, the three-cycle sequence is Utkrama + (Savya → Apasavya → Savya) [USAS].

For the Mṛgaśirā group, which consists of the remaining 8 Apasavya Nakṣatras, the three-cycle sequence is Utkrama (Apasavya → Savya → Apasavya) [UASA]. In all the Apasavya Cakras used, either for the Savya or the Apasavya Nakṣatras, the Candra-Sūrya order is never changed. The fourth place is always reserved for Karka and the fifth for Sūrya, whereas the remaining ten Rāśis are flipped.

When the Savya and Apasavya cycles combine, their ending and joining points manifest regions of danger, which in the parlance of Kālacakra Daśā, gives rise to jumps called the Siṅhavlokana Gati. The complexity does not end here, as we are yet to see the flipping of Karka and Siṅha. The basis of this is that in the Savya group, the sequence of the Rāśis of the Prakāśagrahas is Karka → Siṅha.

On the other hand, in the Apasavya Nakṣatras, the sequence should ideally be Siṅha → Karka, but since this is not allowed, the sequence remains Karka → Siṅha. This gives rise to two Gatis that occur concurrently, the Maṇḍūka Gati and the Marakaṭa Gati. Due to the Karka-Siṅha flipping, the Maṇḍūka Gati occurs between Kanyā → Karka and Siṅha → Mithuna. In this Gati, the Rāśi is jumped to the alternate Rāśi, skipping one Rāśi in between.

The Marakaṭa Gati occurs when there is a sudden change in direction. For instance, in the Apasavya cycle of the Aśvinī group, which is the middle cycle, the sequence should be Kanyā → Siṅha → Karka → Mithuna. However, due to the fixity of Karka → Siṅha, this becomes Kanyā → Karka → Siṅha → Mithuna. This gives rise to the Marakaṭa Gati, which happens when from Kanyā, the Rāśi jumps to Karka, then takes a sudden reversal, comes to Siṅha, and after that jumps to Mithuna. Maṇḍūka means frog, which hops, whereas Marakaṭa means monkey, which abruptly reverses its direction. These sudden changes or jumps give rise to serious troubles in life, danger or even death.

Regarding the Daśā span, Maharṣi Parāśara states in Bṛhatparāśara 46.84. that 5, 21, 7, 9, 10, 16 and 4 years are the Daśā spans of Sūrya, Candra, Maṅgala, Budha, Bṛhaspati, Śukra and Śani. The Daśā span and the lifespan of a person are determined on the basis of this allotment.

For instance, for Aśvinī-1, the nine Navanavāñśas are Meṣa → Vṛṣabha → Mithuna → Karka → Siṅha → Kanyā → Tulā → Vṛścika → Dhanu, which gives rise to 7 → 16 → 9 → 21 → 5 → 9 → 16 → 7 → 10 years, i.e., 100 years. We can say that for one born in Aśvinī-1, the Āyu span is 100 years. According to Maharṣi Parāśara (vide Bṛhatparāśara 46.89.), one born in Meṣa Añśa, the Āyu is 100 years, in Vṛṣabha 85 years, in Mithuna 83 years, in Karka 86 years.

The number of years is the same for Rāśis, situated on the fifth and ninth to them. This Śloka of the Maharṣi endorses that the 9 Rāśis assigned to the Nakṣatra Caraṇas are the Navāñśas, as Maharṣi Parāśara uses the term "Añśa" which is normally used for "Navāñśa". In the detailed narration of these principles below, it is demonstrated how the Āyu of the Nakṣatra Caraṇas is determined.

We can also say that for Savya Nakṣatras, the Āyu assigned to the Caraṇas are Pada1 - 100, Pada2 - 85, Pada3 - 83 and Pada4 - 86. The total is 354 years. For the Apasavya Nakṣatras, the Āyu assigned to the Caraṇas are reversed, i.e., Pada1 - 86, Pada2 - 83, Pada3 - 85 and Pada4 - 100. It is not that one born in a certain Caraṇa, say Aśvinī1, is assigned 100 years always. This only tells us that if one is born in 0° of Aśvinī1, then the default Āyus granted to the native as per the nine Navanavāñśas is 100 years. This only means the Daśā duration and not the longevity of the person.

In real life, however, one can be born in various places of a Nakṣatra Caraṇa, which means that after expiring the remaining Navanavāñśas, the Daśā moves to the next cycle of the Navanavāñśa. For instance, one is born at the end of Aśvinī-1, i.e., the 9th Navanavāñśa of Aśvinī which is Dhanu - this means that after expiring the Dhanu Navanavāñśa, the Daśā moves to Aśvinī-2, which is in Vṛṣabha Navāñśa, and the Daśā sequence is Makara → Kumbha → Mīna → Vṛścika^ → Tulā^ → Kanyā^ → Karka!^ → Siṅha!^ → Mithuna^.

The "^" indicates the Apasavya movement, whereas "!" indicates the luminary switch. We can limit the assignment of the Daśā Rāśis to only nine, which is true for the case of most, but in some cases, it can be extended. Most people touch the Daśā of only one or two Nakṣatra Caraṇa or Navāñśa, whereas only a few who touch three Caraṇas. Depending on the Caraṇa of birth, sometimes one can touch the Caraṇas of two different Nakṣatras.

For instance, in my case - I am born in the last Navanavāñśa of Anurādhā-4 (Meṣa Navāñśa). The last Navanavāñśa of Anurādhā4 is Meṣa, after which the Daśā moves to the 1st Navanavāñśa to Jyeṣṭhā1, which is Mīna. Regarding the crossing of Nakṣatra, the switch cannot happen from Savya Nakṣatra to Apasavya or vice-versa. For instance, after Kṛttikā4, instead of the Daśā moving to Rohini1, it moves to Aśvinī1. For Savya Nakṣatra, the Daśā cycle remains within the Savya Kālacakra, and for Apasavya Nakṣatra, the Daśā cycle remains with the Apasavya Kālacakra.

Regarding the nomenclature of Daśā, Bhukti, etc., there are some minute variations between the classical texts. Maharṣi Parāśara states (vide Bṛhatparāśara 49.6) that in the Kālacakra Daśā of Meṣa in Meṣa Navāñśa, there shall be distress due to troubles caused by the pollution of blood. He further states that in the Daśā of Meṣa in the Vṛṣabha Navāñśa, there is an increase in wealth and agricultural produce.

What can we infer from this? It means that in the Meṣa Navāñśa - Meṣa Navanavāñśa Daśā, there is suffering due to the pollution of blood. Likewise, in the Meṣa Navāñśa - Vṛṣabha Navanavāñśa Daśā, there is an increase in wealth and agricultural produce. Therefore, we can say that the nine Navanavāñśas in a Rāśi (or Nakṣatra Caraṇa) are the Daśās.

To confirm this, let us take another instance. The Maharṣi states in Bṛhatparāśara 49.16-17., that in Siṅha (Navāṅśa), in the Daśā of the Navāṅśa (Navanavāṅśa) of (1) Vṛścika there is distress and disputes, (2) ... Tulā extraordinary gains, (3) ... Kanyā gains of wealth, (4) ... Karka danger from wild animals, (5) ... Siṅha birth of a son, (6) ... Mithuna increase of enemies, (7) ... Vṛṣabha gains from the sale of cattle, (8) ... Meṣa danger from animals and (9) in the Daśā of Mīna Aṅśa journeys to distant places.

In the following table, we notice that in Siṅha Navāṅśa, there are two Daśā sequences. The sequence 1 (Savya Nakṣatra - Bharaṇī group pada1) is Vṛś → Tul → Kan → Kar → Siṅ → Mit → Vṛṣ → Meṣ → Mīn, whereas the sequence 2 (Apasavya Nakṣatra - Rohiṇī group pada4) is Mīn → Meṣ → Vṛṣ → Mit → Siṅ → Kar → Kan → Tul → Vṛś. We notice that, in the explanation of the results, the Maharṣi uses the Savya sequence, i.e., that of Vṛścika, Tulā, Kanyā, etc. I believe the same should also be applied to the Apasavya Nakṣatra, where the Daśās are of the same Navanavāṅśas, but the sequence is reversed.

Table 14: Daśā of Siṅha Navāṅśa

#	Nakṣ	Caraṇa	S/A	Group	Navāṅśa	Mahādaśā									Deha	Jīva
						1	2	3	4	5	6	7	8	9		
5	Bhar	1	S	Bhar	Siṅha	Vṛś	Tul	Kan	Kar	Siṅ	Mit	Vṛṣ	Meṣ	Mīn	Vṛś	Mīn
16	Rohi	4	A	Rohi	Siṅha	Mīn	Meṣ	Vṛṣ	Mit	Siṅ	Kar	Kan	Tul	Vṛś	Vṛś	Mīn
29	Puṣy	1	S	Bhar	Siṅha	Vṛś	Tul	Kan	Kar	Siṅ	Mit	Vṛṣ	Meṣ	Mīn	Vṛś	Mīn
40	Magh	4	A	Rohi	Siṅha	Mīn	Meṣ	Vṛṣ	Mit	Siṅ	Kar	Kan	Tul	Vṛś	Vṛś	Mīn
53	Citr	1	S	Bhar	Siṅha	Vṛś	Tul	Kan	Kar	Siṅ	Mit	Vṛṣ	Meṣ	Mīn	Vṛś	Mīn
64	Viśā	4	A	Rohi	Siṅha	Mīn	Meṣ	Vṛṣ	Mit	Siṅ	Kar	Kan	Tul	Vṛś	Vṛś	Mīn
77	Pūrv	1	S	Bhar	Siṅha	Vṛś	Tul	Kan	Kar	Siṅ	Mit	Vṛṣ	Meṣ	Mīn	Vṛś	Mīn
88	Śrav	4	A	Rohi	Siṅha	Mīn	Meṣ	Vṛṣ	Mit	Siṅ	Kar	Kan	Tul	Vṛś	Vṛś	Mīn
101	Utta	1	S	Bhar	Siṅha	Vṛś	Tul	Kan	Kar	Siṅ	Mit	Vṛṣ	Meṣ	Mīn	Vṛś	Mīn

Now, one might ask, does the Maharṣi cover all Navāṅśa and Navanavāṅśa combinations? Let us verify this using a Navāṅśa, where the Siṅhavlokana Gati is seen, a Gati that happens due to the rendezvous of Savya and Apasavya Cakra. Aśvinī-2 or Vṛṣabha Navāṅśa. We notice that, regardless of whether Vṛṣabha Navāṅśa belongs to Savya or Apasavya Cakra (or Tārā), the Daśā Rāśis (Navanavāṅśas) within the Vṛṣabha Navāṅśa are invariably the same, although their sequence is reversed.

In both the Savya and Apasavya Tārās, the Siṅhavlokana Gati is seen for this Navāṅśa. Regarding Vṛṣabha, Maharṣi Parāśara states (vide Bṛhatparāśara 49.8-10) that in Vṛṣabha (Navāṅśa), Daśā of (1) Makara Navāṅśa

(Navanavāñśa), there shall be a tendency to perform undesirable deeds along with more adverse effects. (2) In the Kumbha Navāñśa, there are profits in business, (3) in the Mīna success in all ventures, (4) in the Daśā of Vṛścika Navāñśa danger from fire, (5) in the Daśā of Tulā Navāñśa recognition from Government and reverence from all, (6) in the Daśā of Kanyā Navāñśa danger from enemies, (7) in the Daśā of Karka Navāñśa distress to wife, (8) in the Daśā of Siṅha Navāñśa diseases of eyes and (9) in the Daśā of Mithuna Navāñśa obstacles in earning a livelihood."

Again, we notice that Maharṣi Parāśara gives the results of the nine Daśās (Navanavāñśas) of Savya Nakṣatra and expects us to apply them for Apasavya Nakṣatras as well.

Table 15: Daśā of Vṛṣabha Navāñśa

#	Nakṣ	Caraṇa	S/A	Group	Navāñśa	Mahādaśā 1	2	3	4	5	6	7	8	9	Deha	Jīva
2	Aśvi	2	S	Aśvi	Vṛṣabha	Mak	Kum	Mīn	Vṛś	Tul	Kan	Kar	Siṅ	Mit	Mak	Mit
19	Mṛga	3	A	Mṛga	Vṛṣabha	Mit	Siṅ	Kar	Kan	Tul	Vṛś	Mīn	Kum	Mak	Mak	Mit
26	Puna	2	S	Aśvi	Vṛṣabha	Mak	Kum	Mīn	Vṛś	Tul	Kan	Kar	Siṅ	Mit	Mak	Mit
43	Pūrv	3	A	Mṛga	Vṛṣabha	Mit	Siṅ	Kar	Kan	Tul	Vṛś	Mīn	Kum	Mak	Mak	Mit
50	Hast	2	S	Aśvi	Vṛṣabha	Mak	Kum	Mīn	Vṛś	Tul	Kan	Kar	Siṅ	Mit	Mak	Mit
67	Anur	3	A	Mṛga	Vṛṣabha	Mit	Siṅ	Kar	Kan	Tul	Vṛś	Mīn	Kum	Mak	Mak	Mit
74	Mūla	2	S	Aśvi	Vṛṣabha	Mak	Kum	Mīn	Vṛś	Tul	Kan	Kar	Siṅ	Mit	Mak	Mit
91	Dhan	3	A	Mṛga	Vṛṣabha	Mit	Siṅ	Kar	Kan	Tul	Vṛś	Mīn	Kum	Mak	Mak	Mit
98	Pūrv	2	S	Aśvi	Vṛṣabha	Mak	Kum	Mīn	Vṛś	Tul	Kan	Kar	Siṅ	Mit	Mak	Mit

Some Ācāryas call the Daśās and Antardaśās differently. Śrī Mantreśvara likes to call the Navāñśa Rāśi as Mahādaśā, whereas the Navanavāñśa Rāśi as the Bhukti or Apahara. In Phaladīpikā 22.5., he states that for one born in the first Caraṇa of Aśvinī, the first Bhukti (subperiod) belongs Meṣa-Maṅgala; the second to Vṛṣabha-Śukra; the third to Mithuna-Budha; the fourth to Karka-Candra; the fifth to Sinha-Sūrya; the sixth to Kanyā-Budha; the seventh to Tulā-Śukra; the eighth to Vṛścika-Maṅgala; and the 9th to Dhanu-Bṛhaspati.

According to Śrī Mantreśvara, for a person born in, say, Anurādhā-4, the Daśā is that of Meṣa, as the Nakṣatra-Caraṇa is mapped to Meṣa Navāñśa. Within Meṣa Daśā, the Bhuktis are in the sequence of Dha → Vṛś → Tul → Kan → Siṅ → Kar → Mit → Vṛṣ → Meṣ. According to this view, one might get in one's lifetime, say one to three Daśā and the periods that we must reckon for deciphering the lifeline should be based on the Bhuktis. Regardless of what we call something as

Navāñśa, Daśā or Bhukti, the concept is the same. For ease of reference, for one born in Anurādhā-4, we shall say that the person is born in Meṣa Navāñśa, but the applicable Daśās are that of Dha → Vṛś → Tul → Kan → Siṅ → Kar → Mit → Vṛṣ → Meṣ. Therefore, a Bhukti, according to Śrī Mantreśvara, is a Mahādaśā in our convention.

Jātakapārijāta also supports our convention. Śrī GK Ojha, in his translation of this text, writes that one who is born in the 1st Caraṇa of Rohiṇī, Maghā, Viśākhā, Śravaṇa has a total Daśā span of 86 years. They are said to be born in Vṛścika Navāñśa, and their sequence of Daśā is Dha → Mak → Kum → Mīn → Meṣ → Vṛṣ → Mit → Siṅ → Kar. Evidently, Śrī Ojha endorses that the person is born in Vṛścika Navāñśa, which is what I have explained before, and the Daśā of such a person is in Dhanu to Karka, that totals up to 86 years.

Again, the basis of this sequence is, however, not clarified, which is what I have clarified in my writing. We shall see that the basis of the Daśā sequence is an alternating sequence of Savya and Apasavya Cakras. The concept of Navanavāñśa is not explained, but it can be inferred when we use this in conjunction with the three-cycle sequence of the Savya and Apasavya Cakras.

After we have determined the Daśā prevailing at birth, the next important step is to determine the Daśā Balance. In this regard, we can utilize the unexpired portion of Candra Nakṣatra. Let us take Aśvinī-1 (Meṣa Navāñśa), whose duration is 100 years. The duration of a Nakṣatra Caraṇa (or Navāñśa) is 200′ (3° 20′), which is allotted to the 100 years. If one is born in 2° of Aśvinī, which is in Aśvinī Caraṇa 1, the unexpired portion is 3° 20′ - 2° = 1° 20′, which is 80′.

The balance portion of the Aśvinī-1 Āyuṣa is 80 / 120 * 100 = 66.67. The expired Daśā is 100 - 66.67 = 33.33. From a Daśā standpoint, the cumulative Daśā periods are Meṣa (7) → Vṛṣabha (23) → Mithuna (32) → Karka (53) → Siṅha (58) → Kanyā (67) → Tulā (83) → Vṛścika (90) → Dhanu (100). Since the elapsed period is 33.33 years, the Daśā must be of Karka Rāśi that starts from the 33rd year and ends in the 53rd year.

The Balance of Karka/Candra Daśā remaining at birth can be known by subtracting the expired Daśā, i.e., 33.33 from 53, which is 19.67 years. The normal duration of Karka Daśā is 21 years, of which 19.67 years is left. After completing the 66.67 years of Aśvinī-1 Daśās, if the native lives longer, he shall move to Aśvinī-2 Daśās, and thus the Daśā continues. Unlike Viñśottarī Daśā, where the Balance of elapsed Nakṣatra is used to determine the Janma Daśā, which is that of the Nakṣatra lord (as per Viñśottarī), in Kālacakra, the Balance of Nakṣatra Caraṇa (or Navāñśa) elapsed is used first to determine the Balance of Nakṣatra Caraṇa Āyuṣa, and after that, the Daśās remaining. Unlike Viñśottarī, the Daśā sequence is not fixed and is affected by the specific Nakṣatra Caraṇa, which is why the method of finding the Daśā balance is different.

The Kālacakra Daśā is dealt with in several classical texts, and important among them are Bṛhatparāśara, Phaladīpikā and Jātakapārijāta. The Daśā also finds a brief mention in the Praśnamārga. While the three classical texts

Bṛhatparāśara, Phaladīpikā and Jātakapārijāta give a detailed exposition of this Daśā, Praśnamārga states this in the context of timing death.

Kālacakra Daśā is certainly an important Āyurdaya Daśā; however, it is also a Phalita Daśā. According to Maharṣi Parāśara, in Mithuna Daśā of Meṣa Navāñśa, there is an advancement of knowledge. In Tulā Daśā of Meṣa Navāñśa, there is a rise in status and authority. These are certainly the results of Phalita and not Āyur Daśā. From Maharṣi Parāśara's narration of the results, it is adequately clear that Kālacakra is also a Phalita Daśā. However, from Āyuṣa standpoint, this is of great use in timing danger, mainly because of its special Gatis, Maṇḍūka, Marakaṭa and Siṅhavlokana, and affliction to its two important entities, the Deha and Jīva.

Praśnamārga 10.8 states that the movement of the Daśā from Mīna to Vṛścika, Kanyā to Karka, Siṅha to Mithuna, Mithuna to Siṅha and Dhanu to Meṣa, shall be a difficult period, as also the subsequent Daśā. Whether the order is regular or otherwise, the Daśā is good if there is no deviation but evil if the "movement" is at the junction of two Rāśis (evidently two Navāñśas).

Praśnamārga 10.9-10 states that, with regards to the Dakṣiṇa (Savya) group of Tārās, the first and last Rāśis indicated by the formula are Deha and Jīva, respectively. At the same time, the reverse is the case with regard to the Vāma (Apasavya) group of Tārās. If Krūras afflict Deha or Jīva, there shall be sickness. If both are afflicted, and the Daśā is also evil, then there shall be death.

Jātakapārijāta 17.7-8 states that "the five Triads beginning from respectively Aśvinī, Punarvasu, Hastā, Mūla, and Pūrvābhādra, reckon the Caraṇas from Meṣa in Pradakṣiṇa order, whereas in the four Triads commencing from Rohiṇī, Maghā, Viśākhā and Śravaṇa, reckon the quarters from Vṛścika in the Apradakṣiṇa order".

Pradakshina means circumambulating around a temple or a Devatā, which is done in a clockwise manner. Apradakṣiṇa is the reverse of that, i.e., Utkrama order. The 27 Nakṣatras are broken into nine groups of three Nakṣatras (Triads) each, like the Navatārā Cakra, whereby five Triads belong to the Savya group and four to the Apasavya group. Five Triads comprise fifteen Nakṣatras, whereas four triads comprise twelve Nakṣatras.

30.1.3.1 CONSTRUCTION

In Bṛhatparāśara 46.54-55, Maharṣi Parāśara explains that we must create two Cakras, called the Savya Cakra and Apasavya Cakra, in the South Indian Kuṇḍalī format. Only this format of the Kuṇḍalī is chosen because it shows us a pattern of the movement of Kāla through the zodiac, Savya and Apasavya, which cannot be easily seen in other formats of Kuṇḍalī, North or East Indian.

Maharṣi Parāśara states thus, "By drawing vertical and horizontal lines, prepare 2 Kuṇḍalīs, Savya and Apasavya, of 12 apartments (koṣṭhas) each. From the second koṣṭha in each Kuṇḍalī fix the Rāśis Meṣa, Vṛṣabha, Mithuna, Karka, Siṅha, Kanyā, Tulā, Vṛścika, Dhanu, Makara, Kumbha, Mīna. Then, Nakṣatras may be incorporated in the manner indicated hereafter. These Kuṇḍalīs, indicative of the 12 Rāśis, are called Kālacakra." Here, the mention is of Savya Kālacakra.

The term Kālacakra is used to define the two Cakras, Savya and Apasavya, where the flow of Kāla is Masculine → Feminine and Feminine → Masculine, respectively. In the Savya Kālacakra shown below, the Rāśis are assigned from Meṣa to Mīna from the second Koṣṭha (apartment). On the other hand, in the Apasavya Kālacakra, the Rāśis are assigned from Vṛścika to Dhanu from the second Koṣṭha (apartment).

Bṛhatparāśara 46.71-72 asks us to prepare a similar chart of 12 Koṣṭhas and from the 2nd Koṣṭha onwards, place the Rāśis from Vṛścika onwards in the reverse order, i.e., Vṛścika → Tulā and so on. This configuration is important because, in this, we are not starting from the eighth Rāśi and moving in reverse order, but we are placing the Rāśis Vṛścika onwards in the second Koṣṭha.

12 Mīna	1 Meṣa	2 Vṛṣabha	3 Mithuna	9 Dhanu	8 Vṛścika	7 Tulā	6 Kanyā
11 Kumbha	SAVYA KĀLACAKRA		4 Karka	10 Makara	APASAVYA KĀLACAKRA		5 Siṅha
10 Makara			5 Siṅha	11 Kumbha			4 Karka
9 Dhanu	8 Vṛścika	7 Tulā	6 Kanyā	12 Mīna	1 Meṣa	2 Vṛṣabha	3 Mithuna

Let us look into another important aspect, which is the assignment of Nakṣatras to this Cakra. Maharṣi explains in Bṛhatparāśara 46.56-58.,

(1) Write Aśvinī, Bharaṇī and Kṛttikā in the Savya Cakra and Rohiṇī, Mṛgaśirā, Ārdrā in the Apasavya.

(2) Then incorporate the three following Nakṣatras, Punarvasu, Puṣya and Aśleṣā in the Savya and Maghā, Pūrvāphālgunī and Uttarāphālgunī in the Apasavya.

(3) Then incorporate the three followings, Hast, Chitra and Swati in the Savya and Viśākhā, Anuradha and Jyeṣṭha in the Apasavya.

(4) Then incorporate Mūla, Pūrvāṣāṛhā and Uttarāṣāṛhā in the Savya and Śravaṇa, Dhaniṣṭhā and Śatabhiṣā in the Apasavya.

(5) Finally, incorporate the last three Nakṣatras, Pūrvābhādra, Uttarābhādra and Revatī, in the Savya Cakra.

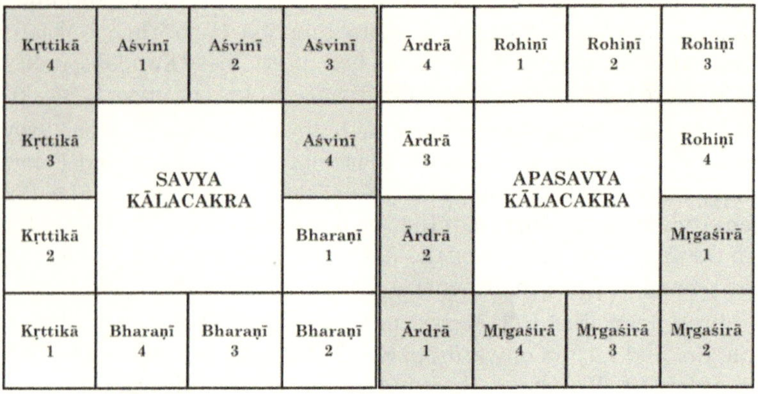
Kṛttikā 4
Aśvinī 1
Aśvinī 2
Aśvinī 3
Ārdrā 4
Rohiṇī 1
Rohiṇī 2
Rohiṇī 3
Kṛttikā 3
SAVYA KĀLACAKRA
Aśvinī 4
Ārdrā 3
APASAVYA KĀLACAKRA
Rohiṇī 4
Kṛttikā 2
Bharaṇī 1
Ārdrā 2
Mṛgaśirā 1
Kṛttikā 1
Bharaṇī 4
Bharaṇī 3
Bharaṇī 2
Ārdrā 1
Mṛgaśirā 4
Mṛgaśirā 3
Mṛgaśirā 2

We notice that the Nakṣatras are grouped into 3 (Triads) and are assigned to Savya and Apasavya groups in sequence. Why is this so? This is because each Nakṣatra has 4 Caraṇas. When all the Caraṇas of the Triads are accumulated, we arrive at 12 Caraṇas, which are precisely mapped to either a Savya or an Apasavya Chakras. Let us take an example to understand this.

The first Triad of Savya Nakṣatra consists of Aśvinī, Bharaṇī, and Kṛttikā, whose Caraṇa can be mapped to twelve Rasis of Savya Kālacakra. In the chart above, we assigned the four Caraṇas of the Nakṣatras from Aśvinī to Kṛttikā from the second Koṣṭha. This gives rise to the mapping of Asvini1 – Meṣa Navāñśa, Asvini2 – Vṛṣabha Navāñśa and so on. For Apasavya Nakṣatras, the napping is Rohini1 – Vṛścika Navāñśa, Rohini2 – Tulā Navāñśa, where the Navāñśas of the same lord is flipped.

Maharṣi Parāśara continues, "Now, there are fifteen Nakṣatras in the Savya and 12 Nakṣatras in the Apasavya. The Caraṇas of Aśvinī, Punarvasu, Hastā, Mūla, Pūrvābhādra, Kṛttikā, Aśleṣā, Svāti, Uttarāṣāṛhā and Revatī of the Savya group should be reckoned in the same manner, as the Caraṇas of Aśvinī".

There are 4 Caraṇas of each Nakṣatra, each of which has a specific treatment in Kālacakra Daśā, that we shall see later. Even within the Savya Group, only certain Nakṣatras are treated in the same manner as Aśvinī. In comparison, others are treated differently, even though they are Savya Nakṣatras. We shall see why! The following table shows the 9 Triads, of which 5 are Savya and 4 are Apasavya.

Table 16

#	Triad	Savya	Apasavya
1	1	Aśvinī	
2		Bharaṇī	
3		Kṛttikā	

#	Triad	Savya	Apasavya
4			Rohiṇī
5	2		Mṛgaśirā
6			Ārdrā
7		Punarvasu	
8	3	Puṣya	
9		Aśleṣā	
10			Maghā
11	4		Pūrvāphālgunī
12			Uttarāphālgunī
13		Hastā	
14	5	Citrā	
15		Svāti	
16			Viśākhā
17	6		Anurādhā
18			Jyeṣṭhā
19		Mūla	
20	7	Pūrvāṣāṛhā	
21		Uttarāṣāṛhā	
22			Śravaṇa
23	8		Dhaniṣṭhā
24			Śatabhiṣā
25		Pūrvābhādra	
26	9	Uttarābhādra	
27		Revatī	

There are five Triads of three Nakṣatras each in the Savya group, totalling fifteen Nakṣatras. On the other hand, there are four Triads of three Nakṣatras in the Apasavya Group, totalling 12 Nakṣatras. The Savya Nakṣatras are Sub-divided into two Subgroups: (1) The Aśvinī Group and (2) The Bharaṇī Group.

There are five Triads of the Savya group. Regarding the Savya Aśvinī group, the first and third Nakṣatras (Aśvinī and Kṛttikā) of the Savya Triads are considered together, denoting ten Nakṣatras (5 * 2). On the other hand, in the Savya Bharaṇī group, the second Nakṣatra of the Savya Triads are considered together, denoting five Nakṣatras.

Table 17

Group	Subgroup	Triad 1	Triad 2	Triad 3	Triad 4	Triad 5
Aśvinī group	**Aśvinī subgroup**	Aśvinī	Punarvasu	Hastā	Mūla	Pūrvābhādra
Bharaṇī group	**Bharaṇī subgroup**	Bharaṇī	Puṣya	Citrā	Pūrvāṣāṛhā	Uttarābhādra
Aśvinī group	**Kṛttikā subgroup**	Kṛttikā	Aśleṣā	Svāti	Uttarāṣāṛhā	Revatī

Like the two groups of Savya, we have two groups of Apasavya, the Apasavya-Rohiṇī group and the Apasavya-Mṛgaśirā group. Bṛhatparāśara 46.72 states that in this chart (Apasavya-Rohiṇī Chart), Deha and Jīva are the same for Rohiṇī, Maghā, Viśākhā and Śravaṇa, as for Rohiṇī.

Bṛhatparāśara 46.77 states that in the 4 Caraṇas of the Apasavya Nakṣatras (Apasavya-Mṛgaśirā group) Mṛgaśirā, Ārdrā, Pūrvāphālgunī, Uttarāphālgunī, Anuradha, Jyeṣṭha, Dhaniṣṭhā and Śatabhiṣā the Deha and Jīva and the Daśā Lords is the same, as for Mṛgaśirā. These two ślokas tell us the Nakṣatras that are grouped under Rohiṇī and Mṛgaśirā groups. There are four Nakṣatras in the Rohiṇī group and right in the Mṛgaśirā group, totalling twelve Apasavya Nakṣatras.

Table 18

Group	Subgroup	Triad 1	Triad 2	Triad 3	Triad 4
Rohiṇī group	**Rohiṇī subgroup**	Rohiṇī	Maghā	Viśākhā	Śravaṇa
Mṛgaśirā group	**Mṛgaśirā subgroup**	Mṛgaśirā	Pūrvāphālgunī	Anurādhā	Dhaniṣṭhā
Mṛgaśirā group	**Ārdrā subgroup**	Ārdrā	Uttarāphālgunī	Jyeṣṭhā	Śatabhiṣā

After the assignment of the Nakṣatras to the Cakras, the next important thing is the determination of Deha and Jīva and the intervening Rāśis. However, before advancing further, let us review the Apasavya Cakra.

In this regarding Maharṣi Parāśara states in Bṛhatparāśara 46.71-72, "O Brāhmaṇa! I have thus given you the description of Savya Cakra. Now, I shall describe Apasavya Cakra. Prepare a similar chart of twelve apartments, and from the second apartment onwards, place the Rāśis from Vṛścika onwards in the reverse order. In this chart, Deha and Jīva would be the same for Rohiṇī, Maghā, Viśākhā and Śravaṇa, as for Rohiṇī."

We notice that, in the Apasavya Kālacakra, the Rāśis belonging to the same Grahas are flipped where the Male and Female Rāśis are exchanged. For instance, Meṣa and Vṛścika belonging to Maṅgala are exchanged. Likewise, Vṛṣabha and Tulā belonging to Śukra are exchanged and so on.

We notice this incredible symmetry when the zodiac commences from Vṛścika and moves to Dhanu! In the figure below, we can see that the zodiac is flipped against an imaginary line crossing 0° Kumbha and 0° Siṅha. The ownership of the two Rāśis by a Graha is based on this flipping of the zodiac. This also explains why the Savya Cakra is called so, meaning Male → Female and the Apasavya is called so, meaning Female → Male.

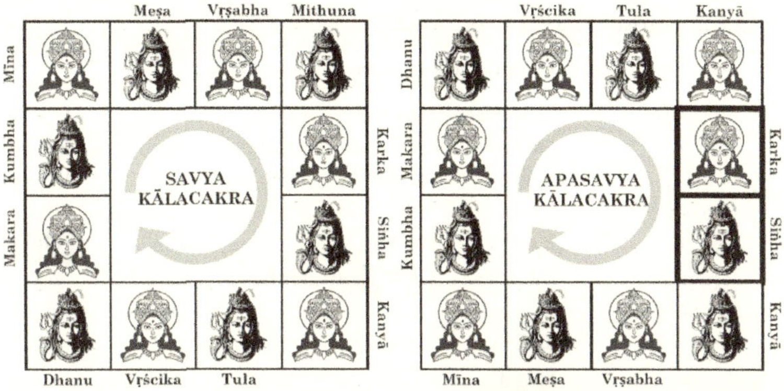

The concept of Kālacakra is based on the **divine manifestation of Ardhanārīśvara**, the form of lord Śiva and Devī Pārvati, in which they complement each other, like Sūrya and Candra, who complement each other as timekeepers. The Grahas are the manifestation of lord Śiva, the lord of the Pañcamahābhūta, the unmanifested.

Like the Ardhanārīśvara form, the Grahas endowed with both Masculine and Feminine forms in the form of their Rāśis. For instance, the Ardhanārīśvara form of Maṅgala is Meṣa-Vṛścika. In the Savya Kālacakra, the flow of Kāla is from Śiva to Śakti. Whereas, in the Apasavya Kālacakra, the flow of Kāla is from Śakti to Śiva. There is only one exception that we must know regarding the Apasavya Kālacakra. In this Kālacakra, the place of Karka and Siṅha are not exchanged.

30.1.3.2 NAKṢATRA CARAṆA NAVĀÑŚA MAPPING

Kālacakra Navāñśa is a special Navāñśa which has two versions. Version one is the Savya Navāñśa and version two is the Apasavya Navāñśa. The Savya Nakṣatras are mapped to the Savya Navāñśa, whereas the Apasavya Nakṣatras are mapped to the Apasavya Navāñśa. Regarding the mapping of Apasavya Nakṣatra Caraṇas to the Apasavya Navāñśa, it is unclear whether the Karka-Siṅha exception is applied.

For instance, for Rohiṇī3, should we jump to Karka or move to Siṅha? Maharṣi Parāśara does not explicitly state this, but this becomes clear when we map the Navanavāñśas to the Navāñśas. In my opinion, this exception should be applied. In the below table, this is indicated.

Table 19: Nakṣatra Caraṇa – Navāñśa mapping

#	Nakṣatra	Kālacakra	Caraṇa 1	Caraṇa 2	Caraṇa 3	Caraṇa 4
1	**Aśvinī**	**Savya**	Meṣa	Vṛṣabha	Mithuna	Karka
2	**Bharaṇī**	**Savya**	Siṅha	Kanyā	Tulā	Vṛścika
3	**Kṛttikā**	**Savya**	Dhanu	Makara	Kumbha	Mīna
4	**Rohiṇī**	**Apasavya**	Vṛścika	Tulā	Kanyā	Karka
5	**Mṛgaśirā**	**Apasavya**	Siṅha	Mithuna	Vṛṣabha	Meṣa
6	**Ārdrā**	**Apasavya**	Mīna	Kumbha	Makara	Dhanu
7	**Punarvasu**	**Savya**	Meṣa	Vṛṣabha	Mithuna	Karka
8	**Puṣya**	**Savya**	Siṅha	Kanyā	Tulā	Vṛścika
9	**Aśleṣā**	**Savya**	Dhanu	Makara	Kumbha	Mīna
10	**Maghā**	**Apasavya**	Vṛścika	Tulā	Kanyā	Karka
11	**Pūrvāphālgunī**	**Apasavya**	Siṅha	Mithuna	Vṛṣabha	Meṣa
12	**Uttarāphālgunī**	**Apasavya**	Mīna	Kumbha	Makara	Dhanu
13	**Hastā**	**Savya**	Meṣa	Vṛṣabha	Mithuna	Karka
14	**Citrā**	**Savya**	Siṅha	Kanyā	Tulā	Vṛścika
15	**Svāti**	**Savya**	Dhanu	Makara	Kumbha	Mīna
16	**Viśākhā**	**Apasavya**	Vṛścika	Tulā	Kanyā	Karka
17	**Anurādhā**	**Apasavya**	Siṅha	Mithuna	Vṛṣabha	Meṣa
18	**Jyeṣṭhā**	**Apasavya**	Mīna	Kumbha	Makara	Dhanu
19	**Mūla**	**Savya**	Meṣa	Vṛṣabha	Mithuna	Karka
20	**Pūrvāṣāṛhā**	**Savya**	Siṅha	Kanyā	Tulā	Vṛścika
21	**Uttarāṣāṛhā**	**Savya**	Dhanu	Makara	Kumbha	Mīna
22	**Śravaṇa**	**Apasavya**	Vṛścika	Tulā	Kanyā	Karka
23	**Dhaniṣṭhā**	**Apasavya**	Siṅha	Mithuna	Vṛṣabha	Meṣa
24	**Śatabhiṣā**	**Apasavya**	Mīna	Kumbha	Makara	Dhanu
25	**Pūrvābhādra**	**Savya**	Meṣa	Vṛṣabha	Mithuna	Karka
26	**Uttarābhādra**	**Savya**	Siṅha	Kanyā	Tulā	Vṛścika
27	**Revatī**	**Savya**	Dhanu	Makara	Kumbha	Mīna

We notice that there is a repetition of the sequence in the above table, which means that they can be compressed. We notice that every seventh Nakṣatra is grouped because the cycle repeats after every six Nakṣatras (three Savya and three Apasavya). Therefore, the 7th Nakṣatra from Aśvinī, i.e., Punarvasu, and the seventh from Punarvasu, i.e., Hastā belong to the same group, which is Aśvinī group. There are six such groups, which consist of 27 Nakṣatras.

There are five Nakṣatras each in Aśvinī, Bharaṇī and Kṛttikā groups, totalling fifteen Nakṣatras, and four Nakṣatras each in Rohiṇī Mṛgaśirā and Ārdrā groups, totalling to 12 Nakṣatras. Based on the Navanavāñśa mapping to the

Navāñśas, Aśvinī and Kṛttikā groups are further aggregated into Aśvinī group and Mṛgaśirā and Ārdrā groups into Mṛgaśirā group.

Table 20: Grouping of Nakṣatras

#	Nakṣ group	Nakṣ	Sav-Apa	Pāda1	Pāda2	Pāda3	Pāda4
1	**Aśvinī**	Aśv, Pun, Has, Mūl, PBh	Sav Aśv	Meṣ	Vṛṣ	Mit	Kar
2	**Bharaṇī**	Bha, Puṣ, Cit, PĀṣ, UBh	Sav Bha	Siṅ	Kan	Tul	Vṛś
3	**Kṛttikā**	Kṛt, Aśl, Svā, UĀṣ, Rev	Sav Aśv	Dha	Mak	Kum	Mīn
4	**Rohiṇī**	Roh, Mag, Viś, Śra	Apa Roh	Vṛś	Tul	Kan	Kar
5	**Mṛgaśirā**	Mṛg, PPh, Anu, Dha	Apa Mṛg	Siṅ	Mit	Vṛṣ	Meṣ
6	**Ārdrā**	Ārd, UPh, Jye, Śat	Apa Mṛg	Mīn	Kum	Mak	Dha

30.1.3.3
THE MAHĀDAŚĀ

Let us now delve deeper into the Mahādaśās, which are constituted by nine Navanavāñśas contained in a Navāñśa (or Nakṣatra Caraṇa). Each Navāñśa has 9 Daśās, and each Daśā has 9 Antardaśā. There are four groups of Nakṣatras, Savya-Aśvinī, Savya-Bharaṇī, Apasavya-Rohiṇī and Apasavya-Mṛgaśirā, and each of them has 4 Caraṇas, which give rise to 16 different sequences of nine Navanavāñśas.

These sequences are formed by alternating cycles of Krama-Savya and Krama-Apasavya for Savya Nakṣatras and Utkrama Savya and Utkrama-Apasavya for Apasavya Nakṣatras. For every 4 Caraṇas of a Nakṣatra, there are 36 Navanavāñśa, which are formed by three cycles of Savya and Apasavya Kālacakra.

As mentioned before, in the Apasavya Kālacakra, the Karka-Siṅha order is fixed; this gives rise to a sequence of Kanyā → Karka → Siṅha → Mithuna (Krama) or Mithuna → Siṅha → Karka → Kanyā (Utkrama). These give rise to the Gatis (jumps) called the Maṇḍūka and Marakaṭa. The jumps from Savya to Apasavya or vice-versa give rise to Siṅhavlokana Gati.

30.1.3.3.1
SAVYA AŚVINĪ GROUP

(AŚVINĪ, PUNARVASU, HASTĀ, MŪLA, PŪRVĀBHĀDRA), (KṚTTIKĀ, AŚLEṢĀ, SVĀTI, UTTARĀṢĀṚHĀ, REVATĪ)

THE SEQUENCE OF THE 3 CYCLES IS
KRAMA-SAVYA → KRAMA-APASAVYA → KRAMA-SAVYA

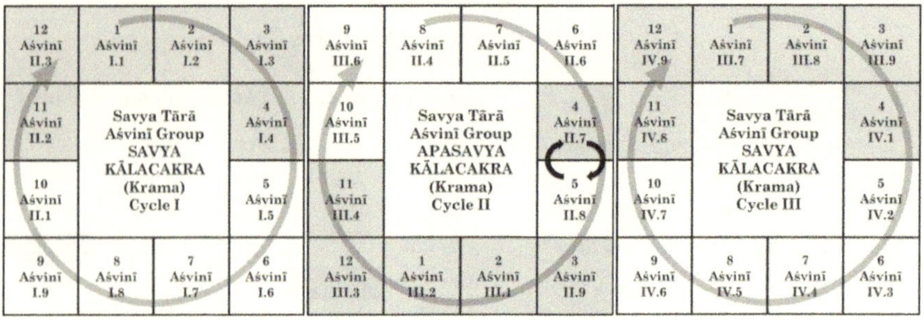

Table 21: Savya-Aśvinī Group

	1 Deha	2	3	4	5	6	7	8	9 Jīva	Age
Pada1	Meṣ	Vṛṣ	Mit	Kar	Siṅ	Kan	Tul	Vṛś	Dha	
	7	16	9	21	5	9	16	7	10	100
Pada2	Mak	Kum	Mīn	Vṛś^	Tul^	Kan^	Kar!^	Siṅ!^	Mit^	
	4	4	10	7	16	9	21	5	9	85
Pada3	Vṛṣ^	Meṣ^	Mīn^	Kum^	Mak^	Dha^	Meṣ	Vṛṣ	Mit	
	16	7	10	4	4	10	7	16	9	83
Pada4	Kar	Siṅ	Kan	Tul	Vṛś	Dha	Mak	Kum	Mīn	
	21	5	9	16	7	10	4	4	10	86

30.1.3.3.2
SAVYA BHARAṆĪ GROUP

BHARAṆĪ, PUṢYA, CITRĀ, PŪRVĀṢĀṚHĀ, UTTARĀBHĀDRA.
THE SEQUENCE OF THE 3 CYCLES IS
KRAMA-APASAVYA → KRAMA-SAVYA → KRAMA-APASAVYA

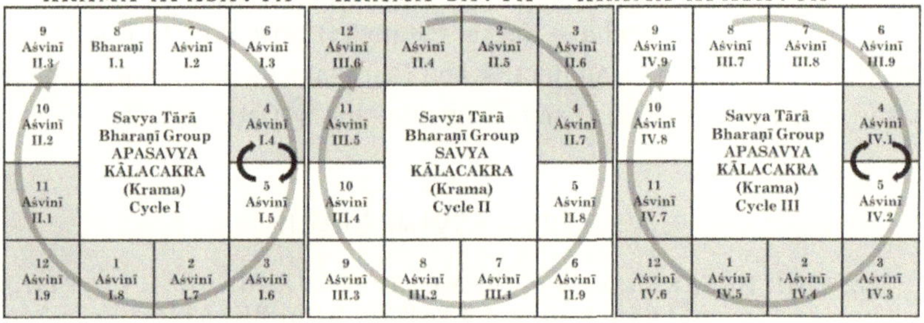

Table 22

	1 Deha	2	3	4	5	6	7	8	9 Jīva	
Pada1	Vṛś^	Tul^	Kan^	Kar!^	Siṅ!^	Mit^	Vṛṣ^	Meṣ^	Mīn^	
	7	16	9	21	5	9	16	7	10	100
Pada2	Kum^	Mak^	Dha^	Meṣ	Vṛṣ	Mit	Kar	Siṅ	Kan	
	4	4	10	7	16	9	21	5	9	85

	1 Deha	2	3	4	5	6	7	8	9 Jīva	
Pada3	Tul	Vṛś	Dha	Mak	Kum	Mīn	Vṛś^	Tul^	Kan^	
	16	7	10	4	4	10	7	16	9	83
Pada4	Kar!^	Siṅ!^	Mit^	Vṛṣ^	Meṣ^	Mīn^	Kum^	Mak^	Dha^	
	21	5	9	16	7	10	4	4	10	86

30.1.3.3.3
APASAVYA ROHIṆĪ GROUP

ROHIṆĪ, MAGHĀ, VIŚĀKHĀ, ŚRAVAṆA

THE SEQUENCE OF THE 3 CYCLES IS

UTKRAMA-APASAVYA → UTKRAMA-SAVYA → UTKRAMA-APASAVYA

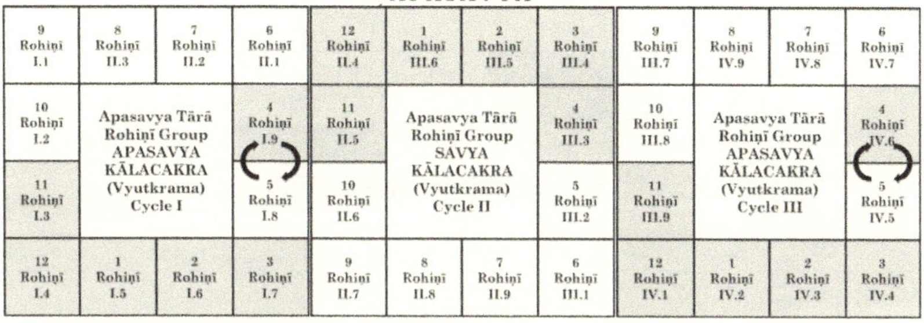
9 Rohiṇī I.1
8 Rohiṇī II.3
7 Rohiṇī II.2
6 Rohiṇī II.1
12 Rohiṇī II.4
1 Rohiṇī III.6
2 Rohiṇī III.5
3 Rohiṇī III.4
9 Rohiṇī III.7
8 Rohiṇī IV.9
7 Rohiṇī IV.8
6 Rohiṇī IV.7
10 Rohiṇī I.2
Apasavya Tārā Rohiṇī Group APASAVYA KĀLACAKRA (Vyutkrama) Cycle I
4 Rohiṇī I.9
11 Rohiṇī II.5
Apasavya Tārā Rohiṇī Group SAVYA KĀLACAKRA (Vyutkrama) Cycle II
4 Rohiṇī III.3
10 Rohiṇī III.8
Apasavya Tārā Rohiṇī Group APASAVYA KĀLACAKRA (Vyutkrama) Cycle III
4 Rohiṇī IV.6
11 Rohiṇī I.3
5 Rohiṇī I.8
10 Rohiṇī II.6
5 Rohiṇī III.2
11 Rohiṇī III.9
5 Rohiṇī IV.5
12 Rohiṇī I.4
1 Rohiṇī I.5
2 Rohiṇī I.6
3 Rohiṇī I.7
9 Rohiṇī II.7
8 Rohiṇī II.8
7 Rohiṇī II.9
6 Rohiṇī III.1
12 Rohiṇī IV.1
1 Rohiṇī IV.2
2 Rohiṇī IV.3
3 Rohiṇī IV.4

Table 23

	1 Jīva	2	3	4	5	6	7	8	9 Deha	
Pada1	Dha	Mak	Kum	Mīn	Meṣ	Vṛṣ	Mit	Siṅ!	Kar!	
	10	4	4	10	7	16	9	5	21	86
Pada2	Kan	Tul	Vṛś	Mīn^	Kum^	Mak^	Dha^	Vṛś^	Tul^	
	9	16	7	10	4	4	10	7	16	83
Pada3	Kan^	Siṅ^	Kar^	Mit^	Vṛṣ^	Meṣ^	Dha	Mak	Kum	
	9	5	21	9	16	7	10	4	4	85
Pada4	Mīn	Meṣ	Vṛṣ	Mit	Siṅ!	Kar!	Kan	Tul	Vṛś	
	10	7	16	9	5	21	9	16	7	100

30.1.3.3.4
APASAVYA MṚGAŚIRĀ GROUP

(MṚGAŚIRĀ, PŪRVĀPHĀLGUNĪ, ANURĀDHĀ, DHANIṢṬHĀ), (ĀRDRĀ, UTTARĀPHĀLGUNĪ, JYEṢṬHĀ, ŚATABHIṢĀ).

THE SEQUENCE OF THE 3 CYCLES IS

UTKRAMA-SAVYA → UTKRAMA-APASAVYA → UTKRAMA-SAVYA

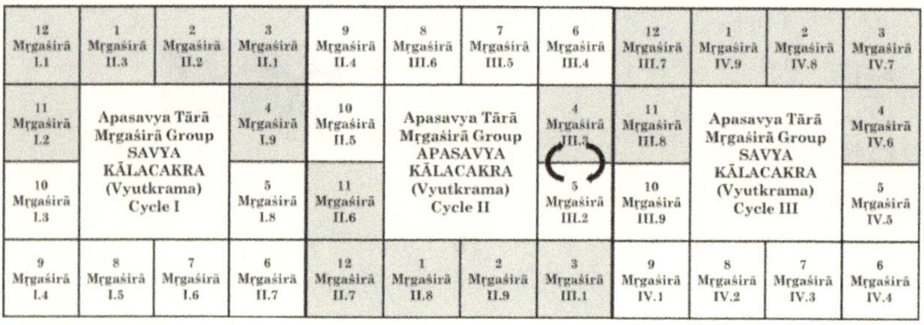
12 Mṛgaśirā I.1
1 Mṛgaśirā II.3
2 Mṛgaśirā II.2
3 Mṛgaśirā II.1
9 Mṛgaśirā II.4
8 Mṛgaśirā III.6
7 Mṛgaśirā III.5
6 Mṛgaśirā III.4
12 Mṛgaśirā III.7
1 Mṛgaśirā IV.9
2 Mṛgaśirā IV.8
3 Mṛgaśirā IV.7
11 Mṛgaśirā I.2
Apasavya Tārā Mṛgaśirā Group SAVYA KĀLACAKRA (Vyutkrama) Cycle I
4 Mṛgaśirā I.9
10 Mṛgaśirā II.5
Apasavya Tārā Mṛgaśirā Group APASAVYA KĀLACAKRA (Vyutkrama) Cycle II
4 Mṛgaśirā III.3
11 Mṛgaśirā III.8
Apasavya Tārā Mṛgaśirā Group SAVYA KĀLACAKRA (Vyutkrama) Cycle III
4 Mṛgaśirā IV.6
10 Mṛgaśirā I.3
5 Mṛgaśirā I.8
11 Mṛgaśirā II.6
5 Mṛgaśirā III.2
10 Mṛgaśirā III.9
5 Mṛgaśirā IV.5
9 Mṛgaśirā I.4
8 Mṛgaśirā I.5
7 Mṛgaśirā I.6
6 Mṛgaśirā II.7
12 Mṛgaśirā II.7
1 Mṛgaśirā II.8
2 Mṛgaśirā II.9
3 Mṛgaśirā III.1
9 Mṛgaśirā IV.1
8 Mṛgaśirā IV.2
7 Mṛgaśirā IV.3
6 Mṛgaśirā IV.4

Table 24

	1 Jīva	2	3	4	5	6	7	8	9 Deha	
Pada1	Mīn^	Kum^	Mak^	Dha^	Vṛś^	Tul^	Kan^	Siṅ^	Kar^	
	10	4	4	10	7	16	9	5	21	86
Pada2	Mit^	Vṛṣ^	Meṣ^	Dha	Mak	Kum	Mīn	Meṣ	Vṛṣ	
	9	16	7	10	4	4	10	7	16	83
Pada3	Mit	Siṅ!	Kar!	Kan	Tul	Vṛś	Mīn^	Kum^	Mak^	
	9	5	21	9	16	7	10	4	4	85
Pada4	Dha^	Vṛś^	Tul^	Kan^	Siṅ^	Kar^	Mit^	Vṛṣ^	Meṣ^	
	10	7	16	9	5	21	9	16	7	100

The table below shows the consolidated information of the 9 Daśās (Navanavāñśas) for one born in any of the 4 Caraṇas of 27 Nakṣatras, i.e., 108 Caraṇas. From this table, one can easily determine the Daśā at birth as well as the forthcoming Daśās. This also gives, at a snapshot level, the classification of Nakṣatras into Savya and Apasavya (S/A), the grouping of the Nakṣatras into Aśvinī, Bharaṇī, Rohiṇī and Mṛgaśirā groups, and the Navāñśas mapped to the Nakṣatra Caraṇas.

As we have seen before, the Navāñśa mapping of the Savya Nakṣatra is from Meṣa to Mīna, whereas for Apasavya Nakṣatra, the mapping is from Vṛścika to Dhanu. Most importantly, the Daśā for the different Caraṇas are marked with KS, KA, US, and UA, which respectively stand for Krama-Savya, Krama-Apasavya, Utkrama-Savya and Utkrama-Apasavya. The difference between the Savya and Apasavya has been previously explained. Now, Krama stands for movement in a regular or clockwise direction, whereas Utkrama stands for reverse or anti-clockwise direction.

For Daśā sequence determination, the counting is done in Krama, i.e., clockwise direction for Savya Nakṣatras (Aśvinī and Bharaṇī groups). In contrast, the counting is Utkrama for Apasavya Nakṣatras (Rohiṇī and Mṛgaśirā groups). We notice that both Savya and Apasavya Nakṣatras have Savya and Apasavya cycles, but Krama is only applicable to Savya and Utkrama Apasavya.

Now, why is it important to know whether the Daśā is Krama or Utkrama, Savya or Apasavya? The Krama-Utkrama order is needed for understanding the sequence, viz., Krama-Savya = Meṣa→ Mīna and Krama-Apasavya = Vṛścika →

Dhanu, which are applicable to Savya Tārās. Whereas Utkrama-Savya = Mīna → Meṣa and Utkrama-Apasavya = Dhanu → Vṛścika, that is applicable to Apasavya Tārās.

The Savya-Apasavya classification is needed in the order of Daśā, Antardaśā, Pratyantardaśā and other subperiods. The Daśā sequence is different for the same Navāñśa, say Meṣa Navāñśa, depending on whether the Navāñśa falls in Savya Cakra or the Apasavya Cakra. For instance, let us take Meṣa Mahādaśā! What should be the Antardaśā sequence of this Daśā? We notice that the Daśā of Aśvinī1 (Meṣa Navāñśa is Meṣ → Vṛṣ → Mit → Kar → Siṅ → Kan → Tul → Vṛś → Dha, whereas the Daśā of Mṛgaśirā4 (also Meṣa Navāñśa) is Dha → Vṛś → Tul → Kan → Siṅ → Kar → Mit → Vṛṣ → Meṣ.

We notice that the sequence is reversed for the same Meṣa Navāñśa. Why? This is because Aśvinī1 Meṣa is Savya-Meṣa, whereas Mṛgaśirā4 Meṣa is Apasavya Meṣa. The Savya-Apasavya classification of the Navāñśa affects the "direction" of the sequence, although the sequence is not altered. In both the cases of Meṣa, the sequence is the same, i.e., Meṣ → Vṛṣ → Mit → Kar → Siṅ → Kan → Tul → Vṛś → Dha, but the direction is reversed.

This principle is followed in Antardaśā and all the subperiods as well. But, for the Antardaśās and other subperiods, the information on which Daśā is not adequate; we also need to know whether the Daśā belongs to Savya or Apasavya Cakra. For Meṣa Navāñśa, this is not a problem because all the Daśā are of Savya quality, but this is not the same for all the other Navāñśas. Let us take Ashvini2, where the cycle changes from Savya to Apasavya.

Ashvini2 is mapped to Vṛṣabha Navāñśa, which has the 9 Navāñśas Mak → Kum → Mīn → Vṛś → Tul → Kan → Kar → Siṅ → Mit. In this sequence, "Mak → Kum → Mīn" belong to Savya Cakra, and "Vṛś → Tul → Kan → Kar → Siṅ → Mit" belong to Apasavya Cakra. Let's find the Antardaśā of Vṛṣabha Daśā. To find the Antardaśā, we must know whether Vṛṣabha is Savya-Vṛṣabha or Apasavya-Vṛṣabha. Since we know that in this sequence, Vṛṣabha is Apasavya, the sequence is Mit → Siṅ → Kar → Kan → Tul → Vṛś → Mīn → Kum → Mak.

In the table below, the Rāśis are denoted by their number, and they are prefixed with K/U for Krama/Utkrama and S/A for Savya/Apasavya. According to the table, Savya Meṣa Daśā, which is denoted by "S1" Navāñśa, the Antardaśā sequence is KS1 → KS2 → KS3 → KS4 → KS5 → KS6 → KS7 → KS8 → KS9. On the other hand, for Apasavya Meṣa, which is denoted by "A1" Navāñśa, the Antardaśā sequence is US9 → US8 → US7 → US6 → US5 → US4 → US3 → US2 → US1. We notice that the sequence is reversed for Apasavya Meṣa. The same logic should be utilized to determine the Pratyantara or further subperiods.

Table 25

#	Nakṣ	Pāda	SA	Grp	D9	Mahādaśā								
						1	2	3	4	5	6	7	8	9
1	Aśv	1	S	Aśv	S1	KS 1	KS 2	KS 3	KS 4	KS 5	KS 6	KS 7	KS 8	KS 9
2	Aśv	2	S	Aśv	S2	KS 10	KS 11	KS 12	KA 8	KA 7	KA 6	KA 4	KA 5	KA 3

#	Nakṣ	Pāda	SA	Grp	D9	Mahādaśā								
						1	2	3	4	5	6	7	8	9
3	Aśv	3	S	Aśv	S3	KA 2	KA 1	KA 12	KA 11	KA 10	KA 9	KS 1	KS 2	KS 3
4	Aśv	4	S	Aśv	S4	KS 4	KS 5	KS 6	KS 7	KS 8	KS 9	KS 10	KS 11	KS 12
5	Bha	1	S	Bha	S5	KA 8	KA 7	KA 6	KA 4	KA 5	KA 3	KA 2	KA 1	KA 12
6	Bha	2	S	Bha	S6	KA 11	KA 10	KA 9	KS 1	KS 2	KS 3	KS 4	KS 5	KS 6
7	Bha	3	S	Bha	S7	KS 7	KS 8	KS 9	KS 10	KS 11	KS 12	KA 8	KA 7	KA 6
8	Bha	4	S	Bha	S8	KA 4	KA 5	KA 3	KA 2	KA 1	KA 12	KA 11	KA 10	KA 9
9	Kṛt	1	S	Aśv	S9	KS 1	KS 2	KS 3	KS 4	KS 5	KS 6	KS 7	KS 8	KS 9
10	Kṛt	2	S	Aśv	S10	KS 10	KS 11	KS 12	KA 8	KA 7	KA 6	KA 4	KA 5	KA 3
11	Kṛt	3	S	Aśv	S11	KA 2	KA 1	KA 12	KA 11	KA 10	KA 9	KS 1	KS 2	KS 3
12	Kṛt	4	S	Aśv	S12	KS 4	KS 5	KS 6	KS 7	KS 8	KS 9	KS 10	KS 11	KS 12
13	Roh	1	A	Roh	A8	UA 9	UA 10	UA 11	UA 12	UA 1	UA 2	UA 3	UA 5	UA 4
14	Roh	2	A	Roh	A7	UA 6	UA 7	UA 8	US 12	US 11	US 10	US 9	US 8	US 7
15	Roh	3	A	Roh	A6	US 6	US 5	US 4	US 3	US 2	US 1	UA 9	UA 10	UA 11
16	Roh	4	A	Roh	A5	UA 12	UA 1	UA 2	UA 3	UA 5	UA 4	UA 6	UA 7	UA 8
17	Mṛg	1	A	Mṛg	A4	US 12	US 11	US 10	US 9	US 8	US 7	US 6	US 5	US 4
18	Mṛg	2	A	Mṛg	A3	US 3	US 2	US 1	UA 9	UA 10	UA 11	UA 12	UA 1	UA 2
19	Mṛg	3	A	Mṛg	A2	UA 3	UA 5	UA 4	UA 6	UA 7	UA 8	US 12	US 11	US 10
20	Mṛg	4	A	Mṛg	A1	US 9	US 8	US 7	US 6	US 5	US 4	US 3	US 2	US 1
21	Ārd	1	A	Mṛg	A12	US 12	US 11	US 10	US 9	US 8	US 7	US 6	US 5	US 4
22	Ārd	2	A	Mṛg	A11	US 3	US 2	US 1	UA 9	UA 10	UA 11	UA 12	UA 1	UA 2
23	Ārd	3	A	Mṛg	A10	UA 3	UA 5	UA 4	UA 6	UA 7	UA 8	US 12	US 11	US 10
24	Ārd	4	A	Mṛg	A9	US 9	US 8	US 7	US 6	US 5	US 4	US 3	US 2	US 1
25	Pun	1	S	Aśv	S1	KS 1	KS 2	KS 3	KS 4	KS 5	KS 6	KS 7	KS 8	KS 9
26	Pun	2	S	Aśv	S2	KS 10	KS 11	KS 12	KA 8	KA 7	KA 6	KA 4	KA 5	KA 3
27	Pun	3	S	Aśv	S3	KA 2	KA 1	KA 12	KA 11	KA 10	KA 9	KS 1	KS 2	KS 3
28	Pun	4	S	Aśv	S4	KS 4	KS 5	KS 6	KS 7	KS 8	KS 9	KS 10	KS 11	KS 12

#	Nakṣ	Pāda	SA	Grp	D9	Mahādaśā 1	2	3	4	5	6	7	8	9
29	Puṣ	1	S	Bha	S5	KA 8	KA 7	KA 6	KA 4	KA 5	KA 3	KA 2	KA 1	KA 12
30	Puṣ	2	S	Bha	S6	KA 11	KA 10	KA 9	KS 1	KS 2	KS 3	KS 4	KS 5	KS 6
31	Puṣ	3	S	Bha	S7	KS 7	KS 8	KS 9	KS 10	KS 11	KS 12	KA 8	KA 7	KA 6
32	Puṣ	4	S	Bha	S8	KA 4	KA 5	KA 3	KA 2	KA 1	KA 12	KA 11	KA 10	KA 9
33	Aśl	1	S	Aśv	S9	KS 1	KS 2	KS 3	KS 4	KS 5	KS 6	KS 7	KS 8	KS 9
34	Aśl	2	S	Aśv	S10	KS 10	KS 11	KS 12	KA 8	KA 7	KA 6	KA 4	KA 5	KA 3
35	Aśl	3	S	Aśv	S11	KA 2	KA 1	KA 12	KA 11	KA 10	KA 9	KS 1	KS 2	KS 3
36	Aśl	4	S	Aśv	S12	KS 4	KS 5	KS 6	KS 7	KS 8	KS 9	KS 10	KS 11	KS 12
37	Mag	1	A	Roh	A8	UA 9	UA 10	UA 11	UA 12	UA 1	UA 2	UA 3	UA 5	UA 4
38	Mag	2	A	Roh	A7	UA 6	UA 7	UA 8	US 12	US 11	US 10	US 9	US 8	US 7
39	Mag	3	A	Roh	A6	US 6	US 5	US 4	US 3	US 2	US 1	UA 9	UA 10	UA 11
40	Mag	4	A	Roh	A5	UA 12	UA 1	UA 2	UA 3	UA 5	UA 4	UA 6	UA 7	UA 8
41	PPh	1	A	Mṛg	A4	US 12	US 11	US 10	US 9	US 8	US 7	US 6	US 5	US 4
42	PPh	2	A	Mṛg	A3	US 3	US 2	US 1	UA 9	UA 10	UA 11	UA 12	UA 1	UA 2
43	PPh	3	A	Mṛg	A2	UA 3	UA 5	UA 4	UA 6	UA 7	UA 8	US 12	US 11	US 10
44	PPh	4	A	Mṛg	A1	US 9	US 8	US 7	US 6	US 5	US 4	US 3	US 2	US 1
45	UPh	1	A	Mṛg	A12	US 12	US 11	US 10	US 9	US 8	US 7	US 6	US 5	US 4
46	UPh	2	A	Mṛg	A11	US 3	US 2	US 1	UA 9	UA 10	UA 11	UA 12	UA 1	UA 2
47	UPh	3	A	Mṛg	A10	UA 3	UA 5	UA 4	UA 6	UA 7	UA 8	US 12	US 11	US 10
48	UPh	4	A	Mṛg	A9	US 9	US 8	US 7	US 6	US 5	US 4	US 3	US 2	US 1
49	Has	1	S	Aśv	S1	KS 1	KS 2	KS 3	KS 4	KS 5	KS 6	KS 7	KS 8	KS 9
50	Has	2	S	Aśv	S2	KS 10	KS 11	KS 12	KA 8	KA 7	KA 6	KA 4	KA 5	KA 3
51	Has	3	S	Aśv	S3	KA 2	KA 1	KA 12	KA 11	KA 10	KA 9	KS 1	KS 2	KS 3
52	Has	4	S	Aśv	S4	KS 4	KS 5	KS 6	KS 7	KS 8	KS 9	KS 10	KS 11	KS 12
53	Cit	1	S	Bha	S5	KA 8	KA 7	KA 6	KA 4	KA 5	KA 3	KA 2	KA 1	KA 12
54	Cit	2	S	Bha	S6	KA 11	KA 10	KA 9	KS 1	KS 2	KS 3	KS 4	KS 5	KS 6
55	Cit	3	S	Bha	S7	KS 7	KS 8	KS 9	KS 10	KS 11	KS 12	KA 8	KA 7	KA 6

#	Nakṣ	Pāda	SA	Grp	D9	Mahādaśā								
						1	2	3	4	5	6	7	8	9
56	Cit	4	S	Bha	S8	KA 4	KA 5	KA 3	KA 2	KA 1	KA 12	KA 11	KA 10	KA 9
57	Svā	1	S	Aśv	S9	KS 1	KS 2	KS 3	KS 4	KS 5	KS 6	KS 7	KS 8	KS 9
58	Svā	2	S	Aśv	S10	KS 10	KS 11	KS 12	KA 8	KA 7	KA 6	KA 4	KA 5	KA 3
59	Svā	3	S	Aśv	S11	KA 2	KA 1	KA 12	KA 11	KA 10	KA 9	KS 1	KS 2	KS 3
60	Svā	4	S	Aśv	S12	KS 4	KS 5	KS 6	KS 7	KS 8	KS 9	KS 10	KS 11	KS 12
61	Viś	1	A	Roh	A8	UA 9	UA 10	UA 11	UA 12	UA 1	UA 2	UA 3	UA 5	UA 4
62	Viś	2	A	Roh	A7	UA 6	UA 7	UA 8	US 12	US 11	US 10	US 9	US 8	US 7
63	Viś	3	A	Roh	A6	US 6	US 5	US 4	US 3	US 2	US 1	UA 9	UA 10	UA 11
64	Viś	4	A	Roh	A5	UA 12	UA 1	UA 2	UA 3	UA 5	UA 4	UA 6	UA 7	UA 8
65	Anu	1	A	Mṛg	A4	US 12	US 11	US 10	US 9	US 8	US 7	US 6	US 5	US 4
66	Anu	2	A	Mṛg	A3	US 3	US 2	US 1	UA 9	UA 10	UA 11	UA 12	UA 1	UA 2
67	Anu	3	A	Mṛg	A2	UA 3	UA 5	UA 4	UA 6	UA 7	UA 8	US 12	US 11	US 10
68	Anu	4	A	Mṛg	A1	US 9	US 8	US 7	US 6	US 5	US 4	US 3	US 2	US 1
69	Jye	1	A	Mṛg	A12	US 12	US 11	US 10	US 9	US 8	US 7	US 6	US 5	US 4
70	Jye	2	A	Mṛg	A11	US 3	US 2	US 1	UA 9	UA 10	UA 11	UA 12	UA 1	UA 2
71	Jye	3	A	Mṛg	A10	UA 3	UA 5	UA 4	UA 6	UA 7	UA 8	US 12	US 11	US 10
72	Jye	4	A	Mṛg	A9	US 9	US 8	US 7	US 6	US 5	US 4	US 3	US 2	US 1
73	Mūl	1	S	Aśv	S1	KS 1	KS 2	KS 3	KS 4	KS 5	KS 6	KS 7	KS 8	KS 9
74	Mūl	2	S	Aśv	S2	KS 10	KS 11	KS 12	KA 8	KA 7	KA 6	KA 4	KA 5	KA 3
75	Mūl	3	S	Aśv	S3	KA 2	KA 1	KA 12	KA 11	KA 10	KA 9	KS 1	KS 2	KS 3
76	Mūl	4	S	Aśv	S4	KS 4	KS 5	KS 6	KS 7	KS 8	KS 9	KS 10	KS 11	KS 12
77	PĀṣ	1	S	Bha	S5	KA 8	KA 7	KA 6	KA 4	KA 5	KA 3	KA 2	KA 1	KA 12
78	PĀṣ	2	S	Bha	S6	KA 11	KA 10	KA 9	KS 1	KS 2	KS 3	KS 4	KS 5	KS 6
79	PĀṣ	3	S	Bha	S7	KS 7	KS 8	KS 9	KS 10	KS 11	KS 12	KA 8	KA 7	KA 6
80	PĀṣ	4	S	Bha	S8	KA 4	KA 5	KA 3	KA 2	KA 1	KA 12	KA 11	KA 10	KA 9
81	UĀṣ	1	S	Aśv	S9	KS 1	KS 2	KS 3	KS 4	KS 5	KS 6	KS 7	KS 8	KS 9

#	Nakṣ	Pāda	SA	Grp	D9	Mahādaśā								
						1	2	3	4	5	6	7	8	9
82	UĀṣ	2	S	Aśv	S10	KS 10	KS 11	KS 12	KA 8	KA 7	KA 6	KA 4	KA 5	KA 3
83	UĀṣ	3	S	Aśv	S11	KA 2	KA 1	KA 12	KA 11	KA 10	KA 9	KS 1	KS 2	KS 3
84	UĀṣ	4	S	Aśv	S12	KS 4	KS 5	KS 6	KS 7	KS 8	KS 9	KS 10	KS 11	KS 12
85	Śra	1	A	Roh	A8	UA 9	UA 10	UA 11	UA 12	UA 1	UA 2	UA 3	UA 5	UA 4
86	Śra	2	A	Roh	A7	UA 6	UA 7	UA 8	US 12	US 11	US 10	US 9	US 8	US 7
87	Śra	3	A	Roh	A6	US 6	US 5	US 4	US 3	US 2	US 1	UA 9	UA 10	UA 11
88	Śra	4	A	Roh	A5	UA 12	UA 1	UA 2	UA 3	UA 5	UA 4	UA 6	UA 7	UA 8
89	Dha	1	A	Mṛg	A4	US 12	US 11	US 10	US 9	US 8	US 7	US 6	US 5	US 4
90	Dha	2	A	Mṛg	A3	US 3	US 2	US 1	UA 9	UA 10	UA 11	UA 12	UA 1	UA 2
91	Dha	3	A	Mṛg	A2	UA 3	UA 5	UA 4	UA 6	UA 7	UA 8	US 12	US 11	US 10
92	Dha	4	A	Mṛg	A1	US 9	US 8	US 7	US 6	US 5	US 4	US 3	US 2	US 1
93	Śat	1	A	Mṛg	A12	US 12	US 11	US 10	US 9	US 8	US 7	US 6	US 5	US 4
94	Śat	2	A	Mṛg	A11	US 3	US 2	US 1	UA 9	UA 10	UA 11	UA 12	UA 1	UA 2
95	Śat	3	A	Mṛg	A10	UA 3	UA 5	UA 4	UA 6	UA 7	UA 8	US 12	US 11	US 10
96	Śat	4	A	Mṛg	A9	US 9	US 8	US 7	US 6	US 5	US 4	US 3	US 2	US 1
97	PBh	1	S	Aśv	S1	KS 1	KS 2	KS 3	KS 4	KS 5	KS 6	KS 7	KS 8	KS 9
98	PBh	2	S	Aśv	S2	KS 10	KS 11	KS 12	KA 8	KA 7	KA 6	KA 4	KA 5	KA 3
99	PBh	3	S	Aśv	S3	KA 2	KA 1	KA 12	KA 11	KA 10	KA 9	KS 1	KS 2	KS 3
100	PBh	4	S	Aśv	S4	KS 4	KS 5	KS 6	KS 7	KS 8	KS 9	KS 10	KS 11	KS 12
101	UBh	1	S	Bha	S5	KA 8	KA 7	KA 6	KA 4	KA 5	KA 3	KA 2	KA 1	KA 12
102	UBh	2	S	Bha	S6	KA 11	KA 10	KA 9	KS 1	KS 2	KS 3	KS 4	KS 5	KS 6
103	UBh	3	S	Bha	S7	KS 7	KS 8	KS 9	KS 10	KS 11	KS 12	KA 8	KA 7	KA 6
104	UBh	4	S	Bha	S8	KA 4	KA 5	KA 3	KA 2	KA 1	KA 12	KA 11	KA 10	KA 9
105	Rev	1	S	Aśv	S9	KS 1	KS 2	KS 3	KS 4	KS 5	KS 6	KS 7	KS 8	KS 9
106	Rev	2	S	Aśv	S10	KS 10	KS 11	KS 12	KA 8	KA 7	KA 6	KA 4	KA 5	KA 3
107	Rev	3	S	Aśv	S11	KA 2	KA 1	KA 12	KA 11	KA 10	KA 9	KS 1	KS 2	KS 3
108	Rev	4	S	Aśv	S12	KS 4	KS 5	KS 6	KS 7	KS 8	KS 9	KS 10	KS 11	KS 12

The above table might appear difficult to understand, as it narrates the sequences in terms of codes KS, KA, US and UA. Therefore, the table is simplified below, where the Rāśi names substitute the codes. The table below is of more practical usage for the determination of the Daśās based on one's Candra Nakṣatra Caraṇa. The table also clearly indicates the Deha and Jīva. For Savya Nakṣatra, the Deha and Jīva are the 1st and the 9th Rāśis, respectively, which is reversed for the Apasavya Nakṣatras.

Table 26

#	Nakṣ	Pāda	SA	Grp	Aṅśa	Mahādaśā									Deha	Jīva
						1	2	3	4	5	6	7	8	9		
1	Aśv	1	S	Aśv	Meṣ	Meṣ	Vṛṣ	Mit	Kar	Siṅ	Kan	Tul	Vṛś	Dha	**Meṣ**	**Dha**
2	Aśv	2	S	Aśv	Vṛṣ	Mak	Kum	Mīn	Vṛś	Tul	Kan	Kar	Siṅ	Mit	**Mak**	**Mit**
3	Aśv	3	S	Aśv	Mit	Vṛṣ	Meṣ	Mīn	Kum	Mak	Dha	Meṣ	Vṛṣ	Mit	**Vṛṣ**	**Mit**
4	Aśv	4	S	Aśv	Kar	Kar	Siṅ	Kan	Tul	Vṛś	Dha	Mak	Kum	Mīn	**Kar**	**Mīn**
5	Bha	1	S	Bha	Siṅ	Vṛś	Tul	Kan	Kar	Siṅ	Mit	Vṛṣ	Meṣ	Mīn	**Vṛś**	**Mīn**
6	Bha	2	S	Bha	Kan	Kum	Mak	Dha	Meṣ	Vṛṣ	Mit	Kar	Siṅ	Kan	**Kum**	**Kan**
7	Bha	3	S	Bha	Tul	Tul	Vṛś	Dha	Mak	Kum	Mīn	Vṛś	Tul	Kan	**Tul**	**Kan**
8	Bha	4	S	Bha	Vṛś	Kar	Siṅ	Mit	Vṛṣ	Meṣ	Mīn	Kum	Mak	Dha	**Kar**	**Dha**
9	Kṛt	1	S	Aśv	Dha	Meṣ	Vṛṣ	Mit	Kar	Siṅ	Kan	Tul	Vṛś	Dha	**Meṣ**	**Dha**
10	Kṛt	2	S	Aśv	Mak	Mak	Kum	Mīn	Vṛś	Tul	Kan	Kar	Siṅ	Mit	**Mak**	**Mit**
11	Kit	3	S	Aśv	Kum	Vṛṣ	Meṣ	Mīn	Kum	Mak	Dha	Meṣ	Vṛṣ	Mit	**Vṛṣ**	**Mit**
12	Kṛt	4	S	Aśv	Mīn	Kar	Siṅ	Kan	Tul	Vṛś	Dha	Mak	Kum	Mīn	**Kar**	**Mīn**
13	Roh	1	A	Roh	Vṛś	Dha	Mak	Kum	Mīn	Meṣ	Vṛṣ	Mit	Siṅ	Kar	**Kar**	**Dha**
14	Roh	2	A	Roh	Tul	Kan	Tul	Vṛś	Mīn	Kum	Mak	Dha	Vṛś	Tul	**Tul**	**Kan**
15	Roh	3	A	Roh	Kan	Kan	Siṅ	Kar	Mit	Vṛṣ	Meṣ	Dha	Mak	Kum	**Kum**	**Kan**
16	Roh	4	A	Roh	Siṅ	Mīn	Meṣ	Vṛṣ	Mit	Siṅ	Kar	Kan	Tul	Vṛś	**Vṛś**	**Mīn**
17	Mṛg	1	A	Mrg	Kar	Mīn	Kum	Mak	Dha	Vṛś	Tul	Kan	Siṅ	Kar	**Kar**	**Mīn**
18	Mṛg	2	A	Mrg	Mit	Mit	Vṛṣ	Meṣ	Dha	Mak	Kum	Mīn	Meṣ	Vṛṣ	**Vṛṣ**	**Mit**
19	Mṛg	3	A	Mrg	Vṛṣ	Mit	Siṅ	Kar	Kan	Tul	Vṛś	Mīn	Kum	Mak	**Mak**	**Mit**
20	Mṛg	4	A	Mrg	Meṣ	Dha	Vṛś	Tul	Kan	Siṅ	Kar	Mit	Vṛṣ	Meṣ	**Meṣ**	**Dha**

#	Nakṣ	Pāda	SA	Grp	Añśa	Mahādaśā 1	2	3	4	5	6	7	8	9	Deha	Jīva
21	Ārd	1	A	Mrg	Mīn	Mīn	Kum	Mak	Dha	Vṛś	Tul	Kan	Siṅ	Kar	Kar	Mīn
22	Ārd	2	A	Mrg	Kum	Mit	Vṛṣ	Meṣ	Dha	Mak	Kum	Mīn	Meṣ	Vṛṣ	Vṛṣ	Mit
23	Ārd	3	A	Mrg	Mak	Mit	Siṅ	Kar	Kan	Tul	Vṛś	Mīn	Kum	Mak	Mak	Mit
24	Ārd	4	A	Mrg	Dha	Dha	Vṛś	Tul	Kan	Siṅ	Kar	Mit	Vṛṣ	Meṣ	Meṣ	Dha
25	Pun	1	S	Aśv	Meṣ	Meṣ	Vṛṣ	Mit	Kar	Siṅ	Kan	Tul	Vṛś	Dha	Meṣ	Dha
26	Pun	2	S	Aśv	Vṛṣ	Mak	Kum	Mīn	Vṛś	Tul	Kan	Kar	Siṅ	Mit	Mak	Mit
27	Pun	3	S	Aśv	Mit	Vṛṣ	Meṣ	Mīn	Kum	Mak	Dha	Meṣ	Vṛṣ	Mit	Vṛṣ	Mit
28	Pun	4	S	Aśv	Kar	Kar	Siṅ	Kan	Tul	Vṛś	Dha	Mak	Kum	Mīn	Kar	Mīn
29	Puṣ	1	S	Bha	Siṅ	Vṛś	Tul	Kan	Kar	Siṅ	Mit	Vṛṣ	Meṣ	Mīn	Vṛś	Mīn
30	Puṣ	2	S	Bha	Kan	Kum	Mak	Dha	Meṣ	Vṛṣ	Mit	Kar	Siṅ	Kan	Kum	Kan
31	Puṣ	3	S	Bha	Tul	Tul	Vṛś	Dha	Mak	Kum	Mīn	Vṛś	Tul	Kan	Tul	Kan
32	Puṣ	4	S	Bha	Vṛś	Kar	Siṅ	Mit	Vṛṣ	Meṣ	Mīn	Kum	Mak	Dha	Kar	Dha
33	Aśl	1	S	Aśv	Dha	Meṣ	Vṛṣ	Mit	Kar	Siṅ	Kan	Tul	Vṛś	Dha	Meṣ	Dha
34	Aśl	2	S	Aśv	Mak	Mak	Kum	Mīn	Vṛś	Tul	Kan	Kar	Siṅ	Mit	Mak	Mit
35	Aśl	3	S	Aśv	Kum	Vṛṣ	Meṣ	Mīn	Kum	Mak	Dha	Meṣ	Vṛṣ	Mit	Vṛṣ	Mit
36	Aśl	4	S	Aśv	Mīn	Kar	Siṅ	Kan	Tul	Vṛś	Dha	Mak	Kum	Mīn	Kar	Mīn
37	Mag	1	A	Roh	Vṛś	Dha	Mak	Kum	Mīn	Meṣ	Vṛṣ	Mit	Siṅ	Kar	Kar	Dha
38	Mag	2	A	Roh	Tul	Kan	Tul	Vṛś	Mīn	Kum	Mak	Dha	Vṛś	Tul	Tul	Kan
39	Mag	3	A	Roh	Kan	Kan	Siṅ	Kar	Mit	Vṛṣ	Meṣ	Dha	Mak	Kum	Kum	Kan
40	Mag	4	A	Roh	Siṅ	Mīn	Meṣ	Vṛṣ	Mit	Siṅ	Kar	Kan	Tul	Vṛś	Vṛś	Mīn
41	PPh	1	A	Mrg	Kar	Mīn	Kum	Mak	Dha	Vṛś	Tul	Kan	Siṅ	Kar	Kar	Mīn
42	PPh	2	A	Mrg	Mit	Mit	Vṛṣ	Meṣ	Dha	Mak	Kum	Mīn	Meṣ	Vṛṣ	Vṛṣ	Mit
43	PPh	3	A	Mrg	Vṛṣ	Mit	Siṅ	Kar	Kan	Tul	Vṛś	Mīn	Kum	Mak	Mak	Mit
44	PPh	4	A	Mrg	Meṣ	Dha	Vṛś	Tul	Kan	Siṅ	Kar	Mit	Vṛṣ	Meṣ	Meṣ	Dha
45	UPh	1	A	Mrg	Mīn	Mīn	Kum	Mak	Dha	Vṛś	Tul	Kan	Siṅ	Kar	Kar	Mīn
46	UPh	2	A	Mrg	Kum	Mit	Vṛṣ	Meṣ	Dha	Mak	Kum	Mīn	Meṣ	Vṛṣ	Vṛṣ	Mit
47	UPh	3	A	Mrg	Mak	Mit	Siṅ	Kar	Kan	Tul	Vṛś	Mīn	Kum	Mak	Mak	Mit

#	Nakṣ	Pāda	SA	Grp	Añśa	Mahādaśā									Deha	Jīva
						1	2	3	4	5	6	7	8	9		
48	UPh	4	A	Mṛg	Dha	Dha	Vṛś	Tul	Kan	Siṅ	Kar	Mit	Vṛṣ	Meṣ	**Meṣ**	**Dha**
49	Has	1	S	Aśv	Meṣ	Meṣ	Vṛṣ	Mit	Kar	Siṅ	Kan	Tul	Vṛś	Dha	**Meṣ**	**Dha**
50	Has	2	S	Aśv	Vṛṣ	Mak	Kum	Mīn	Vṛś	Tul	Kan	Kar	Siṅ	Mit	**Mak**	**Mit**
51	Has	3	S	Aśv	Mit	Vṛṣ	Meṣ	Mīn	Kum	Mak	Dha	Meṣ	Vṛṣ	Mit	**Vṛṣ**	**Mit**
52	Has	4	S	Aśv	Kar	Kar	Siṅ	Kan	Tul	Vṛś	Dha	Mak	Kum	Mīn	**Kar**	**Mīn**
53	Cit	1	S	Bha	Siṅ	Vṛś	Tul	Kan	Kar	Siṅ	Mit	Vṛṣ	Meṣ	Mīn	**Vṛś**	**Mīn**
54	Cit	2	S	Bha	Kan	Kum	Mak	Dha	Meṣ	Vṛṣ	Mit	Kar	Siṅ	Kan	**Kum**	**Kan**
55	Cit	3	S	Bha	Tul	Tul	Vṛś	Dha	Mak	Kum	Mīn	Vṛś	Tul	Kan	**Tul**	**Kan**
56	Cit	4	S	Bha	Vṛś	Kar	Siṅ	Mit	Vṛṣ	Meṣ	Mīn	Kum	Mak	Dha	**Kar**	**Dha**
57	Svā	1	S	Aśv	Dha	Meṣ	Vṛṣ	Mit	Kar	Siṅ	Kan	Tul	Vṛś	Dha	**Meṣ**	**Dha**
58	Svā	2	S	Aśv	Mak	Mak	Kum	Mīn	Vṛś	Tul	Kan	Kar	Siṅ	Mit	**Mak**	**Mit**
59	Svā	3	S	Aśv	Kum	Vṛṣ	Meṣ	Mīn	Kum	Mak	Dha	Meṣ	Vṛṣ	Mit	**Vṛṣ**	**Mit**
60	Svā	4	S	Aśv	Mīn	Kar	Siṅ	Kan	Tul	Vṛś	Dha	Mak	Kum	Mīn	**Kar**	**Mīn**
61	Viś	1	A	Roh	Vṛś	Dha	Mak	Kum	Mīn	Meṣ	Vṛṣ	Mit	Siṅ	Kar	**Kar**	**Dha**
62	Viś	2	A	Roh	Tul	Kan	Tul	Vṛś	Mīn	Kum	Mak	Dha	Vṛś	Tul	**Tul**	**Kan**
63	Viś	3	A	Roh	Kan	Kan	Siṅ	Kar	Mit	Vṛṣ	Meṣ	Dha	Mak	Kum	**Kum**	**Kan**
64	Viś	4	A	Roh	Siṅ	Mīn	Meṣ	Vṛṣ	Mit	Siṅ	Kar	Kan	Tul	Vṛś	**Vṛś**	**Mīn**
65	Anu	1	A	Mṛg	Kar	Mīn	Kum	Mak	Dha	Vṛś	Tul	Kan	Siṅ	Kar	**Kar**	**Mīn**
66	Anu	2	A	Mṛg	Mit	Mit	Vṛṣ	Meṣ	Dha	Mak	Kum	Mīn	Meṣ	Vṛṣ	**Vṛṣ**	**Mit**
67	Anu	3	A	Mṛg	Vṛṣ	Mit	Siṅ	Kar	Kan	Tul	Vṛś	Mīn	Kum	Mak	**Mak**	**Mit**
68	Anu	4	A	Mṛg	Meṣ	Dha	Vṛś	Tul	Kan	Siṅ	Kar	Mit	Vṛṣ	Meṣ	**Meṣ**	**Dha**
69	Jye	1	A	Mṛg	Mīn	Mīn	Kum	Mak	Dha	Vṛś	Tul	Kan	Siṅ	Kar	**Kar**	**Mīn**
70	Jye	2	A	Mṛg	Kum	Mit	Vṛṣ	Meṣ	Dha	Mak	Kum	Mīn	Meṣ	Vṛṣ	**Vṛṣ**	**Mit**
71	Jye	3	A	Mṛg	Mak	Mit	Siṅ	Kar	Kan	Tul	Vṛś	Mīn	Kum	Mak	**Mak**	**Mit**
72	Jye	4	A	Mṛg	Dha	Dha	Vṛś	Tul	Kan	Siṅ	Kar	Mit	Vṛṣ	Meṣ	**Meṣ**	**Dha**
73	Mūl	1	S	Aśv	Meṣ	Meṣ	Vṛṣ	Mit	Kar	Siṅ	Kan	Tul	Vṛś	Dha	**Meṣ**	**Dha**

#	Nakṣ	Pāda	SA	Grp	Aṅśa	Mahādaśā 1	2	3	4	5	6	7	8	9	Deha	Jīva
74	Mūl	2	S	Aśv	Vṛṣ	Mak	Kum	Mīn	Vṛś	Tul	Kan	Kar	Siṅ	Mit	**Mak**	**Mit**
75	Mūl	3	S	Aśv	Mit	Vṛṣ	Meṣ	Mīn	Kum	Mak	Dha	Meṣ	Vṛṣ	Mit	**Vṛṣ**	**Mit**
76	Mūl	4	S	Aśv	Kar	Kar	Siṅ	Kan	Tul	Vṛś	Dha	Mak	Kum	Mīn	**Kar**	**Mīn**
77	PĀṣ	1	S	Bha	Siṅ	Vṛś	Tul	Kan	Kar	Siṅ	Mit	Vṛṣ	Meṣ	Mīn	**Vṛś**	**Mīn**
78	PĀṣ	2	S	Bha	Kan	Kum	Mak	Dha	Meṣ	Vṛṣ	Mit	Kar	Siṅ	Kan	**Kum**	**Kan**
79	PĀṣ	3	S	Bha	Tul	Tul	Vṛś	Dha	Mak	Kum	Mīn	Vṛś	Tul	Kan	**Tul**	**Kan**
80	PĀṣ	4	S	Bha	Vṛś	Kar	Siṅ	Mit	Vṛṣ	Meṣ	Mīn	Kum	Mak	Dha	**Kar**	**Dha**
81	UĀṣ	1	S	Aśv	Dha	Meṣ	Vṛṣ	Mit	Kar	Siṅ	Kan	Tul	Vṛś	Dha	**Meṣ**	**Dha**
82	UĀṣ	2	S	Aśv	Mak	Mak	Kum	Mīn	Vṛś	Tul	Kan	Kar	Siṅ	Mit	**Mak**	**Mit**
83	UĀṣ	3	S	Aśv	Kum	Vṛṣ	Meṣ	Mīn	Kum	Mak	Dha	Meṣ	Vṛṣ	Mit	**Vṛṣ**	**Mit**
84	UĀṣ	4	S	Aśv	Mīn	Kar	Siṅ	Kan	Tul	Vṛś	Dha	Mak	Kum	Mīn	**Kar**	**Mīn**
85	Śra	1	A	Roh	Vṛś	Dha	Mak	Kum	Mīn	Meṣ	Vṛṣ	Mit	Siṅ	Kar	**Kar**	**Dha**
86	Śra	2	A	Roh	Tul	Kan	Tul	Vṛś	Mīn	Kum	Mak	Dha	Vṛś	Tul	**Tul**	**Kan**
87	Śra	3	A	Roh	Kan	Kan	Siṅ	Kar	Mit	Vṛṣ	Meṣ	Dha	Mak	Kum	**Kum**	**Kan**
88	Śra	4	A	Roh	Siṅ	Mīn	Meṣ	Vṛṣ	Mit	Siṅ	Kar	Kan	Tul	Vṛś	**Vṛś**	**Mīn**
89	Dha	1	A	Mṛg	Kar	Mīn	Kum	Mak	Dha	Vṛś	Tul	Kan	Siṅ	Kar	**Kar**	**Mīn**
90	Dha	2	A	Mṛg	Mit	Mit	Vṛṣ	Meṣ	Dha	Mak	Kum	Mīn	Meṣ	Vṛṣ	**Vṛṣ**	**Mit**
91	Dha	3	A	Mṛg	Vṛṣ	Mit	Siṅ	Kar	Kan	Tul	Vṛś	Mīn	Kum	Mak	**Mak**	**Mit**
92	Dha	4	A	Mṛg	Meṣ	Dha	Vṛś	Tul	Kan	Siṅ	Kar	Mit	Vṛṣ	Meṣ	**Meṣ**	**Dha**
93	Śat	1	A	Mṛg	Mīn	Mīn	Kum	Mak	Dha	Vṛś	Tul	Kan	Siṅ	Kar	**Kar**	**Mīn**
94	Śat	2	A	Mṛg	Kum	Mit	Vṛṣ	Meṣ	Dha	Mak	Kum	Mīn	Meṣ	Vṛṣ	**Vṛṣ**	**Mit**
95	Śat	3	A	Mṛg	Mak	Mit	Siṅ	Kar	Kan	Tul	Vṛś	Mīn	Kum	Mak	**Mak**	**Mit**
96	Śat	4	A	Mṛg	Dha	Dha	Vṛś	Tul	Kan	Siṅ	Kar	Mit	Vṛṣ	Meṣ	**Meṣ**	**Dha**
97	PBh	1	S	Aśv	Meṣ	Meṣ	Vṛṣ	Mit	Kar	Siṅ	Kan	Tul	Vṛś	Dha	**Meṣ**	**Dha**
98	PBh	2	S	Aśv	Vṛṣ	Mak	Kum	Mīn	Vṛś	Tul	Kan	Kar	Siṅ	Mit	**Mak**	**Mit**
99	PBh	3	S	Aśv	Mit	Vṛṣ	Meṣ	Mīn	Kum	Mak	Dha	Meṣ	Vṛṣ	Mit	**Vṛṣ**	**Mit**
100	PBh	4	S	Aśv	Kar	Kar	Siṅ	Kan	Tul	Vṛś	Dha	Mak	Kum	Mīn	**Kar**	**Mīn**

#	Na kṣ	Pā da	S A	Gr p	Añ śa	Mahādaśā									De ha	Jīv a
						1	2	3	4	5	6	7	8	9		
10 1	UB h	1	S	B ha	Siṅ	Vṛ ś	Tu l	Ka n	Ka r	Siṅ	Mi t	Vṛ ṣ	Me ṣ	Mī n	**Vṛś**	**Mī n**
10 2	UB h	2	S	B ha	Ka n	Ku m	Ma k	Dh a	Me ṣ	Vṛ ṣ	Mi t	Ka r	Siṅ	Ka n	**Ku m**	**Ka n**
10 3	UB h	3	S	B ha	Tul	Tu l	Vṛ ś	Dh a	Ma k	Ku m	Mī n	Vṛ ś	Tu l	Ka n	**Tul**	**Ka n**
10 4	UB h	4	S	B ha	Vṛś	Ka r	Siṅ	Mi t	Vṛ ṣ	Me ṣ	Mī n	Ku m	Ma k	Dh a	**Ka r**	**D ha**
10 5	Re v	1	S	Aś v	Dh a	Me ṣ	Vṛ ṣ	Mi t	Ka r	Siṅ	Ka n	Tu l	Vṛ ś	Dh a	**Me ṣ**	**D ha**
10 6	Re v	2	S	Aś v	Ma k	Ma k	Ku m	Mī n	Vṛ ś	Tu l	Ka n	Ka r	Siṅ	Mi t	**Ma k**	**Mi t**
10 7	Re v	3	S	Aś v	Ku m	Vṛ ṣ	Me ṣ	Mī n	Ku m	Ma k	Dh a	Me ṣ	Vṛ ṣ	Mi t	**Vṛṣ**	**Mi t**
10 8	Re v	4	S	Aś v	Mī n	Ka r	Siṅ	Ka n	Tu l	Vṛ ś	Dh a	Ma k	Ku m	Mī n	**Ka r**	**Mī n**

To remove any confusion from the counting process, the translations of Maharṣi Parāśara's ślokas are given below. Maharṣi Parāśara states clearly the Daśā sequence and the Deha and Jīva allocations for the 16 different scenarios, four different groups (Aśvinī, Bharaṇī, Rohiṇī, Mṛgaśirā) and 4 Caraṇas. These 16 different Nakṣatra Caraṇa combinations should be used to determine the Daśā sequence for all the 108 Caraṇas. The sequence of the 9 Daśās determines the Āyuṣa allotted to a Nakṣatra Caraṇa or the Navāñśa. To decipher the results, one must take the Daśās along with the Navāñśa to which the Nakṣatra Caraṇa is mapped. That is the basis of the Kālacakra Daśā results that Maharṣi Parāśara narrated in a subsequence section.

BṚHATPARĀŚARA

46.60. In the first Caraṇa of Aśvinī, Meṣa is indicative of Deha, and Dhanu is indicative of Jīva. And the Lords of Meṣa, Vṛṣabha, Mithuna, Karka, Siṅha, Kanyā, Tulā, Vṛścika and Dhanu are Lords of the Daśās in the order, as described before.

46.61. In the second Caraṇa of Aśvinī, Makara is Deha and Mithuna is Jīva, and the Lords of the nine Rāśis from Makara to Mithuna are Lords of the Daśās.

46.62. In the third Caraṇa of the 10 Nakṣatras, beginning from Aśvinī, Vṛṣabha is Deha and Mithuna is Jīva. The Lords of the Rāśis Vṛṣabha, Meṣa, Mīna, Kumbha, Makara, Dhanu, Meṣa, Vṛṣabha and Mithuna are Lords of the Daśās in that order. Notes: The 10 Nakṣatras of Aśvinī group are Aśvinī, Punarvasu, Hastā, Mūla, Pūrvābhādra, Kṛttikā, Aśleṣā, Svāti, Uttarāṣāṛhā, Revatī.

46.63-64. For the fourth Caraṇa of the 10 Nakṣatras, beginning from Aśvinī, Karka is Deha and Mīna is Jīva, and the Lords of the nine Rāśis from Karka to Mīna are the Lords of Daśās.

46.65. In the four Caraṇas of the 5 Nakṣatras, Bharaṇī, Puṣya, Citrā, Pūrvāṣāṛhā and Uttarābhādra, Deha and Jīva are the same, as for Bharaṇī.

46.66. In the first Caraṇa of Bharaṇī Vṛścika is Deha and Mīna is Jīva, and the Lords of the Rāśis Vṛścika, Tulā, Kanyā, Karka, Siṅha, Mithuna, Vṛṣabha, Meṣa and Mīna are the Lords of Daśās in this order.

46.67. In the second Caraṇa of Bharaṇī, Kumbha is Deha and Kanyā is Jīva, and the Lords of Kumbha, Makara, Dhanu, Meṣa, Vṛṣabha, Mithuna, Karka, Siṅha and Kanyā are the Lords of Daśās in that order.

46.68. In the third Caraṇa of Bharaṇī, Tulā is Deha and Kanyā is Jīva, and Lords of the Rāśis Tulā, Vṛścika, Dhanu, Makara, Kumbha, Mīna, Vṛścika, Tulā and Kanyā are the Daśā Lords in this order.

46.69. In the fourth Caraṇa of Bharaṇī, Karka is Deha and Kumbha is Jīva, and the Lords of the Rāśis Karka, Siṅha, Mithuna, Vṛṣabha, Meṣa, Mīna, Kumbha, Makara and Dhanu are the Daśā Lords in this order.

46.73. In the first Caraṇa of Rohiṇī, Karka is Deha and Dhanu is Jīva. The Lords of the Rāśis Dhanu, Makara, Kumbha, Mīna, Meṣa, Vṛṣabha, Mithuna, Siṅha and Tulā are the Daśā Lords in this order.

46.74. In the second Caraṇa of Rohiṇī, Tulā is Deha and Kanyā, the Jīva and the Lords of the Rāśis Kanyā, Tulā, Vṛścika, Mīna, Kumbha, Makara, Dhanu, Vṛścika and Vṛścika is the Daśā Lords.

46.75. In the third Caraṇa of Rohiṇī, Kumbha is Deha and Kanyā Jīva. The Lords of the Rāśis Kanyā, Siṅha, Karka, Mithuna, Vṛṣabha, Meṣa, Dhanu, Makara and Kumbha is the Daśā Lords.

46.76. In the fourth Caraṇa of Rohiṇī, Vṛścika is Deha and Mīna Jīva, and the Lords of the Rāśis Mīna, Meṣa, Vṛṣabha, Mithuna, Siṅha, Karka, Kanyā, Tulā and Vṛścika is the Lords.

46.77. In the four Caraṇas of the Apasavya Nakṣatras Mṛgaśirā, Ārdrā, Pūrvāphālgunī, Uttarāphālgunī, Anurādhā, Jyeṣṭha, Dhaniṣṭhā and Śatabhiṣā the Deha and Jīva and the Daśā Lords is the same, as for Mṛgaśirā.

46.78. In the first Caraṇa of Mṛgaśirā, Karka is Deha and Mīna is Jīva, and the Lords of the Rāśis Mīna, Kumbha, Makara, Dhanu, Vṛścika, Tulā, Kanyā, Siṅha and Karka is the Daśā Lords in this order.

46.79. In the second Caraṇa of Mṛgaśirā, Vṛṣabha is Deha, and Mithuna is Jīva, and the Lords of the Rāśis Mithuna, Vṛṣabha, Meṣa, Dhanu, Makara, Kumbha, Mīna, Meṣa and Vṛṣabha is the Daśā Lords.

46.80. In the third Caraṇa of Mṛgaśirā, Makara is Deha and Mithuna is Jīva, and the Lords of the Rāśis Mithuna, Siṅha, Karka, Kanyā, Tulā, Vṛścika, Mīna, Kumbha and Makara is the Daśā Lords.

46.81. In the fourth Caraṇa of Mṛgaśirā, Meṣa is Deha and Dhanu Jīva, and the Lords of the Rāśis Dhanu, Vṛścika, Tulā, Kanyā, Siṅha, Karka, Mithuna, Vṛṣabha and Meṣa is the Daśā Lords.

Each Nakṣatra group (Aśvinī, Bharaṇī, Rohiṇī and Mṛgaśirā) has a total span of 354 years, which is distributed in similar proportions among each group.

The proportion is 100 - 85 - 83 - 86 for the Savya group, respectively, for Caraṇas 1 to 4. This reversed to 86 - 83 - 85 - 100 in the case of the Apasavya group.

Each Navanavāñśa (Daśā) appears "precisely three times" in a Nakṣatra Group. Although the Daśās appear to be assigned randomly to each Nakṣatra Caraṇa, there is a pattern to it, which we have deciphered. That is why each Rāśi is equally distributed. There are 972 Daśās for 108 Caraṇas, indicating that each Rāśi appears 81 times, which is why the D81 or Navanavāñśa classification of Navāñśa is important.

30.1.3.3.5
DAŚĀ SPANS AND ĀYUṢA

After narrating the Daśā sequence for the Nakṣatra Caraṇas, Maharṣi Parāśara narrates the periods assigned to these Daśās. The span of Daśā is dependent on the years allotted to the Daśārāśi lords. The Daśā spans for the Grahas are Sūrya - 5 years, Candra - 21, Maṅgala - 7 years, Budha - 9 years, Bṛhaspati - 10 years, Śukra - 16 years, and Śani - 4 years. The total duration of a Nakṣatra Caraṇa or Navāñśa is the total of the years allotted to the Navanavāñśas mapped to the Caraṇa.

Some Ācāryas allot the longevity based on the balance of Nakṣatra Caraṇa expired, which is not logically correct. Merely because someone is born in the last portion of a Nakṣatra Caraṇa, we cannot declare that the person shall have Alpāyu. Let me take my case; merely because I was born near the end of Anurādhā-4 does not mean that I was born with Alpāyu. I was born with 3.45 years of Āyuṣa granted by Anurādhā-4, which I have already crossed several years back.

The switching of Nakṣatra Caraṇa, i.e., from Anurādhā-4 to Jyeṣṭhā-1 in this case, does indicate some danger, which can be grave if the transition is not regular. I didn't face the danger because Anurādhā-4 to Jyeṣṭhā-1 is a regular movement from Meṣa to Mīna in reverse regular order. Sometimes, the transitions occur through special Gatis (Siṅhavlokana , Maṇḍūka or Marakaṭa), which are indicative of grave danger, such as that of Bharaṇī-4 to Kṛttikā-1.

We should instead interpret Bṛhatparāśara 46.85-86. in this manner - depending on whether the expired portion is small, moderate or large, the Āyuṣa granted by the Nakṣatra Caraṇa can be small, moderate or long, respectively, but that does not imply that the native shall live that long.

In Bṛhatparāśara 46.87-88., the Maharṣi explains how to find the Navāñśa mapped to a Nakṣatra Caraṇa. Let me take an example of Anurādhā4 to explain this. Anurādhā is the 17th Nakṣatra, and the number of past Nakṣatra is 16. Since the Nakṣatras are grouped into 3, we divide how many such groups have expired, which is arrived at by considering the remainder when the number of expired Nakṣatras is divided by 3.

The remainder, in this case, is 16 / 3 = 5R1 (quotient 5 remainder 1), meaning five cycles are gone, and in the 6th cycle, 1 Nakṣatra is gone. The number of Navāñśas expired in the 6th cycle is arrived at by multiplying the remainder by 4, which is 1 * 4 = 4. Since 4 Navāṃśa (Caraṇas) have expired in the 6th cycle, Anuradha4 is 4 + 4 = 8. Since, Anurādhā is Apasavya, the 8th Navāñśa of Apasavya Cakra is Meṣa (not Vṛścika). This indicates that the native was born in Meṣa Navāñśa. Once the Navāñśa is known, the Daśā balance can be worked out by finding the Navāñśa expired.

Śloka 46.89 gives the Āyuṣa allotted to the different Navāñśas based on their Tattvas. The Agnitattva Navāñśas have 100 years, Pṛthvītattva 85, Vāyutattva 83 years and Jalatattva 86 years. These are derived from the Navanavāñśas assigned to the Navāñśas. We must note that these allotments do not change in the Savya or the Apasavya Cakra because the Navanavāñśas assigned to the Navāñśas in either of the Navāñśas does not change; it is only their order that changes.

In the Apasavya Cakra, the cycle starts with Vṛścika, which is Jalatattva, followed by Vāyutattva, Pṛthvītattva, and Agnitattva, which is why the sequence of the Āyuṣa is reversed, i.e., 86, 83, 85 and 100 years respectively. We notice that the Agnitattva Rāśis are assigned the highest Āyuṣa (100), followed by Jalatattva (86), Pṛthvītattva (85) and Vāyutattva (83).

BṚHATPARĀŚARA

46.83. Maitreya said. O Venerable Maharṣi Parāśara! Now, please guide me about the Daśā spans of the Daśā Lords described by you. Please also demonstrate how the commencement of the Daśā, its elapsed, and the remaining period at the birth is to be calculated.

46.84. Maharṣi Parāśara said. 5, 21, 7, 9, 10, 16 and 4 years are the Daśā spans of Sūrya, Candra, Maṅgala, Budha, Bṛhaspati, Śukra and Śani.

46.85-86. The lifespan of a person is determined from the Caraṇas (Añśas) of the Nakṣatra at the time of birth, or the time of query and the years allotted to the 9 Rāśis, commencing from it (the Nakṣatra Caraṇa). Some sages are of the view that the person enjoys a full life-span (Pūrṇāyu) if his birth is at the commencement of the Caraṇas, middle life-span (Madhyāyu), if the birth is in the middle of the Caraṇas and short life-span (Alpāyu), or face death-like sufferings if the birth is at the end of the Caraṇas of the Nakṣatra.

46.87-88. According to this principle, we should be acquainted with the Caraṇas of the Nakṣatras. Now, I shall tell you how the calculations are made according to the proportion of the Caraṇas of a Nakṣatra. The number of Aśvinī, etc., whichever may be the past Nakṣatras, should be divided by 3. After that, the remainder should be multiplied by 4. To the figure so made available, the Caraṇa of the present Nakṣatra should be added. The product is the Navāñśa from Meṣa onwards.

46.89. The number of years (Pūrṇāyu) is as under. For the Añśa in Meṣa, 100 years; in Vṛṣabha, 85 years; in Mithuna, 83 years; in Karka, 86 years. The number of years is the same for Rāśis, situated on the 5th and 9th to them.

30.1.3.3.6
DAŚĀ PROGRESSION

After completion of the 9 Daśās of the Nakṣatra Caraṇa (Navāñśa) of Candra at birth, the Daśā progresses to the following Caraṇa, and there the 1st Daśā of the Caraṇa commences. For instance, for one is born in Aśvinī1, which is Meṣa Navāñśa, the Daśās are Meṣ → Vṛṣ → Mit → Kar → Siṅ → Kan → Tul → Vṛś → Dha.

The following Nakṣatra Caraṇa is Aśvinī2, which is in Vṛṣabha Navāñśa, and the Daśās are Mak → Kum → Mīn → Vṛś → Tul → Kan → Kar → Siṅ → Mit. Therefore, After the Dhanu Daśā of Aśvinī1, the Daśā moves to Makara Daśā of Aśvinī2. In this context, let us review three different situations.

Table 27

#	Changes	Progression		Result
1	Nakṣatra Caraṇa changes in the same Nakṣatra.	Aśvinī-1 → Aśvinī-2	The 9th Daśā of Aśvinī-1 moves to the 1st Daśā of Aśvinī-2	Aśvinī-1 → Aśvinī-2 Dhanu → Makara
2	Nakṣatra Caraṇa changes to the following Nakṣatra in the same Kālacakra, Savya or Apasavya.	Aśvinī-4 → Bharaṇī-1	The 9th Daśā of Aśvinī-4 moves to the 1st Daśā of Bharaṇī-1	Aśvinī-4 → Bharaṇī-1 Mīna → Vṛṣabha
3	Nakṣatra Caraṇa change to the following Nakṣatra in a different Kālacakra, Savya to Apasavya, or Apasavya to Savya.	Kṛttikā-4 → Rohiṇī-1 **(not allowed)**	The Daśā progression **"cannot"** move across different Kālacakra either from Savya to Apasavya or Apasavya to Savya. The Daśā moves from one Nakṣatra to the next only if they belong to the same Cakra. Therefore, the Daśā movement can happen from Aśvinī → Bharaṇī → Kṛttikā. After Kṛttikā, the Daśā moves back to Aśvinī-1 instead of Rohiṇī-4 because the movement into different Kālacakra is prohibited.	Kṛttikā-4 → Aśvinī-1 Mīna → Meṣa

One might ask, why is the movement across the Chakras prohibited? Why cannot the Daśā progress from Kṛttikā4 to Rohini1? This becomes clear when we minutely scrutinize the movement. 9th Daśā of Kṛttikā4 is Mīna, and the 1st Daśā of Rohiṇī1 is Dhanu. **The Daśā cannot progress from Mīna to Dhanu as this movement is not allowed by Maharṣi Parāśara.**

The progression can happen only through one of the following methods: (1) Sādhāraṇa Gati (regular movement), (2) Siṅhavlokana Gati (trinal jump), (3) Maṇḍūka Gati (alternate Rāśi jump), and (4) Marakaṭa Gati (reverse jump). Therefore, movement from Mīna to Dhanu is not allowed. Essentially, the Savya and Apasavya Kālacakras are independent entities that are contained in themselves, and there is no bridge between these two Kālacakras, which is why the Daśā progression is prohibited between the Kālacakras.

30.1.3.4 THE DAŚĀ BALANCE

We know now that each Nakṣatra Caraṇa of 200 arc-minutes is of either 100y (Agni), 85y (Pṛthvī), 83y (Vāyu) or 86y (Jala) duration. This implies that the Daśā balance at birth can be found by determining the portion of the Nakṣatra Caraṇa yet to be expired. For instance, if one is born in 6° 30' of Meṣa Rāśi, which is 3° 10' of Aśvinī-2, the Nakṣatra Caraṇa yet to be elapsed is 10'. The remaining Daśā is 10 / 200 * 85 = 4.25 years. We know that each Nakṣatra Caraṇa has nine Navanavāñśas (Daśās), contributing to the years allotted to the Nakṣatra Caraṇa.

From this, we can determine the Rāśi for which the Daśā balance is remaining. For Aśvinī-2, the Daśās are Makara (4y), Kumbha (4y), Mīna (10y), Vṛścika (7y), Tulā (16y), Kanyā (9y), Siṅha (5y), Karka (21y), and Mithuna (9y). Since the Daśā balance is 4.25 years, it must be Mithuna Rāśi, which spans the last nine years. Let us follow the calculations in a stepwise method using another example, where Candra's Sphuṭa is 16° 39' of Vṛścika Rāśi.

Table 28

#	Step	Description	Example
1	**Determine Candra's Sphuṭa from the beginning of Meṣa.**	Candrasphuṭa from Meṣa 0° = (Rāśi index - 1) * 30 + Degree + Min / 60 + Sec / 3600	Say Candra's Sphuṭa is 16° 31' 57.29" in Vṛścika Rāśi. This is equal to (8 -1) * 30 + 16 + 31/60 + 57.29/3600 = 226.5326°.
2	**Convert Candra's Sphuṭa arrived above in arc minutes (Kalā).**	Candrasphuṭa in Degree * 60	Here, 226.5326 * 60 = 13591.956'
3	**Divide Candra's Sphuṭa in minutes arrived above by 200 and determine the remainder.**	Candrasphuṭa/ 200 Remainder = Decimals * 200	13591.956 / 200 = 67.95978 Remainder = 0.95978 * 200 = 191.956'.
4	**Determine the Nakṣatra Caraṇa Balance**	200 – remainder	200 - 191.956 = 8.044'
5	**Determine the Daśā Balance**	Nakṣatra Caraṇa Balance / 200 * Navāñśa span	8.044 / 200 * 100 years = 4.022 years = 4 years 0 months 8 days. The Daśā duration for Anurādhā-4 (Meṣa Navāñśa) is 100.

#	Step	Description	Example
			Therefore, we can say that the balance of Daśā at birth is 4y 0m 8d.
6	**Determine the Daśā Rāśi**	The Daśā Rāśi is based in the Navanavāñśas assigned to the Nakṣatra Caraṇa.	Anurādhā-4 is allotted the Navanavāñśas Dhanu (10), Vṛścika (7), Tulā (16), Kanyā (9), Siṅha (5), Karka (21), Mithuna (9), Vṛṣabha (16), Meṣa (7). The last Daśā, of Meṣa, is 7 years, which means that the native is born in Meṣa Daśā, of which 4y 0m 8d left. Adding this to the birthdate, we arrive on **12/8/1978.** Therefore, Meṣa Daśā ended on 12th August 1978, after which Jyeṣṭhā-1 Daśā-1 started. In the computation, I used 360 days a year to arrive at the date.
7	**Determine the Daśā sequence**	Count 9 Daśās from the Daśā at birth	One should be assigned 9 Rāśis for the entire life span. Since Meṣa is the last Rāśi in Anurādhā-4, we should progress to the next Nakṣatra Caraṇa, which is Jyeṣṭhā-1. Jyeṣṭhā-1 is mapped to Apasavya Mīna, the sequence for which is Mīna, Kumbha, Makara, Dhanu, Vṛścika, Tulā, Kanyā, and Siṅha. The total of the Āyus allotted to these Rāśis is 65, and added to it is the Balance of 4.4y. This gives the Kālacakra Āyu of the native as 69.4y = 69y 4m 24d.

Given below are the meanings of the Ślokas given by Maharṣi Parāśara. For the computation, the measurements indicated are in Ghaṭi and Palas of the Nakṣatra Caraṇa. In this computation, we map a Nakṣatra to 60 Ghaṭi, which is sometimes called Nakṣatra Ghaṭi, from which we can find the expired and unexpired portions. If one Nakṣatra is 60 Ghaṭi, one Caraṇa is 60 / 4 = 15 Ghaṭis, which is referred to by the Maharṣi.

When the expired Nakṣatra in Ghaṭi/ Pala is divided by 15, the remainder denotes the unexpired portion of the Nakṣatra Caraṇa. Let us take our example, where one is born in the 16° 31’ 57.29” of Vṛścika Rāśi, which is 13° 11’ 57.29” (13.19925) of Anurādhā Nakṣatra. The Nakṣatra elapsed in Ghaṭi, and Pala is 13.19925/ 13.33333 * 60 = 59.39664 Ghaṭi. The expired Caraṇa can be determined by dividing 59.39664 by 15, which gives us 3.959776, which means 3 Caraṇas and 0.959776 of the 4th Caraṇa has expired.

The Ghaṭi of the present Caraṇa is 0.959776 * 15 = 14.39664. The Daśā expired is 14.39664 / 15 * 100 since Anurādhā-4 is of 100 years duration. This shows that the Daśā expired is 95.9776 years, and the Daśā balance is 100 - 95.9776 = 4.0224 years, i.e., 4y 0m 8d. In Bṛhatparāśara 46.93., the Maharṣi also explains the Navāñśa Kalā method, which I explained above in the stepwise method. Here, 1 Navāñśa is 200 Kalā, and from the Navāñśa elapsed by Candra, we can determine the Daśā Balance, which has been explained above. One can choose either of the methods, as the results are the same. My preference is the Navāñśa Kalā method, as it is less prone to rounding-off issues.

BṚHATPARĀŚARA

46.90-91. Multiply the past Ghaṭis, Palas, etc., of the Caraṇa of the Nakṣatra, in which a person is born, by the existing Daśā years and divide it by 15. The result shall indicate the expired period of the Daśā in years, months, etc. By deducting it from the total number of years allotted, we get the balance of Daśā at birth. The Daśā should be taken as commencing from that Rāśi.

46.92. Multiply the past Ghaṭis, Palas, etc., of the present Caraṇa of the Nakṣatra by the number of years and divide the product by the fourth part of Bhabhog. The years, etc., so obtained may then be deducted from the total Daśā period. The result is the balance of Daśā at birth in years, months, etc.

46.93. The past kalās (minutes) of the Navāñśa, in which Candra may be placed, should be multiplied by the years allotted to the Daśā, and the product should be divided by 200. The resulting years, etc., are the expired portion of the Daśā. By deducting them from the total number of years, the balance of the Daśā at birth is obtained.

30.1.3.5
THE ANTARDAŚĀ

Another significant aspect is the computation of Antardaśā, which is fraught with confusion. This is mainly because Maharṣi Parāśara did not give his guidance on this and left it to our judgement, or perhaps transmission of this knowledge through a bonafide Guru-Śiṣya Paramparā. The problem is unless we understand the basis of the determination of Mahādaśās, the determination of Antardaśā is impossible. What is to be called Antardaśās or Bhukti is also debatable.

While Maharṣi Parāśara and other scholars take the nine Navanavāñśa sequence as the Mahādaśā sequence, Śrī Mantreśvara considers them as the Antardaśās in the Mahādaśās denoted by the Navāñśa in which the nine Navanavāñśa falls. While this is an acceptable idea, for our convention, we use the sequence of nine Navanavāñśa as the Mahādaśās and the subperiods within them as the Antardaśās. Either way, the ślokas of Phaladīpikā do not help us either with the determination of the Antardaśās.

Phaladīpikā 22.13.

The Apahara or Bhukti of any of the Graha constituting a Mahādaśā is thus obtained. Find out the particular mnemonical syllable (out of the nine syllables) composing a formula whose Bhukti is wanted and find out the owner of the Rāśi signified by that syllable. Multiply the number of years assigned to this Graha by the number of years fixed for the Graha whose Mahādaśā is under consideration and divide the product by the total number

of years constituting the Paramāyus of the formula or Cakra. The quotient in years, etc., Shall represent the subperiod required.

In Daśās such as Viñśottarī, the Antardaśā sequence is straightforward, as we merely start with the Mahādaśā lord and progress in the order of the Daśā sequence. For instance, the Mahādaśā sequence of Viñśottarī is Sūrya, Candra, Maṅgala, Rāhu, Bṛhaspati, Śani, Budha, Ketu, Śukra. This means that in the Mahādaśā of Śukra, the Bhuktis are in the order of Śukra, Ketu, Sūrya, Candra, Maṅgala, Rāhu, Bṛhaspati, Śani, Budha.

This is straightforward! Isn't it? However, this is not so for the Mahādaśās in Kālacakra Daśā because there is no fixed sequence. As we have seen before, there are 16 different Mahādaśā sequences, which are derived from 2 (Savya / Apasavya) * 2 (Nakṣatra group) * 4 (Caraṇas). This makes it difficult to determine which sequence to follow for the Antardaśās.

One might argue that we can straightaway use the Daśā sequence to which the Antardaśā belongs. For instance, the Daśā sequence of Aśvinī-2 is Makara → Kumbha → Mīna → Vṛścika → Tulā → Kanyā → Siṅha → Karka → Mithuna. If we were to find the Antardaśā of Mīna Mahādaśā, we could use the same sequence, commencing from Mīna, i.e., Mīna → Vṛścika → Tulā → Kanyā → Siṅha → Karka → Mithuna → Makara → Kumbha.

The Bhukti of the next Daśā i.e., Vṛścika is Vṛścika → Tulā → Kanyā → Siṅha → Karka → Mithuna → Makara → Kumbha → Mīna. In this manner, the Bhukti of all the Daśās can be determined. This might appear logical, but the issue with this is that this does not follow the sequence given by Maharṣi Parāśara for the different Navāñśas.

I believe that the key to understanding the Antardaśā is in the identification of the Daśā Rāśi being in the Savya sequence or the Apasavya sequence. Let us take the Caraṇa-2 of the Savya Aśvinī group (Aśvinī, Punarvasu, Hastā, Mūla, Pūrvābhādra, Kṛttikā, Aśleṣā, Svāti, Uttarāṣāṛhā, Revatī).

In this group, the Mahādaśā sequence for Caraṇa-2 is Makara → Kumbha → Mīna → Vṛścika^ → Tulā^ → Kanyā^ → Siṅha^ → Karka^ → Mithuna^. We notice that the Mahādaśās Makara to Mīna belong to the Savya Kālacakra, and Vṛścika^ to Mithuna^ belong to Apasavya Kālacakra. We can say that for Makara Daśā, the sequence should be based on Savya Kālacakra starting from Makara, i.e., Makara → Kumbha → Mīna → Meṣa → Vṛṣabha → Mithuna → Karka → Siṅha → Kanyā. On the other hand, for Vṛścika Daśā, which is in Apasavya Cakra, the sequence is Vṛścika^ → Tulā^ → Kanyā^ → Karka^ → Siṅha^ → Mithuna^ → Vṛṣabha^ → Meṣa^ → Mīna^. Again, this might appear logical but cannot stand scrutiny.

For instance, regarding the Antardaśā of Makara Daśā, we thought that the sequence should be Makara → Kumbha → Mīna → Meṣa → Vṛṣabha → Mithuna → Karka → Siṅha → Kanyā. However, upon closer examination, we notice that in the Daśā of the Savya-Aśvinī group, after the end of Savya Cakra, the Apasavya

Cakra commences, which means Apasavya Vṛścika should follow Savya Mīna. The following table shows the cycle of 36 Daśās (Navanavāñśas) for the 4 Caraṇas of the Savya-Aśvinī group. Therefore, we cannot say that this approach is foolproof either.

Table 29

	1 Deha	2	3	4	5	6	7	8	9 Jīva
Pada1	Meṣ	Vṛṣ	Mit	Kar	Siṅ	Kan	Tul	Vṛś	Dha
Pada2	Mak	Kum	Mīn	Vṛś^	Tul^	Kan^	Siṅ^	Kar^	Mit^
Pada3	Vṛṣ^	Meṣ^	Mīn^	Kum^	Mak^	Dha^	Meṣ	Vṛṣ	Mit
Pada4	Kar	Siṅ	Kan	Tul	Vṛś	Dha	Mak	Kum	Mīn

After reflecting intently on this matter and with lord Śiva's blessings, suddenly, things started unfolding in my mind. This is the moment of revelation that I narrated at the beginning of this chapter. This is my recommendation, which I think is the most consistent among all. This utilizes the inherent pattern embedded in the Daśā sequence.

We have learnt before that the Daśās are classified into four groups, Savya-Aśvinī, Savya-Bharaṇī, Apasavya-Rohiṇī and Apasavya-Mṛgaśirā, and the cycles of Daśās are (1) Savya-Aśvinī = Krama-Savya → Krama-Apasavya → Krama-Savya, (2) Savya-Bharaṇī = Krama-Apasavya → Krama-Savya → Krama-Apasavya. (3) Apasavya-Rohiṇī = Utkrama-Apasavya → Utkrama-Savya → Utkrama-Apasavya and (4) Apasavya-Mṛgaśirā = Utkrama-Savya → Utkrama-Apasavya → Utkrama-Savya.

All the Nakṣatras fall into these four groups, and they are closed entities in themselves, which is why the four groups are defined. This means that the Nakṣatras in the Aśvinī group, i.e., Aśvinī, Bharaṇī, Kṛttikā, etc., shall always invariably remain within this group, and shall never transcend it. This is a significant point in the entire Kālacakra concept. The Aśvinī, Bharaṇī, Rohiṇī and Mṛgaśirā groups are the fundamental entities, which are self-contained, and what belongs to them shall remain within them.

Now, keeping this principle in mind, let us relook at the Antardaśā sequence again. The Mahādaśā sequence of Aśvinī Caraṇa-2 is Makara → Kumbha → Mīna → Vṛścika^ → Tulā^ → Kanyā^ → Siṅha^ → Karka^ → Mithuna^. Here, Makara to Mīna is from Savya Cakra, whereas Vṛścika^ to Mithuna^ are from Apasavya Cakra. Forgetting for a moment that we want to find the Antardaśā for Makara Daśā, let us ask ourselves that, for Makara Navāñśa, what is the nine Navanavāñśa sequence Maharṣi Parāśara gives.

We find that it is Mak → Kum → Mīn → Vṛś → Tul → Kan → Kar → Siṅ → Mit. Therefore, we should say that for Savya Makara Daśā, the sequence is mentioned above, i.e., Makara to Mithuna. What we are doing is not focusing on the specific sequence of the Daśā in the sequence of 9 Mahādaśās; we are going back to the fundamentals, which is identifying whether the Daśā Navanavāñśa belongs to Savya or Apasavya Cakra, and after that is known, we are finding the nine Navanavāñśas contained within that, and using that as the Antardaśā sequence.

The same principle can be used for Pratyantardaśā, provided we can ascertain whether the concerned Rāśi belong to the Savya or Apasavya Cakra. A better representation of the above Antardaśā sequence using the codes for Savya and Apasavya. Let us start again with Aśvinī Caraṇa-2. Aśvinī-2 falls in Vṛṣabha Navāñśa, which is S2, where "S" denotes Savya Kālacakra, and "2" Vṛṣabha Rāśi.

The Daśā sequence for S2 is S10 → S11 → S12 → A8 → A7 → A6 → A4 → A5 → A3. Here, "S" stands for Savyacakra and numbers for the Rāśis. The Antardaśā sequences for the 9 Mahādaśā of Aśvinī-2 / Savya-Vṛṣabha Navāñśa are as follows:

Table 30: Antardaśās of Savya Vṛṣabha (Aśvinī2)

#	Mahādaśā	1	2	3	4	5	6	7	8	9
1	S10	S10	S11	S12	A8	A7	A6	A4	A5	A3
2	S11	A2	A1	A12	A11	A10	A9	S1	S2	S3
3	S12	S4	S5	S6	S7	S8	S9	S10	S11	S12
4	A8	A9	A10	A11	A12	A1	A2	A3	A5	A4
5	A7	A6	A7	A8	S12	S11	S10	S9	S8	S7
6	A6	S6	S5	S4	S3	S2	S1	A9	A10	A11
7	A4	S12	S11	S10	S9	S8	S7	S6	S5	S4
8	A5	A12	A1	A2	A3	A5	A4	A6	A7	(A8)
9	A3	(S3)	S2	S1	A9	A10	A11	A12	A1	A2

We notice that the ending Antardaśā of a Daśā connects with the Starting Antardaśā of the following Daśā according to the jumps stated by Maharṣi Parāśara. However, there is one violation, which is the ending of Siṅha Daśā (A5) and the starting of Mithuna Daśā (A3), which is because of the *Siṅha-Karka flip* in Apasavya Cakra. The *Siṅha-Karka flip* causes a break in the flow, which is causing the jump from Vṛścika to Dhanu. Otherwise, the jumps would have been according to the allowed jumps of the Maharṣi.

I do not think we can avoid this irregularity in any other manner. But, we can still confidently say that, in all other cases, the jumps occurring between the ending and starting Antardaśās are acceptable. When looking deeper, there are a few other inconsistencies which need deeper study. Still, I firmly believe that the nine Navanavāñśa sequences given for each Navāñśa are the key to defining the Antardaśās.

As per this principle, let's say we want to find the Pratyantardaśā in Makara Daśā, Vṛścika Antardaśā. In the above table, we notice that Vṛścika Antardaśā is denoted as A8, which means it is Vṛścika in the Apasavya Cakra, which the Navanavāñśa sequence is A9 → A10 → A11 → A12 → A1 → A2 → A3 → A5 → A4. Therefore, the Pratyantardaśā starts with Dhanu and moves in Apasavya order to Karka.

For working out the Mahādaśā, Antardaśā, Pratyantardaśā till Prāṇadaśā, we can use the same principle recursively, provided we know whether the Navāñśa is from Savya Kālacakra or Apasavya Kālacakra. The Navanavāñśa allotted to the different Rāśis in the Savya and Apasavya Cakra are summarised in the below table.

The Nakṣatra Caraṇa assigned to the 24 Savya and Apasavya Navāñśas is also mentioned. It hardly matters whether one uses the Navāñśas or the Nakṣatra Caraṇas in computation or delineation of a Kuṇḍalī because, at a fundamental level, they are identical. What is said about Aśvinī also applies to the four Caraṇas of Punarvasu, Hastā, Mūla, and Pūrvābhādra, which are also indicated below.

Table 31

					Navanavāñśa								
SA	Caraṇa	Group	Nakṣatras included	Navāñśa	1	2	3	4	5	6	7	8	9
S	1	Aśvinī	Aśvinī, Punarvasu, Hastā, Mūla, Pūrvābhādra	S1	S1	S2	S3	S4	S5	S6	S7	S8	S9
S	2	Aśvinī		S2	S10	S11	S12	A8	A7	A6	A4	A5	A3
S	3	Aśvinī		S3	A2	A1	A12	A11	A10	A9	S1	S2	S3
S	4	Aśvinī		S4	S4	S5	S6	S7	S8	S9	S10	S11	S12
S	1	Bharaṇī	Bharaṇī, Puṣya, Citrā, Pūrvāṣāṛhā, Uttarābhādra	S5	A8	A7	A6	A4	A5	A3	A2	A1	A12
S	2	Bharaṇī		S6	A11	A10	A9	S1	S2	S3	S4	S5	S6
S	3	Bharaṇī		S7	S7	S8	S9	S10	S11	S12	A8	A7	A6
S	4	Bharaṇī		S8	A4	A5	A3	A2	A1	A12	A11	A10	A9
S	1	Aśvinī	Kṛttikā, Aśleṣā, Svāti, Uttarāṣāṛhā, Revatī	S9	S1	S2	S3	S4	S5	S6	S7	S8	S9
S	2	Aśvinī		S10	S10	S11	S12	A8	A7	A6	A4	A5	A3
S	3	Aśvinī		S11	A2	A1	A12	A11	A10	A9	S1	S2	S3
S	4	Aśvinī		S12	S4	S5	S6	S7	S8	S9	S10	S11	S12
A	1	Rohiṇī	Rohiṇī, Maghā, Viśākhā, Śravaṇa	A8	A9	A10	A11	A12	A1	A2	A3	A5	A4
A	2	Rohiṇī		A7	A6	A7	A8	S12	S11	S10	S9	S8	S7
A	3	Rohiṇī		A6	S6	S5	S4	S3	S2	S1	A9	A10	A11
A	4	Rohiṇī		A5	A12	A1	A2	A3	A5	A4	A6	A7	A8
A	1	Mṛgaśirā	Mṛgaśirā, Pūrvāphālgunī, Anurādhā, Dhaniṣṭhā	A4	S12	S11	S10	S9	S8	S7	S6	S5	S4
A	2	Mṛgaśirā		A3	S3	S2	S1	A9	A10	A11	A12	A1	A2
A	3	Mṛgaśirā		A2	A3	A5	A4	A6	A7	A8	S12	S11	S10
A	4	Mṛgaśirā		A1	S9	S8	S7	S6	S5	S4	S3	S2	S1
A	1	Mṛgaśirā	Ārdrā, Uttarāphālg	A12	S12	S11	S10	S9	S8	S7	S6	S5	S4

									Navanavāñśa				
A	**2**	**Mṛgaśirā**	**unī, Jyeṣṭhā, Śatabhiṣā**	**A11**	S3	S2	S1	A9	A10	A11	A12	A1	A2
A	**3**	**Mṛgaśirā**		**A10**	A3	A5	A4	A6	A7	A8	S12	S11	S10
A	**4**	**Mṛgaśirā**		**A9**	S9	S8	S7	S6	S5	S4	S3	S2	S1

30.1.3.6
DEHA AND JĪVA

To sustain "Life" and "Creation", both "Deha" and "Jīva" need to be aligned and work together in harmony like two wheels of a Cart. If one fails, the sustenance of life becomes difficult. If both fail, life cannot be sustained at all. **Deha** is the Body, which is bounded, limited and has a structure to it. The soul assumes a body in each birth, which becomes the instrument for experiencing the results of previous karma and giving rise to new Karma. Good health, physical well-being, etc., are related to Deha.

On the other hand, **Jīva** is the life force; it is unbounded, unlimited and has no structure to it. It does not have a beginning or an end. It was there from the beginning, and it is there till eternal. It is the soul (Ātma) which assumes different Deha (physical body) in different births. One's drive, motivation, inspiration, energy, etc., are connected with the Jīva. In short, Deha is gross, and Jīva is subtle.

Maharṣi Parāśara (Bṛhatparāśara 46.59-60) states that "I shall describe in detail how the Deha and Jīva should be reckoned in the Caraṇas of the Nakṣatras. In the first Caraṇa of Aśvinī, Meṣa is indicative of Deha, and Dhanu is indicative of Jīva. And the Lords of Meṣa, Vṛṣabha, Mithuna, Karka, Siṅha, Kanyā, Tulā, Vṛścika and Dhanu are Lords of the Daśās in the order, as described before."

Each Nakṣatra Caraṇa is mapped to nine Navanavāñśas, which we can refer to as the chain of 9 Rāśis. The Deha and Jīva Rāśis are always the first and last Rāśi of the chain. All the intervening 7 Rāśis invariably fall within the Deha and Jīva Rāśis. For Aśvinī-1, the Deha is Meṣa and Jīva is Dhanu. For a Navāñśa, the Deha and Jīva are always fixed, and they are the first and last Daśā of the Navāñśa.

For Apasavya Nakṣatra, where the Daśā sequence is reversed, the Deha and Jīva position in the 9-Rāśi chain is also reversed, but they are essentially the same Rāśis. The table below gives the Deha and Jīva for the different Navāñśas. They are not limited only to the Navāñśas but can be used for Daśās, Antardaśās and other subperiods.

Table 32

#	Navāñśa	Deha	Jīva
1	**Meṣa**	Meṣa	Dhanu

#	Navāñśa	Deha	Jīva
2	**Vṛṣabha**	Makara	Mithuna
3	**Mithuna**	Vṛṣabha	Mithuna
4	**Karka**	Karka	Mīna
5	**Siṅha**	Vṛścika	Mīna
6	**Kanyā**	Kumbha	Kanyā
7	**Tulā**	Tulā	Kanyā
8	**Vṛścika**	Karka	Dhanu
9	**Dhanu**	Meṣa	Dhanu
10	**Makara**	Makara	Mithuna
11	**Kumbha**	Vṛṣabha	Mithuna
12	**Mīna**	Karka	Mīna

For one born in Anurādhā-4, the Navāñśa is Meṣa, and the Deha and Jīva are Meṣa and Dhanu, respectively. The Daśā sequence is Dha → Vṛś → Tul → Kan → Siṅ → Kar → Mit → Vṛṣ → Meṣ. Let us know find the Deha and Jīva for Vṛścika Daśā. According to the table above, Karka and Dhanu are the Deha and Jīva for Vṛścika Daśā. The Antardaśā sequence of Vṛścika is Kar → Siṅ → Mit → Vṛṣ → Meṣ → Mīn → Kum → Mak → Dha. Let us now find the Deha and Jīva for Karka Antardaśā.

The Pratyantardaśā sequence for Karka Antardaśā is Mīn → Kum → Mak → Dha → Vṛś → Tul → Kan → Siṅ → Kar, and the Deha and Jīva are Karka and Mīna respectively. In this manner, we can find out not only the Deha and Jīva for the Candra Navāñśa at birth but for every Daśā, Antardaśā till the Deha Antardaśā.

The Navāñśa Deha and Jīva are applicable almost the entire span of life, whereas the Daśā, Antar, etc. Deha and Jīva are applicable for the period of the said Daśā and Antardaśā and thus highly relevant for judging their effects. If the Daśā Deha and Jīva are afflicted, we can expect grave danger or calamity in that Daśā, and so on.

If we look carefully, the following are the only possible combinations of the Deha-Jīva pair. We notice that only Bṛhaspati and Budha are allowed to be Jīva. Bṛhaspati is the life force (Jīva) for Devas, and Budha is the life force (Jīva) for Asuras. Only Candra, Maṅgala, Śukra and Śani allowed to become Deha. Sūrya's Siṅha Rāśi cannot be either a Deha or Jīva. The Deha-Jīva combination is always between the Deva and Asura Group. Candra, Maṅgala and Bṛhaspati are Devas, whereas Śukra, Śani and Budha are Asuras. In each of the Nakṣatra Groups, viz., Aśvinī, Bharaṇī, Rohiṇī and Mṛgaśirā, the Deha-Jīva pairs are mapped to one of the four Caraṇas. In the Savya group viz., Aśvinī, Bharaṇī, the Deha and Jīva appear in the Deha-Jīva order. The order is reversed to Jīva-Deha in the Apasavya group, viz., Rohiṇī, Mṛgaśirā.

Table 33

#	Savya	Apasavya	Deha	Jīva	Dehādhiṣa	Jīvādhiṣa
1	**Aśvinī group 1st Caraṇa**	**Mṛgaśirā group 4th Caraṇa**	Meṣa	Dhanu	Maṅgala	Bṛhaspati

#	Savya	Apasavya	Deha	Jīva	Dehādhiṣa	Jīvādhiṣa
2	Aśvinī group 2nd Caraṇa	Mṛgaśirā group 3rd Caraṇa	Makara	Mithuna	Śani	Budha
3	Aśvinī group 3rd Caraṇa	Mṛgaśirā group 2nd Caraṇa	Vṛṣabha	Mithuna	Śukra	Budha
4	Aśvinī group 4th Caraṇa	Mṛgaśirā group 1st Caraṇa	Karka	Mīna	Candra	Bṛhaspati
5	Bharaṇī group 1st Caraṇa	Rohiṇī group 4th Caraṇa	Vṛścika	Mīna	Maṅgala	Bṛhaspati
6	Bharaṇī group 2nd Caraṇa	Rohiṇī group 3rd Caraṇa	Kumbha	Kanyā	Śani	Budha
7	Bharaṇī group 3rd Caraṇa	Rohiṇī group 2nd Caraṇa	Tulā	Kanyā	Śukra	Budha
8	Bharaṇī group 4th Caraṇa	Rohiṇī group 1st Caraṇa	Karka	Dhanu	Candra	Bṛhaspati

Table 34

#	Deha	Jīva
1	Maṅgala	Bṛhaspati
2	Candra	Bṛhaspati
3	Śukra	Budha
4	Shani	Budha

Here are the translations of the Ślokas of Maharṣi Parāśara

46.82. Maharṣi Parāśara said. O Brāhmaṇa! The description of the Deha and Jīva of the Caraṇas of the Apasavya Nakṣatras and the Daśā Lords is the same, as narrated by Lord Mahādeva to Devī Pārvati.

46.94-95. In the Savya Cakra, the first Añśa is called Deha and the last Jīva. The opposite is the case in the Apasavya Cakra. Therefore, the calculations (of Daśā Balance) should be based on the Deha, etc., in the Savya Cakra and on the Jīva, etc., in Apasavya.

30.1.3.7
GATI OF RĀŚIS IN KĀLACAKRA

The movement of the Daśā through the Kālacakras gives rise to different jumps, which are mainly known as Siṅhavlokana, Maṇḍūka and Marakaṭa. The Siṅhavlokana jump is a trinal jump, whereas Maṇḍūka is an alternate Rāśi jump, and Marakaṭa is a sudden reversal. The regular movement from one Rāśi to the next is not mentioned as a jump, but for ease of reference, I call it Sādhāraṇa Gati. Phaladīpikā calls the Marakaṭa Gati Aśva or Turagagati, implying horses, which suddenly changes its direction, which is seen in the Marakaṭa Gati.

The table below lists the different Gatis that are seen in different Nakṣatras and Caraṇas, which can be used as a ready reference. But this is not required with some practice. Whenever we see that the Daśā jumps to the Trinal Rāśi, mainly Vṛścika to Mīna or Dhanu to Meṣa or vice-versa, the Gati is Siṅhavlokana, when it is between Kanyā → Karka or Siṅha → Mithuna or vice-versa, it is Maṇḍūka Gati. The Marakaṭa Gati appears when there is a sudden reversal in direction caused by Karka-Siṅha in Apasavya Kālacakra.

Phaladīpikā

22.12. In the order of Rasis Vākyakrama, the junctions at the end of Karka, Vṛścika and Mīna give rise to (1) Maṇḍūka Gati, (2) Aśva or Turagagati, and (3) Siṅhavlokana respectively and the Daśās at these intervals cause woeful effects.

Table 35

#	Savya Apasavya group	Caraṇa	Daśā	Gati
1	Savya Aśvinī	2	Mīna → Vṛścika	Siṅhavlokana
2	Savya Aśvinī	2	Kanyā → Karka	Maṇḍūka
3	Savya Aśvinī	2	Siṅha → Mithuna	Maṇḍūka
4	Savya Aśvinī	3	Dhanu → Meṣa	Siṅhavlokana
5	Savya Bharaṇī	1	Kanyā → Karka	Maṇḍūka
6	Savya Bharaṇī	1	Siṅha → Mithuna	Maṇḍūka
7	Savya Bharaṇī	2	Dhanu → Meṣa	Siṅhavlokana
8	Savya Bharaṇī	3	Mīna → Vṛścika	Siṅhavlokana
9	Apasavya Rohiṇī	1	Mithuna → Siṅha	Maṇḍūka
10	Apasavya Rohiṇī	1	Siṅha → Karka	Marakaṭa
11	Apasavya Rohiṇī	1/2	Karka → Kanyā	Maṇḍūka
12	Apasavya Rohiṇī	2	Vṛścika → Mīna	Siṅhavlokana
13	Apasavya Rohiṇī	3	Meṣa → Dhanu	Siṅhavlokana
14	Apasavya Rohiṇī	4	Mithuna → Siṅha	Maṇḍūka
15	Apasavya Rohiṇī	4	Siṅha → Karka	Marakaṭa
16	Apasavya Rohiṇī	4	Karka → Kanyā	Maṇḍūka

#	Savya Apasavya group	Caraṇa	Daśā	Gati
17	Apasavya Mṛgaśirā	2	Meṣa → Dhanu	Siṅhavlokana
18	Apasavya Mṛgaśirā	3	Mithuna → Siṅha	Maṇḍūka
19	Apasavya Mṛgaśirā	3	Siṅha → Karka	Marakaṭa
20	Apasavya Mṛgaśirā	3	Karka → Kanyā	Maṇḍūka
21	Apasavya Mṛgaśirā	3	Vṛścika → Mīna	Siṅhavlokana

BṚHATPARĀŚARA

46.96-98. There are three kinds of movements (Gati) of the Rāśis in the Kālacakra, namely Maṇḍūka, Marakaṭa and Siṅhavlokana. The movement of one Rāśi by jumping over one Rāśi is known as Maṇḍūka Gati. The backward movement to the previous Rāśi is called Marakaṭa Gati. The movement of a Rāśi to the 5th and 9th Rāśi is said to be Siṅhavlokana.

46.99-100. Movement from Kanyā to Karka and from Siṅha to Mithuna is Maṇḍūka Gati. Movement from Siṅha to Karka is Marakaṭa Gati. Movement from Mīna to Vṛścika and from Dhanu to Meṣa is called Siṅhavlokana Gati.

EFFECTS OF DAŚĀS OF RĀŚIS, AS A RESULT OF THESE GATIS

Table 36

#	Savya Apasavya group Caraṇa	Daśā Gati	Generic results	Specific results
1	Savya Aśvinī Caraṇa 2	Mīna → Vṛścika Siṅhavlokana	Possibility of injury from animals, loss of amity with friends, distress to near relations, drowning in a well, fall from animals, the possibility of harm from poison, weapons and diseases and destruction of the residential dwelling.	Suffer from fever
2	Savya Aśvinī Caraṇa 2	Kanyā → Karka Maṇḍūka	Death of the mother or self, trouble from the Government and the possibility of brain fever.	Loss of brothers and kinsmen
3	Savya Aśvinī Caraṇa 2	Karka → Siṅha Marakaṭa	Loss of wealth, agricultural products and animals, death of the father, or an elderly close relation and feeling of lethargy.	Likely death
4	Savya Aśvinī Caraṇa 2	Siṅha → Mithuna Maṇḍūka	Death of the mother or self, trouble from the Government and the possibility of brain fever.	Ill health of the wife
5	Savya Aśvinī Caraṇa 3	Dhanu → Meṣa	Possibility of injury from animals, loss of amity with friends, distress to near relations, drowning in a well, fall from animals, the possibility of harm from	Death of uncles and similar relations

#	Savya Apasavya group Caraṇa	Daśā Gati	Generic results	Specific results
		Siṅhavlokana	poison, weapons and diseases and destruction of the residential dwelling.	
6	Savya-Bharaṇī Caraṇa 1	Kanyā → Karka Maṇḍūka	Death of the mother or self, trouble from the Government and the possibility of brain fever.	Loss of brothers and kinsmen
7	Savya-Bharaṇī Caraṇa 1	Karka → Siṅha Marakaṭa	Loss of wealth, agricultural products and animals, death of the father, or an elderly close relation and feeling of lethargy.	Likely death
8	Savya-Bharaṇī Caraṇa 1	Siṅha → Mithuna Maṇḍūka	Death of the mother or self, trouble from the Government and the possibility of brain fever.	Ill health of the wife
9	Savya-Bharaṇī Caraṇa 2	Dhanu → Meṣa Siṅhavlokana	Possibility of injury from animals, loss of amity with friends, distress to near relations, drowning in a well, fall from animals, the possibility of harm from poison, weapons and diseases and destruction of the residential dwelling.	Death of uncles and similar relations
10	Savya-Bharaṇī Caraṇa 3	Mīna → Vṛścika Siṅhavlokana	Possibility of injury from animals, loss of amity with friends, distress to near relations, drowning in a well, fall from animals, the possibility of harm from poison, weapons and diseases and destruction of the residential dwelling.	Suffer from fever

BṚHATPARĀŚARA

46.101-102. The effects of the Daśā of the Rāśis with Maṇḍūka Gati in the Savya Cakra are distress to friends, relations, parents and elders, and there is likely to be cause for trouble from poison, weapons, thieves and enemies. In the Maṇḍūka Daśā of the Gati of a Rāśi from Siṅha to Mithuna, there is the likelihood of the death of the mother or self, trouble from Government and the possibility of brain fever.

46.103. The effects of the Daśā of Rāśi with Marakaṭa Gati in the Savya Cakra are loss of wealth, agricultural products and animals, death of the father, or an elderly close relation and feeling of lethargy.

46.104-105. The effects of the Daśā of the Rāśis with Siṅhavlokana Gati in the Savya Cakra are the possibility of injury from animals, loss of amity with friends, distress to near relations, drowning in a well, fall from animals, the possibility of harm from poison, weapons and diseases and destruction of the residential dwelling.

Table 37

#	Savya Apasavya group Caraṇa	Daśā Gati	Generic results	Specific results
9	Apasavya Rohiṇī Caraṇa 1	Mithuna → Siṅha Maṇḍūka	Distress to wife and conditions, loss of children, the possibility of feverish conditions and loss of position	Ill health of the wife
10	Apasavya Rohiṇī Caraṇa 1	Siṅha → Karka Marakaṭa	Danger from watery places, loss of position, distress from father, punishment from Government and wandering in the forests	The native may die
11	Apasavya Rohiṇī Caraṇa 1-2	Karka → Kanyā Maṇḍūka	Distress to wife and conditions, loss of children, the possibility of feverish conditions and loss of position	Loss of brothers and kinsmen
12	Apasavya Rohiṇī Caraṇa 2	Vṛścika → Mīna Siṅhavlokana	Destruction of the dwelling and death of the father, etc	Suffer from fever
13	Apasavya Rohiṇī Caraṇa 3	Meṣa → Dhanu Siṅhavlokana	Destruction of the dwelling and death of the father, etc	Death of uncles and similar relations
14	Apasavya Rohiṇī Caraṇa 4	Mithuna → Siṅha Maṇḍūka	Distress to wife and conditions, loss of children, the possibility of feverish conditions and loss of position	Ill health of the wife
15	Apasavya Rohiṇī Caraṇa 4	Siṅha → Karka Marakaṭa	Danger from watery places, loss of position, distress from father, punishment from Government and wandering in the forests	The native may die
16	Apasavya Rohiṇī Caraṇa 4	Karka → Kanyā Maṇḍūka	Distress to wife and conditions, loss of children, the possibility of feverish conditions and loss of position	Loss of brothers and kinsmen
17	Apasavya Mṛgaśirā Caraṇa 2	Meṣa → Dhanu Siṅhavlokana	Destruction of the dwelling and death of the father, etc	Death of uncles and similar relations
18	Apasavya Mṛgaśirā Caraṇa 3	Mithuna → Siṅha Maṇḍūka	Distress to wife and conditions, loss of children, the possibility of feverish conditions and loss of position	Ill health of the wife
19	Apasavya Mṛgaśirā Caraṇa 3	Siṅha → Karka Marakaṭa	Danger from watery places, loss of position, distress from father, punishment from Government and wandering in the forests	The native may die
20	Apasavya Mṛgaśirā Caraṇa 3	Karka → Kanyā Maṇḍūka	Distress to wife and conditions, loss of children, the possibility of feverish conditions and loss of position	Loss of brothers and kinsmen

#	Savya Apasavya group Caraṇa	Daśā Gati	Generic results	Specific results
21	Apasavya Mṛgaśirā Caraṇa 3	Vṛścika → Mīna Siṅhavlokana	Destruction of the dwelling and death of the father, etc.	Suffer from fever

BṚHATPARĀŚARA

46.106-108. In the Daśā of the Rāśis with the Maṇḍūka Gati in the Apasavya Cakra, the effects are distress to the wife and conditions, loss of children, the possibility of feverish conditions and loss of position. In the Daśā of the Rāśis with the Marakaṭa Gati, there may be danger from watery places, loss of position, distress from father, punishment from the Government and wandering in the forests; with the Siṅhavlokana there may be the destruction of the dwelling and death of father etc.

46.109-111. If the movement is from Mīna to Vṛścika, the native may suffer from fever; if from Kanyā to Karka, there may be loss of brothers and kinsmen; if from Siṅha to Mithuna, there may be ill health of the wife; if from Siṅha to Karka, the native may die; if from Dhanu to Meṣa, there may be the death of uncles and similar relations. If the Rāśi is having a Krūrayuti, adverse conditions may be expected in the Daśā of the Rāśi. Favourable effects are felt in its Daśā if the Rāśi is having a Śubhayuti.

30.1.3.8
EFFECTS OF DAŚĀS

BṚHATPARĀŚARA

46.112-113. O Brāhmaṇa! In the Kālacakra Daśā, favourable and unfavourable effects may be predicted after considering the directions of the Rāśis and Grahas.

30.1.3.8.1
KĀLACAKRA AND TRAVEL

BṚHATPARĀŚARA

46.114-119. If the movement is from Kanyā to Karka, good results are realized in places located in the East, and at that time, journeys to the places in the North prove fruitful. Unfavourable effects are felt in places located in the West and the South. It is advisable not to undertake journeys in those directions in the Daśā of these Rāśis. If the movement is from Siṅha to Mithuna, no journey should be undertaken to places located in the East. ...

... However, the journeys to the South-West shall prove fruitful in the Daśā of those Rāśis. If the movement is from Karka to Siṅha, journeys during that period to the South shall prove unfavourable and result in loss, and the native has to return from the South to the West. If the movement is from Mīna to Vṛścika, there shall be distress if the native goes to the North. The same would happen if the movement is from Dhanu to Makara. ...

... There may be ill health, imprisonment, or death if the movement is from Dhanu to Meṣa. There may be gains, comforts, property and marriage if the movement is from Dhanu to Vṛścika. It shall not be advisable to undertake journeys to the West during the related period if the movement is from Siṅha to Karka. Favourable results should be predicted if the Rāśis are yuti with Saumyas and adverse if the Rāśis are yuti with Krūras.

30.1.3.8.2
EFFECTS OF SPECIFIC AÑŚAS

Table 38

#	Navāñśa	Results
1	**Meṣa**	Thief
2	**Vṛṣabha**	Wealthy
3	**Mithuna**	Learned
4	**Karka**	King
5	**Siṅha**	Respected by the King
6	**Kanyā**	Learned
7	**Tulā**	Minister or Advisor
8	**Vṛścika**	Not available
9	**Dhanu**	Sinful
10	**Makara**	Not available
11	**Kumbha**	Businessman
12	**Mīna**	Wealthy

BṚHATPARĀŚARA

46.120-122. According to the Kālacakra mentioned above, the person born in the Añśas of the various Rāśis is, as under. Meṣa Añśa brave and a thief, Vṛṣabha wealthy, Mithuna learned, Karka king, Siṅha respected by the king, Kanyā learned, Tulā minister, or adviser, Dhanu sinful, Kumbha businessman, Mīna wealthy.

30.1.3.8.3
EFFECTS OF DEHA AND JĪVA

BṚHATPARĀŚARA

46.123-128. If the Deha or Jīva Rāśis are yuti with Sūrya, Maṅgala, Śani, or Rāhu, the native shall die. Worse results may be expected if the Deha and Jīva Rāśis are yuti with two or all of them. If there is a malefic in Deha Rāśi, the native suffers ill health; a malefic in a Jīva Rāśi shall make the native very timid. If the Deha or Jīva Rāśi are yuti with two Krūras, there is distress and diseases. ...

... Three Krūras in the Deha or Jīva Rāśi shall cause premature death. Four Krūras in the Deha and Jīva Rāśi shall cause definite death. If Krūras occupy both the Deha and Jīva Rāśis, there is danger from the king and thieves and the death of the native. If Sūrya is in the Deha or Jīva Rāśi, there is danger from fire. ...

... Candra in the Deha or Jīva Rāśi shall cause danger from water, Maṅgala danger from weapons, Budha danger from windy troubles, Śani danger from Gulma (a disease), Rāhu and Ketu danger from poison. If Budha, Bṛhaspati and Śukra occupy the Deha or Jīva Rāśis, the native is wealthy, shall enjoy all kinds of comforts and shall have good health. Mixed results may be expected if both Saumyas and Krūras occupy the Deha and Jīva Rāśis.

46.129-130. In the Daśā of the Rāśis, owned by Krūras, the body and soul is in distress. The effects are favourable in the Daśā of the Rāśis, owned by Saumyas. If a Saumya occupies a Krūra Rāśi, or if a Krūra occupies a Saumya Rāśi, the effects are mixed.

30.1.3.8.4
EFFECTS OF KĀLACAKRA DAŚĀ OF BHĀVAS

Here are the high-level effects of Kālacakra Daśā of the Rāśis in Lagna and other Bhāvas. We must critically examine all which Bhāva the Daśā and Antardaśā Rāśis fall. These Bhāvas become the primary focus in such Daśāntardaśā.

If the Rāśi is owned or occupied by a Saumya or by a Graha in great dignity such as Sva-Ucca-Mitra, then the Bhāva flourishes in such a Daśā. But if the Rāśi is owned or occupied by a Krūra or has a Graha in low dignity, such as Nīca-Śatru, then the Bhāva is ruined, and the native suffers from evils arising from that Bhāva.

Table 39

#	Bhāva	General results	Under Śubha influences	Under Krūra influences
1	Lagna	The body remains healthy, and the native spends life with many kinds of comforts.	Good effects are realized fully. A Graha in dignity: the native is respected by the king or government and acquires wealth.	Likelihood of ill health
2	Dhana	Receives good food, enjoys the happiness of wife and children, gains wealth, achieves progress in the educational sphere, becomes a clever conversationalist and moves into a good society	Good effects are realized fully.	Effects would be of a mixed nature.

#	Bhāva	General results	Under Śubha influences	Under Krūra influences
3	**Sahaja**	Happiness from co-borns, courage, patience, comforts, acquisition of gold, ornaments and clothes and recognition by the king or government,	Good effects are realized fully.	Adverse effects may also be experienced.
4	**Sukha**	Good relations with kinsmen, acquisition of land, houses, or kingdom, conveyances and clothes and enjoyment of sound health	If the Rāśi is Saumya, the good effects are realized in full. If it is a Krūra Rāśi, adverse results are also experienced.	
5	**Mantra**	Being blessed with a wife and children, favours from Government, enjoyment of sound health, good relations with friends, the achievement of fame, good progress in the educational sphere, patience and courage	If the Rāśi is Saumya, the good results are enjoyed in full. If the Rāśi is Krūra, adverse effects are also experienced.	
6	**Śatru**	Danger from the king, fire and weapons and the possibility of suffering from diabetes, Gulma and jaundice	Mitigation of the evil results	Adverse effects are experienced in full
7	**Dārā**	Marriage, marital happiness, being blessed with children, a gain of agricultural products, cows and clothes, favours and recognition from the king and achievement of fame	The beneficial results are experienced in full if the Rāśi is Saumya. Meagre good effects are realized in the case of a Krūra Rāśi.	
8	**Randhra**	Destruction of a residential house, distress, loss of wealth, poverty and danger from enemies	The adverse effects are realized in full if the Rāśi is Krūra. Some mitigation in evil effects may be expected in the case of a Saumya Rāśi.	
9	**Bhāgya**	Not stated	Not stated	Not stated
10	**Karma**	Not stated	Not stated	Not stated
11	**Lābha**	Not stated	Not stated	Not stated
12	**Vyāya**	Not stated	Not stated	Not stated

BṚHATPARĀŚARA

46.131-132. In the Kālacakra Daśā of the Rāśi in Lagna, the body remains healthy, and the native spends life with many kinds of comforts. If the Lagna Rāśi is Saumya, the good effects are realized fully. If the Lagna Rāśi is Krūra, there is a likelihood of ill health. If a Graha in Ucca or Sva Rāśi occupies Lagna, the native is respected by the king or government and acquires wealth.

46.133-134. In the Cakra Daśā of the Rāśi in Dhana, the native receives good food, enjoys the happiness of his wife and children, gains wealth, achieves progress in the educational sphere, becomes a clever conversationalist and moves into good society. If the Rāśi is Saumya, good effects are realized in full; otherwise, the effects would be of a mixed nature.

46.135-136. Happiness from co-borns, bravery, patience, comforts, acquisition of gold, ornaments and clothes and recognition by the king or government are the effects in the Kālacakra Daśā of the Rāśi in Sahaj. If the Rāśi is Saumya, the good results are realized in full; otherwise, adverse effects may also be experienced.

46.137-138. Good relations with kinsmen, acquisition of land, houses, or kingdom, conveyances and clothes and enjoyment of sound health are the effects of the Cakra Daśā of the Rāśi in Bandhu. If the Rāśi is Saumya, the good effects are realized in full. If it is a malefic Rāśi, adverse results are also experienced.

46.139-140. Being blessed with a wife and children, favours from Government, enjoyment of sound health, good relations with friends, the achievement of fame, good progress in the educational sphere, patience and bravery are the effects of the Cakra Daśā of the Rāśi in Putra. If the Rāśi is Saumya, the good results are enjoyed in full. If the Rāśi is Krūra, adverse effects are also experienced.

46.141-142. Danger from the king, fire and weapons and the possibility of suffering from diabetes, Gulma (tumour) and jaundice are the effects of the Cakra Daśā of the Rāśi in 6H. If the Rāśi is Krūra, the above adverse effects are experienced in full. There is some mitigation of the evil effects in the case of a Saumya Rāśi.

46.143-144. Marriage, marital happiness, being blessed with children, a gain of agricultural products, cows and clothes, favours and recognition from the king and achievement of fame are the effects of the Cakra Daśā of the Rāśi in Yuvati. The beneficial results are experienced in full if the Rāśi is Saumya. Meagre good effects are realized in the case of a malefic Rāśi.

46.145-146. Destruction of a residential house, distress, loss of wealth, poverty and danger from enemies are the effects of the Cakra Daśā of the Rāśi in Randhra. The adverse effects are realized in full if the Rāśi is Krūra. Some mitigation in evil effects may be expected in the case of a Saumya Rāśi.

30.1.3.8.5
EFFECTS OF THE KĀLACAKRA

BṚHATPARĀŚARA

49.1-5. Maharṣi Parāśara said. O Brāhmaṇa! I am now going to describe to you the effects of the Kālacakra Daśā. During the Daśā of the Rāśi, owned or occupied by Sūrya, there is ill-health due to blood or bile troubles; ... Candra, there is a gain of wealth and clothes, name and fame and the birth of children; ... Maṅgala, there is bilious fever, gout and wounds; ... Budha, there is the acquisition of wealth and birth of children; ... Bṛhaspati, there is an increase in the number of children, acquisition of wealth and enjoyment; ... Śukra, there is the acquisition of learning, marriage and gain of wealth; ... occupied by Śani, there are all kinds of adverse happenings.

Table 40

#	##	Navāñśa	Daśā	Results	Special Gati
1	1	Meṣa	Meṣa	Distressed due to troubles caused by the pollution of blood	-
2	2	Meṣa	Vṛṣabha	Increase in wealth and agricultural product	-
3	3	Meṣa	Mithuna	Advancement of knowledge	-
4	4	Meṣa	Karka	Acquisition of wealth	-
5	5	Meṣa	Siṅha	Danger from enemies	-
6	6	Meṣa	Kanyā	Distress to wife	-
7	7	Meṣa	Tulā	Kingship	-
8	8	Meṣa	Vṛścika	Death	-
9	9	Meṣa	Dhanu	Acquisition of wealth	-
10	1	Vṛṣabha	Makara	A tendency to perform undesirable deeds along with more adverse effects	-
11	2	Vṛṣabha	Kumbha	Profits in business	-
12	3	Vṛṣabha	Mīna	Success in all ventures	-
13	4	Vṛṣabha	Vṛścika	Danger from fire	Siṅhavlokana
14	5	Vṛṣabha	Tulā	Recognition from the Government and reverence from all	-
15	6	Vṛṣabha	Kanyā	Danger from enemies	-
16	7	Vṛṣabha	Karka	Distress to wife	Maṇḍūka
17	8	Vṛṣabha	Siṅha	Diseases of eyes	Marakaṭa
18	9	Vṛṣabha	Mithuna	Obstacles in earning a livelihood	Maṇḍūka
19	1	Mithuna	Vṛṣabha	Acquisition of wealth	-
20	2	Mithuna	Meṣa	Attacks of fever	-
21	3	Mithuna	Mīna	Affectionate relations with a maternal uncle	-
22	4	Mithuna	Kumbha	Increase in the number of enemies	-
23	5	Mithuna	Makara	Danger from thieves	-

#	##	Navāñśa	Daśā	Results	Special Gati
24	6	Mithuna	Dhanu	Increase in the stock of weapons	-
25	7	Mithuna	Meṣa	(to be verified)	Siṅhavlokana
26	8	Mithuna	Vṛṣabha	Injury by some weapon (to be verified)	-
27	9	Mithuna	Mithuna	Enjoyment	-
28	1	Karka	Karka	Distress	-
29	2	Karka	Siṅha	The displeasure of the sovereign	-
30	3	Karka	Kanyā	Reverence from kinsmen	-
31	4	Karka	Tulā	Beneficence	-
32	5	Karka	Vṛścika	Creation of obstacles by father	-
33	6	Karka	Dhanu	Increase in learning and wealth	-
34	7	Karka	Makara	Danger from water	-
35	8	Karka	Kumbha	Increase in the production of agricultural products	-
36	9	Karka	Mīna	Acquisition of more wealth and enjoyment	-
37	1	Siṅha	Vṛścika	Distress and disputes	Siṅhavlokana
38	2	Siṅha	Tulā	Extraordinary gains	-
39	3	Siṅha	Kanyā	Gains of wealth	-
40	4	Siṅha	Karka	Danger from wild animals	Maṇḍūka
41	5	Siṅha	Siṅha	Birth of a son	Marakaṭa
42	6	Siṅha	Mithuna	Increase of enemies	Maṇḍūka
43	7	Siṅha	Vṛṣabha	Gains from the sale of cattle	-
44	8	Siṅha	Meṣa	Danger from animals	-
45	9	Siṅha	Mīna	Journeys to distant places	-
46	1	Kanyā	Kumbha	Acquisition of wealth	-
47	2	Kanyā	Makara	Financial gains	-
48	3	Kanyā	Dhanu	Mingling with kinsmen	-
49	4	Kanyā	Meṣa	Happiness from mother	Siṅhavlokana
50	5	Kanyā	Vṛṣabha	Birth of children	-
51	6	Kanyā	Mithuna	Increase in enemies	-
52	7	Kanyā	Karka	Love with some woman	-
53	8	Kanyā	Siṅha	Aggravation of diseases	-
54	9	Kanyā	Kanyā	Birth of children	-
55	1	Tulā	Tulā	Financial gains	-
56	2	Tulā	Vṛścika	Good relations with kinsmen	-
57	3	Tulā	Dhanu	Happiness from father	-
58	4	Tulā	Makara	Disputes with mother	-
59	5	Tulā	Kumbha	Birth of a son and financial gains	-
60	6	Tulā	Mīna	Entanglement with enemies	-
61	7	Tulā	Vṛścika	Disputes with women	Siṅhavlokana
62	8	Tulā	Tulā	Danger from water	-
63	9	Tulā	Kanyā	More financial gains	-
64	1	Vṛścika	Karka	Financial gains	Maṇḍūka

#	##	Navāñśa	Daśā	Results	Special Gati
65	2	Vṛścika	Siṅha	Opposition to the king	Marakaṭa
66	3	Vṛścika	Mithuna	Acquisition of land	Maṇḍūka
67	4	Vṛścika	Vṛṣabha	Financial gains	-
68	5	Vṛścika	Meṣa	Danger from reptiles	-
69	6	Vṛścika	Mīna	Danger from water	-
70	7	Vṛścika	Kumbha	Profits in business	-
71	8	Vṛścika	Makara	Possibility of suffering from diseases	-
72	9	Vṛścika	Dhanu	Financial gains	-
73	1	Dhanu	Meṣa	Financial gains	Siṅhavlokana
74	2	Dhanu	Vṛṣabha	Acquisition of more land	-
75	3	Dhanu	Mithuna	Success in ventures	-
76	4	Dhanu	Karka	Success all round	-
77	5	Dhanu	Siṅha	Increase in the accumulated wealth	-
78	6	Dhanu	Kanyā	Disputes	-
79	7	Dhanu	Tulā	Financial gains	-
80	8	Dhanu	Vṛścika	Affliction with diseases	-
81	9	Dhanu	Dhanu	Happiness from children	-
82	1	Makara	Makara	Happiness from children	-
83	2	Makara	Kumbha	A gain of agricultural products	-
84	3	Makara	Mīna	Wellbeing	-
85	4	Makara	Vṛścika	Danger from poison	Siṅhavlokana
86	5	Makara	Tulā	Financial gains	-
87	6	Makara	Kanyā	Increase in enemies	-
88	7	Makara	Karka	Acquisition of property	Maṇḍūka
89	8	Makara	Siṅha	Danger from wild animals	Marakaṭa
90	9	Makara	Mithuna	The danger of falling from a tree	Maṇḍūka
91	1	Kumbha	Vṛṣabha	Financial gains	-
92	2	Kumbha	Meṣa	Diseases of the eyes	-
93	3	Kumbha	Mīna	Journeys to distant places	-
94	4	Kumbha	Kumbha	Increase in wealth	-
95	5	Kumbha	Makara	Success in all kinds of ventures	-
96	6	Kumbha	Dhanu	More enemies	-
97	7	Kumbha	Meṣa	Loss of happiness and enjoyment	Siṅhavlokana
98	8	Kumbha	Vṛṣabha	Death	-
99	9	Kumbha	Mithuna	Wellbeing	-
100	1	Mīna	Karka	Increase in wealth	-
101	2	Mīna	Siṅha	Recognition by Government	-
102	3	Mīna	Kanyā	Financial gains	-
103	4	Mīna	Tulā	Gains from all sources	-
104	5	Mīna	Vṛścika	Fever	-
105	6	Mīna	Dhanu	More enemies	-

#	##	Navāñśa	Daśā	Results	Special Gati
106	7	Mīna	Makara	Conjugal disputes	-
107	8	Mīna	Kumbha	Danger from water	-
108	9	Mīna	Mīna	Good fortune all-round	-

REFERENCES
BṚHATPARĀŚARA

49.6-7. In the Kālacakra Daśā of Meṣa in Meṣa Navāñśa, there is distress due to troubles caused by the pollution of blood. In the Daśā of Meṣa in the Navāñśa of Vṛṣabha, there is an increase in wealth and agricultural products. In the Navāñśa of Mithuna, there is an advancement of knowledge. In the Navāñśa of Karka, there is the acquisition of wealth, in the Siṅha Navāñśa danger from enemies, in the Kanyā distress to wife, in the Tulā kingship, in the Vṛścika death and the Dhanu acquisition of wealth. Such are the effects of the nine Caraṇas of Meṣa. In assessing the net effects, the nature of the Graha occupying the Rāśi should also be considered.

49.8-10. In the Daśā of Makara Navāñśa in Vṛṣabha, there is a tendency to perform undesirable deeds along with more adverse effects. In the Kumbha Navāñśa, there are profits in business, in the Mīna success in all ventures, in the Daśā of Vṛścika Navāñśa danger from fire, in the Daśā of Tulā Navāñśa recognition from Government and reverence from all, in the Daśā of Kanyā Navāñśa danger from enemies, in the Daśā of Karka Navāñśa distress to wife, in the Daśā of Siṅha Navāñśa diseases of eyes and in the Daśā of Mithuna Navāñśa obstacles in earning a livelihood. Such are the effects of the 9 Navāñśas of Vṛṣabha. A similar interpretation should be made of further ślokas on this subject.

49.11-12. In Mithuna in the Daśā of the Vṛṣabha Añśa, there is the acquisition of wealth; in the Daśā of Meṣa Añśa attacks of fever, in the Daśā of Mīna Añśa affectionate relations with a maternal uncle, in the Daśā of Kumbha Añśa increase in the number of enemies, in the Daśā of Makara Añśa danger from thieves, in the Daśā of Dhanu Añśa increase in the stock of weapons, in the Daśā of Vṛṣabha Añśa injury by some weapon and the Daśā of Mithuna Añśa enjoyment.

49.13-15. In Karka in the Daśā of Karka Añśa, there is distress, ... Siṅha displeasure of the sovereign, ... Kanyā reverence from kinsmen, ... Tulā beneficence, ... Vṛścika creation of obstacles by father, ... Dhanu increase of learning and wealth, ... Makara danger from water, ... Kumbha increase in the production of agricultural products and the Daśā of the Mīna Añśa acquisition of more wealth and enjoyment.

49.16-17. In Siṅha in the Daśā of the Navāñśa of Vṛścika there is distress and disputes, ... Tulā extraordinary gains, ... Kanyā gains of wealth, ... Karka danger from wild animals, ... Siṅha birth of a son, ... Mithuna increase of enemies, ... Vṛṣabha gains from the sale of cattle, ... Meṣa danger from animals and in the Daśā of Mīna Añśa journeys to distant places.

49.18-19. In Kanyā in the Daśā of Kumbha Añśa, there is the acquisition of wealth, ... Makara financial gains, ... Dhanu mingling with kinsmen, ... Meṣa happiness from mother, ... Vṛṣabha birth of children, ... Mithuna increase in enemies, ... Karka love with some woman, ... Siṅha aggravation of diseases and in the Daśā of Kanyā Añśa birth of children.

49.20-22. In Tulā in the Daśā of Tulā Añśa, there are financial gains, ... Vṛścika good relations with kinsmen, ... Dhanu happiness from father, ... Makara disputes with mother, ... Kumbha birth of a son and financial gains, ... Mīna entanglement with enemies, ... Vṛścika disputes with women, ... Tulā danger from water and in Daśā of Kanyā Añśa more financial gains.

49.23-24½. In Vṛścika in the Daśā of Karka Añśa, there is financial gains, ... Siṅha opposition to the king, ... Mithuna acquisition of land, ... Vṛṣabha financial gains, ... Meṣa danger from reptiles, ... Mīna danger from water, ... Kumbha profits in business, ... Makara profits in business, ... Makara possibility of suffering from diseases and in the Daśā of Dhanu Añśa financial gains.

49.25-27. In Dhanu in the Daśā of Meṣa Añśa there is financial gains, ... Vṛṣabha acquisition of more land, ... Mithuna success in ventures, ... Karka success all round, ... Siṅha increase in the accumulated wealth, ... Kanyā disputes, ... Tulā financial gains, ... Vṛścika affliction with diseases, ... Dhanu happiness from children.

49.28-29. In Makara in the Daśā of Makara Añśa, there is happiness from children, ... Kumbha gain of agricultural products, ... Mīna wellbeing, ... Vṛścika danger from poison, ... Tulā financial gains, ... Kanyā increase in enemies, ... Karka acquisition of property, ... Siṅha danger from wild animals and in the Daśā of Mithuna Añśa danger of falling from a tree.

49.30-32. In Kumbha in the Daśā of Vṛṣabha Añśa, there are financial gains, ... Meṣa diseases of the eyes, ... Mīna journeys to distant places, ... Kumbha increase in wealth, ... Makara success in all kinds of ventures, ... Dhanu more enemies, ... Meṣa loss of happiness and enjoyment, ... Vṛṣabha death, ... Mithuna wellbeing.

49.33-34½. In Mīna in the Daśā of Karka Añśa, there is an increase in wealth, ... Siṅha recognition by Government, ... Kanyā financial gains, ... Tulā gains from all sources, ... Vṛścika fever, ... Dhanu more enemies, ... Makara conjugal disputes, ... Kumbha danger from water and in the Daśā of Mīna Añśa good fortune all-round. In this manner, on the Kālacakra, prepared on the basis of Caraṇa of the Janma Nakṣatra, the Daśās of the Navāñśa Rāśis and their duration can be assessed, and prediction can be made for the whole life of the native. Appropriate remedial measures (recitation of Mantras, oblations, etc.) should be taken to alleviate the adverse effects caused by malefic Daśās.

49.35-37. The effects of Daśā in Rājayoga, etc., have already been described in Vol. I of this book. The same should be applied judiciously in the Kālacakra. These are, in brief, the effects of Kālacakra Daśā.

PHALADĪPIKĀ

22.1. The Triad of stars reckoned from Aśvinī should be cast by quarters in the Apasavya) or Pradakṣiṇa order from Meṣa to Mīna among the 12 Rasis to which the Navāñśas composing the Triad belong. Again, the 12 quarters of the Triad reckoned from Rohiṇī are to be assigned to the 12 Rasis counted from Vṛścika to Dhanus in the (Savya-reverse, Apradakṣiṇa or anti-clockwise) order.

22.2. Thus, are the Triads of tats reckoned in their order from Aśvinī to be distinguished as Apasavya and Savya). The years assigned to a Graha constitute the Daśā-period of the Rāśi owned by that Graha. This is the peculiarity in the Kālacakra system, say the wise.

22.3. 5, 21, 7, 9, 10, 16, and 4 are the numbers representing the period in years, respectively, of the seven Grahas reckoned from Sūrya and are the means (sources) far feeling the good and bad effects.

22.4. In this Kālacakra system consisting of Daśās, Apaharas, etc., I shall now expound the formulae for the several Nakṣatra Caraṇas from Aśvinī onwards. Every such formula consists of nine syllables indicating by their number (as per Kaṭapayādi) the particular Rāśyāpaharas composing the Daśā of the Nakṣatra Caraṇa under consideration, and consequently, the total life period appertaining to that by means of the year allotted to the several Rāśi owners.

22.5. For these born in the first Caraṇa of Aśvinī, the first subperiod belongs Meṣa-Maṅgala; the second, to Vṛṣabha-Śukra; the third to Mithuna-Budha; the fourth to Karka-Candra; the fifth to Sinha Sūrya; the sixth to Kanyā-Budha; the seventh to Tulā-Śukra; the eighth to Vṛścika-Maṅgala; and the 9th to Dhanu-Bṛhaspati.

For the 2nd Caraṇa of Aśvinī, the subperiods are owned by (1) Makara-Śani, (2) Kumbha-Śani, (3) Mīna-Bṛhaspati, (4) Vṛścika-Maṅgala, (5) Tulā-Śukra, (6) Kanyā-Budha, (7) Karka-Candra, (8) Siṅha-Sūrya and (9) Mithuna-Budha.

For the 3rd Caraṇa of Aśvinī, the subperiods belong to (1) Vṛṣabha-Śukra, (2) Meṣa-Maṅgala, (3) Mīna-Bṛhaspati, (4) Kumbha-Śani, (5) Makara-Śani, (6) Dhanu-Bṛhaspati, (7) Meṣa-Maṅgala, (8) Vṛṣabha-Śukra and (9) Mithuna-Budha.

For the 4th Caraṇa of Aśvinī, the subperiods are owned by (1) Karka-Candra, (2) Siṅha-Sūrya, (3) Kanyā-Budha, (4) Tulā-Śukra, (5) Vṛścika-Maṅgala, (6) Dhanu-Bṛhaspati, (7) Makara-Śani, (8) Kumbha-Śani and (9) Mīna-Bṛhaspati.

22.6. For the 1st Caraṇa of Bharaṇī, the several subperiods are (1) Vṛścika-Maṅgala, (2) Tulā-Śukra, (3) Kanyā-Budha, (4) Karka-Candra, (5) Siṅha-Sūrya, (6) Mithuna-Budha, (7) Vṛṣabha-Śukra, (8) Meṣa-Maṅgala, and (9) Mīna-Bṛhaspati.

For the 2nd Caraṇa of Bharaṇī, the subperiods are (1) Kumbha-Śani, (2) Makara-Śani, (3) Dhanu-Bṛhaspati, (4) Meṣa-Maṅgala, (5) Vṛṣabha-Śukra; (6) Mithuna-Budha, (7) Karka-Candra, (8) Siṅha-Sūrya and (9) Kanyā-Budha.

For the 3rd Caraṇa of Bharaṇī, the subperiods are (1) Tulā-Śukra, (2) Vṛścika-Maṅgala, (3) Dhanu -Bṛhaspati, (4) Makara-Śani, (5) Kumbha-Śani, (6) Mīna-Bṛhaspati, (7) Vṛścika-Maṅgala, (8) Tulā-Śukra and (9) Kanyā-Budha.

For the 4th Caraṇa of Bharaṇī, the subperiods are (1) Karka-Candra, (2) Siṅha-Sūrya, (3) Mithuna-Budha, (4) Vṛṣabha-Śukra, (5) Meṣa-Maṅgala, (6) Mīna-Bṛhaspati, (7) Kumbha-Śani, (8) Makara-Śani, and (9) Dhanu-Bṛhaspati.

22.7. The formulae for Aśvinī and Bharaṇī are described above. The four formulae given for the four Caraṇas of Aśvinī shall also respectively apply to the four Caraṇas of Kṛttikā in the Apasavya-pradakshina Triad. The formulae for Rohiṇī and Mṛgaśirā in the Savya-Triad are stated in the next two Ślokas, and the four formulae given for the four Caraṇas of Mṛgaśirā should also be used again for the four Caraṇas of Ārdrā.

22.8. The sub divisions for the Caraṇa of Rohiṇī are (1) Dhanu-Bṛhaspati, (2) Makara-Śani, (3) Kumbha-Śani, (4) Mīna-Bṛhaspati, (5) Meṣa-Maṅgala, (6) Vṛṣabha -Śukra, (7) Mithuna-Budha, (8) Siṅha-Sūrya and (9) Karka-Candra.

For the 2nd Caraṇa of Rohiṇī, the subperiods are (1) Kanyā-Budha, (2) Tulā-Śukra, (3) Vṛścika-Maṅgala, (4) Mīna-Bṛhaspati, (5) Kumbha-Śani, (6) Makara-Śani, (7) Dhanu-Bṛhaspati, (8) Vṛścika-Maṅgala and (9) Tulā-Śukra.

For the 3rd Caraṇa of Rohiṇī, the subperiods are (1) Kanyā-Budha, (2) Siṅha-Sūrya, (3) Karka-Candra, (4) Mithuna-Budha, (5) Vṛṣabha-Śukra, (6) Meṣa-Maṅgala, (7) Dhanu-Bṛhaspati, (8) Makara-Śani, and (9) Kumbha-Śani.

The 4th Caraṇa of Rohiṇī has the following subperiods (1) Mīna-Bṛhaspati, (2) Meṣa-Maṅgala, (3) Vṛṣabha-Śukra, (4) Mithuna-Budha, (5) Siṅha-Sūrya, (6) Karka-Candra (7) Kanyā-Budha, (8) Tulā-Śukra and (9) Vṛścika-Maṅgala.

22.9. For the 1st Caraṇa of Mṛgaśirā, the subperiods are (1) Mīna-Bṛhaspati, (2) Kumbha-Śani, (3) Makara-Śani, (4) Dhanu-Bṛhaspati, (5) Vṛścika-Maṅgala, (6) Tulā-Śukra, (7) Kanyā-Budha, (8) Siṅha-Sūrya, (9) Karka-Candra.

The subperiods for the 2nd Caraṇa of Mṛgaśirā are (1) Mithuna-Budha, (2) Vṛṣabha-Śukra, (3) Meṣa-Maṅgala, (4) Dhanu-Bṛhaspati, (5) Makara-Śani, (6) Kumbha-Śani, (7) Mīna-Bṛhaspati, (8) Meṣa-Maṅgala and (9) Vṛṣabha-Śukra.

The subperiods for the 3rd Caraṇa of Mṛgaśirā are (1) Mithuna-Budha, (2) Siṅha-Sūrya, (3) Karka-Candra, (4) Kanyā-Budha, 5) Tulā-Śukra, (6) Vṛścika-Maṅgala, (7) Mīna-Bṛhaspati, (8) Kumbha-Śani and (9) Makara-Śani.

The subperiods for the 4th Caraṇa of Mṛgaśirā are (1) Dhanu-Bṛhaspati, (2) Vṛścika-Maṅgala, (3) Tulā-Śukra, (4) Kanyā-Budha (5) Siṅha-Sūrya, (6) Karka-Candra, (7) Mithuna-Budha, (8) Vṛṣabha-Śukra, and (9) Meṣa-Maṅgala.

22.10. The initial Mahādaśā of life belongs to the lord of the Rāśi owning the Nakṣatra Caraṇa occupied by the Candra at the time of birth, being so much of the Rāśi Mahādaśā as corresponds to the Ghaṭis that yet remain of the Nakṣatra Caraṇa. The order of Mahādaśās follows the natural order of the Nakṣatra Caraṇas reckoned from the one described above. This is the opinion, say the sages, held by some (Ācāryas).

22.11. There is a number of formulae, each composed of a number of mnemonic syllables referring to the several Nakṣatra Pad s beginning with the first Caraṇa of Aśvinī and giving Rasis in a certain order. It is with reference to the order of Rasis in these formulae that the Rāśi Mahādaśās of which life is to consist, should be determined. The Vākyakrama men of one school say that should be adhered to.

22.12. In the order of Rasis Vākyakrama, the junctions at the end of Karka, Vṛścika and Mīna give rise to (1) Maṇḍūka Gati, (2) Aśva or Turagagati, and Siṁhavlokana respectively and the Daśās at these intervals cause woeful effects.

22.13. The Apahara or Bhukti of a Graha constituting a Mahādaśā is thus obtained. Find out the particular mnemonical syllable (out of the nine syllables) composing a formula whose Bhukti is wanted and find out the owner of the Rāśi signified by that syllable. Multiply the number of years assigned to this Graha by the number of years fixed for the Graha whose Mahādaśā is under consideration and divide the product by the total number of years constituting the Paramāyus of the formula or Cakra. The quotient in years, etc., Shall represent the subperiod required.

22.14. The total number of years indicated by the sum of the nine mnemonical syllables of any formula represents then the number (in years) of Paramāyus for that formula. Thus, the Paramāyus in years for the 12 Rāśyaṅśas reckoned from Meṣa in an Apasavya Cakra is 100, 85, 83 and 86 repeated thrice, while those for the 17 Rasis Aṅśas reckoned from Vṛścika in a Savya Cakra is the same but in the reverse order; that 86, 83, 85 and 100 repeated thrice.

30.1.3.9
CASE STUDIES

I have presented here three case studies where I have used the year definition as 360 days a year, i.e., the Sāvanavarṣa. I wrote these case studies in the 2018-2019 timeframe when I believed that all Daśās should be based on the Sāvanavarṣa definition of a year.

However, as my research continued, I realized that the Nakṣatra or Graha Daśās, such as Viñśottarī, Aṣṭottarī, etc., should be based on this year definition. But the Rāśi Daśās, such as Sudarśana Cakra, Cara, Sthira Daśā, etc., should be based on Sauravarṣa of mean year duration of 365.2563 days.

Kālacakra is a less used Daśā and also with lesser research. In this Daśā, a small variation of someone's birth time can have a significant impact on the Daśā years. Therefore, this requires significant research. Due to differences in opinions among the scholars, consistent research with the right Daśā definition was not possible before. However, since I have now established the correct approach to casting the Daśā-Antardaśā, I hope that more research takes place for this Daśā moving forward.

In the below examples, I have used the Sāvanavarṣa definition of a year. However, in the discourse section, I have investigated this with a 365.2563 days per year definition (Mean Sauravarṣa). My current standing is that for all Rāśi Daśās, we must use the Sauravarṣa definition. *However, I have chosen to keep the below computations with 360 days definition.*

I intend for the seekers and researchers to continue researching on this subject. My recommendation is to start with Sauravarṣa. Whether one uses Mean or True Sauravarṣa depends on the availability of software. If the software is not available, then I have provided a link to an Excel calculator where the mean Sauravarṣa of 365.2563 days can be used. I would also recommend not to dive deeper into Pratyantar or lower levels since one may get unreliable results. Daśā-Antardaśā is a good level to work out examples!

30.1.3.9.1
SUBHASH CHANDRA BOSE

Śrī Subhash Chandra Bose (23 January 1897 at 12:15, Cuttack, India, 20n30, 85e50) is the founder of the Indian National Army, a great Indian patriot and statesman. He was elected the President of India's Congress Party in 1938, but in 1941, he fled to Germany, then to Malaya, where he set up a *Provisional Government of Free India in 1943.*

It is widely believed that he died in a plane crash on 22nd August 1945; however, this is also highly debatable. Many believed that his death was faked, but the real reason behind that is not yet known. The Rodden Rating for his birth details is "A", which means that we must verify his Candrasphuṭa. The

Candrasphuṭa is Kanyā 7:20:25.95 (157.341). His Janma Nakṣatra is 157.341 * 3/40 = 11.8, which is 12 – Uttarāphālgunī.

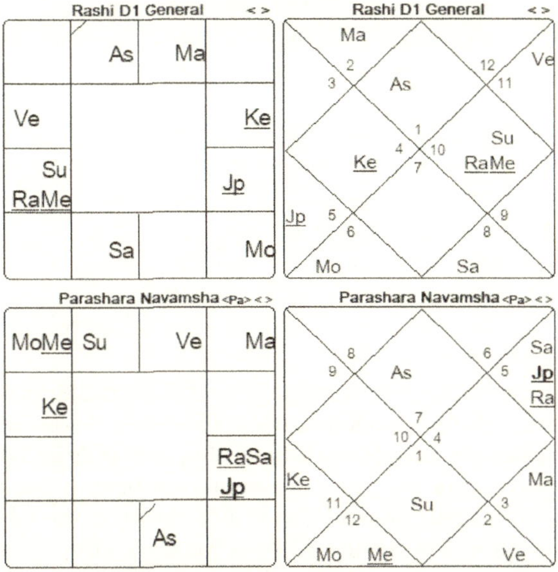

The Nakṣatra Sphuṭa is 0.801 * 40/3 = 10.674°. The Nakṣatra Caraṇa Sphuṭa is arrived as follows: (1) 10.674 * 60 / 200 = 3.202 = 4th Caraṇa and (2) 0.202163 * 200 = 40.433'. He was born in the 4th Caraṇa of Uttarāphālgunī, of which 40.433' has expired. The balance of Nakṣatra Caraṇa is 200 - 40.433 = 159.567'. Uttarāphālgunī is an Apasavya Nakṣatra and is the 3rd Nakṣatra of the 4th Triad, which is Maghā-Pūrvāphālgunī-Uttarāphālgunī. This maps to the 12th Navāñśa of Apasavya Kālacakra, which is Dhanu. Therefore, we can say that Śrī Bose was born in Apasavya Dhanu (A9).

Table 41

					Navanavāñśa								
SA	**Pāda**	**Grp**	**Nakṣ**	**Añśa**	**1**	**2**	**3**	**4**	**5**	**6**	**7**	**8**	**9**
S	**1**	Aśv	**Aśv, Pun, Has, Mūl, PBh**	**S1**	S1	S2	S3	S4	S5	S6	S7	S8	S9
S	**2**	Aśv		**S2**	S10	S11	S12	A8	A7	A6	A4	A5	A3
S	**3**	Aśv		**S3**	A2	A1	A12	A11	A10	A9	S1	S2	S3
S	**4**	Aśv		**S4**	S4	S5	S6	S7	S8	S9	S10	S11	S12
S	**1**	Bha	**Bha, Puṣ, Cit, PĀṣ, UBh**	**S5**	A8	A7	A6	A4	A5	A3	A2	A1	A12
S	**2**	Bha		**S6**	A11	A10	A9	S1	S2	S3	S4	S5	S6
S	**3**	Bha		**S7**	S7	S8	S9	S10	S11	S12	A8	A7	A6
S	**4**	Bha		**S8**	A4	A5	A3	A2	A1	A12	A11	A10	A9
S	**1**	Aśv	**Kṛt, Aśl, Svā, UĀṣ, Rev**	**S9**	S1	S2	S3	S4	S5	S6	S7	S8	S9
S	**2**	Aśv		**S10**	S10	S11	S12	A8	A7	A6	A4	A5	A3
S	**3**	Aśv		**S11**	A2	A1	A12	A11	A10	A9	S1	S2	S3
S	**4**	Aśv		**S12**	S4	S5	S6	S7	S8	S9	S10	S11	S12

				Navanavāñśa									
A	1	Roh	Roh,	**A8**	A9	A10	A11	A12	A1	A2	A3	A5	A4
A	2	Roh	Mag,	**A7**	A6	A7	A8	S12	S11	S10	S9	S8	S7
A	3	Roh	Viś,	**A6**	S6	S5	S4	S3	S2	S1	A9	A10	A11
A	4	Roh	Śra	**A5**	A12	A1	A2	A3	A5	A4	A6	A7	A8
A	1	Mrg	Mrg,	**A4**	S12	S11	S10	S9	S8	S7	S6	S5	S4
A	2	Mrg	PPh,	**A3**	S3	S2	S1	A9	A10	A11	A12	A1	A2
A	3	Mrg	Anu,	**A2**	A3	A5	A4	A6	A7	A8	S12	S11	S10
A	4	Mrg	Dha	**A1**	S9	S8	S7	S6	S5	S4	S3	S2	S1
A	1	Mrg	Ārd,	**A12**	S12	S11	S10	S9	S8	S7	S6	S5	S4
A	2	Mrg	UPh,	**A11**	S3	S2	S1	A9	A10	A11	A12	A1	A2
A	3	Mrg	Jye,	**A10**	A3	A5	A4	A6	A7	A8	S12	S11	S10
A	4	Mrg	Śat	**A9**	S9	S8	S7	S6	S5	S4	S3	S2	S1

From the table, we notice that Uttarāphālgunī falls in the Mrgaśirā group, and the 4th Caraṇa of this group has sequence S9 → S8 → S7 → S6 → S5 → S4 → S3 → S2 → S1. The Daśā starts from Savya-Dhanu (S9) and ends in Savya-Meṣa (S1). Since the Candra Navāñśa is Apasavya-Dhanu, the Deha is the last Rāśi, Meṣa, and the Jīva is the first Rāśi, Dhanu. This is also shown in the table below, which gives us the Deha and Jīva for the 12 Navāñśas. We notice that against Dhanu Navāñśa, the Deha and Jīva are Meṣa and Dhanu respectively.

Table 42

#	Navāñśa	Deha	Jīva	Āyuṣa1	Āyuṣa2
1	**Meṣa**	Meṣa	Dhanu	7	100
2	**Vṛṣabha**	Makara	Mithuna	16	85
3	**Mithuna**	Vṛṣabha	Mithuna	9	83
4	**Karka**	Karka	Mīna	21	86
5	**Siṅha**	Vṛścika	Mīna	5	100
6	**Kanyā**	Kumbha	Kanyā	9	85
7	**Tulā**	Tulā	Kanyā	16	83
8	**Vṛścika**	Karka	Dhanu	7	86
9	**Dhanu**	Meṣa	Dhanu	10	100
10	**Makara**	Makara	Mithuna	4	85
11	**Kumbha**	Vṛṣabha	Mithuna	4	83
12	**Mīna**	Karka	Mīna	10	86

Let us find the Daśā balance and the Daśā prevailing at birth. We found that the Nakṣatra Caraṇa expired is 40.433', and the Āyuṣa of Dhanu Navāñśa is 100 years. This implies that 40.433/200 * 100 = 20.216 years have expired, and 79.784 years remain. Now, when did Dhanu Navāñśa commence in his life?

It must have been 20.216 years before! Isn't it? This works out to be "1877-02-19 15:39:32 IST". We arrived at this derived by 20.216 years or

7277.850 days from the birth date and time. Here we have assumed that one year is 360 days, which I found largely accurate.

Table 43

#	Daśā	Sav Apa	Year	Start	End
1	Dhanu	S	10	19-02-1877	29-12-1886
2	Vṛścika	S	7	29-12-1886	22-11-1893
3	Tulā	S	16	22-11-1893	31-08-1909
4	Kanyā	S	9	31-08-1909	15-07-1918
5	Siṅha	S	5	15-07-1918	19-06-1923
6	Karka	S	21	19-06-1923	29-02-1944
7	Mithuna	S	9	29-02-1944	12-01-1953
8	Vṛṣabha	S	16	12-01-1953	20-10-1968
9	Meṣa	S	7	20-10-1968	14-09-1975

Table 44

#	Daśā code2	Daśā	Year	Duration	Start	End
1	S9	Dhanu	10	3600	19-02-1877	29-12-1886
2	S8	Vṛścika	7	2520	29-12-1886	22-11-1893
3	S7	Tulā	16	5760	22-11-1893	31-08-1909
4	S6	Kanyā	9	3240	31-08-1909	15-07-1918
5	S5	Siṅha	5	1800	15-07-1918	19-06-1923
6	S4	Karka	21	7560	19-06-1923	29-02-1944
7	S3	Mithuna	9	3240	29-02-1944	12-01-1953
8	S2	Vṛṣabha	16	5760	12-01-1953	20-10-1968
9	S1	Meṣa	7	2520	20-10-1968	14-09-1975

Let us now determine which Navāñśa could be fatal for him. When the Daśā, Antar or other subperiods of that Navāñśa are operational, danger to his life could be predicted. We notice that none of the Navāñśas is afflicted because of Deha-Jīva affliction, as for none, both the Deha and Jīva are afflicted. However, Krūras afflict Vṛṣabha, Karka, Vṛścika and Makara, and their periods could be fatal. Among them, Makara is the most afflicted because of Aditya-Caṇḍāla yoga. We can also say that the Deha of Vṛṣabha, Siṅha, Vṛścika, Makara and Karka are also afflicted.

Table 45

#	Navāñśa	Deha	Jīva	Grahas in Deha	Grahas in Jīva
1	Meṣa	Meṣa	Dhanu	-	-
2	Vṛṣabha	Makara	Mithuna	Rāhu, Sūrya, Budha	-
3	Mithuna	Vṛṣabha	Mithuna	-	-
4	Karka	Karka	Mīna	Ketu	-
5	Siṅha	Vṛścika	Mīna	Śani	-
6	Kanyā	Kumbha	Kanyā	Śukra	Candra

#	Navāñśa	Deha	Jīva	Grahas in Deha	Grahas in Jīva
7	**Tulā**	Tulā	Kanyā	-	Candra
8	**Vṛścika**	Karka	Dhanu	Ketu	-
9	**Dhanu**	Meṣa	Dhanu	-	-
10	**Makara**	Makara	Mithuna	Rāhu, Sūrya, Budha	-
11	**Kumbha**	Vṛṣabha	Mithuna	-	-
12	**Mīna**	Karka	Mīna	Ketu	-

Śrī Bose started his Mithuna Daśā on 29-02-1944, and the Antardaśā of this Daśā are given below. From the Daśā table, we notice that Mithuna is a Savya-Mithuna (S3), for which the Daśā sequence is A2 → A1 → A12 → A11 → A10 → A9 → S1 → S2 → S3. He faced grave danger to his life on **22-08-1945**, which is when he is believed to have died in a plane crash. During this time, he was running Mithuna Daśā and Meṣa Antardaśā. Mithuna and Meṣa Rāśi are not afflicted, and their Deha and Jīva are also free from affliction.

This indicates that the claim of his death is spurious. Now, this Daśā is highly sensitive to minor changes to Candrasphuṭa. Since his birth time is debatable, a few minutes of error before and after could be possible. If he were born 2' earlier, his Antardaśā would have been Vṛṣabha. Maṅgala afflicts Vṛṣabha, and Rāhu, Sūrya and Budha also afflict Deha Makara. The affliction to Deha does indicate some danger to his body, but death is less likely because Jīva is not afflicted.

Table 46: Antardaśā

#	Daśā code2	Daśā	Year	Duration	Start	End
1	**A2**	Vṛṣabha	10	324.0	29-02-1944	18-01-1945
2	**A1**	Meṣa	7	226.8	18-01-1945	02-09-1945
3	**A12**	Mīna	16	518.4	02-09-1945	02-02-1947
4	**A11**	Kumbha	9	291.6	02-02-1947	21-11-1947
5	**A10**	Makara	5	162.0	21-11-1947	01-05-1948
6	**A9**	Dhanu	21	680.4	01-05-1948	12-03-1950
7	**S1**	Meṣa	9	291.6	12-03-1950	29-12-1950
8	**S2**	Vṛṣabha	16	518.4	29-12-1950	30-05-1952
9	**S3**	Mithuna	7	226.8	30-05-1952	12-01-1953

30.1.3.9.2
MAHATMA GANDHI

Śrī Mahatma Gandhi's data (2 October 1869 at 07:08:12 LMT, Porbandar, India, 21n38, 69e36) is debatable, as Rodden's rating is "C", which is rectified from approx. time. The time I am considering is 07:25 (GMT+4:38). He was assassinated on 30 January 1948, 5:12 PM, in Delhi, India. The Ayanāñśa used is Ayanāñśa "22:9:4.98" and his Candrasphuṭa is Karka 27:57:36.75 (117.960).

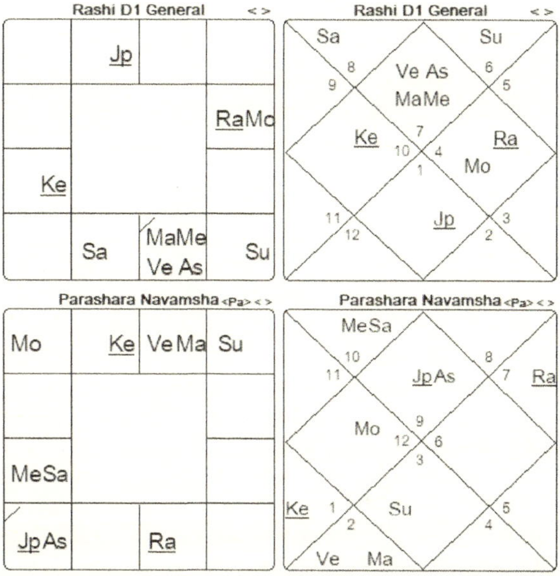

He was born in Aśleṣā-4, an Apasavya Nakṣatra and mapped to Mīna Navāñśa, of 86 years. The Nakṣatra Caraṇa balance is 0.388, the Daśā expired is 33.373, and the balance is 52.627. The Mīna Navāñśa commenced on 1836-11-09 21:27 UT. The Mahādaśās are as follows:

Table 47

#	Daśā code2	Daśā	Year	Duration	Start	End
1	S4	Karka	21	7560	-	-
2	S5	Siṅha	5	1800	-	-
3	S6	Kanyā	9	3240	-	-
4	S7	Tulā	16	5760	-	-
5	S8	Vṛścika	7	2520	-	-
6	S9	Dhanu	10	3600	-	19-11-1903
7	S10	Makara	4	1440	19-11-1903	29-10-1907
8	S11	Kumbha	4	1440	29-10-1907	08-10-1911
9	S12	Mīna	10	3600	08-10-1911	16-08-1921

The first Navāñśa covered his life will 1921, after which he must move into his next Navāñśa Daśā. He is born in the 4th Caraṇa of Aśleṣā Nakṣatra, which ends the Savya Kālacakra. After that, the Daśā must move to the 1st Caraṇa of the same cycle, which is of Punarvasu-1, which is mapped to Meṣa Navāñśa. The Daśā of the previous Navāñśa ended with Mīna, and the new Navāñśa commences with Meṣa. The Daśā transition is smooth from Mīna to Meṣa, indicating no danger during this period. For Savya Meṣa Navāñśa, the Daśā sequence is regular from Meṣa to Dhanu.

Table 48

#	Daśā code2	Daśā	Year	Duration	Start	End
1	S1	Meṣa	7	2520	16-08-1921	10-07-1928
2	S2	Vṛṣabha	16	5760	10-07-1928	17-04-1944
3	S3	Mithuna	9	3240	17-04-1944	01-03-1953
4	S4	Karka	21	7560	01-03-1953	11-11-1973
5	S5	Siṅha	5	1800	11-11-1973	16-10-1978
6	S6	Kanyā	9	3240	16-10-1978	30-08-1987
7	S7	Tulā	16	5760	30-08-1987	07-06-2003
8	S8	Vṛścika	7	2520	07-06-2003	01-05-2010
9	S9	Dhanu	10	3600	01-05-2010	09-03-2020

In the Deha/Jīva chart, we notice that Tulā is considerably afflicted, as here, both the Deha and Jīva are afflicted by Krūras. Among the Rāśis, the afflicted Rāśis are **Karka, Kanyā, Tulā, Vṛścika and Makara**. The dangerous Rāśis are evidently Tulā, followed by Karka, Vṛścika, Makara and Kanyā.

Table 49

#	Navāṅśa	Deha	Jīva	Grahas in Deha	Grahas in Jīva
1	**Meṣa**	Meṣa	Dhanu	Bṛhaspati	-
2	**Vṛṣabha**	Makara	Mithuna	Ketu	-
3	**Mithuna**	Vṛṣabha	Mithuna	-	-
4	**Karka**	Karka	Mīna	Rāhu, Candra	-
5	**Siṅha**	Vṛścika	Mīna	Śani	-
6	**Kanyā**	Kumbha	Kanyā	-	Sūrya
7	**Tulā**	Tulā	Kanyā	Maṅgala, Budha, Śukra	Sūrya
8	**Vṛścika**	Karka	Dhanu	Rāhu, Candra	-
9	**Dhanu**	Meṣa	Dhanu	Bṛhaspati	-
10	**Makara**	Makara	Mithuna	Ketu	-
11	**Kumbha**	Vṛṣabha	Mithuna	-	-
12	**Mīna**	Karka	Mīna	Rāhu, Candra	-

Let us focus on the Mithuna Daśā, which ran from 1944 to 1953. The Antardaśās of this Daśā are given in the below table. Śrī Gandhi passed away on 30 Jan 1948, during which Kumbha Antardaśā Daśā was in progress. Since there are some inaccuracies in his birth time, let us also consider Mīna and Māraka Antardaśā, which are before and after Kumbha. In our assessment of the death inflicting Rāśis, we Mīna and Kumbha are not identified, whereas Makara is indeed identified as a death inflicting Rāśi. Makara has two-prong afflictions: (1) before the Rāśi itself is afflicted, and (2) the Deha of the Rāśi is afflicted. We can adjust the birth time somewhat so that Makara Rāśi Daśā falls during the Jan 1948 timeframe.

Table 50

#	Daśā code2	Daśā	Year	Duration	Start	End
1	A2	Vṛṣabha	7	226.8	17-04-1944	30-11-1944
2	A1	Meṣa	16	518.4	30-11-1944	03-05-1946
3	A12	Mīna	9	291.6	03-05-1946	18-02-1947
4	A11	Kumbha	21	680.4	18-02-1947	30-12-1948
5	A10	Makara	5	162.0	30-12-1948	10-06-1949
6	A9	Dhanu	9	291.6	10-06-1949	28-03-1950
7	S1	Meṣa	16	518.4	28-03-1950	29-08-1951
8	S2	Vṛṣabha	7	226.8	29-08-1951	11-04-1952
9	S3	Mithuna	10	324.0	11-04-1952	01-03-1953

30.1.3.9.3
SARAJIT PODDAR

I am presenting my own Daśā here, not with the intention of revealing my personal experiences, but because I wanted to validate how effective Kālacakra Daśā is for rectification of birth time. I was born in a place where no one was around to deliver me. When my father arrived, bringing someone to attend to my mother, I was already delivered, and no one was present there to record my time.

Based on approximate time, my Janmakuṇḍalī was cast by my uncle, a great Jyotiṣī, and Tantra Mantra Siddha Puruṣa. I was said to be born in Dhanu Lagna, but the Navāñśa Lagna has been doubtful ever since. After much research and experimentation, I settled with Mithuna Navāñśa, with Sūrya in it. I have done detailed Birthtime rectification for my birth and validated the Janma Vighaṭi, Kunda and Prāṇapada, three crucial components at birth that must be in sync.

I think that this is a good case study to verify the birth time based on the computation rules we have defined for the Kālacakra Daśā. I have taken the liberty of zooming down to the Pratyantardaśā level, which is affected by slight variations of the Candrasphuṭa. I also intend to verify the Ayanāñśa, based on which the Candrasphuṭa is derived. The birth details that I use are 14:34:28 IST on 25th August 1974, at Patratu, India (Lon: 85E17, Lat: 23N40).

The Ayanāñśa I use is Sṛṣṭi Ayanāñśa, which for the day is 23°37'0" and Candrasphuṭa Vṛścika 16:31:57.29 (226.533°). The birth occurred in the 8th Navāñśa of Apasavya Kālacakra, in Anurādhā Caraṇa 4, and the Navāñśa is Meṣa Navāñśa. The Nakṣatra Caraṇa expired is 0.960, and the expired Daśā of 100 years of Meṣa is 95.977. The Daśā remaining at birth is 4.023 year of Meṣa Daśā in Meṣa Navāñśa.

After the completion of the 4+ years of Meṣa Daśā of Meṣa Navāñśa, the Daśā moves to the Mīna Navāñśa, where the Daśā commences with Mīna. *The transition from Meṣa Daśā to Mīna Daśā between Meṣa Navāñśa to Mīna Navāñśa is smooth as they are the adjacent Rāśis.* Meṣa governed the first four years of my life. Meṣa is the 5H in the Rāśi Kuṇḍalī from the Janma Lagna and the 6H from the Candra Kuṇḍalī.

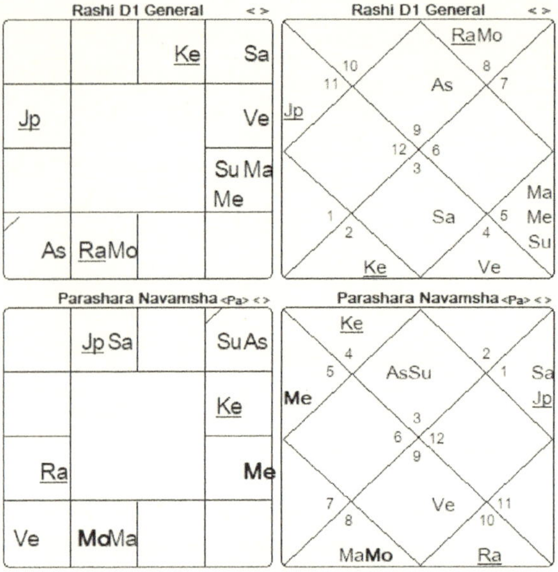

No one afflicts the Rāśi, but the lord Maṅgala is conjunct with his Śatru Budha in Siṅha Rāśi. In the Navāñśa, however, Meṣa is afflicted by the Bṛhaspati and Śani conjunction. Śani is Nīca, indicating health troubles.

Table 51: Daśā cycle 1

#	Daśā code2	Daśā	Year	Duration	Start	End
1	S9	Dhanu	10	3600	-	-
2	S8	Vṛścika	7	2520	-	-
3	S7	Tulā	16	5760	-	29-07-1912
4	S6	Kanyā	9	3240	29-07-1912	12-06-1921
5	S5	Siṅha	5	1800	12-06-1921	17-05-1926
6	S4	Karka	21	7560	17-05-1926	27-01-1947
7	S3	Mithuna	9	3240	27-01-1947	11-12-1955
8	S2	Vṛṣabha	16	5760	11-12-1955	18-09-1971
9	S1	Meṣa	7	2520	18-09-1971	12-08-1978

After Meṣa, the period of the next Navāñśa, Mīna commenced on 12-08-1978, with the Daśā of Mīna. The health trouble continued in the first 3 Daśās of Mīna, viz., Mīna, Kumbha and Makara, and it started improving from Dhanu onwards.

Table 52: Daśā cycle 2

#	Daśā code2	Daśā	Year	Duration	Start	End
1	S12	Mīna	10	3600	12-08-1978	20-06-1988
2	S11	Kumbha	4	1440	20-06-1988	30-05-1992
3	S10	Makara	4	1440	30-05-1992	09-05-1996
4	S9	Dhanu	10	3600	09-05-1996	18-03-2006
5	S8	Vṛścika	7	2520	18-03-2006	09-02-2013
6	S7	Tulā	16	5760	09-02-2013	17-11-2028
7	S6	Kanyā	9	3240	17-11-2028	01-10-2037
8	S5	Siṅha	5	1800	01-10-2037	05-09-2042
9	S4	Karka	21	7560	05-09-2042	18-05-2063

Let us review the affliction to the Rāśis, their Deha and Jīva. We notice that Mithuna is the most afflicted, followed by Siṅha. Vṛṣabha and Vṛścika are significantly afflicted as well. From the list of afflicted Rāśis, it is not clear why I continued to suffer during the initial 3 Daśās, but this can be known from other Daśā, which in this case is Viñśottarī Daśā, in which Budha Daśā was operational till August 1991. Maharṣi Parāśara advised us to use the Triñśāñśa Kuṇḍalī for all kinds of evil, including health troubles.

In the Triñśāñśa Kuṇḍalī, we notice that Makara has the nodes, Kumbha Sūrya, and Mīna Śukra and Candra. Śukra and Candra are Saumyas, but their conjunction is not considered favourable as they are because of water-related health issues. Candra is also the Randhreśa in the Rāśi Kuṇḍalī, which is afflicting Śukra, indicating suffering due to low immunity. In Mīna-Makara, I suffered from Typhoid, which continued for more than two weeks, and it took way too long to recover. This is seen from the presence of Rāhu-Ketu in Makara Triñśāñśa.

Table 53: Deha and Jīva for Rāśis

#	Rāśi	Graha	Deha	Jīva	Grahas in Deha	Grahas in Jīva
1	**Meṣa**	-	Meṣa	Dhanu	-	-
2	**Vṛṣabha**	Ketu	Makara	Mithuna	-	Śani
3	**Mithuna**	Śani	Vṛṣabha	Mithuna	Ketu	Śani
4	**Karka**	Śukra-	Karka	Mīna	Śukra	-
5	**Siṅha**	Sūrya, Maṅgala, Budha	Vṛścika	Mīna	Candra, Rāhu	-
6	**Kanyā**	-	Kumbha	Kanyā	Bṛhaspati	-
7	**Tulā**	-	Tulā	Kanyā	-	-
8	**Vṛścika**	Candra, Rāhu	Karka	Dhanu	Śukra	-
9	**Dhanu**	-	Meṣa	Dhanu	-	-
10	**Makara**	-	Makara	Mithuna	-	Śani
11	**Kumbha**	Bṛhaspati	Vṛṣabha	Mithuna		
12	**Mīna**	-	Karka	Mīna		

I ran Kanyā Antardaśā in Makara Daśā from 06-01-1994 to 01-10-1994, and it was a traumatic period for me. I lost my father on 17-02-1994, and from that time onwards till the end of the Daśā on 09-05-1996, it was a period of untold trouble. Kanyā is not afflicted in the Rāśi Kuṇḍalī, but Maṅgala afflicts its lord in the 9th house. The death of the father can be better seen from other Vargakuṇḍalīs, which shall be covered later. But we do see the troubles due to the Budha-Maṅgala conjunction. In the Triñśāñśa Kuṇḍalī of evils, Budha is afflicted in Karka Rāśi due to the conjunction of Rāhu-Ketu.

Table 54: Antardaśā in Makara Daśā

#	Daśā code2	Daśā	Year	Duration	Start	End
1	S10	Makara	10	167.4	30-05-1992	14-11-1992
2	S11	Kumbha	4	67.0	14-11-1992	20-01-1993
3	S12	Mīna	4	67.0	20-01-1993	28-03-1993
4	A8	Vṛścika	10	167.4	28-03-1993	11-09-1993
5	A7	Tulā	7	117.2	11-09-1993	06-01-1994
6	A6	Kanyā	16	267.9	06-01-1994	01-10-1994
7	A4	Karka	9	150.7	01-10-1994	01-03-1995
8	A5	Siṅha	5	83.7	01-03-1995	24-05-1995
9	A3	Mithuna	21	351.6	24-05-1995	09-05-1996

The Vṛścika Daśā started on 18-03-2006 and ran till 09-02-2013. Nīca Rāhu and Candra considerably afflict Vṛścika. It was an unsettling period, as there were significant uncertainly in my professional life. I worked very long hours to deliver complex projects, but progress was not in sight. My career stagnated for a large part of the period, and my health suffered from fatigue. Vṛścika is the 12th Rāśi from the Lagna and the 1st from Candra Lagna. It contains Candra, the 9th lord from the Candra Lagna, also promising good things in life.

Rāhu in the Lagna, if well-aspected, promises a rise of status, but Rāhu is Nīca, indicating no such promises. The Candra Lagna lord Maṅgala is aspecting the Lagna, and Candra is also powerful due to Śukla Navamī birth, indicating that its Nīcatva is of not much significance. The 9th lord also promises children because it is the 5th from the 5th, which, according to Bhāvāt Bhāvam principle, behaves like the 5th. It was during this period I became the father of two wonderful children, first a daughter and then a son.

The daughter was born in the Karka Antardaśā because Karka is the 9th house, which, as I mentioned above, is capable of blessing one with a child. An adorable daughter of the Rupa of Devī Durgā is born in this Antara. However, due to the conjunction of its lord Candra with Rāhu, the first ten years were of danger. Candra is associated with 10 (Dasabhujā Devī Durgā and Viñśottarī period are ten years). She is named after Devī Durgā. A year later, when I was in Vṛṣabha Antardaśā, I had another blessing; this time, that of a son. The lord of Vṛṣabha, Śukra, is in Karka, again promising another child. Since Śukra is in Pāpakartari yoga, even the son had some danger to his life in his infancy, but not as much as the daughter.

Table 55: Antardaśā in Vṛścika Daśā

#	Daśā code2	Daśā	Year	Duration	Start	End
1	A4	Karka	10	293.0	18-03-2006	05-01-2007
2	A5	Siṅha	4	117.2	05-01-2007	02-05-2007
3	A3	Mithuna	4	117.2	02-05-2007	28-08-2007
4	A2	Vṛṣabha	10	293.0	28-08-2007	16-06-2008
5	A1	Meṣa	7	205.1	16-06-2008	07-01-2009
6	A12	Mīna	16	468.8	07-01-2009	21-04-2010
7	A11	Kumbha	9	263.7	21-04-2010	09-01-2011
8	A10	Makara	5	146.5	09-01-2011	05-06-2011
9	A9	Dhanu	21	615.3	05-06-2011	09-02-2013

It was in Kanyā or Tulā Pratyantardaśā; the daughter was born. I believe she was born in Tulā Pratyantar for the very same reason as Śukra, who is in Karka Rāśi, the 9th from Candra. It was just before Tulā ended she was born. In the Saptāñśa Kuṇḍalī, which is seen for children, Tulā Rāśi is occupied by Rāhu, who is conjunct with 9L Candra in the Rāśikuṇḍalī. Rāhu in Tulā Rāśi that a Śukra, a feminine Graha, owns indicates a fierce form of Devī Durgā, with whose blessings the daughter is born.

Table 56: Pratyantardaśā in Kumbha Daśā

#	Daśā code2	Daśā	Year	Duration	Start	End
1	S12	Mīna	10	34.654	18-03-2006	22-04-2006
2	S11	Kumbha	4	13.862	22-04-2006	06-05-2006
3	S10	Makara	4	13.862	06-05-2006	20-05-2006
4	S9	Dhanu	10	34.654	20-05-2006	23-06-2006
5	S8	Vṛścika	7	24.258	23-06-2006	18-07-2006
6	S7	Tulā	16	55.446	18-07-2006	11-09-2006
7	S6	Kanyā	9	31.188	11-09-2006	12-10-2006
8	S5	Siṅha	5	17.327	12-10-2006	29-10-2006
9	S4	Karka	21	72.773	29-10-2006	10-01-2007

It was near about half an hour after Sūryāsta (Sandhyā Kāla) when the sacred chants of lord Śiva were playing in the delivery room; my son was born in Bharaṇī Nakṣatra. It was Siṅha Pratyantardaśā that was current at that time. Siṅha is the 9th house from the Lagna and conjunct with the 5th lord Maṅgala and aspected by Putrakāraka Bṛhaspati.

Siṅha is a good candidate for promising a son, also because Bṛhaspati, the 2nd and 5th lord from Candra, is also aspecting Siṅha. In the Saptāñśa Kuṇḍalī, Siṅha is occupied by Candra, who is the giver of children in the Kuṇḍalī. We have already identified the role of Candra in the Rāśikuṇḍalī being the 9th lord. The involvement of Candra in Saptāñśa endorses that. It was due to the blessings of lord Somanātha Śiva the Son was born.

Table 57: Pratyantardaśā in Vṛṣabha Dasa

#	Daśā code2	Daśā	Year	Duration	Start	End
1	A3	Mithuna	9	31.555	28-08-2007	28-09-2007
2	A5	Siṅha	5	17.531	28-09-2007	16-10-2007
3	A4	Karka	21	73.629	16-10-2007	28-12-2007
4	A6	Kanyā	9	31.555	28-12-2007	29-01-2008
5	A7	Tulā	16	56.098	29-01-2008	25-03-2008
6	A8	Vṛścika	7	24.543	25-03-2008	19-04-2008
7	S12	Mīna	10	35.062	19-04-2008	24-05-2008
8	S11	Kumbha	4	14.025	24-05-2008	07-06-2008
9	S10	Makara	4	14.025	07-06-2008	21-06-2008

We notice that Kālacakra Daśā is not only a Āyurdaśā but also an excellent Phalita Daśā. But by using this in conjunction with other Phalita Daśā, such as Viñśottarī Daśā, I believe we can attain greater accuracy in timing events. *I used in my computation one year = 360 Sāvana days, as I previously believed that for the timing of events using Daśā, only this measure is relevant. I have ample evidence for the usage of 360 days a year, which is detailed in the chapter of Viñśottarī Daśā.*

However, I encourage the readers to experiment with other year lengths and check which one gives consistently accurate results. The Ayanāñśa I used is the Sṛṣṭi Ayanāñśa, which I have discussed in detail in the Siddhānta section. The value of this Ayanāñśa is 23:37:00 in my case. Its annual rate is "50:17:17.88" sec per tropical year (of 365.2422 days) and "0:8:15.67" sec in a day of 24 hrs. The Zero Ayanāñśa Date is 31-12-283 01:12:00 UT, which makes it close to the Lahiri Ayanāñśa, which is 285 AD. The Lahiri Ayanāñśa for the date of birth is 23:30:10.52, which means 6'49.49" is added to it to get the Ayanāñśa that I used.

30.1.3.10
ADVANCE TOPICS

30.1.3.10.1
APPLICATION TO VARGAS

Vargas are important concepts in Jyotiṣaśāstra, and a detailed assessment of a Kuṇḍalī is not complete without the studies of the Vargas. Now, Kālacakra Daśā is an important Daśā, and according to Maharṣi Parāśara, it is also universally accepted. The question is, how to apply this Daśā system for timing based on the Vargas placements of the Grahas? The idea is actually not difficult and rather straightforward. What Kālacakra Daśā shows is the Rāśi that is active at different times. Let us start with the Candra Navāñśa.

I was born in Anurādhā-4, which is mapped to Meṣa Navāñśa, which is active at birth. However, since I am born near the end of the Navāñśa, the Navāñśa is over nearly after four years, and after that, the next Navāñśa, i.e., Mīna shall commence. What does this show? This shows that Meṣa Navāñśa shall be active for four years, and after that, till the end of life, Mīna Navāñśa shall be active. Now, Mīna Navāñśa is too broad and covers 86 years. How to dissect it and identify the active Navāñśa for a shorter period? For that, the Maharṣi gave us the subdivision of the Navāñśas into the Navanavāñśas!

Let us start with Meṣa Navāñśa, which commences from the birth and ends on 12-08-1978. Within Meṣa, the Navanavāñśa active is also Meṣa, which is the last Daśā of Apasavya Meṣa Navāñśa. After we have identified the Navāñśa and the Navanavāñśa and further subdivisions, we must apply them to all the Varga Kuṇḍalīs. Merely because they are determined based on the Navāñśas, their effects are not limited only to the Navāñśa Varga, but all the Vargas. We can say that during the period of Meṣa Navāñśa and Meṣa Daśā, the Meṣa Rāśi shall vibrate in all the Varga Kuṇḍalīs.

Likewise, the Deha and Jīva of Meṣa, i.e., Meṣa and Dhanu, shall also remain active during this period. Meṣa is the 5H from the Lagna and 6H from Candra, and its lord Maṅgala is well placed in a Mitra Rāśi with Mitra Sūrya, but Śatru Budha. The effects shall be both good and bad, i.e., that of 5th (Trikoṇa - good) and 6th (Dusthāna - bad). In the Navāñśa, Meṣa has Nīca Śani and Vakrī Bṛhaspati. This is not good because Nīca Śani indicates terrible sickness. Imagine, Śani is in Meṣa Rāśi in the Rāśi Kuṇḍalī, which is 5th from the Lagna and 6th from Candra.

This also indicates that the Lagneśa Bṛhaspati is afflicted due to conjunction with Nīca Śani. These all indicate severe health trouble. This is true, as I had to grapple with severe Asthma and suffered bronchitis, pneumonia, etc., during that time. The same Grahas in the 5th also gave me the mindset of philosophy and Sanyāsa, even when I was very young, merely 4-5 years old. I often questioned the purpose of my existence, the nature of life and death, etc., which eventually drew me to Jyotiṣa.

Right now, my active Kālacakra Navāñśa is Mīna. Mīna is the 4th house from the Lagna and the 5th house from Candra, hence a crucial house for knowledge. My entire life is spent in the pursuit of knowledge. I have had a wide interest from a very young age, and I liked to read a wide variety of books. But what attracted me most is the subject of Philosophy, Adhyātma (Spirituality) and Jyotiṣa. In Mīna Navāñśa, Makara Daśā, I completed my Graduation in Agricultural Engineering and became the top scorer in the university.

In Siddhāñśa, we notice Śani in Makara, and Śani is the Kāraka for agriculture, as it involves hard labour. Maṅgala and Śani are the Kāraka for agriculture, where Maṅgala is for land, which is ploughed, whereas Śani denotes the act of ploughing. The following period of Dhanu, which ran from 1996 to 2006, gave me a job in an NGO immediately after my graduation. My work was to help the tribal of Jharkhand, India, conserve their natural resources and boost their agricultural yield through improved agricultural practices.

In the Daśāñśa Kuṇḍalī, Candra is in Dhanu. Candra is the Kāraka for people and an important Graha for social service (Society = Candra). Candra is also in the 12H in the Rāśi Kuṇḍalī, which indicates the dedication of one's time and effort for the upliftment of society. In 1999, I joined the prestigious MBA institute XLRI Jamshedpur to complete my MBA in Human Resources. During this time, I was running Karka, Siṅha and Kanyā Antardaśās in the Dhanu Daśā.

In the Siddhāñśa, Dhanu has Rāhu, Ketu and Bṛhaspati. Bṛhaspati in Svarāśi in Dhanu indicate admission to a prestigious institution, but the nodes there indicate several disturbances, which happened to be true as well. The Karka, Siṅha and Kanyā are associated with Candra and Budha, who are conjunct in Siṅha. These Grahas were instrumental in getting me through the academic rigour of the institute. Candra and Budha conjunction also indicate medicine or other healing disciplines, whereas Siṅha indicates Jyotiṣa. The Daśā is of Dhanu, with Bṛhaspati, and the nodes also indicate heightened interest in Jyotiṣa. It was during this time that I was accepted as Pt. Rath's student. And, under his guidance, my level of Jyotiṣa changed after that.

In Dhanu Daśā Kanyā Antardaśā, I joined an Indian MNC, HCL Infosystems, and moved to Singapore in Tulā Antardaśā. While I was in Singapore, HCL Infosystems was acquired by HCL Technologies, another prestigious Indian MNC. In Daśāñśa Kanyā has Nīca Śukra, indicating a high level of uncertainty when I joined the company, as in 2001, India was going through a short phase of recession, and several job offers rolled out the MBA candidates were not honoured.

There was a phase of uncertainty about whether I would join the company and whether the job was going to be permanent. In Tulā Antardaśā, I moved to Singapore for a three-month project, but after that, I could not return. Tulā contains Nīca Sūrya in Daśāñśa. It is often seen that malefic Grahas or yogas give success only after one leaves one's homeland, as moving to a foreign land often comes with uncertainty and anxiety. Sūrya in Tulā is also aspected by Śani, the 12L from Makara by Daśama-Dṛṣṭi (10th sight) and by Rāhu from 12 by Trikoṇa dṛṣṭi (Trinal aspect. These are strong indicators of relocation to a foreign land.

In Vṛścika Daśā, which started on 18-03-2006, my professional career progressed despite several difficulties. In the Rāśi Kuṇḍalī Vṛścika has Nīca Candra and Rāhu, indicating a period of grave difficulties. In Vṛścika Daśā – Meṣa Antardaśā, I joined Deloitte consulting as the Practice Manager for their SAP Human Capital Management workstream and led several large business transformation projects.

In Daśāñśa Kuṇḍalī, it Meṣa has Maṅgala in Svarāśi. This gives good status and high organisation capacity, like an army general. I started on the 16th of June, exactly the Day the Antardaśā started. I moved to Management consulting in the Mīna-Kumbha period. Mīna is owned by Bṛhaspati, the Kāraka, the Jīva and the Kāraka for human resources and aspected by Candra and Śukra. Śukra is the

Kāraka for management. Kumbha has Rāhu, a powerful administrator and a suave politician.

During this period, my network in the organisation increased manifold. However, given the Daśā is of Vṛścika, my growth didn't happen as much as one would expect, as Vṛścika is afflicted in the Kuṇḍalī. Not only Vṛścika but its Deha, Karka, is also subjected to Pāpakartari yoga, indicating blockages and hurdles. I stayed in Deloitte till Tulā Daśā - Tulā Antardaśā. In Tulā Daśā- Tulā Antardaśā - Dhanu Pratyantardaśā, I joined Ericsson, my current company, as the Head of Workforce Planning and Analytics for a region.

This is a highly Ketu-dominated discipline, as the work involves planning and forecasting, i.e., seeing the future before it happens. Tulā Antardaśā with Sūrya Antardaśā indicates management and administration, whereas Dhanu, which is Ketu's Ucca Rāśi, indicates an analytical discipline. In the Daśāñśa Kuṇḍalī, the lord of Dhanu, i.e., Bṛhaspati conjoined Ketu in Siṅha Rāśi, also indicates management discipline (Sūrya) in human resources (Bṛhaspati) involving Analytics (Ketu).

Right now, when I am writing this article, I am undergoing Tulā-Mīna-Karka. For all knowledge matters, we must look at the Siddhāñśa Kunda, the Kuṇḍalī for Siddhis! In the Siddhāñśa Kuṇḍalī, Tulā has Śukra, Mīna has Maṅgala, and Kāraka is vacant by its lord Candra is with Budha in Siṅha Rāśi. Graha's influences can be fully seen in my writing. Kālacakra Daśā deals with the embrace of two opposing principles, Masculine and Feminine, that are signified by Maṅgala and Śukra, respectively, in my Siddhāñśa Kuṇḍalī. Candra and Sūrya, the Kāraka for mother and father, are also involved. Candra, the lord of Kāraka, is in Siṅha Rāśi, owned by Sūrya, and he conjoins Budha, the Kāraka for Jyotiṣa, in Siṅha Rāśi, the Rāśi of Jyotiṣaśāstra.

30.1.3.10.2
APPLICATION TO RELATIVES

It is relatively straightforward to investigate the Daśā results of an individual from the individual's Kuṇḍalī; it becomes complex and tricky when the principles are extended to the person's relatives. We know how to see the life of those who are connected with us from one's Kuṇḍalī, mainly using the Bhāvas and the Kārakas. For instance, for the father, we should judge his life from the 9th house (10th, according to some) and Sūrya.

Now, how do we use these principles for Kālacakra Daśā? This is not so difficult! Kālacakra Daśā only shows which Rāśis are active at the moment. When the Rāśis are reckoned from the Lagna or the Candra Lagna, we can decipher the events that are likely to be experienced by the natives. When the same Rāśi is examined from the viewpoint of the Lagna and the Kāraka for a relative, the life of the relative can be deciphered.

Say, I lost my father on 17th Feb 1994, who suffered from lung cancer. This happened in Makara Daśā Kanyā Antardaśā, and Siṅha Pratyantar Daśā. Siṅha is the Pitṛ-Lagna because it is the 9th house, and the Rāśi occupied by

Kāraka Sūrya. From the Pitṛ-Lagna, Makara is the 6th house of disease for the father and its lord Śani, the Kāraka for chronic diseases, is in Mithuna Rāśi, indicating respiratory troubles (Mithuna = 3H = Airy = respiration). He had lung cancer. Cancer is also indicated by Śani, which makes one suffer a painful death.

It happened in Kanyā Antardaśā of Makara Daśā. Kanyā is the 2nd house for Pitṛ-Lagna, and Maṅgala afflicts its lord. It is not entirely clear why Kanyā should cause father's demise, but this gets clearer when we delve into the Dvādaśāñśa Kuṇḍalī, where the Pitṛ Lagna is Vṛścika and Budha is the 11th as well as the 8th lord. Being the 8th lord, Budha's placement in the 4th house with Śani, the Kāraka for chronic diseases, indicates affliction to his chest area (4th house).

The affliction of the 8th lord Budha indicated that the Kālacakra period of Budha's Rāśi could cause danger to his life. At that time, Siṅha Pratyantardaśā was current! Siṅha is the Pitṛ-Lagna in the Rāśi Kuṇḍalī and is not conducive to the father's health because of conjunction with Sūrya. Sūrya in the 9th house indicate danger to the father and many times causes early demise. Siṅha has a Sūrya-Maṅgala conjunction in Rāśi Kuṇḍalī, where Maṅgala is the 4th lord. The 4th lord's affliction by Budha indicates affliction to his chest area. In the Dvādaśāñśa Kuṇḍalī, Siṅha is vacant, but the lord Sūrya is in the 9th house, again indicating the danger.

Table 58: Antardaśā in Makara Daśā

#	Daśā code2	Daśā	Year	Duration	Start	End
1	S10	Makara	10	167.4	30-05-1992	14-11-1992
2	S11	Kumbha	4	67.0	14-11-1992	20-01-1993
3	S12	Mīna	4	67.0	20-01-1993	28-03-1993
4	A8	Vṛścika	10	167.4	28-03-1993	11-09-1993
5	A7	Tulā	7	117.2	11-09-1993	06-01-1994
6	A6	Kanyā	16	267.9	06-01-1994	01-10-1994
7	A4	Karka	9	150.7	01-10-1994	01-03-1995
8	A5	Siṅha	5	83.7	01-03-1995	24-05-1995
9	A3	Mithuna	21	351.6	24-05-1995	09-05-1996

Table 59: Pratyantardaśā in Kanyā Antardaśā

#	Daśā code2	Daśā	Year	Duration	Start	End
1	S6	Kanyā	9	28.896	06-01-1994	04-02-1994
2	S5	Siṅha	5	16.053	04-02-1994	20-02-1994
3	S4	Karka	21	67.424	20-02-1994	29-04-1994
4	S3	Mithuna	9	28.896	29-04-1994	28-05-1994
5	S2	Vṛṣabha	16	51.371	28-05-1994	18-07-1994
6	S1	Meṣa	7	22.475	18-07-1994	09-08-1994
7	A9	Dhanu	10	32.107	09-08-1994	11-09-1994

#	Daśā code2	Daśā	Year	Duration	Start	End
8	A10	Makara	4	12.843	11-09-1994	23-09-1994
9	A11	Kumbha	4	12.843	23-09-1994	06-10-1994

30.1.3.10.3
ANTARDAŚĀ JUMPS

The Daśā jumps, or the Gatis, are a crucial aspect of this Daśā. Therefore, this must be understood very well. Although the jumps are clear for the Daśā, it becomes complicated for the Antardaśās and further subperiods. At the Daśā level, the Daśā progression can either be regular (Sādhāraṇa Gati) or have jumps, which are Siṅhavlokana 🦁 Gati (lion jump – to the trines), Maṇḍūka 🐸 Gati (alternate Rāśi jump), and Marakaṭa 🐒 Gati (sudden reversal). The Siṅhavlokana 🦁 Gati happens mainly from Mīna to Vṛścika or Dhanu to Mīna or vice-versa. On the other hand, the Maṇḍūka 🐸 Gati occurs between Siṅha-Mithuna and Karka-Kanyā, and the Marakaṭa 🐒 Gati is always between Siṅha and Kārya. The Maṇḍūka 🐸 and Marakaṭa 🐒 Gati always occur one after the other.

Let us review the several categories of Daśā and Antardaśā jumps and see how many of them violate the Gatis propounded by the Maharṣi. We start with reviewing the Daśā Gati again, as that is the basis of understanding Gati. The Gati occurs within a certain Navāñśa (Nakṣatra Caraṇa) or in the transition from one Caraṇa to the next. Within a Navāñśa, the jump happens when (1) The Savya and Apasavya Cakra meet, causing Siṅhavlokana 🦁 Gati, (2) The Karka-Siṅha exception applies to the Apasavya Cakra, causing Maṇḍūka 🐸 Gati, or (3) there is a sudden reversal of direction because of the Karka-Siṅha exception, causing Marakaṭa 🐒 Gati. Aśvinī-2 has all three kinds of jumps. The jumps also occur at the transition between two Navāñśas. For instance, when the Daśā moves from Aśvinī-4 to Bharaṇī-1, there is a Siṅhavlokana 🦁 Gati, as the Daśā moves from Mīna to Vṛścika. Likewise, when the Daśā moves from Bharaṇī-3 to Bharaṇī-4, there is a Maṇḍūka 🐸 jump. The jumps are highlighted in the tables below.

Table 60: Daśā Gati (Savya Nakṣatra)

Grp	Añśa	Añśa	1	2	3	4	5	6	7	8	9	Middle	End-Start
Aśv	Meṣ	S1	S1	S2	S3	S4	S5	S6	S7	S8	S9	-	-
Aśv	Vṛṣ	S2	S10	S11	S12^	A8^	A7	A6^	A4^	A5^	A3^	🦁🐸🐒	-
Aśv	Mit	S3	A2	A1	A12	A11	A10	A9^	S1^	S2	S3	🦁	-
Aśv	Kar	S4	S4	S5	S6	S7	S8	S9	S10	S11	S12^	-	🦁
Bha	Siṅ	S5	A8^	A7	A6^	A4^	A5^	A3^	A2	A1	A12	🐸🐒	🦁
Bha	Kan	S6	A11	A10	A9^	S1^	S2	S3	S4	S5	S6	🦁	-
Bha	Tul	S7	S7	S8	S9	S10	S11	S12^	A8^	A7	A6^	🦁	🐸
Bha	Vṛś	S8	A4^	A5^	A3^	A2	A1	A12	A11	A10	A9^	-	🐸🦁
Aśv	Dha	S9	S1^	S2	S3	S4	S5	S6	S7	S8	S9	-	🦁
Aśv	Mak	S10	S10	S11	S12^	A8^	A7	A6^	A4^	A5^	A3^	🦁🐸	-

Grp	Añśa	Añśa	1	2	3	4	5	6	7	8	9	Middle	End-Start
Aśv	Kum	S11	A2	A1	A12	A11	A10	A9^	S1^	S2	S3	🦁	-
Aśv	Mīn	S12	S4	S5	S6	S7	S8	S9	S10	S11	S12	-	-

Table 61: Daśā Gati (Apasavya Nakṣatra)

Grp	Añśa	Añśa	1	2	3	4	5	6	7	8	9	Middle	End-Start
Roh	Vṛś	A8	A9	A10	A11	A12	A1	A2	A3^	A5^	A4^	🐸🐒	🐸
Roh	Tul	A7	A6^	A7	A8^	S12^	S11	S10	S9	S8	S7	🦁	🐸
Roh	Kan	A6	S6	S5	S4	S3	S2	S1^	A9^	A10	A11	🦁	-
Roh	Siṅ	A5	A12	A1	A2	A3^	A5^	A4^	A6^	A7	A8^	🐸🐒	🦁
Mṛg	Kar	A4	S12^	S11	S10	S9	S8	S7	S6	S5	S4	-	🦁
Mṛg	Mit	A3	S3	S2	S1^	A9^	A10	A11	A12	A1	A2	🦁	-
Mṛg	Vṛṣ	A2	A3^	A5^	A4^	A6^	A7	A8^	S12^	S11	S10	🦁🐸🐒	-
Mṛg	Meṣ	A1	S9	S8	S7	S6	S5	S4	S3	S2	S1	-	-
Mṛg	Mīn	A12	S12	S11	S10	S9	S8	S7	S6	S5	S4	-	-
Mṛg	Kum	A11	S3	S2	S1^	A9^	A10	A11	A12	A1	A2	🦁	-
Mṛg	Mak	A10	A3^	A5^	A4^	A6^	A7	A8^	S12^	S11	S10	🦁🐸🐒	-
Mṛg	Dha	A9	S9	S8	S7	S6	S5	S4	S3	S2	S1	-	-

The matter becomes complex when we dive into the Antardaśās, or for that matter, subperiods. Let us understand why. When the movement is regular between the Navāñśas, there is no problem, i.e., all the Gatis shall follow what is narrated for the Daśās. For instance, when the transition is between S1 (Savya-Meṣa) and S2 (Savya-Vṛṣabha) Daśās, the jumps are according to what is defined for Meṣa and Vṛṣabha Navāñśas, which is S9 to S10. However, this is not the case for the Daśā jumps.

Let us take the example of Siṅhavlokana 🦁 jump from S1 (Savya-Meṣa) to A9 (Apasavya-Dhanu). In this Daśā transition, Meṣa Daśā ends with Dhanu Antardaśā, while Dhanu Daśā starts with Dhanu Antardaśā. In this case, the Antardaśā stays in the same Navāñśa for two Daśās. Normally, we expect the Antardaśā to move to the next (or another Navāñśa according to specified Gatis), but that does not happen here.

This can be said that the Antardaśā is stagnant, which is not specified by the Maharṣi. Again, when the Daśā moves from Mithuna to Siṅha, which is Maṇḍūka 🐸 Gati, the Antardaśā moves from Vṛṣabha to Mīna. This is a kind of Maṇḍūka 🐸 jump but explicitly specified by the Maharṣi. In the reverse Daśā transition, i.e., from Siṅha to Mithuna, the Antardaśā moves from Vṛścika to Mithuna, which is an eight-house jump, which is a completely new Gati, not described by the Maharṣi.

Table 62: Antardaśā Gati

#	Añśa 1	Añśa 2	Daśā Sequence 1	Daśā sequence 2	Jump	Anomaly
1	S1	A9	S1-S2-S3-S4-S5-S6-S7-S8-S9	S9-S8-S7-S6-S5-S4-S3-S2-S1	S9 → S9	The last period of previous Daśās and the first period of the next Daśā is the same. The Antardaśās is stagnant. The Maharṣi does not specify this.
2	A9	S1	S9-S8-S7-S6-S5-S4-S3-S2-S1	S1-S2-S3-S4-S5-S6-S7-S8-S9	S1 → S1	Same as #1
3	S12	A8	S4-S5-S6-S7-S8-S9-S10-S11-S12	A9-A10-A11-A12-A1-A2-A3-A5-A4	S12 → A9	Siṅhavlokana Gati – No anomaly
4	A8	S12	A9-A10-A11-A12-A1-A2-A3-A5-A4	S4-S5-S6-S7-S8-S9-S10-S11-S12	A4 → A4	Same as #1
5	A3	A5	S3-S2-S1-A9-A10-A11-A12-A1-A2	A12-A1-A2-A3-A5-A4-A6-A7-A8	A2 → A12	Unspecified Maṇḍūka Gati – the Gati from Vṛṣabha to Mīna is not specified by the Maharṣi.
6	A5	A3	A12-A1-A2-A3-A5-A4-A6-A7-A8	S3-S2-S1-A9-A10-A11-A12-A1-A2	A8 → A3	8 Rāśi jumps – The Maharṣi does not specify this.
7	A6	A4	S6-S5-S4-S3-S2-S1-A9-A10-A11	S12-S11-S10-S9-S8-S7-S6-S5-S4	A11→ S12	Sādhāraṇa Gati – No anomaly.
8	A4	A6	S12-S11-S10-S9-S8-S7-S6-S5-S4	S6-S5-S4-S3-S2-S1-A9-A10-A11	S4→S6	Maṇḍūka Gati – No anomaly.

There is no way of knowing whether such anomalous Gatis are allowed or not in the Antardaśā movements. Whatever different scholars shall specify as the sequence of the Antardaśās, there shall always be an element of doubt. This is mainly because, whatever might be the philosophical basis for such specification, one cannot point it to a Śāstra which states it. In a debate, such a situation becomes a case of "my word" vs "your word".

I believe, in such cases, the only way to settle this issue is to test the hypothesis in numerous Kuṇḍalīs and then derive the conclusion. I have tried to give a logical and consistent foundation of the principles that are laid down by the Maharṣi, explaining the rationale of deriving the Daśā sequence and why the sequence must continue in the Antardaśā and further subperiods. But it is only the reflection and experimentation of a sincere seeker that shall lead to the ultimate truth.

—|||—

30.1.4
REFERENCES

30.1.4.1
BṚHATPARĀŚARA

KĀLACAKRA

46.52-53. Maharṣi Parāśara said. O Brāhmaṇa! Now, after making obedience to Lord Śiva, I shall describe the Kālacakra Daśā. Whatever was related by Lord Shiva to Goddess Parvati, is being explained by me for the use of sages to be utilised for the welfare of the people.

46.54-55. By drawing vertical and horizontal lines, prepare 2 Kuṇḍalīs, Savya and Apasvya, of twelve apartments each. From the second apartment in each Kundali fix the Rāśis Meṣa, Vṛṣabha, Mithuna, Karka, Siṅha, Kanyā, Tulā, Vṛścika, Dhanu, Makara, Kumbha, Mīna. Then, Nakṣatras may be incorporated in the manner indicated hereafter. These Kuṇḍalīs, indicative of the twelve Rāśis, are called Kālacakra.

46.56-58. Write Aśvinī, Bharaṇī and Kṛttikā in the Savya Cakra and Rohiṇī, Mṛgaśirā, Ārdrā in the Apasvya. Then incorporate the three following Nakṣatras, Punarvasu, Puṣya and Aśleṣā in the Savya and Maghā, Pūrvāphālgunī and Uttarāphālgunī in the Apasvya. Then incorporate the three following, Hasta, Chitra and Swati in the Savya and Viśākhā, Anurādhā and Jyeṣṭhā in the Apasvya. Then incorporate Mūla, Pūrvāṣāṛhā and Uttarāṣāṛhā in the Savya and Śravaṇa, Dhaniṣṭhā and Śatabhiṣā in the Apasvya. Finally, incorporate the last three Nakṣatras, Pūrvābhādra, Uttarābhādra and Revatī in the Savya Cakra. Now, there will be fifteen Nakṣatras in the Savya and twelve Nakṣatras in the Apasvya (because for the twelve Rāśis, there are twelve Pādas of three Nakṣatras, the Navāñśas). The Pādas of Aśvinī, Punarvasu, Hasta, Mūla, Pūrvābhādra, Kṛttikā, Aśleṣā, Swati, Uttarāṣāṛhā and Revatī of the Savya should be reckoned in the same manner, as the Pādas of Aśvinī.

46.59. Now, I shall describe in detail how the Deha and Jīva should be reckoned in the Pādas of the Nakṣatras.

46.60. In the first Pāda of Aśvinī, Meṣa is indicative of Deha, and Dhanu is indicative of Jīva. And the Lords of Meṣa, Vṛṣabha, Mithuna, Karka, Siṅha, Kanyā, Tulā, Vṛścika and Dhanu are Lords of the Daśās in the order, as described before.

46.61. In the second Pāda of Aśvinī, Makara is Deha and Mithuna is Jīva, and the Lords of the nine Rāśis from Makara to Mithuna are Lords of the Daśās.

46.62. In the third Pāda of the ten Nakṣatras, beginning from Aśvinī, Vṛṣabha is Deha, and Mithuna is Jīva. The Lords of the Rāśis Vṛṣabha, Meṣa, Mīna,

Kumbha, Makara, Dhanu, Meṣa, Vṛṣabha and Mithuna are Lords of the Daśās in that order.

46.63-64. For the fourth Pāda of the ten Nakṣatras, beginning from Aśvinī, Karka is Deha and Mīna is Jīva, and the Lords of the nine Rāśis from Karka to Mīna are the Lords of Daśās.

46.65. In the four Pādas of the five Nakṣatras, Bharaṇī, Puṣya, Chitra, Pūrvāṣāṛhā and Uttarābhādra, Deha and Jīva are the same, as for Bharaṇī.

46.66. In the first Pāda of Bharaṇī, Vṛścika is Deha and Mīna is Jīva, and the Lords of the Rāśis Vṛścika, Tulā, Kanyā, Karka, Siṅha, Mithuna, Vṛṣabha, Meṣa and Mīna are the Lords of Daśās in this order.

46.67. In the second Pāda of Bharaṇī, Kumbha is Deha and Kanyā is Jīva, and the Lords of Kumbha, Makara, Dhanu, Meṣa, Vṛṣabha, Mithuna, Karka, Siṅha and Kanyā are the Lords of Daśās in that order.

46.68. In the third Pāda of Bharaṇī, Tulā is Deha and Kanyā is Jīva and Lords of the Rāśis Tulā, Vṛścika, Dhanu, Makara, Kumbha, Mīna, Vṛścika, Tulā and Kanyā are the Daśā Lords in this order.

46.69. In the fourth Pāda of Bharaṇī, Karka is Deha and Kumbha is Jīva, and the Lords of the Rāśis Karka, Siṅha, Mithuna, Vṛṣabha, Meṣa, Mīna, Kumbha, Makara and Dhanu are the Daśā Lords in this order.

46.71-72. O Brāhmaṇa! I have thus given you the description of Savya Cakra. Now, I shall describe Apasvya Cakra. Prepare a similar chart of twelve apartments, and from the second apartment onwards, place the Rāśis from Vṛścika onwards in the reverse order. In this chart, Deha and Jīva would be the same for Rohiṇī, Maghā, Viśākhā and Śravaṇa as for Rohiṇī.

46.73-76. In the first Pāda of Rohiṇī Karka is Deha and Dhanu is Jīva. The Lords of the Rāśis Dhanu, Makara, Kumbha, Mīna, Meṣa, Vṛṣabha, Mithuna, Siṅha and Tulā will be the Daśā Lords in this order. In the second Tulā will be Deha and Kanyā, the Jīva and the Lords of the Rāśis Kanyā, Tulā, Vṛścika, Mīna, Kumbha, Makara, Dhanu, Vṛścika and Vṛścika will be the Daśā Lords. In the third Kumbha will be Deha and Kanyā Jīva. The Lords of the Rāśis Kanyā, Siṅha, Karka, Mithuna, Vṛṣabha, Meṣa, Dhanu, Makara and Kumbha will be the Daśā Lords. In the fourth Vṛścika will be Deha and Mīna Jīva and the Lords of the Rāśis Mīna, Meṣa, Vṛṣabha, Mithuna, Siṅha, Karka, Kanyā, Tulā and Vṛścika will be the Lords.

46.77. In the four Pādas of the Apasvya Nakṣatras Mṛgaśirā, Ārdrā, Pūrvāphālgunī, Uttarāphālgunī, Anurādhā, Jyeṣṭhā, Dhaniṣṭhā and Śatabhiṣā the Deha and Jīva and the Daśā Lords will be the same, as for Mṛgaśirā.

46.78-81. In the first Pāda of Mṛgaśirā Karka is Deha and Mīna is Jīva, and the Lords of the Rāśis Mīna, Kumbha, Makara, Dhanu, Vṛścika, Tulā, Kanyā, Siṅha and Karka will be the Daśā Lords in this order. In the second Vṛṣabha is Deha and Mithuna is Jīva, and the Lords of the Rāśis Mithuna, Vṛṣabha, Meṣa, Dhanu, Makara, Kumbha, Mīna, Meṣa and Vṛṣabha will be the Daśā Lords. In the third Makara is Deha and Mithuna is Jīva, and the Lords of the Rāśis Mithuna, Siṅha, Karka, Kanyā, Tulā, Vṛścika, Mīna, Kumbha and Makara will be the Daśā Lords. In the fourth Meṣa will be Deha and Dhanu Jīva and the Lords of the Rāśis

Dhanu, Vṛścika, Tulā, Kanyā, Siṅha, Karka, Mithuna, Vṛṣabha and Meṣa will be the Daśā Lords.

46.82. Maharṣi Parāśara said. O Brāhmaṇa! The description of the Deha and Jīva of the Pādas of the Apasvya Nakṣatras and the Daśā Lords is the same, as narrated by Lord Mahādeva to Devī Parvati.

46.83. Maitreya said. O Venerable Maharṣi Parāśara! Now, please guide me about the Daśā spans of the Daśā Lords described by you. Please also demonstrate how the commencement of the Daśā, its elapsed and the remaining periods at the birth are to be calculated.

46.84. Maharṣi Parāśara said five, twenty-one, seven, nine, ten, sixteen and four years are the Daśā spans of Sūrya, Candra, Maṅgala, Budha, Guru, Śukra and Śani.

46.85-86. The span of life of a person is determined from the Pādas (Añśas) of the Nakṣatra at the time of birth or the time of query and the years allotted to the nine Rāśis, commencing from it (the Pāda of the Nakṣatra). Some sages are of the view that the person will enjoy the full span of life (Pūrṇāyu) if his birth is at the commencement of the Pādas, will have a middle span of life (Madhyāyu), if the birth is in the middle of the Pādas and short span of life (Alpāyu), or will face death-like sufferings if the birth is at the end of the Pādas of the Nakṣatra.

46.87-88. According to this principle, we should be acquainted with the Pādas of the Nakṣatras. Now, I shall tell you how the calculations are made according to the proportion of the Pādas of a Nakṣatra. The number of Aśvinī, etc., whichever may be the past Nakṣatras, should be divided by three. After that, the remainder should be multiplied by four. To the figure so made available, the Pāda of the present Nakṣatra should be added. The product will be the Navāñśa from Meṣa onwards.

46.89. The number of years (Pūrṇāyu) is as under. For the Añśa in Meṣa, 100 years; in Vṛṣabha, 85 years; in Mithuna, 83 years; in Karka, 86 years. The number of years will be the same for Rāśis, situated on the 5th and 9th to them.

46.90-91. Multiply the past Ghaṭis, Palas, etc., of the Pāda of the Nakṣatra, in which a person is born, by the existing Daśā years and divide it by fifteen. The result will indicate the elapsed period of the Daśā in years, months, etc. By deducting it from the total number of years allotted, we get the balance of Daśā at birth. The Daśā should be taken as commencing from that Rāśi.

46.92. Multiply the past Ghaṭis, Palas, etc., of the present Pāda of the Nakṣatra by the number of years and divide the product by the fourth part of Bhabhog. The years, etc., so obtained may then be deducted from the total Daśā period. The result will be the balance of Daśā at birth in years, months, etc.

46.93. The past Kalās (minutes) of the Navāñśa, in which Candra may be placed, should be multiplied by the years allotted to the Daśā, and the product should be divided by 200. The resulting years, etc., will be the elapsed portion of the Daśā. By deducting them from the total number of years, the balance of the Daśā at birth is obtained.

46.94-95. In the Savya Cakra, the first Aṅśa is called Deha and the last Jīva. The opposite is the case in the Apasvya Cakra. Therefore, the calculations should be based on the Deha, etc., in the Savya Cakra and on the Jīva, etc., in Apasvya.

Śrī R Sānthānām provides the following example:

We give below the Savya and Apasvya Kālacakra Kuṇḍalīs. For example, the birth is in Mṛgaśirā fourth Pāda. Mṛgaśirā is in the Apasvya Kālacakra. The Lord of Deha is Maṅgala, and that of Jīva is Guru. The Bhayāt of Mṛgaśirā is 58-15 (Ghaṭi-Pala) and Bhabhog is 59-31 (Nakṣatra span of Mṛgaśirā). One-fourth (a Pāda) of the Bhabhog is 14-52-44.

Multiplying this by three will get Ghaṭis of three Pādas, namely 44-38-15. Deducting this from Bhāyat, the past Ghaṭis, Palas, etc., of the fourth Pāda will be 13-36-45. The full Daśā years are 100. Multiplying this by 13-36-45, we get 1361-15 (Ghaṭī-Pala). This divided by 15 will give the elapsed period at birth, namely 90 years and 9 months.

See the Kālacakra. There, we count from Jīva, etc., to Deha. In the fourth Pāda of Mṛgaśirā, Jīva is in Dhanu and Deha in Meṣa. Therefore, by deducting the total of years from Dhanu to Mithuna, namely 77, from 90 years and 9 months, we get the elapsed period of Vṛṣabha, namely 13 years and 9 months. By deducting this from the present 16 years of Śukra, we will get 2 years and 3 months as the balance of Daśā at birth. Accordingly, like Viṅśottarī Daśā, the order of Daśā will be Vṛṣabha, Meṣa, Dhanu, Vṛścika etc.

Śrī R Sānthānām gives another example:

Suppose that at the time of birth of a person in Kṛttikā Nakṣatra, the longitude of Candra is 1r4°50′. This converted into Kalās will be 2090 at birth. The Daśā should be taken as commencing from that. Divide the Kalās by 800 (one Nakṣatra). The result will be the second Nakṣatra, namely Bharaṇī and the remainder will be 490. These will be the past Kalās of Kṛttikā. There are 200 Kalās in one Pāda (Navāṅśa). Divide 490, the past Kalās of Kṛttikā, by 200. We will then get 2, as past Pādas and the remainder 90 will represent the past Kalās of the present Nakṣatra.

By multiplying this by 83, the Daśā years, we will get 7470, which, divided by 200, will indicate the elapsed portion of the Daśā as 37 years, 4 months, and 6 days. By deducting the years of Dehāṅśa, commencing from Vṛṣabha, in the order Vṛṣabha, Meṣa, Mīna, Kumbha (16+7+10+4 = 37), we will get 0 years, 4 months and 6 days. This will be the elapsed portion of Makara. Deducting this from 4, the Daśā period of Makara, we get the balance of the Daśā of Makara, namely 3 years, 7 months, and 24 days. See in this connection the Savya Kālacakra.

GATI OF RĀŚIS IN THE KĀLACAKRA

46.96-98. There are three kinds of movements (Gati) of the Rāśis in the Kālacakra, namely Maṇḍūka, Marakata and Siṅhavalokana. The movement of one Rāśi by jumping over one Rāśi is known as Maṇḍūka Gati. The backward movement to the previous Rāśi is called Marakata Gati. The movement of a Rāśi to the 5th and 9th Rāśi is said to be Siṅhavalokana.

46.99-100. Movement from Kanyā to Karka and from Siṅha to Mithuna is Maṇḍūka Gati. Movement from Siṅha to Karka is Marakata Gati. Movement from Mīna to Vṛścika and from Dhanu to Meṣa is called Siṅhavalokana Gati.

EFFECTS OF GATIS

46.101-102. The effects of the Daśā of the Rāśis with Maṇḍūka Gati in the Savya Cakra are distress to friends, relations, parents and elders, and there is likely to be cause for trouble from poison, weapons, thieves, and enemies. In the Maṇḍūka Daśā of the Gati of a Rāśi from Siṅha to Mithuna, there is the likelihood of the death of the mother or self, trouble from government and the possibility of brain fever.

46.103. The effects of the Daśā of Rāśi with Marakata Gati in the Savya Cakra are loss of wealth, agricultural products and animals, death of the father, or an elderly close relation and feeling of lethargy.

46.104-105. The effects of the Daśā of the Rāśis with Siṅhavalokana Gati in the Savya Cakra are the possibility of injury from animals, loss of amity with friends, distress to near relations, drowning in a well, fall from animals, the possibility of harm from poison, weapons and diseases and destruction of the residential dwelling.

46.106-108. In the Daśā of the Rāśis with the Maṇḍūka Gati in the Apasvya Cakra, the effects will be distress to the wife and conditions, loss of children, the possibility of feverish conditions and loss of position. In the Daśā of the Rāśis with the Marakata Gati, there may be danger from watery places, loss of position, distress from father, punishment from the government and wandering in the forests; with the Siṅhavalokana there may be destruction of the dwelling and death of father etc.

46.109-111. If the movement is from Mīna to Vṛścika, the native may suffer from fever; if from Kanyā to Karka, there may be loss of brothers and kinsmen; if from Siṅha to Mithuna, there may be ill health of the wife; if from Siṅha to Karka, the native may die; if from Dhanu to Meṣa, there may be death of uncles and similar relations. If the Rāśi is yuti with a Krūra, adverse conditions may be expected in the Daśā of the Rāśi. Favourable effects will be felt in its Daśā if the Rāśi is yuti with a Saumya.

46.112-113. O Brāhmaṇa! In the Kālacakra Daśā, favourable and unfavourable effects may be predicted after considering the directions of the Rāśis and Grahas.

46.114-119. If the movement is from Kanyā to Karka, good results are realised in places located in the East and at that time, journeys to the places in the North prove fruitful. Unfavourable effects will be felt in places located in the West and the South. It will be advisable not to undertake journeys in those directions in the Daśā of these Rāśis. If the movement is from Siṅha to Mithuna, no journey should be undertaken to places located in the East. However, the journeys to the South-West will prove fruitful in the Daśā of those Rāśis. If the movement is from Karka to Siṅha, journeys during that period to the South will prove unfavourable and result in loss, and the native has to return from the South to the West. If the movement is from Mīna to Vṛścika, there will be distress if the native goes to the North. The same would happen if the movement is from Dhanu to Makara. There may be ill health, imprisonment, or death if the movement is from Dhanu to Meṣa. There may be gains, comforts, property and marriage if the movement is from Dhanu to Vṛścika. It will not be advisable to undertake journeys to the West during the related period if the movement is from Siṅha to Karka. Favourable results should be predicted if the Rāśis are yuti with Saumyas and adverse if the Rāśis are yuti with Krūras.

46.120-122. According to the Kālacakra mentioned above, the person born in the Añśas of the various Rāśis will be as under. Meṣa Añśa brave and a thief, Vṛṣabha wealthy, Mithuna learned, Karka king, Siṅha respected by the king, Kanyā learned, Tulā minister, or adviser, Dhanu sinful, Kumbha businessman, Mīna wealthy.

46.123-128. If the Deha or Jīva Rāśis are yuti with Sūrya, Maṅgala, Śani, or Rahu, the native will die. Worse results may be expected if the Deha and Jīva Rāśis are yuti with two or all of them. If there is a malefic in Deha Rāśi, the native suffers ill health; a malefic in a Jīva Rāśi will make the native very timid. If the Deha or Jīva Rāśi are yuti with two Krūras, there will be distress and diseases. Three Krūras in the Deha or Jīva Rāśi will cause premature death. Four Krūras in the Deha and Jīva Rāśi will cause definite death. If Krūras occupy both the Deha and Jīva Rāśis, there will be fear from the king and thieves and death of the native. If Sūrya is in the Deha or Jīva Rāśi, there will be danger from fire. Candra in the Deha or Jīva Rāśi will cause danger from water, Maṅgala fear from weapons, Budha fear from windy troubles, Śani fear from Gulma (tumour), Rahu and Ketu fear from poison. If Budha, Guru and Śukra occupy the Deha or Jīva Rāśis, the native will be wealthy, will enjoy all kinds of comforts and will have good health. Mixed results may be expected if both Saumyas and Krūras occupy the Deha and Jīva Rāśis.

46.129-130. In the Daśā of the Rāśis, owned by Krūras, the body and soul will be in distress. The effects will be favourable in the Daśā of the Rāśis, owned by Saumyas. If a Saumya occupies a Krūrarāśi, or if a Krūra occupies a Saumyarāśi, the effects will be of a mixed nature.

EFFECTS OF KĀLACAKRA IN LAGNA AND OTHER BHAVAS

46.131-132. In the Kālacakra Daśā of the Rāśi in Lagna, the body remains healthy, and the native spends life with many kinds of comforts. If the Lagna Rāśi is Saumyarāśi, the good effects are realised fully. If the Lagna Rāśi is a Krūrarāśi, there is likelihood of ill health. If a Graha in Ucca or its Sva Rāśi occupies Lagna, the native is respected by the king or government and acquires wealth.

46.133-134. In the Cakra Daśā of the Rāśi in Dhana, the native receives good food, enjoys the happiness of his wife and children, gains wealth, achieves progress in the educational sphere, becomes a clever conversationalist and moves into good society. If the Rāśi be a benefic, good effects are realised in full; otherwise, the effects would be of a mixed nature.

46.135-136. Happiness from co-borns, bravery, patience, comforts, acquisition of gold, ornaments and clothes and recognition by the king or government are the effects in the Kālacakra Daśā of the Rāśi in Sahaja. If the Rāśi is Saumya, the good results are realised in full; otherwise, adverse effects may also be experienced.

46.137-138. Good relations with kinsmen, acquisition of land, houses, or a kingdom, conveyances and clothes and enjoyment of sound health are the effects of the Cakra Daśā of the Rāśi in Sukha. If the Rāśi is Saumya, the good effects are realised in full. If it is a Krūrarāśi, adverse results are also experienced.

46.139-140. Being blessed with a wife and children, favours from the government, enjoyment of sound health, good relations with friends, achievement of fame, good progress in the educational sphere, patience and bravery are the effects of the Cakra Daśā of the Rāśi in Mantra. If the Rāśi is Saumya, the good results are enjoyed in full. If the Rāśi is a malefic one, adverse effects are also experienced.

46.141-142. Danger from the king, fire and weapons and the possibility of suffering from diabetes, Gulma and jaundice are the effects of the Cakra Daśā of the Rāśi in Ari. If the Rāśi is a malefic one, the above adverse effects will be experienced in full. There will be some mitigation of the evil effects in the case of a Saumyarāśi.

46.143-144. Marriage, marital happiness, being blessed with children, gaining agricultural products, cows and clothes, favours and recognition from the king and achievement of fame are the effects of the Cakra Daśā of the Rāśi in Saptama. The beneficial results will be experienced in full if the Rāśi is Saumya. Meagre good effects will be realised in the case of a Krūrarāśi.

46.145-146. Destruction of a residential house, distress, loss of wealth, poverty and danger from enemies are the effects of the Cakra Daśā of the Rāśi in Randhra. The adverse effects will be realised in full if the Rāśi is Krūra. Some mitigation in evil effects may be expected in the case of a Saumyarāśi.

EFFECTS OF ANTARDAŚĀS IN THE KĀLACAKRA

64.1. Maharṣi Parāśara said. Now, I am going to describe to you the effects of Antardaśās in the Kālacakra Daśā, as related by Lord Shiva to the Goddess Parvati.

64.2. Daśā of Meṣa Añśa. There will be wounds and fever in the Antardaśā of Maṅgala in the Daśā of Meṣa Añśa. In the same Daśā and Antardaśā of the Rāśis, owned by Budha, Śukra, Candra and Guru, all kinds of happiness will be enjoyed. Danger from an enemy will be experienced in the Antardaśā of Sūrya.

64.3-5. Daśā of Vṛṣabha Añśa. Effects, like quarrels and diseases, will be experienced in Antardaśā of Śani. There will be gains of education and physical comfort in the Antardaśā of Guru, going away from home, death, or distress from fevers in the Antardaśā of Maṅgala, and gains of garments, happy association with women in the Antardaśās of the Rāśis, owned by Śukra and Budha. Danger from the king and violent animals may be expected in the Antardaśā of Rāśi, owned by Sūrya.

64.6-10. Daśā of Mithuna Añśa. The effects in the Antardaśās of the Rāśis concerned will be as follows. Śukra - gain of wealth and garments. Maṅgala - death of parents, danger, fever, wounds, and travels to distant places. Guru - increase in intelligence, success in education, opulence and glory, popularity, and affection towards others. Śani - foreign journeys, diseases, fear of death, loss of wealth and kinsmen. Budha - success in education, gains of garments, etc., happiness from wife and children and reverence from all quarters.

64.11-16. Daśā of Karka Añśa. The effects in the various Antardaśās of the Rāśis concerned will be as follows. Candra - happiness from wife and children, gain of wealth and reverence from the public. Sūrya - danger from enemies, animals and the royal family, mental agony, and fear of diseases. Budha and Śukra - happiness from wife, children, and friends, increase in wealth, popularity and name and fame. Maṅgala - danger from poison, weapons, and diseases, like fever. Guru - gains of wealth, physical comfort, and honours from the king. Śani - rheumatism, danger from snakes and scorpions and distress of all kinds.

64.17-21. Daśā of Siṅha Añśa. Maṅgala - diseases of the mouth, bilious fever and danger from weapons. Budha and Śukra - a gain of clothes, happiness from wife and children. Candra - danger from falling from some height, meagre gains of wealth, foreign journeys. Sūrya - danger from enemies, fevers, loss of wisdom, fear of death. Guru - gains of wealth and grains, goodwill of the king and Brāhmaṇas, progress in education.

64.22-26. Daśā of Kanyā Añśa. Śani - many kinds of troubles, travels to distant places, fevers, distress from hunger. Guru - gains of wealth through the goodwill of the king, arrival of friends and kinsmen and success in education. Maṅgala - bilious fever, travels to distant places, danger from fire and weapons. Budha, Śukra and Candra - gains of wealth through sons and employees, many enjoyments. Sūrya - travel to distant lands, danger from diseases, quarrels with kinsmen, danger of assaults by weapons.

64.27-31. Daśā of Tulā Añśa. Śukra - wisdom, comforts, happiness from wife and children and wealth, garments, etc. Maṅgala - distress to father, enmity with friends, danger from a disease of forehead, fevers, poison, weapons, etc. Guru - gain of wealth, acquisition of a kingdom, performance of religious rites, honours from the king and happiness all-round. Śani - travels to distant places, critical diseases, loss in the agricultural sphere, danger from enemies. Budha - the birth of a son, a gain of wealth, happiness from one's wife, joy, the dawn of fortune.

64.32-33. Daśā of Vṛścika Añśa. The following effects will be experienced in the Antardaśās of the Rāśis concerned. Candra, Budha and Śukra - a gain of wealth and grains in different ways, freedom from diseases, and enjoyments of many kinds. Sūrya - danger from enemies, loss of wealth, distress to father, danger from wild and violent animals. Maṅgala - troubles from wind and bile, wounds, danger from fire and weapons. Guru - gains of wealth, grains, and gems, devotion towards deities and Brāhmaṇas, goodwill of the king. Śani - loss of wealth, separation from kinsmen, mental anxiety, danger from enemies, diseases.

64.34-40. Daśā of Dhanu Añśa. The following effects will be derived in the various Antardaśās of the Rāśis, owned by Maṅgala - heartburn, fevers, colds, diseases of the mouth, and many kinds of troubles. Śukra, Budha and Candra - increase in wealth and property and fortune, progress in education, destruction of enemies, happiness from the king. Sūrya - loss of wife and wealth, quarrels, danger from the king, travels to distant lands. Guru - charity, self-mortifications, honours from the king, increase in religious-mindedness, happiness from wife, gain of wealth.

64.41-44. Daśā of Makara Añśa. The following effects will be experienced in the various Antardaśās of the Rāśis, owned by Śani - the wrath of Brāhmaṇas, deities and the king, loss of kinsmen, abandonment of the homeland. Śukra, Budha, Candra, and Guru - devotion towards deities, self-mortification, and honours from the government. Maṅgala - disease of the forehead, assaults on hands and feet, danger from dysentery, blood pollution and bilious troubles. Śani - loss of father and kinsmen, fevers, danger from the king and the enemies.

64.45-49. Daśā of Kumbha Añśa. Śukra - many kinds of educational attainments, gains of property, happiness from wife and children, sound health and increase in wealth. Maṅgala - fevers, danger from fire and enemies, distress from enemies and mental agony. Śani - the danger of troubles from wind, bile and phlegm, quarrels, foreign journeys, the danger of suffering from tuberculosis. Guru - freedom from ill health, happiness, honours from the king and joy. Budha - happiness from wife, children and wealth, joy, increase in good fortune.

64.50-55. Daśā of Mīna Añśa. Candra - increase in wisdom and educational attainments, happiness from wife, freedom from disease, association with friends, joy and happiness. Sūrya - quarrels with kinsmen, danger from thieves, mental agony, loss of position. Budha and Śukra - victory in war, birth of a son, gains of land and cattle, increase in wealth. Maṅgala - bilious troubles, disputes with members of the family, danger from enemies. Guru - gain of wealth and grains, happiness from wife, honours from the king, name, and fame. Śani - loss of wealth, mental agony, abandonment of the homeland on account of associations with prostitutes.

64.56-58. Maharṣi Parāśara said to Maitreya. O Brāhmaṇa! The effects of Antardaśās in the Kālacakra, which have been described above, are based on Savya Cakra. The effects of Antardaśās in the Daśās of the Rāśis in the Apasvya Cakra have to be assessed after considering the benefic and malefic natures of the Lords of the Rāśis. People have to enjoy the good or suffer the bad results, according to their good or bad actions in the previous births. Everybody suffers or enjoys it accordingly. The peculiarity in this respect is that inauspicious results have been ascribed to Krūras. But, if during the Antardaśā, the Graha concerned is a friend of the Daśānātha, the results of the Antardaśā will be favourable. If the Graha concerned is Saumya but an enemy of the Daśānātha, his Antardaśā effects will not prove favourable. This is how the Antardaśā effects have to be analysed, and conclusions arrived at.

EFFECTS OF DAŚĀS OF RĀŚIS IN THE AṄŚAS OF THE VARIOUS RĀŚIS

65.1-3. The following will be the effects in the Daśās of Rāśis in Meṣa Aṅśa. Meṣa - distress from diseases caused by blood pollution, Vṛṣabha - increase in grain production, Mithuna - dawn of knowledge (jñānodaya), Karka - increase in wealth, Siṅha - danger from enemies, Kanyā - happiness from wife, Tulā - ministership, Vṛścika - danger of death, Dhanu - gains of wealth.

65.4-5. Vṛṣabha Aṅśa. Makara - tendency to indulge in sinful actions, Kumbha - profits in business, Mīna - success in all ventures, Vṛścika - danger from fire, Tulā - honours from the king, Kanyā - danger from enemies, Karka - distress to wife, Siṅha - eye troubles, Mithuna - danger from poison.

65.6-8. Mithuna Aṅśa. Vṛṣabha - gains of wealth, Meṣa - fever, Mīna - affectionate relations with a maternal uncle, Kumbha - increase in enemies, Makara - danger from thieves, Dhanu - progress in education, Meṣa - assaults from enemies, Vṛṣabha - quarrels, Mithuna - happiness.

65.9-10. Karka Aṅśa. Karka - enjoyment, Siṅha - danger from the king, Kanyā - happiness from kinsmen, Tulā - good reputation, Vṛścika - distress from father, Dhanu - gain of knowledge and wealth, Makara - disgrace in public, Kumbha - loss in business, Mīna - travels to distant lands.

65.11-13. Siṅha Aṅśa. Vṛścika - quarrels, distress, Tulā - gain of wealth, happiness, Kanyā - increase in wealth and grains, Karka - danger from animals, Siṅha - both happiness and sorrows, Mithuna - increase in enemies, Vṛṣabha - gain of property, happiness, Meṣa - distress, Mīna - long journey.

65.14-15. Kanyā Aṅśa. Kumbha - gain of wealth, Makara - increase in wealth, Dhanu - happiness from brothers, Meṣa - happiness from mother, Vṛṣabha - happiness from sons, Mithuna - danger from enemies, Karka - affectionate relation with wife, Siṅha - increase in ill health, Kanyā - birth of a son.

65.16-18. Tulā Aṅśa. Tulā - gain of wealth, Vṛścika - happiness from brothers, Dhanu - happiness from brothers and uncles, Makara - distress to mother, Kumbha - profits in business, Mīna - gain of property, happiness, Vṛścika - distress to wife, Tulā - danger from water, Kanyā - increase in property and happiness.

65.19-20. Vṛścika Aṅśa. Karka - loss of wealth, Siṅha - danger from government, Mithuna - gain of lands, Vṛṣabha - increase in wealth, Meṣa - distress on account of blood pollution, Mīna - happiness, Kumbha - profits in business, Makara - loss of wealth, Dhanu - gain of property, happiness.

65.21-23. Dhanu Aṅśa. Meṣa - gain of wealth, Vṛṣabha - gain of lands, Mithuna - success in all ventures, Karka - gain of property, happiness, Siṅha - all comforts, Kanyā - quarrels, Tulā - profits in business, Vṛścika - danger from diseases, Dhanu - happiness to sons.

65.24-25. Makara Añśa. Makara - birth of a son, Kumbha - increase in wealth, Mīna - well-being, Vṛścika - danger from animals, Tulā - gain of wealth, Kanyā - danger from enemies, Karka - gain of wealth, Siṅha - danger from enemies, Mithuna - danger from poison.

65.26-28. Kumbha Añśa. Vṛṣabha - increase in wealth, Meṣa - eye troubles, Mīna - travels to distant lands, Kumbha - increase in wealth, Makara - success in all ventures, Dhanu - increase in knowledge and learning, Meṣa - loss of happiness, Vṛṣabha - danger of death, Mithuna - gains of property, happiness.

65.29-31. Mīna Añśa. Karka - increase in wealth, Siṅha - assistance from the king, Kanyā - increase in wealth and grains, Tulā - profits in business, Vṛścika - distress from fever, Dhanu - increase in knowledge and wealth, Makara - antagonism with wife, Kumbha - danger from water, Mīna - all kinds of enjoyments.

65.32. There is no doubt that observance of remedial measures in the form of prescribed Maharṣi Yajñas destroys the evil effects of the inauspicious Daśās and yields happiness.

30.1.4.2
JĀTAKAPĀRIJĀTA

KĀLACAKRA DAŚĀ

17.1-2. Bowing to Śiva, the supreme soul, the prime cause of all things, standing in the centre of the Graha systems and comprehending in his omniscience the 64 branches of knowledge, the all-benign goddess Parvati asked that supreme ruler of all God as follows: "Tell me, O Lord, in detail the entire course of the wheel of time Kālacakra."

17.3. Īśvara said, 'I am of the nature of the Sūrya, and you are declared to be the Candra. The conjunction and opposition of the Sūrya and the Candra bring about the whole universe consisting of mobile and immobile things.

17.4. Draw five straight lines from west to east and five crosswise in such a manner that the interior four squares are left vacant (are not represented in the Cakra). The resulting twelve squares are the twelve celestial signs Meṣa and others, the lords of the east and other points of the compass.

17.5. Wise men say that Maṅgala, Śukra, Budha, Candra, Sūrya, Budha, Śukra, Maṅgala, Guru, Śani, Śani, and Guru are respectively the lords of the signs from Meṣa onwards and also of their Añśas.

17.6. 5, 21, 7, 9, 10, 16 and 4 are the years, respectively, of the 7 Grahas reckoned from the Sūrya. The years of the signs correspond to the years of their lords.

17.7-8. In the 5 triads of Nakṣatras, beginning respectively with Aśvinī, Punarvasu, Hasta, Mula, and Pūrvābhādra reckon the quarters from Meṣa in the Pradakṣiṇa order. In the four triads commencing with Rohiṇī, Maghā, Viśākhā, and Sravana, reckon the quarters from Vṛścika in the Apradakṣiṇa order.

17.9-10. The Cakra consisting of a Dakṣiṇa triad of Nakṣatras should be cast in the Pradakṣiṇa order from Meṣa to Mīna among the 12 Rāśis to which the Navāñśas composing the triad belong. Again, the 12 quarters of the triad called Utara (in contrast with Dakṣiṇa of the previous śloka) are to be assigned to the 12 Rāśis in the Apradakṣiṇa order from Vṛścika to Dhanu. Thus, Dakṣiṇa and Uttara have to be apprehended as distinct from each other.

17.11. Thus, the triads of Nakṣatras reckoned from Aśvinī are to be distinguished as Dakṣiṇa and Uttara just as their padas are reckoned in the Pradakṣiṇa or Apradakṣiṇa order of Rāśis. In the Savya triad, the reckoning begins with Deha. In the Apasavya triad, it begins with Jīva.

17.12. In the Añśas, i.e. quarters of the Nakṣatras representing the houses Meṣa, Vṛṣabha, Mithuna, and Karka, the greatest life is declared to result, being measured respectively by the numbers 100, 85, 83 and 86. The same holds good with respect to the Trikoṇa Rāśis of the four.

17.13-13a. There can thus be a thorough knowledge of the age of a person when what are called Deha and Jīva are previously settled. In the Savya Cakra, the first division of every Rāśi is called Deha, and the last is termed Jīva. In the Apasavya Cakra, this is reversed.

17.13b-14a. When Rāhu, Ketu, Maṅgala, or the Sūrya happen to be in conjunction with Deha and Jīva, there will be death as a consequence thereof; if they happen to be in Deha alone, diseases set in.

17.14b-16. When Budha, Guru and Śukra go to a house which represents Deha or Jīva, then everything tends to happiness and prosperity, and there is an end to sorrow and sadness. When the Deha or the Jīva house is occupied by a mixture of good and bad Grahas, the effect would be of a mixed nature.

17.17. At the time there is a Siṅhavlokana backward glance of a lion, or a Maṇḍūkagati (a frog leap) happens, there is a danger of untimely death from which one is released by an expiation (propitiation).

17.18. When there is a movement from Mīna to Vṛścika (Siṅhavlokana), fever attacks the persons concerned. When there is a jump from Kanyā to Karka (Maṇḍūka), the death taker place of one's mother, relatives, or wife.

17.19. When there is a movement from Karka to Siṅha (after a Maṇḍūkagati), a wise Daivajña should predict a disease due to an ulcer or wound. When there is a movement from Siṅha to Mithuna (Maṇḍūkagati), there will be disease or death of one's wife.

17.20. When the jump from Dhanu to Meṣa, the death of a son or other such relative is to be apprehended. When a Saumya occupies the Rāśis of jumps (Rāśis from which and to where the jump is occurring), there is no danger, but when it has a Krūra, there is danger.

17.21. When there is a jump from Kanya to Karka (Maṇḍūka), the person concerned becomes great during the former portion of it and goes upon a happy trip toward the north.

17.22. When there is a jump from Siṅha to Mithuna, the former portion thereof should be shunned as inauspicious at the commencement of an undertaking, but a trip then in the southwest will be auspicious.

17.23. When there is a jump from Karka to Siṅha in the Savya movement, there is failure of one's business, and sickness comes in its wake. There is a return via southwest towards the south – i.e., there is a passage from Siṅha towards Vṛṣabha through Mithuna.

17.24. When there is a jump from Mīna to Vṛścika (Siṅhavlokana), i.e., in the northern direction, trouble disappears. When the jump is from Dhanu to Meṣa (Siṅhavlokana), the passage is risky; disease and death of a relative may occur.

17.25. When the jump is reversed, i.e., from Meṣa to Dhanu (Siṅhavlokana), there is prosperity, marriage, and other such auspicious events. When Saumyas occupy the Rāśis of jumps, there will be royal favour leading to every kind of prosperity.

17.26. In the case of the Cakra belonging to Meṣa, Dhanu and Siṅha, the lord of the Deha is Maṅgala, and the lord of Jīva is Guru. In the case of the Cakra belonging to Vṛṣabha, Kanyā and Makara, the lord of Deha is Śani, and that of Jīva is Budha. This holds good for Savya Cakra. This is to be taken in reverse order for the Apasavya Cakra.

17.27. In the Savya Cakra, the lord of Deha is Śukra, and the lord of Jīva is Budha in the case of Chakra belonging to Mithuna, Tulā and Kumbha. With respect to the Cakra owned by Karka, Vṛścika and Mīna, the lord of Jīva and Deha are, respectively, Guru and the Candra.

17.28. When Maṅgala, Śani, Sūrya and Rāhu occupy Deha and Jīva separately, death is to be feared. Of this, there can be no doubt when several of them occupy these places.

17.29. The Graha occupying the Deha produces a dangerous ailment, while the one occupying the Jīva brings on great risk. If both the Deha and Jīva are occupied by the Krūras named previously, then undoubtedly, the person becomes a victim.

17.30. With two Krūras in the Deha or Jīva, there will be growing disease; with three of them, there ought to be sudden or untimely death. When all four are present, death sets in.

17.31. Suppose Krūras simultaneously occupy Deha and Jīva. In that case, there is danger from the king, robbers, or other such agencies, but if two Krūras simultaneously occupy them, death undoubtedly occurs.

17.32-33. Damage by fire will result when the Sūrya is in such a position (in Aśubha Deha or Jīva). The Candra in this position will cause injury by conflagration. Maṅgala will bring on hurt inflicted by a deadly weapon. Budha will produce troubles due to flatulence. Guru in such an Aśubha position will cause troubles in the stomach. Śukra will bring on danger by fire; Śani produces colic; Rāhu causes ailments due to venomous bites (of snakes and poisonous insects).

17.34-36. Guru in the third house, Maṅgala in the seventh, Śani in the Janmalagna, Rāhu in the ninth house, the Candra in the tenth, the Sūrya in the twelfth, Budha in the seventh and Śukra in the sixth house are each of them are Maraṇasthāna or death manifestor. When the Graha, which is thus termed Maraṇasthāna, is in Krūrayutidṛṣṭi or occupies a Nīca-Śatru Rāśi or, i.e. deprived of strength, the person concerned comes to grief.

DEHA-JĪVA PHALAM

17.37. Sūrya in Deha or Jīva causes adversities of various sorts, loss of wealth, disease fever, danger from enemies, loss of one's place, bilious afflictions, spleen ailments, diarrhoea, consumption, ear ailments, death of cattle and kinsmen, and the loss of brother or other dear relatives.

17.38. Candra in Deha or Jīva leads to association with one's kinsmen, culminating in the acquisition of a virgin girl (as wife or girlfriend) as a helpmate; to health, ornaments, luxurious apparel, and respect in the land; to acts of gift and the propitiation of Devatās and Brāhmaṇas at baths in holy waters (Gaṅgā, Yamina, Kaveri, Setubandha etc.); to relaxation and pleasant meals.

17.39-40. Maṅgala in Deha or Jīva produces inflammation of the body, disease and dread of fire and robbers, quarrel with kinsmen, death of a brother or other dear relatives, loss of land and treasure, falling off in rank (demotion, humiliation), policy leading to war, colic, piles, leprosy, danger from venomous reptiles and foemen. Fever, smallpox, biliousness, knotty tumour, danger from venomous reptiles, fire, weapons, robbers, enemies, and the king should a wise Daivajña predict in addition, with respect to Maṅgala.

17.41. Budha in Deha or Jīva secures the favour of benevolence, trusted great men, a knowledge of worldly affairs, good manners, an insight into Vedas, philosophy, and science; the acquisition of women, progeny, wives, royal ornaments, luxury goods, elephants, and horses; the increase of discernment, wealth, intellect and fame.

17.42. Guru in Deha or Jīva leads to the many joys of affluence, eminent rank, coronation in the kingdom, the esteem of kings and similar honours, blessings of family life, ornaments, abundant food, wealth, health, fame, victory, and goodwill.

17.43. Śukra in Deha or Jīva secures sexual delight and the society of wine women, the pleasures of pictorial art, fine apparel, wealth, cattle, vehicles, gems and precious stones, musical concerts, dancing parties, lordly magnificence, good fame, great liberality, and association with the virtuous.

17.44. Śani in Deha or Jīva brings about quarrels, bodily pain, death, an affliction of relatives; dread of fire, enemies and ghosts, trouble from venomous reptiles, loss of hone, of wealth, of self-respect; of wife, of children, of homely comforts, of agriculture, of trade and cattle.

17.45. A Daivajña may predict that when Rāhu occupies Deha or Jīva, the person suffers annoyance from enemies, sees their relations in trouble, has to take to a wandering life, is afflicted with paralysis (accompanied by involuntary tremors, a kind of seizure) and have to fear danger from their king.

17.46. When Ketu occupies Deha or Jīva, trouble crops up from thieves, fire and bleeding, poverty, loss of relatives, loss of place and wealth also result.

CAKRADAŚĀ PHALAM

17.47. At the time the Cakradaśā of the Lagna is in progress, the health of the body, much happiness, acquisition of fame, ornaments, dominion, wealth, children, wives, and apparel may be predicted. If the Lagna is in a Saumyarāśi, everything will come off auspiciously; it will be otherwise when the Lagna is in a Krūrarāśi and also when occupied by a Krūra. When the Lagna being in a Saumyarāśi is also occupied by a Saumya, the result will be exceedingly happy. If the Graha in the Lagna be in its svakṣetra, in its Ucca or a Mitra Rāśi and the Cakradaśā of the Lagna be in progress, dominion, wealth and honour from the sovereign will accrue. If, on the other hand, the Graha in the Lagna be Nīca, Asta, or in a Nīca Rāśi, there will be loss of children, wife, and such other dear objects; if the Lagna and its occupants be of a mixed character, the Daivajña should declare the effect to be of a mixed nature.

17.5l-52. During the Cakradaśā of the second house may be expected an increase of wealth and corn, good food, acquisition of children and wives, lands, cattle, honour by the sovereign, attainment of knowledge, eloquence, and amusement in good company. When the Rāśi is Saumya, such good effect as has been said above will follow. It will be otherwise when the Rāśi is Krūra.

17.53-54. When the Cakradaśā of the third house ripens, it will be the good fortune of the person concerned to enjoy much happiness, to get in abundance fruits edible and palatable, to display heroism, firmness, and self-control, to be presented with ear-rings, apparel, and neck-ornaments to attain to dignity and to possess food, drink, and other good things of life in abundance. The Daivajña is to announce good effects when the Rāśi is Saumya.

17.35-57. When the Cakradaśā of the fourth house ripens, the person concerned will get vehicles, ornaments, and new lands in the frontier; make pilgrimages to sacred shrines and the like; obtain conspicuous honour from his community; enjoy the purity of the heart, engage in some great enterprise; be blessed with wife and children; engage in agriculture; acquire new friends and new landed property, new house; derive much happiness; command good health, resources and articles of the toilette such as perfumes, wearing apparel and ornaments. The good things the Daivajña should divine when the Rāśi is Saumya, but all this will be absent when the Rāśi is Krūra.

17.58-60. During the Cakradaśā, the fifth house may be had kingship, honour by the sovereign, acquisition of wives and children, exceeding, stability, sound health, the cherishing of relatives, dispensing of food, acquirement of fame, jubilee and great prosperity, beneficence attainment of wealth, vehicles, wearing apparel and ornaments. The Daivajña should as before predicting the effects properly according as they are due to Saumya or Krūra Rāśi or yutidṛṣṭi of Saumyas or Krūras. He is to add loss of position when the Rāśi is Cara.

17.61-63. During the ripening of the Cakradaśā of the sixth house, the person has to apprehend danger from fire, trouble from thieves, from enemies, from poison, from the sovereign, loss of place, great risk due to gonorrhoea, colic, jaundice and kinsmen ailments, diarrhoea and consumption, ill-fame, loss of wives, wealth, children and relatives, captivity, being put behind the irons, harassment on account of debts and poverty. These will be the effects when the Rāśi is Krūra. The effect will be mixed when the sixth Rāśi is Saumya.

17.64-65. During the ripening of the Cakradaśā of the seventh house may be expected marriage, the joy with a wedded consort, the birth of a son, the pleasures of the table (food) - such as ghee, dal, and sugar; success in agriculture, acquisition of cattle, elephants and ornaments, honour by the sovereign and great renown. When the seventh Rāśi is benefic and is occupied by a Saumya, the good effects spoken of will surely follow.

17.66-67. During the Cakradaśā of the eighth house, there will be much misery, waste of wealth, loss of place, loss of relations, griping pain in the privities and the stomach, poverty, famine, and danger from an enemy. These effects the Daivajña may announce when the Rāśi is Krūra or occupied by a Krūra.

17.68-69. When the Cakradaśā of the ninth house sets in, goodwill certainly results, such as children, friends, wives, wealth, agriculture, Cattle, houses ornaments, an accomplishment of good works and charity, the securing of adherents among men connected with the great men in power. All this will accrue when the Rāśi is Saumya. It will be otherwise when the Rāśi is Krūra.

17.70-71. When the Cakradaśā of the Rāśi of the tenth house is in progress and when that Rāśi is Saumya, the following good things may be predicted by a competent Daivajña: acquisition of a kingdom, honour by a king, good fame, great rejoicing in the society of one's wives, children and relatives, possession of authority, sound health, pleasant recreations in company with good people, the fruit of good works and supremacy.

17.72-73. During the Cakradaśā of the Rāśi of the eleventh house, the person will come into possession of money, health, ornaments and have accession to varied property and household furniture. When Saumyas appear in the Rāśi in question (in Gocara), the Daivajñas declare there will be, as the result thereof, comfort and happiness secured to the females, the children, and the relatives, return from reproductive investments, real prosperity, royal favour, and good fellowship.

17.74-75. When the Cakradaśā of the Rāśi of the twelfth house is in progress, and the Rāśi is Krūra, the following evils may without doubt crop up: bodily suffering, loss of place, encounter with robbers, fire, royal displeasure and the like, trouble from relatives from women and the king; obstruction of activity, exhaustion, loss in agriculture, in cattle and lands; poverty and want of occupation.

17.76. We have thus stated the effect of the Bhāvas from the Lagna to the twelfth, especially pointed out.

17.77-79. In accordance with the strength of the Graha owning a particular Rāśi under consideration, should the Daivajña use suitably the rule enunciated when the lord of the Rāśi in question is possessed of strength occupying a Varga belonging to its Sva-Ucca-Mitra and when the associated Grahas are friendly, and the aspecting ones Saumya the good effects stated already may be announced. But when the lord of the Rāśi has no strength being in its Nīca-Śatru Rāśi, Asta by Sūrya or when it occupies the 6th, 8th, or 12th and the aspecting Grahas or Krūra or Śatru - when such is at birth the state of the Graha owning the Rāśi under consideration - the effect produced by it will be painful.

17.80-81. The effect produced by a Rāśi is of two sorts: bad as well as good. If the Rāśipati is without strength, the person concerned will suffer the evil effects. If the Rāśipati predominates in strength, the effect of the Rāśi will be good, and if the Rāśi is capable of producing good as well as evil, while its lord continues predominant, the good will undoubtedly come to pass.

17.82. If the lord of the Rāśi referred to in the preceding ślokas is in a Cara Rāśi or Añśa, and if a Cara Rāśi produces Kālacakra, the person will have to go to a foreign country.

17.83. In the case adverted to in the preceding Ślokas, the repairing to a foreign country will continue as long as the Cakra in question lasts. Suppose one, and not both, of the above conditions have the characteristics of movability. In that case, the Daivajña should decide the question of the person concerned going to a foreign country or being in his native place, just as the balance of forces tends to the one or the other.

17.84-86. Graha effects which it is possible to foretell, have been described, some of them in the Saṅjñā, i.e., in the chapter on definitions (Adhyāyas 1-2), some in the Karmājīva Adhyāya, some in that treating of the Ashraya yogas (Adhyaya 7), and some in connection with the particular positions of Grahas (Adhyaya 8), with the Rājayoga, Candra yoga, Nabhasa yogas (Adhyāya 7) and the like, and also some as due to good and bad aspects and the combinations in the same bhava of two or more Grahas. An intelligent Daivajña should, by a due exercise of his faculties, consider well these Graha effects as ancient sages have described them and utilise them for making his predictions in connection with the Kālacakra Daśā.

17.87-88. Lay upon the floor a diagram of the Dakṣiṇa Cakra, which begins with Meṣa and ends with Mīna. Also, Draw another diagram on the ground of the Uttarāphālgunī Cakra beginning with Vṛścika and ending with Dhanu in the reverse order. Success or failure can be ascertained, as pointed out by the Rāśis and the Grahas, in a Kuṇḍalī according to their strength. Everybody can have such things foretold in respect to his life in the way that has been pointed out.

17.89-90. Ancient sages have ascertained the progress of Kālacakra to take place in three ways-(1) Maṇḍūkagamana, a frog's leap; (2) Priṣṭatogamana, a going backwards; (3) Siṅhavalokana the glancing of a lion which consists in returning by the way traversed already.

17.91-92a. The second of the three movements mentioned in the previous śloka occurs with respect to the Rāśis Karka and Siṅha. The third, i.e., Siṅhavalokana, is a direct passage between Mīna and Vṛścika, as also between Dhanu and Meṣa either way. The frog's leap is the direct passage between Kanyā and Karka, as well as Siṅha and Mithuna.

17.92b-93a. At the time of Siṅhavalokana, Daivajñas say, there will be suffering caused by fever, loss of place of a loving relative or other such person, distress to persons having the same status as the owner of the Kuṇḍalī in the family, accident in water such as falling in a well, danger from poison, fire of some deadly weapon, and being thrown from a vehicle. All this is likely to happen when the Siṅhavalokana is synchronous with the Daśāchidra, i.e. the Daśā period, Bhukti, Apahara, etc. of an ill-placed Krūra (vide next Sloka).

17.94. The term Daśāchidra, Daivajñas say, is applied to a period when the Daśā of a Krūra, Asta, Nīca or ill-placed Graha is in progress.

17.95. At the time a Maṇḍūkagamana occurs, the death of a revered person or one's parents may happen, or there may be danger from poison, deadly weapons, fire, fever, or incendiary brigands.

17.96. If the Maṇḍūkagamana refers to a Savyacakra, there will be distress to persons in the family holding equal status with the owner of the Kuṇḍalī.

17.97. When the Maṇḍūkagamana is between Siṅha and Mithuna, the Daivajña may predict the death of the mother or the person concerned with a complicated fever or danger from a king or enemy.

17.98-99. In a Siṅhavalokana having reference to a Savyacakra, the evil cropping up will be danger from a quadruped or fire. When there is a Priṣṭatogamana in a Savyacakra, there will be loss of wealth, grain and cattle, disease, or death of a father, or the demise of persons of equal standing.

17.99-100. On the other hand, when the Cakra is Apasavya, and there is a Maṇḍūkapluti, it may occasion illness and trouble to the wife or children of the person concerned or a severe fever to himself, or danger from a beast or an enemy or loss of place. If there is a Siṅhavalokana in an Apasavyacakra, the evil to be dreaded may be loss of place or the death of the person's father.

17.107. suppose there is a Priṣṭatogamana in an Apasavyacakra. In that case, the Daivajña may predict an accident in water, loss of place, loss of father, the incurring the displeasure of a sovereign and the persons having to be taken in consequence to an inaccessible jungle.

17.102. The Nakṣatras Aswini, Krittika, Punarvasu, Aśleṣā, Hastā, Revatī, Mūla, Pūrvābhādra, Uttarāṣāṛhā, and Svāti confirm as the sages say, to the first four of the formulas or the Savyacakra.

17.103. The last four of the formulas for the Savyacakra apply in their order to the four Pādas of the Nakṣatras Citrā, Uttarābhādra, Bharaṇī, Pūrvāṣāṛhā and Puṣya.

17.104. The first four of the formulas, or the Apasavyacakra, are applicable to the Nakṣatras Viśākhā, Rohiṇī, Maghā and Śravaṇa.

17.105. The Nakṣatras Śatabhiṣā, Anurādhā, Jyeṣṭhā, Mṛgaśirā, Dhaniṣṭhā, Uttarāphālgunī, Pūrvāphālgunī and Ārdrā conform to the last four formulas for the Apasavyacakra.

According to Pt V Subrahmaṇya Śāstrī:

Daivajñas are divided into two schools according to their manner of applying these formulas. One class explain that each formula applies to a Nakṣatra Pāda of a particular type and gives the order of the Rāśi-Mahādaśā comprising the entire life represented by the Nakṣatra Pāda and that the subsidiary portions of each Rāśi-Mahādaśā belong to the Rāśis mentioned in the formula.

The Daivajñas of the other class say that each formula is concerned only with the Mahādaśā of the Rāśi owning the corresponding Nakṣatra Pāda (i.e. to which the formula has reference) and the letters in the mnemonic rule indicate the order and the proportionate lengths of the subsidiary periods of the Mahādaśā in question; and that a life consists of several such Rāśi-Mahādaśās following one another in the natural order of the Nakṣatra Pādas the initial Mahādaśā being that of the quarter Nakṣatra occupied by the Candra in the Kuṇḍalī under examination.

An illustration will make the whole thing clear. Take, for instance, the case of the Kuṇḍalī given on page 237 supra.

The Candra's position is 9 Rāśis 14 deg 29 min 39 sec. These, when reduced to minutes, give 17069.65. Dividing this by 800 (the number of minutes of a Nakṣatra), we get 21 Nakṣatras and 269.65 min. The person was born after 269.65 min had passed in the 22nd Nakṣatra viz Śravaṇa, i.e. after 69.65 min had passed in the 2nd quarter of the Nakṣatra, and the Rāśi following this Nakṣatra Pāda is Tulā in the Apasavya Cakra.

The mnemonic formula corresponding to this pada is *taasaadtrakshurnidhir-dasaa,* which, when translated into figures, will become 6-7-8-12-11 10-9-8-7.

According to the first school (69.65/200) * 73 years or 28.90475 years having expired before birth, about 3 years of Vṛścikakuja daśā remain to be passed at the time of birth of the person concerned.

The Mahādaśā that follows next will be that of Mīnaguru, then Kumbhaśani, Makaraśani, Dhanurguru, Vṛścikakuja and Tulāśukra Daśā follow in their order.

The subsidiary portions of each of these Mahādaśās belong to these 9 Rāśis, e.g., the Bhuktis of the 10 years of Mīnaguru Daśā will be:

(1) Mīnaguru: 10 * (10/83), (2) Kumbhaśani: 4 * (10/83), (3) Makaraśani: 4 * (10/83), (4) Dhanurguru: 10 * (10/83), (5) Vṛścikakuja: 7 * (10/83), (6) Tulāśukra 16 * (10/83), (7) Kanyābudha 9 * (10/83), (8) Tulāśukra 16 * (10/83), (9) Vṛścikakuja: 7 * (10/83).

Similarly, for the other Daśās.

The second school will maintain that the initial Mahādaśā of the Kuṇḍalī under reference is that of Tulāśukra, out of which (69.65/200) * 16 or 5'57 years having elapsed already, there are still 10.43 years to be passed and the Mahādaśās to follow are those of Kanyābudha, Siṅharavi, Karkacandra, Mithunabudha, Vṛṣaśukra and so on. The order of the subsidiary periods in each Mahādaśā is that of the Rāśis of the letters in the corresponding formula, e.g. the Bhuktis of the 5 years of Siṅharavi Daśā of the Kuṇḍalī under reference will be:

(1) Mīnaguru: 10 * (5/100), (2) Meṣakuja: 7 * (5/100), (3) Vṛṣaśukra: 16 * (5/100), (4) Mithunabudha: 9 * (5/100), (5) Siṅharavi: 5 * (5/100), (6) Karkacandra 21 * (5/100), (7) Kanyābudha 9 * (5/100), (8) Tulāśukra 16 * (5/100), (9) Vṛścikakuja: 7 * (5/100).

The Daivajñas of Southern India belong to this latter class.

Mantreśvara refers to both the schools in the two following Ślokas:

There are a number of formulas, each composed of a number of mnemonic syllables referring to the several Nakṣatra Pādas beginning with the 1st pada of Aśvinī and giving Rāśis in a certain order. It is with reference to the order of Rāśis in these formulas that the Rāśi-Mahādaśā of which life is to consist should be determined. The Vākyakrama men of the school say that should be adhered to.

The initial Mahādaśā of life belongs to the lord of the Rāśi owning the Nakṣatra-Pāda occupied by the Candra at the time of birth, being so much of the Rāśi-Mahādaśā as corresponds to the ghaṭis that yet remain of the Nakṣatra-Pāda and the order of the Mahādaśās follows the natural order of the Nakṣatra-Pādas reckoned from the one above. This is the opinion, say the sages, held by the other school.

17.106. 5, 21,7,9,10, 16 and 4 are the years, respectively, of the 7 Grahas reckoned from the Sūrya. The year of the Rāśis corresponds to the years of their lords.

17.107. The period of Antardaśā of a Graha in a Mahādaśā is found out by multiplying the latter by the number of years assigned to the Graha and dividing the product by the number of years constituting the entire Ayus of the Cakra. The result will consist of years, months, and days.

17.108. The years assigned to the lord of the main Cakra Daśā should be multiplied into the years for the lord of the Rāśi, of which the Bhukti in the main Daśā is required. The product is to be divided by the maximum life period for the particular Navāñśa to which the Kālacakra belongs. The result in the form of years, months, days, and ghaṭis represents the Bhukti required - it is said in this connection that the lords of Dusthāna produce an abundance of misery and illness.

17.109. The subdivisions (Antardaśā) of a subperiod (Bhukti or Antardaśā treated in its turn as a whole) are to be obtained by multiplying the number of days composing the particular Bhukti chosen by the number of years of the Mahādaśā of the Graha whose Antara is required and dividing the product by the figure representing the maximum Āyus in years for the quarter Nakṣatra concerned. The quotient will be in a day, etc. In this way, the big, small, and smaller divisions of a Graha period styled Dasa, Antardaśā, Antara and Vidaśā may be obtained.

17.110: What is called Sukṣmadaśā, i.e., the subdivisions of a Nakṣatra or Kālacakra Antara, can be obtained by multiplying the figures in Vighaṭis of the Antara in question into the number of years of the Mahādaśā of the Grahas severally and dividing the product by the number of years of the maximum Ayus appropriate to the particular Kālacakra or Nakṣatra pāda under consideration.

17.111. When the pāka of a Graha in the Daśā, Antardaśā, etc. of another Graha is required, multiply the number representing the years of the Mahādaśā of the former into the figure denoting the years, months, days, etc. of the latter and divide the product by the fixed number of years for the maximum Āyuṣa. The quotient will be the pāka required. This rule is to be applied in the case of every pāka that has to be found out.

30.1.4.3
PHALADĪPIKĀ

ĀYURDAYA

13.25: Through the Daśās enunciated by Śrīpati, Aṣṭakavarga, Kālacakra Daśā and the Ududaśā system, a wise man ought to predict the Ayus of the native by the application of suitable rules after a correct calculation of the several planetary positions, careful working, and a minute scrutiny.

KĀLACAKRA DASA

22.1: The triad of Tārās reckoned from Aśvinī should be cast by quarters in the Apasavya) or Pradakṣiṇa order from Meṣa to Mīna among the 12 Rasis to which the Navāñśas composing the triad belong. Again, the 12 quarters of the triad reckoned from Rohiṇī are to be assigned to the 12 Rasis counted from Vṛścika to Dhanus in the (Savya or reverse, Apradakṣiṇa or anticlockwise) order.

22.2: Thus, are the triads of tats reckoned in their order from Aśvinī to be distinguished as Apasavya and Savya). The years assigned to a Graha constitute the Daśā - period of the Rāśi owned by that Graha. This is the peculiarity in the Kālacakra system, say the wise.

22.3: 5, 21, 7, 9, 10, 16, and 4 are the numbers representing the period in years, respectively, of the seven Grahas reckoned from Sūrya and are the means (sources) far feeling the good and bad effects.

22.4: In this Kālacakra system consisting of Daśās, Apaharas, etc., I shall now expound the formulae for the several Nakṣatra padas from Aśvinī onwards. Every such formula consists of nine syllables indicating by their number (as per Kaṭapayādi mnemonics) the particular Rāśyāpaharas composing the Daśā of the Nakṣatrapāda under consideration and consequently the total life period appertaining to that by means of the year allotted to the several Rāśi owners.

22.5: For these born in the first Pāda of Aśvinī, the first subperiod belongs to Meṣakuja; the second to Vṛṣaśukra; the third to Mithunabudha; the fourth to Karkacandra; the fifth to Siṅharavi; the sixth to Kanyābudha; the seventh to Tulāśukra; the 8th to Vṛścikakuja; and the 9th to Dhanurguru. For the 2nd Pāda of Aśvinī, the subperiods are owned by (1) Makaraśani, (2) Kumbhaśani, (3) Mīnaguru, (4) Vṛścikakuja, (5) Tulāśukra, (6) Kanyābudha, (7) Karkacandra, (8) Siṅharavi and (9) Mithunabudha. For the 3rd Pāda of Aśvinī, the subperiods belong to (1) Vṛṣaśukra, (2) MeshaKuja, (3) Mīnaguru, (4) Kumbhaśani, (5) Makaraśani, (6) Dhanurguru, (7) Meṣakuja, (8) Vṛṣaśukra and (9) Mithunabudha. For the 4th Pāda of Aśvinī; the subperiods are owned by (1) Karkacandra, (2) Siṅharavi, (3) Kanyābudha, (4) Tulāśukra, (5) Vṛścikakuja, (6) Dhanurguru, (7) Makaraśani, (8) Kumbhaśani and (9) Mīnaguru.

22.6: For the 1st Pāda of Bharaṇī, the several subperiods are (1) Vṛścikakuja, (2) Tulāśukra, (3) Kanyābudha, (4) Karkacandra, (5) Siṅharavi, (6) Mithunabudha, (7) Vṛṣaśukra, (8) Meṣakuja, and (9) Mīnaguru.

For the 2nd Pāda of Bharaṇī, the subperiods are (1) Kumbhaśani, (2) Makaraśani, (3) Dhanurguru, (4) Meṣakuja, (5) Vṛṣaśukra; (6) Mithunabudha, (7) Karkacandra, (8) Siṅharavi and (9) Kanyābudha.

For the 3rd Pāda of Bharaṇī, the subperiods are (1) Tulāśukra, (2} Vṛścikakuja, (3) Dhanurguru, (4) Makaraśani, (5) Kumbhaśani, (6) Mīnaguru, (7) Vṛścikakuja, (8) Tulāśukra and (9) Kanyābudha.

The subperiods of the 4th Pāda of Bharaṇī are (1) Karkacandra, (2) Siṅharavi, (3) Mithunabudha, (4) Vṛṣaśukra, (5) Meṣakuja, (6) Mīnaguru, (7) Kumbhaśani, (8) Makaraśani, and (9) Dhanurguru.

22.7: The formulae for Aśvinī and Bharaṇī are described above. The four formulae given for the four padas of Aśvinī will also respectively apply to the four padas of Kṛttikā in the Apasavya-Pradakṣiṇa triad. The formulae for Rohiṇī and Mṛgaśirās in the Savya triad are stated in the next two Ślokas, and the four formulae given for the four padas of Mṛgaśirās should also be used again for the four Padas of Ardra.

22.8: The subdivisions for the Pāda of Rohiṇī are (1) Dhanurguru, (2) Makaraśani, (3) Kumbhaśani, (4) Mīnaguru, (5) Meṣakuja, (6) Vṛṣaśukra, (7) Mithunabudha, (8) Siṅharavi and (9) Karkacandra:

For the 2nd Pāda of Rohiṇī, the subperiods are (1) Kanyābudha, (2) Tulāśukra, (3) Vṛścikakuja, (4) Mīnaguru, (5) Kumbhaśani, (6) Makaraśani, (7) Dhanurguru, (8) Vṛścikakuja and (9) Tulāśukra.

For the 3rd Pāda of Rohiṇī, the subperiods are (1) Kanyābudha, (2) Siṅharavi, (3) Karka - Chadra, (4) Mithunabudha, (5) Vṛṣaśukra, (6) Meṣakuja, (7) Dhanurguru, (8) Makaraśani, and (9) Kumbhaśani.

The 4th Pāda of Rohiṇī has the following subperiods (1) Mīnaguru, (2) Meṣakuja, (3) Vṛṣaśukra, (4) Mithunabudha, (5) Siṅharavi, (6) Karkacandra (7) Kanyābudha, (8) Tulāśukra and (9) Vṛścikakuja.

22.9: For the 1st Pāda of Mṛgaśirās, the subperiods are (1) Mīnaguru, (2) Kumbhaśani, (3) Makaraśani, (4) Dhanurguru, (5) Vṛścikakuja, (6) Tulāśukra, (7) Kanyābudha, (8) Siṅharavi, (9) Karkacandra.

The subperiods for the 2nd Pāda of Mṛgaśirās are (1) Mithunabudha, (2) Vṛṣaśukra, (3) Meṣakuja, (4) Dhanurguru, (5) Makaraśani, (6) Kumbhaśani, (7) Mīnaguru, (8) Meṣakuja and (9) Vṛṣaśukra.

The 3rd Pāda of Mṛgaśirās has the following subperiods (1) Mithunabudha, (2) Siṁharavi, (3) Karkacandra, (4) Kanyābudha, (5) Tulāśukra, (6) Vṛścikakuja, (7) Mīnaguru, (8) Kumbhaśani and (9) Makaraśani.

The subperiods for the 4th Pāda of Mṛgaśirās are (1) Dhanurguru, (2) Vṛścikakuja, (3) Tulāśukra, (4) Kanyābudha (5) Siṁharavi, (6) Karkacandra, (7) Mithunabudha, (8) Vṛṣaśukra, and (9) Meṣakuja.

22.10: The initial Mahādaśā of life belongs to the lord, of the Rāśi owning the Nakṣatra Pāda occupied by Candra at the time of birth, being so much of the Rāśi Mahādaśā as corresponds to the Ghaṭis that yet remain of the Nakṣatra Pāda. The order of Mahādaśās follows the natural order of the Nakṣatra padas reckoned from the one above. This is the opinion, say the sages, held by some (Daivajñas).

22.11: There are a number of formulae, each composed of a number of mnemonic syllables referring to the several Nakṣatra Pad s beginning with the first Pāda of Aśvinī and giving Rasis in a certain order. It is with reference to the order of Rasis in these formulae that the Rāśi Mahādaśās of which life is to consist, should be determined. The Vākyakrama men of one school say that should be adhered to.

22.12: ln the order of Rasis Vākyakrama, the junctions at the end of Karka, Vṛścika and Mīna give rise to (1) Maṇḍūkagati, (2) Aśva or Turagagati, and Siṁhavalokana respectively and the Daśās at these intervals cause woeful effects.

22.13: The Apahara or Bhukti of any of the Graha constituting a Mahādaśā is thus obtained. Find out the particular mnemonical syllable (out of the nine syllables) composing a formula whose Bhukti is wanted and find out the owner of the Rāśi signified by that syllable. Multiply the number of years assigned to this Graha by the number of years fixed for the Graha whose Mahādaśā is under consideration and divide the product by the total number of years constituting the entire Āyuṣa of the formula or Chakra. The quotient in years, etc., Will represent the sub-period required.

22.14: The total number of years indicated by the sum of the nine mnemonical syllables of any formula represents the number (in years) of Parama Āyuṣa for that formula. Thus, the Parama Āyuṣa in years for the 12 Rāśyaṅśas reckoned from Meṣa in an Apasavya Chakra will be 100, 85, 83 and 86 repeated thrice, while those for the 17 Rasis Aṅśas reckoned from Vṛścika in a Savya Chakra will be the same but in the reverse order; that 86, 83, 85 and 100 repeated thrice.

22.15: Whatever effects have been declared before by me in the case of the several Mahādaśās, the same should be stated by a wise Daivajña in the case of these Daśās also.

22.16: Ascertain the 5th, 8th, and 4th Tārā from Janmārkṣa, i.e., the Tārā occupied by Candra at the time of a person's birth. Cycles of Daśās are calculated from every one of these as the starting point. The Daśā counted from the 5th is called Utpanna; that from the 8th, Adhana; that from the 4th, Mahādaśā. If the Daśās in these cycles have their ends tallying with each other or with the end of the Daśā taken in the same order from Janmārkṣa, i.e., giving the same number of years, months, etc., it is a sign that the life of the person concerned is to end with the Daśā. In the case of people endowed with short, long and medium lives, the demise will happen at the close of the Daśā of the 3rd, 7th and 5th Tārā, respectively counted from the Janmatārā they being called respectively.

22.17: 1, 2, 9, 20, 18, 20, and 50 are the figures indicating the number of years prescribed respectively for Candra, Maṅgala, Budha, Śukra, Bṛhaspati, Sūrya and Śani in the Naisargika daśā system. The Daśās play their part in the order given here according to the natural strength of the Grahas concerned. The Yavanas are of the opinion that the Lagna Daśā, which is benefic, comes after these Daśās. However, others do not approve of this method.

22.18: The Rāśis, degrees, minutes, etc., of a Graha, should be converted into minutes, and as many multiplies of 2400 as may be found necessary should be subtracted from the same. The remainder represents the Āyuṣkalās of the Graha. The same should be divided by 200. The quotient gives the number of years, months, and days in the Añśāyurdaya contribution towards the lifespan by a Graha according to its Degree, etc., according to Satyācārya. If the Graha be retrograde or in exaltation, this quotient has to be trebled; If the Graha be in his own Rāśi or Navāñśa, Dreṣkāṇa or Vargottama, the Āyurdaya has to be doubled; if in depression, it has to be reduced by half. If the Graha be eclipsed, then also the reduction is half. But this last reduction will not apply to Śukra and Śani.

22.19: When Krūras occupy the six Bhavas counted backwards from the 12th, the whole, a half, a third, a fourth, a fifth and sixth, respectively, of their Āyurdaya is lost. When benefic Grahas occupy such positions, the loss is half of that incurred in the case of malefic ones. When several Grahas are in a Bhāva, only the strongest of them causes a reduction in the Āyurdaya. All Grahas except Maṅgala loses a third of their Āyurdaya when in inimical houses. The number of years contributed by the Lagna, according to Satyācārya's view, corresponds to the number of its Navāñśas that have risen. Even if the Lagna be strong or of medium strength, the same rule holds.

22.20: The rule of Satyācārya is preferable (to that laid down by Maya or Jīvaśarmā). But, some make the process inconsistent and unwarrantable by a series of multiplications. The dictum of the Ācāryas (Satyācārya and others) is the following:

(1) When several multiplications crop up, only one and that the highest, is to be gone through. For instance, when a Graha is in its Svarāśi, its Ucca and Vakrī motion, the Āyurdaya is not to be doubled first, and then the result trebled and the second result further trebled. According to the rule, the Āyurdaya should be trebled one for all.

(2) Again, when there are several reductions applicable, only one and the greatest should be made. For instance, a Graha may be in an Śatrurāśi and may be Asta by Sūrya. It is enough if the reduction by half, i.e., Astāṅgata reduction, is made.

22.21: The aggregate number of Piṇḍāyurdaya years assigned to the several Grahas from Sūrya onwards (in their highest exaltation point) are respectively 19,25,15,12,15,21 and 0. All the reduction should be gone through as before. When a malefic Graha is present in the Lagna, take only the minutes, seconds, etc., indicating the Lagna, leaving out the Rāśis. Multiply the total Āyuṣa by this and divide by 360. This result should reduce the whole Āyurdaya. If the Lagna be aspected by a benefic, the period to be subtracted will be only half of the above result. So, say those well versed in the Āyurdaya system.

22.22: In the Piṇḍāyurdaya system when the Añśa (Lagna Navāñśa) is strong, the Lagna Āyuṣa (or Lagna Daśā) corresponds to the Lagna Navāñśa. When the Lagna (Rāśi) is strong, the number of years, for Lagna - Āyuṣa corresponds to the number signified by the Rāśi, etc, counted from Meṣa, and not the Lagna Navāñśa.

22.23: The years assigned to the several Grahas in śloka 22.21 are to be adopted in full when they are in exaltation. When a Graha is in its depression point, the period assigned to it is reduced by half; when it occupies an intermediate position, the reduction is to be proportionate, say the wise.

22.24: The Piṇḍāyurdaya system is advocated as the best by Manittha, Chanakya, Maya and others. But Satyācārya has pronounced this method to be faulty, and Varāhamihira also has made similar pronouncement.

22.25: Jīvaśarmā lays down in accordance with his doctrine that the maximum period of life given by each Graha from Sūrya onwards is one-seventh of the maximum aggregate period (120 years and 5 days). In this Āyurdaya also, all the reductions are enjoined. The Lagna Āyuṣa also should be calculated in the same way as in the other systems.

22.26: The full period of life in the case of men has been declared as 120 years (12 * 10) by some. Others there are who have stated that the full lifespan will be the time taken by Śani to make 3 complete revolutions (in his orbit). There is a third school that says that the full life period of a man is the time taken by Candra for making 1000 revolutions. But we are of the opinion that the full period of man's life in this Kaliyuga is only 100 years, as stated in the Vedas.

22.27: Of the Lagna, Sūrya and Candra, whichever is strongest will have its Daśā first. Then will come the Daśā of the Grahas in Kendra and other positions. When several occupy together any one of these positions, the precedence will be given to the Graha, which predominates in strength. When they happen to be of equal strength, that which gives a longer period, in years of Āyurdaya, will have its turn first. When there is equality even in regard to the number of years of Āyurdaya of the Grahas, that which rises first after being eclipsed by Sūrya gets its Daśā prior to its fellows.

If such Grahas should, however, have a chance to have equal strength, equal Āyurdaya and equal rising after their conjunction with Sūrya, then that Graha, which is anterior in the general order of precedence among the significators, would rule the Daśā in question, and this general order of precedence is usually taken to be (1) the Lagna, (2) Sūrya, (3) Candra, (4) Maṅgala, (5) Budha, (6) Bṛhaspati, (7) Śukra and (8) Śani.

The strength of any Graha for this purpose is obtained by multiplying the position by the distance of the Graha from its nearest Bhāvasandhi and dividing the product by the distance between the Bhāvāñśa and one of its Sandhis.

22.28: Añśāyurdaya is to be calculated upon the predominance in strength of the Lagna; Piṇḍāyurdaya upon Sūrya's superiority in strength and Naisargikayurdaya when Candra's power is strongest: We shall now state what should be done when the three (Lagna, Sūrya and Candra) are of equal strength.

22.29: Add the three Ayurdayas and divide the sum by 3. The quotient will be the Āyurdaya required. If only two of them are strong, add the two Ayurdayas and take half the result. When the three Grahas are all weak, adopt the method advocated by Jīvaśarmā for finding out the Āyurdaya.

22.30: The Kālacakra Daśā system has to be resorted to only when the lord of the Navāñśa occupied by Candra is strong. The Daśā calculation, as per the Nakṣatra method, is always considered the best.

22.31: The full period of life in the case of men and elephants is given as 120 years and 5 days, while in that of horses, it is 32 years. It is 25 in the case of asses and camels and 24 for bulls and buffaloes. Twelve years are allotted for dogs and 16 for sheep and the like.

22.32: This Āyuṣa lifespan has been declared by wise men with respect to only those who are engaged in the practice of virtuous actions, who keep their senses under control, who eat a wholesome diet, who are devoted to the Brāhmaṇas and the Devatās and who preserve the landmarks of character and conduct peculiar to their high families.

Thus ends the 22nd Adhyāya on "Kālacakra Daśā, etc." in the work Phaladīpikā composed by Mantreśvara.

30.1.4.4
PRAŚNAMĀRGA

KALACHAKRA DAŚĀ

10.8. The beginning of the Daśā 'movement', from Meena to Vrischika, Kanyā to Karka, Siṅha to Mithuna, Mithuna to Simha and Dhanus to Meṣa, will be a difficult period as also the subsequent Daśā. Whether the order is regular or otherwise, the Daśā 'movement' will be good if there is no deviation but evil if the 'movement' is at the junction of two Rasis.

10.9-10. In regard to the Dakṣiṇa (clockwise) group of Nakṣatras, the first and last 'signs' indicated by the formula are Deha and Jīva, respectively. At the same time, the reverse will be the case in regard to the Vāma (anticlockwise) group of Nakṣatras. If Krūras afflict Deha or Jīva, there will be sickness. If both are afflicted and the Daśā is also evil, then there will be death.

Dr BV Raman gives his reflections here:

In the above three ślokas, the reference is to Kālacakra Daśā. Here, I propose to make only a few observations on this system. For more details, reference may be made to standard treatises or my forthcoming book, Kalachakra Daśā.

The 27 Nakṣatra are divided into two groups: the Dakṣiṇa (Savya) group, where the reckoning is clockwise and the Vāma (Apasavya) group, where the reckoning is anticlockwise: the former group consisting of five triads of Nakṣatras and the latter four triads. For those born, say in the first Pāda of Aśvinī, Punarvasu, or Hastā, the Daśās run in the order of Meṣakuja, Vṛṣaśukra, etc., up to Dhanurguru.

For those born in the second Pāda of the same Nakṣatras, the succession of Daśās would be in the order of Makaraśani, Kumbhaśani, Mīnaguru, Vṛścikakuja, Tulāśukra, Kanyābudha, Karkacandra, Siṅharavi and Mithunabudha. Here, it will be seen that the movement or 'jump' of the Daśā is from Mīna to Vṛścika, Kanyā to Karka and also Siṅha to Mithuna, and hence, deviating. The junctions of the Daśās mentioned above are harmful. The three important movements indicative of extremely bad results are Siṅhavalokana (Mīna to Vṛścika) or Maṇḍūkagamana (Kanyā to Karka) and Priṣṭatogamana (Siṅha to Mithuna). These ślokas will prove useful to those who are familiar with the Kālacakra system of directing.

—III—

30.2
THE DISCOURSE

Jayanta: Guruji, you dedicated this book to Ādi Śaṅkarācārya. Kindly tell us about him.

Ācārya: I am eager to discuss his life and philosophy, but let us start with understanding his Kuṇḍalī. There is much controversy, and modern historians try to place his birth in 788 A.D., much later than the Indian Historians.

Jayanta: So, in which year was he born?

Ācārya: We shall discuss about that. But let us start by examining what Dr Raman says about his birth. The following is excerpted from his book "Notable Horoscopes". This is a good starting point.

> A learned Indian scholar who has written a book entitled Life and Teachings of Śaṅkarācārya says that "in all this confusion of evidence, it is safe to assume that Śaṅkara flourished sometime between the middle of the seventh and the first quarter of the ninth centuries". On what grounds he has come to this conclusion has not been made clear.
>
> There is no doubt confusion prevails regarding the year of Śaṅkara's birth. Still, much of it could have been avoided if some of these scholars had taken the trouble to carefully examine all the relevant literature bearing on Śaṅkara's life and times, free from any prepossessions which are a concomitant of Western education.
>
> A careful study of such authorities as oankaravtjayas of Mādhavācārya, Anandagiri and Chidvilasa, Punyasloka Manjari and the Guru Paramparā list preserved in Śringerī Mutt reveals that Śaṅkara was born definitely before Christ and not in the 7th or 8th century AD. as oriental scholars - Indian and European - have made out It looks as though these scholars have confused Ādi Śaṅkara with his name-sake Abhinava Śaṅkara who was the Guru of Kamakoti Pīṭha and the 36th in succession to Ādi Śaṅkara.
>
> This Abhinava Śaṅkara, a very learned and pious man, was born in 788 A.D. in the cyclic year Bhava, solar month Vṛṣabha, on the 10th day of the bright half. It is said that like Ādi Śaṅkara, this Abhinava Śaṅkara also toured all over India, held discussions with learned men and conquered them intellectually. He died in 839 A.D.
>
> Almost all authorities are unanimous that Ādi Śaṅkara was born on Vaisakha Suddha Pañcamī at midday. *suklapaksheshu panchamyam tithyam bhaskaravasave: madhyanhechobhijinnama muhurta subhaveekshate.* As regards the year, Sukhacharya's Brihat Śaṅkara Vijaya and Chidvilasa's Śaṅkara Vijaya make it clear that Śaṅkara's birth took place in Kaliyuga 2593, Sunday, Vaisakha Śukla Pañcamī, in Punarvasu Nakṣatra, at midday, when the Sun was in Aries, the

> Moon in Punarvasu last quarter and when Jupiter, Saturn and Mars were in Kendras, exalted or in own house, Śukra was exalted, and Budha was with Sūrya.
>
> This date corresponds to 3rd April 509 B.C., the Vāra being Somavāra. Unfortunately, except in regard to Sūrya and Budha, the positions of other Grahas (Sūrya 20°; Candra 71°42'; Maṅgala 252°18'; Budha 7°6'; Guru 225°30'; Śukra 37°18'; Śani 338°12'; and Rāhu 41°18') do not tally with those suggested in the authorities.
>
> As Prof. B. Suryanarain Rao says: "According to the records of Śringerī Mutt (Guru Paramparā Patti) which are well preserved and reliable", Śaṅkara was born on the 5th day of the bright half of the lunar month of Vaisakha of the cyclic year Eswara in Vikrama 14. This corresponds to 25th March 44 B.C. I am inclined to give greater weight to the reliability of this date as it is given in the lists preserved by the Gurus of Śringerī, and consequently, there was no chance of their having been tampered with.
>
> Śaṅkara's Guru was Govindapada, who is said to have been begotten by his Kṣatriya wife, the great Vikramāditya. Śaṅkara must, therefore, have lived about the time of Vikramāditya.

Jayanta: So, Dr Raman believes Ādi Śaṅkarācārya was born on 25th March 44 B.C. What do you believe?

Ācārya: I believe that Ādi Śaṅkara was born much earlier. Let us examine that.

Ādi Śaṅkara established four Pīṭhas in the four Cardinal directions of India, presided by four Śaṅkarācāryas. They are Śringerī Śāradā Pīṭhaṃ in the South (Karnataka), Dvārakā Śāradā Pīṭhaṃ (Gujarat, Dwarka) in the West, Purī Govardhanmaṭha Pīṭhaṃ (Odisha, Puri) in the East, and Badri Jyotirmaṭha Pīṭhaṃ (Uttarakhand) in the North.

Let us examine what these Pīṭhas have to say about this Ādiguru Śrī Śaṅkara.

The following is from Purī Govardhanmaṭha Pīṭhaṃ:

https://www.govardhanpeeth.org/en/

Around 507 B.C., there descended on the sacred, deeply adorable soil of this holy land, a personality extraordinary who, by the sheer force of his matchless erudition, enlightened the whole world. He was none other than Ācārya Ādi Śaṅkara, a very embodiment of Lord Śiva, tenth in the line of Guru traceable back to Śrīmān Nārāyaṇa himself. He had dispelled all the dark forces that were hitting hard at the very foundation of Sanātana Dharma. He flew the banner of Sanātana Dharma, thus establishing its invulnerability once and for all. All this he accomplished solely by his all-too-rare spiritual wisdom, lustre, and strength, in short, his spiritual process.

His holiness Ādi Śaṅkarācārya was born in Kaladi village of Kerala. His father's name was Śivaguru, and his mother's name was Sati Āryambā. He was a Nambūdiri Brāhmaṇa by caste. He was born on *Yudhisthir Sambat 2631* in 507 B.C. on Vaiśākha Śukla Pañcamī on Ravivāra. His thread ceremony took place at the age of 5 years. Taking his mother's blessings, he left home to take a life of

Sanyāsa, initiated by Śrī Govindapadācārya on the auspicious day in the Kārtika Māsa on Devothana Ekādaśī. From the age of 5 to 8 years, Ācārya Śaṅkara learnt the Vedas, Vedāṅga, Dharma Śāstra, Purāṇa, Itihāsa, Budhagama etc. According to Sanātana Dharma and Śiva Purana, Hindus call Ādi Śaṅkarācārya as the reincarnation of Lord Śiva. According to Ādi Śaṅkarācārya philosophy, all four Pīṭha's Ācārya are known as Śaṅkarācārya.

Ācārya Śaṅkara, within a short span of sixteen years, re-established Sanātana Dharma after overcoming not only Buddhism but other directionless religions. His holy body left in demise at the age of 32 years in the year 2663, says 475 B.C., on the holy day of Kārtika Pūrṇimā.

The following is the delineation of Ācārya Śaṅkara's birth according to Dvārakā Śāradā Pīṭha:

The following is from Dvārakā Śāradā Pīṭhaṃ:

https://shreesharadapithmathdwarka.org/

वैदिक सनातन धर्म की पुनर्स्थापना करने वाले महान दार्शनिक आदि शंकराचार्य का जन्म भारत के केरल प्रांत में एर्णाकुलम जिले के ग्राम काल्टी में ईसा पूर्व सन् 507 वैशाख शु० 5 के दिन हुआ था। उनके पिता का नाम शिवगुरू तथा माता का नाम आर्याम्बा था। 8 वर्ष की आयु में पूज्यपाद गोविन्द भगवत्पाद से कार्तिक शु० 11 को सन्यास ग्रहण किया। उन्होंने प्रस्थानत्रयी आदि पर भाष्यों की रचना की। आचार्य शंकर का आविर्भाव ऐसी विषम परिस्थिति में हुआ, जब सनातन हिन्दु धर्म बलहीन, विध्वंश और विच्छिन्न हो गया था तथा विदेशी आक्रमण हो रहे थे। बनाया। उन्होंने 16 वर्ष की आयु में महान कार्यों को सम्पादित उन्होंने अपनी विद्वता एवं तप बल से बौद्ध विद्वानों को पराजित किया। श्री मंडन मिश्र जैसे विद्वानों को भी उन्होंने शास्त्रार्थ में पराजित कर शिष्य किया।

राजा सुधन्वा को प्रभावित कर उन्हें शिष्य बनाया। आदि गुरू शंकराचार्य जी ने 32 वर्ष के संक्षिप्त जीवन काल में भारत वर्ष के सुदूर जनपदों का भ्रमण कर वैदिक सनातन हिन्दू धर्म का व्यापक प्रचार-प्रसार किया। सुप्तप्राय समाज को जागृत किया। अपने जीवन काल में उन्होंने अनेकों ग्रंथ लिखे तथा मंदिरों का जीर्णोद्वार कराया। धर्म की सत्ता निरंतर बनी रहे और आध्यात्मिक मूल्यों का उत्कर्ष होता रहे इस दृष्टि से महान भविष्य दृष्टा ने भारत वर्ष के 4 धार्मिक केन्द्रों में मठों की स्थापना की। मठाम्नाय महानुशासन में आचार्य श्री ने कहा है - "कृते विश्व गुरू ब्रम्हा त्रेतायां ऋषि सप्तमः। द्वापरे व्यास एवं स्यात्, कलावत्र भवाभ्यहम्॥" अर्थात् सतयुग में ब्रह्म, त्रेता में वशिष्ठ, द्वापर में वेद व्यास और कलयुग में भगवान शंकर ही विश्वगुरू हैं।

उनके द्वारा स्थापित चारों पीठों के आचार्य शंकराचार्य की पद्वी से विभूषित होते हैं। उन्होंने पूर्व में पुरूषोत्तम क्षेत्र पुरी में ऋग्वेद से सम्बन्धित पूर्वाम्नाय गोवर्धनमठ की, दक्षिण में रामेश्वरम् में स्थित कर्नाटक के श्रृंगेरी में यजुर्वेद से सम्बद्ध दक्षिणाम्नाय की, गुजरात में द्वारिकापुरी (सामवेद) श्री शारदामठ एवं बद्रीनाथ क्षेत्र में उत्तर में ज्योतिर्मठ (अथर्ववेद) की स्थापना की। इसके अनुक्रम में उन्होंने पुरी में पद्मपाद महाभाग को, दक्षिण में हस्तामलकाचार्य को, पश्चिम में सुरेश्वर महाभाग को (मण्डल मिश्र) तथा उत्तर में तोटकायार्य महाभाग को शंकरचार्य के पद पर प्रतिष्ठित किया।

उन्होंने अल्प समय में ही बौद्ध कापालिक, नास्तिकवाद, पाखँडवाद का खंडनकर, धर्म नियंत्रित पक्षपात विहीन शोषण विनिर्मुक्त वैदिक शासनतन्त्र की स्थापना की तथा भारत को अखंड भारत के रूप में प्रतिष्ठित किया। 32 वर्ष की आयु में लीला संवरण कर समाधि ली।

आचार्य शंकर के समय भारत राजनैतिक, धार्मिक, सामाजिक दृष्टि से अनेक ईकाईयों में बंटा था। आवागमन भी कष्ट साध्य था- संचार साधन भी सीमित थे। अपने सन्यासी शिष्यों को वन, पर्वत, अरण्य तीर्थ, आश्रम, गिरि, पुरी, भारती, सागर एवं सरस्वती इन 10 भागों में विभक्त किया। ये सन्यासी अपने-अपने क्षेत्र में विचरण कर धर्म प्रचार के द्वारा समाज को संगठित करें, इस दृष्टि से क्षेत्र का विभाजन किया। गोवर्धन पीठ पुरी की स्थापना श्री शंकराचार्य जी द्वारा ईशा पूर्व सन् 486 के कार्तिक मास में की गई। इस पीठ के 145 वें शंकराचार्य स्वामी श्रीनिश्चनानन्द सरस्वती जी महाराज हैं।

आद्य शंकराचार्य ने विधान किया कि उनके द्वारा स्थापित 4 पीठों के पीठाधीश्वर उनके प्रतिभूति समझे जावेंगे। चार पीठों में शंकराचार्यों की परम्परा अनवरत चली आ रही है। हिन्दु धर्म के संरक्षण और उन्नयन में चारों पीठ की भूमिका महत्वपूर्ण है। आज भी शंकराचार्य जी की पीठ राष्ट्रीय एकता की वैजयन्ती फहरा रही है। आद्य शंकराचार्य सनातन धर्म की विश्व व्यापी महानता के उदार प्रवक्ता थे। उन्होंने वैदिक धर्म को अनंत युगों का स्थायित्व देकर उसे अत्यंत सुदृढ़ नींव प्रदान किया। हिन्दु धर्म का दर्शन चिरस्थायी है और सम्पूर्ण विश्व के लिये मंगलकारी है।

आद्य शंकराचार्य भगवान की आदर्श परम्परा के अनुसार पुरी पीठाधीश्वर जगद्गुरू शंकराचार्य स्वामी श्री निश्चलानन्द सरस्वती जी महाराज ने अन्यों के हित का ध्यान रखते हुए हिन्दुओं के अस्तित्व एवं आदर्श की रक्षा, देश की सुरक्षा तथा अखंडता के लिए धर्मसंघ पीठ परिषद, आदित्य वाहिनी एवं आनंद वाहिनी नामक संस्था का गठन किया है, जिसके माध्यम से पूरे भारत वर्ष में सार्वभौम सनातन धर्म का प्रचार-प्रसार निरन्तर जारी है।

The following is from Badrikāśrama Jyotirmaṭha Pīṭhaṃ
https://shreejyotirmathah.org/

आज से लगभग 2522 वर्ष पूर्व केरल प्रदेश के कालटी नामक ग्राम में माता आर्याम्बा और पिता शिवगुरु से भगवान् शंकर ने देवताओं की प्रार्थना एवं माता-पिता की तपस्या से बालक शंकर के रूप में अवतरित हुए। बाल्यकाल से ही आपकी अद्भुत प्रतिभा बड़े बड़े विद्वानों को चमत्कृत करती रही। दो वर्ष की अल्पायु में ही आप मातृभाषा के विद्वान् बनकर उसमें साहित्य रचना करने लगे थे। उनकी इस प्रतिभा से प्रभावित होकर केरल के तत्कालीन नरेश राजशेखर ने उन्हें राजदरबार में सम्मानित करने हेतु आमन्त्रित किया । परन्तु बालक शंकर ने अपनी विद्याभ्यास की व्यस्तता बनाकर राजसेवकों को विनय पूर्वक वापस कर दिया । तब राजा स्वयं बालक शंकर का दर्शन करने आया और उनकी अलौकिक प्रतिभा का दर्सन कर अभिभूत हुआ।

आचार्य शंकर के बारे में प्रसिद्धि है कि उन्होंने आठ वर्ष की अवस्था में चारों वेद, बारह वर्ष में सभी शास्त्रों का अध्ययन कर लिया था और उनके द्वारा रचा गया भाष्य जो कि लोक में शांकरभाष्य के नाम से प्रसिद्ध है, का प्रणयन उन्होंने सोलह वर्ष की अवस्था में ही कर दिया था। वे लोकोत्तर प्रतिभा के धनी थे । आठ वर्ष की आयु में ही उन्हें ज्ञान की प्राप्ति हो गई थी और वे माता से आज्ञा लेकर नर्मदा तट स्थित गोविन्दपादाचार्य जी से संन्यास ग्रहण कर शंकर भगवत्पाद के रूप में प्रतिष्ठित हुए थे ।

आचार्य शंकर ने चार बार पैदल ही सारे देश का भ्रमण किया था और स्थान स्थान पर अपने ज्ञान के आलोक से लोगों को प्रभावित किया था । जहाँ वैचारिक मतभेद था उसे उन्होंने शास्त्रार्थ द्वारा निरस्त किया और सारे देश में एक ही सत्य सनातन धर्म की प्रतिस्थापना की । उनके

समय में 72 सम्प्रदायों में सारा समाज बंट चुका था और मुख्य रूप से बौद्ध मतानुयायी वैदिक मत के विपरीत चलने को लोगों को प्रेरित कर रहे थे। ऐसे समय में आचार्य शंकर ने मतवादों का निरास करते हुए अद्वैत मत की प्रतिष्ठा की। उनके द्वारा दश उपनिषदों और गीता तथा ब्रह्मसूत्र पर किया गया भाष्य अत्यन्त प्रसिद्ध है।

The following is from Badrikāśrama Jyotirmaṭha Pīṭhaṃ

https://sringeri.net/

Jagadguru Śrī Ādi Śaṅkara Bhagavatpāda established the first of the four Amnaya Pīṭhaṃs at Śringerī more than twelve centuries ago to foster the sacred tradition of Sanatana Dharma.

Hallowed for all times by Sage Ṛsyaśringa, who stayed and performed Tapas here, Śringerī attracted the great Ācārya with a remarkable sight.

Tradition has it that after the Ācārya had dispersed all the non-Vaidika creeds prevailing in the country, He was on the look-out for a convenient and holy place where he could establish an institution to spread the truths of Advaita Vedānta. When the Ācārya came to Śringerī, he saw an unusual sight on the banks of the Tunga. A cobra was seen spreading out its hood over a frog in labour pains to give it a shadow from the scorching mid-day sun. Struck with the sanctity of the place, which could infuse love between natural adversaries, the Ācārya chose this very location to establish His first Maṭha.

The *Mādhavīya Śaṅkara Digvijayam* describes that the Ācārya came across many virtuous people at Śringerī and taught them the doctrine of Advaita. He then invoked the Divinity of Knowledge, Devī Śāradā and consecrated an icon of the Devī. Thus, the Pīṭhaṃ He founded at Śringerī in South India for fostering the Vedas and the sacred tradition of Sanatana Dharma came to be known as the Dakṣiṇamnaya Śrī Śāradā Pīṭhaṃ.

The Ācārya appointed his prime disciple, Śrī Sureśvarācārya, as the first Ācārya of the Pīṭhaṃ. Since then, the Pīṭhaṃ has been blessed with an unbroken Guru Paramparā, a garland of spiritual masters and Jivanmuktas representing Śrī Ādi Śaṅkarācārya. The succeeding Ācāryas has led a life of such austere penance that it has led disciples to adore in them the radiance of Śrī Ādi Śaṅkara Himself.

Besides being a centre of spiritual power, Śringerī also came to be known as a great place of traditional learning owing to the presence of Devī Śāradā and the erudition of the Ācāryas of the Pīṭhaṃ. The Ācāryas were instrumental in bringing forth commentaries on the Vedas and in further expounding the Bhaśyas of Śrī Ādi Śaṅkarācārya. The Ācāryas also wrote a number of independent works related to Advaita besides producing a number of hymns underlining their ardent devotion to the non-dual "Supreme" worshipped in diverse forms. The Pīṭhaṃ thus came to be regarded as the Vyākhyanā Siṅhāsana, The Throne of Transcendental Wisdom. Consequently, the Birudavali hails the Ācārya as the occupier of this throne. Many regard Devī Śāradā Herself to be moving in the form of the presiding Ācārya of the Pīṭhaṃ.

In the 14th century, royal patronage to the Pīṭhaṃ began with the founding of the famous Vijayanagar empire under the divine guidance of the 12th

Ācārya, Jagadguru Śrī Vidyaranya. The austerity of the Ācārya influenced the rulers to such an extent that they began ruling in the name of the Ācārya and granted the Pīṭhaṃ the rights over secular administration of the land. At the rulers' request, the Ācārya began conducting a Durbar during the Navarātri festival - an occasion deemed by the rulers to honour their Guru. Subsequently, the Ācārya came to be known as the Karnataka Siṅhāsana Pratisthāpanācārya, and the Pīṭhaṃ became a mighty institution - a Samsthānam and is known to this day as the Jagadguru Śaṅkarācārya Mahāsamsthānam, Dakṣiṇamnaya Śrī Śāradā Pīṭhaṃ at Śringerī. Over the succeeding centuries, a number of empires and rulers, including the Mysore Maharajahs Hyder Ali and Tipu Sultan, the Nizam of Hyderabad, the Peshwas and the Keladi rulers and Travancore Rajas were drawn towards the Pīṭhaṃ and respected the Ācārya as their Guru.

Śrī Vidyaranya Mahāsvāmi being accorded royal honour in the Adda-Pallaki by the Vijayanagara Emperors, Harihara and Bukkaraya. A 17th-century painting based on the mural at Virupaksha temple at Hampi. This tradition has continued since then and is followed even today.

In the recent past, the Śāradā Pīṭhaṃ has shone through the lives of the Ācāryas - Jagadguru Śrī Sacchidananda Śivābhinava Nṛsiṅha Bhāratī Mahāsvāmigal, the re-discoverer of Śrī Ādi Śaṅkara's birthplace at Kalady and the founder of the famous Pāthaśāla at Śringerī; followed by the renowned Jivanmukta, Jagadguru Śrī Chandrasekhara Bhāratī Mahāsvāmigal; succeeded by the crest jewel of Yogis, Jagadguru Śrī Abhinava Vidyātirtha Mahāsvāmigal. They have all left indelible impressions in the hearts of the disciples.

With such a rich history associated with Śrī Ādi Śaṅkarācārya's first and foremost Pīṭhaṃ, many wonder at the aptness of the Ācārya's choice of locating the Pīṭhaṃ at Śringerī, a spot replete with a holy past, and bountiful with natural splendour and serenity.

Today, the Śringerī Śāradā Pīṭhaṃ bedecked with an unbroken chain of Ācāryas continues to uphold the principles of Sanatana Dharma with the 36th Ācārya Jagadguru Śaṅkarācārya Śrī Śrī Bhāratī Tirtha Mahāsvāmiji acting as a treasure of spiritual wisdom and peace for all seekers.

Jayanta: It appears that different Pīṭhas have different timing of Ādi Śaṅkarācārya. Śringerī Maṭha states that it is 1200 years back, which is near 800 CE.

Ācārya: Yes, they have different opinions. But among them, the Puri Pīṭha appears more authentic. They have retained the list of their successive Ācāryas, which you can check on their website. The list is from Kālī 2617 (-484) to the current date.

Jayanta: This shows that Ādi Śaṅkara must have been born before -484 CE.

Ācārya: Since the esteemed Ācārya lived for 32 years, the 507 BCE birthdate appears more reliable. But let us not jump to conclusions and examine all the information we have at our disposal.

Jayanta: Let us investigate further, Guruji!

Ācārya: While researching on this, I came across this poste by Śmt Jayasree Saranathan on "Date of Ādi Śaṅkarācārya" at https://jayasree-saranathan.medium.com/date-of-adi-shankaracharya-39540f22d8d8. Here she quoted Citsukhācārya. This one given by Citsukhācārya and quoted by N. Mahaliṅgam in his book and also produced with the exact verse by T.S. Nārāyaṇa Sastry (pp. 39, 40). She provides a snip of the verse and the Kuṇḍalī. The snip quotes "of Chitsukha's work, we have complete details with regard to the date of Śaṅkara:"

ततः सा दशमे मासे संपूर्गशुभलक्षणे । षर्डिंशे शतके श्रीमद्युधिष्ठिरशकस्य वै ॥ एकत्रिंशेऽथ वर्षे तु हायने नन्दने शुभे । मेषराशिं गते सूर्ये वैशाखे मासि शोभने ॥ शुक्लपक्षे च पश्चभ्यां तिथ्यां भास्करवासरे । पुनर्वसुगते चन्द्रे लग्ने कर्कटकाह्वये ॥ मध्याह्ने चाऽभिजिन्नाममुहूर्ते शोभनेक्षिते । स्वोच्चस्थे केन्द्रसंस्थे च गुरौ मन्देकुजेरवौ ॥ निजतुङ्गगते शुक्रे, रविणा सङ्गते बुधे । प्रासूत तनयं साध्वी गिरिजेव षडाननम् ॥ (12 to 16).

"Then in the tenth month of her pregnancy which was fraught with all auspicious signs, in the year **2631 of the Yudhiṣthira Saka, in the auspicious year Nandana, on Sunday the 5th day of the bright half of the auspicious month Vaiśākha**, when Sūrya was in, and Candra was in Punarvasu Nakṣatra, in the Kataka Lagna, just at mid-day, in the Abhijit Muhurta, with the Lagna aspected by Śubha Grahas, when Guru, Sani, Maṅgala and Sūrya were in Kendra and Ucca, when Śukra was Ucca, and when the auspicious Budha was with Sūrya, the chaste Āryambā gave birth to a son even as Pārvati gave birth to the glorious Shanmukha." 2631 Yudhiṣṭhira Saka corresponds to 2593 Kali or 509 B.C.

The reconstructed Kuṇḍalī gives the following Graha positions: Lagna-Guru in Karka, Śani in Tulā, Maṅgala in Makara, Śukra in Mīna, Sūrya-Budha in Meṣa and Candra in Mithuna.

Jayanta: The reconstructed Kuṇḍalī appears to be like Śrī Rāma's with only the difference of Candra in 12H in Mithuna (in Punarvasu).

Ācārya: Yes, that is right.

Jayanta: What is Yudhiṣṭhira Śākā?

Ācārya: Wikipedia states:

युधिष्ठिर संवत् या युधिष्ठिर शक की शुरूवात ईसा पूर्व ३१३८-३९ में हुई थी। इसे भारत के महान सम्राट पाण्डु पुत्र युधिष्ठिर ने प्रवर्तित किया था। युधिष्ठिर - संवत् महाभारत के घोर संग्राम के पश्चात् महाराज युधिष्ठिर के सिंहासन पर आरूढ़ होने के समय से आरम्भ होता है । कलियुग के आरम्भ से ३७ वर्ष पूर्व यह संवत् आरंभ हुआ था। महाभारत युद्ध समाप्ति के १८ दिन बाद इस शक का आरंभ किया गया था।

So Yudhiṣṭhira Era = Kālī – 37 = -3101 – 37 = -3138

Looking up this information, we find that the Era started on Jan 12, -3138 at Sunrise (7:23 LMT Ujjain), Śubhakṛti Caitra Śukla Pratipada, Guruvara, Revatī Nakṣatra. The Kuṇḍalī of the Era is as follows:

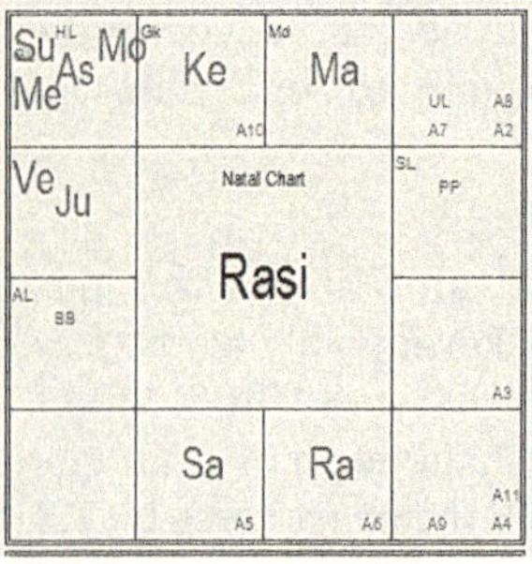

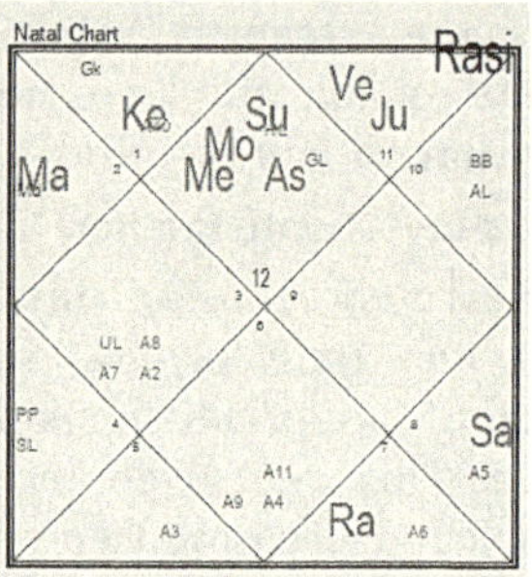

2631 Yudhiṣṭhira Śākā is -507 CE (2631 – 3188). This is what is provided by Śrī Govardhan Maṭha of Puri.

He was born in Nandana Vaiśākha Śukla Pañcamī on a Ravivāra in 2631 Yudhiṣṭhira Śākā. This corresponds to March 28, -508. He was said to be born near 12:00 at Abhijit Muhūrta.

His birth details are as follows:

March 28, -508; 12:00 LMT; 5:05:44 East; 76 E 26', 10 N 10'; Kaladi, India; Nandana – Vaiśākha; Śukla Pañcamī (Ju) (70.50% left); Somavāra (Mo); Ārdrā (Ra) (76.15% left); Sukarman Yoga (Ma) (38.84% left); Bava Karaṇa (Su) (41.00% left); Śukra Horā; Maṅgala Kāla; Sūryodaya 6:02; Sūryāsta 18:06; Janma Ghaṭis: 14.914; Ayanāñśa 349-07-53.48; Sidereal Time: 0:23:13.

The Kuṇḍalī is as follows:

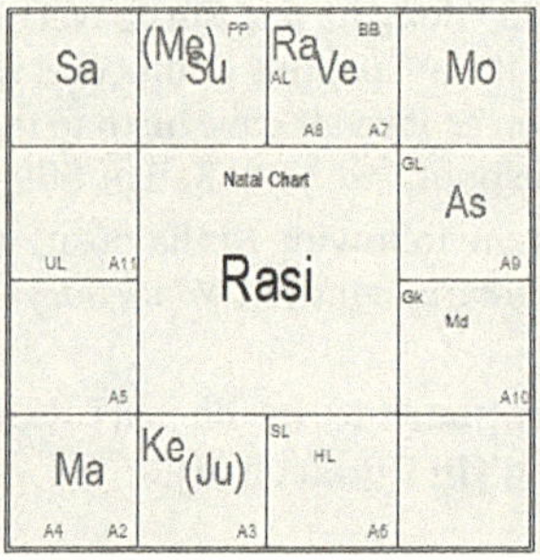

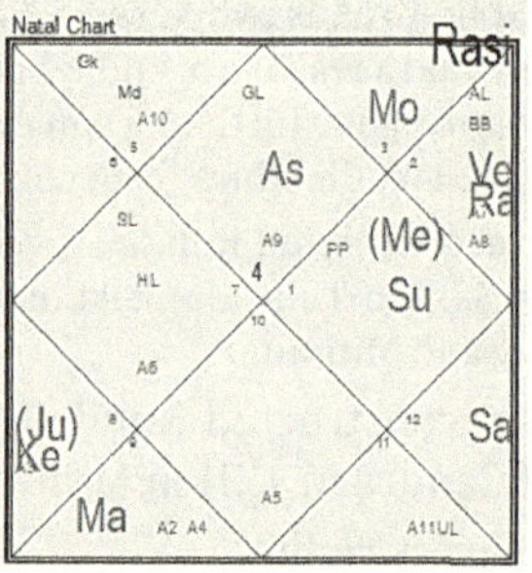

The following are the positions of the Grahas as per True Citrāpakṣa Ayanāñśa.

Lagna 20°22'31.04"; Sūrya 18°24'26.36"; Candra 9°56'50.68"; Maṅgala 10°17'05.86"; Budha (R) 5°38'34.29"; Guru (R) 14°06'39.58"; Śukra 5°43'05.84"; Śani 6°54'53.77"; Rāhu 9°48'09.66"; Ketu 9°48'09.66".

Kailāśa: According to this, he was born in Ārdrā. Was he not born in Punarvasu?

Ācārya: Where does the Punarvasu start?

Kailāśa: Mithuna has the last 2 Pada of Mṛgaśirā, 4 Pada of Ārdrā and the first 3 Pādas of Punarvasu. It must start after 6 Pādas of Mṛgaśirā and Ārdrā, which is 20°20'.

Ācārya: His Candra was in 10th degree, and the gap between its position and where it should be is 10 degrees. Therefore, it can't be an error in Ayanāñśa. If we accept this date, then we must forgo the claim that he was born in Punarvasu.

Kailāśa: How about other Graha positions besides Sūrya-Budha and Candra? They also do not match. Guru is in Vṛścika and Śani in Mīna. According to the Kuṇḍalī provided in the text, Śani should be in Tulā and Guru in Karka.

Ācārya: Let us focus on the Pañcāṅga details, such as Nandana Year, Vaiśākha Śukla Pañcamī, Candra in Punarvasu and Ravivāra. Normally, one would not go wrong with these details. The Graha positions are affected by the Siddhānta computations, so we can't be sure what source they used to get these positions.

Kailāśa: Noted Guruji. How do we search for that?

Ācārya: Let us examine all the Nandhana Years from -508 onwards. They occur in a cycle of 60 years. So, we can check every successive year by adding 60 to them. For Vaishaka Māsa, Sūrya should be in Meṣa, which should be in the March-April timeframe. The years are -508, -448, -388, -328, -268, -208, -148, -88 and -28. Let us see in which year Candra was in Punarvasu on Vaishaka Śukla Pañcamī at Noon.

The details are as follows for Nandana Vaiśākha Śukla Pañcamī:

-508: Mar 28: Ārdrā, Somavāra

-448: Mar 27: Ārdrā, Bṛhaspativāra

-388: Mar 23: Mṛgaśirā, Śukravāra

-328: Mar 19: Mṛgaśirā, Śanivāra

-268: Mar 17: Adhika Vaiśākha: Mṛgaśirā, Somavāra; Nīja Vaiśākha: Apr 15: Punarvasu, Maṅgalavāra.

-208: Apr 13: Punarvasu, Śukravāra

-148: Apr 11: Punarvasu, Ravivāra

-88: Apr 8: Ārdrā, Somavāra

-28: Apr 4: Ārdrā, Maṅgalavāra

What do you notice here?

Kailāśa: It appears that on the Nandana Varṣa, on Vaiśākha Śukla Pañcamī day, the Nakṣatra were Mṛgaśirā, Ārdrā or Punarvasu. It was Punarvasu in -268, -208 and -148. But only in -148 it fell on Ravivāra. Was he born in -148?

Ācārya: If we were to accept that he was born in Ravivāra and Punarvasu Nakṣatra, then we are not left with any choice. We are forced to accept -148, which is 360 years away from the traditional year of -508. However, if we can accept that he was born on Ārdrā and Somavāra, we can also accept that he was born in -508. In all cases, however, he could be born in Karka Lagna in Abhijit Muhūrta, which coincides with Midday.

Kailāśa: What are the Graha positions in -148?

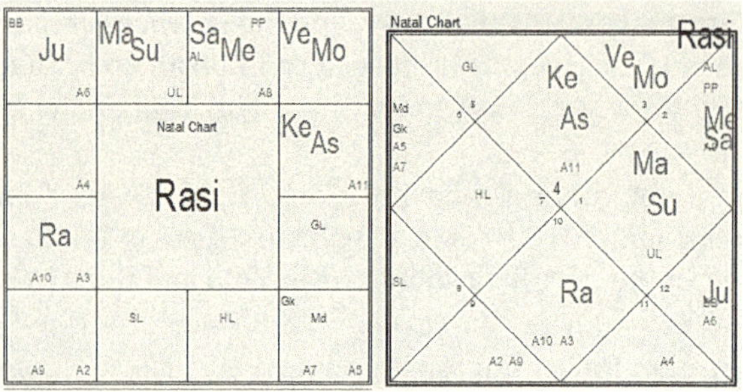

Ācārya: In the Kuṇḍalī, Guru is in Svarāśi, Sūrya is Ucca in 10H but with Maṅgala. Budha is separated from Sūrya but is with Śani. Śani is in Mitrarāśi, Vṛṣabha. Śukra is in a Mitrarāśi, Mithuna, and Candra is in 12H in Punarvasu. Lagna in Karka with Ketu. There is powerful Pravrājya Yoga in the Kuṇḍalī, so it could be the true Janmakuṇḍalī of Ādi Śaṅkarācārya.

The birth details are:

April 11, -148; 12:00 LMT, TZ 5:06 E; 76 E 26', 10 N 10', Kaladi, India; Nandana - Vaiśākha; Śukla Panchami (Ju) (26.94% left); Ravivāra (Su); Punarvasu (Ju) (73.53% left); Śūla yoga (Ju) (72.82% left); Balava Karaṇa (Mo) (53.87% left); Maṅgala Horā (5 min sign: Sg); Śukra Kāla; Sūryodaya: 5:53:51 (5.893); Sūryāsta: 18:05:30 (18.087); Janma Ghaṭī: 15.2563; Ayanāñśa: 354-00-21.96.

The time of birth could be based on Abhijit Muhūrta of the day and need not be at Noon. Abhijit is the 8th muhurta of the day. Abhijit ending time = Sūryodaya + Muhūrta Index/15 * Dinamāna = Sūryodaya + Muhūrta Index/15 * Dinamāna. Dinamāna = 18.087 - 5.893 = 12.194. Abhijit =5.893 + 8/15^12.194 = 12.396 = 12:23:46. The Muhūrta duration of the day was 12.194/15 = 0.813 hr = 00:48:47. The Muhūrta started at 12.396 - 0.813 = 11.583 = 11:34:59. So it is possible that Ādi Śaṅkara was born between 11:35 and 12:23.

Jayanta: Guruji, how can we conclusively establish that he was born in 149 BC instead of 509 BC?

Kailāśa: Gurubhrāta, why did you take 149 BC instead of -148?

Jayanta: That is because 149BC is written as -148 because, in the Gregorian calendar, there is no 0. So, year 0 is written as 1BC, -1 as 2BC and so on. In this manner, -148 is 149 BC, and -508 is 509 BC. Similarly, Kālī Yuga is 23 Jan -3101 but is written as 23 Jan -3102 BC.

Ācārya: For conclusive evidence, I suggest you read the article by Śmt Jayashree Saranathan, who has provided several other details. The article is at https://jayasree-saranathan.medium.com/date-of-adi-shankaracharya-39540f22d8d8.

Kailāśa: So, should we consider -148 as the year of Ādi Śaṅkara's birth?

Ācārya: We should be open to both years -508 and -148 and try to uncover more evidence. I cannot reject -508 easily because of the list of successive Śaṅkarācāryas in Govardhan Maṭha Puri. However, if we accept that, we must also accept that Ādi Śaṅkara was born on a Somavāra and Ārdrā Nakṣatra as against the conventional wisdom of Ravivāra and Punarvasu Nakṣatra.

Following are more details to corroborate Ādi Śaṅkara's lifetime. I excerpted this from "https://bharatbhumika.blogspot.com/2017/05/the-timeline-of-adi-sankaracharya.html"

> The Brihat Śaṅkara Vijaya of Śrī Chitsukhacharya states that Ādi Śaṅkarācārya, having adorned the Earth for 32 years, attained the state of eternal happiness in Yudhiṣṭhira Saka 2663.
>
> The Prachina Śaṅkara Vijaya of Anandagiri states that Ādi Śaṅkarācārya cast off his mortal body in the year 2625 of the Kali Yuga.
>
> The Punyaslokamanjari of Śrī Sadasivendra Sarasvati states that Ādi Śaṅkarācārya passed away at the age of 32 on the 11th day (Ekādaśī) of the bright half (Śukla Pakṣa) of the month of Vaisakha of the year Raktākṣī in 2625 of the Kaliyuga.
>
> The Śaṅkara Vijaya Kavya of Vyasachaliya states that 'on one occasion, on an Ekādaśī day which was especially dear to the Supreme Nārāyaṇa, the giver of final beatitude, in the bright half of the month of Vaisakha of the year Raktākṣī in 2625 of Kaliyuga, the great Guru (Ādi Śaṅkarācārya) suddenly longed to cast off his mortal body.
>
> The Śaṅkara Vijaya Kavya of Vyasachaliya states, 'In the auspicious year Nandana corresponding to 2593 of the Kaliyuga, while Sūrya was on his northern course (Uttarayana), on Śukla Pakṣa Pañcamī of the month of Vaiśākha (Meṣa) on Ravivāra in combination with Punarvasu, the Nakṣatra presided over by Aditi, and in an auspicious Yoga, and an auspicious Lagna (Karka) with auspicious Grahas and aspected by Saumyas, when Sūrya, Maṅgala and Śani were in their exaltation and Guru in Kendra, the chaste lady (Āryambā), wife of Śivaguru, without any pain of labour, gave birth to a son (Ādi Śaṅkarācārya).
>
> The Śaṅkara Digvijaya of Madhava-Vidyaranya states that as per the records of Śringerī Maṭha, Ādi Śaṅkarācārya was born in the 14th year of the reign of Vikramāditya.
>
> The Nepali chronology of Sūryavaṅśi (solar dynasty) kings states that the first king of this dynasty came to the throne in the year 1389 of the Kaliyuga, while the 23rd king is said to have been coronated 2700 years after the Kaliyuga. The 27th king is said to have come to the throne in Harsha Samvat 119. Ādi Śaṅkarācārya is said to have visited Nepal during the reign of Vṛṣadeva Varma, the 18th king.
>
> The Jina Vijaya states that:
>
> Kumārila Bhaṭṭa was born in the year 2077 of the Yudhiṣṭhira Saka and fell from his Jain teacher's grace in the year 2109.
>
> Śaṅkarācārya's death occurred in the year 2157 in the Yudhiṣṭhira Saka.
>
> When 15 years had elapsed from his birth, Ādi Śaṅkarācārya met Bhattacharya for the first and last time.
>
> We can use the information above to arrive at Ādi Śaṅkarācārya's traditional timeline:

Ādi Śaṅkarācārya passed away in Yudhiṣṭhira Saka 2663 or Kaliyuga 2625. With the traditional date of 3102 BCE as the onset of the Kaliyuga, the year of Ādi Śaṅkarācārya's death works out to 477 BCE. This means Yudhiṣṭhira Saka started in 477 + 2663 = 3140 BCE.

We know that the Mahabharata war took place 36 years before Lord Kṛṣṇa's death in 3102 BCE. So, the war would have taken place in 3102 + 36 = 3138 BCE. Yudhiṣṭhira was crowned king after the war, so it is not unreasonable to expect that the Yudhiṣṭhira Saka is reckoned to the round date of 3140 BCE.

With a lifespan of 32 years, Ādi Śaṅkarācārya's birth year should be 477 + 32 = 509 BCE, which works out to 3102 - 509 = 2593 Kali Yuga.

The scribe Al-Beruni (who accompanied Mahmud Ghaznavi during his invasions of India) mentions the Śrī Harsha Vikramāditya era to have begun in 457 BCE, which gives us the following timeline for the Nepal royal dynasty: 1st king (1389 Kaliyuga = 1713 BCE) ® 23rd king (2700 Kaliyuga = 402 BCE) ® 27th king (119 Harsha = 338 BCE). Using the above timeline, Vrishadeva Varma, the 18th king of the dynasty, would be placed in ~500 BCE. This supports our chronology for Ādi Śaṅkarācārya (509 – 477 BCE).

With Śrī Harsha Vikramāditya dying in 457 BCE, he and Śaṅkarācārya (509 to 477 BCE) must have been contemporaries, justifying the Śaṅkara Digvijaya's comment that Ādi Śaṅkarācārya was born during the reign of Vikramāditya (and the legend that Ādi Śaṅkarācārya was contemporaneous with Vikramāditya and Bhartrihari).

The Vetala Panchavimshati – the story of the legendary king Vikramāditya of Ujjayini and his dialogues with a Vetala (spirit) – states: 18 Philosophy, says Śaṅkarācārya, is either the gift of nature or the reward of study. The text, whose central character is based on either Śrī Harsha Vikramāditya of Ujjayini (of the 457 BCE era) or an unknown Vikramāditya of the Vikram Samvat of 57 BCE, should not be aware of any Śaṅkarācārya if Ādi Śaṅkarācārya was born in 788 CE.

In his book 'The Age of Śaṅkara,' T.S. Nārāyaṇa Sastry says that Jains and Buddhists uniformly place their Yudhiṣṭhira Saka 468 years after the commencement of the Kali Yuga. So, the Jina Vijaya's date of Ādi Śaṅkarācārya's death in 2157 Yudhiṣṭhira Saka works out to 477 BCE (= 2157+468 = 2625 Kaliyuga), which matches the traditional date from Hindu sources.

We can calculate Kumārila Bhaṭṭa's birth to have occurred in 557 BCE (= 3102 – (2077 + 468)) and the meeting of Ādi Śaṅkarācārya and Kumārila Bhaṭṭa to have occurred in 509-15 = 494 BCE, giving a lifespan of 63 years to Kumārila Bhaṭṭa (557 – 494 BCE).

Mahavira, the 24th Tirthankara of the Jains, is said to have attained Nirvāṇa 470 years before the Vikrama era of 57 BCE. Since Mahavira is believed to have died at the age of 72, his lifespan works out to 599 – 527 BCE. This, as expected from the Jina Vijaya, makes Mahavira a contemporary of Kumārila Bhaṭṭa.

Jayanta: The Punyaslokamanjari of Śrī Sadasivendra Sarasvati states that Ādi Śaṅkarācārya passed away at the age of 32 on Śukla Ekādaśī of Vaiśākha of the year Raktākṣī in 2625 of the Kaliyuga. From which can't we find Śaṅkarācārya's timeline?

Ācārya: Kālī 2625 = -3101 + 2625 = -476 (477BC). This corresponds to the following Kuṇḍalī.

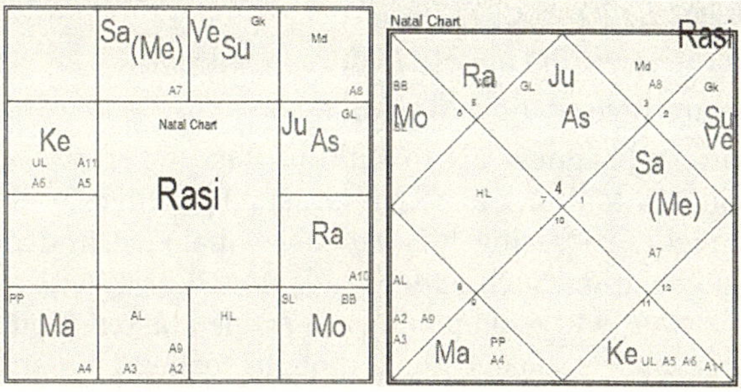

I assumed the time to be near midday when Lagna was in Karka with Ucca Guru. The details of his Puṇya (passing away) are April 11, -476; 11:48 LMT; TZ 5:18:52 (East of GMT); 79 E 43', 12 N 50'; Kañchipuram, India; Rākṣasi Varṣa; Vaiśākha Māsa; Śukla Ekādaśī; Śukravāra; Hastā Nakṣatra.

So, until we have better knowledge of his time, we should believe that *Ādi Śaṅkara was born on March 28, -508, and left his mortal remains on April 11, -476, and lived for 32 years.* This corresponds to 509-477 BCE. There are some discrepancies with his birth details, such as Punarvasu and Ravivāra, which could be an error in recording his details. This error could have occurred when someone tried to tally his birth details of Nandana Varṣa, Vaiśākha Śukla Pañcamī with the actual date in the calendar.

Jayanta: Guruji, can we study Ādi Śaṅkara's Kuṇḍalī?

Ācārya: Let us examine the Kuṇḍalī based on his birth in March 28, -508. What are the salient features of the Kuṇḍalī?

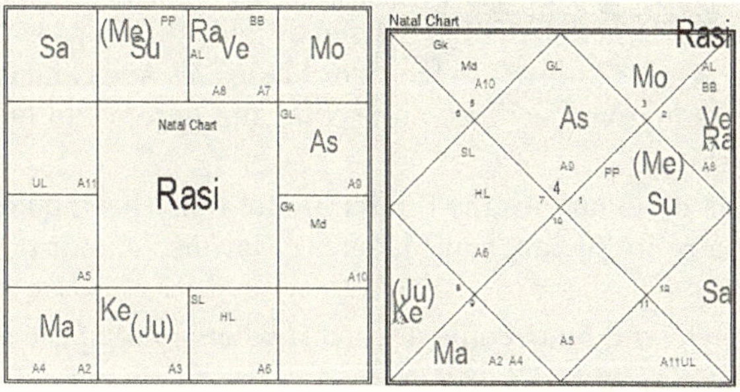

Jayanta: He is born in in Ārdrā Nakṣatra. Rudra rules Ārdrā. Ādi Śaṅkara was the incarnation of Mahādeva Śaṅkara. This makes sense.

Ācārya: That is a good point indeed. Do you know that Śrī Lakṣmaṇa, brother of Śrī Rāma, was the Avatāra of Ādi Śeṣa, and therefore, born in Āśleṣā. Sometimes, the Avatāras are born in the Tārās of the Devatās.

Jayanta: That is interesting. The Lagneśa Candra is in 12H of Mokṣa. This indicates that he was willing to give up his comforts of life. Lagna is dṛṣṭied by Guru from Vṛścika, the Rāśi of the occult and Siddhis. Guru is with Ketu forming Śiva Yoga.

Kailāśa: Guruji, the Yoga formation is in 5H, the Mantra Bhāva, indicating his mind in divine contemplation. It is in deep contemplation since the Yoga is occurring in Vṛścika Rāśi.

Āratī: What is the effect of Lagneśa Candra in Mithuna?

Ācārya: There are several indications of this.

Because Candra and Lagneśa are in Mithuna Rāśi, the effects of Mithuna will be predominant in his. Mithuna is a Dvisvarāśi and owned by Budha, the intelligent Graha of thought processing. It is the Rāśi of dialogue, as denoted by a couple engaged in a conversation. Such a person adept in Śāstras, with a scientific outlook, a messenger, clever, witty, eloquent, with refined tastes, fond of music, creative, capable, dexterous, persuasive and a thought reader. So many of these indications can be found in Ādi Śaṅkara.

In his Kuṇḍalī Sūrya is the Ātmakāraka, and in Gopurāñśa, indicating an exalted soul. Ātmakāraka Sūrya is also Ucca in Rāśi and in Kanyā Navāñśa. Kanyā Navāñśa indicates humility. 9L is in Siṅhasanāñśa, indicating his great spiritual merit. All Grahas except Candra, Budha and Rāhu are in Pārijātāñśa. He was indeed a great soul born to this world.

Jayanta: Guruji, what made him a Sanyāsi at such a young age?

Ācārya: For Sanyāsa Yoga, we must examine Janmeśa (Candra's dispositor) and Śani, the Sanyāsa Kāraka.

Remember the three Yogas:

(1) If Janmeśa is dṛṣṭied by no one but dṛṣṭies Śani, the native gets initiated into the holy order of the Graha, who is stronger amongst the two.

(2) If Janmeśa is devoid of strength and is dṛṣṭied only by Śani, the native becomes initiated into the holy order, signified by Śani.

(3) If Candra is in Śani's Dreṣkāṇa dṛṣṭied by Śani, this Yoga is formed. A similar Yoga is formed when Candra is in Śani's or Maṅgala's Añśa and dṛṣṭied by Śani. In these cases, the native becomes an ascetic and enters the holy order, signified by Śani.

Kailāśa: In this case, Janmeśa is Budha in Meṣa and has no connection with Śani. Also, Candra is not in Śani's or Maṅgala's Navāñśa. Candra is also not in Śani's Dreṣkāṇa.

Āratī: Guruji, why did he become a Sanyāsi when none of the Yogas are applicable?

Ācārya: A special Yoga is applicable in this case because he was not an ordinary Sanyāsi but an illustrious Sanyāsi and initiator of a holy order. He organized the Sanyāsis into different classes and established the four Śaṅkara Maṭhas.

For such Jātaka, Maharṣi Parāśara states: When Guru, Candra and Lagna are dṛṣṭied by Śani and Guru occupies the 9th, the person, born in the Rājayoga, will become a holy illustrious founder of a system of philosophy or holy order.

You cannot apply such Yogas verbatim and understand their key components, which are:

(1) Śani's influence on three bodies, viz., Lagna, Candra and Guru. This can occur in several ways, some of which are:

_ Lagna-Candra in Śani's Rāśi in Lagna, dṛṣṭied by Guru

_ Lagna is owned by Candra, who is in Śani's Rāśi with Guru

_ Candra in Lagna in Guru's Rāśi and dṛṣṭied by Śani.

_ Śani in Trikoṇa to Lagna, Guru and Candra.

(2) Guru must influence 9H by ownership, placement or dṛṣṭi.

Kailāśa: Guruji, this makes sense. I can see the connection now in Ādi Śaṅkara's case. In his Kuṇḍalī:

(1) Lagna is owned by Candra and in Śani's Trikoṇa. Therefore, Lagna is under Śani's influence. Śani has Tripāda dṛṣṭi on Candra and Dvipāda dṛṣṭi on Lagna.

(2) Śani is in Guru's Rāśi and Guru's Trikoṇa. Therefore, Śani has a strong influence on Guru. Śani has Dvipāda dṛṣṭi on Guru.

(3) Guru owns 9H and also aspects it with Pūrṇadṛṣṭi. Therefore, Guru has a predominant influence on 9H.

Āratī: But Śani is not aspecting Candra and Lagna?

Ācārya: Āratī, you must not forget about the Pāda Dṛṣṭis.

_ All Grahas have *Tripāda* (three quarter or 75%) dṛṣṭi on Caturasra (4H-8H). Maṅgala has Pūrṇa dṛṣṭi on these places.

_ All Grahas have *Dvipāda* (two quarter or 50%) dṛṣṭi on Koṇa (5H-9H). Guru has Pūrṇa dṛṣṭi on these places.

_ All Grahas have *Ekpāda* (one quarter or 25%) dṛṣṭi on Koṇa (3H-10H). Śani has Pūrṇa dṛṣṭi on these places.

_ All Grahas have *Pūrṇadṛṣṭi* (four quarter or 100%) dṛṣṭi on Saptama (7H).

_ Grahas have no dṛṣṭi on 2H, 12H, 11H, and 6H. Therefore, they are called shadow houses.

Āratī: This makes sense now. So, the summary of the Yoga is that.

(1) Śani has a strong influence on Lagna, Candra and Guru.

(2) Guru has a strong influence on 9H.

Ācārya: You got it. Do remember another Yoga of Maharṣi Parāśara.

When Śani is 9H and without any dṛṣṭi, the person, possessed of Rājayoga, will take himself to the holy order before becoming a King. If there is no Rājayoga, the native becomes an ascetic.

Jayanta: This also appears to apply Ādi Śaṅkara's Kuṇḍalī because Śani is in his 9H but has dṛṣṭi from Maṅgala and Guru. He also has Rājayoga conferred by Ucca Sūrya in 10H.

Ācārya: He was indeed a King among the ascetics. He was not a worldly king because Sūrya was subject to Pāpakartari by Śani and Rāhu. He relinquished his Rājayoga. There is another Rājayoga formed by mutual dṛṣṭi between Candra and Maṅgala, the Lagneśa and Pañcameśa. None of these Yogas are applicable since he relinquished his position as a supreme authority of people but became an authority of Śāstras.

Jayanta: Why so?

Ācārya: Look at the Ātmakāraka. Even though Ātmakāraka is Ucca, it is under Pāpakartari, indicating that he relinquished his kingly position. Besides, Lagneśa is in 12H, indicating relinquishing his worldly affairs. If not so, when he possessed the body of Amaraka, the King, he could have lived a life of luxury and splendour till his end. But he chose not to and focused on his pursuit of knowledge.

Kailāśa: It seems like some people cannot become king, but some people choose not to become a King.

Ācārya: You are right, Kailāśa.

Āratī: Why did he lose his father very early?

Jayanta: That is straightforward. Examine Sūrya and the ninth house.

(1) Sūrya is subject to Pāpakartari.

(2) 9H has 8L Śani.

(3) 9L Guru is in Vṛścika with Ketu.

(4) 9H from Sūrya has Maṅgala, a Krūra.

He lost his father when he was very young, i.e., only four.

Ācārya: Also examine the Daśā.

Jayanta: He lost his father in Rāhu-Śani or Rāhu-Budha as per Viñśottarī.

Āratī: Why?

Jayanta: Let us examine the Māraka for father.

From Sūrya, Mārakas are Rāhu and Śukra.

From 9H, the Mārakas are Sūrya, Budha and Maṅgala.

So, it is likely that his father died in Rāhu-Budha.

Ācārya: How about his Dvādaśāñśa?

Jayanta: Without a precise birth time, it isn't easy to see Dvādaśāñśa. But let me still try. I think his Dvādaśāñśa Lagna could be in Dhanu.

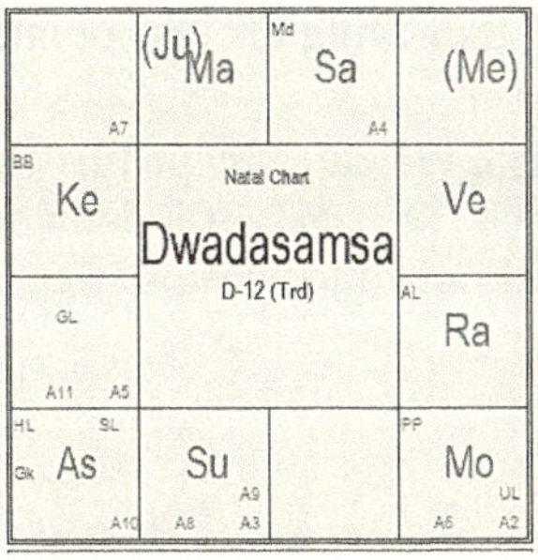

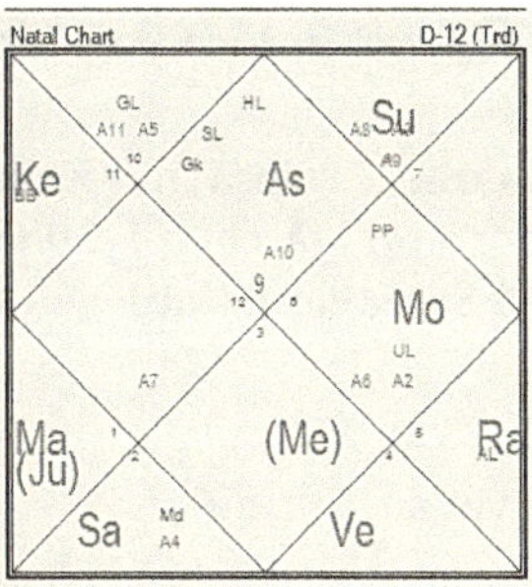

Kailāśa: Why do you think so?

Jayanta: because of the following reasons:

(1) His Dvādaśāñśa Lagna is in 6H from Rāśi Lagna, indicating separation or loss of parents.

(2) In his Dvādaśāñśa, 9H has Rāhu, and its lord Sūrya is in 12H in Vṛścika. Placement in Vṛścika indicates danger. Also, placement in 12H is not good. His mother was fine because 4L Guru is in 5H with 5L Maṅgala, while 4H is vacant.

Kailāśa: If Rāhu was in 9H, how was his father a Prakāṇḍa Paṇḍita (a great scholar)?

Ācārya: Rāhu has ten heads like Rāvaṇa and can give exceedingly high knowledge. In some respects, he is like Guru. The reason why he was a great scholar was because Guru dṛṣṭies 9H Siṅha and 9L Sūrya in Vṛścika. Vṛścika is the Rāśi of the occult and Siddhis, besides being a violent Rāśi.

Kailāśa: What should be his Navāñśa then?

Jayanta: If we fix the Dvādaśāñśa Lagna to Dhanu, the only option we have is Vṛścika Navāñśa. The Navāñśa Kuṇḍalī is shown below. Navāñśa Lagna in Vṛścika with Guru in it indicates a great Paṇḍita, knowledgeable in deep knowledge of the Śāstras. Vṛścika shows a deep well, and his knowledge was indeed very deep, like a well. He had several supernatural powers and Siddhis, offered by Vṛścika Navāñśa Lagna. Guru is also the 9L of Rāśi Kuṇḍalī, and his presence in Navāñśa Lagna indicates birth from a divine blessing.

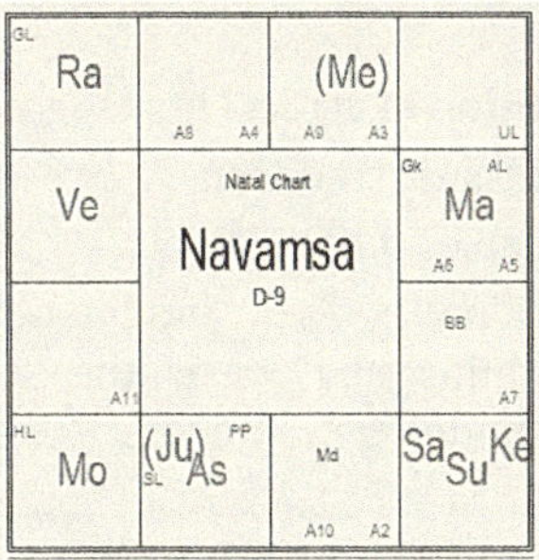

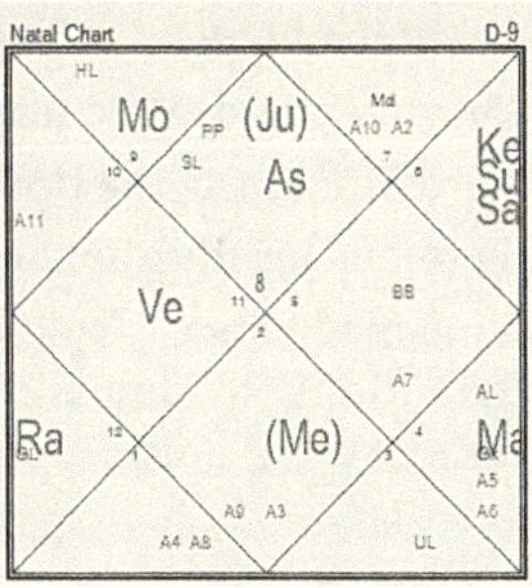

Kailāśa: Yes, He was a great Paṇḍita, and the Navāñśa Lagna makes sense. Also, Lagna's Koṇa has Rāhu in Mīna Rāśi showing great knowledge of the

Maharṣis, and Maṅgala in 9H in Nīca position, indicating his loss of father at an early age.

Ācārya: Well done, Jayanta and Kailāśa. We can accept this Kuṇḍalī as genuine, i.e., he was born on March 28, -508 at 11:36 LMT, at Kaladi, on a Śukla Pañcamī in Ārdrās and Somavāra. Until we find new information, we can accept this Kuṇḍalī.

Jayanta: Dhanyavād, Guruji!

Kailāśa: Dhanyavād, Guruji!

Jayanta: Guruji, I am interested in learning more about Vedānta since we are discussing Ādi Śaṅkara, the foremost among the Vedantists.

Ācārya: Vedānta is also known as Uttara Mīmāṃsā. It is one of the six orthodox schools of Vaidika philosophy.

Sunidhi: What are these six orthodox schools of Vaidika philosophy?

Ācārya: Vaidika philosophy is the foundation of Sanātana Dharma. It is called *darśana* "दर्शन" from the Sanskrit root *dṛś* दृश meaning "to see, to experience".

The Vaidika philosophy consists of six schools of thoughts called *ṣaḍdarśana* "षड्दर्शन", *sāṃkhya* "सांख्य", yoga, "योग", nyāya न्याय, vaiṣeśika "वैषेशिक", *mīmāṃsā* "मीमांसा" and *vedānta* वेदान्त. These are called the āstika आस्तिक philosophical traditions. They accept the Vedas as an authoritative source of knowledge.

The Indian philosophy also yielded philosophical systems that share concepts with āstika philosophies but rejected the Vedas; these have been called nāstika "नास्तिक" (non-orthodox) philosophies; they include Buddhism, Jainism, Chārvāka, Ājīvika, and others, which are thus classified under Indian but not Vaidika philosophy.

The six Āstika schools of philosophies are:

Nyāya, the school of logic

Vaiśeṣika, the atomist school

Sāṃkhya, the enumeration school

Yoga, the school of Patañjali

Mīmāṃsā or Purva Mīmāṃsā the tradition of critical investigation

Vedānta or Uttara Mīmāṃsā, the Upaniṣadic tradition.

Sunidhi: Kindly tell us briefly about each of these schools.

Ācārya: Nyāya means "justice", "rules", "method", or "judgment". Nyāya's most significant contributions to Indian philosophy were the systematic development of the theory of logic, methodology, and its treatises on epistemology.

Nyāya school's epistemology accepts four out of six Pramanas as reliable means of gaining knowledge:

Pratyakṣa (perception)

Anumāṇa (inference)

Upamāna (comparison and analogy)

Śabda (word, testimony of past or present reliable experts).

In its metaphysics, Nyāya school is closer to Vaiśeṣika than others.

It holds that human suffering results from mistakes or defects produced by activity under wrong knowledge (ignorance), and Mokṣa (liberation) is gained through right knowledge. Nyāya concerns itself with epistemology, which is the reliable means to gain correct knowledge and to remove wrong notions. False knowledge is not merely ignorance to the followers of this school; it includes delusion. Correct knowledge is discovering and overcoming one's delusions and understanding the true nature of soul, self, and reality.

The followers of this school approached philosophy as a form of direct realism, stating that *anything that really exists is, in principle, humanly knowable.* To them, correct knowledge and understanding are different from simple, reflexive cognition; it requires Anuvyavasaya "अनुव्यवसाय", that is cross-examination of cognition, reflective cognition of what one thinks one knows. An influential collection of texts on logic and reason is the Nyāya Sūtras, attributed to Aksapada Gautama.

Nyāya school resembles in some of its methodology and human suffering foundations of Buddhism; however, a key difference between the two is that Buddhism believes that there is neither a soul nor self. Nyāya schools, like some other schools of Hinduism such as Dvaita and Viśiṣṭādvaita, believe that there is a soul and self, with mokṣa as a state of removal of ignorance, wrong knowledge, the gain of correct knowledge, and unimpeded continuation of self.

Sunidhi: Dhanyavād Guruji, how about the Vaiśeṣika school?

Ācārya: the Vaiśeṣika was an independent philosophy in its early stages with its metaphysics, epistemology, logic, ethics, and soteriology. Over time, the Vaiśeṣika school became similar in its philosophical procedures, ethical conclusions, and soteriology to the Nyāya school but retained its differences in epistemology and metaphysics.

The epistemology of the Vaiśeṣika school accepted only two reliable means to knowledge: direct observation and inference. The Vaiśeṣika school consider their scriptures, the Vedas, as indisputable and valid means to knowledge.

The Vaiśeṣika school is known for its insights into naturalism. It is a form of atomism in natural philosophy. It postulated that all objects in the physical universe are reducible to paramāṇu (atoms), and one's experiences are derived from the interplay of substance (a function of atoms, their number, and their spatial arrangements), quality, activity, commonness, particularity, and inherence. Everything is composed of atoms; qualities emerge from aggregates of atoms; cosmic forces predetermine the aggregation and nature of these atoms.

According to the Vaiśeṣika school, knowledge and liberation were achievable by a complete understanding of the world of experience. Vaiśeṣika Darśana was founded by Kaṇāda Kaśyapa.

Sunidhi: Kindly tell us about Sāṃkhya, Guruji!

Ācārya: views reality as composed of two independent principles, Puruṣa and Prakṛti. Puruṣa is the consciousness witness. It is absolute, independent, free, beyond perception, above any experience by mind or senses, and impossible to describe in words.

Unmanifest Prakṛti is matter or nature. It is inactive, unconscious, and is a balance of the three Guṇas (innate tendencies), namely sattva, rajas, and tamas. When Prakṛti comes into contact with Puruṣa, it manifests, evolving twenty-three tattvas, namely intellect (mahat), ego (ahamkara), mind (manas); the five sensory capacities known as ears, skin, eyes, tongue and nose; the five action capacities vak: speech (voice), pani: grasping (hands), pāda: walking (feet), pāyu: excretion (anus) and upastha: procreation (genitals); and the five "subtle elements" or "modes of sensory content" (tanmatras), from which the five "gross elements" or "forms of perceptual objects" (earth, water, fire, air and space) emerge, in turn giving rise to the manifestation of sensory experience and cognition.

Jiva ('a living being') is the state in which Puruṣa is bonded to Prakṛti. The human experience is an interplay of the two, Puruṣa being conscious of the various combinations of cognitive activities. The end of the bondage of Puruṣa to Prakṛti is called Mokṣa (liberation) or Kaivalya (final destination).

Sāṃkhya's epistemology accepts three of six Pramāṇas ('proofs') as the only reliable means of gaining knowledge, as does yoga. These are pratyakṣa ('perception'), anumāṇa ('inference') and śabda (āptavacana, meaning, 'word/ testimony of reliable sources'). Sometimes described as one of the rationalist schools of Indian philosophy, it relies exclusively on reason.

While Sāṃkhya-like speculations are found in the Ṛgveda and early Upaniṣads, the Sāṃkhya ideas are found in the Upaniṣads, the Bhagavadgītā, and the Mokṣadharma section of the Mahābhārata. It was related to the early ascetic traditions and meditation, spiritual practices, religious cosmology, and methods of reasoning that result in liberating knowledge (vidya, Jñāna, viveka) that end the cycle of duḥkha (suffering) and rebirth, allowing for "a great variety of philosophical formulations". The defining method of Sāṃkhya was established with the Sāṃkhyakārikā.

Sāṃkhya is strongly related to the Yoga school, for which it forms the theoretical foundation, and it has influenced other schools of Vaidika philosophy.

Sunidhi: Dhanyavād Guruji. Kindly tell us about the Mīmāṃsā school

Ācārya: Mīmāṃsā means "reflection" or "critical investigation" and thus refers to a tradition of contemplation which reflected on the meanings of certain Vaidika texts.

This tradition is also known as Pūrva-Mīmāṃsā because of its focus on the earlier (pūrva) Vaidika texts dealing with ritual actions, and similarly as Karma-Mīmāṃsā due to its focus on ritual action (karma). This school is known for its philosophical theories on the nature of Dharma, based on hermeneutics (the branch of knowledge that deals with the interpretation of scriptures) of the Vedas, especially the Brāḥmanas and Saṃhitas.

The Mīmāṃsā school was foundational and influential for the Vedāntic schools, which were also known as Uttara-Mīmāṃsā for their focus on the "later" (*uttara*) portions of the Vedas, the Upaniṣads. While both "earlier" and "later" Mīmāṃsā investigate the aim of human action, they do so with different attitudes towards the necessity of ritual practice.

Mīmāṃsā has several sub-schools, each defined by its Pramāṇa.

The Prabhākara sub-school, which takes its name from the seventh-century philosopher Prabhākara, described the five epistemically reliable means to gaining knowledge: pratyakṣa or perception; anumāna or inference; upamāṇa, comparison and analogy; arthāpatti, the use of postulation and derivation from circumstances; and śabda, the word or testimony of past or present reliable experts.

The Bhāṭṭa sub-school, from philosopher Kumārila Bhaṭṭa, added a sixth means to its canon; anupalabdhi meant non-perception, or proof by the absence of cognition (e.g., the lack of gunpowder on a suspect's hand).

The school of Mīmāṃsā consists of both atheistic and theistic doctrines, but the school showed little interest in a systematic examination of the existence of God. Rather, it held that the soul is an eternal, omnipresent, inherently active spiritual essence and focused on the epistemology and metaphysics of Dharma.

For the Mīmāṃsā school, Dharma meant rituals and social duties, not Devas, because Devas existed only in name. The Mīmāṃsā followers also held that Vedas are "eternal, author-less, and infallible", that Vaidika injunctions and mantras in rituals are prescriptive kārya or actions, and the rituals are of primary importance and merit. They considered the Upaniṣads and other texts related to self-knowledge and spirituality as a subsidiary, a philosophical view that Vedānta disagreed with.

While their deep analysis of language and linguistics influenced other schools of Vaidika Philosophy, their views were not shared by others. The followers of this school considered the purpose and power of language to prescribe the proper and correct usage clearly. In contrast, the Vedānta followers extended the scope and value of language as a tool also to describe, develop and derive. The Mīmāṃsā followers considered orderly, law-driven, procedural life as the central purpose and noblest necessity of Dharma and society, and divine sustenance means to that end.

The Mīmāṃsā school is a form of philosophical realism. A key text of the Mīmāṃsā school is the Mīmāṃsā Sūtra of Jaimini.

Sunidhi: Dhanyavād Guruji. Kindly tell us about Vedānta.

Ācārya: "Vedānta" means "conclusion of the Vedas" and encompasses the ideas that emerged from, or were aligned with, the speculations and enumerations contained in the Upaniṣads, with a focus on Jñāna and Mokṣa. Vedānta developed into many schools, all of which base their ideas on the authority of a common group of texts called the Prasthānatrayī, translated as "the three sources": the Upaniṣads, the Brahmasūtras, and the Bhagavad Gītā.

All Vedānta schools contain extensive discussions on ontology, soteriology, and epistemology, even as there is much disagreement among the various schools. Independently considered, they may seem completely disparate due to the pronounced differences in thoughts and reasoning.

The main schools of Vedānta are:

Bhedābheda or Dvaitādvaita (difference and non-difference)

Advaita (non-dualism)

Viśiṣṭādvaita (qualified non-dualism)

Tattvavada (Dvaita) (dualism)

Suddhadvaita (pure non-dualism)

Acintya-Bhedābheda (inconceivable difference and non-difference).

Modern developments in Vedānta include Neo-Vedānta and the philosophy of the Swaminarayan Sampradāya.

Most major Vedānta schools, except Advaita Vedānta and Neo-Vedānta, are related to Vaiṣṇavism and emphasize Bhakti to God, understood as Viṣṇu or a related manifestation. Advaita Vedānta, on the other hand, emphasizes Jñāna and Jñāna Yoga over theistic devotion. While the monism of Advaita has attracted considerable attention in the West due to the influence of modern Hindus like Svāmi Vivekānanda and Ramana Maharṣi, most of the other Vedānta traditions focus on Vaiṣṇava theology.

Vedānta means the end of the Vedas and refers to the Upaniṣads. It is concerned with the Jñānakāṇḍa or knowledge section of the Vedas, i.e., the Upaniṣads. The meaning of Vedānta expanded later to encompass the different philosophical traditions that are based on the Prasthanatrayi.

Vedānta is also called Uttara Mīmāṃsā, which means the "latter enquiry" or "higher enquiry" and is often contrasted with Pūrva Mīmāṃsā, the "former enquiry" or "primary enquiry". Pūrva Mīmāṃsā deals with the Karmakāṇḍa or ritualistic section (the Samhita and Brahmanas) in the Vedas, while Uttara Mīmāṃsā concerns itself with the deeper questions of existence and meaning.

The crucial features of Vedānta are:

(1) Vedānta is the pursuit of knowledge into the Brahman and the Ātman.

(2) The Upaniṣads, the Bhagavadgītā, and the Brahmasūtras constitute the basis of Vedānta (known as the three canonical sources).

(3) Scripture (Śruti) is the main reliable source of knowledge (Pramāṇa).

(4) Brahman exists as the unchanging material cause and instrumental cause of the world. The exception is that Dvaita Vedānta does not hold Brahman to be the material cause but only the efficient cause.

(5) The Ātman is the agent of its acts (karma) and the recipient of the consequences of these actions.

(6) Belief in rebirth (Samsāra) and the desirability of release from the cycle of rebirths (Mokṣa).

The primary Upaniṣads, the Bhagavadgītā and the Brahmasūtras, are the foundational scriptures in Vedānta. All schools of Vedānta propound their philosophy by interpreting these texts, collectively called the Prasthānatrayī, literally three sources.

The Upaniṣads, or Śruti prasthāna, are considered the Śruti, the "heard" (and repeated) foundation of Vedānta.

The Brahmasūtras, or the Nyāya or Yukti, is considered the reason-based foundation of Vedānta.

The Bhagavadgītā, or Smṛti prasthāna, is considered the Smṛti (remembered) foundation of Vedānta.

All prominent Vedantic teachers, including Śaṅkara, Bhāskara, Ramanuja, Madhva, Nimbārka, and Vallabha, wrote commentaries on these three sources.

The Brahmasūtras of Bādarāyaṇa serve as a synthesis of the teachings found in the diverse Upaniṣads. While there may have been other similar syntheses in the past, only the Brahmasūtras have survived to the present day. The Bhagavadgītā, with its syncretism of Sāṃkhya, Yoga, and Upaniṣadic thought, has also been a significant influence on Vedantic thought.

The Vedānta followers agree that the Śrutis (Vedas and Upaniṣads) are the sole means of knowing (Pramāṇa) regarding spiritual matters (which are beyond perception and inference). In this regard, Ācārya Rāmānuja states:

A theory that rests exclusively on human concepts may, at some other time or place, be refuted by arguments devised by cleverer people. The conclusion is that with regard to supernatural matters, Śrutis alone is the epistemic authority and that reasoning is to be used only in support of Śrutis [Śrī Bhāṣya 2.1.12].

For specific sub-schools of Vedānta, other texts may be equally complimentary. For example, for "Advaita" Vedānta, the works of Ādi Śaṅkara are central. For the "Dvaita" Vaiṣṇava schools of Vedānta, the Bhāgavata Purāṇa is particularly crucial. The Bhāgavata Purāṇa is one of the most widely commented upon works in Vedānta. This text is so central to the Kṛṣṇa-cantered Vedānta schools that Ācārya Vallabha added the Bhāgavata Purāṇa as a fourth text to the Prasthānatrayī.

Vedānta philosophies discuss three fundamental metaphysical concepts and their interrelations.

Brahman: the ultimate reality

Ātman: the individual soul, self

Jagat: the empirical world, the ever-changing physical universe, body, and matter

Ācārya Śaṅkara, in formulating Advaita, talks of two conceptions of Brahman: The higher Brahman as an undifferentiated Being and a lower Brahman endowed with qualities as the creator of the universe:

Parā Brahman: The undifferentiated, absolute, infinite, transcendental, supra-relational Brahman beyond all thought and speech is defined as parā, nirviśeṣa, or nirguṇa Brahman and is the Absolute.

Aparā Brahman: The Brahman with qualities defined as aparā or Saguṇa Brahman. The Saguṇa Brahman is endowed with attributes and represents the personal God of religion.

Ācārya Ramanuja, in formulating Viśiṣṭādvaita, rejects Nirguṇa - that the undifferentiated Absolute is inconceivable - and adopts a theistic interpretation of the Upaniṣads, accepting Brahman as Īśvara, the personal God who is the seat of all auspicious attributes, as the One reality. The Īśvara of Viśiṣṭādvaita is accessible to the devotee yet remains the Absolute, with differentiated attributes.

Ācārya Madhva, in expounding Dvaita philosophy, maintains that Viṣṇu is the supreme Īśvara, thus identifying the Brahman, or absolute reality, of the Upaniṣads with a personal Devatā, as Ācārya Ramanuja had done before him.

Ācārya Nimbārka, in his Dvaitādvaita philosophy, accepted the Brahman both as Nirguṇa and as Saguṇa.

Ācārya Vallabha, in his Śuddhādvaita philosophy, not only accepts the triple ontological essence of the Brahman but also His manifestation as personal Īśvara, as matter, and as individual souls.

Jayanta: In the different philosophies of Vedānta, what are the relationships of the Ātman (Jīvātmā) and Brahman (Īśvara)?

Ācārya: According to Advaita Vedānta philosophy of Śaṅkarācārya, Ātman is identical to Brahman, and there is no difference. The perception of the difference between them is an illusion.

According to Viśiṣṭādvaita philosophy of Rāmanujācārya, Ātman is different from Brahman, though eternally connected with Him as His mode. The oneness of the Brahman is understood in the sense of an organic unity (*vishistaikya*). Brahman alone, as organically related to all Ātman and the material universe (*jagat*), is the one Ultimate Reality.

According to the Dvaita philosophy of Mādhavācārya, the Ātman is totally and always different from Brahman.

According to Śuddhādvaita of Ācārya Vallbhācārya, the Ātman and Brahman are identical; both, along with the changing empirically observed universe being Kṛṣṇa.

Jayanta: Guruji, you did not explain Acintya Bhedābheda. Kindly elaborate on that.

Ācārya: Acintya Bhedābheda represents the philosophy of inconceivable one-ness and difference. Acintya means 'inconceivable', *bheda* translates as 'difference', and *abheda* translates as 'non-difference'. Śrī Chaitanya Mahāprabhu, the founder of Gaudiya Vaiṣṇavism, propounds this philosophy.

The Gaudiya Vaiṣṇava Sampradāya employs the term in relation to the relationship of creation and creator (Kṛṣṇa, Svayam Bhagavan), between Īśvara and his energies. This differentiates the Gaudiya Sampradāya from the other Vaishnava Sampradāyas. It can be understood as an integration of the Dvaita Advaita of Mādhavācārya and Viśiṣṭādvaita of Ramanujācārya.

Jayanta: What is the Epistemological basis of Vedānta? The Vedānta schools recognize six epistemic means.

Ācārya: Pramāṇa means "proof", "that which is the means of valid knowledge". It encompasses the study of reliable and valid means by which human beings gain accurate, true knowledge. The focus of Pramāṇa is the manner in which correct knowledge can be acquired, how one knows or does not know, and to what extent knowledge pertinent about someone or something can be acquired. The Hindu texts identify six Pramāṇas as correct means of accurate knowledge and truths:

(1) Pratyakṣa (perception)

(2) Anumāṇa (inference)

(3) Upamāṇa (comparison and analogy)

(4) Arthāpatti (postulation, derivation from circumstances)

(5) Anupalabdi (non-perception, negative/cognitive proof)

(6) Śabda (scriptural testimony/ verbal testimony of past or present reliable experts).

The different schools of Vedānta have historically disagreed as to which of the six are epistemologically valid. For example, while Advaita Vedānta accepts all six Pramāṇas, Viśiṣṭādvaita and Dvaita accept only three Pramāṇas (perception, inference, and testimony).

Advaita considers Pratyakṣa (perception) as the most reliable source of knowledge. Śabda, the scriptural evidence, is considered secondary except for matters related to Brahman, where it is the only evidence. In Viśiṣṭādvaita and Dvaita, Śabda, the scriptural testimony, is considered the most authentic means of knowledge.

All schools of Vedānta subscribe to the theory of Satkāryavāda, which means that the effect is pre-existent in the cause. But there are two different views on the status of the "effect", that is, the world. Most schools of Vedānta, as well as Sāṃkhya, support Pariṇāmavada, the idea that the world is a real transformation (Pariṇāma) of Brahman.

The Brahmasūtras espouse the realist Pariṇāmavāda, which appears to have been the view most common among early Vedantins". In contrast to Bādarāyaṇa, Ādi Śaṅkara and Advaita Vedantists hold a different view,

Vivartavāda, which says that the effect, the world, is merely an unreal (Vivarta) transformation of its cause, Brahman.

Sunidhi: Guruji, kindly elaborate on the different schools of Vedānta.

Ācārya: First, let us understand the reason behind the different schools of Vedānta. Even though the Upaniṣads provide the ultimate truth, different Ācāryas have different philosophical inquiries presenting arguments for or against them. Differing interpretations of the Upaniṣads and their synthesis, the Brahmasūtras, led to the development of different schools of Vedānta over time.

The Bhandarkar Oriental Research Institute conducted a comprehensive comparative analysis of the Brahmasūtra commentaries by Ācāryas Śaṅkara Nimbārka, Ramanuja, Vallabha, and Madhva. In his conclusion, they determined that Nimbārka 's and Ramanuja's commentaries provide the most accurate interpretation of the Brahmasūtras, considering both the passages that emphasize unity and those that emphasize diversity.

Although "Advaita" Vedānta is the most well-known school of Vedānta and is sometimes perceived as the sole representation of Vedantic thought, with Śaṅkara being a follower of Śaiva Sampradāya, scholars believe that the true essence of Vedānta lies within the Vaiṣṇava Sampradāyas and can be considered a discourse within the broad framework of Vaiṣṇavism. Four Vaiṣṇava Sampradāyas are considered to be of special significance based on the teachings of Ramanuja, Madhva, Vallabha, and Nimbārka.

Sunidhi: Guruji, kindly elaborate on the Vedānta schools.

Ācārya: They are as follows:

(1) Advaita of Ādi Śaṅkarācārya

(2) Śuddhādvaita of Vallabhācārya

(3) Viśiṣṭādvaita of Rāmanujacharya

(4) Dvaita or Tattvavāda of Mādhavācārya

(5) Dvaitādvaita of Nimbārkācārya

(6) Achintya Bhedābheda of Śrī Chaitanya Mahāprabhu

(7) Akṣara-Puruṣottama of Śrī Svāmināraỵaṇa

Let me briefly explain them now:

Advaita Vedānta: Non-Dualism

Advaita Vedānta is propounded by Gaudapāda and Ādi Śaṅkara, espouses non-dualism. Brahman is held to be the sole unchanging metaphysical reality and identical to the individual Ātman. The physical world, on the other hand, is always changing empirical Māyā. The absolute and infinite Ātman-Brahman is realized by a process of negating everything relative, finite, empirical and changing.

The school accepts no duality, no limited individual Ātman, and no separate unlimited cosmic soul (Parabrahman). All souls and their existence across space and time are considered to be the same oneness. Spiritual liberation in Advaita is the full comprehension and realization of oneness, that one's unchanging Ātman is the same as the Ātman in everyone else, as well as being identical to Brahman.

Śuddhādvaita: Pure Non-Dualism

Vallabhācārya propounds Śuddhādvaita, states that the entire universe is real and is subtly Brahman only in the form of Kṛṣṇa. Vallabhācārya agreed with Advaita Vedānta's ontology but emphasized that Prakṛti (empirical world, body) is not separate from the Brahman but just another manifestation of the latter. Everything, everyone, everywhere - soul and body, living and non-living, Jīva and matter - is the eternal Kṛṣṇa.

The way to Kṛṣṇa, in this school, is bhakti. Vallabha opposed the renunciation of monistic Sanyāsa as ineffective and advocated the path of devotion (bhakti) rather than knowledge (Jñāna). The goal of bhakti is to turn away from ego, self-centeredness, and deception and to turn towards the eternal Kṛṣṇa in everything, continually offering freedom from Samsāra.

Viśiṣṭādvaita Vedānta: Qualified Non-Dualism

Viśiṣṭādvaita is propounded by Rāmanujacharya. It asserts that Ātman and Brahman (Viṣṇu) are different, a difference that is never transcended. With this qualification, Rāmanujacharya also affirmed monism by saying that there is unity of all Ātman and that the individual Ātman has the potential to realize identity with the Brahman. Viśiṣṭādvaita is a qualified non-dualistic school of Vedānta and, like Advaita, begins by assuming that all souls can hope for and achieve the state of blissful liberation.

On the relation between Brahman and the world of matter (Prakṛti), Viśiṣṭādvaita states both are two different absolutes, both metaphysically true and real, neither is false or illusive and that Saguṇa Brahman with attributes is also real. Ramanuja states that Īśvara, like man, has both Ātman and Śarīra, and the world of matter is the glory of God's body. The path to Brahman (Viṣṇu), according to Ramanuja, is devotion to godliness and constant remembrance of the beauty and love of the personal god (bhakti of Saguṇa Brahman).

Dvaita: Dualism

Mādhavācārya propounds Dvaita or Tattvavāda. It is based on the premise of realism. Dvaita means dualism and was later applied to Madhvācārya's philosophy (originally called Tattvavāda). In this philosophy, Ātman and Brahman (Viṣṇu) are understood as two completely different entities. Brahman is the creator of the universe, perfect in knowledge, perfect in knowing, perfect in its power, and distinct from souls, distinct from matter.

In Dvaita Vedānta, an individual soul must feel attraction, love, attachment, and complete devotional surrender to Viṣṇu for salvation, and it is only His grace that leads to redemption and salvation. Madhva believed that some souls are eternally damned, a view not found in Advaita and Viśiṣṭādvaita Vedānta. While the Viśiṣṭādvaita Vedānta asserted "qualitative monism and quantitative pluralism of souls", Madhva asserted both "qualitative and quantitative pluralism of souls".

Dvaitādvaita Vedānta: Dualistic Non-Dualism

Dvaitādvaita is propounded by Nimbārka. Brahman, Ātman (*cit*) and matter or the universe (*acit*) are considered as three equally real and co-eternal realities. Brahman is the controller (*niyanta*), the soul is the enjoyer (bhokta), and the material universe is the object enjoyed (bhogya). The Brahman is Kṛṣṇa, the ultimate cause who is omniscient, omnipotent, all-pervading Being.

He is the efficient cause of the universe because, as Lord of Karma and internal ruler of Ātmās, He brings about creation so that the individual Ātmās can reap the consequences of their karma. Brahman is considered to be the material cause of the universe because creation was a manifestation of His powers of Ātman (cit) and matter (acit); creation is a transformation (pariṇāma) of Īśvara's powers. He can be realized only through a constant effort to merge oneself with His nature through meditation and devotion.

Bhedābheda Vedānta: Difference In Non-Difference

Bhedābheda means "difference and non-difference" and is more a tradition than a school of Vedānta. This Sampradāya emphasizes that Ātman is both different and not different from Brahman. Notable figures in this school are Bhartriprapancha, Nimbārka, who founded the Dvaitādvaita school; Bhāskara, Ramanuja's teacher Yādavaprakāśa; Chaitanya, who founded the Acintya Bhedābheda Sampradāya, and Vijñānabhikṣu.

Acintya-Bhedābheda: Inconceivable Difference In Non-Difference

Chaitanya Mahāprabhu was the prime exponent of Acintya-Bhedābheda. In Acintya means 'inconceivable'. Acintya-Bhedābheda represents the philosophy of "inconceivable difference in non-difference" in relation to the non-dual reality of Brahman-Ātman, which it calls Kṛṣṇa, svayam Bhagavan. The notion of "inconceivability" is used to reconcile apparently contradictory notions in Upaniṣadic teachings.

This school asserts that Kṛṣṇa is Bhagavan of the bhakti yogins, the Brahman of the Jñāna yogins, and has a divine potency that is inconceivable. He is all-pervading and thus in all parts of the universe (non-difference), yet he is inconceivably more (difference). This school is at the foundation of the Gaudiya Vaiṣṇava religious tradition.

Akṣara-Puruṣottama: The Word and Nārāyaṇa

The Swaminarayan Darshana, also called Akshar-Purushottam Darśana by the Bochasanwasi Śrī Akṣara Puruṣottama Swaminarayan Sanstha (BAPS), was propounded by Swaminarayan and is rooted in Ramanuja's Viśiṣṭādvaita. It asserts that Parabrahman (Puruṣottama, Nārāyaṇa) and Akṣarabrahman are two distinct eternal realities. Adherents believe that they can achieve Mokṣa by becoming Akṣararūpa (or Brahmarūpa), that is, by attaining qualities similar to Akṣara (or Akṣarabrahman) and worshipping Puruṣottama (Nārāyaṇa).

Jayanta: Guruji, how has the Vedānta philosophy emerged in the modern world?

Ācārya: Vedānta, adopting ideas from other Āstika Darśanas, became the most prominent school of Hinduism. Vedānta traditions led to the development of many traditions in Hinduism. Śrī Vaiṣṇavism of south and southeastern India is based on Ramanuja's Viśiṣṭādvaita Vedānta. Ramananda led to the Vaiṣṇava Bhakti Movement in north, east, central, and west India. This movement draws its philosophical basis from Viśiṣṭādvaita. A large number of devotional Vaiṣṇavism traditions of East India and North India. Particularly, the Braj region, west and central India are based on various sub-schools of Bhedābheda Vedānta. Advaita Vedānta influenced Kṛṣṇa Vaiṣṇavism in the northeastern state of Assam. The Madhva school of Vaiṣṇavism found in coastal Karnataka is based on Dvaita Vedānta.

Āgamas, the classical literature of Śaivism, though independent in origin, shows Vedānta association and premises. Of the ninety-two Āgamas, ten are Dvaita texts, eighteen Bhedābheda, and sixty-four Advaita texts. While the Bhairava Śāstras are monistic, Śiva Śāstras are dualistic. Scholars find the link between Gaudapāda's Advaita Vedānta and Kashmir Śaivism evident and natural. Tirumular, the Tamil Śaiva Siddhanta scholar credited with creating "Vedānta-Siddhānta, a synthesis of Advaita Vedānta and Śaiva Siddhānta, stated, "becoming Śiva is the goal of Vedānta and Siddhānta; all other goals are secondary to it and are vain."

Śāktism, where a Devī is considered identical to Brahman, has similarly flowered from a synthesis of Advaita (Devī as Parabrahman) and Dvaita premises of Sāṃkhya-Yoga Darśanas, sometimes referred to as Śāktādvaitavāda, the path of non-dualistic Śakti.

Kailāśa: Guruji, how have the Upaniṣadic thoughts influenced the modern scientific thoughts?

Ācārya: They have immense influences. Let us understand them from the thoughts and reflections of modern physicists.

In the early 1900s, scientists discovered that subatomic particles such as electrons exhibited behaviours that went against the expectations of classical physics. Explaining this behaviour required formulating theories and principles of *quantum mechanics*. These natural laws accurately predicted the behaviour of electrons and other subatomic particles.

Some of the most renowned physicists in history include *Einstein, Niels Bohr, Erwin Schrödinger, and Werner Heisenberg*. However, these scientists and others would soon discover that the newcomer, while unveiling new theoretical and technological possibilities, also made some peculiar predictions. For instance, it enabled electrons to pass through barriers, particles to occupy multiple locations simultaneously, black holes to gradually disappear, and the exchange of information between observers at speeds exceeding that of light.

This was a pivotal moment in history when the field of physics was experiencing significant turmoil. There was a disruption to the familiar classical picture of reality, replaced by one that seemed too crazy to be true. However, this new perspective explained numerous experimental observations that the old one couldn't. Einstein, Bohr, Schrödinger, Heisenberg, and other renowned physicists were greatly concerned by the profound implications of this. They were confronted with a personal quandary: whether to embrace an outlandish theory that yielded results or abandon it in favour of an intuitive theory that proved ineffective.

They realised that their understanding that the world we perceive is not the ultimate reality but rather a construct within our consciousness was not entirely original. In the Upaniṣads, they discovered resonances with their theories, providing a philosophical grounding to navigate the profound implications of quantum mechanics.

The development of quantum physics was driven by a series of perplexing observations that revealed the unpredictable nature of light. In 1865, James Maxwell demonstrated that light could be represented as electromagnetic waves. In 1905, Albert Einstein presented his findings on the photoelectric effect, suggesting that light consists of minuscule particles known as photons. In 1924, Louis de Broglie, a French aristocrat, put forth a revolutionary idea that challenged conventional views by suggesting that all matter displays wave-like characteristics. This proposition, which explores the wave-particle duality, has sparked numerous debates that question the fundamental aspects of reality itself.

In classical physics, microscopic particles such as electrons are considered to be solid spherical balls of matter. Quantum physics presents a completely different perspective that may seem unfamiliar to us. According to scientific findings, the position of an electron is not fixed but rather exists within a spread-out range of possibilities. When attempting to observe the electron, it is more likely to be found in a denser region of the cloud rather than a sparser one.

The wave function can mathematically represent this cloud. At the core of quantum physics lies an equation that dictates the evolution of a wave function over time. In 1926, Erwin Schrödinger came up with the equation that is now known as Schrödinger's equation.

Science writers delight in depicting the contrast between the world described by quantum physics and the world we experience through our senses. Given the composition of macroscopic objects, such as trees and cars, which consist of microscopic particles like atoms and molecules, it follows that these macroscopic objects should exhibit wave-like behaviour. However, our personal experiences do not align with this. So, at what point does something transition from wave-like behaviour to particle-like behaviour? It is quite intriguing how this phenomenon occurs when we make observations.

As per the Copenhagen interpretation of quantum mechanics, the act of observation leads to the transformation of an object from its quantum state to the familiar classical form. The collapse of the wave function suggests that the reality we perceive is dependent on our presence as observers. Just like a physicist, an observer doesn't simply watch reality unfold but actively shapes it.

If left undisturbed, objects would maintain their wave-like nature until they are subjected to observation. In a thought-provoking manner, Einstein encapsulated the peculiarities of quantum physics by posing a question to a friend: "Does the Moon only exist when I observe it?"

The Upaniṣads explore the concept of subjective reality. The Upaniṣads are a compilation of ancient Sanskrit texts that have been passed down through generations of teachers and students for centuries. Just as a physicist studies the laws of the universe, the Upaniṣads delve into the nature of reality, the mind, and the self.

In 1918, Schrödinger came across Indian philosophy through the works of the German philosopher Arthur Schopenhauer. With great enthusiasm, Schopenhauer proclaimed that the study of the Upaniṣads is the most beneficial and uplifting pursuit in the entire world. "It has brought immense comfort to my existence. It will bring me comfort in my final moments."

The Upaniṣads explore the connection between the Brahman and the Ātman. Brahman represents the universal self or the ultimate singular reality. The Ātman is the inner essence of the individual, the core of their being. The Upaniṣads emphasise the concept of *tat tvam asi*, highlighting the unity between the Brahman and the Ātman. There exists a single universal self, and we are all interconnected with it.

The Isha Upaniṣad asserts, "the Brahman forms everything that is living or non-living ... the wise man knows that all beings are identical with his self, and his self is the self of all beings."

This thought captivated Schrödinger. He had named his dog Ātman. It is also said that his conference talks would sometimes conclude with the statement 'Ātman=Brahman', which he humorously referred to as the second Schrödinger's equation. After their relationship came to an end, Sheila May, the Irish artist, expressed her deep connection with him in a heartfelt letter. She described how she saw a profound sense of life and shared consciousness in his eyes, transcending the boundaries of individuality. You can love me for the rest of your life, but we are now two separate individuals.

Quantum physics bridges the divide between the observer and the observed. According to the Upaniṣads, there is a profound connection between the observer and the observed. In his 1944 book, *What is Life*, Schrödinger explored a unique line of thinking. Considering the possibility that our observations shape the world, it would imply the existence of countless parallel worlds, each tailored to every individual. Why is it that our worlds appear to be identical? Does an event in my world also occur in yours? What is the reason behind the synchronisation of these worlds?

He discovered his answer once more within the Upaniṣads. "There is clearly only one option," he stated, "which is the merging of minds or consciousness." The apparent multiplicity is merely an illusion; in reality, there exists only one mind. This is the teaching of the Upaniṣads.

According to the Upaniṣads, Brahman is the sole existence. Everything we observe in our surroundings is an illusion, a result of our limited understanding and imperfect perception. According to the Chandogya Upaniṣad, everything is Brahman. Everything originates from Brahman, everything returns to Brahman, and Brahman upholds everything.

In this passage, Schrödinger discusses the concept of a singular entity that appears as multiple aspects due to a deceptive illusion. He draws a parallel between this illusion and the effect created by a gallery of mirrors.

Quantum physics asserts that reality is composed of waves, and the concept of wave-particle duality emerges from the act of observation. Just as a physicist would explain, our perception of reality is limited, causing us only to see an incomplete version of the true wave nature of reality. This reduction is what we refer to as the collapse of the wave function. The rise of Māyā aligns perfectly with the downfall.

Schrödinger deeply embraced the fundamental teachings of the Upaniṣads. He states, "Myriads of suns, surrounded by possibly inhabited planets, multiplicity of galaxies, each one with its myriads of suns... According to me, all these things are Māyā."

The Upaniṣads provide insights into the emergence of reality from consciousness. However, consciousness cannot be located within our bodies as a physical substance or organ. Given this scenario, it is worth considering how a non-material consciousness can engage with and influence our physical bodies. Where exactly does the mind interact with matter? This question has been a source of great debate among philosophers for centuries.

Given our inability to find a satisfactory explanation for this perplexing interaction, we are faced with a seemingly straightforward decision: either consciousness or reality is non-existent.

The Upaniṣads present a perspective that leans towards idealism - suggesting that consciousness is self-existent and that the physical world is contingent upon it. There is no objective reality that exists independently of the observer. Many physicists, including Schrödinger, expressed their support for this perspective and expressed frustration with the reluctance of Western thought to embrace it. They believed that this doctrine was often dismissed as fantastic and unscientific despite its potential.

According to his analysis, the mind-body problem revolves around our never-ending search for the elusive point at which the mind influences matter or vice versa. He wrote, "is our fruitless quest for the place where mind acts on matter or vice-versa... The material world has only been constructed at the price of taking the self, that is, the mind, out of it, removing it; the mind is not part of it; obviously, therefore, it can neither act on it nor be acted on by any of its parts."

Schrödinger found great inspiration in the Upaniṣads. He enthusiastically shared his thoughts with everyone he encountered and made dedicated efforts to integrate them into his daily routine. The inscription on his tombstone states, "... So all Being is the "one and only" Being; And that it continues to be when someone dies; [this] tells you that he did not cease to be."

Schrödinger thought that Western thought should carefully incorporate ideas from Indian philosophy. As he wrote, "I do believe that this is precisely the point where our present way of thinking does need to be amended, perhaps by a bit of blood-transfusion from Eastern thought. That will not be easy; we must beware of blunders — blood transfusion always needs great precaution to prevent clotting. We do not wish to lose the logical precision that our scientific thought has reached, and that is unparalleled anywhere at any epoch."

Kailāśa: Dhanyavād Guruji.

Ācārya: Let us examine the quotes of some of the leading physicists on Vedānta and Upaniṣads.

Erwin Schrödinger

Erwin Schrödinger (12 August 1887 - 4 January 1961) was a Nobel Prize-winning Austrian and naturalized Irish physicist who developed fundamental results in quantum theory. In particular, he is recognized for postulating the Schrödinger equation. This equation provides a way to calculate the wave function of a system and how it changes dynamically in time. He coined the term "quantum entanglement" and was the earliest to discuss it, doing so in 1932.

He wrote many works on various aspects of physics: statistical mechanics and thermodynamics, physics of dielectrics, colour theory, electrodynamics, general relativity, and cosmology, and he made several attempts to construct a unified field theory. In his book *What Is Life*, Schrödinger addressed the problems of genetics, looking at the phenomenon of life from the point of view of physics. He also paid great attention to the philosophical aspects of science, ancient and oriental philosophical concepts, ethics, and religion. He also wrote on philosophy and theoretical biology. In popular culture, he is best known for his "Schrödinger's cat" thought experiment.

Spending most of his life as an academic with positions at various universities, Schrödinger, along with Paul Dirac, won the Nobel Prize in Physics in 1933 for his work on quantum mechanics; the same year, he left Germany due to his opposition to Nazism. In his personal life, he lived with both his wife and his mistress which may have led to problems causing him to leave his position at Oxford. Subsequently, until 1938, he had a position in Graz, Austria, until the Nazi takeover when he fled, finally finding a long-term arrangement in Dublin, Ireland, where he remained until retirement in 1955, and where he pursued several sexual relationships with minors.

He quotes:

> "It is relatively easy to sweep away the whole of metaphysics, as Kant did. The slightest puff in its direction blows it away, and what was needed was

not so much a powerful pair of lungs to provide the blast as a powerful dose of courage to turn it against so timelessly venerable a house of cards.

But you must not think that what has then been achieved is the actual elimination of metaphysics from the empirical content of human knowledge. In fact, if we cut out all metaphysics, it will be found to be vastly more difficult, indeed probably quite impossible, to give any intelligible account of even the most circumscribed area of specialisation within any specialised science you, please. Metaphysics includes, amongst other things — to take just one quite crude example — the unquestioning acceptance of a more-than-physical — that is, transcendental — significance in a large number of thin sheets of wood-pulp covered with black marks such as are now before you... A real elimination of metaphysics means taking the soul out of both art and science, turning them into skeletons incapable of any further development."

"The Bhagavad Gita... is the most beautiful philosophical song existing in any known tongue."

"This life of yours which you are living is not merely a piece of this entire existence, but in a certain sense the whole; only this whole is not so constituted that it can be surveyed in one single glance. This, as we know, is what the Brāhmaṇas express in that sacred, mystic formula which is yet really so simple and so clear: *tat tvam asi*, this is you. Or, again, in such words as "I am in the east and the west, I am above and below, I am this entire world." [Schrödinger, 'Meine Weltansicht' (My View of the World), 1961]

"The multiplicity is only apparent. This is the doctrine of the Upaniṣads. And not of the Upaniṣads only. The mystical experience of the union with God regularly leads to this view unless strong prejudices stand in the West." [Erwin Schrödinger, What is Life? p. 129, Cambridge University Press]

"From the early great Upaniṣads, the recognition Ātman = Brahman (the personal self-equals the omnipresent, all-comprehending eternal self) was in Indian thought considered, far from being blasphemous, to represent, the quintessence of deepest insight into the happenings of the world. The striving of all the scholars of Vedānta was, after having learned to pronounce with their lips, really to assimilate in their minds this grandest of all thoughts." [From an essay on determinism and free will]

"Most of my ideas and theories are heavily influenced by Vedānta".

"There is no kind of framework within which we can find consciousness in the plural; this is simply something we construct because of the temporal plurality of individuals, but it is a false construction... The only solution to this conflict insofar as any is available to us at all lies in the ancient wisdom of the Upaniṣad." (Mein Leben, Meine Weltansicht [My Life, My World View] (1961), Chapter 4)

Werner Heisenberg

Werner Karl Heisenberg (5 December 1901 - 1 February 1976) was a German theoretical physicist, one of the main pioneers of the theory of quantum mechanics, and a principal scientist in the Nazi nuclear weapons program during World War II. He published his Umdeutung paper in 1925, a major reinterpretation of old quantum theory. In the subsequent series of papers with

Max Born and Pascual Jordan, during the same year, his matrix formulation of quantum mechanics was substantially elaborated. He is known for the uncertainty principle, which he published in 1927. Heisenberg was awarded the 1932 Nobel Prize in Physics "for the creation of quantum mechanics".

Heisenberg also made contributions to the theories of the hydrodynamics of turbulent flows, the atomic nucleus, ferromagnetism, cosmic rays, and subatomic particles. He was also instrumental in planning the first West German nuclear reactor at Karlsruhe, together with a research reactor in Munich, in 1957.

Following World War II, he was appointed director of the Kaiser Wilhelm Institute for Physics, which soon after was renamed the Max Planck Institute for Physics. He was the director of the institute until it was moved to Munich in 1958. He then became director of the Max Planck Institute for Physics and Astrophysics from 1960 to 1970.

Heisenberg was also president of the German Research Council, chairman of the Commission for Atomic Physics, chairman of the Nuclear Physics Working Group, and president of the Alexander von Humboldt Foundation.

He quotes:

> In Uncommon Wisdom: Conversations With Remarkable People (1988), Frtjof Capra writes about the conversation between Rabindranath Tagore and Werner Heisenberg: "He began to see that the recognition of relativity, interconnectedness, and impermanence as fundamental aspects of physical reality, which had been so difficult for himself and his fellow physicists, was the very basis of Indian spiritual traditions."
>
> In The Holographic Paradigm (pg. 217-218), there is a text that talks about Renee Weber's interview with Fritjof Capra. Capra states that Schrödinger, in speaking about Heisenberg, has said: "I had several discussions with Heisenberg. I lived in England then [circa 1972], and I visited him several times in Munich and showed him the whole manuscript chapter by chapter. He was very interested and very open, and he told me something that I think is not known publicly because he never published it. He said that he was well aware of these parallels. While he was working on quantum theory, he went to India to lecture and was a guest of Tagore. He talked a lot with Tagore about Indian philosophy. Heisenberg told me that these talks had helped him a lot with his work in physics because they showed him that all these new ideas in quantum physics were, in fact, not all that crazy. He realized there was, in fact, a whole culture that subscribed to very similar ideas. Heisenberg said that this was a great help for him. Niels Bohr had a similar experience when he went to China."
>
> "After the conversations about Indian philosophy, some of the ideas of Quantum Physics that had seemed so crazy suddenly made more sense."
>
> "Quantum theory will not look ridiculous to people who have read Vedānta."

Robert Oppenheimer

J. Robert Oppenheimer (22 April 1904 – 18 February 1967) was an American theoretical physicist. He was director of the Manhattan Project's Los

Alamos Laboratory during World War II and is often called the "father of the atomic bomb".

Born in New York City, Oppenheimer earned a Bachelor of Arts degree in chemistry from Harvard University in 1925 and a doctorate in physics from the University of Göttingen in Germany in 1927, where he studied under Max Born. After research at other institutions, he joined the physics department at the University of California, Berkeley, where he became a full professor in 1936.

He made significant contributions to theoretical physics, including achievements in quantum mechanics and nuclear physics, such as the *Born-Oppenheimer* approximation for molecular wave functions, work on the theory of electrons and positrons, the *Oppenheimer-Phillips* process in nuclear fusion, and early work on quantum tunnelling. With his students, he also made contributions to the theory of neutron stars and black holes, quantum field theory, and the interactions of cosmic rays.

In 1942, Oppenheimer was recruited to work on the Manhattan Project. In 1943, he was appointed director of the project's Los Alamos Laboratory in New Mexico, tasked with developing the first nuclear weapons. His leadership and scientific expertise were instrumental in the project's success. On July 16, 1945, he was present at the first test of the atomic bomb, Trinity. In August 1945, the weapons were used against Japan in the bombings of Hiroshima and Nagasaki, the only use of nuclear weapons in an armed conflict.

In 1947, Oppenheimer became the director of the Institute for Advanced Study in Princeton, New Jersey, and chaired the influential General Advisory Committee of the newly created U.S. Atomic Energy Commission. He lobbied for international control of nuclear power to avert nuclear proliferation and a nuclear arms race with the Soviet Union.

He opposed the development of the hydrogen bomb during a 1949–1950 governmental debate on the question. Subsequently, he took positions on defence-related issues that provoked the ire of some U.S. government and military factions. During the second Red Scare, Oppenheimer's stances, together with his past associations with the Communist Party USA, led to the revocation of his security clearance following a 1954 security hearing.

This effectively ended his access to the government's atomic secrets and his career as a nuclear physicist. Also stripped of his direct political influence, Oppenheimer nevertheless continued to lecture, write, and work in physics. In 1963, as a gesture of political rehabilitation, he was given the Enrico Fermi Award. He died four years later of throat cancer. In 2022, the federal government vacated the 1954 revocation of his security clearance.

He quotes:

> "Access to the Vedas is the greatest privilege this century may claim over all previous centuries."
>
> The general notions about human understanding... which are illustrated by discoveries in atomic physics, are not in the nature of things wholly

unfamiliar, wholly unheard of or new. Even in our own culture, they have a history, and in Buddhist and Hindu thought, a more considerable and central place. What we shall find [in modern physics] is an exemplification, an encouragement, and a refinement of old wisdom.

The juxtaposition of Western civilization's most terrifying scientific achievement with the most dazzling description of the mystical experience given to us by the Bhagavad Gita, India's greatest literary monument.

The Bhagavad Gita... is the most beautiful philosophical song existing in any known tongue." ["Sacred Jewels of Yoga: Wisdom from India's Beloved Scriptures, Teachers, Masters, and Monks"]

It is the only religion in which the time scales correspond to those of modern scientific cosmology.

Niels Bohr

Niels Henrik David Bohr (7 October 1885 - 18 November 1962) was a Danish physicist who made foundational contributions to understanding atomic structure and quantum theory, for which he received the Nobel Prize in Physics in 1922. Bohr was also a philosopher and a promoter of scientific research.

Bohr developed the Bohr model of the atom, in which he proposed that energy levels of electrons are discrete and that the electrons revolve in stable orbits around the atomic nucleus but can jump from one energy level (or orbit) to another. Although other models have supplanted the Bohr model, its underlying principles remain valid. He conceived the principle of complementarity: that items could be separately analysed in terms of contradictory properties, like behaving as a wave or a stream of particles. The notion of complementarity dominated Bohr's thinking in both science and philosophy.

Bohr founded the Institute of Theoretical Physics at the University of Copenhagen, now known as the Niels Bohr Institute, which opened in 1920. Bohr mentored and collaborated with physicists, including Hans Kramers, Oskar Klein, George de Hevesy, and Werner Heisenberg. He predicted the properties of a new zirconium-like element, which was named hafnium, after the Latin name for Copenhagen, where it was discovered. Later, the synthetic element bohrium was named after him.

During the 1930s, Bohr helped refugees from Nazism. After the Germans occupied Denmark, he met with Heisenberg, who had become the head of the German nuclear weapon project. In September 1943, word reached Bohr that he was about to be arrested by the Germans, so he fled to Sweden. From there, he was flown to Britain, where he joined the British Tube Alloys nuclear weapons project and was part of the British mission to the Manhattan Project. After the war, Bohr called for international cooperation on nuclear energy. He was involved with the establishment of CERN and the Research Establishment Risø of the Danish Atomic Energy Commission. He became the first chairman of the Nordic Institute for Theoretical Physics in 1957.

He quotes:

"I go into the Upaniṣads to ask questions."

Carl Sagan

Carl Edward Sagan (9 November 1934 - 20 December 1996) was an American astronomer and science communicator. His best-known scientific contribution is his research on the possibility of extraterrestrial life, including experimental demonstration of the production of amino acids from basic chemicals by exposure to light. He assembled the first physical messages sent into space, the Pioneer plaque and the Voyager Golden Record, which were universal messages that could potentially be understood by any extraterrestrial intelligence that might find them. He argued in favour of the hypothesis, which has since been accepted, that the high surface temperatures of Venus are the result of the greenhouse effect.

Initially an assistant professor at Harvard, Sagan later moved to Cornell, where he spent most of his career. He published more than 600 scientific papers and articles and was the author, co-author, or editor of more than 20 books. He wrote many popular science books, such as The Dragons of Eden, Broca's Brain, Pale Blue Dot, and The Demon-Haunted World. He also co-wrote and narrated the award-winning 1980 television series Cosmos: A Personal Voyage, which became the most widely watched series in the history of American public television: Cosmos has been seen by at least 500 million people in 60 countries. A book, also called Cosmos, was published to accompany the series. Sagan also wrote a science-fiction novel, published in 1985, called Contact, which became the basis for the 1997 film Contact. His papers, comprising 595,000 items, are archived in the Library of Congress.

Sagan was a popular public advocate of sceptical scientific inquiry and the scientific method; he pioneered the field of exobiology and promoted the *Search for Extra-terrestrial Intelligent* life (SETI). He spent most of his career as a professor of astronomy at Cornell University, where he directed the Laboratory for Planetary Studies. Sagan and his works received numerous awards and honours, including the NASA Distinguished Public Service Medal, the National Academy of Sciences Public Welfare Medal, the Pulitzer Prize for General Non-Fiction (for his book The Dragons of Eden), and (for Cosmos: A Personal Voyage), two Emmy Awards, the Peabody Award, and the Hugo Award. He married three times and had five children. After developing myelodysplasia, Sagan died of pneumonia at the age of 62 on December 20, 1996.

He quotes:

> "The Hindu religion is the only one of the world's great faiths dedicated to the idea that the Cosmos itself undergoes an immense, indeed an innate, number of deaths and rebirths. It is the only religion in which the time scales correspond to those of modern scientific cosmology. Its cycles run from our ordinary day and night to a day and night of Brahma, 8.64 billion years long. Longer than the age of the Earth or the Sun and about half the time since the Big Bang. And there are much longer time scales still." [Carl Sagan, Cosmos]
>
> "The most elegant and sublime of these is a representation of the creation of the universe at the beginning of each cosmic cycle, a motif known as

the cosmic dance of Lord Śiva. The god called in this manifestation Nataraja, the Dance King. In the upper right hand is a drum whose sound is the sound of creation. In the upper left hand is a tongue of flame, a reminder that the universe, now newly created, billions of years from now, will be utterly destroyed." [Carl Sagan, Cosmos, pg. 213-214]

A millennium before Europeans were willing to divest themselves of the Biblical idea that the world was a few thousand years old, the Mayans were thinking of millions and the Hindus billions." [Carl Sagan, Cosmos, pg 213-214]

Nikola Tesla

Nikola Tesla (10 July 1856 - 7 January 1943) was a Serbian-American inventor, electrical engineer, mechanical engineer, and futurist. He is known for his contributions to the design of the modern alternating current (AC) electricity supply system.

Born and raised in the Austrian Empire, Tesla first studied engineering and physics in the 1870s without receiving a degree. He then gained practical experience in the early 1880s working in telephony and at Continental Edison in the new electric power industry. In 1884, he emigrated to the United States, where he became a naturalized citizen. He worked for a short time at the Edison Machine Works in New York City before he struck out on his own. With the help of partners to finance and market his ideas, Tesla set up laboratories and companies in New York to develop a range of electrical and mechanical devices. His AC induction motor and related polyphase AC patents, licensed by Westinghouse Electric in 1888, earned him a considerable amount of money and became the cornerstone of the polyphase system which that company eventually marketed.

Attempting to develop inventions he could patent and market, Tesla conducted a range of experiments with mechanical oscillators/generators, electrical discharge tubes, and early X-ray imaging. He also built a wirelessly controlled boat, one of the first ever exhibited. Tesla became well known as an inventor and demonstrated his achievements to celebrities and wealthy patrons at his lab and was noted for his showmanship at public lectures. Throughout the 1890s, Tesla pursued his ideas for wireless lighting and worldwide wireless electric power distribution in his high-voltage, high-frequency power experiments in New York and Colorado Springs. In 1893, he made pronouncements on the possibility of wireless communication with his devices. Tesla tried to put these ideas to practical use in his unfinished Wardenclyffe Tower project, an intercontinental wireless communication and power transmitter but ran out of funding before he could complete it.

After Wardenclyffe, Tesla experimented with a series of inventions in the 1910s and 1920s with varying degrees of success. Having spent most of his money, Tesla lived in a series of New York hotels, leaving behind unpaid bills. He died in New York City in January 1943. Tesla's work fell into relative obscurity following his death until 1960, when the General Conference on Weights and Measures named the International System of Units (SI) measurement of magnetic flux density the Tesla in his honour. There has been a resurgence in popular interest in Tesla since the 1990s.

He quotes:

> "All perceptible matter comes from a primary substance, or tenuity beyond conception, filling all space, the Akasha or aluminiferous ether, which is acted upon by the life-giving Prana or creative force, calling into existence, in never-ending cycles, all things and phenomena." [Man's Greatest Achievement, John J. O'Neal., & Prodigal Genius, The Life of Nikola Tesla, 1944]

Kailāśa: Dhanyavād Guruji. Let us discuss the life of Ādi Śaṅkara.

Ācārya: Absolutely, Ādi Śaṅkara is known for harmonizing reading of the Śāstras with liberating knowledge of the self at its core, synthesizing the Advaita Vedānta teachings of his time.

Over 300 texts are attributed to him, including commentaries (Bhāṣya), introductory topical expositions (Prakaraṇa Grantha) and poetry (Stotra). Some of them are likely to be written by admirers or scholars with an eponymous name. Works known to be written by Śaṅkara himself are the Brahmasūtrabhāśya, his commentaries on ten Mukhya Upaniṣads, his commentary on the Bhagavad Gita, and the Upadeśasāhasrī. The authenticity of Śaṅkara being the author of Vivekacūḍāmaṇi is debated.

The central concern of Śaṅkara's writings is the liberating knowledge of the true identity of Jīvātmā as Ātman-Brahman, considering the Upaniṣads as an independent means of knowledge beyond the ritually-oriented Mīmāṃsā - the critical investigation of the Vedas.

Śaṅkara has an unparalleled status in the tradition of Advaita Vedānta, but his influence on Hindu intellectual thought has been questioned. Until the 10th century, Śaṅkara was overshadowed by his older contemporary Maṇḍana Miśra, and there is no mention of him in concurring Hindu, Buddhist, or Jain sources until the 11th century.

Hagiographies dating from the 14th-17th centuries worshipped him as a ruler-renunciate, travelling on a Digvijaya (conquest of the four quarters) across the Indian subcontinent to propagate his philosophy, defeating his opponents in theological debates. These hagiographies portray him as the founding four Maṭhas, and Ādi Śaṅkara also came to be regarded as the organiser of the Daśanāmī monastic order and the unifier of the Shanmata tradition of worship. The title of Śaṅkarācārya, used by heads of certain monasteries in India, is derived from his name.

Śaṅkara is most known for his systematic reviews and commentaries (Bhaśyas) on ancient Indian texts. Śaṅkara's masterpiece of commentary is the Brahmasūtrabhāśya (literally, commentary on Brahmasūtra), a fundamental text of the Vedānta school of Hinduism.

Most of his commentaries on the ten Mukhya (principal) Upaniṣads are considered authentic by scholars, and these are Bhāśya on Bṛhadāraṇyaka, Chandogya, Aitareya, Taittiriya, the Kena, Īśā, Katha, Mundaka, and Praśna. The authenticity of the commentary on the Mandukya Upaniṣad and Gaudapada's Madukyakārika are debated.

Other authentic works of Śaṅkara include commentaries on the Bhagavadgītā (Prasthanatrayi Bhāśya). His Vivarana (tertiary notes) on the commentary by Vedavyāsa on Yogasūtra, as well as those on Apastamba Dharmasūtras (*adhyatama-patala-bhāśya*), are accepted by scholars as authentic works of Śaṅkara. Among the Stotra, the Dakshinamurti Stotra, the Bhajagovinda Stotra, the Shivanandalahari, the Carpatapanjarika, the Viṣṇusatpadi, the Harimide, the Dashashloki, and the Kṛṣṇastaka are likely to be authentic.

Śaṅkara also authored Upadeśasahasri, his most important original philosophical work. Of other original Prakaranas (treatises), seventy-six works are attributed to Śaṅkara. Modern-era Indian scholars accept five and thirty-nine works, respectively, as authentic.

Śaṅkara's stotras considered authentic include those dedicated to Kṛṣṇa and one to Śiva – often considered two different sects within Hinduism. Scholars suggest that these Stotra are not sectarian but essentially Advaitic and reach for a unified, universal view of Vedānta.

Śaṅkara's commentary on the Brahmasūtras is the oldest surviving. However, in that commentary, he mentions older commentaries like those of Dravida, Bhartrprapancha and others which are either lost or yet to be found.

Commentaries on Nṛsiṅha-Purvatatapaniya and Shveshvatara Upaniṣads are attributed to Śaṅkara, but their authenticity is debated. Similarly, commentaries on several early and later Upaniṣads attributed to Śaṅkara are debated; these include Kaushitaki, Maitri, Kaivalya, Paramahamsa, Sakatayana, Mandala Brahmana, Maha Nārāyaṇa and Gopalatapaniya. However, in Brahmasūtra-Bhāśya, Śaṅkara cites some of these Upaniṣads as he develops his arguments. Still, the historical notes left by his companions and disciples, along with major differences in style and the content of the commentaries on later Upaniṣad have led scholars to conclude that the commentaries on later Upaniṣads were not Śaṅkara's work.

The authenticity of Śaṅkara being the author of Vivekacūḍāmaṇi is debated, though it is closely interwoven into the spiritual heritage of Śaṅkara.

The Aparokshanubhuti and Atmabodha are also attributed to Śaṅkara as his original philosophical treatises, but this is uncertain. Scholars have some reservations that Śaṅkara completely authored the compendium *Sarvadarśanasiddhānta Sangraha* because of differences in style and thematic inconsistencies in parts. Similarly, Gayatri-Bhāśya is doubted to be Śaṅkara's work. Other commentaries that are doubted as Śaṅkara's work include those on Uttaragita, Sivagita, Brahmagita, Lalitashasranama, Sutasamhita and Sandhyabhāśya. The commentary on the Tantric work Lalitatrisatibhāśya attributed to Śaṅkara is also doubted.

Śaṅkara is widely credited with commentaries on other scriptural works, such as the Viṣṇusahasranāma and the Sānatsujātiya, but both these are considered fictional by scholars who have expressed doubts. Hastamalakiya-

Bhāśya is also widely believed in India to be Śaṅkara's work, and it is included in the Samata edition of Śaṅkara's works, but some scholars doubt it.

Śaṅkara has been described as influenced by Śaivism and Śāktism. Still, his works and philosophy suggest greater overlap with Vaiṣṇavism, the influence of the Yoga school of Hinduism, but most distinctly express his Advaitin convictions with a monistic view of spirituality, and his commentaries mark a turn from realism to idealism.

According to Śaṅkara, the one unchanging entity (Brahman) alone is real, while changing entities do not have absolute existence. Śaṅkara's primary objective was to explain how Mokṣa is attained in this life by recognizing the true identity of jīvātmā as Ātman-Brahman, as mediated by the Mahāvākyas, especially *tat tvam asi*, "That you are." Correct knowledge of jīvātmā and Ātman-Brahman is the attainment of Brahman, immortality, and leads to Mokṣa from suffering and Samsāra, the cycle of rebirth.

Śaṅkara recognized the means of knowledge, but his thematic focus was upon metaphysics and soteriology, and he took for granted the Pramāṇas, that is, epistemology or "means to gain knowledge, reasoning methods that empower one to gain reliable knowledge".

Śaṅkara was born in Kaladi in the southern Indian state of Kerala, in a village named. He was born to Nambudiri Brāhmaṇa parents. His parents were an aged, childless couple who led a devout life of service to the poor. They named their child Śaṅkara, meaning "giver of prosperity". His father died while Śaṅkara was very young. Śaṅkara's Upanayana, the thread ceremony and the initiation into student life, had to be delayed due to the death of his father and was then performed by his mother.

He was attracted to the life of Sanyāsa from early childhood. His mother disapproved. At age eight going to a river with his mother, to bathe, and a crocodile caught him. Śaṅkara called out to his mother to permit him to become a Sanyāsi or else the crocodile would kill him. The mother agrees, and Śaṅkara is freed and leaves his home for education. He reaches a Śaiva monastery along a river in a north-central state of India and becomes the disciple of a teacher named Govinda Bhagavatpāda.

The accounts diverge in detail about the first meeting between Śaṅkara and his Guru, where they met, as well as what happened later. Several texts suggest Śaṅkara schooling with Govindapada happened along the river Narmadā in Omkareshwar, a few places it along river Gaṅgā in Kāśi as well as Badari (Badrinātha in the Himalayas).

The sources also vary in their description of where he went, who he met and debated and many other details of his life. Most mention Śaṅkara studying the Vedas, Upaniṣads and Brahmasūtra with Govindapada, and Śaṅkara authoring several key works in his youth while he was studying with his teacher.

It is with his teacher, Govinda, that Śaṅkara studied Gaudapadiya Kārikā, as Govinda was himself taught by Gaudapāda. Most also mention a meeting with scholars of the Mīmāṃsā school of Hinduism, namely Kumārila and Prabhakara, as well as Maṇḍana and various Buddhists, in Śāstrārtha (debates).

Different and widely inconsistent accounts of his life include diverse journeys, pilgrimages, public debates, installation of yantras and Liṅgams, as well as the founding of monastic centres in north, east, west, and south India. While the details and chronology vary, most sources present Śaṅkara as travelling widely within India, Gujarat to Bengal, and participating in public philosophical debates with different Āstika schools of Hindu philosophy, as well as Nāstika traditions such as Buddhists, Jains, Arhatas, Saugatas, and Charvakas.

The sources credit him with starting several Maṭha (monasteries), but this is uncertain. Ten monastic orders in different parts of India are generally attributed to Śaṅkara's travel-inspired Sanyāsi schools, each with Advaita notions, of which four have continued in his tradition: Bhāratī (Śringerī), Sarasvati (Kañchi), Tirtha and Asramin (Dvaraka).

Other monasteries that record Śaṅkara's visit include Giri, Puri, Vana, Aranya, Parvata, and Sagara - all names traceable to the Āśrama system in Vaidika literature.

Śaṅkara had a number of disciple scholars during his travels, including Padmapadacharya (also called Sanandana, associated with the text Atmabodha), Sureśvaracharya, Totakācārya, Hastamalakacharya, Chitsukha, Prthividhara, Chidvilasayati, Bodhendra, Brahmendra, Sadananda and others, who authored their literature on Śaṅkara and Advaita Vedānta.

According to sources supported by four maṭhas, Ādi Śaṅkara died at Kedarnath in the northern Indian state of Uttarakhand, a Hindu pilgrimage site in the Himalayas. Texts say that he was last seen by his disciples behind the Kedarnath temple, walking in the Himalayas until he was not traced. Some texts locate his death in alternate locations such as Kañchipuram (Tamil Nadu) and somewhere in the state of Kerala. According to the source related to the monastery of Kañchi, Ādi Śaṅkara died at Kañchi, which I believe to be more authentic.

Śaṅkara is regarded as the founder of the Daśanāmī Sampradāya of Hindu monasticism and the Pañcayatana Pujā and Ṣaṇmata of the Smarta tradition.

According to tradition, Ādi Śaṅkara organised the Hindu monks of these ten sects or names under four Maṭhas, with the headquarters at Dvārakā in the West, Jagannātha Puri in the East, Śringerī in the South, and Badrikāśrama in the North. Each Maṭha was headed by one of his four main disciples, who each continued the Vedānta Sampradaya.

Traditionally, Śaṅkara is regarded as the greatest teacher and reformer of the Smarta sampradaya, which is one of four major sampradaya of Hinduism. According to scholars, Śaṅkara established the nondualist interpretation of the Upaniṣads as the touchstone of a revived Smarta sampradaya:

Practically, Śaṅkara fostered a reunion between Advaita and Smarta, which by his time had not only continued to defend the Varṇāśrama Dharma as defining the path of Karma but had developed the practice of Pañcayatana Pujā as a solution to varied and conflicting devotional practices. Thus, one could worship any one of five deities (Viṣṇu, Śiva, Durgā, Sūrya, Gaṇeśa) as one's Iṣṭadevatā. Ṣaṇmata system includes Skanda under its fold.

Sunidhi: Kindly tell the legend of his birth and childhood.

Ācārya: Very well!

Several centuries back, lived a devout Brāhmaṇa named Vidyādhirāja at Kaladi in Kerala. His family home was in Śivapuram, a village about three miles southeast of Kumbakonam in Tamil Nadu. There was a Śiva temple in this village. In this temple, the Varāha Avatāra of Viṣṇu worshipped Śiva. The name of the presiding deity of the temple was "Śivagurunātha". Vidyadhiraja's son was "Śivaguru", named after the Lord of Sivapuram. Vidyādhirāja got Śivaguru married to Āryambā from Melpazhur, twenty miles southeast of Ernakulam in Kerala.

Śivaguru and his wife, Āryambā, spent their life in Pujā, giving alms to the poor and performing other good deeds. But they were childless and deeply longed for a child. This childless couple went to Trichur and performed Pujā to Lord Vadakkunathan (Śiva) at Vṛṣabhacaleśvara temple for 48 days and prayed for a son.

Satisfied with their devotion, Lord Śiva appeared in their dreams and told them, "I am extremely happy with your devotion, and I will grant your wish. But tell me whether you want many ordinary children or one extremely intelligent son who will live for only a short period." The couple asked the Lord to decide for them what was good for them.

Lord Dakṣiṇāmurti was pleased with the reply and granted them a boon of one intelligent but short-lived son. Time passed, and a son was born to Āryambā in the Vasanta Ṛtu at noon under the Ārdrā Nakṣatra. As Lord Śiva had already promised that he would be born for the benefit of the world, the child was named Śaṅkara.

Śivaguru was delighted to find that the dream in which he had a boon from Śiva had indeed come true. He saw that his son was of a divine lineage and bore the marks of an incarnation. The mark of the wheel on the infant Śaṅkara's head, the impress of the third eye on the forehead, and the sign of the Triśūla on the shoulders made wise men decide that he was an incarnation of Śiva. Those who visited immediately realized that the child was not an ordinary child.

Śaṅkara was an infant prodigy. He displayed extraordinary intelligence even when he was a child. By his third year finished reading many books and only listening to the readings and chanting of the Vedas, the Vedānta, the Rāmāyaṇa, the Mahābhārata and the Purāṇas and learnt them by heart. He was a Śrutidhara, one who could repeat in full all that he heard just once.

Śivaguru was extremely happy to find his son endowed with divine powers. He wanted to perform the boy's Upanayana in his fifth year and then send him to the Gurukula for study. But Śivaguru died before he could have the Upanayana done. After the bereavement in the family, Āryambā moved to her father's house for some days. But she remembered the last wish of her husband. As soon as Śaṅkara reached his fifth year, she returned to her home and performed Śaṅkara's Upanayana as per the Śāstras. After that, she sent Śaṅkara to the Gurukula to study.

Śaṅkara's Guru was charmed by his devotion to learning. The correctness of Śaṅkara's pronunciation of words and the sharpness of his intellect fascinated everyone. In a short span of two years, Śaṅkara was proficient in the Upaniṣads, Purāṇas, Itihāsas and Vedas. He also mastered the various philosophical systems like Nyāya, Sāṃkhya, Yoga and Vaiśeṣika. It was like Devaguru Bṛhaspati incarnated in him.

In accordance with the Gurukula rules, Brahmacāri Śaṅkara used to go out for Bhikṣa (alms) every day. One day, he went to the house of a poor Brāhmaṇa. That day, they did not even have a handful of rice. The housewife, not knowing what to do, gave Śaṅkara an Amla, an Indian gooseberry. With tears, she told him of their condition. This deeply moved Śaṅkara. Moved by their plight, he spontaneously composed and sang a Stotra to Devī Mahālakṣmī, the Devī of wealth.

The Stotra, consisting of eighteen ślokas, known as "Kanakadhārā", moved Devī Mahālakṣmī. She appeared before him and said, "My dear child, the members of this poor family, in their past lives, did not perform any meritorious acts. How will I bestow on them wealth?" Śaṅkara then replied to the Mother, "Dear Mother, this lady just now gave me an Amla fruit when she had nothing else. That, by itself, is a worthy act. If you wish to favour me, please free this family from poverty." Moved by Ādi Śaṅkara's devotion and the act of generosity of the Brāhmaṇa's wife, the Devī showered a stream of gold within the hut of his poor Brāhmaṇa.

Āratī: Gurudeva, kindly tell us the Stotra, which removed the poverty of the Brāhmaṇa.

Ācārya: Here it is:

अङ्गं हरेः पुलकभूषणमाश्रयन्ती भृङ्गाङ्गनेव मुकुलाभरणं तमालम् ।
अङ्गीकृताखिल-विभूतिरपाङ्गलीला माङ्गल्यदास्तु मम मङ्गलदेवतायाः ॥१॥

Salutations to Mā Lakṣmī, who dwells like a delightful ornament within Hari, like bees that are attracted to the half-open buds of the black Tamala tree and decorate them with their humming sound. The one who carries within her the affluence of the entire world and showers wealth through her divine glance. May that glance bring auspiciousness and prosperity into my life.

मुग्धा मुहुर्विदधती वदने मुरारेः प्रेमत्रपाप्रणिहितानि गतागतानि ।
माला दृशोर्मधुकरीव महोत्पले या सा मे श्रियं दिशतु सागरसम्भवायाः ॥२॥

Salutations to Mā Lakṣmī, whose glances are directed towards the face of Hari. Charmed by his face, her glances are filled with love and bashfulness as they return to his face time and again. Her glances are like the honeybees that hover around the huge water lily. She who has risen from the ocean of milk, may she bestow her glance filled with good fortune upon me.

विश्वामरेन्द्रपदविभ्रमदानदक्षम् आनन्दहेतुरधिकं मुरविद्विषोऽपि ।

ईषन्निषीदतु मयि क्षणमीक्षणार्धम् इन्दीवरोदरसहोदरमिन्दिरायाः ॥३॥

Salutations to Mā Lakṣmī, she, who with a mere side glance, could grant the exalted position of the King of the three worlds to Indra. This made the enemy of Madhu, who is the Supreme Bliss, overwhelmed with joy. I pray that a glance through the splendour of those half-closed eyes resembling blue lotuses could rest on me, for just a moment.

आमीलिताक्षमधिगम्य मुदा मुकुन्दम् आनन्दकन्दमनिमेषमनङ्गतन्त्रम् ।

आकेकरस्थितकनीनिकपक्ष्मनेत्रं भूत्यै भवेन्मम भुजङ्गशयाङ्गनायाः ॥४॥

Salutations to Mā Lakṣmī, who has captured the joyous face of Mukunda through her fully opened eyes, her gaze remaining on his ecstatic face with closed eyes. Her glance is filled with happiness and love. Let a glance that lavishes Mukunda, he who rests on the snake, from the corner of her eyes, come to rest on me.

बाह्वन्तरे मधुजितः श्रितकौस्तुभे या हारावलीव हरिनीलमयी विभाति ।

कामप्रदा भगवतोऽपि कटाक्षमाला कल्याणमावहतु मे कमलालयायाः ॥५॥

Salutations to Mā Lakṣmī, who resides in the heart of the conqueror of the demon Madhu, where lies the Kausthuba Maṇi, an exceedingly valuable gem. Her glances shine like a bluish-yellow string of pearls that raise love in Hari. Through her string of side glances, may the one who resides in lotuses bless me with those side glances, touch my life, and bring auspiciousness and wealth to me.

कालाम्बुदालिललितोरसि कैटभारेर्धाराधरे स्फुरति या तडिदङ्गनेव ।

मातुः समस्तजगतां महनीयमूर्तिर्भद्राणि मे दिशतु भार्गवनन्दनायाः ॥६॥

Salutations to Mā Lakṣmī, she who hovers like a bee, like a streak of lightning flashing over the bosom that resembles a black cloudy sky, the bosom of one who killed Kaiṭabha. The gracious mother of the whole universe, the daughter of the mighty Sage Bhargava. May her auspicious form touch my life and bring me prosperity.

प्राप्तं पदं प्रथमतः किल यत्प्रभावान्माङ्गल्यभाजि मधुमाथिनि मन्मथेन ।

मय्यापतेत्तदिह मन्थरमीक्षणार्धमन्दालसं च मकरालयकन्यकायाः ॥७॥

Salutations to Mā Lakṣmī, through whose power Manmatha, the Kāma Devatā, was able to reach the one who slew Madhu, Hari, who is always connected with the one who bestows happiness. May the power from the glance of that kind and gentle half-open eyes, full of love and blessings, a glance so soft, of the daughter of the ocean, fall upon me.

दद्याद् दयानुपवनो द्रविणाम्बुधाराम् अस्मिन्नकिञ्चनविहङ्गशिशौ विषण्णे ।
दुष्कर्मघर्ममपनीय चिराय दूरं नारायणप्रणयिनीनयनाम्बुवाहः ॥८॥

Salutations to Mā Lakṣmī, and may she bestow the wind of her mercy and shower her wealth on this destitute, helpless like the child of a bird, driven by poverty. May she remove the impact of the burden of sins from my life. May she bestow the shower of rain of mercy from her eyes, she, the beloved of Nārāyaṇa.

इष्टा विशिष्टमतयोऽपि यया दयार्द्रदृष्ट्या त्रिविष्टपपदं सुलभं लभन्ते ।
दृष्टिः प्रहृष्टकमलोदरदीप्तिरिष्टां पुष्टिं कृषीष्ट मम पुष्करविष्टरायाः ॥९॥

Salutations to Mā Lakṣmī. With just her divine glance, even the most difficult desires, like attaining a place in heaven, can be achieved. This is the power of her moist, compassionate eyes, the kindest eyes one can ever see. Her glance that bears the splendour of a lotus in bloom, that magical, joyous moment; may it come my way. May the merciful glance of the one seated in a lotus nourish my wishes.

गीर्देवतेति गरुडध्वजसुन्दरीति शाकम्भरीति शशिशेखरवल्लभेति ।
सृष्टिस्थितिप्रलयकेलिषु संस्थितायै तस्यै नमस्त्रिभुवनैकगुरोस्तरुण्यै ॥१०॥

Salutations to Mā Lakṣmī. She is the Devī of Knowledge and Speech. She is the beautiful consort of the one who carries Garuda as his emblem. She who sustains everyone with nature and vegetation, the beloved and consort of the one with the crescent moon. She, who observes the divine play of creation, maintenance, and destruction. The youthful consort of the Guru of all the worlds, the three worlds offer her their revered salutations.

श्रुत्यै नमोऽस्तु शुभकर्मफलप्रसूत्यै रत्यै नमोऽस्तु रमणीयगुणार्णवायै ।
शक्त्यै नमोऽस्तु शतपत्रनिकेतनायै पुष्ट्यै नमोऽस्तु पुरुषोत्तमवल्लभायै ॥११॥

Salutations to Mā Lakṣmī, she who symbolizes the Vedas, that help produce auspicious and positive results in life. She who is Rathi, an ocean of good qualities. She who is revered as Shakti, one who resides in the abode of hundred petals. Salutations to you, as the one who nourishes, the Devī of plenty, the beloved of Purushottama.

नमोऽस्तु नालीकनिभाननायै नमोऽस्तु दुग्धोदधिजन्मभूत्यै ।
नमोऽस्तु सोमामृतसोदरायै नमोऽस्तु नारायणवल्लभायै ॥१२॥

Salutations to Mā Lakṣmī, the one who has the face of a lotus in full bloom. Salutations to you, the one born of the ocean of milk, along with the moon and the divine nectar. Salutations to you, the most beloved of Nārāyaṇa.

सम्पत्कराणि सकलेन्द्रियनन्दनानि साम्राज्यदानविभवानि सरोरुहाक्षि ।
त्वद्वन्दनानि दुरिताहरणोद्यतानि मामेव मातरनिशं कलयन्तु मान्ये ॥१३॥

Salutations to Mā Lakṣmī. To the one whose lotus eyes are the cause of all prosperity and who is the cause of great joy in all senses. She of the lotus eyes who has the power to bestow kingdoms. Singing your glories brings forth your grace that removes all difficulties, miseries, and sins from our lives. Mother, may I always be blessed to serve you and sing your glories.

यत्कटाक्षसमुपासनाविधिः सेवकस्य सकलार्थसम्पदः ।

संतनोति वचनाङ्गमानसैस्त्वां मुरारिहृदयेश्वरीं भजे ॥१४॥

Salutations to Mā Lakṣmī. The worship of your side glance that is blessed by the entire wealth and prosperity you bestow upon me. May my thoughts, words, and deeds be enveloped by your worship, you who are the beloved Devī residing in the heart of Murari.

सरसिजनिलये सरोजहस्ते धवलतमांशुकगन्धमाल्यशोभे ।

भगवति हरिवल्लभे मनोज्ञे त्रिभुवनभूतिकरि प्रसीद मह्यम् ॥१५॥

Salutations to Mā Lakṣmī. She who abides in the lotus and holds the lotus in her hands. She who is dressed in dazzling white and is adorned with the most fragrant garlands and radiates a divine aura. She who is the most beloved of Hari and the source of immense happiness and is captivating. She who is the source of prosperity and well-being for all three worlds. O Mother, please grace me with your compassion.

दिग्घस्तिभिः कनककुम्भमुखावसृष्टस्वर्वाहिनीविमलचारुजलप्लुताङ्गीम् ।

प्रातर्नमामि जगतां जननीमशेषलोकाधिनाथगृहिणीममृताब्धिपुत्रीम् ॥१६॥

Salutations to Mā Lakṣmī. She, who is bathed by the holy waters of the Gaṅgā that flows from heaven, is showered from all directions in golden pitchers by the eight elephants. The water is pure and flows from the celestial region and beautifies her. I salute the Mother of the eternal universe early in the morning, she who is the consort of the Supreme Being, the Preserver, and the daughter of the ocean that gives nectar.

कमले कमलाक्षवल्लभे त्वं करुणापूरतरङ्गितैरपाङ्गैः ।

अवलोकय मामकिञ्चनानां प्रथमं पात्रमकृत्रिमं दयायाः ॥१७॥

Salutations to Mā Lakṣmī. She, who is the lotus-eyed of her beloved Hari. She, whose eyes are filled with kindness and compassion, please look at me, this utterly destitute, and make me the first, deserving to be in the path of your unconditional compassion.

स्तुवन्ति ये स्तुतिभिरमूभिरन्वहं त्रयीमयीं त्रिभुवनमातरं रमाम् ।

गुणाधिका गुरुतरभाग्यभागिनो भवन्ति ते भुवि बुधभाविताशयाः ॥१८॥

Salutations to Mā Lakṣmī. Those who sing this hymn every day and glorify; She, who is the Supreme Devī, the embodiment of the Vedas, the Mother of the three worlds, will receive blessings of virtues in abundance. They shall be blessed to have the wise in their destiny and will become wise by her awakening of their wisdom.

Āratī: Dhanyavād Guruji.

Sunidhi: Guruji, kindly continue Ādi Śaṅkara's childhood legend.

Ācārya: While even the very intelligent students took at least twenty years to acquire mastery of all scriptures, Śaṅkara was able to acquire that mastery in just two years with the blessings of his Guru. Hence, Śaṅkara was permitted to return home long before the expiry of the prescribed term at the Gurukula.

Śaṅkara, as a Brahmachari, now lived at home and devoted himself to learning and teaching. He continued to study various philosophical systems that existed at that time. But it was the serving of his mother that was for him his all-important duty and his greatest discipline. He ensured his mother's comfort and happiness by attending to her and serving her.

Śaṅkara's measureless proficiency in studies and uncommon skill in instructing brought him much renown, and within a few days, his fame spread on all corners. Even aged scholars in large numbers began to come to him for a deeper study of the scriptures.

Śaṅkara's early life was marked by several miracles that indicated his inherent divinity. Ādi Śaṅkara's mother, the devout Āryambā, used to go every day for a bath to the river Pūrṇa, a sacred river. The river was far off from Śaṅkara's house; even then, Devī Aryamba used to go to the river every day steadfastly. On her way back home, she offered worship at the shrine of Keśava, her Kula Devatā. Once, on a hot summer day, Āryambā went to the river as usual, but even after a long time, she did not return home.

Śaṅkara went in search of her. As he was walking along the riverbank, he saw her lying unconscious due to exhaustion. In deep misery, he wept profusely and started nursing his mother back to her senses and then slowly led her way back home.

Śaṅkara was ardently devoted to his mother, and no words can portray his feelings on seeing the condition of his mother. All in tears, he sent forth a prayer to God, saying, "Lord, You are indeed omnipotent. If You only wish, anything is possible. I cannot bear to see the suffering of my mother. Be gracious and bring the river closer to our house. Then, there will be no more suffering for my mother." He was immersed in this prayer incessantly, day and night.

The All-merciful Lord responded to the prayers of Śaṅkara. During the night, it rained so heavily that the river changed its course. Breaking through its north bank, the Pūrṇa River began to flow by the side of Śaṅkara's house. Even today, one can see the river has taken an uncharacteristic turn towards the Maṭha shrine in Kaladi. This is one of the miracles that made him noted among his people.

Sunidhi: That is so enlightening. Kindly tell us the circumstances in which he embraced Sanyāsa.

Ācārya: The tale of the crocodile and his mother granting him permission of Sanyāsa is widely known. Let me tell you the legend.

As Śaṅkara's divine quality spread all around, many people came to see him, even from far-off places. Many scholars wanted to hear his exposition of the Śāstras.

One day, a few Jyotiṣīs arrived at Śaṅkara's home. After discussing the Śāstras, the Jyotiṣīs expressed a desire to look into the Ādi Śaṅkara's Kuṇḍalī. On examining the Kuṇḍalī, they said that death might overtake him in his eighth or sixteenth or thirty-second year.

On hearing this, Aryamba was deeply distressed and sadly informed Śaṅkara about it. Śaṅkara had just entered his eighth year then. It was not the time to leave the world, but Śaṅkara realised that it was time to leave his mother and home. He knew that he must embrace Sanyāsa to attain knowledge of Truth. He knew that without the knowledge of Truth, there was no possibility of achieving Mokṣa. Śaṅkara sensed an opportunity now to talk to his mother.

"The Lord had told you before I was born that I would live shortly. So why do you worry? You cannot change the Divine Order. So, why not bravely accept that?"

He said, "In your earlier births, you gave birth to so many children. What is your connection with them now?"

Śaṅkara continued: "After rains, one sees a lot of bubbles on the surface of the water. Some bubbles are attached for some time. Afterwards, they vanish one by one and merge with the water. We are also like those bubbles. We must leave one day and merge with the absolute reality".

Aryamba was amazed at her son's speech! But she did not want to understand anything Śaṅkara said. "Is this the way to talk to your Mother? Your father is no more; you will go away; then what will I do? Please pray that I should die. If you do, I am sure it will happen. I will go to your father, even though I cannot see you married and enjoy my grandchildren." She said sobbingly.

Śaṅkara realized the futility of the conversation with his mother as that would only prolong her agony. Notwithstanding his desire to embrace Sanyāsa, he waited patiently for a reasonable time.

One day, he bolstered courage and told her of his intention to embrace Sanyāsa. Aryamba started weeping. Embracing him, she said, "My dear child, is it right for you to speak such a thing? You are such a tender sapling now. If you become a Sanyāsi and walk out of home, who is there to look after me? Who will take me to places of pilgrimage? Who will perform my funeral rites when I die? No, no, my dear, as long I am alive, you cannot become a Sanyāsi."

Śaṅkara remained quiet. There seemed to be no way out of the situation. Śaṅkara prayed with an earnest heart to the Lord, requesting him to make it possible for him to take Sanyāsa. Śaṅkara wanted to embrace Sanyāsa only with his mother's permission. He patiently waited.

One day, early in the morning, Śaṅkara asked his mother to accompany him to the Pūrṇa river for a bath, now that the river was very close to their house.

While Śaṅkara was having a bath, suddenly, everyone heard a scream: "Help! ".

It was Śaṅkara's scream.

Aryamba responded: "What happened, Śaṅkara? "

"Ah! My leg! Something is pulling it! Help me!"

Aryamba saw a crocodile pulling her son's leg. She spontaneously shouted for help. But the crocodile continued to pull him down to deeper waters. In between the tussle, Śaṅkara said, "Mother, only you can save me.

Aryamba responded immediately. "Tell me, son, what can I do? How do I save you?"

"Give me permission for my rebirth, I will be saved" - Śaṅkara.

Aryamba pondered, "The crocodile will eat my son anyway, then why is my son asking for permission for a rebirth?"

She responded, "Son, I don't understand what you are saying. I will do anything to save you".

Śaṅkara said, "Mother, rebirth need not happen only after death. If I totally change the path of my life, i.e., change to the life of a Sanyāsi, that will also be a rebirth. So, if you permit me to become a Sanyāsi, that will be my rebirth. Mother, why don't we test that? In any case, I am going to be swallowed by this crocodile."

The crocodile had pulled him further.

She thought, "I gave birth to this child after a lot of prayers. Is this the way to lose my child? Is this the time to think? Is there any hope of saving my child?".

Aryamba had no other option!

Finally, Aryamba responded with great difficulty, "My son, so be it. You become a Sanyāsi, or whoever you want. As long as you are safe and living anywhere in this world, I permit you." She sobbed bitterly and fainted.

Śaṅkara chanted the mantras to become a Sanyāsi and embraced Sanyāsa.

Immediately, the crocodile released him. Śaṅkara came out of the water as a Sanyāsi. He was not a complete Sanyāsi yet. Now, he needed to go through a formal Sanyāsa Dikṣa.

Immediately after Śaṅkara came out of the water, a Gandharva (divine musician) appeared from the water where the crocodile was and spoke to Śaṅkara: "Years ago, I was into bad habits and was enjoying in a riverbed when Maharṣi Durvāsā passed by. I ignored him totally, and he became very angry and cursed me to be a crocodile.

He also said that the only way for me to get back to being a Gandharva was to hold the Lotus feet of Lord Śiva when he visited this river sometime in future. Because of this act today, I am free of my Śrāpa and you from the wordly life." After saying this, the Gandharva disappeared.

By then, Aryamba regained her consciousness. With her motherly affection, she told Śaṅkara: "Come, my son, let us go home".

Śaṅkara said:

"Home? Just a few minutes ago, you told me that I can embrace Sanyāsa. You know that Sanyāsis have no home. How can I go with you?"

For a moment Aryamba thought that she only had a bad dream. But she soon realised that it was all real. Profusely weeping, she said, "What is this that you say, my boy? You are but a child; how indeed can you renounce home now? How can I renounce my son born out of so much of prayers?"

Śaṅkara did not loosen his resolve. He quietly said:

"Who do you think saved me from becoming a prey to the crocodile? That Īśvara will look after everything".

"I am the one born of your womb. I know how much you sacrificed to have me as your son. I will never forget that you opted for one intelligent son instead of many ordinary children. I know you have nobody except me to love you in this world."

"What have you achieved besides sadness and sorrow in your life? Before I was born, you dearly longed for a child. Then you suffered for nine months, bearing me. Then you were sad because your son was going to live only for a short while. Later, you were sad about losing your husband. Leaving me in Gurukula, you suffered because you were all alone. For how long do you want to continue this suffering?"

"Like how I have to perform my duties to my mother, I have my duties to the World. I cannot postpone it to a period 'after you'. I did not ask for Sanyāsa, only for me. If you renounce me, you will also find peace. The sadness and sorrow will not be there any longer for you. The peace and fulfilment you will get in this sacrifice cannot be obtained through any other means, including having me with you or by accumulating more wealth."

"Please do not grieve. The whole world will be my home hereafter. All those who will initiate me into the sacred path will be my fathers. All women who give me Bhikṣa will be my mothers. By realizing the Ātman, I will gain peace, and that peace will be my spouse. All my disciples will be my sons".

Disappointed, Aryamba said: "You are my only son. You have to perform the rites of your father and forefathers. Who will perform my final rites?"

Śaṅkara said: "As per the Śāstras if one is diligent as a Sanyāsi, it is said that his forefathers to twenty-one generations would get Mokṣa. However, I promise you that during your last moments, when you think of me, I shall, wherever I may be at that time, know of it. And I shall reach you. Before you leave your mortal frame, I will help you to have a vision of your Iṣṭadevatā. That indeed will be the essence of all pilgrimages for you."

The circumstances which attended Śaṅkara's birth remerged into Aryamba's memory, and he realized its inevitability. In a voice choked with emotion, she said, "So be it, my son; I bless you that you attain your desired goal."

Ādi Śaṅkara realized the results of his earnest prayers to Īśvara to embrace Sanyāsa. By Īśvara's grace, Aryamba's was filled with an ineffable joy. She would no longer hinder her son's ascending to the absolute Brahman. Śaṅkara then prostrated at the feet of his mother as per Śāstraic injunctions.

After receiving her blessings from his mother, Śaṅkara walked out to have a view of the Kuladevatā Śrī Keśava. And Sūrya soon rose to view on the eastern horizon. An eight-year-old boy full of dispassion and having cast off his mother's affectionate shelter now went about in the eternal quest, the search for the ultimate truth.

Those who saw this shaven-headed boy clad in a Sanyāsi's robe with Daṇḍa and Kamaṇḍalu in hand fixated by their gaze on this resplendent boy. Loving mothers who saw him shed silent tears thinking of his mother. Śaṅkara was unaffected by things he heard or saw. He was unaffected by the curious glances, compassionate sighs, and eager queries. He was solely focused on the supreme Spirit and Reality.

Meditating with a one-pointed mind on the All-pervading Supreme Energy, the soul behind all creation, he walked on. He would cover long distances on foot, ask for Bhikṣa, accept the food, rest, and walk on.

Sunidhi: How did he meet his Guru?

Ācārya: In the quest for Truth, he passed through many villages, towns, and cities, crossed many fields and meadows, wild animal-infested forests, hills, rivers, and rivulets and strode along many unknown paths. Śaṅkara finally reached Omkārnātha by the Narmadā river. There, he learnt that a great Yogī, Govinda Bhagavatpāda, had been living in an ecstatic trance for many years in a cave. Śaṅkara's heart was filled with indescribable ecstasy.

Advancing a short distance, Śaṅkara met a few old Sanyāsis who lived near the caves at Omkārnātha, and he enquired them of Govinda Bhagavatpāda.

This boy, at an age when others of his years were still playing with toys and battling with learning Akṣaras, had come alone and on foot, all the way from home in far off South, in search of a Guru!

An old Sanyāsi told Śaṅkara, "Child, The Yogī Govinda Bhagavatpāda, lives in that cave. He has been in a trance for a long time. We have been waiting here and have grown old in waiting. Blessed indeed are you, child! Commendable is your Guru Bhakti."

Śaṅkara got a positive response from the old Sanyāsi when he asked if he could have a Darśana of the Yogī inside the cave. Immediately, Śaṅkara prostrated before the caves. He was waiting for instructions to enter the caves.

With tears welling up from within and flowing down his tender cheeks, he stood with folded hands and started praying. All of a sudden, he heard a voice, loud and clear, from inside the cave, "Who is there?"

Śaṅkara's heart was flooded with an inexpressible sublime bliss driven by a powerful urge of devotional emotion. He answered spontaneously, singing the Daśaślokī.

न भूमिर्न तोयं न तेजो न वायुः न खं नेन्द्रियं वा न तेषां समूहः ।
अनेकान्तिकत्वात् सुषुप्त्येकसिद्धः तदेकोऽवशिष्टः शिवः केवलोऽहम् ॥ १॥

Neither earth, nor water, nor fire, nor air, nor ether, nor sense-organ, nor their aggregate (am I) because they are transient. That which is the one established in sleep, that one which remains (after the sublation of all else) - that auspicious absolute (self) I am.

न वर्णा न वर्णाश्रमाचारधर्मा न मे धारणाध्यानयोगादयोऽपि ।

अनात्माश्रयाहंममाध्यासहानात्तदेकोऽवशिष्टः शिवः केवलोऽहम् ॥ २॥

Neither the castes, nor the rules of conduct relating to the castes and stages of life, nor even concentration, meditation, yoga, etc., pertain to me; for the superimposition of 'I' and 'mine' which is dependent on the non-self has been destroyer. That one which remains (after the sublation of all else) - that auspicious absolute (self) I am.

न माता पिता वा न देवा न लोका न वेदा न यज्ञा न तीर्थं ब्रुवन्ति ।

सुषुप्तौ निरस्तातिशून्यात्मकत्वात्तदेकोऽवशिष्टः शिवः केवलोऽहम् ॥ ३॥

Neither mother, nor father, nor the Gods, nor the worlds, nor the Vedas, nor the sacrifices, nor place of pilgrimage are there, they say, in sleep. Because (in sleep) there is not absolute void either, that one which remains (after the sublation of all else) - that auspicious absolute (self) I am.

न साङ्ख्यं न शैवं न तत्पाञ्चरात्रं न जैनं न मीमांसकादेर्मतं वा ।

विशिष्टानुभूत्या विशुद्धात्मकत्वात्तदेकोऽवशिष्टः शिवः केवलोऽहम् ॥ ४॥

Neither the Sankhya, nor the Śaiva, nor the Pañcarātra, nor the Jaina, nor the Mīmāṃsā, etc. (are valid doctrines); for, by unique experience (it is shown that) the Self is extremely pure. That one which remains (after the sublation of all else) - that auspicious absolute (self) I am.

न चोर्ध्वं न चाधो न चान्तर्न बाह्यं न मध्यं न तिर्यङ् न पूर्वाऽपरा दिक् ।

वियद्व्यापकत्वादखण्डैकरूपः तदेकोऽवशिष्टः शिवः केवलोऽहम् ॥ ५॥

Neither above, nor below, nor inside, nor outside, nor in the middle, nor athwart, nor in the eastern nor in the western direction (am I). Since I am all-pervading like ether, I am undivided by nature. That one which remains (after the sublation of all else) 0 that auspicious absolute (self) I am.

न शुक्लं न कृष्णं न रक्तं न पीतं न कुब्जं न पीनं न ह्रस्वं न दीर्घम् ।

अरूपं तथा ज्योतिराकारकत्वात्तदेकोऽवशिष्टः शिवः केवलोऽहम् ॥ ६॥

Neither white, nor black, nor red, nor yellow, neither small, nor large, neither short, nor long (am I); likewise (I am) without form; for I am of the nature of light. That one which remains (after the negation of all else) - that auspicious absolute (self) I am.

न शास्ता न शास्त्रं न शिष्यो न शिक्षा न च त्वं न चाहं न चायं प्रपञ्चः ।

स्वरूपावबोधो विकल्पासहिष्णुः तदेकोऽवशिष्टः शिवः केवलोऽहम् ॥ ७॥

Neither preceptor, nor scripture (there is), neither pupil nor instruction; neither you nor I, nor this universe. The awareness of one's nature does not admit of alternatives. That one which remains (after the sublation of all else) that auspicious absolute (self) I am.

न जाग्रन् न मे स्वप्नको वा सुषुप्तिः न विश्वो न वा तैजसः प्राज्ञको वा ।
अविद्यात्मकत्वात् त्रयाणां तुरीयः तदेकोऽवशिष्टः शिवः केवलोऽहम् ॥ ८॥

Neither the state of waking nor that of dream nor that of deep-sleep is for me; neither the Viśva nor the Tejasa nor the Prajñā (am I). Since the three are of the nature of lack of awareness, I am the Fourth. That one which remains (after the sublation of all else) - that auspicious absolute (self) I am.

अपि व्यापकत्वात् हितत्त्वप्रयोगात्स्वतः सिद्धभावादनन्याश्रयत्वात् ।
जगत् तुच्छमेतत् समस्तं तदन्यत्तदेकोऽवशिष्टः शिवः केवलोऽहम् ॥ ९॥

Because that (the Self) is all-pervasive, the true goal, of self-established nature, and not dependent on anything else, this entire universe which is different from that is unreal. That one which remains (after the sublation of all else) - that auspicious absolute (self) I am.

न चैकं तदन्यद् द्वितीयं कुतः स्यात् न केवलत्वं न चाकेवलत्वम् ।
न शून्यं न चाशून्यमद्वैतकत्वात् कथं सर्ववेदान्तसिद्धं ब्रवीमि ॥ १०॥

That (self) is not even one; how can a second, as different from that be? There is not (for it) absoluteness, nor non-absoluteness. Neither the void nor the non-void is it because it is the non-dual (reality). How can I describe that which is established by all the Vedāntas?

॥ इति श्रीमद् शंकराचार्यविरचितं दशश्लोकी समाप्तं ॥

Śaṅkara also gave out these ślokas to His disciples before leaving this world, when they asked Him to instruct them on the ideas to be contemplated and meditated upon.

Śaṅkara prostrated before the great Sage, Govinda Bhagavatpāda, and said:

"You are certainly the Sage Patañjali, the personification of Yoga Śāstra. You are born of the great Nāga, Ādi Śeṣa. Like the drums of Mahādeva, you sound and resound supreme wisdom. Your glory is infinite. You have perfection, having imbibed the total knowledge from Śrī Gaudapāda, the disciple of Śukadeva, the son of Vedavyāsa. I plead you to accept me as your Śiṣya and bestow on me the knowledge of Brahman. Please accept the prayer of this earnest seeker by showing him how to realize the Absolute Truth."

Govinda Bhagavatpāda was protecting the wealth of Jñāna and had been waiting to hand it over to the owner. And he knew the time had come for the handing over. At an Śubha Muhūrta, Śaṅkara was accepted as a Śiṣya by esteemed Govinda Bhagavatpāda, who initiated him into the Paramahamsa order of Sanyāsa.

Śaṅkara now becomes Śrī Śaṅkarācārya.

Govinda Bhagavatpāda started to instruct the discipline of Yoga to Śrī Śaṅkarācārya. The course of studies started with Hatha Yoga in the first year. Hatha yoga prepares the body for the spiritual path via physical and breathing exercises and asceticism. It prepares and conditions the body so that the mind can practice meditation to overcome obstacles. Ādi Śaṅkarācārya effortlessly mastered the Hatha Yoga in the first year.

Govinda Bhagavatpāda then taught Rāja Yoga, the science of disciplining the mind. Rāja Yoga is the king of all Yogas, and it is concerned with the mind. It transcends the physical body. The Yogī, sitting in a comfortable posture, watches his mind and silences his thoughts. He stills the mind, restrains the thoughts and enters into the thoughtless state. Śrī Śaṅkara mastered this discipline in the second year.

Due to his ascetic effort and transcending his physical and mental boundaries, he attained several psychic powers like telepathy, clairvoyance, movement in space unseen and Icchāmṛtyu "इच्छामृत्यु", death at will.

In this third year, Govinda Bhagavatpāda initiated his Śiṣya into the exalted discipline of Jñāna Yoga, the Realization of Ultimate Reality through Knowledge. Jñāna Yoga is the road to perfection since it helps the Yogī perceive Truth in its entirety without any trappings. It involves (1) Developing precise awareness of the mind, the body, and the Ātman, (2) Purification of the body and the mind through self-discipline, and (3) Acquiring true awareness of the world around and beyond. Knowledge of Sat (Truth) and Asat (Falsehood), and (4) Practicing elimination of thought process.

By practising Jñāna Yoga, Śrī Śaṅkara (a) became free from all illusions and delusions, (b) became remarkably clear-minded and fearless, (c) became not stained by any longings, high or low, (d) became qualified to make the bold leap into the Impersonal 'beyond', and (c) lost all sense of individuality in the ocean of Infinity.

Govinda Bhagavatpāda made Śrī Śaṅkara undergo the duly regulated scheme of Sravana-Manana-Nidhidhyasana. This involves (a) hearing the spiritual truths and secrets from the mouth of the Guru, (b) investigating and discussing them, and (c) constant contemplation of them.

Govinda Bhagavatpāda established Śrī Śaṅkara in the higher planes of spiritual striving and truth-experiencing. He found that Śrī Śaṅkara's spiritual practice and education were completed, and he had reached the highest state. He needed no more training and no further instruction. He had become firmly established in Self-Knowledge. But Śrī Śaṅkara never demonstrated his Siddhis out of vanity. He was full of compassion for serving humanity.

Realising that his training of Śrī Śaṅkara had been completed, Govinda Bhagavatpāda felt that it was time for his departure from the world. He addressed Śrī Śaṅkara calmly:

"My son, you are born with a divine mandate to re-establish the Vaidika Dharma. You are not meant to merely swim safely across the waters of life and death. You have already done that as naturally as a fish swimming in water. Now, you must help others to do the swimming across. See reflections of Rama, Kṛṣṇa and Vyāsa in yourself. Now my work is completed. I have passed on to you the

Jñāna, which I inherited from my Guru. You are destined to accomplish much more."

Śrī Śaṅkara acknowledged His Guru's orders with silent consent.

On an auspicious Muhūrta, Govinda Bhagavatpāda smilingly cast off his mortal remain in Samādhi. The Śiṣyas performed the last rites on the banks of Narmadā in devotion befitting an exalted Yogī.

Sunidhi: What happened next?

Ācārya: Ādi Śaṅkara, along with a few other Sanyāsis, proceeded to Kāśi as his Guru had ordained. Kāśi lies between two holy rivers, Varana to the North and Asi, which joins the Gaṅgā in the South. It is called Kāśi because it is believed that supreme brilliance shines here and lights the way to Heaven.

With the holy Gaṅgā on one side, Śrī Śaṅkara was having the Darśana of Lord Viśvanātha and Devī Viśālākṣī every day. He was soon 'discovered' as an enlightened person. Earnest seekers flocked around Him in increasing numbers. He began teaching them the Absolute Truth. Within a short time, his vast learning, unusual gifts of exposition, astounding intellectual keenness, and charming personality became widely known. Scholars and monks belonging to diverse philosophical sects and owing allegiance to various systems of thought like Jaina and Buddha approached Śrī Śaṅkara and had their doubts cleared on the Absolute Truth.

Thus, His life task of re-establishing the Vaidika Dharma in the world had its auspicious beginning in Kāśi. Many scholars enter into debate with Śrī Śaṅkara to establish the superiority of their viewpoints. He patiently heard them and defeated them in arguments with his irrefutable reasoning. In the presence of the genius of the Young-Sanyāsi, others aspiring for victory were humbled, and they felt blessed to realise the Truth.

One day, a Brāhmaṇa youth named Sanandana from South India arrived at Kāśi. For many years, he had been in search of a Guru who would put him on the sure path to Absolute Knowledge. He heard of Śrī Śaṅkara's uncommon genius, developed a high regard for Him, and requested him to be his Guru. Śaṅkara surveyed the youth and, after putting a few queries, permitted him to stay with him.

After some time, Sanandana begged Śrī Śaṅkara to initiate him into Sanyāsa, to which Śrī Śaṅkara obliged. Thus, Sanandana became the first Sanyāsi disciple to Śrī Śaṅkara.

Śrī Śaṅkara thus became Guru Śrī Śaṅkarācārya.

Sanandana, as a boy, had developed a religious turn of mind and went to a hill called Ahobala in the south to realise God. He had engaged himself in the worship of Lord Nṛsiṅha; the Lion headed Avatāra of Lord Viṣṇu.

One day, a hunter came to him and asked him, "Why are you living alone in this uninhabited forest?" He told the hunter that he was looking for a creature with a lion's face and a human body. He asked the hunter to help him find it. The hunter returned after a while with an image of Nṛsiṅha wrapped in green leaves.

Sanandana prostrated before this image and prayed. Lord Nṛsiṅha appeared before Sanandana, asking him, "Dear child, ask for a boon." Sanandana asked for 'Abhaya', and "It is also my wish that whenever I remember you, you shall appear and help me out of my difficulty." "Be it so," said the Lord and disappeared.

Sanandana was highly devoted to his Guru. He constantly stayed by the side of Śaṅkarācārya, serving his Guru. Endowed with superior intelligence and a deep knowledge of the scriptures, he was able to win the complete confidence of his Guru and soon became his favourite.

The other disciples, human as they were, looked at Sanandana with jealousy. This did not escape Ācārya's eye. And strangely he made everyone understand and concede the superiority of Sanandana.

One day, Sanandana had reached the other side of the river on some errand. He had crossed the river by means of a bridge close by. Desiring to give to all an exhibition of his unequalled Guru Bhakti, Ācārya cried out in a loud voice, "O Sanandana, come to me at once!"

This fright-filled call of his Guru disturbed Sanandana a great deal. He felt for sure that his master was in some danger and needed immediate help. But he saw that getting to the opposite bank of the river by walking over the bridge would mean a waste of time. The call of his Guru was a distress signal and had to be responded to immediately. He was in no mood to calculate and count the pros and cons of his action. And so, he answered his Guru's call by simply getting into the river and walking.

The water was cold, and the current was strong enough to sweep away even an elephant. But in Sanandana's mind, there was no river to be crossed, no cold to be borne, no danger to be faced. Only the call of the Guru sounded in his ears, and only the need to be near his Guru as quickly as possible was in his mind. He was utterly oblivious to every other consideration.

The onlookers were sure that he would sink in the water and perish. They raised shouts of alarm and waved at him, warning him. Sanandana was deaf and blind to everything. And then, a miracle happened. He did not sink. At every step of his foot bloomed a lotus and supported him, and he crossed the river walking on the bed of lotuses. Sanandana ran breathlessly and stood before Ācārya for his commands.

The other disciples stood amazed at this supernatural happening and were dumbfounded. Then, pointing to Sanandana, Ācārya addressed his other disciples, "You have now witnessed what immense grace the Devī Bhagavati has on Sanandana. Henceforth, we will call him Padmapāda, the lotus-footed". Padmapāda, with a sense of humility and a spirit of dedication, bowed again and again at the holy feet of Śrī Śaṅkarācārya.

One day, Śrī Śaṅkarācārya, accompanied by his disciples, was proceeding to the Gaṅgā for a bath. On the way, He saw a pathetic sight. A young woman was crying loudly and soliciting help. A dead body, possibly of her husband, lay on the ground, its head resting on her lap. She wanted proper performance of the funeral rites of her departed husband. She had been sitting with a corpse in such a way that the narrow path leading to the river was totally blocked.

Śrī Śaṅkarācārya requested the woman to move the corpse to one side of the pathway so that He could proceed to the river. The women could not pay attention to Śrī Śaṅkarācārya's words. On being repeatedly requested by Him to move the body to one side of the pathway, the woman responded by telling him, "Why, Great Soul, why do you not yourself ask the corpse to move aside?"

The Guru responded to her in a voice choked with compassion, "Mother, I understand your grief. However, can a corpse ever move of its own accord?"

The woman then fixed her gaze on Śrī Śaṅkarācārya and spoke, "You best of Sanyāsis, you say that it is the one and only Brahman who is the sole authority of the universe and Śakti is indifferent. Is this not so? When Brahman is present everywhere, why should not the corpse move? Brahman is present there, too."

The Guru stood astonished and began to think over what she said. And all of a sudden, both the woman and the corpse disappeared! He experienced the sportive play of the Great Devī, Mahāmāyā, who is Śakti or the 'Prime Energy'. It was because of her glance that earth and heaven throbbed. Prostrating, The Guru began to sing in praise of the Devī Tripurāsundarī, the sole refuge of the universe:

He spontaneously venerated her with Bhavānyaṣṭakam.

Sunidhi: Kindly tell us about that, Guruji!

Ācārya: Here you go. This is one of my favourite Stotras.

न पुत्रो न पुत्री न भृत्यो न भर्ता ।

न जाया न विद्या न वृत्तिर्ममैव

गतिस्त्वं गतिस्त्वं त्वमेका भवानि ॥१॥

Neither the mother nor the father, neither the relation nor the friend, neither the son nor the daughter, neither the servant nor the husband, neither the wife nor the knowledge, and neither my sole occupation is my refuges that I can depend, oh, Bhāvāni. So, O Devī, you are my refuge and my only refuge, Bhāvāni.

भवाब्धावपारे महादुःखभीरु

पपात प्रकामी प्रलोभी प्रमत्तः ।

कुसंसारपाशप्रबद्धः सदाहं

गतिस्त्वं गतिस्त्वं त्वमेका भवानि ॥२॥

I am in this ocean of birth and death, i am a coward, who dare not face sorrow, i am filled with lust and sin, i am filled with greed and desire, and tied i am, by this useless life that i lead. So, O Devī, you are my refuge and my only refuge, Bhāvāni.

न जानामि दानं न च ध्यानयोगं

न जानामि तन्त्रं न च स्तोत्रमन्त्रम् ।

न जानामि पूजां न च न्यासयोगं
गतिस्त्वं गतिस्त्वं त्वमेका भवानि ॥३॥

Neither do i know how to give, nor do i know how to meditate, neither do i know tantra, nor do i know stanzas of prayer, neither do i know how to worship, nor do i know the art of yoga. So, O Devī, you are my refuge and my only refuge, Bhāvāni.

न जानामि पुण्यं न जानामि तीर्थं
न जानामि मुक्तिं लयं वा कदाचित् ।
न जानामि भक्तिं व्रतं वापि मात
र्गतिस्त्वं गतिस्त्वं त्वमेका भवानि ॥४॥

Know I not how to be righteous, know I not the way to the places sacred, know I not methods of salvation, know I not how to merge my mind with god, know I not the art of devotion, know I not how to practice austerities, oh, mother. So, O Devī, you are my refuge and my only refuge, Bhāvāni.

कुकर्मी कुसङ्गी कुबुद्धिः कुदासः
कुलाचारहीनः कदाचारलीनः ।
कुदृष्टिः कुवाक्यप्रबन्धः सदाहं
गतिस्त्वं गतिस्त्वं त्वमेका भवानि ॥५॥

Perform I bad actions, keep I the company of bad ones, think I bad and sinful thoughts, serve I bad masters, belong I to a bad family, immersed I am in sinful acts, see I with bad intentions, write I collection of bad words, always and always. So, O Devī, you are my refuge and my only refuge, Bhāvāni.

प्रजेशं रमेशं महेशं सुरेशं
दिनेशं निशीथेश्वरं वा कदाचित् ।
न जानामि चान्यत् सदाहं शरण्ये
गतिस्त्वं गतिस्त्वं त्वमेका भवानि ॥६॥

Neither do I know the creator, nor the lord of Lakṣmī, neither do I know the lord of all, nor do I know the lord of devas, neither do I know the god who makes the day, nor the god who rules at night, neither do I know any other gods, O Devī to whom I bow always. So, O Devī, you are my refuge and my only refuge, Bhāvāni.

विवादे विषादे प्रमादे प्रवासे
जले चानले पर्वते शत्रुमध्ये ।
अरण्ये शरण्ये सदा मां प्रपाहि
गतिस्त्वं गतिस्त्वं त्वमेका भवानि ॥७॥

While I am in a heated argument, while I am immersed in sorrow, while I am suffering an accident, while I am travelling far off, while I am in water or fire, while I am on the top of a mountain, while enemies surround me, and while I am in a deep forest, O Devī, I always bow before thee. So, O Devī, you are my refuge and my only refuge, Bhāvāni.

अनाथो दरिद्रो जरारोगयुक्तो
महाक्षीणदीनः सदा जाड्यवक्त्रः ।
विपत्तौ प्रविष्टः प्रनष्टः सदाहं
गतिस्त्वं गतिस्त्वं त्वमेका भवानि ॥८॥

While being an orphan, while being extremely poor, affected by the disease of old age, while I am terribly tired, while I am in a pitiful state, with problems swallowing me, and while I suffer serious dangers, I always bow before thee. So, O Devī, you are my refuge and my only refuge, Bhāvāni.

Sunidhi: What happened next?

Ācārya: Śrī Śaṅkarācārya understood that the Devī Supreme, whom the Lord Himself worshipped, had made him realise her magnanimous glory and grace. She was the Creator, the Preserver, and the Destroyer of this universe, and it was She again who bestowed material abundance.

He had already experienced that the individual Soul (Jiva) and the Infinite Soul (Brahman) were identical. He now understood that the Brahman was just a witness, a mere spectator and no more. The authorship of the universe was that of Śakti, The Prime Energy.

Śrī Śaṅkarācārya understood that remaining immersed in deep meditation would not help him to accomplish his life's purpose. He would have to work out a practical application to life and labour on earth of his experience of Absolute Reality. Only then would he become the meaningful living embodiment.

Sunidhi: Did he have similar experiences with Lord Mahādeva also?

Ācārya: Certainly! When Mother Bhāvāni played Her Līlā in the life of Śaṅkara, would Mahādeva, the consort of Bhāvāni, be left behind? On another day, when Śrī Śaṅkarācārya with his Śiṣyas was going to bath in the holy Gaṅgā, he saw a Caṇḍāla (an untouchable). He had four fat dogs held on a leash and was approaching drunkenly from the opposite direction.

Finding no other way of avoiding a confrontation with him, Śrī Śaṅkarācārya addressed him and said, "Oh, you Caṇḍāla, step aside with your dogs, and let us go". The Caṇḍāla did not heed his words and continued to advance. Śrī Śaṅkarācārya, in a somewhat excited voice, cried out again, "Stop, fellow, stop. Leave a passage free for us". The terrible-looking Caṇḍāla burst out: "Whom are you asking to move aside, Sir? Are you demanding the self to do so or the body to do so? The Self is omnipresent, non-active, ever pure by nature. Instead, if you ask the physical body to move aside, you know that the body is inert matter; how can it move aside at all?

"Moreover, in what respect is your body distinct and different from any other body? You say that you are firmly established and rooted in the Supreme Truth, and there is One non-dual entity, 'One without a Second'. I see that your claim is false; you are indulging in plain talk. Is there any difference between a

Caṇḍāla and a Brāhmaṇa from the viewpoint of the knower of the Truth? Is Sūrya reflected in the waters of Gaṅgā any different from Sūrya reflected in a dirty water pool? Is this your knowledge of the all-ness and the Absolute Reality?"

Sunidhi: This is incredibly profound. What happened next?

Ācārya: Hearing these words of the Caṇḍāla, charged with wisdom, Śrī Śaṅkarācārya was both amazed and ashamed. He clearly perceived that this was the play of the Divine. He remembered what Kṛṣṇa had said in Bhagavadgītā 5.18.

विद्याविनयसंपन्ने ब्राह्मणे गवि हस्तिनि ।

शुनि चैव श्वपाके च पण्डिताः समदर्शिनः ॥

A wise man sees with an equal eye the learned and cultured Brāhmaṇa, the cow, the elephant, the dog, the outcaste.

Immediately, Śrī Śaṅkarācārya folded his palms in adoration and spoke prayerfully, "He who perceives all beings with an awareness of "sameness" and acts with that perception of sameness in all, he indeed is my Guru. You Caṇḍāla are my Guru. I bow down at your holy feet a million times".

All of a sudden, the Caṇḍāla and his dogs disappeared. But Śrī Śaṅkarācārya saw the Divine form of the glorious Lord of the Universe, Śrī Mahādeva. The Lord stood before him in all glory holding in His hands the four Vedas. These eternal scriptures were what Śrī Śaṅkarācārya had seen as dogs before. He bowed down at the feet of the Great Lord and spontaneously sang the मनीषापञ्चकं Manīṣāpañcakaṃ Stotra.

Sunidhi: Guruji, kindly tell us about this Manīṣāpañcakaṃ Stotra.

In the Stotra, the first couple of ślokas are about the question of the Caṇḍāla. The response of Ādi Śaṅkara follows that. In the Manīṣāpañcakaṃ Stotra, in the first four ślokas, the non-duality as specified in the four Vedas is glorified. The fifth śloka glorifies the Pranava Mantra, 'OM', which includes the four Vedas.

The Caṇḍāla asked:

सत्याचार्यस्य गमने कदाचिन्मुक्ति दायकम् ।

काशीक्शेत्रं प्रति सह गौर्या मार्गे तु शङ्करम् ॥

अन्त्यवेषधरं दृष्ट्वा गच्छ गच्छेति चाब्रवीत् ।

शङ्करःसोऽपि चाण्डलस्तं पुनः प्राह शङ्करम् ॥

अन्नमयादन्नमयमथवा चैतन्यमेव चैतन्यात् ।

यतिवर दूरीकर्तुं वाञ्छसि किं ब्रूहि गच्छ गच्छेति ॥

O great Sanyāsi! Tell me. Do you want me to keep a distance from you, by uttering 'go away' 'go away' taking me to be an outcaste? Is it addressed from one body made of food to another body made of food, or is it consciousness from consciousness - which, O, the best among Sanyāsis, you wish should go away, by saying "go away, go away"? Do tell me.

प्रत्यग्वस्तुनि निस्तरङ्गसहजानन्दावबोधाम्बुधौ
विप्रोऽयं श्वपचोऽयमित्यपि महान्कोऽयं विभेदभ्रमः ।
किं गङ्गाम्बुनि बिम्बितेऽम्बरमणौ चाण्डालवीथीपयः
पूरे वाऽन्तरमस्ति काञ्चनघटीमृत्कुम्भयोर्वाऽम्बरे ॥

Answer me. While the Supreme Being is reflected in every object as the Sūrya's reflection could be seen in the peaceful waveless water bodies, why this doubting confusion and differentiation, i.e. whether one is a Brāhmaṇa or an outcaste? Who is the superior one, etc? Is there any difference in the reflection of Sūrya in the waters of the Gaṅgā or the water present in the street of an outcaste?

Likewise, is there any difference when the water- containers happen to be golden vessels and earthen pots?

Immediately Śaṅkarācārya realises the presence of the Lord Śaṅkara before him who has apparently shown Himself with a view to removing the last vestige of imperfection in His Śiṣya and reels off the following five Ślokas - constituting 'Manīṣāpañcakaṃ'- ending with a further stanza in the form of an epilogue.

जाग्रत्स्वप्नसुषुप्तिषु स्फुटतरा या संविदुज्जृम्भते
या ब्रह्मादिपिपीलिकान्ततनुषु प्रोता जगत्साक्षिणी ।
सैवाहं न च दृश्यवस्त्विति दृढप्रज्ञापि यस्यास्ति चे-
च्चाण्डालोऽस्तु स तु द्विजोऽस्तु गुरुरित्येषा मनीषा मम ॥ १॥

If one is convinced firmly that he is that very Ātman which manifests itself in all the conditions of sleep, wakefulness and dream, in all the objects from the great Brahmā (the creator) to the tiny ant and which is also the vibrant but invisible, witnesser of all, then as per my clear conclusion, he is the great Guru, be he a twice-born (Brāhmaṇa) or an outcaste (Caṇḍāla).

ब्रह्मैवाहमिदं जगच्च सकलं चिन्मात्रविस्तारितं
सर्वं चैतदविद्यया त्रिगुणयाऽशेषं मया कल्पितम् ।
इत्थं यस्य दृढा मतिः सुखतरे नित्ये परे निर्मले
चाण्डालोऽस्तु स तु द्विजोऽस्तु गुरुरित्येषा मनीषा मम ॥ २॥

I am quite convinced that he is the great Master, be he a Brāhmaṇa or an outcaste, who, dwelling on the pure and infinite Brahman thinks of himself as that very Brahman, of whose manifestation the whole Universe is, though apparently the Universe is assumed to consist of different things, due to ignorance and the three Guṇas, Sattva, Rajas, and Tamas.

शश्वन्नश्वरमेव विश्वमखिलं निश्चित्य वाचा गुरो-
र्नित्यं ब्रह्म निरन्तरं विमृशता निर्व्याजशान्तात्मना ।
भूतं भावि च दुष्कृतं प्रदहता संविन्मये पावके
प्रारब्धाय समर्पितं स्ववपुरित्येषा मनीषा मम ॥ ३॥

I am fully convinced by the Guru's words that the entire Universe is a transitory illusion and that the human body is given to constantly meditate on the infinite and Supreme Being with a serene and unquestioning mind and thus to burn in that Sacred Fire the sins with which the human is born.

या तिर्यङ्नरदेवताभिरहमित्यन्तः स्फुटा गृह्यते
यद्भासा हृदयाक्षदेहविषया भान्ति स्वतोऽचेतनाः ।
तां भास्यैः पिहितार्कमण्डलनिभां स्फूर्तिं सदा भावय-
न्योगी निर्वृतमानसो हि गुरुरित्येषा मनीषा मम ॥ ४॥

In my considered opinion that Yogī is great who has clearly grasped within himself the truth and quality of the Supreme Being through which all our activities are performed and whose effulgence is hidden by ignorance of an ordinary person even as the Sūrya's halo is concealed by the clouds.

यत्सौख्याम्बुधिलेशलेशत इमे शक्रादयो निर्वृता
यच्चित्ते नितरां प्रशान्तकलने लब्ध्वा मुनिर्निर्वृतः ।
यस्मिन्नित्यसुखाम्बुधौ गलितधीर्ब्रह्मैव न ब्रह्मविद्
यः कश्चित्स सुरेन्द्रवन्दितपदो नूनं मनीषा मम ॥ ५॥

I am convinced that whoever has his mind dwelling upon the Great Being who is being worshipped by Indra and other gods and is thus completely at peace with himself has not only understood Brahman, but he is himself that great Brahman!

दासस्तेऽहं देहदृष्ट्याऽस्मि शंभो
जातस्तेंऽशो जीवदृष्ट्या त्रिदृष्टे ।
सर्वस्याऽऽत्मन्नात्मदृष्ट्या त्वमेवे-
त्येवं मे धीर्निश्चिता सर्वशास्त्रैः ॥

O Lord! In the form of body, I am your servant. In the form of life, O three-eyed one, I am part of yourself. In the form of soul, you are within me and in every other soul. I have arrived at this conclusion through my intellect and on the authority of the various scriptures.

॥ इति श्रीमच्छङ्करभगवतः कृतौ मनीषापञ्चकं सम्पूर्णम् ॥

Sunidhi: Kindly continue with Ādi Śaṅkara's legend.

Ācārya: Pleased by this Stotra, Lord Mahādeva placed his hand on Śaṅkara's head and said: "Child, I am pleased. I wish that you work towards the re-establishment of Vaidika Dharma on earth, the Spiritual Discipline described in the Vedas. You must give out a flawless meaning of Vedānta and remove duality and darkness. You must write out a commentary on the Brahmasūtra of Vyāsa and firmly establish that knowledge of Brahman. You have to preach the Vaidika Dharma in such a way as to make it available to all". Mahādeva then disappeared!

Soon after, as per the wishes of Mahādeva, Ācārya was explaining to his Śiṣyas the commentary on the Brahmasūtras when an aged Brāhmaṇa entered the place. The lesson was stopped as the venerable old man stepped in, and everyone there got up and, with great reverence, requested him to take a seat.

Without taking the offered seat, the old man queried: "I hear that a certain Sanyāsi here gives a detailed explanation of the Brahmasūtras. Can you tell me where he is?"

The disciples answered: "This is our Guru Śaṅkarācārya, who has all the Śāstras in his memory, and they are all at his fingertips. He has written a commentary on the Brahmasūtras, which has silenced all critics. He is now teaching us that valuable treasure".

Then the old man took a seat and requested the Ācārya: "They call you the commentator on the Brahmasūtra composed by Vedavyāsa. Well, I want to see if your commentary agrees with my interpretation. Please tell me the meaning of the first section of the third chapter".

Everyone was stunned by the authority of the old man's poser of the question.

With great humility, Ācārya said: "To all masters who know the meaning of the Sūtras, I offer my salutations. I have no such egoistic feeling that I am a great comprehender of the Sūtras. I shall try to answer all your questions".

With these words, Ācārya started giving out a correct explanation of the Sūtra that the old man had asked. Ācārya found in the old man a very powerful contestant. Hardly had the Ācārya put forth a point with his unmatched brilliance, the old man cut short with what struck everyone as an unassailable objection.

With great steadiness, Ācārya met the old man's objections with replies, strikingly sensible and impressively rational. But the old man would not be silenced. He would put forth another argument, only to draw out a more powerful counter-argument from Śrī Śaṅkarācārya.

Indeed, this battle of wits went on and on. In this volley of dialogue, the whole of the Brahmasūtras, the four Vedas, many scriptures, and various philosophies all came in for analysis, elucidation, research and summing up.

The combatants were far removed in age from each other but so alike in wisdom and learning. The astoundingly deep scholarship, the astonishing power of memory, the limitless sweep of intellect, the rare depths of introspection, and the powerful skill in debate made the disciples dazed and dumbfounded as the entertaining warfare went on.

The Himalayan debate raged for several days. Padmapāda, who had followed this clash of high talent with keen understanding, approached the Ācārya in private and asked him, "Master, who other than Vedavyāsa can possess all this superior scholarship, this sharp intellect and this great skill of debate? Is it possible that he is Vedavyāsa in the disguise of an old man, and we stand outwitted as to his real identity?"

The next day, Ācārya addressed the old man: "Great soul, we have been eager to know who you are. All of us believe that you are indeed Vedavyāsa. If our feeling is right, please accept our salutations".

The spontaneity and sincerity of Ācārya's words touched the Brāhmaṇa deeply, and he told the Ācārya that his inference was correct and that he was indeed Vedavyāsa.

Ācārya and all the disciples prostrated before Śrī Vedavyāsa. Placing his hand on Ācārya's bowed head, the greatest of the sages blessed the young Sanyāsi.

Ādi Śaṅkara spontaneously composed the following in praise of the great Maharṣi.

व्यासं वसिष्ठनप्तारं शक्तेः पौत्रमकल्मषम् ।

पराशरात्मजं वन्दे शुकतातं तपोनिधिम् ॥

"I bow down to Sage Vyāsa, the son of Parāśara, the grandson of Vasishta, who is free from impurities, and the father of Shuka, a treasure trove of austerity."

व्यासाय विष्णुरूपाय व्यासरूपाय विष्णवे ।

नमो वै ब्रह्मनिधये वासिष्ठाय नमो नमः ॥

"I bow to Vyāsa who is the form of Viṣṇu, and to Viṣṇu who is the form of Vyāsa. Salutations to the treasure of Brahman, salutations again and again to Vaśiṣṭha."

कृष्णद्वैपायनं व्यासं सर्वलोकहिते रतम् ।

वेदाब्जभास्करं वन्दे शमादिनिलयं मुनिम् ॥

"I salute Vyāsa, the son of Parāśara, who is devoted to the well-being of all beings, Sūrya who illuminates the lotus of the Vedas, and the Sage who dwells in tranquillity and other virtues."

वेदव्यासं स्वात्मरूपं सत्यसन्धं परायणम् ।

शान्तं जितेन्द्रियक्रोधं सशिष्यं प्रणमाम्यहम् ॥

"I bow down to Sage Vyāsa, who is the embodiment of the Vedas, the abode of truth, and the ultimate refuge. He is peaceful, free from anger, and has conquered his senses. With disciples, I offer my salutations."

अचतुर्वदनो ब्रह्मा द्विबाहुरपरो हरिः ।

अफाललोचनः शम्भुः भगवान् बादरायणः ॥

"Brahmā, who has four faces, Viṣṇu, who has two arms, Śiva, who has three eyes and is without a wife, And the Lord, Bādarāyaṇa, Vyāsa, the son of Parāśara."

शङ्करं शङ्कराचार्यं केशवं बादरायणम् ।

सूत्रभाष्यकृतौ वन्दे भगवन्तौ पुनः पुनः ॥

"I bow again and again to Śaṅkara (Śiva), to Adi Śaṅkarācārya, to Kesava (Viṣṇu), and to Bādarāyaṇa (Vyāsa), the authors of the sūtras and their commentaries."

ब्रह्मसूत्रकृते तस्मै वेदव्यासाय वेधसे ।

ज्ञानशक्त्यवताराय नमो भगवतो हरेः ॥

"I offer my salutations to the blessed Vyāsa, the compiler of the Vedas, who authored the Brahma Sutras. He is the incarnation of the power of knowledge, and I bow to the divine Lord Hari."

व्यासः समस्तधर्माणां वक्ता मुनिवरेडितः ।

चिरञ्जीवी दीर्घमायुर्ददातु जटिलो मम ॥

"Vyāsa, praised by the best among sages, is the expounder of all dharmas. May the long-lived Vyāsa, the knotted-haired Sage, grant me a long life."

प्रज्ञाबलेन तपसा चतुर्वेदविभाजकः ।

कृष्णद्वैपायनो यश्च तस्मै श्रीगुरवे नमः ॥

"I bow to the revered Guru who, with the strength of wisdom and austerity, divided the four Vedas, and to Krishna Dvaipāyana Vyāsa."

जटाधरस्तपोनिष्ठः शुद्धयोगो जितेन्द्रियः ।

कृष्णाजिनधरः कृष्णस्तस्मै श्रीगुरवे नमः ॥

"I bow to the revered Guru, who wears matted locks, is steadfast in austerity, practices pure yoga, and has conquered the senses. He who wears the garment of deerskin, Kṛṣṇa, I offer my salutations."

भारतस्य विधाता च द्वितीय इव यो हरिः ।

हरिभक्तिपरो यश्च तस्मै श्रीगुरवे नमः ॥

"I bow to the revered Guru who is like the second creator of Bharata (India), and who is devoted to Hari (Viṣṇu). He who is devoted to the worship of Hari, I offer my salutations."

जयति पराशरसूनुः सत्यवतीहृदयनन्दनो व्यासः ।

यस्यास्य कमलगलितं भारतममृतं जगत्पिबति ॥

"Victory to the son of Parāśara, the joy of Satyavati's heart, Vyāsa! By whose composition, the nectar of Bharata (India), sweet as the lotus, is drunk by the world."

वेदविभागविधात्रे विमलाय ब्रह्मणे नमो विश्वदृशे ।

सकलधृतिहेतुसाधनसूत्रसृजे सत्यवत्यभिव्यक्तिमते ॥

"I bow to the pure Brahman, the divider of the Vedas, the seer of the universe. The one who manifests the expression of Satyavati, the creator of the thread of means for upholding all righteousness."

वेदान्तवाक्यकुसुमानि समानि चारु

जग्रन्थ सूत्रनिचयेन मनोहरेण ।

मोक्षार्थिलोकहितकामनया मुनिर्यः

तं बादरायणमहं प्रणमामि भक्त्या ॥

"I bow with devotion to Sage Bādarāyaṇa, who, with the enchanting collection of sutras, wove the beautiful flowers of Vedantic statements, which are equal and pleasing. The Sage, desiring the welfare of the world and liberation seekers, created them."

Āratī: Guruji, who is Sage Bādarāyaṇa, and how is he related to Maharṣi Vyāsa?

Ācārya: Sage Bādarāyaṇa is another name for Maharṣi Vyāsa. He is revered in Hindu tradition as the compiler of the Vedas, the author of the Mahabharata, and the composer of the Brahma Sutras or Vedānta Sutras.

Various names often refer to Vyāsa in different contexts. "Vyāsa" itself means "compiler" or "arranger," indicating his role in compiling and arranging the Vedas. "Bādarāyaṇa" is another name for Vyāsa, derived from the place where he is believed to have resided for some time, which is Badri or Badrikāśrama.

So, Sage Bādarāyaṇa is none other than Maharṣi Vyāsa, both referring to the same revered figure in Hindu tradition, known for his immense contribution to Vaidika literature and philosophy.

Āratī: Kindly tell us the legend of the birth of Maharṣi Parāśara and Maharṣi Vyāsa.

Ācārya: The birth legend of Maharṣi Parāśara is recounted in various Sanātana texts, particularly in the Purāṇas and the Mahābhārata. Parāśara is considered one of the greatest sages of Sanātana Sanskṛti, renowned for his contributions to Jyotiṣa and as the author of the Viṣṇu Purāṇa and Parāśara Smṛti.

Parāśara once halted for a night in a little hamlet on the banks of the river Yamunā. He was put up in the house of the fisherman chieftain Deśarāja. When dawn broke, the chief asked his daughter, Matsyagandhā, whose name means "one with the smell of fish", to ferry the sage to his next destination. When on the ferry, Parāśara was attracted by the beautiful girl and asked her to fulfil his desire to give a son to her. Matsyagandhā refused, fearing the other people and sages who were standing on the bank of the river on the other side.

He then created an island within the river with his mystic power and asked her to land the boat there. On reaching the other side, the sage once again chanted the mantra to make her pregnant, but she declared that her body stank and Parāśara granted her the boon that the finest fragrance may emit from her person. She was, after that, known as Satyavati (enlivened with truth).

The powers of the sage transformed Matsyagandhā into Yojanagandhā, whose fragrance can be smelled from across a yojana. She now smelled of musk. Then, she insisted that the act of getting a child was not appropriate in broad daylight, as her father and others would see them from the other bank; they should wait till night. The sage, with his powers, shrouded the entire area in fog.

Before Parāśara gave her a child, Satyavati again interrupted him to say that he would enjoy his child and depart, leaving her shamed in society. She asked Parāśara to promise her that the childbirth would be a secret and her secret intact; the son born from their union would be as famous as the great sage, and her fragrance and youth would be eternal.

Parāśara granted her these wishes and was satiated by the beautiful Satyavati. Parāśara then gave her a child who was a son called Kṛṣṇa Dvaipāyana was born, who was dark-complexioned and hence may be called by the name Kṛṣṇa and also the name Dvaipāyana, meaning 'island-born'.

He later compiled the classic Vaidika literature of India, and so is called Vyāsa, who is the seventeenth incarnation of Lord Viṣṇu. Leaving Satyavati, Parāśara proceeded to perform Tapasyā. Later, Vyāsa also became a Ṛṣi, and Satyavati returned to her father's house and, in due course, married Śāntanu.

In Anushasana Parva of Mahābhārata, Parāśara told Yudhisthira that he prayed to Śiva. He desired to obtain a son with great ascetic merit, endued with superior energy, earn worldwide fame, and arrange the Vedas. Śiva appeared and granted him his wishes, and in addition, he told him that his son Kṛṣṇa would be one of the Saptarṣis of Savarni manvantara, be immortal by being free of diseases, and he would be the friend of Indra.

Āratī: How about the birth legend of Maharṣi Parāśara?

Ācārya: Maharṣi Parāśara's father was Maharṣi Śakti. Maharṣi Śakti was the son of Maharṣi Vaśiṣṭha and Devī Arundhati. Maharṣi Śakti died in his early age. This made Maharṣi Vaśiṣṭha (Parāśara's grandfather) live in his hermitage with Devī Adṛśyantī (Parāśara's mother).

Vaśiṣṭha heard the chanting of the Vedas, and Adṛśyantī told him that Vaidika hymn sounds were coming from his grandchild, Parāśara, who was developing in her womb. Vaśiṣṭha was happy to hear this. Adṛśyantī gave birth to a son, and the child grew up to become Parāśara.

Parāśara was raised by his grandfather Vaśiṣṭha because he lost his father at an early age. His father, Śakti, was on a journey and came across an angry Rākṣasa who had once been a king but was turned into a demon as a curse from Vaśiṣṭha feeding on human flesh. The demon devoured Parāśara's father. In the Viṣṇu Purāṇa, Parāśara speaks about his anger from this:

I had heard that a Rākṣasa employed by Vishvāmitra had devoured my father: violent anger seized me, and I commenced a sacrifice for the destruction of the Rākṣasas: hundreds of them were reduced to ashes by the rite when, as they were about to be entirely exterminated, my grandfather Vaśiṣṭha said to me: Enough, my child; let your wrath be appeased: the Rākṣasas are not culpable: your father's death was the work of destiny.

Anger is the passion of fools; it becometh not a wise man. By whom, it may be asked, is anyone killed? Every man reaps the consequences of his acts. Anger, my son, is the destruction of all that man obtains by arduous exertions, fame, and devout austerities and prevents the attainment of heaven or emancipation. The chief sages always shun wrath: be not subject to its influence, my child. Let no more of these unoffending spirits of darkness be consumed. Mercy is the might of the righteous.

Āratī: Why did Parāśara Muni limp?

Ācārya: Parāśara lived with his grandfather, Vaśiṣṭha, till he completed his education and then, because of differences with his grandfather, left his Āśrama and founded a new one on the banks of Yamunā. Sage Vaśiṣṭha believed in the supremacy of the Trayi-Vidya, i.e. the Vedas were only three-fold- Rig Yajur and Sama. He refused to give equal status to the followers of Atharvaveda.

Parāśara, however, believed that the Atharvaveda, without which the mind and body could be cured- deserved equal importance. Hence, he left his grandfather's Āśrama and founded a new one. All his life, he went in search of the great sage Jabali - who was said to be the only person who knew the Atharvaveda completely. But during his lifetime he could never meet the great sage. Many years later, his son Vedavyāsa not only met and learnt all Atharvaveda stotras from Jabali but also married the sage's daughter.

Unfortunately, an evil king - a descendant of Kartavirya Arjuna - went on a rampage, killing Brāhmaṇas, plundering Āśramas and prosecuting people. This was just before Santanu came to the throne.

Parāśara tried to stop the king by the ascetic powers and almost succeeded, but during the encounter, he suffered an accident to his leg. He remained lame for the rest of his life.

Āratī: Why did Maharṣi Vishvāmitra plot to kill sage Vashistha's son, Maharṣi Śakti?

Ācārya: Vishvāmitra was the son of King Gadhi and hence was a Kṣatriya. After his father dies, he becomes the king. Once, when he was wandering in the forest for hunting and had become very weak due to thirst and hunger, he reached the hermitage of Maharṣi Vaśiṣṭha.

Mahabharata Adi Parva describes that Maharṣi Vaśiṣṭha welcomed him and his army appropriately by the grace of the divine cow Kāmadhenu. Kāmadhenu could fulfil all demands of anyone. After seeing that cow, King Vishvāmitra wanted her.

He says to Maharṣi Vaśiṣṭha, 'O Brahmana, O great Muni, give me you Kāmadhenu in exchange for ten thousand mudras, or my kingdom.

But sage Vaśiṣṭha has refused to give the cow. He said, 'O sinless one, this cow has been kept by me for the sake of the gods, guests, and the Pitris, as also for my sacrifices. I cannot give her in exchange for even thy kingdom.

After that, there was a great battle between Vishvāmitra and Vaśiṣṭha. And finally, sage Vaśiṣṭha was victorious. Vishvāmitra thought that a Brāhmaṇa had more power than a Kṣatriya. He decided to become a Brahmarṣi.

Vishvāmitra, beholding this wonderful feat that resulted from Brāhmaṇa's prowess, became disgusted with Kṣatriya prowess and said, 'O, fie on Kshatriya prowess! Brahmana prowess is true prowess! In judging strength and weakness, I see that asceticism is true strength.' Saying this, the monarch, abandoning his large domains and regal splendour and turning his back upon all pleasures, set his mind on asceticism. Crowned with success in asceticism and filling the three worlds with the heat of his ascetic penances, he afflicted all creatures and finally became a Brahmana. The son of Kusika at last drank Soma with Indra himself (in Heaven).

Later in the text, the story of Maharṣi Vaśiṣṭha's son is described. Maharṣi Vaśiṣṭha has a hundred sons; the eldest of them is Śakti.

Once, there was a king named Kalmashapada of the Ikshvaku race who was unequalled on earth for prowess. One day, the king went from his capital into the woods for purposes of hunting, and this grinder of foes pierced with his arrows many deer and wild boars. And in those deep woods, the king also slew many rhinoceroses.

Engaged in sport for some length of time, the monarch became very much tired and at last he gave up the chase, desiring to rest awhile. "The great Vishvāmitra, endued with energy, had, a little while ago, desired to make that monarch his disciple. As the monarch, afflicted with hunger and thirst, was proceeding through the woods, he came across the best of Ṛṣis, the illustrious son of Vaśiṣṭha, coming along the same path.

The king, ever victorious in battle, saw that Muni bearing the name of Śakti, that illustrious propagator of Vaśiṣṭha's race, the eldest of the high-souled Vaśiṣṭha's hundred sons, coming along from opposite direction. The king, beholding him, said, 'Stand out of our way.'

The Ṛṣi, addressing the monarch in a conciliatory manner, said unto him sweetly, 'O king, this is my way. This is the eternal rule of morality indicated in every treatise on duty and religion, viz., that a king should ever make way for Brahmanas.' Thus, they addressed each other, respecting their right of way. 'Stand aside, stand aside' were the words they said unto each other. The Ṛṣi, who was in the right, did not yield, nor did the king yield to him from pride and anger.

That best of monarchs, enraged at the Ṛṣi, refusing to yield him the way, acted like a Rākṣasa, striking him with his whip. Thus whipped by the monarch, that best of Ṛṣis, the son of Vaśiṣṭha, was deprived of his senses by anger and speedily cursed that first of monarchs, saying, 'O worst of kings, since thou persecutest like a Rākṣasa an ascetic, thou shalt from this day, became a Rākṣasa subsisting on human flesh! Hence, thou worst of kings! thou shalt wander over the earth, affecting human form!' Thus did the Ṛṣi Sakti, endued with great prowess, speak unto king Kalmashapada.

At this time, Vishvāmitra, between whom and Vaśiṣṭha there was a dispute about the discipleship of Kalmashapada, approached the place where that monarch and Vaśiṣṭha's son were. Vishvāmitra, the Ṛṣi of severe ascetic penances, of great energy, approached the pair (Kalmashapada and Śakti), knowing by his spiritual insight that they had been thus quarrelling with each other.

After the curse had been pronounced, the best of monarchs knew that Ṛṣi to be Vaśiṣṭha's son and equal unto Vaśiṣṭha himself in energy. Vishvāmitra, desirous of benefiting himself, remained on that spot, concealed from the sight of both by making himself invisible. Then that best of monarchs, thus cursed by Śakti, desiring to propitiate the Ṛṣi, began to plead him humbly.

Vishvāmitra, ascertaining the disposition of the king and fearing that the difference might be made up, ordered a Rākṣasa to enter the body of the king. A

Rākṣasa of the name of Kinkara then entered the monarch's body in obedience to Śakti's curse and Vishvāmitra's command. And knowing that the Rākṣasa had possessed himself of the monarch, that best of Ṛṣis, Vishvāmitra, then left the spot and went away.

After that, the Rākṣasa first killed sage Śakti and then his younger brothers. A little while after, the king deprived of all his senses by the Rākṣasa within him, beholding Śakti who had cursed him, said, 'Because thou hast pronounced on me this extraordinary curse, therefore, I shall begin my life of cannibalism by devouring thee.' Having said this, the king immediately slew Śakti and ate him up like a tiger eating the animal it was fond of.

After Śakti, Vishvāmitra repeatedly urged the Rākṣasa, who was within the monarch, against the other sons of Vaśiṣṭha. Like a wrathful lion devouring small animals, the Rākṣasa in the King's body soon devoured the other sons of the illustrious Vaśiṣṭha that were junior to Śakti in age. But Vaśiṣṭha, learning that all his sons had been caused to be slain by Vishvāmitra, patiently bore his grief like the great mountain that bears the earth. That best of Munis, that foremost of intelligent men, was resolved rather to sacrifice his own life than exterminate in anger the race of Kauśikas (Vishvāmitra's race).

Āratī: Dhanyavād Guruji.

Sunidhi: Kindly tell us what happened after the meeting of Ādi Śaṅkara and Maharṣi Vedavyāsa.

Ācārya: Śrī Vedavyāsa expressed great joy upon discovering Ācārya's true identity and deep understanding. Seated at Ācārya's invitation, he praised, "Your wisdom has truly captivated me. You possess divine gifts unmatched by any on earth or in heaven. No one else could have answered my queries as you did. Among spiritual teachers, you are unrivalled."

"I came here upon learning of your commentary on my Sūtras," continued Vedavyāsa. "I am convinced of your capability for this task. Like the radiant Sūrya dispelling darkness, you will spread the brilliance of Advaita and eradicate ignorance."

"I urge you to continue your noble work," he added. "You must write commentaries on the Śrutis and the Smṛtis."

Ācārya humbly responded, "I have already fulfilled that task," and presented his other works to Vedavyāsa. Impressed, Vedavyāsa exclaimed, "Your work is indeed remarkable! I am thoroughly delighted."

In the midst of this joyous atmosphere, Ācārya made a solemn request to Vedavyāsa: "Sir, I have completed all that you asked of me. Please permit me to renounce my mortal form in your presence."

Padmapāda and the other disciples were shocked into silence. However, Vedavyāsa intervened, informing Ācārya that his mission was far from over. He bestowed upon Ācārya a boon of extended life, emphasizing his pivotal role in spreading scriptural truth and Advaita philosophy.

Vedavyāsa instructed Ācārya to first engage in debate with Kumārila Bhaṭṭa and then travel across the land to confront and convince opposing scholars. He emphasized the importance of harmonizing different schools of thought and firmly establishing Vedānta. Vedavyāsa departed, leaving the disciples relieved and joyful at the prospect of Ācārya's prolonged life.

Eager to fulfil Vedavyāsa's instructions, Ācārya set out to conquer Kumārila, recognizing him as a formidable opponent renowned for his philosophical prowess.

Sunidhi: Kindly tell us about Kumārila Bhaṭṭa.

Ācārya: Kumārila Bhaṭṭa was a scholar of Mīmāṃsā school of philosophy. He is famous for many of his various theses on Mīmāṃsā, such as Mīmāṃsā-Śloka-Varttikā. Kumārila was a staunch believer in the supreme validity of the Vaidika injunction, a champion of Pūrva-Mīmāṃsā and a Karmakāṇḍi. The Varttikā is mainly written as a sub-commentary of Sabara's commentary on Jaimini's Purva Mīmāṃsā Sūtras. Some scholars classify his philosophy as *existential realism.*

Āratī: What is existential realism?

Ācārya: Existential realism is a philosophical perspective that explores the nature of existence and reality. It combines elements of existentialism, which emphasizes *individual existence, freedom, and choice*, with realism, which holds that there is an *objective reality independent of human perception*.

In existential realism, reality is seen as both objective and subjective. It acknowledges that there is an external reality that exists independently of human perception and interpretation. It also recognizes that our subjective experiences and perspectives shape our understanding of reality.

Existential realism suggests that while there is an objective reality, our perception of it is filtered through our individual experiences, beliefs, and interpretations. It emphasizes the importance of acknowledging both the objective and subjective aspects of reality in order to gain a more comprehensive understanding of existence.

It seeks to reconcile the objective and subjective aspects of reality, recognizing the complexity of human experience and the limitations of our understanding.

Āratī: Dhanyavād, Guruji.

Sunidhi: Kindly continue with Kumārila Bhaṭṭa, Guruji.

Scholars differ as regards Kumārila Bhaṭṭa's views on a personal God. Some scholars believe that Bhaṭṭa promoted a personal God (Saguṇa Brahman), which conflicts with the Mīmāṃsā school. In his Varttikā, Kumārila Bhaṭṭa goes to great lengths to argue against the theory of a creator God and holds that the actions enjoined in the Veda had definite results without an external interference of Devatās.

Kumārila is also credited with the logical formulation of the Mīmāṃsā belief that the Vedas are unauthored (Apauruṣeya). In particular, he is known for his defence of Vaidika ritualism against medieval Buddhist idealism. His work strongly influenced other schools of Indian philosophy, with the exception that while Mīmāṃsā considers the Upaniṣads to be subservient to the Vedas, the Vedānta school does not think so.

The birthplace of Kumārila Bhaṭṭa is uncertain. According to the 16th-century Buddhist scholar Tārānātha, Kumārila was a native of South India. However, Anandagiri's Śaṅkara-Vijaya states that Kumārila came from "the North" (udagdeśāt) and debated the Buddhists and the Jains in the South.

Another theory is that he came from eastern India, specifically Kāmarūpa (present-day Assam). Sesa's Sarvasiddhāntarahasya uses the eastern title Bhaṭṭācārya for him. His writings indicate that he was familiar with the production of silk, which was common in present-day Assam. Yet another theory is that he comes from Mithila, which has a similar culture to Assam and produced another scholar on the subject, Maṇḍana Miśra.

Kumārila Bhaṭṭa and his followers in the Mīmāṃsā tradition known as Bhāṭṭas argued for a strongly compositional view of semantics called abhihitānvaya or "designation of what has been denoted." In this view, the meaning of a sentence was understood only after understanding first the meanings of individual words. Word referents were independent, complete objects. He also used several Tamil words in his works, including one of the earliest mentions of the name Dravida in North Indian sources, found in his Tantravarttikā.

The view mentioned above of sentence meaning was debated over some seven or eight centuries by the followers of the Prabhākara school within Mīmāṃsā, who argued that words do not directly designate meaning. Rather, word meanings are understood as already connected with other words (anvitābhidhāna, anvita = connected; abhidhāna = denotation). This view was influenced by the holistic arguments of Bhartṛhari's sphoṭa theory. Essentially, the Prābhākaras argued that sentence meanings are grasped directly from perceptual and contextual cues, skipping the stage of grasping the individual word meanings singly.

In his text Ślokavarttikā, Kumārila Bhaṭṭa argues that cognitions are intrinsically valid (*svatah pramanya*): It should be understood that all Pramāṇas have the property of being Pramāṇas intrinsically; for a capacity not already existing by itself (*svatah*) cannot be produced by anything else. Kumārila argues against the need for second-order justification before accepting cognitions as valid.

Kumārila Bhaṭṭa is known for his defence of Vaidika ritualism against medieval Buddhist idealism. With the aim to prove the superiority of Vaidika scripture, Kumārila Bhaṭṭa presented several novel arguments:

"Buddhist (or Jain) scripture could not be correct because it had several grammatical lapses." Thus, he presents his argument:

The scriptures of Buddhists and Jains are composed in overwhelmingly incorrect (asadhu) language, words of the Magadha or Dakshinatya languages, or even their dialects (*tadopabhramsa*). Therefore, false compositions (*asannibandhana*) cannot possibly be true knowledge (*śāstra*). By contrast, the very form itself (the well-assembled language) of the Veda proves its authority to be independent and absolute.

Every extant school held some Śāstra to be correct. To show that the Veda was the only correct Śāstra, Kumārila said that "the absence of an author would safeguard the Veda against all reproach" (Apauruṣeya). There was "no way to prove any of the contents of Buddhist scriptures directly as wrong in spirit" unless one challenges the legitimacy and eternal nature of the scripture itself. It is well known that the Pali Canon was composed after the Buddha's Parinirvāṇa. Further, even if they were the Buddha's words, they were not eternal or unauthored like the Vedas.

The Sautrantika Buddhist school believed that the universe was momentary (kshanika). Kumārila said that this was absurd, given that the universe does not disappear every moment. No matter how small one would define the duration of a moment, one could divide the moment into infinitely further parts. Kumārila argues: "If the universe does not exist between moments, then in which of these moments does it exist?" Because a moment could be infinitesimally small, Bhaṭṭa argued that the Buddhist was claiming that the universe was non-existent.

The Determination of Perception (*pratyaksha pariccheda*). Some scholars believe that Kumārila's understanding of Buddhist philosophy was far greater than that of any other non-Buddhist philosopher of his time.

The *Mādhavīya Śaṅkara Digvijayam*, a work on the life of Śaṅkara, claims that Śaṅkara challenged Bhaṭṭa to a debate on his deathbed. Kumārila Bhaṭṭa could not debate Śaṅkara as he was punishing himself for having disrespected his Buddhist teacher by defeating him in a debate using the Vedas by self-immolation at the banks of Gaṅgā at Prayagraj and instead directed him to argue with his student Maṇḍana Miśra in Māhiṣmatī. He said:

You will find a home at whose gates there are a number of caged parrots discussing abstract topics like - 'Do the Vedas have self-validity, or do they depend on some external authority for their validity? Are karmas capable of yielding their fruits directly, or do they require the intervention of God to do so? Is the world eternal, or is it a mere appearance?' Where you find the caged parrots discussing such abstruse philosophical problems, you will know that you have reached Maṇḍana's place.

Sunidhi: Tell us more about the encounter of Ādi Śaṅkara with Kumārila Bhaṭṭa.

Ācārya: Kumārila held a firm belief that in order to refute any philosophical school of thought effectively, one must thoroughly grasp its principles and practices. Hence, when confronted with the challenge of combatting Buddhism, he deemed it necessary to immerse himself in its teachings. Concealing his true identity, Kumārila entered a Buddhist school as a humble disciple, driven by a genuine desire to comprehend the intricacies of Buddhist philosophy.

During his time as a Buddhist pupil, Kumārila faced a pivotal moment when his teacher began disparaging the sacred Vedas. Filled with anguish at this denigration of the revered scriptures, Kumārila could not remain silent. Thus ensued a profound intellectual duel between teacher and pupil, a clash of ideologies marked by sharp wit and rigorous argumentation.

With relentless determination, Kumārila systematically dismantled each of his teacher's arguments, demonstrating the indisputable authority of the Vedas. Incensed by Kumārila's bold critique, the teacher, in a fit of rage, ordered his pupil's execution by throwing him from the roof of the building.

As Kumārila plummeted towards what seemed like a certain death, he invoked the protective power of the Vedas, calling upon their truth to safeguard his life. Miraculously, he survived the fall, albeit at the cost of losing one eye. Reflecting upon this harrowing experience, Kumārila realized the profound significance of unwavering faith. His momentary hesitation, indicated by the word "if," proved costly, underscoring the importance of absolute conviction.

Undeterred by adversity, Kumārila channelled his newfound resolve into fervently promoting Vaidika Dharma. With zeal and conviction, he embarked on a mission to revive and reaffirm the authenticity of Vaidika teachings wherever he went. His intellectual prowess and unwavering dedication enabled him to not only challenge Buddhism but also to confront and triumph over other rival philosophical schools, including Jainism.

Kumārila's legacy extended beyond his prowess as a debater; he emerged as a prolific writer, wielding his pen with authority to expound upon the intricacies of Mīmāṃsā philosophy. His life's journey exemplified resilience, faith, and an unyielding commitment to upholding the sanctity of Vaidika Sampradāya amidst the intellectual tumult of his time.

Śrī Śaṅkarācārya set out to meet this Kumārila Bhaṭṭa at Prayāga. Prayāga is now Triveni, where the rivers Gaṅgā, Yamunā and the subterranean Sarasvatī unite.

He desired to visit and worship at the many holy spots on the banks of the sacred Yamunā and so moved along the Yamunā towards the direction of Prayāga. On the way, he touched Kurukṣetra, the site of the Mahābhārata battle where the Gita was born.

He reached Bṛndāvana, the playground of Śrī Kṛṣṇa's childhood. The Ācārya went to see many spots associated with Kṛṣṇa's childhood and visited the famous temples in the region. At the shrine of Lord Kṛṣṇa, he was moved by his divine love for the Supreme Guru of Gita and reverentially offered a sweet hymn at the feet of Kṛṣṇa.

Upon arriving in Prayāga, Ācārya was greeted with disquieting news: Kumārila Bhaṭṭa, the renowned scholar, had embarked on a harrowing act of self-immolation, a penance for deceiving his own Guru many years prior. His transgression? Masquerading as a disciple to learn Buddhist philosophy. Despite the gravity of his sin, Ācārya's foremost intention in visiting Prayāga was to engage in discourse with Kumārila. Learning of Kumārila's relentless commitment to atone for his wrongdoing through the agonizing husk-fire ritual, Ācārya resolved to confront him.

Upon reaching the site where Kumārila was already engulfed in flames, Ācārya seized the opportunity to expound the profound tenets of Advaita philosophy to him. Amidst the searing heat and impending tragedy, Ācārya delineated the essence of Advaita, contrasting it with the opposing Mīmāṃsā school of thought.

Ācārya elucidated that Advaita emphasizes the transformative power of Vaidika Karma in purifying the soul, leading one towards the realization of Īśvara through Bhakti, and ultimately merging with the infinite Brahman through the pursuit of Jñāna. In contrast, Mīmāṃsā disregards the Upaniṣads and posits that liberation (Mokṣa) can be attained solely through the performance of Karma, devoid of any necessity for divine intervention or devotion.

Drawing from sacred scriptures like the Upaniṣads, Brahmasūtras, and Bhagavadgītā, Ācārya underscored the foundational principle of non-duality in Advaita. He articulated how the individual soul (Ātman) is fundamentally identical to the supreme reality (Parabrahman), as revealed by profound Vaidika aphorisms such as "*tat tvam asi*" and "*aham brahmāsmi*". The attainment of this sublime realization, though profoundly challenging, offers a glimpse into the ultimate truth beyond the veil of illusion.

Employing vivid analogies, Ācārya illuminated the intricacies of Advaita philosophy to Kumārila. Through examples such as mistaking a rope for a snake in darkness, he emphasized the transient nature of illusion and the underlying reality upon which it rests. Despite Kumārila's physical agony amidst the husk fire, he expressed his newfound conviction in Advaita. He entrusted the propagation of this profound wisdom to his disciple, Maṇḍana Miśra, residing in Mahishmati.

With a heavy heart yet unwavering determination, Ācārya bid farewell to Prayāga alongside his Śiṣyas, setting forth on a journey to confront Maṇḍana Miśra.

Sunidhi: Kindly tell us about the account of his debate with Maṇḍana Miśra.

Ācārya: Maṇḍana Miśra was a philosopher who wrote on the Mīmāṃsā and Advaita systems. He was an avid follower of Karma Mīmāṃsā and Karmakāṇḍa. He was a contemporary of Adi Śaṅkara, who became his disciple. He is often identified with Sureśvara, though the scholars debate the authenticity. Still, the official Śringerī documents recognise Maṇḍana Miśra as Sureśvara.

Maṇḍana Miśra was a student of the Mīmāṃsā scholar Kumārila Bhaṭṭa. He wrote several treatises on Mīmāṃsā, but also a work on Advaita, the Brahmasiddhi. Maṇḍana Miśra probably was more influential in the Advaita Vedānta tradition than is usually acknowledged.

His influence was such that some regard this work to have "set forth a non-Śaṅkara brand of Advaita." The "theory of error" set forth in the Brahmasiddhi became the normative Advaita Vedānta theory of error. According to Maṇḍana Miśra, errors are opportunities because they "lead to truth", and full correct knowledge requires that not only should one understand the truth but also examine and understand errors as well as what is not truth.

His student Vachaspati Miśra, who is believed to have been an incarnation of Śaṅkara to popularize the Advaita view, wrote the Bhāmatī, a commentary on Śaṅkara's Brahmasūtra Bhāśya, and the *Brahmatattvasamikṣa*, a commentary on Maṇḍana Miśra's Brahmasiddhi. Maṇḍana Miśra mainly inspired his thoughts, and he harmonises Śaṅkara's thoughts with that of Maṇḍana Miśra's.

Maṇḍana Miśra's influence and status can also be discerned in a popular legend about his debate with Ādi Śaṅkara. According to legend described in biographies of Śaṅkara, Ādi Śaṅkara debated with Maṇḍana Miśra. The vanquished would become a disciple of the victor and accept his school of thought. According to this legend, Śaṅkara defeated Maṇḍana Miśra, and as agreed, Maṇḍana became a disciple of Śaṅkara and assumed the name Sureśvara. According to the Advaita Vedānta tradition, Maṇḍana Miśra, along with Hastāmalaka, Padmapāda, and Totakācārya, was one of the four main disciples of Śaṅkara and was the first head of Śringerī Maṭha, one of the four Maṭhas that Śaṅkara later established.

Maṇḍana Miśra has often been identified with Sureśvara. Sureśvara and Maṇḍana Miśra were contemporaries of Śaṅkara. A strong tradition in Hinduism states that he started life as a Mīmāṃsāka became a Sanyāsa and an Advaitin after Maṇḍana Miśra and his wife Ubhaya Bhāratī were defeated by Śaṅkara in a debate and was given the yogapatta or monastic name "Sureśvara".

According to Kuppuswami Śāstrī, it is not likely that Maṇḍana Miśra, the author of Brahmasiddhi, is identical with Sureśvara. Still, the tradition is correct in describing Maṇḍana Miśra and Śaṅkara as contemporaries. His critical edition of the Brahmasiddhi also points out that the name Maṇḍana Miśra is both a title and a first name, which is a possible cause for the confusion of personalities. Maṇḍana Miśra's brand of Advaita differs in certain critical details from that of Śaṅkara, whereas Sureśvara's thought is very faithful to that of Śaṅkara.

According to Maṇḍana Miśra, the individual Jīva is the locus of avidya, whereas Sureśvara contents that avidya regarding Brahman is located in Brahman. These two different stances are also reflected in the opposing positions of the Bhāmatī school and the Vivarana school. According to him, the knowledge which arises from the Mahāvākya is insufficient for liberation. Only the direct realisation of Brahma is liberating, which can only be attained by meditation. According to Sureśvara, this knowledge is directly liberating, while meditation is, at best, a useful aid.

R. Balasubramanian disagrees with the arguments of Kuppuswami Śāstrī and others, arguing that there is no conclusive evidence available to prove that Maṇḍana, the author of the Brahmasiddhi, is different from Sureśvara, the author of the Naiṣkarmyasiddhi and the Vārtikas.

Maṇḍana Miśra received the best of traditional training at the feet of Kumārila Bhaṭṭa and perfected his scholarship. He settled at Mahishmatipura as a householder with his wife Ubhaya Bhāratī (sister of Kumārila Bhaṭṭa). They were an ideal couple, each of them equal to the other in all branches of learning, ethical character, and strict observation of Vaidika injunctions. Ubhaya Bhāratī was supposed to be an Avatāra of Devī of learning, Sarasvatī Devī, as Maṇḍana Miśra was supposed to be an Avatāra of Brahma. His scholarship and the reverence in which he was held earned him the honorific epithet of "Maṇḍana Miśra". His real name was Viśvarūpa.

Maṇḍana Miśra was a distinguished practitioner of the Purva Mīmāṃsā philosophy. The Mīmāṃsā philosophy is mainly derived from the Karmakāṇḍa portion of the Vedas and emphasizes the importance of rituals. In this school of thought, a particular ritual is done, and the results are achieved instantaneously. It displays a straightforward cause-and-effect relationship if practised accurately.

When Ādi Śaṅkara reached the mansion of Maṇḍana Miśra, it was found bolted from inside. Ādi Śaṅkara, as a Sanyāsi, had no right of admission into a house found closed. Such are the rules of Smṛti, which govern the daily conduct of traditional Sanyāsis. Ādi Śaṅkara pondered a little. He had firmly decided to redeem Maṇḍana Miśra from the rigidity of dogmatic ritualism. Therefore, he felt like using his extraordinary Yogic powers and entered the house through the closed door.

Maṇḍana Miśra had an innate dislike for Sanyāsis because of his staunch belief in ritualism; he believed that only those who wished to escape the rigours of Vaidika injunctions found a refuge in the Sanyāsa Āśrama. Moreover, when Ādi Śaṅkara entered the house, it was a time when the presence of a Sanyāsi was most unwelcome. Maṇḍana Miśra was performing a Śrāddha, and the Brāhmaṇas were about to be fed. The entry of Sanyāsi at such a time caused a disturbance, and Maṇḍana Miśra was infuriated.

There were heated arguments between them. The Brāhmaṇas found the situation going out of control. They wished to set it right. They suggested to Maṇḍana Miśra to invite Ādi Śaṅkara for Bhikṣa (alms), seeing him as a bhokta occupying Viṣṇu Sthāna in the ceremony. Staunch ritualist as he was, Maṇḍana Miśra was fully bent on saving the ritual. He invited Ādi Śaṅkara accordingly.

But Ādi Śaṅkara declined to accept the invitation. He explained to Maṇḍana Miśra that he did not come for Bhikṣā of the edibles but for a Vāda Bhikṣa, a controversial debate in philosophy. Maṇḍana Miśra, who had never met his match in learning before, was willing to a dialectical fight. He gladly welcomed it. The Śrāddha was allowed to be finished as ordained. The debate was fixed for the next day.

Maṇḍana Miśra was a perfect and adept ritualist who preached widely. The young and charming Advaita Vedāntin, Ādi Śaṅkara, on his country-wide tour, was eager to debate with Maṇḍana Miśra, who was by then already old. Maṇḍana Miśra reasoned that since he had spent more than half his life learning and preaching Mīmāṃsā, it would be unfair to debate with a youngster in his twenties who barely had any experience.

Hence, with the intention of being fair to Śaṅkara, Miśra allowed Śaṅkara to choose his judge. Śaṅkara had heard greatly about Miśra's righteousness and appreciated him for his act of fairness. But he was quick to decide that none but Maṇḍana Miśra's wife herself could be the most appropriate judge for this debate. To make the dispute more purposeful, they agreed to a bet. If Śaṅkara loses in the debate, He would become a disciple of Maṇḍana Miśra and get married in the life. If Maṇḍana Miśra loses, he should become Sanyāsi and disciple of Śaṅkara.

The debate endured for seventeen days, but on the eighteenth day, Maṇḍana displayed signs of distress and agitation. Despite being a renowned scholar, he sweated profusely. Observing this, Ubhaya Bhāratī, his caring wife, felt deeply distressed. Suppressing her emotions, she adhered to her commitment to honesty and, in a decisive moment, publicly declared, "My husband has been defeated in the debate." The audience was left stunned by her bold proclamation.

Ubhaya Bhāratī's moral courage shone brilliantly, captivating all with her unparalleled impartiality and unwavering objectivity. Maṇḍana gracefully accepted his defeat, finding solace in its resolution. Freed from mental conflict and emotional strain, he humbly bowed before the Ācārya, expressing his complete surrender. "Venerable monk," he began, "I am devoid of doubts, hesitations, or reservations. With a clear conscience, I earnestly seek your guidance to become your Śiṣya. If you deem me worthy and capable of embracing a life of absolute renunciation, I implore you to initiate me into the monastic order."

Ubhaya Bhāratī, having observed silently for a time, found her emotions overwhelming her. Unwilling to part from her husband, she turned to the Ācārya and spoke: "Sir, my husband's defeat is not yet absolute. It is written in the scriptures that a wife is half of her husband's soul. While I acknowledge your victory over him, you must also overcome me, the other half of my husband, before claiming him as your disciple. I am compelled to challenge you to a debate."

The Ācārya found himself facing an unexpected situation. Ubhaya Bhāratī's proposal to debate caught him off guard. After a moment of consideration, he replied, "Mother, esteemed scholars do not typically engage in debates with women."

She responded pointedly, "Why do you harbour a condescending attitude towards women? Surely, you are aware that the esteemed sage

Yājñavalkya engaged in debate with Gārgi, and Rājarṣi Janaka debated with the knowledgeable woman Sulabha. If such esteemed figures could engage in debate with women, why should you refuse when I challenge you? If you decline, then you must acknowledge your defeat."

The Ācārya realized he could not evade this determined yet gracious woman. Driven by his mission, which transcended personal acclaim, he reluctantly agreed to the debate with the impartial arbitrator. Waste no time; the debate commenced between the wandering ascetic and the housewife with fervour.

Ubhaya Bhāratī passionately aligned herself with her husband's philosophy and engaged fervently in debate. As the discussion delved deeper into intricate and complex topics, her articulate style, profound scholarship, analytical prowess, and unwavering self-assurance left the Ācārya in awe. Recognizing her as a formidable opponent of equal brilliance, he proceeded cautiously. Over seventeen days, Ubhaya Bhāratī posed numerous challenging questions across various philosophical realms, to which the Ācārya responded with original and compelling answers.

As the debate seemingly had no end in sight, Ubhaya Bhāratī realized that victory over the monk in the domain of Veda and Advaita was unattainable. On the eighteenth day, she sprung a surprise on the Ācārya, driven solely by her desire to retain her husband. Unfettered by the discomfort she may cause to the ascetic, who had renounced worldly pleasures, she continued to press on with her inquiries in front of her husband.

She inquired, "What indicators and characteristics define romantic passion? How many classifications exist within the realm of erotic science? Where are the focal points of erotic passion located within the body? What actions manifest this passion, and what actions quell it? How does passion fluctuate in the male and female bodies during the Śukla and Kṛṣṇa Pakṣa of Candra?"

Ācārya was taken aback, pausing in silence for a moment. Then he responded, "Mother, please direct your inquiries towards scriptures, and I shall provide answers accordingly. Why do you pose such questions to a celibate monk?"

Ubhaya Bhāratī's response was swift, "O greatest of monks, is not the study of eroticism also a valid field of knowledge? As a monk, you may claim renunciation of worldly desires, but have you truly relinquished the desire to excel in debates? If you are a genuine ascetic, you should have mastery over the senses and have conquered passions. Why should a mere discussion on eroticism disturb your tranquillity?"

Ācārya remained silent. She pressed on, "Mastering passions such as lust and anger come through true understanding. If a simple discourse on eroticism unsettles your mind, it suggests a lack of firm grasp on the knowledge of truth. Therefore, you are unfit to be my husband's Guru."

Ubhaya Bhāratī's words carried weight, revealing her determination to retain her husband. Ācārya listened intently, his gaze fixed downwards in contemplation. He found himself in a dire predicament. Answering the questions risked branding him as a fraudulent ascetic, tarnishing the very title of 'Sanyāsi'. Yet, remaining silent would result in defeat in the debate, forcing him back into a life he could not justify. It was a profound dilemma, unlike any he had encountered before, leaving him in a state of profound embarrassment.

Mother Śaradā was revealing her divine essence, orchestrating a sublime drama that showcased the power of Parāśaktī. Without her, even the deities such as Śiva, Viṣṇu, and others would lose their essence and significance. Praise be to Śrī Śaradā, Śrī Rājarājeśvarī, Devī Kāmākṣi, Śrī Mahālakṣmī, Śrī Tripurasundarī!

The Ācārya overcame his initial surprise at the unexpected questions and prepared himself to confront the challenging situation. With a serene demeanour devoid of anger or resentment, he addressed her with a smile, saying, "Mother, I am a celibate monk. The fundamental discipline for a monk, as prescribed by the scriptures, is the complete renunciation of lust and all its associated tendencies. I am not driven by a desire to win debates, as you suggested. My purpose here is not to triumph over others but to fulfil my mission of Loka Saṅgraha, of which this debate is but a small part."

Ācārya said, "Responding verbally to your inquiries would compromise the sanctity of monasticism. Therefore, I propose to transfer to another physical form and then address your questions by composing a written work. Do you agree to this arrangement?" Ubhaya Bhāratī accepted Ācārya's proposal, granting him a month to fulfil his commitment. She thus postponed the inevitable for a month.

For the first time since posing the 'challenging' questions, Ubhaya Bhāratī lifted her head to gaze at Śrī Śaṅkarācārya. The eternally serene Ācārya met her gaze. However, instead of evoking devotion as before, his gaze instilled a sense of trepidation in Ubhaya Bhāratī.

Ācārya departed from the city of Mahishmati, seeking solace in the tranquillity of a dense forest, accompanied by his disciples. Suddenly, they came across a man reclining beneath a tree. Thoughts raced through their minds: "He must possess great courage to sleep so peacefully in this forest, unaccompanied and seemingly free from worries. Could there be no lurking danger?"

Their concerns were unfounded, for the man was already beyond harm's reach - he was deceased. Ācārya discovered that he was none other than King Amaraka, who had ventured into the woods for a hunting expedition only to meet an untimely demise.

Though the king's demise was tragic, Ācārya perceived it as an opportunity. He confided in Padmapāda, saying, "Listen, Padmapāda, this presents a remarkable chance for me. I shall promptly inhabit the king's body, assume the role of Amaraka temporarily, seek answers to all of Ubhaya Bhāratī's inquiries, and then return. During my absence, please safeguard..." He hesitated at the term "my body" before continuing, "Please safeguard the body in a secluded cave. The soul remains unaffected by this action of mine, and the body shall remain pure."

Padmapāda hesitated, his concerns evident. Anxiously, he attempted to dissuade Ācārya. "Please reconsider, Ācārya," he urged. "Assuming the role of a married man may tarnish your reputation as a Sanyāsi. And what of the consequences? What if..."

Ācārya interrupted reassuringly, "Do not fret, Padmapāda. You may perceive this as a challenging role for a Sanyāsi, but there will come a time when I shall undertake a role even more demanding. You must brace yourself and remain steadfast."

With resolve, Ācārya continued, "Ensure the careful guardianship of this apparently lifeless body within the cave. In a month, I shall return to inhabit it once more." Utilizing his Yogic prowess of Parakāyā Praveśa, Ācārya then merged his consciousness into the king's body.

Upon his return to the palace, the King exhibited a profound transformation in his demeanour. He attended to the needs of his people diligently, addressing their concerns and resolving issues. He generously extended assistance to the impoverished, frequented temples with devotion, and displayed a keen interest in poetry, among other pursuits. No longer was he deemed 'a tyrant king'; instead, he emerged as a benevolent ruler.

Meanwhile, Ācārya, inhabiting the king's body, summoned scholars well-versed in the science of eroticism. Delving into the writings on sexuality by sage Vātsyāyana and exploring various commentaries, he acquired comprehensive expertise on the subject. Additionally, he honed his practical skills in the art of eroticism. With his unparalleled intellect, Ācārya authored an authoritative treatise on eroticism, surpassing all of Ubhaya Bhāratī's inquiries. Padmapāda, in disguise, arranged a meeting with King Amaraka and obtained the manuscript from him clandestinely.

Meanwhile, the erudite ministers grew wary of the king's sudden transformation. How could such a notorious personality undergo such a dramatic change overnight? Their suspicions led them to uncover the truth of Parakāyā Praveśa. Delighted with the benevolent rule of the king, they wished for him to remain in his current form indefinitely without reverting to his original body.

Believing that the destruction of the original body would secure the king's perpetual reign, they located the body of Ācārya concealed in the caves. Swiftly, the ministers commanded their men to cremate the Sanyāsi's body. Padmapāda and his companions, disguised, approached the king and communicated cryptically, conveying dual meanings. The Ācārya within the king's body discerned the concealed message instantly.

As the soul of Ācārya departed from the King's body, leaving the King lifeless, it sought out its original form. Meanwhile, the ministers' men set fire to Ācārya's body, which quickly began to burn. When Ācārya's Ātmā reached its former body, it found the right hand already consumed by the flames.

Undeterred, Ācārya rose from the funeral pyre. At the behest of Padmapāda, Ācārya recited a hymn extolling Lord Lakṣmī Nṛsiṁha, known as the Lakṣmī Nṛsiṁha Stotra.

Each stanza ends with "*mama dehi karāvalambam*", meaning, 'O Lord Lakṣmī Nṛsiṁha, provide me the support of your hands'.

The charred hand was swiftly saved through the divine grace of Lord Lakṣmī Nṛsiṁha, who bestowed his blessings upon this devout follower reminiscent of Prahlada. Expressing gratitude to the Lord, the Ācārya then journeyed back to the city of Mahishmati, prepared to face Ubhaya Bhāratī.

Maṇḍana eagerly anticipated Ācārya's return, having already committed himself to the mentorship of Ācārya in his mind. Maṇḍana stood out among Ācārya's disciples. In contrast, others approached the Guru conventionally, with homage and respect, and received his benevolence through plea; Maṇḍana had persevered fiercely to earn the Guru's favour.

Upon Ācārya's arrival, Maṇḍana and Ubhaya Bhāratī extended a heartfelt welcome. Addressing Ubhaya Bhāratī, Ācārya presented the promised book, stating, "Mother Bhāratī, here is the answer to all your questions; please accept it."

Ubhaya Bhāratī meticulously perused the book from cover to cover, deeply impressed by its quality. The treatise delved into the realm of Jyotiṣa, exploring the conception, evolution, and reproduction of humanity based on specific conditions prescribed by ancient Ṛṣis. It also elucidated principles concerning human anatomy, mental and moral attributes, aesthetic and psychological inclinations, as well as the dynamics of interpersonal relationships influenced by celestial alignments. This comprehensive work, titled Amarakam, encompassed a wide array of topics pertinent to human existence.

Ubhaya Bhāratī addressed the Ācārya, saying, "Esteemed one, your triumph is truly complete now. My husband will embrace discipleship and monastic life under your guidance. As for me, I shall return to my eternal realm of Satyaloka, thus concluding my incarnation as Ubhaya Bhāratī."

In reverence, the Ācārya bowed before her, extolling her divine virtues. He remarked, "Beloved Mother Bhāratī, you have descended upon the earth to impart celestial wisdom. I recognize you as none other than Devī Sarasvatī. If you were to depart from this earthly realm now, knowledge itself would vanish from the world. Therefore, I request you to remain here for a while longer."

Devī Sarasvatī extended an offer to grant a boon to the Ācārya. He humbly requested her presence alongside him until he could consecrate her divine grace at a suitable location. She consented to his plea with one condition: he must not look back during their journey to ascertain if she followed. Should he glance back, she would remain at that spot.

Accepting the condition, the Ācārya proceeded to initiate Maṇḍana into Sanyāsa according to tradition. Maṇḍana relinquished his former name, assuming the new name Sureśvarācārya.

Sunidhi: Kindly tell us the Lakṣmī Nṛsiṅha Stotra, which Ādi Śaṅkara sang in the account mentioned above.

श्रीमत्पयोनिधिनिकेतन चक्रपाणे
भोगीन्द्रभोगमणिरञ्जितपुण्यमूर्ते ।
योगीश शाश्वत शरण्य भवाब्धिपोत
लक्ष्मीनृसिंह मम देहि करावलम्बम् ॥१॥

Salutations to the divine Śrī Lakṣmī Nṛsiṅha, who dwells upon the Ocean of Milk, brimming with beauty and auspiciousness, bearing a radiant discus in His hand... With His countenance illuminated by the divine light emanating from the gems adorning the serpent Adi Sesha's hoods... He is the sovereign of yoga, eternal and the sanctuary for devotees like a boat amidst the ocean of worldly existence... O Lakṣmī Nṛsiṅha, kindly grant me Your refuge, embracing me with Your divine hands.

ब्रह्मेन्द्ररुद्रमरुदर्ककिरीटकोटि
सङ्घट्टिताङ्घ्रिकमलामलकान्तिकान्त ।
लक्ष्मीलसत्कुचसरोरुहराजहंस
लक्ष्मीनृसिंह मम देहि करावलम्बम् ॥२॥

Salutations to the revered Śrī Lakṣmī Nṛsiṅha, before whom countless adorned heads of Brahma, Rudra, the Maruts (Wind-Gods), and the Sun-God gather... Longing to attain His resplendence, they converge at His stainless, pure feet... He is akin to a majestic swan gracefully gliding on the lake within the heart of Devī Lakṣmī... O Lakṣmī Nṛsiṅha, I implore Your refuge, cradling me within Your divine hands.

संसारघोरगहने चरतो मुरारे
मारोग्रभीकरमृगप्रवरार्दितस्य ।
आर्तस्य मत्सरनिदाघनिपीडितस्य
लक्ष्मीनृसिंह मम देहि करावलम्बम् ॥३॥

Salutations to the venerable Śrī Lakṣmī Nṛsiṅha, in this dense forest of worldly existence, I roam, O Murari, vanquisher of the demon Mura... Numerous formidable and ferocious desires assail me in this Samsāri wilderness, instilling profound fear... I am deeply wounded and distressed amidst the selfishness and zeal of this existence... O Lakṣmī Nṛsiṅha, extend to me Your refuge, embracing me with Your divine hands.

संसारकूपमतिघोरमगाधमूलं
सम्प्राप्य दुःखशतसर्पसमाकुलस्य ।
दीनस्य देव कृपणापदमागतस्य
लक्ष्मीनृसिंह मम देहि करावलम्बम् ॥४॥

Salutations to the revered Śrī Lakṣmī Nṛsiṅha, in this daunting well of worldly existence, its depths unfathomable... I have descended, where hundreds of serpents of sorrows coil... To this wretched soul, O Deva, plagued by various calamities... O Lakṣmī Nṛsiṅha, I implore Your refuge, clasping me within Your divine hands.

संसारसागरविशालकरालकाल

नक्रग्रहग्रसननिग्रहविग्रहस्य ।

व्यग्रस्य रागरसनोर्मिनिपीडितस्य

लक्ष्मीनृसिंह मम देहि करावलम्बम् ॥५॥

Salutations to the esteemed Śrī Lakṣmī Nṛsiṅha in this vast ocean of worldly existence, where time, akin to a crocodile, relentlessly devours all... My life is entangled, consumed like Rāhu eclipsing and consuming the planet, akin to the moon... While my senses, immersed in the waves of passion's juice, slowly deplete my vitality... O Lakṣmī Nṛsiṅha, extend to me Your refuge, embracing me with Your divine hands.

संसारवृक्षमघबीजमनन्तकर्म

शाखाशतं करणपत्रमनङ्गपुष्पम् ।

आरुह्य दुःखफलितं पततो दयालो

लक्ष्मीनृसिंह मम देहि करावलम्बम् ॥६॥

Salutations to the revered Śrī Lakṣmī Nṛsiṅha in this tree of worldly existence where evil is the seed, and endless activities are its myriad branches... The senses are its leaves, and passion (Ananga or Kamadeva) is its flower... Having climbed this tree of samsara and tasted its fruits of sorrows, I now descend, O Compassionate One... O Lakṣmī Nṛsiṅha, grant me Your refuge, cradling me within Your divine hands.

संसारसर्पघनवक्त्रभयोग्रतीव्र

दंष्ट्राकरालविषदग्धविनष्टमूर्तेः ।

नागारिवाहन सुधाब्धिनिवास शौरे

लक्ष्मीनृसिंह मम देहि करावलम्बम् ॥७॥

Salutations to the esteemed Śrī Lakṣmī Nṛsiṅha, facing this all-consuming serpent of worldly existence with its dreadful visage and sharp fangs... It has scorched and overpowered me with its potent poison... O You who ride upon the enemy of serpents, Garuda, capable of slaying the serpents of samsara, O Dweller in the ocean of nectar, which can heal the burnt... O Shauri, Viṣṇu... O Lakṣmī Nṛsiṅha, bestow upon me Your refuge, embracing me with Your divine hands.

संसारदावदहनातुरभीकरोरु

ज्वालावलीभिरतिदग्धतनूरुहस्य ।

त्वत्पादपद्मसरसीशरणागतस्य

लक्ष्मीनृसिंह मम देहि करावलम्बम् ॥८॥

Salutations to the revered Śrī Lakṣmī Nṛsiṅha, the burning heat of this worldly existence instils fear and inflicts suffering upon us... Its scorching flames consume every part of my being... Your lotus feet are like a cool lake offering refuge to the scorched souls... O Lakṣmī Nṛsiṅha, grant me Your refuge, enfold me within Your divine hands.

संसारजालपतितस्य जगन्निवास

सर्वेन्द्रियार्तवडिशार्थझषोपमस्य ।

प्रोत्खण्डितप्रचुरतालुकमस्तकस्य

लक्ष्मीनृसिंह मम देहि करावलम्बम् ॥९॥

Salutations to the revered Śrī Lakṣmī Nṛsiṅha, like one who dwells in this world and has become entangled in the net of worldly attachments... Whose every sense organ is afflicted akin to a hooked fish... Whose very palate and head are deeply torn by the numerous hooks of sensory desires... Such is my condition... O Lakṣmī Nṛsiṅha, please grant me Your refuge, embracing me with Your divine hands.

संसारभीकरकरीन्द्रकराभिघात

निष्पिष्टमर्मवपुषः सकलार्तिनाश ।

प्राणप्रयाणभवभीतिसमाकुलस्य

लक्ष्मीनृसिंह मम देहि करावलम्बम् ॥१०॥

Salutations to the revered Śrī Lakṣmī Nṛsiṅha; this worldly existence, akin to a colossal and fearsome elephant, has struck me with its trunk... Crushing my very core beneath its feet... O Lord, You, the most beautiful and annihilator of all pains... To me, filled with the dread of death in this realm... O Lakṣmī Nṛsiṅha, please extend Your refuge to me, embracing me with Your divine hands.

अन्धस्य मे हृतविवेकमहाधनस्य

चोरैः प्रभो बलिभिरिन्द्रियनामधेयैः ।

मोहान्धकूपकुहरे विनिपातितस्य

लक्ष्मीनृसिंह मम देहि करावलम्बम् ॥११॥

Salutations to the revered Śrī Lakṣmī Nṛsiṅha, my blindness caused by the theft of discernment, the precious wealth of viveka... Seized away by the incessant demands of the senses, prompting for constant indulgences... Has plunged my life into the dark well of delusion... O Lakṣmī Nṛsiṅha, please bestow upon me Your refuge, cradling me within Your divine hands.

लक्ष्मीपते कमलनाभ सुरेश विष्णो

वैकुण्ठ कृष्ण मधुसूदन पुष्कराक्ष ।

ब्रह्मण्य केशव जनार्दन वासुदेव

देवेश देहि कृपणस्य करावलम्बम् ॥१२॥

Salutations to the revered Śrī Lakṣmī Nṛsiṅha, O Lakshmipati, consort of Devī Lakṣmī, O Kamalanābha, adorned with a lotus on the navel, O Sureśa, lord of the Suras, O Viṣṇu, O Vaikuntha, O Kṛṣṇa, O Madhusudana, O Puṣkarākṣa, with lotus eyes, O Brahmaṇya, O Keśava, O Janārdana, O Vāsudeva, O Deveśa, lord of Devas... Please grant refuge to this pitiful one, holding me with Your divine hands.

यन्माययोर्जितवपुःप्रचुरप्रवाह
मग्नार्थमत्र निवहोरुकरावलम्बम् ।
लक्ष्मीनृसिंहचरणाब्जमधुव्रतेन
स्तोत्रं कृतं सुखकरं भुवि शङ्करेण ॥१३॥

Salutations to the revered Śrī Lakṣmī Nṛsiṅha, whose beautiful form is strengthened by the power of Maya originating from the divine source, flowing with abundant divinity. For the sake of rescuing those immersed in delusion, the all-encompassing hand of refuge of Lakṣmī Nṛsiṅha has been extended from the same divine source. By immersing oneself in the nectar of Śrī Lakṣmī Nṛsiṅha's lotus feet. This Stotra is composed by Ādi Śaṅkarācārya, bringing great joy to those who deeply meditate upon it in this world.

Sunidhi: What happened after Ādi Śaṅkara defeated Maṇḍana Miśra?

Ācārya: The journey southward commenced as Ācārya and his followers traversed the path, accompanied by Devī Sarasvatī. Upon reaching a sandy area near the merging point of the Tunga and Bhadra rivers, Devī Sarasvatī's anklets got stuck in the sand, silencing their delicate chimes. Until then, Ācārya had relied on the sound of these bells to confirm her presence. With the tinkling ceased, Ācārya glanced back, only to find her halted there. At that moment, he sanctified her as Śaradā, right at that spot, in a standing posture.

Ācārya then set out on Digvijaya - a campaign of conquest in the cultural and spiritual field of Bhāratavarṣa, covering all parts. After that, Ācārya arrived at Śrīśailam in Andra Pradesh. He visited the shrine of Śrī Mallikarjuna and Devī Bhramarāmbā.

He sang a prayer in praise of Mahādeva. Seeing the radiant and loving face of the Devī, Ācārya burst out into a hymn in praise of Mā Bhramarāmbā. Ācārya also established a Śrīcakra in the sanctum sanctorum of Śrī Devī.

Śrīśailam was the stronghold of the dreaded Kāpālikas. Kāpālikas carried a skull with them according to all accounts, thus imitating Bhairava, the Brahman-slayer. According to orthodox prescriptions, a Brahman-slayer had to expiate for his sin by living outside society for 12 years, carrying a skull as an alms bowl and a skull-topped staff.

In a stricter sense, it denotes a particular Śaiva ascetic order closely related to the Lākulas and the Pāśupatas. In a wider meaning, it refers to a (usually Śākta) tantric practitioner who adopts the observance and possibly other practices of the original Kāpālikas.

From the *Mattavilāsaprahasana*, we learn that Kāpālikas were to discard or distribute their possessions (*saṃvibhāga*) in the manner of other ascetic orders. They wore a loincloth (*kaupīna*) to cover themselves. They kept only their *bhairavic* attributes, which included the skull-bowl and perhaps a snakeskin (*ahicamma*, representing one of Śiva's attributes, the snake) for the Brahmanical Yajñopavīta. Unlike other Sanyāsa Sampradāyas, Kāpālikas seem to have allowed women to receive full initiation.

The Kāpālikas were perhaps the most notorious Śaiva ascetics of classical India. They were known for their cremation ground rituals and for wandering around with a skull for an alms bowl. The skull (kapāla), their most conspicuous attribute, also provided their name. But the Kāpālikas are also designated as Somasiddhāntins, "Those of the Soma Doctrine", or the "Soma People with the Skull".

With their accustomed fury and thoroughness, they declared war on the Ācārya and his philosophy. But the Ācārya baffled them by the soundness and the force of Advaitic philosophy.

The king *Krakaca* harboured deep resentment towards Ācārya, prompting him to enlist Ugrabhairava, the leader of the *Kāpālikas* in Śrīśailam, with the sinister task of eliminating Ācārya. Ugrabhairava was highly skilled in the art of deception. Under the guise of a sincere seeker, he approached Ācārya, humbly bowing at his feet and expressing a desire to become his disciple. Despite his omniscience, Ācārya granted Ugrabhairava's request, admitting him into the esteemed circle of his disciples.

Ugrabhairava's conduct and steadfast dedication captivated all those who crossed paths with him. One day, as Ācārya was deep in meditation, Ugrabhairava approached him, prostrating himself at his feet and shedding tears. When Ācārya inquired about the reason for his distress, Ugrabhairava spoke:

"My lord, I perceive your true nature. You are a magnificent soul, akin to Śiva himself, overflowing with compassion and benevolence. You embody countless virtues without end. I implore you to grant just one wish of mine, thus bestowing purpose upon my human existence."

Ācārya replied, "Noble one, express your desire openly. I shall fulfil your wish."

Ugrabhairava responded, "Throughout my life, I have dedicated myself to various spiritual practices, aiming to prove myself worthy of dwelling in the realm of Lord Śiva. Through my penance, I earned the Lord's favour, and he granted me a boon. According to the boon, my desire will be granted upon performing a Homa to Rudra, with the condition that the head of a True Sanyāsi is sacrificed. Since receiving this boon, I have tirelessly searched far and wide for such a Sanyāsi, yet my efforts have been in vain. However, you possess omniscience. If you consent to assist me, my human existence will find its purpose fulfilled."

Despite Ācārya's earnest attempts to impart profound wisdom on the philosophy of true knowledge, Ugrabhairava remained obstinate to his pleas.

Instead, he continued to weep and implore, "Lord, you understand that I am not capable of grasping the teachings of Advaita and retaining them. I am elderly, and my days are numbered. Now, it is up to you to show me mercy. It is said that the great sage, Dadhichi, attained eternal glory by sacrificing his body for Indra's cause. Similarly, by relinquishing your transient form for my sake, you will achieve enduring renown."

Ācārya gradually came to believe that it was appropriate for his temporary form to contribute to a virtuous deed. Furthermore, he understood that everything was subject to the divine will, and true wisdom lay in allowing events to unfold according to divine decree. With this realization, he promptly expressed his willingness to Ugrabhairava's request.

Ugrabhairava responded, "Master, I will ensure that the sacrifice is carried out cautiously without your disciples becoming aware of it. Nearby, in the forest, there lies an abandoned shrine of Bhairava. I will make all the necessary arrangements there. On the upcoming Amāvasyā, at midnight, you may come to the shrine. No one will be privy to any of these proceedings."

Ācārya agreed to the plan. On the designated day, he proceeded to the sacrificial site where Ugrabhairava awaited. Confirming Ugrabhairava's readiness, Ācārya assumed the Padmasana position, closed his eyes, and began meditating, granting permission for the ritualistic sacrifice of his own life.

Filled with satisfaction, Ugrabhairava drew his sword, thinking, "I am about to eliminate the greatest adversary of my faith from this world. By performing this service to my religion, I will reap abundant rewards." With this conviction, he hurled the sword towards Ācārya.

On that fateful Amāvasyā night, while the Ācārya proceeded quietly to the site of sacrifice, Padmapāda lay asleep alongside the other disciples. Suddenly, he was overcome by a dreadful dream. In this vision, he witnessed someone ruthlessly severing the head of his revered Guru, Ādi Śaṅkarācārya. Shocked and disoriented, Padmapāda awoke, unsure of how to respond to such a distressing revelation. In his moment of confusion, he recalled the boon bestowed upon him by Lord Nṛsiṅha.

[Lord Nṛsiṅha manifested before Sanandana, addressing him tenderly, "Beloved child, request a boon from me." Sanandana promptly sought the boon of 'Abhaya', meaning fearlessness, and added, "It is also my earnest desire that whenever I invoke your remembrance, you shall appear and aid me in overcoming my tribulations." Graciously, the Lord granted, "So be it."]

As soon as Padmapāda invoked the memory of the Lord, Nṛsiṅha not only materialized before him but also infused into Padmapāda's being. With newfound strength, Padmapāda sprang from his bed and swiftly made his way to the designated sacrificial spot.

There, he witnessed Ugrabhairava brandishing the sword and preparing to strike Ācārya. In a split second, Padmapāda, now possessed by Nṛsiṅha, intercepted the sword. With a mighty roar akin to a lion's, he swiftly tore open Ugrabhairava's heart with his razor-sharp claws, just as he had done with Hiranyakashipu in the mythic tales. The thunderous reverberation of his roar echoed throughout Śrīśailam, signifying the triumph of divine justice.

Ācārya's eyes fluttered open upon hearing the resounding noise. To his astonishment, he beheld a breathtaking sight. "Could this be Lord Lakshmi Nṛsiṅha? Is that not Hiranya's body adorning his neck like a garland?" he pondered in disbelief. Ācārya rubbed his eyes to gain a clearer view of the extraordinary spectacle, only to find Padmapāda standing in place of the Lord. At the same time, the lifeless form of Ugrabhairava lay sprawled nearby, stained with blood.

By the time Padmapāda regained consciousness, he found himself bewildered and disoriented. He confessed that he had no recollection of the events that transpired save for the disturbing dream and the invocation of his beloved deity. Padmapāda's quick thinking and presence of mind had unknowingly spared the life of Śrī Śaṅkarācārya, as divine intervention had worked through him.

While at Śrīśailam, Śrī Śaṅkarācārya composed some exquisite verses in praise of Lord Mallikarjuna. Sample this composition, known as Śivānandalahari:

"What can I offer you, Īśvara?" Ācārya mused, addressing the divine. "You, who possess everything, what gift can I present to you? Very well, I offer you my heart..." he continued, only to be interrupted by the divine's imminent approach to accept even that. Surprised, Ācārya remarked, "Look at him. I presumed he was affluent... yet he possesses no riches! Clad in elephant skin adorned with a snake around his neck, he claims to consume poison as sustenance. He asks me, 'You have given me your heart; what can I offer you in return?' Lord, grant me the devotion that perpetually fixates on your lotus feet."

With reverence, Ācārya bowed before Lord Mallikarjuna, the divine figure who serves as a bridge for traversing the formidable ocean of Samskara, perpetually residing atop the Śrīśailam hill.

From Śrīśailam, Ācārya and his disciples went to Ahobilam to pay respects to the Lord Nṛsiṅha, who saved Ācārya's life. There, he composed the famous Lakṣmī Nṛsiṅha Pañcaratnam.

Sunidhi: Where is Ahobilam?

Ācārya: Ahobilam is a town and holy site in the Nandyal district in Andhra Pradesh, India. Picturesque hills of the Eastern Ghats with several mountain hills and gorges surround it. It is the centre of worship of Lord Nṛsiṅha, to whom nine temples and other shrines are dedicated. The main village and a temple complex are at Lower Ahobilam. Upper Ahobilam, about 8 kilometres to the east, has more temples in a steep gorge.

The main Nṛsiṅha Svāmi temples at each site were built or expanded by the emperors of Vijayanagara in the 15th and 16th centuries, then sacked by the Mughals in 1578, then restored and expanded at various times, up to the present day. As they stand, they are a mixture of work from all these periods.

Indeed, it is fascinating to observe the dynamic exchange of knowledge and devotion between the Guru, Śrī Śaṅkarācārya, and his disciple, Padmapāda. While Padmapāda imbibed the teachings of Advaita, Bhakti, and Jñāna from his revered Guru, Śrī Śaṅkarācārya, it is equally remarkable that the Guru himself acquired the fervent devotion to Lord Nṛsiṅha from his devoted disciple, Padmapāda.

The successive Śaṅkarācārya of the lineage of Adi Śaṅkara have continued to worship Nṛsiṅha. In addition to worshipping Mahā Tripurasundarī and Śrī Candramauḷīśvara as the main Devatās, Lakṣmī Nṛsiṅha Upasana has also been traditionally followed by the Ācāryas.

Śrī Śaṅkarācārya's Digvijayam continued towards south. In Karnataka, along with his disciples, he visited a Vaiṣṇava temple.

Kailāśa: Guruji, kindly tell us about the legend of Hastāmalakācārya.

In the village of Sriveli, where the revered Ācārya had set up camp, resided a destitute Brāhmaṇa who arrived with his young son, who was both deaf and mute.

With tears welling in his eyes, the father confided in the Ācārya: "I went through great hardship to conduct his Upanayana ceremony, yet my son remains unable to utter a single word. He has not grasped even the basics of the alphabet, let alone the ability to read the Vedas and other sacred texts. Never once has he called out to me or his mother. He fails to communicate his hunger or thirst. You, revered one, are known for your boundless compassion. I pray you to shower your grace upon him and restore him to normalcy."

The Ācārya gazed upon the boy and gently inquired: "Dear child, who are you? Where do you journey? What is your name?" Without hesitation, the boy met the Ācārya's gaze and responded in a melodic tone, articulating in verse:

"I am neither human nor divine,
Nor Yakṣa, nor castes of any line.
Neither Brāhmaṇa, nor Kṣatriya's son,
Nor trader, nor touched by the lowest one.
Not Brahmacāri, nor the householder's role,
Nor hermit in the forest, nor a seeker of soul.
I am that ever self-aware, whole."

The boy, who had been mute since birth, responding to the Ācārya's inquiries with a verse revealing the essence of the Self, was a phenomenon beyond understanding. The verse echoed the Ācārya's own experience when his Guru, Govinda Bhagavatpāda, posed the question, "Who are you?"

The boy's father, overwhelmed with joy, couldn't comprehend the meaning of his son's words. He was elated that his son had begun speaking and didn't delve deeper into understanding. Filled with pride, he humbly bowed before the Ācārya, expressing his gratitude, and then departed with his son.

Upon returning home, the father eagerly invited the townsfolk to witness his son's newfound ability to hear and speak. However, the boy remained unable to hear or speak. Disheartened, the father speculated that perhaps the blessing from the Sanyāsi had only lasted for a brief period. With a hopeful heart, he brought his son once again to the Ācārya.

Before the Ācārya once more, the boy spoke fluently yet again, a miracle unfolding before their eyes. "Your son is not meant for you; leave him with me," declared the Ācārya. With solemn agreement, the parents entrusted their son into the care of the Ācārya. Though conflicted by the thought that their son was with them when he was mute, yet not with them when he was restored, they departed for home, a sense of fulfilment enveloping their hearts.

Under the guidance of the Ācārya, the boy was initiated into the ascetic path of Sanyāsa and bestowed the name Hastāmalaka. The verse that came out first from the boy when he started to talk was known as Hastāmalakiyam Stotra.

Kailāśa: Kindly tell us about the Hastāmalakiyam Stotra.

Ācārya: It is as follows:

कस्त्वं शिशो कस्य कुतोऽसि गन्ता किं नाम ते त्वं कुत आगतोऽसि ।
एतन्मयोक्तं वद चार्भक त्वं मत्प्रीतये प्रीति विवर्धनोऽसि ॥ १॥

Who are you, O child? Whose are you? Wherefrom have you come? What is your name, and where are you going? Tell me all this, O little one. Your affectionate words increase my affection for you.

हस्तामलक उवाच ।
नाहं मनुष्यो न च देव-यक्षौ न ब्राह्मण-क्षत्रिय-वैश्य-शूद्राः ।
न ब्रह्मचारी न गृही वनस्थो भिक्षुर्न चाहं निजबोध रूपः ॥ २॥

Hastāmalaka said: I am not a human, nor a deity or a yaksha. I am neither a Brāhmaṇa, nor a Kṣatriya, Vaiśya, or Śudra. I am not a celibate, nor a householder, nor one in the forest dwelling stage, nor a beggar. I am none of these; my true nature is that of pure consciousness.

निमित्तं मनश्चक्षुरादि प्रवृत्तौ निरस्ताखिलोपाधिराकाशकल्पः ।
रविर्लोकचेष्टानिमित्तं यथा यः स नित्योपलब्धिस्वरूपोऽहमात्मा ॥ ३॥

As Sūrya is the cause of the activity of the eyes and other senses, and yet is devoid of all adjuncts, being like space, and as it is the cause of all the movements in the world, similarly, I am the eternal Self, the substratum of constant self-awareness, which is the cause of all mental activities and perceptions, but itself is unaffected by any of them.

यमग्न्युष्णवन्नित्यबोध स्वरूपं मनश्चक्षुरादीन्यबोधात्मकानि ।
प्रवर्तन्त आश्रित्य निष्कम्पमेकं स नित्योपलब्धिस्वरूपोऽहमात्मा ॥ ४॥

Like fire, which is inherently hot and always knows its own nature, and which causes the cognition of the mind and other senses, I am the eternal Self, steadfast and unwavering, upon whom all activities depend.

मुखाभासको दर्पणे दृश्यमानो मुखत्वात् पृथक्त्वेन नैवास्ति वस्तु ।

चिदाभासको धीषु जीवोऽपि तद्वत् स नित्योपलब्धिस्वरूपोऽहमात्मा ॥ ५॥

Just as an object seen in a mirror appears separate due to the reflection on the mirror's surface, but in reality, there is no separate existence, similarly, the individual self appears to exist separately due to the reflection of consciousness in the intellect. Yet, like the eternal Self, I am the substratum of constant self-awareness.

यथा दर्पणाभाव आभासहानौ मुखं विद्यते कल्पनाहीनमेकम् ।

तथा धी वियोगे निराभासको यः स नित्योपलब्धिस्वरूपोऽहमात्मा ॥ ६॥

Just as in the absence of a mirror, there is no reflection of the face, and only one exists without any imagination, similarly, in the absence of intellect, the Self devoid of reflection shines forth as the eternal substratum of constant self-awareness.

मनश्चक्षुरादेर्वियुक्तः स्वयं यो मनश्चक्षुरादेर्मनश्चक्षुरादिः ।

मनश्चक्षुरादेरगम्यस्वरूपः स नित्योपलब्धिस्वरूपोऽहमात्मा ॥ ७॥

Independent of the mind and the eyes, the Self itself is not the mind nor the eyes. Being beyond the reach of the mind and the eyes, the Self, of the nature of unapproachable awareness, shines forth as the eternal substratum of constant self-awareness.

य एको विभाति स्वतः शुद्धचेताः प्रकाशस्वरूपोऽपि नानेव धीषु ।

शरावोदकस्थो यथा भानुरेकः स नित्योपलब्धिस्वरूपोऽहमात्मा ॥ ८॥

Just as Sūrya, though of the nature of light, shines independently as the only illuminator, not divided among the various objects, similarly, the Self, of the nature of pure consciousness, shines forth as the eternal substratum of constant self-awareness.

यथाऽनेकचक्षुः प्रकाशो रविर्न क्रमेण प्रकाशीकरोति प्रकाश्यम् ।

अनेका धियो यस्तथैकः प्रबोधः स नित्योपलब्धिस्वरूपोऽहमात्मा ॥ ९॥

Just as Sūrya, the illuminator of many eyes, does not sequentially illuminate each object one by one but shines forth simultaneously, similarly, the single consciousness, the illuminator of many intellects, is the constant substratum of self-awareness.

विवस्वत् प्रभातं यथा रूपमक्षं प्रगृह्णाति नाभातमेवं विवस्वान् ।

यदाभात आभासयत्यक्षमेकः स नित्योपलब्धिस्वरूपोऽहमात्मा ॥ १०॥

Just as Sūrya, assuming various forms, grasps the whole world without itself undergoing any change, similarly, the one consciousness, shining forth, illumines all objects without itself being affected by them, is the eternal substratum of constant self-awareness.

यथा सूर्य एकोऽप्स्वनेकश्चलासु स्थिरास्वप्यनन्यद्विभाव्यस्वरूपः ।

चलासु प्रभिन्नः सुधीष्वेक एव स नित्योपलब्धिस्वरूपोऽहमात्मा ॥ ११॥

Just as Sūrya, though one, appears as many in the moving and still waters, yet remains unchanged and distinct from them, similarly, the one consciousness, though appearing as diverse in the fluctuating intellects, remains constant and is the eternal substratum of constant self-awareness.

घनच्छन्नदृष्टिर्घनच्छन्नमर्कम् यथा निष्प्रभं मन्यते चातिमूढः ।

तथा बद्धवद्भाति यो मूढ-दृष्टेः स नित्योपलब्धिस्वरूपोऽहमात्मा ॥ १२॥

Just as a dense fog obstructs the vision of Sūrya and fools consider it as devoid of radiance, similarly, to the deluded vision bound by ignorance, the eternal substratum of constant self-awareness appears obscured.

समस्तेषु वस्तुष्वनुस्यूतमेकं समस्तानि वस्तूनि यन्न स्पृशन्ति ।

वियद्वत्सदा शुद्धमच्छस्वरूपं स नित्योपलब्धिस्वरूपोऽहमात्मा ॥ १३॥

The one, pure and immutable, pervading all objects but untouched by any, like space, is the eternal substratum of constant self-awareness.

उपाधौ यथा भेदता सन्मणीनां तथा भेदता बुद्धिभेदेषु तेऽपि ।

यथा चन्द्रिकाणां जले चञ्चलत्वं तथा चञ्चलत्वं तवापीह विष्णो ॥ १४॥

Just as there is differentiation in the gems due to their settings, and likewise in the intellects due to their limitations, similarly, just as the moon's reflection appears unsteady in water, likewise, your apparent instability.

॥ इति श्रीहस्तामलकाचार्यरचितं हस्तामलकसंवादस्तोत्रं सम्पूर्णम् ॥

Kailāśa: Dhanyavād, Guruji for the elaboration of the Stotra.

Sunidhi: Guruji, kindly continue with Ādi Śaṅkara's legend.

Ācārya: Ādi Śaṅkara, along with his disciples, was walking along the Tungabhadra river during a hot summer day when he watched a marvellous sight!

A pregnant frog was struggling in the blazing sun to be delivered of its offspring. A cobra, the natural enemy of frogs, raised its hood to provide the frog with shelter and protection from the ravages of the tropical sun.

The Ācārya was greatly moved by the sight of the venomous snake protecting its arch-rival. If there was paradise on earth, it was there, where the cobra and the frog lived in mutual amity and peace. Even natural animosities did not exist, he thought.

Called Śriṅgagiri (now *Sringeri*), the place had also been the sacred abode of sage Ṛṣyaśriṅga.

Both the rivers Tunga and Badra were flowing there. A popular saying about the river Tunga was, "Tunga Pāna Gaṅgā Snāna". That is, drinking the water of this sacred river had the same effect as taking a dip in the holy Gaṅgā. The place was expressive of the lofty spiritual atmosphere prevailing there.

Since Śrī Śaṅkarācārya had consecrated Śaradā Devī in that same place, He decided to establish his first monastery there.

Ācārya started the task of building up the spiritual lives of everyone there through expositions of his commentaries and other scriptures through his religious instruction and spiritual discourses. Gradually, a fine temple and a monastery were built.

Śaradā Parameśvarī, the chief deity here, is much more than just an aspect of Devī Sarasvatī. She is Tripurasundarī, the triple form of Lakṣmī-Sarasvatī-Gauri. She is the supreme queen, Rājarājeśvarī.

The Ācārya also established various other Devatās like Bhadrakālī, Hanuman, Gaṇeśa and Bhairava for the protection of the place.

Thus, Ācārya established the Sringeri Maṭha, the first of the monasteries, with stability lasting over hundreds of decades for the infinite good of the world.

The establishment of the Sringeri Maṭha by the Ācārya is, in many ways, a very significant event in the spiritual history of Bhāratavarṣa.

Staying in Sringeri, the Ācārya wrote many books full of instructions with the spirit of renunciation.

Sunidhi: Kindly tell us about Totakācārya.

A young man named Giri, lacking proficiency in reading and writing, dedicated himself to serving his Guru, Ācārya. Besides attending to Ācārya's needs, Giri readily assisted the other disciples. In no time, he endeared himself to everyone, especially Ācārya. The Ācārya's disciples were highly educated and proficient in scriptural exposition and debate. In comparison, Giri's knowledge paled. However, his devotion to his Guru was unmatched.

During scripture lessons led by the Ācārya, Giri would respectfully sit close by, listening attentively to every word spoken. One day, Śrī Śaṅkarācārya remained silent during the scheduled scripture teaching session. The disciples had gathered, awaiting his guidance. Sensing the anticipation, Padmapāda spoke up: "We are eagerly waiting for you to commence the teachings."

The Ācārya responded, "Please be patient, and let Giri also join us." Padmapāda expressed surprise, saying, "Giri is indeed a remarkable boy, but can he grasp anything from the scriptures? In terms of intellect, this Giri seems as inert as an object, incapable of comprehending the Upaniṣads."

After washing his Guru's garments in the nearby river, Giri began his walk back. Suddenly, a burst of song and dance overcame him! Magnificent verses, brimming with rhythm, effortlessly flowed from his mouth.

The renowned hymn composed by Giri in praise of Śrī Śaṅkarācārya is called Totakāṣṭakam. This exquisite poem is crafted in the Totaka Chhanda meter, a form that even esteemed composers found challenging to grasp. Everyone was astonished to hear these verses, expressed in pristine Sanskrit and resonating with profound meaning.

Despite feeling ashamed, Padmapāda praised Giri for his remarkable dedication to the Ācārya. He humbly prostrated before the Ācārya, regretting his earlier remarks about Giri. On an auspicious day, the Ācārya initiated Giri into Sanyāsa, bestowing upon him the name Totakācārya.

Sunidhi: Dhanyavād Guruji.

Āratī: Guruji, by this time, was the mother Aryamba of Ādi Śaṅkara alive? Ādi Śaṅkara promised to visit her at her last moment. Didn't he?

Ācārya: Yes, his mother's ending time came near.

One day, while it was the time for teaching, Ādi Śaṅkarācārya was deeply immersed in meditation. His disciples sensed that he was engaged in a profound dialogue, even within his meditation. Concerned, they observed his serene face, filled with worry.

Meanwhile, in Kaladi, Aryamba lay very ill, her thoughts consumed by her son. Through the power of telepathy, the Ācārya heard her silent plea. He swiftly entered into meditation and beseeched Śrī Kṛṣṇa to manifest before his mother.

Ādi Śaṅkara addressed Śrī Kṛṣṇa, saying, "My mother is on her deathbed, longing for my presence. I have made her a promise to be by her side at her final moment. Without delay, I must go to her." With his Yogic powers, the Ācārya swiftly traversed to Kaladi to be with his mother.

Aryamba, in a state of semi-consciousness, found herself lost in memories of her time with her son, Śaṅkara. Longing to see him one last time, she heard his voice and slowly opened her eyes. To her astonishment, she discovered herself lying in the comforting embrace of her beloved Śaṅkara.

"Staying steadfast in this life has not been in vain," she thought. "I have not only seen my son, but I have also felt his presence and now I can hear his sweet voice as well."

"O mother, O mother, can you see me? It's your Śaṅkara. I've journeyed far to be with you, O mother," he gently spoke.

"Śaṅkara! How could I not recognize you? You promised to come to me in my final days when I call upon you. But to think of you, I must have forgotten you, Śaṅkara! Yet, I didn't wish to disturb you. So, I tried to push you out of my mind! Oh! But I couldn't, Śaṅkara. Why did you abandon your duties and come to me?" Aryamba wished to express these sentiments but found herself unable to do so in her current state.

The Ācārya understood her unspoken words. "O mother, I have also lived the life you envisioned! I was once a King, O mother. For a whole month, I experienced kingship! Yet, I find greater joy as a Sanyāsi. True happiness resides within oneself and cannot be sought externally."

Aryamba, incapacitated to comprehend, was, as per her wish, Ācārya invoked Lord Śiva. The Lord dispatched his messengers to transport Aryamba to Śiva Loka. However, upon beholding the fearsome appearance of the messengers adorned with snakes and tridents, Aryamba was seized with fright. "Śaṅkara! They appear so terrifying! I refuse to go with them," she exclaimed.

The Ācārya then turned his focus to Nārāyaṇa in meditation, and soon the Lord, adorned with the conch, discus, mace, and lotus, manifested before Aryamba. Overjoyed at the sight of her beloved deity, Aryamba bestowed abundant blessings upon her son.

By that time, the messengers of Lord Viṣṇu had arrived in a magnificent flying chariot. It seemed as though Aryamba's home had been transfigured into Vaikuntha, the divine abode of Viṣṇu. Subsequently, the messengers transported her soul on the flying chariot to Viṣṇu Loka. Thus, Aryamba attained the divine presence of the Lord at his lotus feet.

The Ācārya regarded himself as truly blessed to have been present by Aryamba's side in her final moments, facilitating her salvation by enabling her to behold her beloved deity.

Meanwhile, Ācārya wrote Mātṛ Pañcakam about Mother.

Āratī: Kindly tell us more about it.

Ācārya: It is as follows:

॥अथ श्री मातृपञ्चकम् ॥

मुक्तामणि त्वं नयनं ममेति
राजेति जीवेति चिर सुत त्वम् ।
इत्युक्तवत्यास्तव वाचि मातः
ददाम्यहं तण्डुलमेव शुष्कम् ॥ १॥

In your tender embrace, those words gently whispered: "You are the treasure of my gaze, my beloved prince, may your days be abundant, my son!" Oh Mother! Now, I present merely parched grains of rice.

अम्बेति तातेति शिवेति तस्मिन्
प्रसूतिकाले यदवोच उच्चैः ।
कृष्णेति गोविन्द हरे मुकुन्द
इति जनन्यै अहो रचितोऽयमञ्जलिः ॥ २॥

In the moment of your birth, your cries echoed: "Mother!! Father!! Śiva!! Kṛṣṇa! Govinda! Hare! Mukunda!" To that mother, I humbly bow with hands clasped in reverence.

आस्तां तावदियं प्रसूतिसमये दुर्वारशूलव्यथा
नैरुच्यं तनुशोषणं मलमयी शय्या च सांवत्सरी ।
एकस्यापि न गर्भभारभरणक्लेशस्य यस्याक्षमः
दातुं निष्कृतिमुन्नतोऽपि तनयस्तस्यै जनन्यै नमः ॥ ३॥

During the moments of my birth, O mother! you endured excruciating pain. Not a word did you utter of your bodily torment nor of the agony endured lying in bed for nearly a year. For even a fraction of the suffering you bore during pregnancy, O mother! a son finds himself incapable of offering redemption. To that mother, I bow in deep reverence!

गुरुकुलमुपसृत्य स्वप्नकाले तु दृष्ट्वा
यतिसमुचितवेशं प्रारुदो मां त्वमुच्चैः ।
गुरुकुलमथ सर्वं प्रारुदत्ते समक्षं

सपदि चरणयोस्ते मातरस्तु प्रणामः ॥ ४॥

In a dream, when you beheld me garbed as an ascetic, you cried out and rushed to the school to find me. The entire school then wept in unison before you. At your feet, O mother! I humbly offer my respects!

न दत्तं मातस्ते मरणसमये तोयमपिवा

स्वधा वा नो दत्ता मरणदिवसे श्राद्धविधिना ।

न जप्त्वा मातस्ते मरणसमये तारकमनु-

रकाले सम्प्राप्ते मयि कुरु दयां मातुरतुलाम् ॥ ५॥

At the hour of your departure, O mother! I failed to offer you water, nor did I perform the necessary rites on the day of your passing. I neglected to recite the mantra that guides one across this worldly ocean. Alas! I have arrived belatedly! O mother! Grant me your unmatched mercy.

In our scriptures, the position of the Mother is elevated even above that of the Devatās. A Sanyāsi who has renounced worldly attachments is permitted to bow before his mother. There exists no mantra greater than Gāyatrī and no Devatā superior to the Mother. The Ācārya's devotion to his mother stems from the Brahman consciousness intertwined with Bhakti.

Kailāśa: Did he perform his mother's funeral rites as he promised?

Ācārya:

Ādi Śaṅkara, mindful of his promise to his mother, began her funeral rites. By that time, all the villagers had gathered. The Ācārya declared, "I will conduct her last rites. Though it may not be customary for a Sanyāsi, it is my duty and heartfelt wish to fulfil her final rites."

The villagers called him a cheat and a hypocrite. They said, "You, being a monk, have no relationship with anyone. You have no right to perform the funeral rites of your mother. We will never allow you to do that".

The illiterate villagers refused to heed the words of Jagatguru Śrī Śaṅkarācārya. They departed in anger and forbade anyone from assisting the Ācārya in conducting the funeral rites. Left alone, the Ācārya remained with the body of his mother.

Despite the Ācārya being the Jagatguru could not avoid this difficult situation presented before him by the Samsāra. The Ācārya bore his mother's body with immense difficulty. There were no mantras, no cries, no customary rituals, no water, no fire... Everything was Śaṅkara, Śaṅkara, Śaṅkara...

He could only carry her as far as the garden yard behind the house. There, he laid her body down. Looking up, he muttered: "Hey Agni Bhagwan! Until now, I have not offered you ghee or wood according to household Dharma. But now, I offer you the holier body of my mother. Please accept her!" Instantly, the fire consumed her body, returning it to its rightful place.

Sunidhi: What a difficult situation, but beautiful last rites for the mother.

Ācārya: Indeed. Such was the greatness of Ādi Śaṅkara.

Sunidhi: Kindly tell us about Śaṅkara Smṛti.

Ācārya: It was about how to live a righteous life.

Ādi Śaṅkara found himself in Kaladi, his birth village, where he conducted his mother's funeral rites. Meanwhile, King Rājasekhara, who had encountered the Ācārya when he was merely eight years old, learned of his presence in Kaladi. Witnessing a significant decline in social norms, the king contemplated social reform. Recognizing the arrival of the Ācārya as an opportune moment, he resolved to implement social reform under the guidance and instructions of the revered teacher.

The King approached the Ācārya and outlined his plan. In agreement with the king's proposal, the Ācārya responded, "Very well, I shall draft a concise code. You should then discuss its merits and flaws with the scholars here before implementing it. This will promote the well-being of the people."

Subsequently, a book comprising sixty-four principles was composed. Delighted, the king read it repeatedly. The book was titled Śaṅkara Smṛti, signifying 'the code of Śaṅkara'.

The king gathered an assembly of scholars to evaluate the merits and shortcomings of the code. The Ācārya participated in the deliberations. The scholars contended that the principles proposed by the Ācārya contradicted scripture and posed a threat to society. As the debate ensued, the divine radiance of the Ācārya gradually silenced the scholars. However, despite being subdued, they remained steadfast in their refusal to concede defeat.

In a novel attempt to assert their stance, the scholars organized two simultaneous meetings, each nearly fifty miles apart, on the same day and at the same time. They separately informed the king that they challenged the Ācārya to a debate. If he could defeat them, they would accept his code. The Ācārya accepted the challenge.

On the appointed day, under the king's leadership, the Ācārya adeptly responded to the numerous questions posed by the scholars, silencing them all. It became evident that the code he formulated aligned with the scriptures, including the Vedas and Puranas.

The scholars were astonished by the myriad quotations from scriptures effortlessly recalled by the Ācārya, demonstrating his remarkable memory. Though they admitted defeat, they remained hopeful that the other meeting would rule in their favour, as the Ācārya was engaged in debate elsewhere and couldn't possibly be present.

However, using his Yogic Siddhis, the Ācārya multiplied himself and appeared at the other meeting at the appointed hour. He addressed all queries and dispelled doubts, leaving the scholars speechless. Despite acknowledging their defeat, they believed they had won since the Ācārya couldn't have attended the other meeting.

When news of both meetings spread, everyone was astonished. Bowing before the young Ācārya with such supernatural abilities, the scholars accepted his code and agreed to implement it in society.

Kailāśa: Kindly tell us how Ādi Śaṅkara recovered the lost creation of King Rājasekhara.

Ācārya: King Rājasekhara became a devoted disciple of the Ācārya. One day, the Ācārya inquired about the progress of the king's literary works and if he had authored any new books. Sighing, the king replied, "No, sir, I have abandoned it. It is a tragic tale. The three plays that I once shared with you long ago have been consumed by fire. The grief of this loss has left me bereft of the desire to write any new plays."

Expressing empathy for the king's loss, the Ācārya consoled him, saying, "I understand your sentiments. Long ago, you shared your plays with me, and I was so captivated by them that I remember every detail from beginning to end. I shall dictate from my memory, and you may transcribe them, thus restoring the texts."

The king and his attendants diligently transcribed the Ācārya's dictation of the three plays. Upon reading the texts, the king discovered that the Ācārya had dictated precisely the same words he had once written. Overwhelmed with gratitude and reverence, the king bowed repeatedly at the Ācārya's feet.

Sunidhi: Guruji, kindly tell us about the episode of Śrī Guruvāyūr.

Ācārya: Guruvāyūr is a temple town in the Thrissur district of Kerala, India. It houses the Guruvāyūr Śrī Kṛṣṇa Temple. According to Hindu legend, the deity Kṛṣṇa is said to have asked a deity and a sage to take the Mūrti from his temple in Dvaraka before a flood destroyed it and established it in Kerala.

Accordingly, the Mūrti of Kṛṣṇa is believed to have been brought by the Vāyudeva and Devaguru Bṛhaspati and was placed in Guruvāyūr. Guru refers to the title of Bṛhaspati, and Vāyu refers to Vāyudeva.

Guruvāyūr Ekādaśī is a special occasion here. Of the twenty-four Ekādaśīs in a Lunar year, the Vṛścika Māsa Śukla Ekādaśī has special significance in Guruvāyūr temple. A memorial honour for Gajarājan Keśavan is conducted in Guruvāyūr.

The Karanavar, or head of the elephant family, places a wreath at the statue of Keshavan in front of Sreevalsam guest house, and all the other elephants stand around and pay obeisance.

On Ekādaśī day, the Udayāstamāna Pūjā is conducted by the Devaswom itself. After the morning Siveli procession, on Ekādaśī, there is a grand elephant procession to the Parthasarathi temple since it is regarded as Gītopadeśam Day also. On Ekādaśī after night pooja, the famous Ekādaśī Vilakku with elephant procession takes place and provides a fitting finale to the festival.

It was Ekādaśī, the auspicious day of the Vṛścika Māsa Śukla Ekādaśī, coinciding with Gītopadeśam Day when Lord Kṛṣṇa imparted the Gītā to Arjuna. The Ācārya wanted to get back to Sringeri, and He invoked his Yogic Siddhis to fly in space.

While above Guruvāyūr, he saw the Siveli procession of the Lord Kṛṣṇa on the northern side of the Nadapandal of the temple. He felt sorry for the crowd that did not know about the Brahman in the self and were rushing to see an image outside of the self!

In the blink of an eye, the Ācārya suddenly fell to the ground before the Lord! Quickly regaining his composure, the Ācārya beheld the Lord in all His magnificence. Understanding the reason for his sudden fall, the Ācārya humbly prostrated before the Lord, seeking forgiveness. The Lord then revealed that acts such as temple worship, chanting the Lord's name, and listening to religious discourses were cherished expressions of devotion to Him. The small aperture in the roof above the northwest courtyard of the Guruvāyūr Temple serves as a memorial to this sacred event.

The Ācārya chanted 8 slokas in praise of Govinda, known as Govinda Ashtakam.

He formulated the elaborate Pujā routines at the temple. He said that on Ekādaśī day, there should be a grand festival with dawn to dusk worship. Even today, the system of daily rites at the temple is practised in accordance with the directions given by Śrī Śaṅkarācārya.

Sunidhi: Kindly tell us about the creation of Pañcapādikā by Padmapāda.

Ācārya: While at Sringeri, the Ācārya had requested Sureśvara to write the explanatory notes on his commentary of Brahmasūtra Bhāśya.

Padmapāda and the other disciples were aware that Sureśvara possessed expertise in the Mīmāṃsā system and had transitioned to Advaita from it. They feared that he might advocate for the superiority of the Mīmāṃsā system and misinterpret the significance of the Ācārya's commentaries. Additionally, Sureśvara had embraced Sanyāsa after initially leading a household life, contrasting with the other disciples who were Brahmacāris. These differences created a tense atmosphere among them.

The Ācārya, sensing the discomfort among the disciples, instructed Sureśvara to cease his current work and instead focus on writing about Advaita Vedānta. He then entrusted Padmapāda with the task of composing explanatory notes based on the teachings previously imparted to Sureśvara.

Sureśvara diligently penned an authoritative philosophical treatise on Brahman and the self. Upon reading it, the Ācārya was overjoyed. He was deeply impressed by Sureśvara's profound understanding of Advaita, his extensive scholarship, eloquent writing style, adept use of language to convey meaning, his adept dismantling of opposing viewpoints with unassailable logic, and the powerful manner in which he established his conclusions.

The other disciples, including Padmapāda, held a great appreciation for Sureśvara's scholarly contribution. There were no doubts among them regarding Sureśvara's profound knowledge or his dedication to Advaita Vedānta. Although Padmapāda had not yet finished his work, he presented to the Ācārya whatever he had written thus far. The Ācārya commended Padmapāda's efforts and bestowed upon the collection of notes the name "Vijayadindima," blessing him to complete the work.

Feeling burdened by guilt over the incident involving Sureśvara's work, Padmapāda sought to atone for his perceived transgression. With the blessings of his Guru, he embarked on a pilgrimage to Holy Rāmeśvaram, accompanied by a few fellow disciples. By this time, Padmapāda had nearly completed the Vijayadindima.

During their journey, Padmapāda stopped to visit his maternal uncle in Śrīraṅgam. He shared with his uncle about his revered Guru and engaged in deep discussions on the scriptures. Padmapāda's uncle, himself a learned scholar and follower of the Dvaita philosophy, participated actively in the discourse.

Padmapāda's exceptional reasoning and logic gradually persuaded his uncle to reconsider his own beliefs. Impressed by Padmapāda's arguments, his uncle humbly requested to borrow the book Vijayadindima so that he could study and gain a deeper understanding of Advaita philosophy. He pledged to return the book to Padmapāda upon his return from Rāmeśvaram.

Despite the agreement, Padmapāda's wicked uncle found himself unable to counter the profound insights and arguments presented in Vijayadindima through debate. Recognizing that the publication of the book would pose a formidable challenge to Dvaita philosophy, he resolved to destroy it. However, he did not want Padmapāda to discover his treachery.

In his deviousness, the uncle concealed Vijayadindima inside his house and set fire to the building, ensuring the destruction of the book along with his dwelling.

Upon his return, Padmapāda was devastated to learn of the fire and the subsequent destruction of Vijayadindima. Overwhelmed by shock and grief, his sense of guilt intensified. Without delay, he departed from the place, filled with a deep longing to reunite with his Guru, the Ācārya.

Padmapāda recounted his journey and the heartbreaking loss of Vijayadindima to the Ācārya. In response, the Ācārya offered solace to his disciple, saying, "Do not dwell in futile sorrow. The bitter fruits of past actions are inevitable. It is wiser to endure the pain that cannot be remedied patiently. There is no need for distress over the destruction of your works. You had previously read to me the explanatory notes on the first five sutras, and I still remember them vividly. I will dictate from my memory, and you may transcribe them."

Padmapāda diligently transcribed the notes on the five sutras from the Ācārya's dictation, creating Pañcapādikā. Through this process, his mind found tranquillity, and both mental and physical exhaustion dissipated completely. In spirit and body, he experienced a profound purification.

Sunidhi: What happened next? Did he continue his Digvijaya yatra?

Ācārya: Indeed, he did that. Ādi Śaṅkara and His four distinguished disciples, Sureśvara, Padmapāda, Hastāmalaka and Totakācārya and a number of His devotees continued the Digvijaya yatra towards the south.

The entourage arrived at Chidambaram, a sacred site deeply associated with Nataraja, the cosmic form of Lord Śiva performing the Ananda Tāṇḍavam, the Dance of Bliss.

The Nataraja Mūrti is housed within the sacred confines of the Citsabhā. Positioned behind this iconic figure is a darkened backdrop, symbolizing the veiled presence of the Ākāśa Liṅga. Though physically imperceptible, the concept of an unseen Liṅga adorned with resplendent Bilva garlands underscores the profound belief in the presence of all within the void. It is in this enigmatic portrayal, known as the Chidambara Rahasya or the Secret of Chidambaram that devotees worship Śiva in a manifestation transcending physical form. Accessible via five silver-plated steps, reminiscent of the Pañcākṣari mantra: na-ma-śi-vā-ya, the Citsabhā serves as a testament to the boundless nature of divinity.

In that temple, the Ācārya devoutly worshipped Lord Śiva. It is believed that he attained a profound understanding of the secrets of Śrīyantra and Śrīcakra meditation within its sacred confines. During his meditation, he envisioned through his inner eye, known as Jñānadṛṣṭi, the formless and yet manifest sphaṭika Liṅga—transcending attributes yet imbued with them—that he would later install in the temple.

Subsequently, the Ācārya embarked on a journey to another esteemed temple situated at Thiruvidaimarudur, nestled within the Tanjavur district. This temple is renowned for housing the revered Mahaliṅgam, the name bestowed upon the Liṅga within its sanctum. According to tradition, this liṅgam stands amidst two other significant Liṅgams, namely Mallikarjuna and Putarjuna, hence earning the appellation Madhyarjuna.

Ācārya engaged in profound debates on Advaita philosophy, triumphing over numerous scholars at Thiruvidaimarudur. Upon the conclusion of the debates, he invited them to enter the temple premises. As they approached the Sanctum Santorum, a resounding voice reverberated, proclaiming, "Satyam is Advaita." This declaration echoed thrice, accompanied by a miraculous manifestation—a hand emerged from the Liṅga, affirming the truth. Moved by this divine revelation, the scholars embraced the principle of Advaita and acknowledged Śrī Śaṅkarācārya as their revered Guru.

Śrī Śaṅkarācārya then visited Thiruvanaikaval, near Tiruchirapalli. The temple is named after the elephant, which is believed to have worshipped Lord Śiva here. Installed under an ancient Jambu tree, the Liṅga is partially submerged in water and meant to represent God incarnate as water.

Within this temple, the presence of Devī Akhilandeśvari emanated formidable power, overwhelming those who sought her divine sight with her intense aura. To mitigate her fierceness, the Ācārya crafted two sets of earrings known as Tatankam and offered them to the Devī. With the presentation of these adornments, the intensity of the Devī's demeanour lessened. The Ācārya then proceeded to worship both Śrī Jampukeśvarar and Śrī Akhilandeśvari. Subsequently, he journeyed to the nearby Śrīraṅgam.

Śrīraṅgam boasts an impressive array of 22 gopurams, among which stands the remarkable thirteen-tiered Rajagopuram towering at a height of 236 feet, making it the tallest in India. Situated on an islet formed by the convergence of the Kaveri and Kollidam rivers, the temple holds a significant position. Legend has it that Śrī Śaṅkarācārya himself installed a Yantra known as Janākarṣaṇa Yantra within its precincts to draw pilgrims. After spending several days in prayer and delivering profound Advaita discourses at Śrīraṅgam, Ādi Śaṅkara continued his journey southward.

Śrī Śaṅkarācārya and His disciples reached Madurai after visiting many temples along their way from Śrīraṅgam. The sprawling Mīnākṣi Sundareśvarar temple in Madurai is being considered as one of the world's wonders. The Ācārya worshipped Mīnākṣi and composed Mīnākṣi Pañcaratnam and Mīnākṣi stotram here.

From Madurai, Ādi Śaṅkara and his companions embarked towards Thiruvananthapuram. En route, they toured temples, engaged with locals, and disseminated the teachings of Advaita philosophy. The majestic Śrī Anantha Padmanabha Swamy Temple in Thiruvananthapuram, dedicated to Lord Viṣṇu, with its towering 100-foot 'gopuram', left a profound impression. Ācārya Śaṅkara resided in Thiruvananthapuram, devoutly worshipping the Lord and engaging in scholarly discussions on Advaita philosophy with various learned individuals.

Ādi Śaṅkara proceeded towards the southernmost point of India. However, during his journey, the Ācārya fell ill from the strain of extensive travel. Despite his ailment, he pressed on with his pilgrimage and finally reached Kanyakumari, where the Bay of Bengal, the Arabian Sea, and the Indian Ocean converge. Kanyakumari translates to "a virgin," signifying purity. The temple overlooking the coastline is dedicated to Devī Kanyā. She adorns a dazzling diamond nose ring that glimmers out towards the sea. Ācārya Śaṅkara humbly prostrated before the Devī and offered his reverence.

From Kanyakumari, Ācārya journeyed northward towards Tiruchendur. Along the way, he paused at the Suchindram Temple, dedicated to a Devatā embodying the collective energies of Śiva, Viṣṇu, and Brahma. Despite his ongoing illness, Ācārya Śaṅkara, accompanied by his disciples and devotees, eventually arrived at Tiruchendur.

Tiruchendur stands among the six Arupadai Veedu shrines of Murugan, nestled along the seashore at the southernmost tip of India, near Tirunelveli and Kanyakumari. Unlike the other five Padaiveedu shrines situated atop hills, Tiruchendur rests beside the sea, embraced by its waters to the north and east. Here, Śrī Śaṅkarācārya engaged in meditation upon Lord Subrahmaṇya and composed the Subrahmanya Bhujangam. In his composition, the Ācārya declared: "Just by beholding your sacred ashes (Vibhuti), all afflictions shall be healed." Remarkably, the Ācārya himself experienced recovery from his ailment when he recited his composition in the presence of Lord Subrahmaṇya.

The group proceeded northward to Rāmeśvaram, where they encountered the Rāmanātha Temple. This temple, often referred to as the Kāśi of the south, is renowned for housing one of the twelve Jyotirliṅgas. Ācārya Śaṅkara partook in a sacred bath at the convergence of Mahodadhi (Bay of Bengal) and Ratnakara (Arabian Sea). Accessing the Sanctum Sanctorum effortlessly, he conducted the Abhiṣeka ceremony for Rāmanātha Svāmi using water from the Gaṅgā, performed Bilva Pujā, and engaged in meditation. Additionally, he paid homage to Śrī Parvathavardhini.

Ācārya visited the Kodaṇḍarāmasvāmi Temple, where Vibhishna, Ravana's brother, surrendered to Rāma. He then journeyed to Dhanushkodi and Rāmasetu. Remaining in Rāmeśvaram for two months, Ācārya solidified its status as the principal Kṣetra for the Sringeri Maṭha.

Ācārya embarked on his journey towards North India to propagate the Advaita philosophy. En route to Tirupathi, he arrived at Śrīkālahasti. The temple there venerates Śiva and symbolizes Vāyu among the Pañcabhūta Sthalams, which celebrate Śiva as the embodiment of the primary elements. The temple's unique feature is the presence of Vayu, demonstrated by a perpetual flame that flickers despite the absence of any openings for air. Remarkably, the shrine is situated thirty feet below ground level.

In ancient times, the Liṅgam was revered by a spider, a cobra, and an elephant. The spider worshipped the Lord by weaving a web over the Liṅgam, the snake by placing a gem atop it, and the elephant by bathing the Liṅgam with water from its trunk. It is said that all three creatures attained Mokṣa, liberation, through their devout worship of the Lord. The name of the place, Śrīkālahasti, reflects their contributions: Śrī (spider), Kāla (cobra), and Hasti (elephant). The Ācārya worshipped the Lord at Śrīkālahasti and left for Tirupati.

The Ācārya beheld the divine form of Lord Veṅkaṭeśa, the eternal auspicious Śrīnivāsa. Within the sacred icon, he perceived the presence of Keśava, Nārāyaṇa, Govinda, Viṣṇu, Madhusudhana, Trivikrama, Vamana, Sridhara, Hṛṣīkeśa, Padmanabha, and Dāmodara - encapsulating all the manifestations of the Lord. Suddenly, he discerned a Liṅgam atop the Lord's head, portraying Viṣṇu bearing Śiva. This revelation unveiled the golden crown adorning Śrī Balaji. The Ācārya reverently worshipped the Lord and immersed himself in meditation upon Him.

Śrī Śaṅkarācārya instituted the Dhanākarṣaṇa Yantra at this temple to draw prosperity. The Ācārya eloquently documented all his encounters with Śrī Venkatesa in exquisite verses, composing the Śrī Viṣṇu Padadi Kesanta Varnana Stotram.

During his pilgrimage, Śrī Śaṅkarācārya disseminated the fundamentals of Pañcayatana Pujā, making a significant contribution to Sanatana Vaidika dharma. He expounded that Brahman could manifest in five primary forms: Śiva, Viṣṇu, Sūrya, Gaṇeśa, and Durgā. Individuals could select one of these deities as their principal focus of worship based on their preferences, predispositions, and qualifications. The remaining four deities could be revered as auxiliary Devatās supporting the chosen deity.

The Ācārya continued his journey into Andhra Pradesh, traversing numerous locations and disseminating the wisdom of Brahman and the Self. Eventually, he reached the sacred city of Puri in Orissa. Upon entering the renowned Jagannath temple, he was surprised to find the altar empty.

He discovered that during the tumultuous period of oppression by Kālayavana, who sought to eradicate all Yadavas, including Kṛṣṇa, the priests of the temple had buried the casket containing the wooden image of Lord Jagannath along the banks of Chilika Lake. Subsequently, amidst Buddhist attacks that ensued, the casket was further relocated. However, with the assistance of a benevolent king, a multitude of Salagrama stones were installed, and the rites of worship were reinstated upon the same altar.

The Ācārya, overwhelmed with profound sadness upon witnessing the empty altar devoid of the image of Jagannātha, immersed himself in intense meditation along the banks of the lake. Following his contemplation, he addressed the people, conveying: "The casket housing the idols rests buried beneath the largest banyan tree on the eastern banks of the lake. If that precise location is excavated, the casket shall be unearthed."

The people diligently excavated the designated spot and, to their astonishment, uncovered the casket. Joyous celebrations ensued among the gathered crowd. With great pomp and splendour, the casket was transported to Puri. On an auspicious day, amid immense joy and reverence, the image of the Lord was ceremoniously installed in the shrine of Jagannātha.

Additionally, the Ācārya established Govardhan Maṭha in Puri to propagate Vaidika Dharma. At the Jagannath temple, he composed the Jagannātha Aṣṭakam, a hymn glorifying the Lord.

Ācārya proceeded on a westward journey towards Saurashtra and reached the Godāvari River near Nasik in Maharashtra. There, he visited the Tryambakeśvara temple, which houses one of the twelve Jyotirliṅgas. A remarkable aspect of this Jyotirliṅga is its three faces, representing the divine trinity of Brahma, Viṣṇu, and Śiva. The term "Tryambaka" signifies the "three-eyed one," referring to Lord Śiva, with "tri" meaning "three" and "ambak" meaning "eye."

The Ācārya devoutly worshipped the Lord and engaged in deep meditation upon Tryambakeśvara. He actively participated in detailed discussions with the local populace, imparting knowledge on the principles of bhakti (devotion) and the significance of proper worship.

Ācārya then proceeded to Pandharpur, renowned for its Vithoba temple situated on the banks of the river. Vithoba is a manifestation of Kṛṣṇa, with Rukmini as his consort. The name Vithala signifies "One who stands on a brick," as the Lord is depicted standing on a small stone platform within the temple. The deity's idol stands at a height of 3-1/2 feet, with an inverted lotus beneath the platform. In his composition, Panduranga Āṣṭakam, Śrī Śaṅkarācārya beautifully described the Lord as 'Parabrahma Liṅgam'.

Śrī Ācārya proceeded on his journey to Ujjain, home to another Jyotirliṅga Temple. Ujjain, situated on the banks of the river Shipra in Madhya Pradesh, is renowned as one of the revered Śiva Kṣetrams. Accompanied by his disciples, the Ācārya paid homage to the deity Mahākāleśvara. He expressed his reverence through a charming hymn composed in the deity's honour, his profound devotion deeply touching the hearts of all present.

Witnessing the Ācārya's humble and unassuming lifestyle, the people became intrigued and eager to learn more about him and the principles of Advaita philosophy. Responding to their curiosity, the Ācārya engaged in debates with renowned scholars on Advaita philosophy, ultimately emerging victorious and winning them over with his persuasive arguments and profound wisdom.

Śrī Ācārya then continued his pilgrimage to Somanātha, located on the south coast of Saurashtra in Gujarat. The temple, a magnificent sight to behold, is dedicated to the revered deities Somanātha and Someśvar, with the Śiva Liṅgam enshrined here being one of the Jyotirliṅgas. After offering worship to Lord Somanātha, Ācārya and his disciples proceeded to Dvarakā.

In Dvarakā, the Ācārya established a Pīṭha. To empower this sacred seat, he designated Kālikādevī as the presiding Devī and Siddeśvara as the primary deity. Thus, the Pīṭha came to be known as Dvarakā Kalika Pīṭha.

After founding the Maṭha at Dvarakā, the Ācārya remained there for a period, diligently organizing the worship rituals. He then resumed his journey, venturing towards Rajasthan and Sindh. In Rajasthan, he visited Pushkar, a revered pilgrimage site dedicated to Brahma. Travelling through villages and towns, he visited numerous shrines, receiving great honour and respect at each stop.

His profound teachings on Advaita Vedānta deeply impacted followers of various beliefs, leading them to embrace and follow the path of Advaita after listening to the Ācārya's enlightening discourses.

The Ācārya journeyed through Puruṣapura (Peshawar) and the Bahlika[1] region (undivided Punjab), eventually arriving in the country of Gandhara, located between Kabul and Peshawar. Buddhism held a significant influence in this region. The Ācārya, responding to the earnest quest for truth among the people, imparted teachings on the Vaidika path, fulfilling their aspirations and encouraging them to embrace this ancient wisdom. Puruṣa

---

[1] Bahlika is mentioned in Atharvaveda, Mahabharata, Ramayana, Puranas, Vartikka of Katyayana, Brhatsamhita, Amarkosha etc. and in the ancient Inscriptions. The other variations of Bahlika are Bahli, Balhika, Vahlika, Valhika, Bahlava, Bahlam, Bahlim, Bahlayana and Bahluva. According to the Bhuvanakosha section of the Puranas, Bahlika was a Janapada located in the Udichya (Uttarapatha) division. Some hymns of Atharvaveda invoke the fever to go to the Gandharis, Mahavrsas (a tribe of Punjab), Mujavants and, further off, to the Bahlikas. Mujavant is the name of a hill (and the people) located in Hindukush or Pamir.

The Ācārya engaged in profound debates with Buddhist teachers, demonstrating that Lord Buddha's spiritual teachings were in harmony with Vaidika injunctions and that Buddha himself achieved the highest form of enlightenment. Through his discussions, the Ācārya expounded the truths of the Vedas and the principles of spiritual practice. He highlighted that misunderstandings regarding Lord Buddha's instructions and life had led Buddhists to propagate theories contrary to the Vedas.

The Ācārya achieved spiritual triumph in the region of Kamboja, situated on the banks of the Kabul River, as well as in various other areas north of Kashmir, including those in what is now known as Pakistan-occupied Kashmir. Enduring vast deserts, towering peaks, and formidable rivers, he eventually arrived in Kashmir.

Kashmir held great significance as a centre of Hindu culture during that era. It was adorned with eminent scholars from across India and sincere spiritual seekers, enriching the grandeur of the region. Additionally, Kashmir was revered as the sacred abode of Śaradā, the Devī of learning and fine arts.

Inside the Śaradā Devī temple resided the Sarvajna Pīṭha, the revered seat of omniscience. Guarded by renowned scholars hailing from diverse regions of India, this pedestal remained unoccupied. Any scholar aspiring to ascend the Pīṭha would have to demonstrate comprehensive knowledge, surpassing challenges posed by scholars representing various sects and faiths. The authority to ascend the Pīṭha would be granted only through the unanimous agreement of all the scholars present.

Śrī Ācārya approached the temple and expressed his eagerness to engage in debates with the scholars present. Representatives from various philosophical traditions, including Vaiśeṣikas, followers of Sāṃkhya attributed to Kapila, proponents of Nyāya associated with Gautama, adherents of Mīmāṃsā attributed to Jaimini, Buddhists, Jains, and other erudite intellectuals, participated in discussions with the Ācārya on a wide array of subjects.

At the conclusion of the debates, all the scholars, in unison, acknowledged, "You are a boundless ocean of knowledge and learning. Your mastery encompasses all scriptures and branches of learning. We consider it a great honour to have engaged in debate with you, even in defeat. We unanimously invite you to ascend the Pīṭha."

Śrī Ācārya offered worship to the Devī Śaradā with a melodious Śloka. At that sacred moment, a celestial voice resonated from the heavens: "Dear son Śaṅkara, I am delighted with you. Today, I confer upon you the title of Sarvajna (all-knowing). You alone are deserving of occupying this Pīṭha." It was the divine voice of Śaradā, the mother of the universe, echoing throughout the temple.

Upon hearing the divine voice, the Ācārya humbly prostrated before the Devī. This extraordinary occurrence left everyone convinced of the living presence of the Devī at that sacred site. Seated upon the Pīṭha, the Ācārya elucidated the true essence of the great Devī Parāśaktī, satisfying the hearts and minds of all those in attendance.

During his sojourn in Kashmir, the Ācārya imparted teachings on Advaita, Brahman, and the Self to the general populace. He formally initiated numerous deserving individuals into the worship of Devī Śaradā, basing his teachings on Advaita Vedānta. After this period of spiritual instruction and initiation, Śrī Ācārya resumed his journey, proceeding onwards to Srinagar.

In Srinagar, the Ācārya learned of the Tāntrikas' involvement in the practice of human sacrifice. He initiated a debate with them, elucidating the genuine essence of spirituality and scriptures and correcting their misguided beliefs. After extensive discussions, the Tāntrikas acknowledged the wisdom of the Ācārya and renounced the ritual of human sacrifice. They even dismantled the stone altar used for these sacrifices. The profound transformation brought about by the Ācārya's teachings was comprehensive and far-reaching.

Gopaditya, the King of Kashmir, honoured the Ācārya by naming a hill after him, known as 'Śaṅkara Giri'. Presently, this hill is referred to as the 'Takhti Sulaiman Hills'. Additionally, the king erected a temple dedicated to Śrī Śaṅkarācārya atop this hill. After this gesture of reverence, Śrī Śaṅkarācārya resumed his journey towards Kailāśa and eventually arrived in Haridwar.

Indeed, Haridwar holds significant mythological importance as the gateway to the Himalayas. According to legend, Bhagiratha, a king, brought the sacred river Ganga down to the earth, leading her to flow through Haridwar. This act was undertaken to cleanse the ashes of his ancestors, who had been reduced to ashes by the curse of the sage Kapila. A place known as Kapilastana in Haridwar is believed to be the site of Kapila's Āśrama, marking the spot where this significant event occurred.

Upon reaching Hṛṣīkeśa, Śrī Ācārya visited the Yajñeśvara Mahāviṣṇu Temple. To his surprise, upon entering the sanctum, he discovered that the pedestal was bare and devoid of any divine image or arrangements for worship. Upon inquiry, he learned that long ago, due to the turmoil caused by bandits, the priests of the temple had hidden the image of Śrī Viṣṇu deep within the holy waters of the Ganga. Despite extensive efforts to recover the Mūrti, it remained elusive and could not be located.

After a moment of contemplation, Śrī Ācārya entered into deep meditation. In his profound trance, he located the Mūrti of Śrī Viṣṇu. Walking a short distance along the banks of the Ganga, he pointed to a specific spot and instructed the people to excavate below the riverbed to retrieve the Mūrti. To the astonishment of all, the image was discovered intact. On an auspicious day, Śrī Śaṅkarācārya presided over the reinstatement of the image in the Sanctum Sanctorum, conducting all the requisite religious rites. With this divine task fulfilled, he resumed his pilgrimage and continued onwards towards the sacred destination of Badrinātha.

Close to Hṛṣīkeśa, Śrī Ācārya visited Lakṣmaṇa Jhoola, a site associated with the religious austerities undertaken by Vidura. According to legend, Lakshmana, the brother of Lord Rama, crossed the river at this location using a hanging bridge made of jute. Continuing his journey, Śrī Ācārya arrived at Vyāsāśrama and Devaprayāga. Here, he paid reverence at the temples dedicated to Ganesa, Śrī Rama and Sita, as well as Hara and Pārvati.

Śrī Śaṅkarācārya and his disciples reached Badrinātha, where the majestic snow-covered peaks of Nara and Nārāyaṇa towered on two sides, radiating the glory of ancient times. Nearby, the river Alakananda flowed majestically, adding to the serene ambience. Adjacent to the temple of Nārāyaṇa, there were hot springs where Śrī Ācārya and his disciples bathed before proceeding to the shrine of Badrinārāyaṇa.

However, upon reaching the shrine, they found that the four-armed Mūrti of Badrinārāyaṇa was absent, and instead, a Salagrama stone was being worshipped in its place.

As in another temple, here, too, the image had been concealed by the forefathers of the priests to safeguard it from bandits. Despite extensive efforts to recover the image, it remained elusive. Consequently, the Lord had been worshipped through the symbol of the sacred Salagrama stone.

Upon learning this, Śrī Ācārya became deeply contemplative and immersed himself in meditation. Upon returning to normal consciousness, he made his way towards the Nāradakuṇḍa springs. Despite the dangerous undercurrents that had claimed many lives, Śrī Ācārya descended into the waters. Remarkably, he emerged from the springs holding in his hands a four-armed image of Nārāyaṇa.

Upon bringing the Mūrti out of the water and closely examining it, Śrī Ācārya found no distinctive features indicating its divine nature. Thus, he returned it to the water and dived into the Nārāyaṇakuṇḍa once again, retrieving another Mūrti. However, even this one lacked any discernible divine qualities. Undeterred, Śrī Ācārya dove into the waters for a third time and retrieved yet another Mūrti.

Just as he was about to return it to the water, a voice intervened, declaring, "I am Badrinātha, consecrated by Brahma in the past. Give this divine Mūrti its rightful place." This divine revelation halted Śrī Ācārya's actions and affirmed the sacred identity of the Mūrti.

The Ācārya reverently bowed before the Mūrti and, following the prescribed rituals, performed the ceremonial bathing of the image. With his own sacred hands, he installed the Nārāyaṇa Mūrti in the shrine, ensuring its rightful place. Moved by divine inspiration, Śrī Ācārya composed and recited the Shat-Padi stotram, offering profound praise to the Lord Badrinātha.

An installation performed by Śrī Ācārya signified the transmission of a potent spiritual current whose efficacy would endure for countless generations. Entrusting the responsibility of worshipping the newly installed deity to a deserving group of his followers, Śrī Ācārya meticulously outlined the procedures for the worship, ensuring that the sacred rites would be carried out with utmost reverence and devotion.

Śrī Śaṅkarācārya established Joshimaṭh, one of the five Maṭhas, marking a significant spiritual centre. Situated approximately fourteen kilometres from Helang on the route to Badrinātha, it was at this sacred site that the Ācārya attained enlightenment and composed the illustrious work Śrī Śaṅkara Bhāśya.

In addition to founding the Maṭha, Śrī Ācārya constructed a temple dedicated to Lord Nṛsiṅha, the divine protector, and performed the consecration rites, infusing the place with divine sanctity and spiritual vibrancy.

Ācārya embarked on a pilgrimage to various sacred sites, including Viṣṇu Prayāga, Brahmakuṇḍa, Viṣṇukuṇḍa, and Śivakuṇḍa, among others, before reaching Kedarnath. There, Śrī Śaṅkarācārya paid homage to Lord Śiva and meticulously formulated worship protocols for future generations to observe.

The backdrop of the temple was adorned with majestic snow-clad peaks, marking the onset of the Himalayan range. It was amidst these mountains that Śrī Ācārya identified Kailāśa, the sacred abode of Lord Śiva.

Śrī Śaṅkarācārya, guided by divine inspiration, discerned the path leading to Kailāśa, the heavenly abode. With a heart filled with reverence and anticipation, he embarked on the arduous journey towards the earthly manifestation of Heaven, Mount Meru, known as Kailāśa.

After a journey filled with spiritual significance and inner transformation, Śrī Śaṅkarācārya finally arrived at Kailāśa, the celestial sanctuary, the abode of Lord Śiva himself.

On the summit of Kailāśa Peak, amidst a lush garden adorned with radiant jewels and garlands and filled with diverse trees, creepers, and blossoming flowers, stood a pedestal adorned with pure gems. Surrounding this exquisite scene were attendants engaged in soft murmurs and conversation.

Seated upon this pedestal were Bhagavan Mahādeva, the Great God, and his divine consort, Umā Devī. They were accompanied by Brahma, Indra, and Viṣṇu, alongside Bṛhaspati and Śukra, along with numerous Brāhmaṇas, Ṛṣis, Siddhas, and Gandharvas. The Lord, adorned with a crescent moon and wielding a trident, bestowed blessings with one hand and dispelled fear with the other, exuding divine grace. His consort, Devī, adorned with shining ornaments, emanated beauty and tranquillity.

Śrī Ācārya was blessed with the divine vision of Lord Parameśvara and Devī Parvathi, witnessing their divine presence both individually and in the Ardhanārīśvara form, where they are united as one. Filled with reverence and devotion, Śrī Ācārya offered adoration to Devī and Parameśvara by singing hymns such as the "*śivapādādikeśāntavarṇana stotram*" and the "*śivakeśādi-pādāntavarṇana stotram*," extolling their divine attributes and offering heartfelt praise.

Indeed, Śrī Ācārya's hymns exemplify the poetic tradition of describing Devīs from their divine head to their lotus feet and Puruṣa Devatās from their feet to their radiant heads. Blessed with divine grace and inspiration by Parvathi and

Parameśvara, Śrī Ācārya's poetic prowess shone brightly, enabling him to compose such sublime and beautiful hymns. His verses resonate with profound devotion and reverence, capturing the sublime beauty and attributes of the divine beings he worshipped.

Devī Umā and Lord Maheśvara bestowed their divine gaze upon Śrī Ācārya, who, like a celestial nectar, disseminated the profound teachings of Advaita from the vast ocean of Vedānta, enriching the universe with spiritual wisdom. Pleased beyond measure by Ācārya's prayers and devotion, the Lord blessed him abundantly.

In a gesture of divine grace, Lord Parameśvara presented Śrī Ācārya with five Sphaṭika Liṅgams, entrusting him with the sacred duty of arranging their worship for the welfare of the universe. The Lord imparted detailed instructions on the mode of worship for these Liṅgams, ensuring their sanctity and efficacy.

Additionally, Lord Parameśvara bestowed upon Śrī Ācārya the palm-leaf manuscript of Saundaryalaharī, a hymn composed by Śiva himself in praise of Parāśaktī, the Divine Mother. Reverently, Śrī Ācārya bowed before the Lord and Devī, offering heartfelt praises through the enchanting verses of Umā Maheśvara Stotram before taking his leave, carrying with him the divine blessings and sacred treasures bestowed upon him.

According to the saying, "God gives a boon, but there is a Nandikeśvara in between," Nandikeśvara, the celestial attendant of Lord Śiva, intervened when Śrī Ācārya was departing from Kailāśa with the Pañca Liṅgams and Saundaryalaharī. Misinterpreting the situation as potential looting of Kailāśa's treasures, Nandikeśvara impulsively leapt upon Śrī Ācārya to seize the sacred items.

In the ensuing commotion, Nandikeśvara managed to obtain the last fifty-one ślokas of Saundaryalaharī and became enchanted by their beauty. He became so absorbed in the divine verses that he forgot about Śrī Ācārya, the remaining portion of the Saundaryalaharī, and the Pañca Liṅgams. Meanwhile, Śrī Śaṅkarācārya returned with the first forty-nine ślokas of Saundaryalaharī and the Liṅgams, completing his mission despite the interruption.

Ācārya, feeling saddened by the loss of half of Saundaryalaharī, sought solace in prayer. In response to his earnest prayer, Umā Devī, the Divine Mother, blessed him with the divine inspiration to write the remaining ślokas and complete the hymn himself, thus ensuring its entirety and perfection.

Additionally, the five Liṅgams that Ācārya received from Lord Śiva held profound significance. They were the Mukti-Liṅgam, representing liberation; Vara-Liṅgam, symbolizing blessings; Mokṣa-Liṅgam, signifying emancipation; Bhoga-Liṅgam, representing worldly enjoyment; and Yoga-Liṅgam, symbolizing spiritual union and transcendence.

These Liṅgams bestowed upon Ācārya by Lord Śiva held immense spiritual power and significance, enriching his spiritual journey and teachings. These consecrations imbued these sacred sites with heightened spiritual significance and divine energy, enriching the spiritual journey of devotees.

The Bhoga-Liṅgam, symbolizing worldly enjoyment and fulfilment, was consecrated At Sringeri, the ancient seat of learning and spirituality.

The Yoga-Liṅgam, symbolizing spiritual union and transcendence, was consecrated at Kañchipuram, a revered pilgrimage place in Tamil Nadu.

The Vāra-Liṅgam, representing blessings, was consecrated at Neelakantha Kṣetram in Nepal, bestowing divine grace upon devotees.

The Mokṣa-Liṅgam, symbolizing spiritual liberation, was consecrated at Chidambaram, a revered site in south India. During a previous visit to Chidambaram, Ācārya had a vision of the Sphaṭika Liṅgam, which inspired this consecration.

The Mukti-Liṅgam, symbolizing liberation, was consecrated by Ācārya at Badrinātha, a sacred pilgrimage site in the Himalayas.

Upon arrival in Nepal from Kailāśa, Śrī Śaṅkarācārya was received with great reverence by the king and his entourage. Bestowing blessings upon the king and offering him valuable counsel, the revered Ācārya proceeded to the sacred temple of Śrī Paśupatinātha.

To his dismay, he discovered that the worship of Paśupatinātha had been halted due to the influence of Buddhism, and the sanctity of the shrine had been tarnished. Religious adversaries had desecrated the temple by littering it with refuse and impurities.

Following the directives of the revered Ācārya, his disciples diligently undertook the task of purifying the temple premises, thereby reinstating the sanctity of the sacred site. Residing within the temple courtyard for days, Śrī Śaṅkarācārya personally oversaw the restoration efforts, ensuring that the glory of the temple was fully revived. Additionally, he established the proper rites of worship and commenced delivering enlightening discourses to the gathered populace.

Under the influence of Śrī Śaṅkarācārya's divine presence and teachings, the Buddhist intruders eventually withdrew from Nepal without confronting him directly, thus allowing the restoration of orthodox Hindu practices in the region.

Under the divine guidance of Śrī Śaṅkarācārya, the auspicious consecration ceremony of the Vara-Liṅgam was conducted in the temple, marking a significant milestone in the spiritual revival of Nepal. With the rekindling of Sanatana Vaidika Dharma, the entire nation experienced a profound resurgence of spiritual vibrancy, fostering a renewed connection to ancient traditions and practices.

Śrī Ācārya took it upon himself to impart essential teachings on daily duties and deity worship to the people, ensuring that spiritual knowledge was disseminated widely across the land. Encouraged by the king's keen interest in these sacred activities, the momentum of Vaidika and Vedantic learning gained considerable traction throughout Nepal.

In response to Śrī Śaṅkarācārya's divine influence, various centres dedicated to the study of Vedas and scriptures were established across the region, serving as focal points for the dissemination of sacred knowledge and fostering a deepened understanding of Sanatana Dharma among the populace.

Śrī Śaṅkarācārya's journey continued as he returned to Prayag, a place of profound significance where the sacred confluence of the Gaṅgā, Yamunā, and Sarasvatī rivers, known as Triveni, holds spiritual resonance. Immersing himself in the divine ambience of this revered site, he bore witness to the grandeur of the Kumbha Melā, a congregation of pilgrims from far and wide.

Ācārya defeated the powers of the Vāmacāris. He was unscathed, overcame hundreds of obstacles, and spread the glory of Vedānta all over Nepal.

During the Kumbha Melā, Śrī Ācārya engaged in enlightening discussions with numerous Sanyāsis representing various sects and divisions across Bhāratavarṣa. With a spirit of openness and understanding, he shared insights into Sanatana Vaidika Dharma and the profound philosophy of Advaita, fostering meaningful dialogues and establishing harmonious connections with fellow seekers of truth.

Through these interactions, Śrī Śaṅkarācārya exemplified the essence of unity in diversity, transcending sectarian boundaries to emphasize the underlying unity of all spiritual paths. His wisdom and guidance enriched the spiritual tapestry of the Kumbh Mela, inspiring seekers to delve deeper into the eternal truths of Vedānta and the profound teachings of Advaita philosophy.

Śrī Śaṅkarācārya's profound vision and organizational skills extended to the realm of Sanyāsis, where he devised a systematic framework for their classification and governance. Designating ten distinct divisions known as Daśanāmī, he bestowed upon each order a unique identity and purpose, fostering unity and cooperation among the ascetic community.

The ten divisions, namely Tirtha, Āśrama, Vana, Araṇya, Giri, Parvata, Sāgara, Sarasvatī, Bharati, and Puri, each represented a sacred aspect of the spiritual journey, guiding Sanyāsis through various stages of their ascetic life. By organizing Sanyāsis into these cohesive groups, Śrī Ācārya ensured a harmonious blend of diversity and unity within the ascetic community.

With meticulous attention to detail, Śrī Śaṅkarācārya established rituals, rites, and protocols for each division, laying the foundation for a structured and disciplined way of life for Sanyāsis. Through this reorganization, he sought to enhance the effectiveness of their spiritual practices and foster collaboration in their pursuit of truth.

Having completed this noble endeavour, Śrī Śaṅkarācārya embarked on another journey to Kāśi, the Mokṣapuri, furthering his mission to spread the light of Advaita philosophy and uphold the sanctity of Sanatana Vaidika Dharma.

Śrī Śaṅkarācārya visited Kāśi, then again and visited the Vishvanātha temple. He worshipped the Lord and offered His prayers. Here, Śrī Śaṅkarācārya composed and sang "Bhaja Govindam". In Bhaja Govindam, Ācārya eulogises His Guru, Śrī Govinda Bhagavatpāda, in the name of Lord Govinda.

His indirect message to the non-believers, materialists and wholly worldly-minded is, "All secular knowledge and earthly acquisitions which you acquire now will not help you at the time of death. Only seeking the Lord will give peace".

In Kāśi, the renowned seat of spirituality and learning, Śrī Ācārya's divine inspiration gave rise to profound compositions, including the Kāśi Pañcakam and the Annapurna Stotram, which celebrated the sacredness of the city and offered homage to the benevolent Devī Annapurna.

From Kāśi, Śrī Śaṅkarācārya proceeded to Gaya, a revered pilgrimage destination renowned for its significance in offering oblations to ancestors. Here, devout individuals sought the blessings of Śrī Viṣṇu to ensure the liberation and spiritual upliftment of their departed forefathers, thereby continuing the age-old tradition of honouring ancestral spirits with reverence and devotion.

At the site where Lord Buddha attained enlightenment, a temple enshrined an image of Buddha, serving as a sacred pilgrimage destination for Buddhists. Śrī Ācārya, in his Dasāvatāra Stotra, had recognized Lord Buddha as one of the ten incarnations of Viṣṇu. According to his teachings, Lord Buddha achieved enlightenment through spiritual practices aligned with the Vaidika path, emphasizing the harmony between diverse spiritual traditions and the underlying unity of spiritual realization.

Śrī Ācārya clarified that the concept of Nirvana, as taught originally by Lord Buddha, and Mokṣa, as described in Vedānta, are synonymous, both representing a state of liberation and ultimate bliss. However, over time, the original teachings of Lord Buddha were misinterpreted by later followers, leading to divergent interpretations within Buddhist sects. Śrī Ācārya played a crucial role in reforming these sects and reinstating the true essence of Buddha's teachings, emphasizing the commonality and unity of spiritual realization across different traditions.

The acceptance of Buddha as an incarnation of Śrī Nārāyaṇa by Śrī Ācārya had a profound impact on the Buddhist religion. The recognition of Buddha as an avatar of Viṣṇu weakened the foundations of Buddhism, leading to a resurgence of Vaidika Dharma in the region. In Gaya and surrounding areas, people from various social backgrounds embraced the worship of Buddha as an incarnation of Viṣṇu. This shift towards Vaidika Dharma attracted large numbers of individuals, fostering a renewed interest in the Vaidika tradition and its teachings.

Śrī Ācārya's teachings had a profound impact on Bengal, where Buddhist and Hindu Tantrikas held significant influence. Prior to his arrival, knowledge of the Vedas was scarce, and many were unaware of its existence. However, through the efforts of the Ācārya and his disciples, the Sanatana Vaidika Dharma began to take root in Bengal. Hindu scriptures were introduced and disseminated across different parts of the region, gradually replacing the dominance of Tantric practices. Householders started worshipping deities such as Śiva and Kali, following the guidance of the Ācārya's disciples. Scholars were drawn to the profound exposition of scriptures and the elucidation of Vaidika principles by the Ācārya. Ultimately, Śrī Śaṅkarācārya became widely recognized and revered as the living incarnation of the divine by the people of Bengal.

Upon reaching Assam, Śrī Śaṅkarācārya was faced with a significant challenge. Accompanied by his disciples and a multitude of devotees, he was received with great reverence by the ruler of Assam. After bestowing blessings upon the king, the Ācārya, escorted by the king himself, made his way to the base of Kamagiri hill, the sacred abode of the Devī Kāmākhyā, renowned in the Purāṇas. With solemnity and devotion, the Ācārya ascended the hill and performed the sacred rites of worship at the shrine of Parashakti.

The Ācārya and his disciples gave instructions in Vaidika dharma to the people of Assam. Those days, all over Assam, the Tāntrikas were predominant. They were accomplished in charms and spells and were skilled in the rites of destruction, mental distraction and bringing the opponent into subjugation.

Śrī Śaṅkarācārya diligently worked with the Tāntrikas, guiding them away from the practices of black magic and urging them to abandon pursuits for petty gains. He redirected their focus towards Advaita, making it the sole objective of Tantra. With patience and wisdom, he instructed them on the proper practices of Tantra, emphasizing the need for selflessness and complete devotion to Parāśaktī. Having reformed their approach, the Ācārya initiated them into the Dakṣiṇācāra mode of worship of the Devī. This transformation led to a surge in people's adherence to Vaidika dharma as they became engrossed in the worship of the divine Mother.

The opposition from certain Tāntrikas to the transformation of their practices by the Ācārya was met with a challenge. They questioned his authority to alter their tantric traditions, firmly believing that Devī Kamakhya was the deity of their tantric practices. They expressed disbelief that she remained silent amid these changes. In their resistance, they resorted to invoking "Abhicāra," a form of occult practice aimed at causing harm or misfortune to someone.

As the black magic took its toll on the Ācārya's health, his disciples grew increasingly concerned. Despite his declining condition, he persisted in his discourses and interactions with people. Recognizing the severity of the situation, Padmapāda, one of his devoted disciples, fervently prayed to Lord Lakshmi Nṛsiṅha for assistance. In response to Padmapāda's prayers, the Lord appeared before him and imparted instructions on how to counteract the effects of the black magic spell afflicting the Ācārya.

Under Padmapāda's guidance, a counter-black-magic incantation was invoked, effectively curing the Ācārya of his affliction. However, the same spell proved fatal to those Tāntrikas who had initiated the Abhicāra against him. This dramatic turn of events spread rapidly, leading to widespread recognition of the Ācārya and his disciples. As word of the incident spread, many began to acknowledge the supremacy of the Advaita system.

Taking advantage of this newfound attention, Śrī Śaṅkarācārya once again engaged with the people of Assam, highlighting the shortcomings in their Tāntrika practices and offering guidance on how to reform and improve their traditions. Through his teachings and guidance, he sought to steer them towards a path of spiritual growth and enlightenment aligned with the principles of Advaita Vedānta.

Śrī Śaṅkarācārya's journey took him once again to North Bengal, where he encountered Murari Miśra and Dharma Gupta, renowned scholars of Mīmāṃsā philosophy. Upon learning that Maṇḍana, the eminent Mīmāṃsaka, was accompanying the Ācārya as his disciple, they abandoned any hopes of engaging in debate.

Instead, the Ācārya patiently elucidated the points of divergence between the conclusions of Vedānta and those of Mīmāṃsā. Through his teachings, Murari Miśra and Dharma Gupta came to appreciate the profound insights of Advaita Vedānta, ultimately embracing it as their path of spiritual pursuit. Thus, another pair of distinguished scholars was won over by the clarity and profundity of Śrī Śaṅkarācārya's teachings.

The Yogi, emanating an aura of divine brilliance, approached Śrī Śaṅkarācārya as he sat in meditation along the banks of the Ganga. His presence filled the surroundings with an ethereal light, captivating the attention of all who beheld him. With a countenance serene and imposing, adorned with matted locks of hair, the Yogi exuded an unmistakable air of spirituality and wisdom.

Upon witnessing this celestial visitor, Śrī Śaṅkarācārya humbly rose from his seat and reverentially bowed down before the divine figure, pleading him to be seated. The meeting between the two luminaries, each embodying profound spiritual stature, held the promise of profound dialogue and spiritual communion.

In a voice resonating with grace and charm, the divine visitor, none other than Gaudapāda, the revered Parama Guru of Śrī Śaṅkarācārya, addressed him with affection and reverence. With a benevolent gaze, he bestowed his blessings upon the Ācārya, acknowledging his attainment of supreme knowledge and his tireless efforts in guiding countless souls across the turbulent seas of ignorance and duality.

"Dearest son," Gaudapāda began, his words carrying the weight of divine wisdom, "your accomplishments have brought me immense joy. Like a steadfast boat ferrying travellers across a river, you have served as a beacon of enlightenment for multitudes. Know that I am Gaudapāda, your Parama Guru, and I have come here today to bless you."

With his palms joined reverently above his head, the Ācārya humbly addressed the illustrious Gaudapāda, expressing gratitude for his benevolent gaze and the blessings bestowed upon him. "O great Guru, ocean of kindness," he spoke with utmost reverence, "your blessings will fortify me with strength. The mere sight of your divine presence is a profound blessing in itself."

Pleased by the Ācārya's words, brimming with humility and devotion, Śrī Gaudapāda blessed him with a gracious smile. Later, as the evening descended, the Ācārya joyously shared the account of his divine encounter with his disciples, filling their hearts with awe and reverence.

At Tiruvottiyur, Śrī Śaṅkarācārya arrived and sanctified the land with his divine presence. He undertook the consecration of the Sphaṭika Liṅgam (Yoga-Liṅgam) at this sacred site, bestowing his blessings upon the devotees gathered there. After completing the rituals, the Ācārya continued his journey southward, spreading the light of Advaita Vedānta and revitalizing the spiritual fabric of the land with each step.

Śrī Śaṅkarācārya's visit to the Tiruvotriyur temple marked a significant transformation in its rituals and worship practices. By putting an end to the ritual of offering sacrifices at the Amman shrine, he ushered in a new era of non-violent and spiritually uplifting practices. Additionally, his initiation of a Śrīcakra symbolized the introduction of a potent spiritual symbol that would inspire devotion and elevate consciousness among the devotees.

Moreover, by transforming the fierce form of Devī into a graceful and kind one, Śrī Śaṅkarācārya emphasized the compassionate aspect of the divine feminine. This shift from fear to love in the devotees' perception of the Devī facilitated a deeper and more harmonious relationship with the divine.

Overall, Śrī Śaṅkarācārya's interventions at the Tiruvottiyur temple brought about spiritual renewal and upliftment, aligning the worship practices more closely with the principles of Advaita Vedānta and fostering a sense of peace and reverence among the devotees.

Śrī Śaṅkarācārya's actions in Mangadu further demonstrate his profound spiritual insight and compassionate nature. By appointing a Kerala Nambūdiri to perform Pujā at the shrine, he ensured that the worship would be conducted with the utmost sincerity and adherence to tradition.

The composition of the Tripurasundarī Aṣṭakam added another layer of spiritual depth to the temple's worship, praising the divine mother in eight verses of devotion and reverence.

Moreover, Śrī Śaṅkarācārya's installation and consecration of an Ardha-Meru Śrīcakra in front of the Devī in Mangadu exemplified his ability to harness divine energies for the benefit of the people. By nullifying the heat emanating from the Homakuṇḍa through this sacred ritual, he brought relief and comfort to the devotees, showcasing his mastery over spiritual practices and his commitment to serving humanity.

The Śrīcakra installed by Śrī Śaṅkarācārya in Mangadu is imbued with profound symbolism and spiritual significance. Its base in the shape of a tortoise symbolizes stability and longevity, while the three steps represent the ascent from the physical to the metaphysical realms. The 16-petal lotus and yantra signify the unfolding of divine consciousness and the harmonization of cosmic forces.

The 43 triangles within the Śrīcakra correspond to the various aspects of the divine, representing the 43 devatas or deities. Each triangle embodies specific attributes and energies that contribute to the divine manifestation. Furthermore, the use of eight different herbs in its construction underscores the holistic and purifying nature of the Śrīcakra's influence.

As Śrī Śaṅkarācārya journeyed from Mangadu to Kañchi, his spiritual legacy continued to reverberate, leaving behind sacred symbols and practices that would inspire generations to come.

King Rājasenā's warm welcome and the reverence shown by the local scholars exemplify the widespread recognition of Śrī Śaṅkarācārya's spiritual eminence and his profound impact on society. His visit to the sacred shrines of Kañchi, including those dedicated to Devī Kāmākṣi, Śrī Ekāmbaranātha, and Śrī Varadarāja, reflects his devotion to the divine and his commitment to upholding the spiritual traditions of the land.

By staying at the Muktimaṇḍapa in the temple of Viśveśvara and spending time on the banks of the Sarvatīrtham Kuṇḍa, Śrī Śaṅkarācārya further deepened his connection with the spiritual energies of Kañchi, contributing to the sanctity and vibrancy of the sacred city.

The Ācārya's vision for remodelling Kañchi in the form of a Srichakra underscores the profound spiritual symbolism inherent in the city's layout. By reconstructing the temples of Ekāmbaranātha, Kāmākṣi, and Varadarāja according to his instructions, King Rājasenā demonstrated his commitment to honouring the spiritual heritage of Kañchi and aligning the city with divine principles.

The division of Kañchi into twin cities, Śiva-Kañchi and Viṣṇu-Kañchi, with the Kāmākṣi temple at the centre, symbolizes the harmonious coexistence of different aspects of the divine within the city's sacred precincts. The arrangement also facilitates the circumambulation of Ekāmbaranātha and Varadarāja Mūrtis around the central Kāmākṣi temple during festivals, further enhancing the spiritual significance of the city's layout.

Additionally, the sanctum of the Kāmākṣi temple serving as the Bindu of the Śrīcakra emphasizes the central role of divine energy represented by the Devī Kāmākṣi in the spiritual fabric of Kañchi. This holistic approach to city planning reflects a profound understanding of sacred geometry and the integration of spiritual principles into urban design.

The consecration of the Prithivi Liṅgam at Śrī Ekāmbaranātha in Śiva-Kañchi and Śrī Varadarāja in Viṣṇu-Kañchi by Śrī Śaṅkarācārya marks the culmination of the spiritual transformation initiated by the remodelling of Kañchi City. These consecrations symbolize the infusion of divine energy into the city's sacred spaces, ensuring that they serve as centres of spiritual nourishment and upliftment for generations to come.

In addition to consecrating the temples, Śrī Śaṅkarācārya's installation of a Śrīcakra in front of the Temple of Devī Kāmākṣi further enhances the spiritual ambience of Kañchi. The presence of the Śrīcakra serves as a focal point for devotion and meditation, amplifying the divine vibrations emanating from the temple and fostering a deeper connection with the Devī Kāmākṣi.

By consecrating both the temples and the Śrīcakra, Śrī Śaṅkarācārya ensures that Kañchi becomes a veritable abode of divine grace and spiritual fulfilment, drawing devotees from far and wide to experience the transformative power of sacred worship and spiritual practice within its sacred precincts.

The transformation of Devī Kāmākṣi from Ugra Svarūpini to Śānta Svarūpini, orchestrated by Śrī Śaṅkarācārya, reflects the Ācārya's profound spiritual vision and his ability to invoke divine grace for the welfare of the people. By ensuring that the Devī remains in a peaceful and tranquil form within the temple premises, Śrī Śaṅkarācārya establishes an atmosphere of harmony and spiritual serenity in Kañchi, benefiting all who come to seek her blessings.

The establishment of the Sarvajña Pīṭha at Kañchi further solidifies the city's status as a centre of spiritual knowledge and wisdom. This seat of learning serves as a beacon of enlightenment, attracting scholars and seekers from far and wide to engage in the study and contemplation of the sacred scriptures and the teachings of Advaita Vedānta.

The divine debate between Śrī Sarasvatī Devī and Śrī Śaṅkarācārya exemplifies the depth of the Ācārya's wisdom and his mastery over the scriptures. Through this exchange, Śrī Sarasvatī Devī herself acknowledges the greatness of Śrī Śaṅkarācārya's intellect and bestows upon him the name 'Sarasvatī,' affirming his status as a repository of knowledge and wisdom.

In all these endeavours, Śrī Śaṅkarācārya demonstrates his unwavering commitment to the propagation of Sanātana Dharma and the upliftment of humanity, leaving an indelible mark on the spiritual landscape of Kañchi and beyond.

Realizing the need to reach out to the common people and impart the teachings of Sanātana Dharma in a manner accessible to all, Śrī Śaṅkarācārya made the visionary decision to establish a separate Pīṭha dedicated to this noble cause. This new institution would serve as a platform to disseminate spiritual knowledge and moral values among the masses, irrespective of their background or social status.

With the same zeal and dedication that characterized his other endeavours, Śrī Śaṅkarācārya embarked on the establishment of this new Pīṭha, ensuring that it would be inclusive and welcoming to people from all walks of life. He envisioned a place where the timeless wisdom of Sanātana Dharma would be shared through simple yet profound teachings, making it relevant and applicable to the everyday lives of ordinary individuals.

Through the establishment of this Pīṭha, Śrī Śaṅkarācārya aimed to instil a sense of spiritual awareness and ethical conduct in the hearts and minds of people across the land. By offering guidance on righteous living and the path to spiritual fulfilment, he sought to uplift and inspire individuals to lead lives of virtue, compassion, and wisdom.

In this way, Śrī Śaṅkarācārya's commitment to the welfare of humanity extended beyond the realm of scholarly discourse to encompass the uplifting of the common man, ensuring that no one was left untouched by the transformative power of Sanātana Dharma.

Establishing the Kamakoti Pīṭha as the apex institution to represent the essence of the Vedas and the significance of the Pranava Mantra, Śrī Śaṅkarācārya demonstrated his deep understanding of the spiritual heritage of Bharat. By choosing the name "Indra Saraswathi" for himself as the first Peetaathipathi of the Śrī Kañchi Kamakoti Pīṭha, he symbolized the divine union of knowledge, power, wisdom, and strength.

The name "Saraswathi" bestowed upon him by Devī Saraswathi herself signified his embodiment of learning, scholarship, and eloquence, attributes associated with the Devī of wisdom. On the other hand, the title "Indra," conferred upon him by Lord Indra, highlighted his leadership, authority, and ability to inspire and guide others on the path of righteousness.

As "Indra Saraswathi," Śrī Śaṅkarācārya exemplified the harmonious fusion of intellect and action, spirituality and worldly engagement. Through his role as the Head of the Kamakoti Pīṭha, he aimed to disseminate the timeless teachings of Sanātana Dharma far and wide, guiding humanity towards spiritual evolution and upliftment.

In assuming this position, Śrī Śaṅkarācārya embraced the responsibility of preserving and propagating the sacred knowledge of the Vedas, as well as nurturing the spiritual welfare of all beings. His tenure as the first Peetaathipathi of the Kamakoti Pīṭha marked the beginning of a legacy of spiritual leadership and service that continues to inspire seekers of truth and wisdom to this day.

The incident you described showcases Śrī Śaṅkarācārya's profound spiritual power and his ability to command respect even from celestial beings like Indra. By invoking the Ashwini Devas to cure Sureśvara and then protecting them from Indra's wrath, he demonstrated his mastery over divine forces and his compassionate nature.

Indra's recognition of Śrī Śaṅkarācārya's authority by bowing down to him and bestowing upon him the title "Indra" is symbolic of the Ācārya's spiritual supremacy. It signifies the acknowledgement of his divine mission and his role as a guiding light for humanity.

In this episode, Śrī Śaṅkarācārya's intervention not only saved Sureśvara but also showcased his divine grace and his ability to maintain harmony and balance even among celestial beings. It emphasizes the reverence and admiration accorded to him by both mortals and gods alike, highlighting his universal significance as a spiritual luminary and a beacon of enlightenment.

The act of consecrating the Yoga Liṅgam, also known as Śrī Candramauḷīśvara, at the Kamakoti Pīṭha by Śrī Śaṅkarācārya signifies the integration of spiritual energy into the seat of spiritual authority. This act ensures that the divine presence of Candramauḷīśvara, along with Śrī Maha Tripurāsundarī as the Śakti, blesses the spiritual endeavours of the Pīṭha.

Śrī Śaṅkarācārya's directive to his successors at Kañchi to take Candramauḷīśvara to various places for worship underscores the universality and accessibility of divine worship. By spreading the worship of Candramauḷīśvara across different locations, the Ācārya ensures that devotees from all regions have the opportunity to connect with and receive the blessings of this sacred deity.

This act reflects the Ācārya's vision of promoting spiritual harmony and inclusivity, transcending geographical boundaries, and ensuring that the divine presence of Candramauḷīśvara is accessible to all devotees regardless of their location. It reinforces the idea that divine worship is not confined to a specific place but can be experienced and embraced by all those who seek spiritual enlightenment and guidance.

The establishment of proper worship rituals for Śrī Maha Tripurāsundarī and Śrī Candramauḷīśvara by Śrī Śaṅkarācārya signifies his dedication to ensuring the spiritual well-being of his followers and the promotion of devotional practices. His exemplary devotion and meticulous Pujā rituals inspired countless individuals in Kañchi to deepen their spiritual practices, leading to a profound sense of bhakti (devotion) that permeated the city.

In addition to Kañchi, Śrī Śaṅkarācārya also established the Govardhana Pīṭha at Puri to oversee spiritual matters in Eastern Bharat. This Pīṭha represented the Rig Veda, with the Mahāvākya "*prajñānam brahma*" (Supreme knowledge is Brahman). The presiding deity was Viṣṇu Jagannātha, accompanied by his śakti, Vimala, and the sacred tirtha was Mahodhadhi, the Bay of Bengal. The head of this Pīṭha was titled Vana or Aranya, symbolizing the spiritual connection with the forest or wilderness, where seekers often retreat for deeper contemplation and communion with the divine.

The Śaradā Pīṭha at Sringeri was entrusted with the spiritual welfare of Southern Bharat. Representing the Yajurveda, its guiding Mahāvākya is "*aham brahmasmi*". The presiding deity is Candramauḷīśvara, accompanied by his śakti, Śaradā. The sacred tirtha associated with this Pīṭha is the Tungabhadra river. The head of this Pīṭha held titles such as Bhārati, Sarasvatī, and Puri.

For Western Bharat, the Kālikā Pīṭha at Dvarakā was established, representing the Saama Veda, with the Mahāvākya "*tat tvam asi*". Lord Siddeśvara and Mahākālī are worshipped here, with the Gomati River serving as the sacred tirtha. The head of this Pīṭha holds titles such as Tīrtha and Āśrama.

In Northern Bharat, the Jyotir Pīṭha at Badrinātha took responsibility, representing the Atharva Veda, with the Mahāvākya "*ayam ātma brahma*". Lord Nārāyaṇa and his śakti, Puranagiri, are revered here, with the Alaknanda River as the sacred tirtha. The head of this Pīṭha holds titles such as Giri and Parvata.

Śrī Śaṅkarācārya thus established very firmly the paths of Bhakti, Karma and Jnana as per the Advaita Vedānta.

Indeed, in just thirty-two years, Śrī Śaṅkarācārya embodied a unique convergence of qualities rarely seen in a single individual. He epitomized the union of a sage and a saint, blending profound wisdom with spiritual devotion. As a philosopher, he delved deep into the mysteries of existence, while his unwavering devotion marked him as a true mystic. His works, both original compositions and commentaries, showcased his versatility as a writer and thinker.

Śrī Śaṅkarācārya was a bridge between tradition and innovation, honouring the ancient wisdom of the Vedas while introducing new insights and interpretations. He established and integrated various spiritual centres, bringing unity amidst diversity. Despite his intense renunciation, he engaged in tireless activity for the upliftment of humanity, leaving an indelible mark on the spiritual landscape of Bharat. Truly, he stands as a towering figure, embodying the highest ideals of human potential.

As Śrī Śaṅkarācārya sat in meditation before Devī Kāmākṣi, surrounded by His disciples and devotees, the atmosphere was charged with spiritual fervour. The air resonated with the chanting of Upaniṣads, the singing of His praise, and the melodic bhajans offered by various groups. Each voice blended harmoniously, creating a symphony of devotion that filled the temple precincts.

Amidst this divine ambience, Śrī Ācārya's serene countenance radiated an otherworldly aura, signalling His imminent departure from the mortal realm. His actions and demeanour hinted at His imminent transcendence beyond the confines of the materialistic world. Aware of the profound significance of this moment, His disciples and devotees remained in respectful silence, their hearts filled with reverence and devotion for their beloved Guru.

In the presence of Devī Kāmākṣi, the divine Mother, and surrounded by the devoted assembly, Śrī Śaṅkarācārya prepared to embark on His final journey, leaving behind a legacy of wisdom, compassion, and spiritual enlightenment for generations to come.

In that sacred moment within the hallowed precincts of the Kāmākṣi Temple, the divine presence of Śrī Śaṅkarācārya illuminated the surroundings with a transcendent glow. As His eyes met those of the gracious Kāmākṣi, it was a poignant exchange, a final communion between Guru and Devi, signifying His readiness to merge into the eternal embrace of the Supreme Brahman.

Within the radiant glow of the Śrīcakra, where the divine energies converged, Śrī Kameśvara, the embodiment of serene tranquillity, sat upon the Brahmasana Pīṭha. Beside Him, adorned with blazing eyes of grace, sat the resplendent Kāmākṣi, her divine presence filling the sanctum with divine radiance.

As Śrī Śaṅkarācārya's lips moved in solemn invocation, the verses of the Tripurasundarī Vedapada Stavam resonated through the temple halls, casting off the shackles of His mortal, subtle, and causal bodies one by one. With each syllable, He drew closer to the ultimate liberation, the sublime union with the Supreme Brahman, Satchidānanda.

In that sacred moment of transcendence, the earthly form of Śrī Śaṅkarācārya dissolved into the boundless expanse of divine consciousness, leaving behind a legacy of profound wisdom, compassion, and spiritual illumination that would continue to guide humanity for ages to come.

As Śrī Śaṅkarācārya, in the form of divine light, gracefully approached the sanctum sanctorum of Devī Kāmākṣi, each step resonated with the sacred vibrations of transcendence. With every movement, His luminous form radiated an aura of sublime purity, drawing closer to the radiant presence of the Divine Mother.

Within the sanctum, the divine effulgence of Devī Kāmākṣi illuminated the space with unparalleled brilliance, her form enveloped in a celestial glow that transcended earthly realms. As Śrī Śaṅkarācārya's divine light merged with hers, the two luminous energies converged in a divine union, symbolizing the ultimate merging of the individual soul with the Supreme.

In this sacred moment of sublime union, the boundaries between the devotee and the Divine dissolved into the boundless expanse of divine consciousness, as Śrī Śaṅkarācārya merged seamlessly with the radiant brilliance of Devī Kāmākṣi. In this eternal embrace, the Jyoti of Śrī Śaṅkarācārya merged with the brighter luminosity of the Divine Mother, symbolizing the ultimate attainment of oneness with the Supreme.

Ādi Śaṅkara merged into Parabrahman, the Absolute Truth!

Kailāśa: Did Ādi Śaṅkara not pass away in Kedarnātha?

Ācārya: Some people believe so. But he likely spent his last moment with Devī Kāmākṣi in Kanchipuram.

KĀLACAKRA DAŚĀ

Jayanta: Guruji, can we discuss Kālacakra Daśā now.

Ācārya: Of course, it is a very important Daśā. Different Daśā systems originated from different Devatās. Lord Śiva is the originator of the Kālacakra Daśā system. In Bṛhatparāśara 46.52-53, Maharṣi Parāśara states that he explains Lord Śiva narrates this Daśā to Devī Pārvati for the welfare of the people.

However, before learning Kālacakra Daśā, one must learn about Kāla Daśā and Cakra Daśā.

Kailāśa: Why are there three Daśās, Kāla, Cakra and Kālacakra?

Ācārya: Each Daśā presents a specific scope and offers a method to delineate a person's life. They are useful in delineating a specific area of life. Some of them are applicable based on the presence of a certain Yoga in a Kuṇḍalī.

For instance, Aṣṭottarī Daśā is applicable when Rāhu is in a Kendrakoṇa to Lagneśa. But it must not be in the Lagna.

Sunidhi: Then it must be applicable to your Kuṇḍalī because:

(1) Rāhu is not in the Lagna.

(2) Rāhu is in a Kendra to Lagneśa.

Ācārya: Yes. That is right. However, there are other Daśās, such as Viñśottarī, Sudarśana Cakra and Cara, which are applicable to all Kuṇḍalīs. They can be used for delineating someone's entire life.

However, there are Daśās, such as Sthira, Śūla, Brahmā, etc., which are used for longevity purposes only. Yet, other Daśās, such as Piṇḍa, Añśa, and Nisarga, are used for delineating longevity and one's entire life.

Sunidhi: How about Kālacakra Daśā?

Ācārya: Maharṣi Parāśara did not specify any condition for the application of the Kālacakra Daśā. However, other Ācāryas have different opinions.

Ācārya Mantreśvara states that Kālacakra Daśā should be applied when the ruler Navāñśa occupied by the Candra is stronger than the Rāśi. But this is not a widely accepted view. We should apply this Daśā in all cases, like Viñśottarī.

Sunidhi: Noted, Guruji.

Kailāśa: Kindly continue with Kāla and Cakra Daśās.

Ācārya: Here is the elaboration of the Kāla Daśā. For details of this Daśā, refer to Bṛhatparāśara 46.44-49. This is dependent on the Prātaḥ Sandhyā (morning twilight) and Sāyaṁ Sandhyā (evening twilight). There are 60 Ghaṭis in a day, commencing with Sūryodaya. The Sūryodaya is defined as the sight of Sūrya's semi-disk. Due to the scattering of Sūrya's Raśmis, the Prātaḥ Sandhyā or Dawn appears before the geometric Sunrise, which coincides with the rise of Sūrya's centre in the eastern horizon. It is called Civil twilight or Civil dawn.

Civil twilight is the time when the geometric centre of Sūrya is between the horizon and 6° below the horizon. It is the period when enough natural light remains that artificial light in towns and cities is not needed. Under clear weather conditions, civil twilight approximates the limit at which solar illumination suffices for the human eye to distinguish terrestrial objects clearly. Enough illumination renders artificial sources unnecessary for most outdoor activities. At civil dawn and civil dusk, sunlight clearly defines the horizon while the brightest stars and planets can appear. As observed from the Earth, sky-gazers know Śukra, the brightest Graha, as the "morning star" or "evening star" because they can see it during civil twilight.

Kailāśa: So, the Sūryodaya in Jyotiṣa is defined by the appearance of Sūrya's Raśmi on the horizon instead of the coincidence of Sūrya's centre with the eastern horizon. Right!

Ācārya: That is right. Similarly, the Sāyaṁ Sandhyā (or Sūryāsta) occurs when Sūrya is much below the western Horizon, as that marks the disappearance of Sūrya's Raśmi, and evening lights must be turned on.

Kailāśa: How to check this in software like Jagannātha Horā?

Ācārya: Go to Preferences > Related to Calculations > Sunrise, Sunset & Special Lagna Definitions. In the "What is the meaning of Sunrise" field, select the option "The tip of Sun's disk appears to be on the eastern horizon".

Kailāśa: Noted, Guruji. Kindly continue with the delineation of Kāla Daśā.

Ācārya: 5 Ghaṭis before and after Sūryodaya is the Prātaḥ Sandhyā. Similarly, 5 Ghaṭis before and after Sūryāsta are Sāyaṁ Sandhyā. Each Sandhyā is of 10 Ghaṭis. The Sandhyās are of 20 Ghaṭis. The Prātaḥ Sandhyā is called Khaṇḍa, and Sāyaṁ Sandhya is called Suddha. What remains is 40 Ghaṭis, of which 20 Ghaṭis of the day and 20 Ghaṭis of the night. The 20 Ghaṭis of the night are called Pūrṇa, and the 20 Ghaṭis of the day is called Mugdha.

Sunidhi: So, the day is divided into four parts:

(1) Khaṇḍa: Prātaḥ Sandhyā: 10 Ghaṭis

(2) Mugdha: daytime: 20 Ghaṭis

(3) Śuddha: Sāyaṁ Sandhyā: 10 Ghaṭis

(4) Pūrṇa: Nighttime: 20 Ghaṭis

So, they constitute the 60 Ghaṭis.

Ācārya: That is right.

If the birth is in Pūrṇa or Mugdha, its past Ghaṭis should be multiplied by 2, and the product should be divided by 15.

The figure so arrived at should be converted into years, months etc.

By multiplying it by the serial number of Sūrya and other Grahas in their normal order, we will get the Kāla Daśā of the nine Grahas.

If the birth is during Sandhya, then its past Ghaṭis should be multiplied by 4 and the product divided by 15.

The figure so arrived at in terms of years, months, etc., should be multiplied by the serial number of Sūrya and the other Grahas to get the Kāla Daśā of the nine Grahas.

Kailāśa: Kindly illustrate this with an example.

Ācārya: Let us compute this Daśā for my Kuṇḍalī. I am born at 14:34:28 (14.574 hrs), while the Sūryodaya is at 5:28:6 (5.468) and Sūryāsta 18:13:47 (18.230).

Dinamāna = 18.230 - 5.468 = 12.762

Rātrimāna = 24 - 12.762 = 11.238

Here, I have approximated the Ahorātramāna (full day) as 24 hrs.

The Dinamāna must be divided into 5:20:5 for the Khaṇḍa, Mugdha, and Pūrṇa sections. This totals 30 Ghaṭis of Dinamāna.

This gives us 5/30 * 12.762: 20/30 * 12.762: 5/30 * 12.762 = 2.127: 8.508: 2.127 for the day section.

Similarly, the Rātrimāna must be divided into 5:20:5 for the Śuddha, Pūrṇa, and Khaṇḍa sections. This totals 30 Ghaṭis of Rātrimāna.

This gives us 5/30 * 11.238: 20/30 * 11.238: 5/30 * 11.238 = 1.873: 7.492: 1.873 for the night section.

Kailāśa: So, how to determine your birth Daśā?

Ācārya: The person is born at 14.574.

Kailāśa: What is the time of birth in Ghaṭis?

Ācārya: (14.574 - Sūryodaya) / Dinamāna * 30 = (14.574 - 5.468) / 12.762 * 30 = 21.406. The breakdown of Dinamāna is 5:20:5, and in cumulative terms, it is 5:25:30 for Khaṇḍa: Mugdha: Śuddha. 21.406 is in the Mugdha section.

Kailāśa: How much of Mugdha is expired?

Ācārya: Mugdha expired is (21.406 – 5) / 20 * 100 = 16.406 / 20 * 100 = 82.03%. This also gives the duration of the person's life.

Kailāśa: How to determine the Daśā of the Grahas?

Ācārya: You must follow the following steps:

(1) If the birth is in Purṇa or Mugdha, its past Ghaṭis should be multiplied by two, and the product should be divided by 15. Call this "Base period".

(2) By multiplying it (Base period) by the serial number of Sūrya and other Grahas in their normal order, we shall get the Kāla Daśā of these Grahas.

(3) Find the total longevity by multiplying the Base period by 45.

Let us apply this in the given Kuṇḍalī.

(1) The expired Ghaṭis = 21.406 – 5 = 16.406. Base period = 16.406 * 2 / 15 = 2.187y.

(2) The Daśā of the Grahas is as follows:

Sūrya = 1 * 2.187 = 2.187

Candra = 2 * 2.187 = 4.375

Maṅgala = 3 * 2.187 = 6.562

Budha = 4 * 2.187 = 8.750

Guru = 5 * 2.187 = 10.937

Śukra = 6 * 2.187 = 13.125

Śani = 7 * 2.187 = 15.312

Rāhu = 8 * 2.187 = 17.500

Ketu = 9 * 2.187 = 19.687

(3) The total of the Daśā periods are 2.187 + 4.375 + 6.562 + 8.750 + 10.937 + 13.125 + 15.312 + 17.500 + 19.687 = 98.436. You can also find this from the % of Mugdha expired. Longevity = 82.03% * 120 = 98.436. This can also be found using the formula Base period * 45 = 2.187 * 45 = 98.436.

The cumulative Daśā period is Sūrya 2.187, Candra 6.562, Maṅgala 13.125, Budha 21.875, Guru 32.812, Śukra 45.937, Śani 61.249, Rāhu 78.749, Ketu 98.436. These are the ending ages of the Daśās.

Kailāśa: Right now, you are in your 51st year, which means you are in Śani Daśā, which will end in 61.249y. Right?

Ācārya: Yes, that is right. I am in Śani Kāla Daśā.

Kailāśa: What is the definition of the Daśāvarṣa here?

Ācārya: You need to experiment with this. But I suppose it is 360 days a year, called the Sāvana Varṣa. This is because the human life of 120 years is made up of 360 days a year, which equals 43200 days. According to Varāhamihira, the maximum duration of human life is 120y 5d, which is 43205 days. Scholars such as Ācārya Vaidyanātha suggest that the Sāvana Varṣa must be converted to Sauravarṣa by multiplying 360 and dividing by 365 (an approximation of Saurya Varṣa, which is precisely 365.2563).

Kailāśa: Guruji, how accurate is this longevity computation?

Ācārya: You cannot mindlessly rely on this, as there are other methods of longevity as well. Longevity is one of the most complex areas of Jyotiṣa, and you can assess it by considering multiple factors. No one factor is singularly reliable.

Kailāśa: What is the use of Kāla Daśā?

Ācārya: It could be a general purpose Daśā, as nothing specific is stated for its usage.

Sunidhi: How is Antardaśā found for this Daśā?

Ācārya: Nothing is specified for this. But there are two options.

(1) The Antardaśā sequence is fixed Sūrya to Rāhu in Vāra order.

(2) The Antardaśā sequence commences from Daśā Graha and follows the Vāra order. This is like the Viñśottarī.

Sunidhi: How about the Antardaśā period?

Ācārya: You can use the formula Daśāvarṣa/45 * Graha index. Graha index is Sūrya 1, Candra 2, Maṅgala 3, Budha 4, Guru 5, Śukra 6, Śani 7, Rāhu 8 and Ketu 9, i.e., the Vāra order.

Sunidhi: Noted Guruji. Is this Daśā available in any software?

Ācārya: Yes. Jagannātha Horā has this Daśā and is accurate.

Sunidhi: Dhanyavād, Guruji.

Kailāśa: What is next, Guruji?

Ācārya: Let us examine the Cakra Daśā.

Kailāśa: We are looking forward to it, Guruji!

Ācārya: This Daśā also uses the breakdown of a day into the Sandhyās, daytime and nighttime, as we have seen in the case of Kāla Daśā.

This is straightforward as the Daśā commences per the following rules:

(1) Daytime: Mugdha: Lagneśa's Rāśi

(2) Nighttime: Pūrṇa: Lagna's Rāśi

(3) Sandhyā: Khaṇḍa/Śuddha: Second Rāśi from the Lagna.

Once you have decided on the commencing Rāśi, you progress the Daśā of the twelve Rāśis in regular order. Suppose the commencing Rāśi is Kumbha, then Daśā progresses in sequence Kumbha, Mīna, Meṣa, ..., Makara. Each Daśā is ten years old.

Kailāśa: Can you demonstrate this?

Ācārya: Sure. Let us apply this in the same Kuṇḍalī as above. The person is born in the Mugdha section of the day.

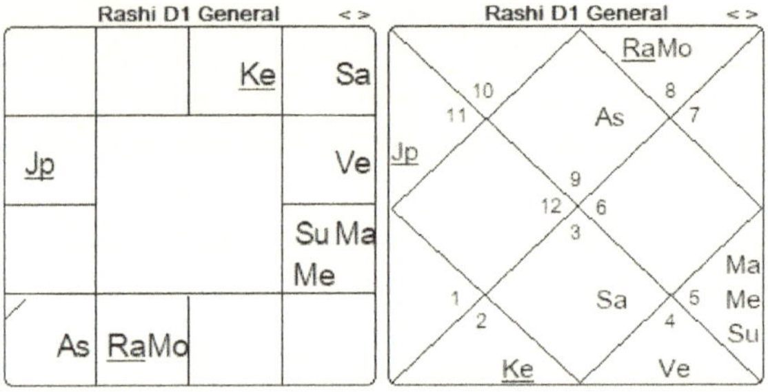

The Daśā should commence from Lagneśa's Rāśi. Lagneśa is Guru, in Kumbha. Therefore, the Daśā commences from Kumbha. The following is from Jagannātha Horā.

Kumbha: 1974-08-25 — 1984-08-25

Mīna: 1984-08-25 — 1994-08-25

Meṣa: 1994-08-25 — 2004-08-25

Vṛṣabha: 2004-08-25 — 2014-08-25<<

Mithuna: 2014-08-25 — 2024-08-25

Karka: 2024-08-25 — 2034-08-25

Siṅha: 2034-08-25 — 2044-08-25

Kanyā: 2044-08-25 — 2054-08-26

Tulā: 2054-08-26 — 2064-08-25

Vṛścika: 2064-08-25 — 2074-08-26

Dhanu: 2074-08-26 — 2084-08-25

Makara: 2084-08-25 — 2094-08-26

Kailāśa: What is the definition of Daśāvarṣa here?

Ācārya: Since it is a Rāśidaśā, we must consider the True Sidereal Year as the definition of the year. It is based on Sūrya's passage through the Rāśis.

Kailāśa: How about the Antardaśā?

Ācārya: For Rāśidaśās, Maharṣi Parāśara states that the Antardaśā commences from the Rāśi held by the Daśeśa (Daśārāśi lord). This is also called the Daśā Pākarāśi.

Kailāśa: Dhanyavād Guruji. Where this Daśā is used?

Ācārya: Maharṣi Parāśara has not specified this. So, I believe this is a general purpose Daśā, similar to Cara and Sudarśana Cakra Daśā.

Kailāśa: Should we consider the first Daśā based on the balance of the Daśā principle, or it should always be 10 years?

Ācārya: Since Maharṣi has not specified the Balance of Daśā, it should be 10 years. It is like Sudarśana Cakra Daśā, which is always 1 year for the Lagna Bhāva. It is not based on the Lagnasphuṭa. We must apply the same principle here, i.e., the first Daśā is of 10 years.

Kailāśa: Noted, Guruji! Did you find this Daśā useful?

Ācārya: I have found limited applicability of this Daśā. But let me share some principles which I uncovered.

(1) Cakra Daśā should be used along with Sudarśana Cakra Daśā.

(2) In Sudarśana Cakra Daśā, we have one year allotted to each Rāśi in succession, with the first year ruling the first house, the second year, the second house and so on. But their overall results are governed by the Daśaka Rāśi.

(3) The Daśaka or decade Rāśi is allotted ten years each so that, in one's entire lifetime of 120 years, one experiences all twelve Rāśis.

(4) In a conventional sense, the Daśaka Rāśi is counted from Lagna to the twelfth house. However, instead, we can consider the Daśaka Rāśi based on Cakra Daśā.

Let me explain this with an example.

The native got married and had the birth of two children in Vṛṣabha Cakra Daśā. Vṛṣabha is the Daśaka Rāśi.

These are the Sudarśana Cakra Daśā from 1998 to 2010, following the True Solar Year definition.

1H: 1998-08-25 — 1999-08-26

2H: 1999-08-26 — 2000-08-25

3H: 2000-08-25 — 2001-08-25

4H: 2001-08-25 — 2002-08-25

5H: 2002-08-25 — 2003-08-26

6H: 2003-08-26 — 2004-08-25

7H: 2004-08-25 — 2005-08-25 << marriage

8H: 2005-08-25 — 2006-08-25

9H: 2006-08-25 — 2007-08-26 << first child

10H: 2007-08-26 — 2008-08-25 << second child

11H: 2008-08-25 — 2009-08-25

12H: 2009-08-25 — 2010-08-25

What are the effects of Vṛṣabha Daśaka Rāśi?

Consider Vṛṣabha as the Daśālagna. Vṛṣabha has Ketu, indicating health troubles and mental stress. Lagneśa Śukra is in 3H aspecting 9H in Pāpakartari.

This shows challenges and excessive hardwork as if things are stuck (Pāpakartari).

Grahas in Kendras manifest things. All four Kendras are occupied. Lagna has Ketu, 4H has Maṅgala-Sūrya-Budha, 7H has Rāhu-Candra and 10H has Vakrī Guru. Things one gets (reward) are seen from Grahas involved with Koṇas, or Bhāvas occupied by the Koṇeśas.

9L Śani in 2H (family) aspecting 4L (house), spouse (7L) and 2L-5L Budha (children) in Siṅha. 5L is conjoined 4L and 7L in Siṅha. Gain of house, spouse and children are indicated.

In Sudarśana Cakra Daśā, marriage occurred in 7H, which makes sense. 7H (from Lagna) is Vṛṣabha, which is 2H from Daśaka Lagna, indicating the growth of the family. The first child is born in 9H (Siṅha), which contains 5L from Daśaka Lagna, indicating the birth of the first child. The second child is born in 10H (Kanyā), which is 5H from Daśaka Lagna.

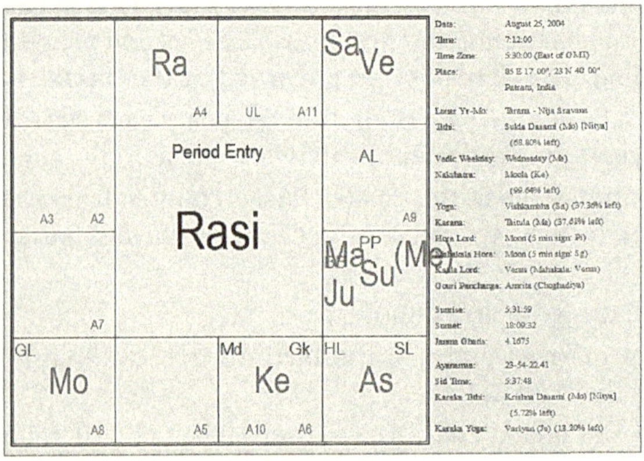

Let us examine the Daśāpraveśa Cakra of the Vṛṣabha Cakra Daśā. Focus on the Daśālagna Vṛṣabha and focus on the Grahas in Kendrakoṇas and their lords. Lagneśa Śukra is in 2H with 9L Śani, indicating growth in the family. Maṅgala-Sūrya-Budha in Siṅha as in the Janmakuṇḍalī. Santāna Kāraka Guru in Siṅha with 5L in a Kendra (4H). 7L Maṅgala is also in 4H conjunct with 5L and dṛṣṭied by 9L, indicating marriage.

Overall, the events of marriage and children could be seen from the Cakra Daśā used in conjunction with the Sudarśana Cakra Daśā.

KĀLACAKRA DAŚĀ

Kailāśa: Dhanyavād Guruji! Let us continue with Kālacakra Daśā.

Ācārya: The fundamental principle of this system is that the time flows in two directions in Kālacakra, viz., Savya and Apasavya.

Āratī: What is Savya and Apasavya.

Ācārya: Savya is masculine and Apasavya is feminine.

Sunidhi: Some scholars say that Savya is zodiacal direction and Apasavya is anti-zodiacal. Savya is forward, and Apasavya is reverse.

There are two zodiacs in Kālacakra, Savya and Apasavya.

Ācārya: Normally, that is so. But using that concept here will confuse you. We will use it elsewhere. The zodiacal and anti-zodiacal directions are called Krama and Utkrama. There are two directions of motion (called Kramas) in Kālacakra, Krama and Utkrama.

Combined with Savya and Apasavya, they give rise to four combinations:

Savya-Krama

Savya-Utkrama

Apasavya-Krama

Apasavya-Utkrama

Sunidhi: What are the differences between the Savya and Apasavya zodiacs?

Ācārya: In both zodiacs, the first Rāśi is of Maṅgala, and the last Rāśi is of Guru. But the method of reckoning is different.

Savya Cakra = Meṣa to Mīna; Meṣa-Vṛṣabha-Mithuna..., Mīna

Apasavya Cakra = Vṛścika to Dhanu; Vṛścika-Tulā-Kanyā..., Dhanu

Savya Cakra is governed by Puruṣa, Lord Śiva.

Apasavya Cakra is governed by Prakṛti, Devī Śakti.

Sunidhi: This makes sense now. What is the difference between Krama and Utkrama?

Krama = Maṅgala to Guru; Maṅgala-Śukra-Budha-Candra-Sūrya-Budha-Śukra-Maṅgala- Guru -Śani-Śani- Guru.

Utkrama = Guru-Śani-Śani-Guru-Maṅgala-Śukra-Budha-Sūrya-Candra-Budha-Śukra-Maṅgala.

Sunidhi: Why do we have the two pairs, Savya-Apasavya and Krama-Utkrama?

Ācārya: While the Savya-Apasavya pair denotes the reversal of Masculinity-Femininity, the Krama-Utkrama pair denotes the reversal of direction.

Sunidhi: How to combine the two?

Ācārya: Let us examine them:

Savya-Krama: *Masculine-Regular:* Meṣa to Mīna: Meṣa-Vṛṣabha-Mithuna-Karka-Siṅha-Kanyā-Tulā-Vṛścika-Dhanu-Makara-Kumbha-Mīna.

Savya-Utkrama: *Masculine-Reverse:* Mīna to Meṣa: Mīna-Kumbha-Makara-Dhanu-Vṛścika-Tulā-Kanyā-Siṅha-Karka-Mithuna-Vṛṣabha-Meṣa.

Apasavya-Krama: *Feminine-Regular:* Vṛścika to Dhanu: Vṛścika-Tulā-Kanyā-Siṅha-Karka-Mithuna-Vṛṣabha-Meṣa-Mīna-Kumbha-Makara-Dhanu.

Apasavya-Utkrama: *Feminine-Reverse:* Dhanu to Vṛścika: Dhanu-Makara-Kumbha-Mīna-Meṣa-Vṛṣabha-Mithuna-Karka-Siṅha-Kanyā-Tulā-Vṛścika

Sunidhi: It appears that for masculine, the regular is zodiacal motion, and the reverse is anti-zodiacal motion. But it is the reverse for feminine, i.e., the regular is anti-zodiacal motion, and the reverse is zodiacal motion. Why is that so?

Ācārya: That is because, for masculinity, the regular direction is zodiacal. But for femininity, the regular direction is anti-zodiacal. This is how the universe has conceived masculinity and femininity.

Sunidhi: How is this concept used in Kālacakra Daśā?

Ācārya: This Daśā is complex because the Daśā order is not fixed and depends on certain conditions. In the heart of this Daśā, there are two Kālacakras, the Savya and Apasavya Kālacakra.

Sunidhi: I understand that, Guruji. You already explained this before.

Ācārya: The Savya Kālacakra is the normal zodiac that is in vogue. Normally, we do not use the Apasavya Kālacakra.

The Apasavya Kālacakra is the mirror image of the Savya Kālacakra, which is arrived at by dividing the zodiac by an imaginary line passing through the zero-degree Kumbha and Siṅha and then flipping the two halves.

This is better understood when the Kuṇḍalī is drawn in the South-Indian format, which is what Maharṣi Parāśara recommends.

Sunidhi: It isn't easy to understand, Guruji. Kindly elaborate on this concept.

Ācārya: The following is the Savya Kālacakra.

12 Mīna	1 Meṣa	2 Vṛṣabha	3 Mithuna
11 Kumbha	SAVYA KĀLACAKRA		4 Karka
10 Makara			5 Siṅha
9 Dhanu	8 Vṛścika	7 Tulā	6 Kanyā

Sunidhi: This is clear, as this is what we use regularly. How about the Apasavya Kālacakra.

Ācārya: This is what the Apasavya Kālacakra looks like.

9 Dhanu
8 Vṛścika
7 Tulā
6 Kanyā
10 Makara
APASAVYA KĀLACAKRA
5 Siṅha
11 Kumbha
4 Karka
12 Mīna
1 Meṣa
2 Vṛṣabha
3 Mithuna

Sunidhi: Why did you flip the Rāśis between the top and bottom halves of the zodiac?

Ācārya: This is how the Apasavya Kālacakra is. You need to break your preconceived notions and think about the Apasavya Kālacakra in this manner. This is the fundamental concept of Kālacakra Daśā, which people fail to catch.

Sunidhi: What is their correspondence with the Nakṣatras? As far as I know, there are Savya and Apasavya Nakṣatra pairs.

Ācārya: Good question. The 12 Rāśis of the zodiac are mapped to the Nakṣatra Pādas. So, we need to map 12 Rāśis to 12 Nakṣatra Pādas. Now, tell me, how many Nakṣatra are involved here?

Sunidhi: One Nakṣatra has four Pādas, so twelve Pādas must be mapped to three Nakṣatra. Isn't it?

Ācārya: You are right. Each zodiac, Savya and Apasavya, are mapped to sets of three Nakṣatras. This is another fundamental concept.

Sunidhi: Kindly explain this, Guruji.

Ācārya: Aśvinī-Bharaṇī-Kṛttikā is three consecutive Nakṣatras that are mapped to Meṣa to Mīna in the Savya (Krama) Kālacakra.

Sunidhi: So, it means, Meṣa-Vṛṣabha-Mithuna-Karka-Siṅha-Kanyā-Tulā-Vṛścika-Dhanu-Makara-Kumbha-Mīna are mapped to Aśvinī1-Aśvinī2-Aśvinī3-Aśvinī4-Bharaṇī1-Bharaṇī2-Bharaṇī3-Bharaṇī4-Kṛttikā1-Kṛttikā2-Kṛttikā3-Kṛttikā4. Is that right?

Ācārya: That is absolutely correct. The three Nakṣatra combinations are called a Triad or Tritārā. Now, let us examine the case of Apasavya Kālacakra. Rohiṇī-Mṛgaśirā-Ārdrā is a Apasavya Triad.

Sunidhi: So, they are mapped to Vṛścika to Dhanu, in the Apasavya (Krama) Kālacakra. Is that right?

Ācārya: You are right. Now, tell me their mapping, like you did for Savya Kālacakra.

Sunidhi: The sequence of Apasavya "Krama" Kālacakra is Vṛścika-Tulā-Kanyā-Siṅha-Karka-Mithuna-Vṛṣabha-Meṣa-Mīna-Kumbha-Makara-Dhanu. The Nakṣatra mapping is Rohiṇī1-Rohiṇī2-Rohiṇī3-Rohiṇī4-Mṛgaśirā1-Mṛgaśirā2-Mṛgaśirā3-Mṛgaśirā4-Ārdrā1-Ārdrā2-Ārdrā3-Ārdrā4.

Sunidhi: Guruji, kindly tell us about the Savya and Apasavya Nakṣatra Triads.

Ācārya: The Nakṣatras alternate between the Savya and Apasavya Triads.

Sunidhi: Since there are three Nakṣatras in a Triad, how many Triads should there be?

Ācārya: There are 27 Nakṣatra. This means that there must be nine Triads.

Ācārya: That is correct. Of the nine Triads, five are Savya, and four are Apasavya. Can you tell me why?

Kailāśa: Guruji, let me try.

Ācārya: Sure, go ahead.

Kailāśa: I think there are two reasons behind that.

(1) Five is an odd number and, therefore, Masculine. So, it is related to Savya. Four is an even number and, therefore, Feminine. So, it is related to Apasavya.

(2) If we put them into a sequence, it is Savya-Apasavya-Savya-Apasavya-Savya-Apasavya-Savya-Apasavya-Savya. This indicates that Savya occurs five times, and Apasavya occurs four times.

Ācārya: That is indeed a very good answer. Very well done!

Kailāśa: Dhanyavād, Guruji. Kindly tell us how to use the Nakṣatra Caraṇa mapping with Navāñśa here.

Ācārya: Good question. Tell me whether these Savya and Apasavya Kālacakras are mapped to Rāśi or Navāñśa Cakras.

Kailāśa: Kindly clarify, Guruji. From our general knowledge, the Nakṣatra Caraṇas should be mapped to Navāñśa.

Ācārya: You are right. Maharṣi Parāśara nowhere explicitly states that the Nakṣatra Pādas are mapped to Rāśi Cakras.

We know that each Nakṣatra Caraṇa is precisely mapped to a Navāñśa. If we disregard this crucial point, I believe we miss the core concept of Kālacakra.

Because of the Nakṣatra Caraṇa mapping, we must use the Savya and Apasavya Cakras as Navāñśa Kuṇḍalī and not Rāśi Kuṇḍalī.

Kailāśa: Guruji, this makes sense. Kindly elaborate further.

Ācārya: Each Nakṣatra has four Caraṇas, which means the three Nakṣatras in the Aśvinī-Bharaṇī-Kṛttikā Triad, having twelve Caraṇas are precisely mapped to the twelve Navāñśas of the Savya Cakra.

On the other hand, the twelve Caraṇas of the three Nakṣatras, Rohiṇī-Mṛgaśirā-Ārdrā Triad, are mapped to the twelve Navāñśas of the Apasavya Cakra.

Kailāśa: This makes sense.

Ācārya: Therefore, in a Savya Cakra (Navāñśa), the mapping is Aśvinī1 – Meṣa, Ashvini2 – Vṛṣabha, Aśvinī3 – Mithuna, Aśvinī4 – Karka and so on.

Similarly, in a Apasavya Cakra (Navāñśa), the mapping is Rohiṇī1 - Vṛścika, Rohiṇī2 - Tulā, Rohiṇī3 - Kanyā, Rohiṇī4 - Siṅha and so on.

Sunidhi: Dhanyavād Guruji.

Ācārya: This is the fundamental design of the Kālacakra.

Suppose one is born in Aśvinī4; we should say that the person is born in Savya Karka Navāñśa. Why?

Sunidhi: That is because Aśvinī is a Savya Nakṣatra. So, it should be mapped to Savya Kālacakra Navāñśa. This is the fourth Rāśi from Meṣa, which is Karka. Is that right?

Ācārya: That is perfect. Can you tell me the mapping of all the Savya Triads?

Sunidhi: Let me try. Here is the mapping of the Savya Navāñśa. I have denoted the Nakṣatra by their number, i.e., Aśvinī is N1, Bharaṇī is N2 and so on. So N1-1 means Aśvinī1, N1-2 is Aśvinī2 and so on.

Table 63: Savya Navāñśa

Navāñśa	Triad1	Triad3	Triad5	Triad7	Triad9
Meṣa	N1-1	N7-1	N13-1	N19-1	N25-1
Vṛṣabha	N1-2	N7-2	N13-2	N19-2	N25-2
Mithuna	N1-3	N7-3	N13-3	N19-3	N25-3
Karka	N1-4	N7-4	N13-4	N19-4	N25-4
Siṅha	N2-1	N8-1	N14-1	N20-1	N26-1
Kanyā	N2-2	N8-2	N14-2	N20-2	N26-2
Tulā	N2-3	N8-3	N14-3	N20-3	N26-3
Vṛścika	N2-4	N8-4	N14-4	N20-4	N26-4
Dhanu	N3-1	N9-1	N15-1	N21-1	N27-1
Makara	N3-2	N9-2	N15-2	N21-2	N27-2
Kumbha	N3-3	N9-3	N15-3	N21-3	N27-3
Mīna	N3-4	N9-4	N15-4	N21-4	N27-4

Ācārya: Perfect. Now, show the mapping of the Apasavya Navāñśa.

Sunidhi: Here it is.

Table 64

Navāñśa	Triad2	Triad4	Triad6	Triad8
Vṛścika	N4-1	N10-1	N16-1	N22-1
Tulā	N4-2	N10-2	N16-2	N22-2
Kanyā	N4-3	N10-3	N16-3	N22-3
Siṅha	N4-4	N10-4	N16-4	N22-4
Karka	N5-1	N11-1	N17-1	N23-1
Mithuna	N5-2	N11-2	N17-2	N23-2
Vṛṣabha	N5-3	N11-3	N17-3	N23-3
Meṣa	N5-4	N11-4	N17-4	N23-4
Mīna	N6-1	N12-1	N18-1	N24-1
Kumbha	N6-2	N12-2	N18-2	N24-2

Navāñśa	Triad2	Triad4	Triad6	Triad8
Makara	N6-3	N12-3	N18-3	N24-3
Dhanu	N6-4	N12-4	N18-4	N24-4

Ācārya: Well done, Sunidhi. This is perfect.

Sunidhi: Dhanyavād, Guruji.

Ācārya: Now, let us understand some patterns.

When we do the mapping of the Nakṣatra Caraṇas to either the Savya or Apasavya Kālacakras, we arrive at *six distinct groups* having the same mapping.

For instance, for the Nakṣatras Aśvinī, Punarvasu, Hastā, Mūla, Pūrvābhādra, the Caraṇa 1 to 4 are respectively mapped to Meṣa, Vṛṣabha, Mithuna and Karka Navāñśas. We can say that the five Nakṣatras, Aśvinī, Punarvasu, Hastā, Mūla, and Pūrvābhādra, belong to the Aśvinī group.

Sunidhi: It is unclear. Could you elaborate on this?

Ācārya: It should be clear if you see the below figure.

Navāñśa	Triad1	Triad3	Triad5	Triad7	Triad9
Meṣa	N1-1	N7-1	N13-1	N19-1	N25-1
Vṛṣabha	N1-2	N7-2	N13-2	N19-2	N25-2
Mithuna	N1-3	N7-3	N13-3	N19-3	N25-3
Karka	N1-4	N7-4	N13-4	N19-4	N25-4
Siṅha	N2-1	N8-1	N14-1	N20-1	N26-1
Kanyā	N2-2	N8-2	N14-2	N20-2	N26-2
Tulā	N2-3	N8-3	N14-3	N20-3	N26-3
Vṛścika	N2-4	N8-4	N14-4	N20-4	N26-4
Dhanu	N3-1	N9-1	N15-1	N21-1	N27-1
Makara	N3-2	N9-2	N15-2	N21-2	N27-2
Kumbha	N3-3	N9-3	N15-3	N21-3	N27-3
Mina	N3-4	N9-4	N15-4	N21-4	N27-4

Sunidhi: Oh! I see now what you meant. For Nakṣatra 1Aśvinī, 7Punarvasu, 13Hastā, 19Mūla and 25Pūrvābhādra, the four Caraṇas are mapped to Meṣa to Karka Navāñśa. You are saying that they belong to the Aśvinī group.

Ācārya: You got it. Similarly, we have the Bharaṇī group. Below is the figure for the Bharaṇī group.

Navāñśa	Triad1	Triad3	Triad5	Triad7	Triad9
Meṣa	N1-1	N7-1	N13-1	N19-1	N25-1
Vṛṣabha	N1-2	N7-2	N13-2	N19-2	N25-2
Mithuna	N1-3	N7-3	N13-3	N19-3	N25-3
Karka	N1-4	N7-4	N13-4	N19-4	N25-4
Siṅha	N2-1	N8-1	N14-1	N20-1	N26-1
Kanyā	N2-2	N8-2	N14-2	N20-2	N26-2
Tulā	N2-3	N8-3	N14-3	N20-3	N26-3
Vṛścika	N2-4	N8-4	N14-4	N20-4	N26-4
Dhanu	N3-1	N9-1	N15-1	N21-1	N27-1
Makara	N3-2	N9-2	N15-2	N21-2	N27-2
Kumbha	N3-3	N9-3	N15-3	N21-3	N27-3
Mina	N3-4	N9-4	N15-4	N21-4	N27-4

Sunidhi: I see now. So, the Bharaṇī group Nakṣatra Caraṇas are mapped to Siṅha to Vṛścika Navāñśa. This group contains the Nakṣatras 2Bharaṇī, 8Puṣya, 14Citrā, 20Pūrvāṣāṛhā and 26Uttarābhādra. Isn't it?

Ācārya: There you go. You got it. There are six such groups. 3 in Savya and 3 in Apasavya.

In each Savya group, there are five Nakṣatra = 3 * 5 = 15 Nakṣatra.

In each Apasavya group, there are four Nakṣatra = 3 * 4 = 12 Nakṣatra.

Total, Savya + Apasavya = 15 + 12 = 27 Nakṣatra.

Sunidhi: I see now. Can we examine the Nakṣatra in a figure form?

Ācārya: Why don't you give it a try?

Sunidhi: Let me try. The below table shows the six groups with the highlighted ones indicating the Savya group.

Table 65

#	Group	Nakṣ1	Nakṣ2	Nakṣ3	Nakṣ4	Nakṣ5
1	(S) Aśvinī	Aśvinī	Punarvasu	Hastā	Mūla	Pūrvābhādra
2	(S) Bharaṇī	Bharaṇī	Puṣya	Citrā	Pūrvāṣāṛhā	Uttarābhādra
3	(S) Kṛttikā	Kṛttikā	Aśleṣā	Svāti	Uttarāṣāṛhā	Revatī
4	(A) Rohiṇī	Rohiṇī	Maghā	Viśākhā	Śravaṇa	
5	(A) Mṛgaśirā	Mṛgaśirā	Pūrvāphālgunī	Anurādhā	Dhaniṣṭhā	
6	(A) Ārdrā	Ārdrā	Uttarāphālgunī	Jyeṣṭhā	Śatabhiṣā	

Ācārya: You are absolutely correct. Very well done!

Therefore, we have six groups, (1) Aśvinī^, (2) Bharaṇī^, (3) Kṛttikā^, (4) Rohiṇī, (5) Mṛgaśirā, and (6) Ārdrā. The ones marked with "^" are Savya, and the remaining three are Apasavya. Each Savya group has five Nakṣatras – they are the Pentads. Each Apasavya group has four Nakṣatras – they are the Quads.

Kailāśa: So, the 27 Nakṣatras are classified under three Savya and three Apasavya groups. Isn't it?

Ācārya: Yes, you have understood it.

The 6 Groups are further reduced to 4 groups, led by Aśvinī, Bharaṇī, Rohiṇī and Mṛgaśirā Nakṣatras.

Kailāśa: How is this so?

Ācārya: It is done in the following manner:

Savya-Aśvinī and Savya-Kṛttikā groups are grouped into "Savya-Aśvinī" group. Likewise, the Apasavya-Mṛgaśirā and Apasavya-Ārdrā groups are grouped into the "Apasavya-Mṛgaśirā" group.

Savya-Bharaṇī and Apasavya-Rohiṇī groups stay unchanged.

This is how it looks in the figure.

Table 66

#	Group	Nakṣ1	Nakṣ2	Nakṣ3	Nakṣ4	Nakṣ5
1	(S) Aśvinī	Aśvinī	Punarvasu	Hastā	Mūla	Pūrvābhādra
2	(S) Bharaṇī	Bharaṇī	Puṣya	Citrā	Pūrvāṣāṛhā	Uttarābhādra
3	(S) Kṛttikā	Kṛttikā	Aśleṣā	Svāti	Uttarāṣāṛhā	Revatī
4	(A) Rohiṇī	Rohiṇī	Maghā	Viśākhā	Śravaṇa	
5	(A) Mṛgaśirā	Mṛgaśirā	Pūrvāphālgunī	Anurādhā	Dhaniṣṭhā	
6	(A) Ārdrā	Ārdrā	Uttarāphālgunī	Jyeṣṭhā	Śatabhiṣā	

Sunidhi: So, we have four groups now.

(1) *Savya-Aśvinī: 10 Nakṣatras:* Aśvinī, Punarvasu, Hastā, Mūla, Pūrvābhādra, Kṛttikā, Aśleṣā, Svāti, Uttarāṣāṛhā, Revatī

(2) *Savya-Bharaṇī: 5 Nakṣatras:* Bharaṇī, Puṣya, Citrā, Pūrvāṣāṛhā, Uttarābhādra

(3) *Apasavya-Rohiṇī: 4 Nakṣatras:* Rohiṇī, Maghā, Viśākhā, Śravaṇa

(4) *Apasavya-Mṛgaśirā: 8 Nakṣatras:* Mṛgaśirā, Pūrvāphālgunī, Anurādhā, Dhaniṣṭhā, Ārdrā, Uttarāphālgunī, Jyeṣṭhā, Śatabhiṣā

Ācārya: Yes, that is correct!

Sunidhi: What is next?

Ācārya: Now, we must understand the concept of Navanavāñśas.

Kailāśa: Does this mean subdividing a Navāñśa into nine parts?

Ācārya: Yes, you are right. Each Navāñśa in the Savya or Apasavya Cakra contains 9 Daśās, which represent nine Navanavāñśas. The Navanavāñśas are the Navāñśas within Navāñśas.

Kailāśa: Why must we do that?

Ācārya: This is to understand two crucial concepts, the Deha and Jīva.

The understanding of the Deha and Jīva requires the understanding of the Navanavāñśas assigned to a Navāñśa.

Besides the Savya and Apasavya Cakra, the concept of Navanavāñśa is the second crucial structural design of the Kālacakra.

The sequence of Kālacakra Daśā and two important entities, the Deha and Jīva, are based on this Navanavāñśa sequence.

Maharṣi Parāśara narrates the sequence of nine Navanavāñśas for each Navāñśa. Since each Navāñśa maps to a Nakṣatra Caraṇas, there are nine subdivisions of a Nakṣatra Caraṇa, which are the Navanavāñśas.

Kailāśa: This is interesting Guruji. Do you mean to say each Nakṣatra Caraṇa has nine Daśās? So, if someone is born Anurādhā4, he will have a specific sequence of Daśās based on the Navanavāñśas?

Ācārya: Yes, that is how it is. The first in the Daśā sequence is the Deha, and the last one is the Jīva. This sequence of Navanavāñśa, Deha and Jīva governs one's life.

Let us see what Maharṣi Parāśara states.

Bṛhatparāśara 46.60 states that Aśvinī1 is mapped to Meṣa Navāñśa (Savya Kālacakra), with Meṣa Deha and Dhanu Jīva.

The Navanavāñśas of Meṣa Navāṃśa are (1) Meṣa, (2) Vṛṣabha, (3) Mithuna, (4) Karka, (5) Siṅha, (6) Kanyā, (7) Tulā, (8) Vṛścika and (9) Dhanu and these denote the 9 Daśās of Aśvinī1 or Meṣa Navāñśa.

Although the Navanavāñśas is stated for all the Nakṣatra Caraṇas, the rationale for deriving them is not clarified by Maharṣi Parāśara. But I will try to provide the rational basis for the derivation of the Navanavāñśas.

Kailāśa: We are eager to learn about it, Guruji.

Ācārya: Through the grace of Lord Mahādeva, I found that the assignment of Navanavāñśas is based on alternating Savya and Apasavya Cakras.

Let us take the example of Aśvinī Nakṣatras. There are four Caraṇas of Aśvinī that are mapped to 4 Navāñśas (Meṣa to Karka).

Each of these Caraṇas (Navāñśas) has nine Navanavāñśas. So, how many Navanavāñśas in four Caraṇas of Aśvinī?

Kailāśa: 4 Caraṇas * 9 Navanavāñśas = 36 Navanavāñśas. Right?

Ācārya: Yes, the thirty-six Navanavāñśas are mapped to three cycles of twelve Rāśis. So, it is about circumnutating the Rāśicakra three times.

Kailāśa: Kindly elaborate further.

Ācārya: Maharṣi Parāśara states in 46.60-64:

In Aśvinī1, Meṣa is Deha and Dhanu is Jīva. The Daśā sequence is Savya-Krama, i.e., Meṣa-Vṛṣabha...Dhanu.

In Aśvinī2, the Daśā commences from the next Rāśi from Dhanu. Here Deha is Makara and Jīva is Mithuna. The Daśā sequence Savya-Utkrama i.e., Makara-Dhanu... Mithuna.

In Aśvinī3, Vṛṣabha is Deha and Mithun is Jiva. The Daśā sequence Savya-Utkrama i.e., Vṛṣabha, Meṣa, Mīna, Kumbha, Makara, Dhanu, Meṣa, Vṛṣabha and Mithuna.

In Aśvinī4, Karka is Deha and Mīna is Jiva. The Daśā sequence Savya-Krama i.e., Karka, Siṅha..., Mīna.

Kailāśa: Why is the sequence of Aśvinī3 jumped from Dhanu to Meṣa? That does not make sense.

Ācārya: That is called a jumping of Rāśi, or Viśeṣa Gati. I will explain it later. But let me explain why this is happening and how to decode the pattern.

It is Utkrama order, and therefore, the sequence is Vṛṣabha, Meṣa... Dhanu. The sequence of Savya Cakra is Meṣa to Dhanu. So, the sequence for four Pādas of Aśvinī are:

Aśvinī1 Krama: Meṣa... Dhanu

Aśvinī2 Utkrama: Makara...Mithuna.

Aśvinī3 Utkrama: Vṛṣabha...Dhanu + Meṣa...Vṛṣabha.

Aśvinī4 Krama: Karka... Mīna

I will help in decoding the basis of this sequence later.

Ācārya: We must note the following:

Cycle 1 is Savya: the sequence of Navanavāñśas is from Meṣa to Mīna

Cycle 2 is Apasavya: the sequence of Navanavāñśas is from Vṛścika to Dhanu.

Cycle 3 is Savya: the sequence of Navanavāñśas is from Meṣa to Mīna

The three-cycle sequence is *Krama+(Savya-Apasavya-Savya).*

This sequence applies to the ten Nakṣatras of Savya-Aśvinī group: Aśvinī, Punarvasu, Hastā, Mūla, Pūrvābhādra, Kṛttikā, Aśleṣā, Svāti, Uttarāṣāṛhā, Revatī.

Kailāśa: Is the sequence different for other groups such as the Savya-Bharaṇī group (Bharaṇī, Puṣya, Citrā, Pūrvāṣāṛhā, Uttarābhādra)?

Ācārya: Yes, it is different.

In the Savya-Bharaṇī group, consisting of five Nakṣatras, Bharaṇī, Puṣya, Citrā, Pūrvāṣāṛhā, Uttarābhādra, the three-cycle sequence is *Krama+ (Apasavya-Savya-Apasavya).*

Kailāśa: Noted, Guruji!

Ācārya: So far, we have seen the sequence for Savya Nakṣatras, Savya-Aśvinī (10 Nakṣatras) and Savya-Bharaṇī (5 Nakṣatras).

This is different for the twelve Apasavya Nakṣatras:

(1) *Apasavya-Rohiṇī: 4 Nakṣatras:* Rohiṇī, Maghā, Viśākhā, Śravaṇa

(2) *Apasavya-Mṛgaśirā: 8 Nakṣatras:* Mṛgaśirā, Pūrvāphālgunī, Anurādhā, Dhaniṣṭhā, Ārdrā, Uttarāphālgunī, Jyeṣṭhā, Śatabhiṣā

In the case of the twelve Apasavya Nakṣatras, we notice a reversal (Utkrama).

The Savya-Krama sequence is Meṣa → Mīna.

The Apasavya-Krama sequence is Vṛścika → Dhanu.

Kailāśa: Noted, Guruji. I am waiting for further elaboration.

Ācārya:

The Utkrama sequence reverses the sequence. Therefore:

The Savya-Utkrama sequence transforms from Meṣa-Mīna to Mīna-Meṣa.

The Apasavya-Utkrama sequence transforms from Vṛścika-Dhanu to Dhanu-Vṛścika.

For the Apasavya-Rohiṇī group, the three-cycle sequence is *Utkrama+ (Savya- Apasavya-Savya*).

For the Mṛgaśirā group, the three-cycle sequence is *Utkrama+(Apasavya-Savya-Apasavya).*

Sunidhi: Let me summarise this:

(1) *Savya-Aśvinī: 10 Nakṣatras:* Aśvinī, Punarvasu, Hastā, Mūla, Pūrvābhādra, Kṛttikā, Aśleṣā, Svāti, Uttarāṣāṛhā, Revatī: *Krama+(Savya-Apasavya-Savya)* = KSAS.

(2) *Savya-Bharaṇī: 5 Nakṣatras:* Bharaṇī, Puṣya, Citrā, Pūrvāṣāṛhā, Uttarābhādra: *Krama+ (Apasavya-Savya-Apasavya)* = KASA.

(3) *Apasavya-Rohiṇī: 4 Nakṣatras:* Rohiṇī, Maghā, Viśākhā, Śravaṇa: *Utkrama+ (Apasavya-Savya-Apasavya) = UASA.*

(4) *Apasavya-Mṛgaśirā: 8 Nakṣatras:* Mṛgaśirā, Pūrvāphālgunī, Anurādhā, Dhaniṣṭhā, Ārdrā, Uttarāphālgunī, Jyeṣṭhā, Śatabhiṣā: *Utkrama+(Savya-Apasavya-Savya) = USAS.*

Kailāśa: It appears that we must remember the *mnemonics*:

SAS = *aspuhamupbkrassvuare* = KSAS

SBH = *bhpucipaub* = KASA

ARO = *romavisr*= UASA

AMR = *mrarppupanjydhsa* = USAS

Ācārya: That is a good idea. You can always keep this as a small reference note with yourself so that you can recall them when needed.

Kailāśa: What is next, Guruji?

Ācārya: We shall now focus on the Candra-Sūrya reversal.

Kailāśa: What does that mean?

Ācārya: There is a reversal of their Rāśis in a specific condition. We shall examine that. Remember the two rules:

Apasavya Cakra rule: In Apasavya Cakras used for either the Savya or Apasavya Nakṣatras, the Candra-Sūrya order is "never" reversed. The fourth place is reserved for Karka and the fifth place for Sūrya, whereas the remaining 10 Rāśis are flipped.

Kailāśa: Wow, that is a revelation. Do you mean in Apasavya Cakra, all Rāśis are flipped in the horizontal axis, but Karka and Siṅha are not?

Ācārya: That is indeed the case. The "True" Apasavya Cakra is shown below. You can see that Karka and Siṅha are not flipped.

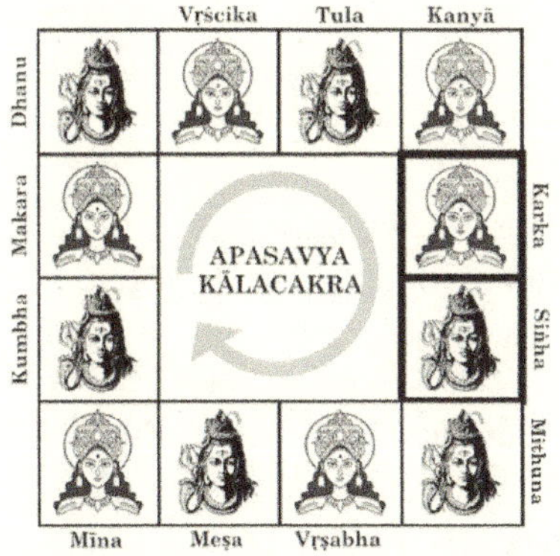

The Savya Cakra is regular, as shown below. In this, as usual, Karka and Siṅha are aligned to the fourth and fifth Rāśi.

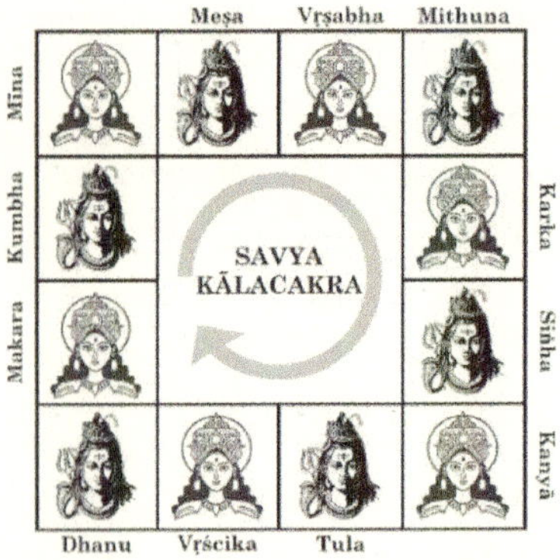

When the Savya and Apasavya cycles combine, their ending and joining points manifest regions of danger due to discontinuity and special jumps such as Siṅhavlokana Gati. *Siṅhavlokana Gati* is like a lion is watching and ready to pounce on its Prey.

Kailāśa: Noted, Guruji. There are also other Gatis as well. Isn't it?

Ācārya: Yes, we shall examine all of them.

Now, focusing on the progression of the Rāśis and the Gatis. It is a complex system. The complexity does not end with the Siṅhavlokana Gati. We are yet to see the flipping of Karka and Siṅha. The basis of this is that in the Savya group, the sequence of the Rāśis of the Prakāśagrahas is Karka → Siṅha.

Kailāśa: Noted, Guruji!

Ācārya: In the Apasavya Nakṣatras, the sequence should ideally be Siṅha → Karka, but since this is not allowed, the sequence remains Karka → Siṅha.

This gives rise to two Gatis that occur concurrently, the Maṇḍūka Gati and the Marakaṭa Gati. Maṇḍūka Gati is like a frog's jump, and Marakaṭa Gati is like a monkey's jump.

Kailāśa: What is the reasoning for the Maṇḍūka Gati?

Ācārya: Due to the Karka-Siṅha flipping (in Apasavya Cakra), the Maṇḍūka Gati occurs between Kanyā → Karka and Siṅha → Mithuna. In this Gati, the Rāśi is jumped to the *alternate Rāśi*, skipping one Rāśi in between.

Kailāśa: Dhanyavād, Guruji! You have explained Siṅhavlokana and Maṇḍūka Gati. How about Marakaṭa Gati?

Ācārya: The Marakaṭa Gati occurs when there is a sudden change in direction.

For instance, in the Apasavya cycle of the Aśvinī group, which is the middle cycle (in the *Savya-Apasavya-Savya* cycles), the sequence should ideally be Kanyā-Siṅha-Karka-Mithuna.

However, due to the fixity of Karka-Siṅha (*in Apasavya Cakra*), this becomes Kanyā-Karka-Siṅha-Mithuna. This gives rise to the Marakaṭa Gati, which happens between Kanyā to Karka (*Maṇḍūka*), then a sudden reversal from Karka to Siṅha (*Marakaṭa*), and after that from Siṅha to Mithuna (*Maṇḍūka*).

The *Marakaṭa* Gati always occurs with *Maṇḍūka* Gati.

Maṇḍūka means frog, which *hops* and *Marakaṭa* means monkey, which *abruptly reverses its direction*. These sudden changes or jumps give rise to serious troubles in life, danger or even death.

Kailāśa: Noted, Guruji. Kindly tell us about the Daśā durations in this Daśā.

Ācārya: Regarding the Daśā durations, Maharṣi Parāśara states in Bṛhatparāśara 46.84 that 5, 21, 7, 9, 10, 16 and 4 years are the Daśā durations of Sūrya, Candra, Maṅgala, Budha, Bṛhaspati, Śukra and Śani.

Sūrya 5, Candra 21, Maṅgala 7, Budha 9, Bṛhaspati 10, Śukra 16 and Śani 4.

Based on this the Daśā duration of the Rāśis are Meṣa 7, Vṛṣabha 16, Mithuna 9, Karka 21, Siṅha 5, Kanyā 9, Tulā 16, Vṛścika 7, Dhanu 10, Makara 4, Kumbha 4, Mīna 10.

Kailāśa: Is this the basis for the longevity allotted to different Nakṣatra Pādas?

Ācārya: That is how it is. The Daśā duration and the lifespan of a person are determined on the basis of this allotment.

For instance, for Aśvinī1, the Navanavāñśas are Meṣa-Vṛṣabha-Mithuna-Karka-Siṅha-Kanyā-Tulā-Vṛścika-Dhanu, which gives rise to 7-16-9-21-5-9-16-7-10 years, i.e., 100 years.

Kailāśa: Does this mean that for one born in Aśvinī1, the Āyu span is 100 years?

Ācārya: According to Maharṣi Parāśara (46.89.), one born in Meṣa Añśa, the Āyu is 100 years, in Vṛṣabha 85 years, in Mithuna 83 years, in Karka 86 years. This is based on the Navanavāñśas assigned to them, the Nakṣatra Caraṇas or the Navāñśas.

Kailāśa: Is this how we determine the Āyuṣas for the different Nakṣatra Pādas?

Ācārya: We can notice the following pattern:

(1) For Savya Nakṣatras, the Āyuṣa allotted to the Caraṇas are I - 100, II - 85, III - 83 and IV - 86. The total is 354 years.

(2) For the Apasavya Nakṣatras, the Āyuṣa allotted to the Caraṇas are reversed, i.e., I - 86, II - 83, III - 85 and IV - 100.

Kailāśa: But it does not make sense that everyone born in Aśvinī1 should have Āyuṣa of 100 years.

Ācārya: It is not that one born in a certain Caraṇa, say Aśvinī1, is always assigned 100 years.

This only tells us that if one is born in 0° of Aśvinī1, then the default Āyus granted to the native as per the Navanavāñśas is 100 years.

This only means the Daśā duration and not the longevity of the person.

Kailāśa: Then how to apply this knowledge to real Kuṇḍalīs?

Ācārya: In real Kuṇḍalīs, one can be born in various points of a Nakṣatra Caraṇa, which means that after expiring the remaining Navanavāñśas, the Daśā moves to the next cycle of the Navanavāñśa.

Kailāśa: It is unclear. Kindly elaborate.

Ācārya: Suppose one is born at the end of Aśvinī1, i.e., the 9th Navanavāñśa of Aśvinī1, which is Dhanu. This merely means that after elapsing the Dhanu Navanavāñśa, the Daśā moves to Aśvinī2, which is in Vṛṣabha Navāñśa (of Savya Kālacakra), and the Daśā sequence is Makara-Kumbha-Mīna-Vṛścika^-Tulā^-Kanyā^-Karka!^-Siṅha!^-Mithuna^.

Kailāśa: What do "!" and "^" indicate in the Navanavāñśa sequence?

Ācārya: "^" indicates the Apasavya movement, whereas "!" indicates the luminary switch. The Luminary switch is the switching of Karka and Siṅha.

Kailāśa: Does this mean that everyone experiences 9 Navāñśas (9 Daśās)?

Ācārya: Normally, we can limit the assignment of the Daśā Rāśis to only 9, which is true for the case of most, but in some cases, it can extend.

Most people touch the Daśā of only one or two Nakṣatra Caraṇa (Navāñśa), whereas a few can touch three Caraṇas.

Kailāśa: So, this means, depending on the Caraṇa of birth, one can touch the Caraṇas of one or two different Nakṣatras. Right?

Ācārya: Yes, that is right! Let me give an example.

In my case - I am born in the last Navanavāñśa of Anurādhā4 (Meṣa Kālacakra Navāñśa). The last Navanavāñśa of Anurādhā4 (Meṣa) is Meṣa, after which the Daśā moves to the 1st Navanavāñśa to Jyeṣṭhā1 (Apasavya *Dhanu* Kālacakra Navāñśa), which is Mīna.

Kailāśa: Noted, Guruji!

Ācārya: Now, regarding the crossing of Nakṣatra, the switch cannot happen from Savya to Apasavya Nakṣatra or vice-versa.

For instance, after Kṛttikā4, instead of the Daśā moving to Rohini1, it moves to Aśvinī1.

For Savya Nakṣatra, the Daśā cycle remains within the Savya Kālacakra, and for Apasavya Nakṣatra, the Daśā cycle remains with the Apasavya Kālacakra.

Kailāśa: Noted, Guruji!

Ācārya: Regarding the nomenclature of Daśā, Bhukti, etc., there are some minute variations between the classical texts.

Maharṣi Parāśara states (49.6) that in the Kālacakra Daśā of Meṣa in Meṣa Navāñśa, there shall be distress due to troubles caused by the pollution of blood. He further states that in the Daśā of Meṣa in the Vṛṣabha Navāñśa, there is an increase in wealth and agricultural produce.

What can we infer from this?

Kailāśa: What, Guruji?

Ācārya: It means that in the Meṣa Navāñśa - Meṣa Daśā (Navanavāñśa), there is suffering due to the pollution of blood.

Similarly, in the Meṣa Navāñśa - Vṛṣabha Daśā (Navanavāñśa), there is an increase in wealth and agricultural produce.

Kailāśa: Doesn't it mean that the nine Navanavāñśas in a Navāñśa (or Nakṣatra Caraṇa) are the Daśās?

Ācārya: You got it!

To confirm this, let us take another instance. The Maharṣi states (49.16-17) that in Siṅha (Navāñśa), in the Daśā of the Navāñśa (Navanavāñśa) of:

(1) ... Vṛścika: there is distress and disputes,

(2) ... Tulā: extraordinary gains,

(3) ... Kanyā: gains of wealth,

(4) ... Karka: danger from wild animals,

(5) ... Siṅha: the birth of a son,

(6) ... Mithuna: increase of enemies,

(7) ... Vṛṣabha: gains from the sale of cattle,

(8) ... Meṣa: danger from animals and

(9) ... Mīna: journeys to distant places.

Kailāśa: Now, I can understand this.

Ācārya: In the following table, we notice that in Siṅha Navāñśa, there are two Daśā sequences.

Sequence 1 (*Savya-Bharaṇī group pada1*) is Vṛś-Tul-Kan-Kar-Siṅ-Mit-Vṛṣ-Meṣ-Mīn.

Sequence 2 (*Apasavya-Rohiṇī group pada4*) is Mīn-Meṣ-Vṛṣ-Mit-Siṅ-Kar-Kan-Tul-Vṛś.

We notice that, in the explanation of the results, for Savya Nakṣatra, the Maharṣi uses the Savya-Utkrama, i.e., that of Vṛścika-Tulā-Kanyā...Mithuna. I believe the same should also be applied to the Apasavya Nakṣatra, for the Daśās are of the same Navanavāñśa (Siṅha in this case). Still, the sequence is reversed (Utkramāpasavya).

Table 67: Daśā of Siṅha Navāñśa

#	Nakṣ	Car	S/A	Group	Navāñśa	Mahādaśā									Deha	Jīva
						1	2	3	4	5	6	7	8	9		
5	***Bhar***	*1*	*S*	*Bhar*	***Siṅha***	*Vṛś*	*Tul*	*Kan*	*Kar*	*Siṅ*	*Mit*	*Vṛṣ*	*Meṣ*	*Mīn*	*Vṛś*	*Mīn*
16	Rohi	4	A	Rohi	**Siṅha**	Mīn	Meṣ	Vṛṣ	Mit	Siṅ	Kar	Kan	Tul	Vṛś	Vṛś	Mīn
29	***Puṣy***	*1*	*S*	*Bhar*	***Siṅha***	*Vṛś*	*Tul*	*Kan*	*Kar*	*Siṅ*	*Mit*	*Vṛṣ*	*Meṣ*	*Mīn*	*Vṛś*	*Mīn*
40	Magh	4	A	Rohi	**Siṅha**	Mīn	Meṣ	Vṛṣ	Mit	Siṅ	Kar	Kan	Tul	Vṛś	Vṛś	Mīn

#	Nakṣ	Car	S/A	Group	Navāñśa	Mahādaśā 1	2	3	4	5	6	7	8	9	Deha	Jīva
53	*Citr*	*1*	*S*	*Bhar*	*Siṅha*	*Vṛś*	*Tul*	*Kan*	*Kar*	*Siṅ*	*Mit*	*Vṛṣ*	*Meṣ*	*Mīn*	*Vṛś*	*Mīn*
64	Viśā	4	A	Rohi	Siṅha	Mīn	Meṣ	Vṛṣ	Mit	Siṅ	Kar	Kan	Tul	Vṛś	Vṛś	Mīn
77	*Pūrv*	*1*	*S*	*Bhar*	*Siṅha*	*Vṛś*	*Tul*	*Kan*	*Kar*	*Siṅ*	*Mit*	*Vṛṣ*	*Meṣ*	*Mīn*	*Vṛś*	*Mīn*
88	Śrav	4	A	Rohi	Siṅha	Mīn	Meṣ	Vṛṣ	Mit	Siṅ	Kar	Kan	Tul	Vṛś	Vṛś	Mīn
101	*Utta*	*1*	*S*	*Bhar*	*Siṅha*	*Vṛś*	*Tul*	*Kan*	*Kar*	*Siṅ*	*Mit*	*Vṛṣ*	*Meṣ*	*Mīn*	*Vṛś*	*Mīn*

Kailāśa: Does this mean that each Navāñśa has two Navāñśa sequences for Savya and Apasavya Nakṣatras?

Ācārya: Yes. If the Navāñśa falls in a Savya Nakṣatra, the first sequence is applied. Instead, if the same Navāñśa falls in an Apasavya Nakṣatra, the second sequence is used.

Savya Tārā: Sequence 1

Apasavya Tārā: Sequence 2: Reverse of Sequence 1.

Kailāśa: Does the Maharṣi cover all Navāñśa and Navanavāñśa combinations?

Ācārya: Let us verify this using a Navāñśa, where the Siṅhavlokana Gati is seen, a Gati that happens due to the meeting of Savya and Apasavya Cakra.

This is seen in Aśvinī2 (Vṛṣabha Navāñśa).

We notice that, regardless of whether Vṛṣabha Navāñśa belongs to Savya or Apasavya Tārā, the Daśā Rāśis (Navanavāñśas) within the Vṛṣabha Navāñśa are invariably the same but as expected the sequence is reversed.

Kailāśa: Noted, Guruji. So, it is established that the Navanavāñśas sequence for a Navāñśa is "always" the same, but it is reversed for the Apasavya Tārā.

Ācārya: That is right!

In both the Savya and Apasavya Tārās, the Siṅhavlokana Gati is seen for Vṛṣabha Navāñśa.

Kailāśa: What is the Śāstraic reference to that?

Ācārya: Regarding Vṛṣabha, Maharṣi Parāśara states (49.8-10.) that in Vṛṣabha (Navāñśa):

(1) In the Makara Navāñśa (*read this as Navanavāñśa*) Daśā, there shall be a tendency to perform undesirable deeds along with more adverse effects.

(2) In the Kumbha Navāñśa, there are profits in business,

(3) In the Mīna Navāñśa success in all ventures,

(4) In the Vṛścika Navāñśa, danger from fire,

(5) In the Tulā Navāñśa, recognition from the Government and reverence from all,

(6) In the Kanyā Navāñśa, danger from enemies,

(7) In the Daśā of Karka Navāñśa, distress to the wife,

(8) In the Siṅha Navāñśa, diseases of the eyes and

(9) In the Mithuna Navāñśa, obstacles in earning a livelihood."

Again, notice that Maharṣi Parāśara gives the results of the nine Daśās (Navanavāñśas) of Savya Tārā and expects us to apply them for Apasavya Tārā (in reverse).

Table 68: Daśā of Vṛṣabha Navāñśa

#	Na kṣ	C ar	S/ A	Gro up	Navā ñśa	Mahādaśā 1	 2	 3	 4	 5	 6	 7	 8	 9	De ha	Jī va
2	***Aśv i***	*2*	*S*	*Aśvi*	***Vṛṣa bha***	*M ak*	*Ku m*	*Mī n*	*Vṛ ś*	*T ul*	*K an*	*K ar*	*Siṅ*	*Mi t*	*Ma k*	*Mi t*
1 9	**Mṛ ga**	3	A	Mṛg a	**Vṛṣa bha**	Mi t	Si ṅ	K ar	Ka n	T ul	Vṛ ś	Mī n	Ku m	M ak	Ma k	Mi t
2 6	***Pu na***	*2*	*S*	*Aśvi*	***Vṛṣa bha***	*M ak*	*Ku m*	*Mī n*	*Vṛ ś*	*T ul*	*K an*	*K ar*	*Siṅ*	*Mi t*	*Ma k*	*Mi t*
4 3	**Pū rv**	3	A	Mṛg a	**Vṛṣa bha**	Mi t	Si ṅ	K ar	Ka n	T ul	Vṛ ś	Mī n	Ku m	M ak	Ma k	Mi t
5 0	***Ha st***	*2*	*S*	*Aśvi*	***Vṛṣa bha***	*M ak*	*Ku m*	*Mī n*	*Vṛ ś*	*T ul*	*K an*	*K ar*	*Siṅ*	*Mi t*	*Ma k*	*Mi t*
6 7	**An ur**	3	A	Mṛg a	**Vṛṣa bha**	Mi t	Si ṅ	K ar	Ka n	T ul	Vṛ ś	Mī n	Ku m	M ak	Ma k	Mi t
7 4	***Mū la***	*2*	*S*	*Aśvi*	***Vṛṣa bha***	*M ak*	*Ku m*	*Mī n*	*Vṛ ś*	*T ul*	*K an*	*K ar*	*Siṅ*	*Mi t*	*Ma k*	*Mi t*
9 1	**Dh an**	3	A	Mṛg a	**Vṛṣa bha**	Mi t	Si ṅ	K ar	Ka n	T ul	Vṛ ś	Mī n	Ku m	M ak	Ma k	Mi t
9 8	***Pūr v***	*2*	*S*	*Aśvi*	***Vṛṣa bha***	*M ak*	*Ku m*	*Mī n*	*Vṛ ś*	*T ul*	*K an*	*K ar*	*Siṅ*	*Mi t*	*Ma k*	*Mi t*

Kailāśa: Noted, Guruji!

Ācārya: Some Ācāryas call the Daśās and Antardaśās differently. Śrī Mantreśvara likes to call the Navāñśa Rāśi as Mahādaśā, whereas the Navanavāñśa Rāśi as the Bhukti or Apahara.

In Phaladīpikā 22.5, he states that for one born in the first Caraṇa of Aśvinī, the first Bhukti belongs to Meṣa-Maṅgala; the second to Vṛṣabha-Śukra; the third to Mithuna-Budha; the fourth to Karka-Candra; the fifth to Sinha-Sūrya; the sixth to Kanyā-Budha; the seventh to Tulā-Śukra; the eighth to Vṛścika-Maṅgala; and the 9th to Dhanu-Bṛhaspati.

According to Śrī Mantreśvara, for a person born in, say, Anurādhā4, the Daśā is that of Meṣa, as the Nakṣatra-Caraṇa is mapped to Meṣa Navāñśa. Within Meṣa Daśā, the Bhuktis are in the sequence of Dha-Vṛś-Tul-Kan-Siṅ-Kar-Mit-Vṛṣ-Meṣ.

Kailāśa: Oh! This is interesting. But the concept is the same; only the nomenclature is different.

Ācārya: According to this view, one might get in one's lifetime, say 1 to 3 Daśā and the periods that we must reckon for deciphering the lifeline should be based on the Bhuktis.

Kailāśa: That makes sense.

Ācārya: Regardless of what we call something Navāñśa, Daśā or Bhukti, the concept is the same.

For ease of reference and consistency, for one born in Anurādhā4, we should say that:

(1) The person is born in Meṣa Navāñśa

(2) The applicable Daśās are that of Dha-Vṛś-Tul-Kan-Siṅ-Kar-Mit-Vṛṣ-Meṣ.

Therefore, a Bhukti, according to Śrī Mantreśvara, is a Mahādaśā in our convention. Daśā of Śrī Mantreśvara is called Navāñśa in our convention.

Kailāśa: What convention do other scholars follow?

Ācārya: Jātakapārijāta also supports our convention. Śrī GK Ojha, in his translation of this text, writes that one who is born in the 1st Caraṇa of Rohiṇī, Maghā, Viśākhā, Śravaṇa has a total Daśā span of 86 years.

They are said to be born in Vṛścika Navāñśa, and their sequence of Daśā is Dha-Mak-Kum-Mīn-Meṣ-Vṛṣ-Mit-Siṅ-Kar.

Evidently, Śrī Ojha endorses that the person is born in Vṛścika Navāñśa, which is what I have explained before, and the Daśā of such a person is in Dhanu to Karka, that totals up to 86 years.

Kailāśa: Noted, Guruji.

Ācārya: Again, the basis of this sequence is not clarified, which I have clarified in this discussion. We shall see that the basis of the Daśā sequence is an alternating sequence of Savya and Apasavya Cakras. The concept of Navanavāñśa is not explained, but it can be inferred when we use this in conjunction with the three-cycle sequence of the Savya and Apasavya Cakras.

Kailāśa: How to determine the Daśā balance at birth?

Ācārya: After we have determined the Daśā prevailing at birth, the next important step is to determine the Daśā Balance.

In this regard, we can utilize the unexpired portion of Candra Nakṣatra. Let us take Aśvinī1 (Meṣa Navāñśa), whose duration is 100 years. The duration of a Nakṣatra Caraṇa (or Navāñśa) is 200' (3°20'), which is allotted to the 100 years.

If one is born in 1°6'40" (1.111°) of Aśvinī, which is in Aśvinī1, the unexpired portion is 3.333 - 1.111° = 2.222°, which is 133.33'.

The balance portion of the Aśvinī1 Āyuṣa is 133.33 / 200 * 100 = 66.67. The expired Daśā is 100 - 66.67 = 33.33. From a Daśā standpoint, the cumulative Daśā periods are Meṣa (7) → Vṛṣabha (23) → Mithuna (32) → Karka (53) → Siṅha (58) → Kanyā (67) → Tulā (83) → Vṛścika (90) → Dhanu (100). Since the expiration period is 33.33 years, the Daśā must be of Karka Rāśi that starts from the 33rd year and ends in the 53rd year.

The Balance of Karka-Candra Daśā remaining at birth can be known by subtracting the expired Daśā, i.e., 33.33 from 53, which is 19.67 years.

The normal duration of Karka Daśā is 21 years, of which 19.67 years is left. After completing the 66.67 years (Daśā balance) of Aśvinī1 Daśās, if the native lives longer, he shall move to Aśvinī2 Daśās, and thus the Daśā continues.

Kailāśa: This makes sense now. The method of finding Daśā balance is different from Viñśottarī.

Ācārya: Yes, that is so!

In Viñśottarī Daśā, the Balance of elapsed Nakṣatra is used to determine the Janma Daśā, which is that of Janmatārā Pati (*janma tāreśa*).

In Kālacakra, the Balance of Nakṣatra Caraṇa (or Navāñśa) elapsed is used first to determine the Balance of Nakṣatra Caraṇa Āyuṣa. After that, the Daśās remaining is determined.

Unlike Viñśottarī, in Kālacakra Daśā, the Daśā sequence is "not fixed" and is affected by the Nakṣatra Caraṇa of Candra. This is the reason why the method of finding the Daśā balance is different.

Kailāśa: Dhanyavād Guruji. Kindly tell us about Deha and Jīva.

Ācārya: In a Navanavāñśa sequence, the first Daśārāśi is Deha, and the last Daśārāśi is Jīva. For instance, for Aśvinī1, the Data sequence is Meṣa-Vṛṣabha-Mithuna-Karka-Siṅha-Kanyā-Tulā-Vṛścika-Dhanu. Here, Meṣa is Deha and Dhanu is Jīva.

Kailāśa: Noted, Guruji.

Sunidhi: I have some questions regarding the Daśā sequence. Appreciate it if you could clarify.

Ācārya: Indeed, go ahead.

Sunidhi: Kindly explain the ślokas of Maharṣi Parāśara.

46.60: In Aśvinī1, Meṣa is Deha, and Dhanu is Jiva (life). And the Lords of Meṣa, Vṛṣabha, Mithuna, Karka, Siṅha, Kanyā, Tulā, Vṛścika and Dhanu are Lords of the Daśās in the order.

Ācārya: I have explained this before. For Aśvinī1, Meṣa-Vṛṣabha...Dhanu is the Daśā sequence, where Meṣa is Deha and Dhanu is Jīva. This is quite straightforward.

Sunidhi: Kindly explain the next śloka.

46.61: In Ashvini2, Makara is Deha, Mithun is Jiva, and the Lords of the nine Rāśis from Makara to Mithuna are Lords of the Daśās.

Ācārya: This is the Savya-Aśvinī group, for which the sequence is KSAS.

Sunidhi: What does that mean? Kindly explain.

Ācārya: This means *Krama + (Savya-Apasavya-Savya)*. Let me explain further.

The Savya and Apasavya sequence for the twelve Rāśis are.

Table 69

	1	2	3	4	5	6	7	8	9	10	11	12
Savya	Meṣ	Vṛṣ	Mit	Kar	Siṅ	Kan	Tul	Vṛś	Dha	Mak	Kum	Mīn
Apasavya	Vṛś	Tul	Kan	Kar	Siṅ	Mit	Vṛṣ	Meṣ	Mīn	Kum	Mak	Dha

Now, each Nakṣatra has four Caraṇas. Each Caraṇa has nine Navanavāñśas. So, each Nakṣatra has thirty-six Navanavāñśas. This equals three cycles of the zodiac.

For the Savya-Aśvinī group, which includes ten Nakṣatras, the three-cycle sequence is Krama + (Savya-Apasavya-Savya). Let us arrange the Rāśis in this order. In the below table, the Apasavya Sequence is shown with a "^" mark and shaded in grey.

Table 70: Savya-Aśvinī group (KSAS)

Caraṇa	1 Deha	2	3	4	5	6	7	8	9 Jīva
I	Meṣ	Vṛṣ	Mit	Kar	Siṅ	Kan	Tul	Vṛś	Dha
II	Mak	Kum	Mīn	Vṛś^	Tul^	Kan^	Kar^	Siṅ^	Mit^
III	Vṛṣ^	Meṣ^	Mīn^	Kum^	Mak^	Dha^	Meṣ	Vṛṣ	Mit
IV	Kar	Siṅ	Kan	Tul	Vṛś	Dha	Mak	Kum	Mīn

What does this show?

Sunidhi: Now, it is clear why the Navanavāñśa sequence for Aśvinī2 is Makara to Mithuna. I can see why Makara is Deha and Mithuna is Jīva. Let us examine the third Pāda of Aśvinī as per Maharṣi Parāśara.

46.62. For Aśvinī3, Vṛṣabha is Deha, and Mithuna is Jiva. The Lords of the Rāśis Vṛṣabha, Meṣa, Mīna, Kumbha, Makara, Dhanu, Meṣa, Vṛṣabha and Mithuna are Lords of the Daśās in that order.

Ācārya: Does this match the sequence that is presented above?

Sunidhi: Yes, it does! Now, it makes sense. Let us examine the next śloka.

46.63-64. For Aśvinī4 (and its group of ten Nakṣatras), Karka is Deha and Mīna is Jiva, and the Lords of the nine Rāśis from Karka to Mīna are the Lords of Daśās.

Ācārya: This also makes sense now. Isn't it?

Sunidhi: It does. Let us check the Bharaṇī group of five Nakṣatras (Bharani, Pushya, Chitra, Pūrvāṣāṛhā and Uttarābhādra).

Ācārya: What is the formula for Bharaṇī?

Sunidhi: The formulae you mentioned above are:

SAS = 10N = *aspuhamupbkrassvuare* = KSAS

SBH = 5N = *bhpucipaub* = KASA

ARO = 4N = *romavisr* = UASA

AMR = 8N = *mrarppupanjydhsa* = USAS

Ācārya: Very good. You now see the use of the formula I have mentioned above.

Sunidhi: Yes, I can see their use now. For Bharaṇī, it is SBH = *bhpucipaub* = KASA.

So, for Savya-Bharaṇī, it is Krama + (Apasavya-Savya-Apasavya).

Ācārya: Can you build the Nakṣatra Caraṇa table?

Sunidhi: Yes, I can do so.

Let us start with the Savya-Apasavya table.

Table 71

	1	2	3	4	5	6	7	8	9	10	11	12
Savya	Meṣ	Vṛṣ	Mit	Kar	Siṅ	Kan	Tul	Vṛś	Dha	Mak	Kum	Mīn
Apasavya	Vṛś	Tul	Kan	Kar	Siṅ	Mit	Vṛṣ	Meṣ	Mīn	Kum	Mak	Dha

Now, let us create the Caraṇa table for the five Nakṣatra of the Savya-Bharaṇī group. The Apasavya Cakra is marked with "^" and shaded in grey.

Table 72

Caraṇa	1 Deha	2	3	4	5	6	7	8	9 Jīva
I	Vṛś^	Tul^	Kan^	*Kar^*	*Siṅ^*	Mit^	Vṛṣ^	Meṣ^	Mīn^
II	Kum^	Mak^	Dha^	Meṣ	Vṛṣ	Mit	Kar	Siṅ	Kan
III	Tul	Vṛś	Dha	Mak	Kum	Mīn	Vṛś^	Tul^	Kan^
IV	*Kar^*	*Siṅ^*	Mit^	Vṛṣ^	Meṣ^	Mīn^	Kum^	Mak^	Dha^

Ācārya: Let us apply them to Maharṣi Parāśara's ślokas. He states in 46.65, In the four Padas of the 5 Nakṣatras, Bharani, Pushya, Chitra, Pūrvāṣāṛhā and Uttarābhādra, Deha and Jiva are the same, as for Bharaṇī.

Sunidhi: This makes sense and is what we arrived before. The next śloka is:

46.66. In Bharaṇī1, Vṛścika is Deha and Mīna is Jiva, and the Lords of the Rāśis Vṛścika, Tulā, Kanyā, *Karka, Siṅha,* Mithuna, Vṛṣabha, Meṣa and Mīna are the Lords of Daśās in this order.

Ācārya: Do you see the sequence jumped from Kanyā to Karka and then to Siṅha? It is the Maṇḍūka-Marakaṭa Gati case.

Sunidhi: Yes, I can see that now. I now understand that it is because, in Apasavya Cakra, Karka and Siṅha are not flipped. Karka is always in the fourth place, and Siṅha in the fifth place.

Ācārya: There you go. You have fully understood the concept. Who are the Deha and Jīva?

Sunidhi: Deha is the first Rāśi, and Jīva is the last in the Navanavāñśa sequence. In this case, Deha is Vṛścika and Jīva is Mīna. The next śloka is:

46.67. In Bharaṇī2, Kumbha is Deha and Kanyā is Jiva, and the Lords of Kumbha, Makara, *Dhanu, Meṣa,* Vṛṣabha, Mithuna, Karka, Siṅha and Kanyā are the Lords of Daśās in that order.

Ācārya: Do you see the Siṅhavlokana Gati here?

Sunidhi: Yes, Guruji, I can see the jump between Dhanu and Meṣa.

Ācārya: Very good. You have learnt to see the special jumps or Gatis.

Sunidhi: Dhanyavād, for all your guidance. The next śloka is:

46.68. In Bharaṇī3, Tulā is Deha and Kanyā is Jiva and Lords of the Rāśis Tulā, Vṛścika, Dhanu, Makara, Kumbha, *Mīna, Vṛścika,* Tulā and Kanyā are the Daśā Lords in this order.

Ācārya: Can you see the Siṅhavlokana Gati here?

Sunidhi: Yes, it is between Mīna and Vṛścika. You mentioned before that the Siṅhavlokana Gati occurs when there is a transition between Savya and Apasavya Cakra. I can see that clearly.

Ācārya: How about the next śloka?

46.69. In Bharaṇī4, Karka is Deha and Kumbha is Jiva, and the Lords of the Rāśis Karka, Siṅha, Mithuna, Vṛṣabha, Meṣa, Mīna, Kumbha, Makara and Dhanu are the Daśā Lords in this order.

Sunidhi: Here also, the Karka-Siṅha exception can be seen. If there was no exception in Apasavya Cakra, the Daśā should have started from Siṅha because that should have come after Kanyā. But due to the fixity of Karka-Siṅha Rāśis, Kanyā is followed by Karka and, after that, Siṅha.

Ācārya: You have understood well the concept of Śiva (Siṅha) and Śakti (Karka) and their position in the Kālacakra. Their position is immutable. Everything else revolves around them.

Sunidhi: Let us now examine the Apasavya Cakra.

Ācārya: Let us do that. There are two formulae for Apasavya as well. What are they?

Sunidhi: They are:

ARO = 4N = *romavisr* = USAS

AMR = 8N = *mrarppupanjydhsa* = UASA

The first one is the Apasavya-Rohiṇī group consisting of four Nakṣatras. The second one is the Apasavya-Mṛgaśirā group consisting of eight Nakṣatra.

The Maharṣi states:

46.71-72. O Brāhmaṇa! I have thus given you the description of Savya Cakra. Now, I shall describe the Apasavya Cakra. Prepare a similar chart of twelve apartments, and from the second apartment onwards, place the Rāśis from Vṛścika onwards in the reverse order. In this chart, Deha and Jīva would be the same for Rohiṇī, Maghā, Viśākhā and Śravaṇa, as for Rohini.

Ācārya: Why not construct the table for Apasavya-Rohiṇī? Remember, the sequence is in Utkrama (reverse order).

Sunidhi: Let me try. The Savya and Apasavya in the Krama sequence are as follows.

Table 73: Krama sequence

	1	2	3	4	5	6	7	8	9	10	11	12
Savya	Meṣ	Vṛṣ	Mit	Kar	Siṅ	Kan	Tul	Vṛś	Dha	Mak	Kum	Mīn
Apasavya	Vṛś	Tul	Kan	Kar	Siṅ	Mit	Vṛṣ	Meṣ	Mīn	Kum	Mak	Dha

In Utkrama sequence, they are:

Table 74: Utkrama sequence

	1	2	3	4	5	6	7	8	9	10	11	12
Savya	Mīn	Kum	Mak	Dha	Vṛś	Tul	Kan	Siṅ	Kar	Mit	Vṛṣ	Meṣ
Apasavya	Dha	Mak	Kum	Mīn	Meṣ	Vṛṣ	Mit	Siṅ	Kar	Kan	Tul	Vṛś

Now, let me construct the Nakṣatra Pāda table. Apasavya-Rohiṇī is UASA = Utkrama+(Apasavya-Savya-Apasavya). In the below table, Apasavya is marked with "^" and highlighted in grey.

Table 75

Caraṇa	1 Jīva	2	3	4	5	6	7	8	9 Deha
I	Dha^	Mak^	Kum^	Mīn^	Meṣ^	Vṛṣ^	Mit^	Siṅ^	Kar^
II	Kan^	Tul^	Vṛś^	Mīn	Kum	Mak	Dha	Vṛś	Tul
III	Kan	Siṅ	Kar	Mit	Vṛṣ	Meṣ	Dha^	Mak^	Kum^
IV	Mīn^	Meṣ^	Vṛṣ^	Mit^	Siṅ^	Kar^	Kan^	Tul^	Vṛś^

Ācārya: Very well. You can apply them in Maharṣi's Parāśara's ślokas.

Sunidhi: Maharṣi Parāśara states:

46.73. In Rohiṇī1 Karka is Deha and Dhanu is Jiva. The Lords of the Rāśis Dhanu, Makara, Kumbha, Mīna, Meṣa, Vṛṣabha, Mithuna, Siṅha and Karka will be the Daśā Lords.

Ācārya: This matches your derived Daśā sequence. But why are the Deha and Jīva different?

Sunidhi: It appears that in Apasavya Nakṣatra, the Deha-Jīva order is reversed. This means the first Daśā is of Jīva, and the last Daśā is of Deha. I can also see that Mithuna is followed by Siṅha and then Karka, again proving the concept of Karka-Siṅha fixity of the Rāśis.

Ācārya: You got it right. Apasavya is feminine, and therefore, the order is reversed.

Sunidhi: Dhanyavād, for endorsing that. Now, the next śloka states:

46.74. In Rohiṇī2, Tulā is Deha and Kanyā is Jīva. The Lords of the Rāśis Kanyā, Tulā, Vṛścika, Mīna, Kumbha, Makara, Dhanu, Vṛścika and Tulā will be the Daśā Lords.

This precisely matches the sequence we derived above.

Ācārya: Well done. Now, check the remaining two Pādas.

Sunidhi: The ślokas for the next Pādas are as follows:

46.75. In Rohiṇī3, Kumbha is Deha and Kanyā is Jiva. The Lords of the Rāśis Kanyā, Siṅha, Karka, Mithuna, Vṛṣabha, Meṣa, Dhanu, Makara and Kumbha will be the Daśā Lords.

46.76. In Rohiṇī4, Vṛścika is Deha and Mīna Jiva, and the Lords of the Rāśis Mīna, Meṣa, Vṛṣabha, Mithuna, Siṅha, Karka, Kanyā, Tulā and Vṛścika will be the Lords.

They all match what we derived before.

Ācārya: Let us focus on Apasavya-Mṛgaśirā group. What is the formula for that?

Sunidhi: The formula for AMR = 8N = *mrarppupanjydhsa* = USAS. So, it is *Utkrama + (Savya-Apasavya-Savya).*

Ācārya: Why don't you derive the Nakṣatra Pāda table?

Sunidhi: The Utkrama Savya-Apasavya table is as follows:

Table 76

	1	2	3	4	5	6	7	8	9	10	11	12
Savya	Mīn	Kum	Mak	Dha	Vṛś	Tul	Kan	Siṅ	Kar	Mit	Vṛṣ	Meṣ
Apasavya	Dha	Mak	Kum	Mīn	Meṣ	Vṛṣ	Mit	Siṅ	Kar	Kan	Tul	Vṛś

The Nakṣatra Pāda table is as follows:

Table 77

	1 Jīva	2	3	4	5	6	7	8	9 Deha
Pada1	Mīn	Kum	Mak	Dha	Vṛś	Tul	Kan	Siṅ	Kar
Pada2	Mit	Vṛṣ	Meṣ	Dha^	Mak^	Kum^	Mīn^	Meṣ^	Vṛṣ^
Pada3	Mit^	Siṅ^	Kar^	Kan^	Tul^	Vṛś^	Mīn	Kum	Mak
Pada4	Dha	Vṛś	Tul	Kan	Siṅ	Kar	Mit	Vṛṣ	Meṣ

Maharṣi Parāśara states the following on the applicability of the Apasavya-Mṛgaśirā. As per the formula, the Nakṣatra associated with this is *mrarppupanjydhsa, i.e., mr-ar-pp-up-an-jy-dh-sa (Mṛgaśirā, Ardra, Pūrvāphālgunī, Uttarāphālgunī, Anurādhā, Jyeṣṭha, Dhaniṣṭhā and Śatabhiṣā).*

46.77. In the four Padas of the Apasavya Nakṣatras Mṛgaśirā, Ardra, Pūrvāphālgunī, Uttarāphālgunī, Anurādhā, Jyeṣṭha, Dhaniṣṭhā and Śatabhiṣā the Deha and Jiva and the Daśā Lords will be the same, as for Mṛgaśirā.

This is precisely what is included in the formula. You have explained before how these Nakṣatra are derived.

The following is the Navanavāñśa sequence for the four Caraṇas of the Apasavya-Mṛgaśirā group.

46.78. In Mṛgaśirā1, Karka is Deha and Mīna is Jīva. The Lords of the Rāśis Mīna, Kumbha, Makara, Dhanu, Vṛścika, Tulā, Kanyā, Siṅha and Karka will be the Dasha Lords.

46.79. In Mṛgaśirā2, Vṛṣabha is Deha and Mithuna is Jīva. The Lords of the Rāśis Mithuna, Vṛṣabha, Meṣa, Dhanu, Makara, Kumbha, Mīna, Meṣa and Vṛṣabha will be the Dasha Lords.

46.80. In Mṛgaśirā3, Makara is Deha and Mithuna is Jīva. The Lords of the Rāśis Mithuna, Siṅha, Karka, Kanyā, Tulā, Vṛścika, Mīna, Kumbha and Makara will be the Dasha Lords.

46.81. In Mṛgaśirā4, Meṣa is Deha and Dhanu is Jīva. The Lords of the Rāśis Dhanu, Vṛścika, Tulā, Kanyā, Siṅha, Karka, Mithuna, Vṛṣabha and Meṣa will be the Dasha Lords.

They all match our tables.

Ācārya: Very well done, Sunidhi.

Sunidhi: Dhanyavād, Guruji. With the method you have explained, it makes complete sense how the Navanavāñśa sequence is derived.

Kailāśa: Gurudeva, you have successfully decoded the reasoning behind the Navanavāñśa sequence. I have always wondered about the rationale behind the sequences. It wasn't easy to make sense since there were so many unexplainable jumps.

Ācārya: Indeed Kailāśa. It is not easy to decipher that. I could do it only due to the divine grace of Lord Mahādeva, who ignited a spark in me so that I could see how the sequences are derived. I hope the world will appreciate the effort in explaining the hidden concepts behind this outstanding Daśā system.

Jayanta: Dhanyavād, Guruji. The sequence makes complete sense now.

Āratī: Dhanyavād, Guruji for the elaboration. It has been an enlightening experience.

Kailāśa: The Kālacakra Daśā is dealt with in several classical texts, and important among them are Bṛhatparāśara, Phaladīpikā and Jātakapārijāta. The Daśā also finds a brief mention in the Praśnamārga.

While the three classical texts Bṛhatparāśara, Phaladīpikā and Jātakapārijāta give a detailed exposition of this Daśā, Praśnamārga states this in the context of timing death.

Jayanta: How to use this Daśā, Gurudeva?

Ācārya: Kālacakra Daśā is verily an important Āyurdaya Daśā as per Praśnamārga. However, it is also a Phalita Daśā.

According to Maharṣi Parāśara, in Mithuna Daśā of Meṣa Navāñśa, there is an advancement of knowledge. In Tulā Daśā of Meṣa Navāñśa, there is a rise in status and authority.

These are certainly the results of Phalita and not Āyur Daśā.

From Maharṣi Parāśara's narration of the results, it is adequately clear that Kālacakra is also a Phalita Daśā.

From Āyuṣa standpoint, this is of great use in timing danger, mainly because of its Viśeṣa Gatis, Maṇḍūka 🐸, Marakaṭa 🐒 and Siṅhavlokana 🦁, and affliction to its two important entities, the Deha and Jīva.

Jayanta: That makes sense, Gurudeva.

Ācārya: Let us examine some important ślokas from the Śāstras.

Praśnamārga 10.8 states that the movement of the Daśā from (1) Mīna to Vṛścika, (2) Kanyā to Karka, (3) Siṅha to Mithuna, (4) Mithuna to Siṅha and (5) Dhanu to Meṣa shall be a *difficult period*, as also the subsequent Daśā. Whether the order is regular or otherwise, the Daśā is good if there is no deviation but evil if the "movement" is at the junction of two Rāśis (evidently two Navāñśas).

Praśnamārga 10.9-10 states that, with regards to the Dakṣiṇa (Savya) group of Tārās, the first and last Rāśis indicated by the formula are Deha and Jīva, respectively. At the same time, the reverse is the case with regard to the Vāma (Apasavya) group of Tārās. *If Krūras afflict Deha or Jīva, there shall be sickness. If both are afflicted, and the Daśā is also evil, then there shall be death.*

Jātakapārijāta 17.7-8 states that "the five Triads beginning from respectively Aśvinī, Punarvasu, Hastā, Mūla, and Pūrvābhādra, reckon the Caraṇas from Meṣa in Pradakṣiṇa order, whereas in the four Triads commencing from Rohiṇī, Maghā, Viśākhā and Śravaṇa, reckon the quarters from Vṛścika in the Apradakṣiṇa order".

Jayanta: Noted, Guruji. You have already explained them. Now, they make sense.

Ācārya: Pradakṣiṇa means circumambulating around a temple or a Devatā, which is done in a clockwise manner. Apradakṣiṇa is the reverse of that, i.e., Utkrama order. The twenty-seven Nakṣatras are classified into nine groups of three Nakṣatras (Triad or Tritārā) each, like the Navatārā Cakra, whereby five Triads belong to the Savya group and four to the Apasavya group. Five triads comprise fifteen Nakṣatras, whereas four triads comprise twelve Nakṣatras.

Jayanta: Noted, Guruji.

Āratī: Guruji, what is Kālacakra Navāñśa?

Ācārya: The Kālacakra Navāñśa is based on the Nakṣatra Pāda mapping to Navāñśa based on Savya and Apasavya designation. The following is the mapping of the Navāñśas for the different Rāśis.

Table 78: Kālacakra Navāñśa

Rāśi	1	2	3	4	5	6	7	8	9
Meṣ	Meṣ	Vṛṣ	Mit	Kar	Siṅ	Kan	Tul	Vṛś	Dha
Vṛṣ	Mak	Kum	Mīn	Vṛś^	Tul^	Kan^	Siṅ^	Kar^	Mit^
Mit	Vṛṣ^	Meṣ^	Mīn^	Kum^	Mak^	Dha^	Meṣ	Vṛṣ	Mit
Kar	Kar	Siṅ	Kan	Tul	Vṛś	Dha	Mak	Kum	Mīn
Siṅ	Vṛś^	Tul^	Kan^	Siṅ^	Kar^	Mit^	Vṛṣ^	Meṣ^	Mīn^
Kan	Kum^	Mak^	Dha^	Meṣ	Vṛṣ	Mit	Kar	Siṅ	Kan
Tul	Tul	Vṛś	Dha	Mak	Kum	Mīn	Vṛś^	Tul^	Kan^
Vṛś	Siṅ^	Kar^	Mit^	Vṛṣ^	Meṣ^	Mīn^	Kum^	Mak^	Dha^
Dha	Meṣ	Vṛṣ	Mit	Kar	Siṅ	Kan	Tul	Vṛś	Dha
Mak	Mak	Kum	Mīn	Vṛś^	Tul^	Kan^	Siṅ^	Kar^	Mit^
Kum	Vṛṣ^	Meṣ^	Mīn^	Kum^	Mak^	Dha^	Meṣ	Vṛṣ	Mit
Mīn	Kar	Siṅ	Kan	Tul	Vṛś	Dha	Mak	Kum	Mīn

Āratī: It appears that out of 108 Nakṣatra Pādas:

48 Pādas are of Apasavya Nakṣatras (marked with * and highlighted in grey). There are 12 Apasavya Nakṣatras.

60 Pādas are of Savya Nakṣatras. There are 15 Savya Nakṣatras.

Ācārya: That is right. The Savya and Apasavya Triads alternate in sequence. There are five Triads of Savya Nakṣatra and four Triads of Apasavya Nakṣatra.

Āratī: Noted Guruji. It seems you have "not" retained the Karka-Siṅha exception in the Apasavya Kālacakra.

Ācārya: Yes, you are right. That is only used in the Navanavāñśa and not the Navāñśa. Therefore, in Apasavya Cakra, the sequence is reversed.

Table 79

	1	2	3	4	5	6	7	8	9	10	11	12
S	Meṣ	Vṛṣ	Mit	Kar	Siṅ	Kan	Tul	Vṛś	Dha	Mak	Kum	Mīn
A	Vṛś ^	Tul ^	Kan ^	Kar ^	Siṅ ^	Mit ^	Vṛṣ ^	Meṣ ^	Mīn ^	Kum ^	Mak ^	Dha ^

Āratī: Is there a way to remember the Kālacakra Navāñśa?

Ācārya: Yes, there is. Follow the following steps:

(1) Find the Navāñśa position of the Grahas as per normal reckoning.

(2) If the Graha is in an Apasavya Nakṣatra, then flip it to the other Rāśi of the Navāñśa lord.

(3) For Karka-Siṅha, use them interchangeably.

Āratī: Noted, Guruji!

Kailāśa: Gurudeva, you have covered the sequences for the four groups of Nakṣatra. Kindly provide all of them in one place for ease of reference.

Ācārya: Alright. Here you go. You need to find the table to which a Nakṣatra belongs and apply them accordingly.

Table 80: Nakṣatra Table

	Nakṣatra	Table	Nakṣatra	Table	Nakṣatra	Table
1	Aśvinī	I	Maghā	III	Mūla	I
2	Bharaṇī	II	Pūrvāphālgunī	IV	Pūrvāṣāṛhā	II
3	Kṛttikā	I	Uttarāphālgunī	IV	Uttarāṣāṛhā	I
4	Rohiṇī	III	Hastā	I	Śravaṇa	III
5	Mṛgaśirā	IV	Citrā	II	Dhaniṣṭhā	IV
6	Ārdrā	IV	Svāti	I	Śatabhiṣā	IV
7	Punarvasu	I	Viśākhā	III	Pūrvābhādra	I
8	Puṣya	II	Anurādhā	IV	Uttarābhādra	II
9	Aśleṣā	I	Jyeṣṭhā	IV	Revatī	I

(1) *Savya-Aśvinī: 10 Nakṣatras:* Aśvinī, Punarvasu, Hastā, Mūla, Pūrvābhādra, Kṛttikā, Aśleṣā, Svāti, Uttarāṣāṛhā, Revatī: *Krama+(Savya-Apasavya-Savya)* = KSAS.

Table 81: Table I

Caraṇa	1 Deha	2	3	4	5	6	7	8	9 Jīva	Age
I	Meṣ	Vṛṣ	Mit	Kar	Siṅ	Kan	Tul	Vṛś	Dha	100
II	Mak	Kum	Mīn	Vṛś^	Tul^	Kan^	Kar^	Siṅ^	Mit^	85
III	Vṛṣ^	Meṣ^	Mīn^	Kum^	Mak^	Dha^	Meṣ	Vṛṣ	Mit	83
IV	Kar	Siṅ	Kan	Tul	Vṛś	Dha	Mak	Kum	Mīn	86

(2) *Savya-Bharaṇī: 5 Nakṣatras:* Bharaṇī, Puṣya, Citrā, Pūrvāṣāṛhā, Uttarābhādra: *Krama+ (Apasavya-Savya-Apasavya)* = KASA.

Table 82: Table II

Caraṇa	1 Deha	2	3	4	5	6	7	8	9 Jīva	Age
I	Vṛś^	Tul^	Kan^	*Kar^*	*Siṅ^*	Mit^	Vṛṣ^	Meṣ^	Mīn^	100
II	Kum^	Mak^	Dha^	Meṣ	Vṛṣ	Mit	Kar	Siṅ	Kan	85
III	Tul	Vṛś	Dha	Mak	Kum	Mīn	Vṛś^	Tul^	Kan^	83
IV	*Kar^*	*Siṅ^*	Mit^	Vṛṣ^	Meṣ^	Mīn^	Kum^	Mak^	Dha^	86

(3) *Apasavya-Rohiṇī: 4 Nakṣatras:* Rohiṇī, Maghā, Viśākhā, Śravaṇa: *Utkrama+ (Apasavya-Savya-Apasavya) = UASA.*

Table 83: Table III

Caraṇa	1 Jīva	2	3	4	5	6	7	8	9 Deha	Age
I	Dha^	Mak^	Kum^	Mīn^	Meṣ^	Vṛṣ^	Mit^	Siṅ^	Kar^	86
II	Kan^	Tul^	Vṛś^	Mīn	Kum	Mak	Dha	Vṛś	Tul	83
III	Kan	Siṅ	Kar	Mit	Vṛṣ	Meṣ	Dha^	Mak^	Kum^	85
IV	Mīn^	Meṣ^	Vṛṣ^	Mit^	Siṅ^	Kar^	Kan^	Tul^	Vṛś^	100

(4) *Apasavya-Mṛgaśirā: 8 Nakṣatras:* Mṛgaśirā, Pūrvāphālgunī, Anurādhā, Dhaniṣṭhā, Ārdrā, Uttarāphālgunī, Jyeṣṭhā, Śatabhiṣā: *Utkrama+(Savya-Apasavya-Savya) = USAS.*

Table 84: Table IV

	1 Jīva	2	3	4	5	6	7	8	9 Deha	Age
Pada1	Mīn	Kum	Mak	Dha	Vṛś	Tul	Kan	Siṅ	Kar	86
Pada2	Mit	Vṛṣ	Meṣ	Dha^	Mak^	Kum^	Mīn^	Meṣ^	Vṛṣ^	83
Pada3	Mit^	Siṅ^	Kar^	Kan^	Tul^	Vṛś^	Mīn	Kum	Mak	85
Pada4	Dha	Vṛś	Tul	Kan	Siṅ	Kar	Mit	Vṛṣ	Meṣ	100

Arati: Guruji, Kindly give an example of how to use the tables.

Ācārya: Suppose we wish to find the Navanavāñśa sequence for Svāmi Vivekānanda. In his Kuṇḍalī, Candra is in Hastā3. In the Nakṣatra Table, we find Table I against Hastā. In Table 1, against Pāda 3, we find the following sequence.

Vṛṣ^-Meṣ^-Mīn^-Kum^-Mak^-Dha^-Meṣ-Vṛṣ-Mit

Therefore, his Daśā sequence is this.

Āratī: I can understand now. Kindly tell us the longevity associated with different Navāñśas in Kālacakra Navāñśa.

Ācārya: To find the Longevity associated with Nakṣatra Pāda, you will need to apply the following pattern:

Table 85

Nakṣatra	Pāda1	Pāda2	Pāda3	Pāda4
Savya	100	85	83	86
Apasavya	86	83	85	100

Applying these to the Nakṣatra Pādas, we have the following longevity mapped to the nine different Navāñśas of the twelve Rāśis.

Table 86

Rāśi	1	2	3	4	5	6	7	8	9
Meṣ	100	85	83	86	100	85	83	86	100
Vṛṣ	85	83	86	86	83	85	100	86	83
Mit	85	100	86	83	85	100	100	85	83
Kar	86	100	85	83	86	100	85	83	86
Siṅ	86	83	85	100	86	83	85	100	86
Kan	83	85	100	100	85	83	86	100	85
Tul	83	86	100	85	83	86	86	83	85
Vṛś	100	86	83	85	100	86	83	85	100
Dha	100	85	83	86	100	85	83	86	100
Mak	85	83	86	86	83	85	100	86	83
Kum	85	100	86	83	85	100	100	85	83
Mīn	86	100	85	83	86	100	85	83	86

Āratī: Guruji, is there a pattern to it?

Ācārya: Yes, there is indeed a pattern. Each Rāśi has a specified Āyuṣa. They are as follows:

86	**100**	**85**	**83**
83			**86**
85			**100**
100	**86**	**83**	**85**

It also means the following:

(1) Agni Navāñśa 100

(2) Pṛthvī Navāñśa 85

(3) Vāyu Navāñśa 83

(4) Jala Navāñśa 86

Let us take an example. In my Kuṇḍalī, Candra is in Anurādhā4. This falls in Meṣa Kālacakra Navāñśa. Meṣa is an Agni Navāñśa; therefore, it has 100y longevity. The Navanavāñśa sequence Dha-Vṛś-Tul-Kan-Siṅ-Kar-Mit-Vṛṣ-Meṣ also adds up to 100y.

Āratī: Noted, Guruji!

Ācārya: Let's take another example – the fourth Pāda of Rohiṇī. It is a Apasavya Nakṣatra. It is mapped to Karka Navāñśa in regular Navāñśa. Since it is an Apasavya Nakṣatra, it is flipped to Siṅha. Siṅha is an Agni Navāñśa, so its longevity should be 100y.

In the above Nakṣatra Table, Rohiṇī's Table is III. In Table III, the Pāda 4 sequence is Mīn^-Meṣ^-Vṛṣ^-Mit^-Siṅ^-Kar^-Kan^-Tul^-Vṛś^, which is 100y. So, our computation matched.

Āratī: Yes, Guruji!

Let's take another example - Mṛgaśirā1. In regular Navāñśa, it is mapped to Siṅha. In Kālacakra Navāñśa, it is flipped to Karka since Mṛgaśirā is Apasavya. Karka is Jala Navāñśa; therefore, its longevity is 86. In Nakṣatra Table, Mṛgaśirā is IV. In Table IV, Pāda 1, the sequence is Mīn-Kum-Mak-Dha-Vṛś-Tul-Kan-Siṅ-Kar, and longevity is 86. So, in both cases, it matches.

So, what we have derived so far is correct.

Āratī: Noted, Guruji. This is very helpful.

Sunidhi: Guruji, kindly tell us how to find the Daśā balance at birth. It was somewhat confusing when you explained it before.

Ācārya: No problem. Let us use the case of Svāmi Vivekānanda.

His Candra is in Hastā3 in 17°27'23" (17.456). Hastā is a Savya Nakṣatra. In regular Navāñśa, Candra is in Mithuna, which should remain as such as it is in a Savya Nakṣatra. Mithuna is a Vāyu Navāñśa, and its longevity is 83.

In Nakṣatra Table it is in Table I. In Table 1, Caraṇa 3, the sequence is Vṛṣ^-Meṣ^-Mīn^-Kum^-Mak^-Dha^-Meṣ-Vṛṣ-Mit of longevity 83.

The ages of the Rāśis are:

Table 87

1	2	3	4	5	6	7	8	9	10	11	12
Meṣ	Vṛṣ	Mit	Kar	Siṅ	Kan	Tul	Vṛś	Dha	Mak	Kum	Mīn
7	16	9	21	5	9	16	7	10	4	4	10

The ages allotted to the Navanavāñśas of Mithuna Rāśi are:

Table 88

Caraṇa	1 Deha	2	3	4	5	6	7	8	9 Jīva
III	**Vṛṣ^**	**Meṣ^**	**Mīn^**	**Kum^**	**Mak^**	**Dha^**	**Meṣ**	**Vṛṣ**	**Mit**
Age	16	7	10	4	4	10	7	16	9
Cum Age	16	23	33	37	41	51	58	74	83

This means that Mithuna Navāñśa is divided into 83 units. One Nakṣatra Pāda is 3°20' (3.333). Candra is in the 6th Navāñśa. 5 Navāñśa is 16°40' (16.667). The Nakṣatra pada expired is 17.456 - 16.667 = 0.789. The longevity expired is

0.789 / 3.333 * 83 = 19.648. This shows that Vṛṣabha Daśā is gone, and he is Meṣa Daśā. The balance of Meṣa remaining is 23 - 19.648 = 3.352. After that, he will continue Mīna-Kumbha...Vṛṣabha in that sequence.

Sunidhi: Dhanyavād Guruji. It is clear now.

Kailāśa: Kindly tell us how to compute the Antardaśās in this Daśā.

Ācārya: That is one of the most confounding parts of Kālacakra Daśā. Let me try to explain this. In Daśās such as Viṅśottarī, the Antardaśā sequence is straightforward, as we merely start with the Mahādaśā lord and progress in the order of the Daśā sequence.

For instance, the Mahādaśā sequence of Viṅśottarī is Sūrya, Candra, Maṅgala, Rāhu, Bṛhaspati, Śani, Budha, Ketu, Śukra. This means that in Śukra Daśā, the Bhuktis are in the order of Śukra, Ketu, Sūrya, Candra, Maṅgala, Rāhu, Bṛhaspati, Śani, Budha. This is straightforward! Isn't it?

Kailāśa: Yes, that is straightforward. Can't we apply the same concept in Kālacakra Daśā?

Ācārya: No, this is not so for the Mahādaśās in Kālacakra Daśā because there is no fixed sequence. As we have seen before, there are 16 different Mahādaśā sequences, which are derived from 2 (Savya-Apasavya) * 2 (Nakṣatra group) * 4 (Caraṇas). This makes it difficult to determine which sequence to follow for the Antardaśās.

Kailāśa: Can't we use the Daśā sequence to which the Antardaśā belongs?

For instance, the Daśā sequence of Aśvinī2 is Makara-Kumbha-Mīna-Vṛścika-Tulā-Kanyā-Siṅha-Karka-Mithuna. If we were to find the Antardaśā of Mīna Mahādaśā, we could use the same sequence, commencing from Mīna, i.e., Mīna-Vṛścika-Tulā-Kanyā-Siṅha-Karka-Mithuna-Makara-Kumbha.

Similarly, the Bhukti of the next Daśā i.e., Vṛścika is Vṛścika-Tulā-Kanyā-Siṅha-Karka-Mithuna-Makara-Kumbha-Mīna. In this manner, the Bhukti of all the Daśās can be determined.

Ācārya: This might appear logical, but the issue with this is that *this does not follow the sequence* given by Maharṣi Parāśara for the different Navāṅśas.

Kailāśa: Then what method should we employ in finding the Antardaśās?

Ācārya: I believe that the key to understanding the Antardaśā is in the identification of the Daśā Rāśi being in the Savya or Apasavya Kālacakra.

Suppose we take the Caraṇa2 of the Savya-Aśvinī group (*Aśvinī, Punarvasu, Hastā, Mūla, Pūrvābhādra, Kṛttikā, Aśleṣā, Svāti, Uttarāṣāṛhā, Revatī*).

For this, the Daśā sequence is Makara-Kumbha-Mīna-*Vṛścika^-Tulā^-Kanyā^-Siṅha^-Karka^-Mithuna^*. We notice that the Daśās Makara-Mīna belong to the Savya Kālacakra, and *Vṛścika^-Mithuna^* belong to Apasavya Kālacakra.

Therefore, for Makara Daśā, the sequence could be based on Savya Kālacakra starting from Makara, i.e., Makara-Kumbha-Mīna-Meṣa-Vṛṣabha-Mithuna-Karka-Siṅha-Kanyā.

On the other hand, for Vṛścika Daśā, which is in Apasavya Cakra, the sequence is Vṛścika^-Tulā^-Kanyā^-Karka^-Siṅha^-Mithuna^-Vṛṣabha^-Meṣa^-Mīna^.

Kailāśa: It makes sense. Can't we use this approach?

Ācārya: Again, this might appear logical but cannot stand scrutiny.

Kailāśa: Why?

Ācārya: To understand, let us take the Antardaśās of Makara Daśā.

We thought that the sequence should be Makara-Kumbha-Mīna-Meṣa-Vṛṣabha-Mithuna-Karka-Siṅha-Kanyā. Right?

Kailāśa: Yes, Guruji.

Ācārya: To understand see the Daśā sequence for the four Pādas of Aśvinī group.

Table 89

Caraṇa	1 Deha	2	3	4	5	6	7	8	9 Jīva	Age
I	Meṣ	Vṛṣ	Mit	Kar	Siṅ	Kan	Tul	Vṛś	Dha	100
II	Mak	Kum	Mīn	Vṛś^	Tul^	Kan^	Kar^	Siṅ^	Mit^	85
III	Vṛṣ^	Meṣ^	Mīn^	Kum^	Mak^	Dha^	Meṣ	Vṛṣ	Mit	83
IV	Kar	Siṅ	Kan	Tul	Vṛś	Dha	Mak	Kum	Mīn	86

Kailāśa: What about it?

Ācārya: Don't you see that after Savya Mīna, we must have Apasavya Vṛścika?

Kailāśa: So?

Ācārya: Then how can we have this sequence: Makara-Kumbha-Mīna-*Meṣa-Vṛṣabha-Mithuna-Karka-Siṅha-Kanyā*? Here Savya Meṣa follows Savya Mīna? This is not one of the approved sequences. Therefore, we "cannot" accept this sequence and this approach.

Kailāśa: Then what is the way out?

Ācārya: After reflecting intently on this matter and with lord Śiva's grace, suddenly things started unfolding in my mind. This is the moment of revelation that I narrated at the beginning of this chapter. I am providing my recommendation, which I think is the most consistent approach.

Kailāśa: What is its basis, Guruji?

Ācārya: This utilizes the inherent pattern embedded in the Daśā sequence.

Kailāśa: Noted. Kindly elaborate, Guruji.

Ācārya: We have learnt before that the Daśās are classified into four groups, and their cycles of the Daśās are:

Savya-Aśvinī: *Krama+(Savya-Apasavya-Savya)* = KSAS.

Savya-Bharaṇī: *Krama+ (Apasavya-Savya-Apasavya)* = KASA.

Apasavya-Rohiṇī: *Utkrama+ (Apasavya-Savya-Apasavya) = UASA.*

Apasavya-Mṛgaśirā: *Utkrama+(Savya-Apasavya-Savya) = USAS*

Kailāśa: Yes, Guruji! You have explained this before. How to use this knowledge here?

Ācārya: All the Nakṣatras fall into the two Kālacakras, Savya and Apasavya, and they are *self-contained systems in themselves*, which is why the two Kālacakras are defined.

Kailāśa: What do you mean by *self-contained system*?

Ācārya: All sequences must continue within the Kālacakra. For example. The sequences of Savya Kālacakra (say Aśvinī-Bharaṇī-Kṛttikā) are:

Aśvinī

I: Meṣ-Vṛṣ-Mit-Kar-Siṅ-Kan-Tul-Vṛś-Dha

II: Mak-Kum-Mīn-Vṛś^-Tul^-Kan^-Kar^-Siṅ^-Mit^

III: Vṛṣ^-Meṣ^-Mīn^-Kum^-Mak^-Dha^-Meṣ-Vṛṣ-Mit

IV: Kar-Siṅ-Kan-Tul-Vṛś-Dha-Mak-Kum-Mīn

Bharaṇī

I: Vṛś^-Tul^-Kan^-Kar^-Siṅ^-Mit^-Vṛṣ^-Meṣ^-Mīn^

II: Kum^-Mak^-Dha^-Meṣ-Vṛṣ-Mit-Kar-Siṅ-Kan

III: Tul-Vṛś-Dha-Mak-Kum-Mīn-Vṛś^-Tul^-Kan^

IV: Kar^-Siṅ^-Mit^-Vṛṣ^-Meṣ^-Mīn^-Kum^-Mak^-Dha^

Kṛttikā (same as Aśvinī)

I: Meṣ-Vṛṣ-Mit-Kar-Siṅ-Kan-Tul-Vṛś-Dha

II: Mak-Kum-Mīn-Vṛś^-Tul^-Kan^-Kar^-Siṅ^-Mit^

III: Vṛṣ^-Meṣ^-Mīn^-Kum^-Mak^-Dha^-Meṣ-Vṛṣ-Mit

IV: Kar-Siṅ-Kan-Tul-Vṛś-Dha-Mak-Kum-Mīn

There are twelve Pādas mapped to the twelve Navāṅśas. They constitute the Savya Kālacakra, which represents a self-contained whole. Therefore, the sequence of the Daśās is Meṣa [I] - Vṛṣabha [II] - Mithuna [III] - Karka [IV] - Siṅha [I] - Kanyā [II] - Tulā [III] - Vṛścika [IV]-Dhanu [I]-Makara [II] – Kumbha [III] - Mīna [IV]. After Meṣa (Aśvinī1) follows Vṛṣabha (Aśvinī2), after Karka (Aśvinī4) follows Siṅha (Bharaṇī1), after Vṛścika (Bharaṇī4) follows Dhanu (Kṛttikā1) and so on.

Kailāśa: What happens after Mīna (Kṛttikā4)? Would the Daśā move to Rohiṇī1?

Ācārya: No. That is where the concept of *self-contained* whole comes in. Rohiṇī1 falls in Apasavya Cakra. The Daśā cannot move from Savya to Apasavya. The Daśā of Savya Janmatārā Nakṣatra must move into Savya Kālacakra.

Kailāśa: Is that so?

Ācārya: Because the Savya Navāṅśas must remain within the boundaries of Savya Kālacakra.

Kailāśa: I do not understand. Can you explain it further?

Ācārya: Suppose, Kṛttikā4 is followed by Rohiṇī1. Let us examine their Daśās. Kṛttikā4 (Mīna Navāñśa) Navanavāñśa is Kar-Siṅ-Kan-Tul-Vṛś-Dha-Mak-Kum-Mīn. Rohiṇī1 (Vṛścika Navāñśa) Navanavāñśa is Dha^-Mak^-Kum^-Mīn^-Meṣ^-Vṛṣ^-Mit^-Siṅ^-Kar^. The movement is from Mīn to Dha^. *This is not one of the acceptable jumps.*

Kailāśa: I see now, why do you say that after Mīna, we should move to Meṣa. This will represent the Navanavāñśas Kar-Siṅ-Kan-Tul-Vṛś-Dha-Mak-Kum-Mīn and Meṣ-Vṛṣ-Mit-Kar-Siṅ-Kan-Tul-Vṛś-Dha respectively. So Mīna is followed by Meṣa, which makes sense.

Ācārya: The following figure diagrammatically represents the Savya Kālacakra flow of Navāñśas and the Daśās (Navanavāñśas) within them.

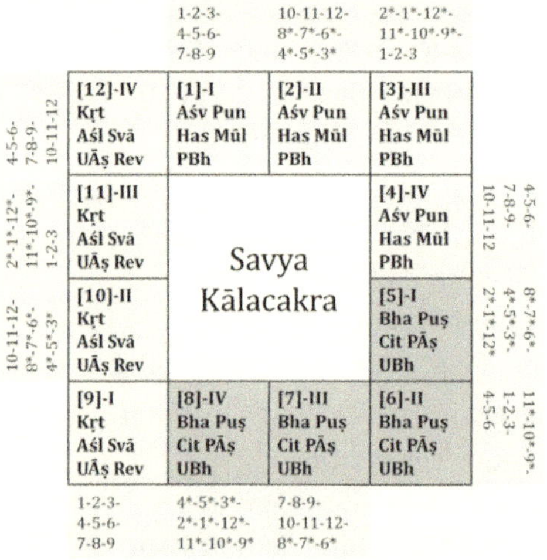

Kailāśa: Can we take the example of the ending of Apasavya Kālacakra and the beginning of Savya Kālacakra, i.e., the reverse of the above?

Ācārya: Let us do that. Ārdrā4 is the last Nakṣatra of Rohiṇī-Mṛgaśirā-Ārdrā Triad. Apasavya Kālacakra starts with Vṛścika and ends with Dhanu. So Ārdrā4 Navāñśa is Dhanu. Dhanu Navanavāñśa sequence is Dha-Vṛś-Tul-Kan-Siṅ-Kar-Mit-Vṛṣ-Meṣ. Suppose after Ārdrā4, the Daśā moves to Punarvasu1 in Savya Nakṣatra.

Savya Nakṣatra stars with Meṣa and ends with Mīna. So Punarvasu1 is mapped to Meṣa Navāñśa. Meṣa Navanavāñśa sequence is Meṣ-Vṛṣ-Mit-Kar-Siṅ-Kan-Tul-Vṛś-Dha. So, the Daśā will move from Meṣa (Ardra4) to Meṣa (Punarvasu1). Does that make logical sense?

Kailāśa: No, Guruji. It does not make sense.

Ācārya: But if the Daśā moved from Apasavya Dhanu to Apasavya Vṛścika, the Daśā sequence would have moved from Dha-Vṛś-Tul-Kan-Siṅ-Kar-Mit-Vṛṣ-Meṣ to Dha^-Mak^-Kum^-Mīn^-Meṣ^-Vṛṣ^-Mit^-Siṅ^-Kar^. So, the Daśā would move from Meṣa (Ardra4) to Dhanu (Rohiṇī1). The movement from Meṣa to Dhanu is allowed, and it is called the Siṅhavlokana jump).

Kailāśa: This makes sense now, Guruji.

Ācārya: The following figure diagrammatically represents the Apasavya Kālacakra flow of Navāñśas and the Daśās (Navanavāñśas) within them.

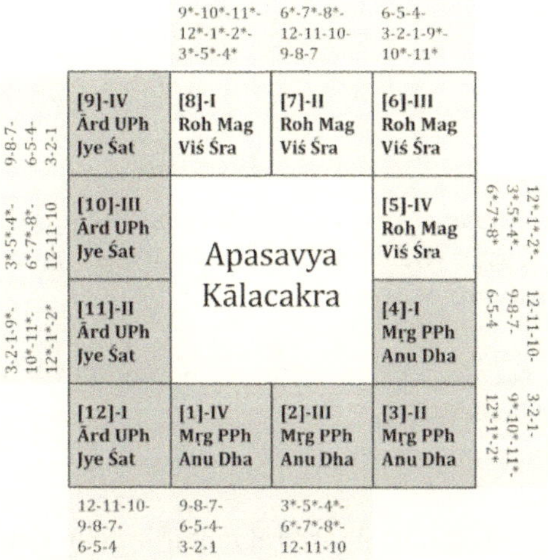

Kailāśa: Noted, Guruji.

Ācārya: This means that the Nakṣatras in the Savya Kālacakra, i.e., Aśvinī, Bharaṇī, Kṛttikā etc., shall always invariably remain within the Kālacakra, and shall *never transcend it.*

This is a significant point in the entire Kālacakra concept.

The Kālacakras are the fundamental entities which are self-contained, and what belongs to them shall remain within them.

Kailāśa: Noted, Guruji. It means the two Kālacakras you have given above are all self-contained entities, and the Daśā-Antardaśā sequence must rotate within them. They cannot break their boundaries and move to another sequence.

Ācārya: Yes, you have understood it perfectly. You cannot break their boundaries and jump between the Kālacakras.

Always remember the following formulae:

For Savya Kālacakra: SAS-KSAS — SBH-KASA — SAS-KSAS

For Apasavya Kālacakra: ARO-UASA — AMR-USAS — AMR-USAS.

These formulae are the cornerstone of Kālacakra Daśā.

Kailāśa: Noted, Guruji!

Ācārya: Now, keeping this principle behind our mind, let us relook at the Antardaśā sequence again.

The Mahādaśā sequence of Aśvinī2 (Vṛṣabha Navāñśa) is Makara-Kumbha-Mīna-Vṛścika^-Tulā^-Kanyā^-Siṅha^-Karka^-Mithuna^. In the Daśā or

Navanavāñśa sequence, *Makara to Mīna* is from Savya Cakra, whereas *Vṛścika^ to Mithuna^* are from Apasavya Cakra.

Suppose we wish to find the Savya Makara, the first Daśā in Aśvinī2. For that, tell me the Navanavāñśa sequence for Savya Makara as per Maharṣi Parāśara.

Kailāśa: It is Mak-Kum-Mīn-Vṛś^-Tul^-Kan^-Kar^-Siṅ^-Mit^.

Ācārya: Very good Kailāśa.

Therefore, for Savya Makara Daśā, Antardaśā sequence is what you have mentioned above.

Kailāśa: Noted, Guruji.

Ācārya: What we are doing is not focusing on the specific sequence of the Daśā in the sequence of nine Daśās (Navanavāñśas); we are going back to the fundamentals, which is identifying whether the Daśā belongs to Savya or Apasavya Cakra.

After that, we find the Navanavāñśas contained within that Navāñśa and use that as the Antardaśā sequence.

Kailāśa: Can we use the same concept in Pratyantardaśā?

Ācārya: Good question Kailāśa.

The same approach should be used for Pratyantardaśā. In that case, we will only need to ascertain whether the Daśā belongs to the Savya or Apasavya Cakra.

Āratī: Guruji, you have found the Navanavāñśa sequence for Savya Makara as Mak-Kum-Mīn-Vṛś^-Tul^-Kan^-Kar^-Siṅ^-Mit^. How to find this sequence for all the Navāñśas?

Ācārya: That is based on the four Caraṇas of the Aśvinī-Bharaṇī-Rohiṇī-Mṛgaśirā group of Nakṣatra. For ease of reference, I am providing them here.

Here, SAS1 means Savya-Aśvinī-Caraṇa1. SBH1 means Savya-Bharaṇī-Caraṇa1. ARO1 means Apasavya-Rohiṇī-Caraṇa1. And AMR1 means Apasavya Mṛgaśirā-Caraṇa1. Similarly, you must understand the remaining Caraṇas.

Table 90

Nav āñśa	Savya Kālacakra	Nava Navāñśa	Apasavya^ Kālacakra	Nava Navāñśa
1	**Meṣa**	SAS1	**Vṛścika^**	ARO1
2	**Vṛṣabha**	SAS2	**Tulā^**	ARO2
3	**Mithuna**	SAS3	**Kanyā^**	ARO3
4	**Karka**	SAS4	**Siṅha^**	ARO4
5	**Siṅha**	SBH1	**Karka^**	AMR1
6	**Kanyā**	SBH2	**Mithuna^**	AMR2
7	**Tulā**	SBH3	**Vṛṣabha^**	AMR3
8	**Vṛścika**	SBH4	**Meṣa^**	AMR4
9	**Dhanu**	SAS1	**Mīna^**	AMR1

Nav āñśa	Savya Kālacakra	Nava Navāñśa	Apasavya^ Kālacakra	Nava Navāñśa
10	Makara	SAS2	Kumbha^	AMR2
11	Kumbha	SAS3	Makara^	AMR3
12	Mīna	SAS4	Mīna^	AMR4

Āratī: Kindly put the Navanavāñśas in the place of the codes SAS1, SAS2 and so on. It will help with the reference.

Ācārya: Kailāśa. Can you do it?

Kailāśa: Certainly, Guruji. Here it is!

Table 91

Nav āñśa	Savya Kālacakra	Nava Navāñśa	Apasavya^ Kālacakra	Nava Navāñśa
1	Meṣa	Meṣ-Vṛṣ-Mit-Kar-Siṅ-Kan-Tul-Vṛś-Dha	Vṛścika^	Dha^-Mak^-Kum^-Mīn^-Meṣ^-Vṛṣ^-Mit^-Siṅ^-Kar^
2	Vṛṣabha	Mak-Kum-Mīn-Vṛś^-Tul^-Kan^-Kar^-Siṅ^-Mit^	Tulā^	Kan^-Tul^-Vṛś^-Mīn-Kum-Mak-Dha-Vṛś-Tul
3	Mithuna	Vṛṣ^-Meṣ^-Mīn^-Kum^-Mak^-Dha^-Meṣ-Vṛṣ-Mit	Kanyā^	Kan-Siṅ-Kar-Mit-Vṛṣ-Meṣ-Dha^-Mak^-Kum^
4	Karka	Kar-Siṅ-Kan-Tul-Vṛś-Dha-Mak-Kum-Mīn	Siṅha^	Mīn^-Meṣ^-Vṛṣ^-Mit^-Siṅ^-Kar^-Kan^-Tul^-Vṛś^
5	Siṅha	Vṛś^-Tul^-Kan^-Kar^-Siṅ^-Mit^-Vṛṣ^-Meṣ^-Mīn^	Karka^	Mīn-Kum-Mak-Dha-Vṛś-Tul-Kan-Siṅ-Kar
6	Kanyā	Kum^-Mak^-Dha^-Meṣ-Vṛṣ-Mit-Kar-Siṅ-Kan	Mithuna^	Mit-Vṛṣ-Meṣ-Dha^-Mak^-Kum^-Mīn^-Meṣ^-Vṛṣ^
7	Tulā	Tul-Vṛś-Dha-Mak-Kum-Mīn-Vṛś^-Tul^-Kan^	Vṛṣabha^	Mit^-Siṅ^-Kar^-Kan^-Tul^-Vṛś^-Mīn-Kum-Mak
8	Vṛścika	Kar^-Siṅ^-Mit^-Vṛṣ^-Meṣ^-Mīn^-Kum^-Mak^-Dha^	Meṣa^	Dha-Vṛś-Tul-Kan-Siṅ-Kar-Mit-Vṛṣ-Meṣ
9	Dhanu	Meṣ-Vṛṣ-Mit-Kar-Siṅ-Kan-Tul-Vṛś-Dha	Mīna^	Mīn-Kum-Mak-Dha-Vṛś-Tul-Kan-Siṅ-Kar
10	Makara	Mak-Kum-Mīn-Vṛś^-Tul^-Kan^-Kar^-Siṅ^-Mit^	Kumbha^	Mit-Vṛṣ-Meṣ-Dha^-Mak^-Kum^-Mīn^-Meṣ^-Vṛṣ^
11	Kumbha	Vṛṣ^-Meṣ^-Mīn^-Kum^-Mak^-Dha^-Meṣ-Vṛṣ-Mit	Makara^	Mit^-Siṅ^-Kar^-Kan^-Tul^-Vṛś^-Mīn-Kum-Mak
12	Mīna	Kar-Siṅ-Kan-Tul-Vṛś-Dha-Mak-Kum-Mīn	Dhanu^	Dha-Vṛś-Tul-Kan-Siṅ-Kar-Mit-Vṛṣ-Meṣ

Ācārya: Very well, Kailāśa. Āratī, you can easily refer to the Navanavāñśa sequences for different Savya and Apasavya Rāśis.

Āratī: Dhanyavād Guruji.

Kailāśa: Guruji, we can further compress the table as per the following:

Table 92

Navāñśa	Savya Kālacakra	Nava Navāñśa
1	Meṣa	Meṣ-Vṛṣ-Mit-Kar-Siṅ-Kan-Tul-Vṛś-Dha
2	Vṛṣabha	Mak-Kum-Mīn-Vṛś^-Tul^-Kan^-Kar^-Siṅ^-Mit^

Navāñśa	Savya Kālacakra	Nava Navāñśa
3	Mithuna	Vṛṣ^-Meṣ^-Mīn^-Kum^-Mak^-Dha^-Meṣ-Vṛṣ-Mit
4	Karka	Kar-Siṅ-Kan-Tul-Vṛś-Dha-Mak-Kum-Mīn
5	Siṅha	Vṛś^-Tul^-Kan^-Kar^-Siṅ^-Mit^-Vṛṣ^-Meṣ^-Mīn^
6	Kanyā	Kum^-Mak^-Dha^-Meṣ-Vṛṣ-Mit-Kar-Siṅ-Kan
7	Tulā	Tul-Vṛś-Dha-Mak-Kum-Mīn-Vṛś^-Tul^-Kan^
8	Vṛścika	Kar^-Siṅ^-Mit^-Vṛṣ^-Meṣ^-Mīn^-Kum^-Mak^-Dha^
9	Dhanu	Meṣ-Vṛṣ-Mit-Kar-Siṅ-Kan-Tul-Vṛś-Dha
10	Makara	Mak-Kum-Mīn-Vṛś^-Tul^-Kan^-Kar^-Siṅ^-Mit^
11	Kumbha	Vṛṣ^-Meṣ^-Mīn^-Kum^-Mak^-Dha^-Meṣ-Vṛṣ-Mit
12	Mīna	Kar-Siṅ-Kan-Tul-Vṛś-Dha-Mak-Kum-Mīn

Ācārya: Glad that you have noticed the pattern. For everyone, kindly clarify the pattern for Apasavya Cakra.

Kailāśa: Guruji, for Apasavya, the sequence is just reversed. Suppose for Savya Meṣa Kālacakra, the sequence is Meṣ-Vṛṣ-Mit-Kar-Siṅ-Kan-Tul-Vṛś-Dha. For Apasavya Meṣa Kālacakra, the sequence is Dha-Vṛś-Tul-Kan-Siṅ-Kar-Mit-Vṛṣ-Meṣ.

Let us take another example. For Savya Vṛṣabha, the sequence is Mak-Kum-Mīn-Vṛś^-Tul^-Kan^-Kar^-Siṅ^-Mit^. For Apasavya Vṛṣabha, the sequence is Mit^-Siṅ^-Kar^-Kan^-Tul^-Vṛś^-Mīn-Kum-Mak, which is the reverse of Savya.

Ācārya: You have made an outstanding discovery.

Kailāśa: It also means that the Deha and Jīva for all the Kālacakras are fixed.

Table 93

Navāñśa	Savya Kālacakra	Nava Navāñśa	Deha	Jīva
1	Meṣa	Meṣ-Vṛṣ-Mit-Kar-Siṅ-Kan-Tul-Vṛś-Dha	Meṣa	Dha
2	Vṛṣabha	Mak-Kum-Mīn-Vṛś^-Tul^-Kan^-Kar^-Siṅ^-Mit^	Mak	Mit
3	Mithuna	Vṛṣ^-Meṣ^-Mīn^-Kum^-Mak^-Dha^-Meṣ-Vṛṣ-Mit	Vṛṣ	Mit
4	Karka	Kar-Siṅ-Kan-Tul-Vṛś-Dha-Mak-Kum-Mīn	Kar	Mīn
5	Siṅha	Vṛś^-Tul^-Kan^-Kar^-Siṅ^-Mit^-Vṛṣ^-Meṣ^-Mīn^	Vṛś	Mīn
6	Kanyā	Kum^-Mak^-Dha^-Meṣ-Vṛṣ-Mit-Kar-Siṅ-Kan	Kum	Kan
7	Tulā	Tul-Vṛś-Dha-Mak-Kum-Mīn-Vṛś^-Tul^-Kan^	Tul	Kan
8	Vṛścika	Kar^-Siṅ^-Mit^-Vṛṣ^-Meṣ^-Mīn^-Kum^-Mak^-Dha^	Kar	Dha
9	Dhanu	Meṣ-Vṛṣ-Mit-Kar-Siṅ-Kan-Tul-Vṛś-Dha	Meṣ	Dha
10	Makara	Mak-Kum-Mīn-Vṛś^-Tul^-Kan^-Kar^-Siṅ^-Mit^	Mak	Mit
11	Kumbha	Vṛṣ^-Meṣ^-Mīn^-Kum^-Mak^-Dha^-Meṣ-Vṛṣ-Mit	Vṛṣ	Mit
12	Mīna	Kar-Siṅ-Kan-Tul-Vṛś-Dha-Mak-Kum-Mīn	Kar	Mīn

Ācārya: Jayanta, do you see the pattern in Deha and Jīva?

Jayanta: Certainly, I can see it. All the Dehas fall in Cara and Sthira Rāśi, but all the Jīvas fall in Dvisvabhāva Rāśis. Also, the Jīvas always fall in pairs except Meṣa and Mīna.

Ācārya: Glad you have noticed that.

Āratī: Dhanyavād, Guruji and Gurubhrāta.

Ācārya: A better representation of the above Antardaśā sequence is using the codes for Savya and Apasavya. Let us start again with Aśvinī2. Aśvinī2 falls in Vṛṣabha Navāñśa, which is S2, where "S" denotes Savya Kālacakra, and "2" Vṛṣabha.

The Daśā sequence for S2 is S10 - S11 - S12 - A8 - A7 - A6 - A4 - A5 - A3. Here, "S" stands for Savyacakra and numbers for the Rāśis. The Antardaśā sequences for the nine Daśās of Aśvinī2 or Savya-Vṛṣabha Navāñśa are as follows:

Table 94: Antardaśās of Savya Vṛṣabha (Ashvini2)

#	Daśā	Antar 1	Antar 2	Antar 3	Antar 4	Antar 5	Antar 6	Antar 7	Antar 8	Antar 9
1	S10	S10	S11	S12	A8	A7	A6	A4	A5	A3
2	S11	A2	A1	A12	A11	A10	A9	S1	S2	S3
3	S12	S4	S5	S6	S7	S8	S9	S10	S11	S12
4	A8	A9	A10	A11	A12	A1	A2	A3	A5	A4
5	A7	A6	A7	A8	S12	S11	S10	S9	S8	S7
6	A6	S6	S5	S4	S3	S2	S1	A9	A10	A11
7	A4	S12	S11	S10	S9	S8	S7	S6	S5	S4
8	A5	A12	A1	A2	A3	A5	A4	A6	A7	(A8)
9	A3	(S3)	S2	S1	A9	A10	A11	A12	A1	A2

In this sequence ending Antardaśā of a Daśā connects with the starting Antardaśā of the next Daśā following the jumps stated by Maharṣi Parāśara.

Kailāśa: Noted, Guruji.

Ācārya: We notice one violation here, which is a jump A8-S3 (Vṛścika-Mithuna), Siṅha Daśā (A5) and beginning of Mithuna Daśā (A3). There is no concept of 6-8 Rāśi jump in Kālacakra Daśā. The *Siṅha-Karka flip* in Apasavya Cakra causes this.

The *Siṅha-Karka flip* causes a break in the flow, which is causing the jump from Vṛścika to Mithuna.

Kailāśa: What does this mean?

Ācārya: Suppose someone is ending Apasavya Siṅha Daśā and moving to Apasavya Mithuna Daśā. The last Antardaśā of Siṅha is Vṛścika, and the first Antardaśā of Mithuna is Mithuna. The Antardaśā will jump from Vṛścika to Mithuna, which is the eighth house jump. Maharṣi Parāśara only allows a 5H-9H jump (Siṅhavlokana), 3H-11H jump (Maṇḍūka), and 12H jump (Marakaṭa). The 6H-8H jump is not mentioned.

Kailāśa: So, what do we do?

Ācārya: There is no way we can avoid this irregularity. We can infer that such jumps can bring danger to someone's life.

But we can still confidently say that, in all other cases, the jumps occurring between the Antardaśās are acceptable.

Kailāśa: Noted, Guruji!

Ācārya: When looking deeper, there are a few other inconsistencies which need deeper study, but I firmly believe that the Navanavāñśa sequence given for each Navāñśa is the key to defining the Antardaśās.

Kailāśa: Noted, Guruji!

Ācārya: Let us apply this principle to determining Pratyantardaśās.

Suppose we want to find the Pratyantardaśā in Makara Daśā, Vṛścika Antardaśā. In the above table, we notice that Vṛścika Antardaśā is denoted as A8, which means Apasavya Vṛścika. The Navanavāñśa sequence for Apasavya Vṛścika is A9 - A10 - A11 - A12 - A1 - A2 - A3 - A5 - A4.

Therefore, the Pratyantardaśā starts with Dhanu (A9) and moves in Apasavya order to Karka (A4).

Kailāśa: Noted, Guruji! Can this principle be used for further sub-level Daśās?

Ācārya: Certainly, we can use this for Mahādaśā, Antardaśā, and Pratyantardaśā till Prāṇadaśā, we can use the same principle for all subdivisions, provided we know whether the Navāñśa is from Savya or Apasavya Kālacakra.

Kailāśa: This makes sense.

Ācārya: For ease of reference, the Navanavāñśas allotted to the different Rāśis in the Savya and Apasavya Cakra are summarised in the table below.

The Nakṣatra Caraṇa assigned to the 24 Savya and Apasavya Navāñśas is also mentioned. It hardly matters whether one uses the Navāñśas or the Nakṣatra Caraṇas in computation or delineation of a Kuṇḍalī because, at a fundamental level, they are identical. What is said about Aśvinī also applies to the four Caraṇas of Punarvasu, Hastā, Mūla, and Pūrvābhādra, which are also indicated below.

Table 95

				Navanavāñśa								
SA	Pāda	Group	Navāñśa	1	2	3	4	5	6	7	8	9
S	1	**S-Aśvinī**	**S1**	S1	S2	S3	S4	S5	S6	S7	S8	S9
S	2	**S-Aśvinī**	**S2**	S10	S11	S12	A8	A7	A6	A4	A5	A3
S	3	**S-Aśvinī**	**S3**	A2	A1	A12	A11	A10	A9	S1	S2	S3
S	4	**S-Aśvinī**	**S4**	S4	S5	S6	S7	S8	S9	S10	S11	S12
S	1	**S-Bharaṇī**	**S5**	A8	A7	A6	A4	A5	A3	A2	A1	A12
S	2	**S-Bharaṇī**	**S6**	A11	A10	A9	S1	S2	S3	S4	S5	S6
S	3	**S-Bharaṇī**	**S7**	S7	S8	S9	S10	S11	S12	A8	A7	A6
S	4	**S-Bharaṇī**	**S8**	A4	A5	A3	A2	A1	A12	A11	A10	A9
S	1	**S-Aśvinī**	**S9**	S1	S2	S3	S4	S5	S6	S7	S8	S9
S	2	**S-Aśvinī**	**S10**	S10	S11	S12	A8	A7	A6	A4	A5	A3
S	3	**S-Aśvinī**	**S11**	A2	A1	A12	A11	A10	A9	S1	S2	S3
S	4	**S-Aśvinī**	**S12**	S4	S5	S6	S7	S8	S9	S10	S11	S12

				Navanavāñśa								
A	**1**	**A-Rohiṇī**	**A8**	A9	A10	A11	A12	A1	A2	A3	A5	A4
A	**2**	**A-Rohiṇī**	**A7**	A6	A7	A8	S12	S11	S10	S9	S8	S7
A	**3**	**A-Rohiṇī**	**A6**	S6	S5	S4	S3	S2	S1	A9	A10	A11
A	**4**	**A-Rohiṇī**	**A5**	A12	A1	A2	A3	A5	A4	A6	A7	A8
A	**1**	**A-Mṛgaśirā**	**A4**	S12	S11	S10	S9	S8	S7	S6	S5	S4
A	**2**	**A-Mṛgaśirā**	**A3**	S3	S2	S1	A9	A10	A11	A12	A1	A2
A	**3**	**A-Mṛgaśirā**	**A2**	A3	A5	A4	A6	A7	A8	S12	S11	S10
A	**4**	**A-Mṛgaśirā**	**A1**	S9	S8	S7	S6	S5	S4	S3	S2	S1
A	**1**	**A-Mṛgaśirā**	**A12**	S12	S11	S10	S9	S8	S7	S6	S5	S4
A	**2**	**A-Mṛgaśirā**	**A11**	S3	S2	S1	A9	A10	A11	A12	A1	A2
A	**3**	**A-Mṛgaśirā**	**A10**	A3	A5	A4	A6	A7	A8	S12	S11	S10
A	**4**	**A-Mṛgaśirā**	**A9**	S9	S8	S7	S6	S5	S4	S3	S2	S1

Kailāśa: Dhanyavād Guruji. This is similar to the reference table you have given above regarding the Navanavāñśas of the twelve Navāñśas of Savya and twelve Navāñśas of Apasavya Cakra.

Ācārya: Yes, this is another method of reckoning the same. From this table, you will know which Navāñśa a Nakṣatra Pāda maps to, whether that is in Savya or Apasavya Navāñśa, and what Daśā sequence is assigned to that. After that, you can find the Antardaśās, Pratyantardaśās till Prāṇa Daśā in Kālacakra Daśā.

If you are unsure which group a Nakṣatra belongs to, you can use the following reference table:

Table 96

#	Nakṣatra	Group	Nakṣatra	Group	Nakṣatra	Group
1	**Aśvinī**	S-Aśvinī	**Maghā**	A-Rohiṇī	**Mūla**	S-Aśvinī
2	**Bharaṇī**	S-Bharaṇī	**Pūrvāphālgunī**	A-Mṛgaśirā	**Pūrvāṣāṛhā**	S-Bharaṇī
3	**Kṛttikā**	S-Aśvinī	**Uttarāphālgunī**	A-Mṛgaśirā	**Uttarāṣāṛhā**	S-Aśvinī
4	**Rohiṇī**	A-Rohiṇī	**Hastā**	S-Aśvinī	**Śravaṇa**	A-Rohiṇī
5	**Mṛgaśirā**	A-Mṛgaśirā	**Citrā**	S-Bharaṇī	**Dhaniṣṭhā**	A-Mṛgaśirā
6	**Ārdrā**	A-Mṛgaśirā	**Svāti**	S-Aśvinī	**Śatabhiṣā**	A-Mṛgaśirā
7	**Punarvasu**	S-Aśvinī	**Viśākhā**	A-Rohiṇī	**Pūrvābhādra**	S-Aśvinī
8	**Puṣya**	S-Bharaṇī	**Anurādhā**	A-Mṛgaśirā	**Uttarābhādra**	S-Bharaṇī
9	**Aśleṣā**	S-Aśvinī	**Jyeṣṭhā**	A-Mṛgaśirā	**Revatī**	S-Aśvinī

Kailāśa: This makes it crystal clear. Dhanyavād Guruji!

Sunidhi: Āratī: Dhanyavād Guruji. We can understand the Daśā now.

Jayanta: This has been an enlightening session on the Kālacakra Daśā. Kindly tell us how to use this Daśā.

Ācārya: In the absence of software, this becomes tedious to do it by hand. But I will show you with some worked out examples.

But before we go into the examples, let us understand the principles of judging this Daśā.

Jayanta: We are looking forward to it, Guruji!

Ācārya: Here are the principles:

Firstly, treat this as a Rāśi Daśā instead of a Graha Daśā.

Jayanta: Why is this a Rāśi Daśā and not a Graha Daśā? Isn't it based on Candra's sphuṭa?

Ācārya: It is a Rāśi Daśā because its Name contains Cakra, which stands for Bhacakra. Besides, Kālacakra is the zodiac, and therefore, it is a Rāśi Daśā. Even though Candra's sphuṭa determines the Daśā balance at birth, the Daśās are of the Navanavāñśas, which are Rāśis. Therefore, it is certainly a Rāśidaśā.

Jayanta: I have a doubt. If it is a Rāśidaśā, why must we determine the Daśā balance at birth? Why can't we use Candra's Nakṣatra Pāda to determine the applicable Navanavāñśa but not use Candrasphuṭa to find the Daśā balance? Don't we use a similar concept in Cara and Sudarśana Cakra Daśā? In these two Daśās, we use Lagna to find the commencing Rāśi but do not use Lagnasphuṭa.

Shouldn't this be the case even in Kālacakra Daśā?

Ācārya: You have a valid point.

Jayanta: Even in Cakra Daśā, the birth in different Sandhyās, etc., is used for determining the commencing Rāśi, but it is not mentioned to find the Daśā Balance at birth. It states each Daśā is ten years. That's all.

Ācārya: That is a valid point. However, for Kālacakra Daśā, Maharṣi states the following:

46.85-86. The longevity of a person is determined from the Pādas of the Nakṣatra at the time of birth, or the time of query and the years allotted to the 9 Rāśis commencing from it. Some sages are of the view that the person will enjoy Pūrṇāyu if his birth is at the commencement of the Pādas. It will be Madhyāyu if the birth is in the middle of the Pādas. It is Alpāyu or will face death-like sufferings if the birth is at the end of the Pādas.

What does it mean?

It means that depending on the location of Candra in the Nakṣatra Pāda, the longevity is proportionally allotted. This is the Daśā Balance. If someone is born at the beginning of a Nakṣatra Pāda, full longevity of that Pāda is granted. However, if someone is born at the end of the Pāda, only some is granted. Isn't this the Daśā balance?

Kailāśa: That makes sense, Guruji!

Ācārya: Besides, Maharṣi Parāśara clearly specifies the following:

46.90-91. Multiply the past Ghaṭis, Palas, etc., of the Nakṣatra Pāda in which a person is born by the existing Daśā years and divide it by 15. The result will indicate the elapsed period of the Daśā in years, months, etc. By deducting it from the total number of years allotted, we get the balance of Daśā at birth. The Daśā should be taken as commencing from that Rāśi.

46.92. Multiply the past Ghaṭis, Palas, etc., of the present Pāda of the Nakṣatra by the number of years and divide the product by the fourth part of

Bhabhog. The years, etc., so obtained may then be deducted from the total Daśā period. The result will be the balance of Daśā at birth in years, months, etc.

46.93. The past Kalās of the Navāñśa, in which Candra may be placed, should be multiplied by the years allotted to the Daśā, and the product should be divided by 200. The resulting years, etc., will be the expired portion of the Daśā. By deducting them from the total number of years, the balance of the Daśā at birth is obtained.

Kailāśa: This is adequately clear why we must find the Daśā balance.

Ācārya: Each Nakṣatra Pāda has 9 Rāśis (Navanavāñśas). You must find how much Nakṣatra Pāda (or Navāñśa) has elapsed, and you must commence the Daśā from the Rāśi so arrived. This is clearly stated in 46.91. The approach I have explained above to find the Janma Daśā from the appropriate Navanavāñśa is based on Maharṣi's Parāśara's instructions.

Kailāśa: Noted, Guruji!

Ācārya: Let us focus on Deha and Jīva. Each Nakṣatra Pāda has a Deha and a Jīva. For a Savya Nakṣatra, the first Navanavāñśa is Deha, and the last one is Jīva. For an Apasavya Nakṣatra, the first Navanavāñśa is Jīva, and the last one is Deha.

Kailāśa: What is the rule for Deha and Jīva?

Ācārya: If the Deha and Jīva Rāśi are afflicted, then the duration of the Navāñśa is ruined.

Kailāśa: But the duration of a Nakṣatra Pāda or Navāñśa is almost the entire life of the person. That is not practical to determine someone's mishaps and dangers in life.

Ācārya: You are right. Therefore, we must find the Deha and Jīva for every Daśā.

Kailāśa: Kindly elaborate on how we do that.

Ācārya: Suppose someone is running the Daśā of Apasavya Meṣa. The Navanavāñśa sequence for this is Dha-Vṛś-Tul-Kan-Siṅ-Kar-Mit-Vṛṣ-Meṣ. This means Meṣa is Deha, and Dhanu is Jīva. If these two Rāśis are afflicted, then Meṣa Daśā will be fatal for the native.

Kailāśa: Ok. I understand now. So, we must find the Deha and Jīva for every Daśā.

Ācārya: You should find them for every Daśā, Antardaśā till Prāṇa Daśā. It is the same concept.

You can use the Deha and Jīva based on this table for every Daśā and its subdivisions. Also, their subdivisions will be based on the Navanavāñśa.

Also note that if the Daśā is of Apasavya Kālacakra, the Navanavāñśa sequence is reversed, but the Deha and Jīva remain the same for both Savya and Apasavya Kālacakra.

Table 97

Navāñśa	Savya Kālacakra	Nava Navāñśa	Deha	Jīva
1	**Meṣa**	Meṣ-Vṛṣ-Mit-Kar-Siṅ-Kan-Tul-Vṛś-Dha	**Meṣa**	**Dha**
2	**Vṛṣabha**	Mak-Kum-Mīn-Vṛś^-Tul^-Kan^-Kar^-Siṅ^-Mit^	**Mak**	**Mit**
3	**Mithuna**	Vṛṣ^-Meṣ^-Mīn^-Kum^-Mak^-Dha^-Meṣ-Vṛṣ-Mit	**Vṛṣ**	**Mit**
4	**Karka**	Kar-Siṅ-Kan-Tul-Vṛś-Dha-Mak-Kum-Mīn	**Kar**	**Mīn**
5	**Siṅha**	Vṛś^-Tul^-Kan^-Kar^-Siṅ^-Mit^-Vṛṣ^-Meṣ^-Mīn^	**Vṛś**	**Mīn**
6	**Kanyā**	Kum^-Mak^-Dha^-Meṣ-Vṛṣ-Mit-Kar-Siṅ-Kan	**Kum**	**Kan**
7	**Tulā**	Tul-Vṛś-Dha-Mak-Kum-Mīn-Vṛś^-Tul^-Kan^	**Tul**	**Kan**
8	**Vṛścika**	Kar^-Siṅ^-Mit^-Vṛṣ^-Meṣ^-Mīn^-Kum^-Mak^-Dha^	**Kar**	**Dha**
9	**Dhanu**	Meṣ-Vṛṣ-Mit-Kar-Siṅ-Kan-Tul-Vṛś-Dha	**Meṣ**	**Dha**
10	**Makara**	Mak-Kum-Mīn-Vṛś^-Tul^-Kan^-Kar^-Siṅ^-Mit^	**Mak**	**Mit**
11	**Kumbha**	Vṛṣ^-Meṣ^-Mīn^-Kum^-Mak^-Dha^-Meṣ-Vṛṣ-Mit	**Vṛṣ**	**Mit**
12	**Mīna**	Kar-Siṅ-Kan-Tul-Vṛś-Dha-Mak-Kum-Mīn	**Kar**	**Mīn**

Kailāśa: Dhanyavād, Guruji. This makes the Kālacakra Daśā adequately clear. We will only need this table for all our computations.

Ācārya: Also note that you will need the following three tables as well.

(1) Nakṣatra Navāñśa mapping

(2) Rāśi duration

(3) Navāñśa Āyuṣa

The following is the Nakṣatra-Navāñśa mapping table.

Table 98: Nakṣatra-Navāñśa mapping

#	Nakṣatra	I	II	III	IV
1	**Aśvinī**	**Meṣa**	**Vṛṣabha**	**Mithuna**	**Karka**
2	**Bharaṇī**	**Siṅha**	**Kanyā**	**Tulā**	**Vṛścika**
3	**Kṛttikā**	**Dhanu**	**Makara**	**Kumbha**	**Mīna**
4	Rohiṇī^	Vṛścika^	Tulā^	Kanyā^	Siṅha^
5	Mṛgaśirā^	Karka^	Mithuna^	Vṛṣabha^	Meṣa^
6	Ārdrā^	Mīna^	Kumbha^	Makara^	Dhanu^
7	**Punarvasu**	**Meṣa**	**Vṛṣabha**	**Mithuna**	**Karka**
8	**Puṣya**	**Siṅha**	**Kanyā**	**Tulā**	**Vṛścika**
9	**Aśleṣā**	**Dhanu**	**Makara**	**Kumbha**	**Mīna**
10	Maghā^	Vṛścika^	Tulā^	Kanyā^	Siṅha^
11	Pūrvāphālgunī^	Karka^	Mithuna^	Vṛṣabha^	Meṣa^
12	Uttarāphālgunī^	Mīna^	Kumbha^	Makara^	Dhanu^
13	**Hastā**	**Meṣa**	**Vṛṣabha**	**Mithuna**	**Karka**
14	**Citrā**	**Siṅha**	**Kanyā**	**Tulā**	**Vṛścika**
15	**Svāti**	**Dhanu**	**Makara**	**Kumbha**	**Mīna**
16	Viśākhā^	Vṛścika^	Tulā^	Kanyā^	Siṅha^
17	Anurādhā^	Karka^	Mithuna^	Vṛṣabha^	Meṣa^

#	Nakṣatra	I	II	III	IV
18	Jyeṣṭhā^	Mīna^	Kumbha^	Makara^	Dhanu^
19	**Mūla**	**Meṣa**	**Vṛṣabha**	**Mithuna**	**Karka**
20	**Pūrvāṣāṛhā**	**Siṅha**	**Kanyā**	**Tulā**	**Vṛścika**
21	**Uttarāṣāṛhā**	**Dhanu**	**Makara**	**Kumbha**	**Mīna**
22	Śravaṇa^	Vṛścika^	Tulā^	Kanyā^	Siṅha^
23	Dhaniṣṭhā^	Karka^	Mithuna^	Vṛṣabha^	Meṣa^
24	Śatabhiṣā^	Mīna^	Kumbha^	Makara^	Dhanu^
25	**Pūrvābhādra**	**Meṣa**	**Vṛṣabha**	**Mithuna**	**Karka**
26	**Uttarābhādra**	**Siṅha**	**Kanyā**	**Tulā**	**Vṛścika**
27	**Revatī**	**Dhanu**	**Makara**	**Kumbha**	**Mīna**

The following is the Rāśi duration table.

Table 99

1	2	3	4	5	6	7	8	9	10	11	12
Meṣ	**Vṛṣ**	**Mit**	**Kar**	**Siṅ**	**Kan**	**Tul**	**Vṛś**	**Dha**	**Mak**	**Kum**	**Mīn**
7	16	9	21	5	9	16	7	10	4	4	10

The following is the Navāñśa Āyuṣa table.

Table 100

1	2	3	4	5	6	7	8	9	10	11	12
Meṣ	**Vṛṣ**	**Mit**	**Kar**	**Siṅ**	**Kan**	**Tul**	**Vṛś**	**Dha**	**Mak**	**Kum**	**Mīn**
100	85	83	86	**100**	85	83	86	**100**	85	83	86

If you have these four tables, you can compute the entire Kālacakra Daśā by hand.

Kailāśa: You have explained before that we do not need the Nakṣatra Navāñśa mapping table. Because after drawing the regular Navāñśa, we merely need to flip the Navāñśas for the Apasavya Nakṣatra. Isn't it?

Ācārya: You are right. But you can use the Nakṣatra-Navāñśa mapping table as a quick reference guide.

Kailāśa: Noted, Guruji!

Sunidhi: Guruji, let us do some case studies.

Ācārya: Before that, let us walk through the rules of assessment. We started that before but didn't complete it.

Jayanta: That makes sense, Guruji. Let us go through the rules.

Ācārya: They are as follows:

Kālacakra Daśā is a Rāśi Daśā; therefore, the Rāśi Daśā rules are applicable.

For every Daśā, first, determine how well the Deha and Jīva Rāśis are. The results of the entire Daśā are dependent on this.

In judging the results, always following this sequence: Graha in the Bhāva, Graha aspecting the Bhāva, the placement of the Bhāveśa. This is the precedence of activation of results. Let us call these Grahas "Prāṇi Graha". Prāṇi means active or becoming lively.

In a Daśā, the events manifest due to the following rules:

The Naisargika and Bhāvavat Kārakatvas of a Prāṇi Graha. For instance, for Kanyā Lagna, if 7L Guru is in the Kālacakra Daśā Rāśi, then in such Daśā, there can be childbirth (Naisārgika Kārakatva of Guru) or marriage (Bhāvavat Kārakatva of Guru).

You must consider the Bhāvavat Kārakatvas of the Prāṇi Graha from Janma Lagna and Daśā Lagna. In the above example, suppose the Daśā is of Vṛṣabha Lagna and Guru is the eighth and eleventh lord. In that case, the results of the eighth and eleventh will also be experienced.

The results, favourable or unfavourable, are dependent on the dignity of the Prāṇi Graha.

A Graha is favourable if the Graha is in Sva-Ucca-Mūla-Mitra Rāśi-Añśa, subject to Śubha or Śubhakartari Yoga, not defeated in a Graha Yuddha or not Asta. Śubha Yoga is formed when Saumyas are in 2H or 12H from the Graha.

A Graha is unfavourable if the Graha is in Nīca-Śatru Rāśi-Añśa, subject to Aśubha or Pāpakartari Yoga, defeated in a Graha Yuddha or Asta. Aśubha Yoga is formed when Saumyas are in 2H or 12H from the Graha.

You must consider the Graha placements from the Daśālagna. If Saumyas are in Kendrakoṇa and Krūras are in the third or sixth, the Daśā is favourable. If either Saumyas or Krūras in the eleventh, then the Daśā is favourable. Saumyas outside Kendrakoṇa-Dhana and Krūras in these places make the Daśās painful. Krūras are excruciatingly painful in Mokṣatrikoṇa (4-8-12) from the Daśālagna. Krūras simultaneously occupying Dhana and Randhra can cause fatality.

You must examine the Gocara through the Daśārāśi. If there is Saumya Gocara, the results are favourable. If Krūras transit the Daśārāśi, then the results are unfavourable.

The Daśārāśi with a high Aṣṭakavarga score in Sarvāṣṭakavarga is favourable.

You must examine the Daśārāśi in Aṣṭakavarga of all the Grahas. If the Daśārāśi has a high Aṣṭakavarga score in the Bhinnāṣṭakavarga of a Graha, good results of that Graha manifest. If the Daśārāśi has a low Aṣṭakavarga score in the Bhinnāṣṭakavarga of a Graha, then there are unfavourable results of that Graha. You should mainly focus on Naisārgika Kārakatvas of the Grahas.

Āratī: Guruji, kindly tell us the effects of Bhāvas based on favourable or unfavourable placements.

Ācārya: I have mentioned above that good effects of a Bhāva manifest of the Daśārāśi have good Grahas, or Daśārāśi lord is well placed. The affected Bhāva is based on the Bhāva occupied by the Daśārāśi, the Graha in Daśārāśi, the Graha aspecting the Daśārāśi, and the Bhāva held by the Daśārāśi lord (Daśeśa).

The high-level effects of a favourable and unfavourable Bhāva are as follows:

Lagna: 1H:

Favourable: General comfort, success, good health, financial prosperity, fame, promotions to higher positions, rise of eminence, happily placed in life, physically strong, brilliant appearance, increase of prosperity with time like Śuklapakṣa Candra.

Unfavourable: Failure, head disease, sorrows, dishonour, displacement, financial losses, bodily pains, discomforts, imprisonment, living incognito, suffering from fear, danger, anxiety, and disease, suffer loss of near and dear ones, loss of position and misfortunes.

Dhana: 2H:

Favourable: Increase in family wealth, gains of utensils, family amity and happiness, success or acquisition to family, acquisition of good daughters, good meals, wealth through teaching and eloquence, admiration in an assembly.

Unfavourable: Loss of ancestral property, facial diseases, sickness in family members, right eye ailment, loss of utensils, behaving stupidly in a public assembly, not being true to his word or his family, receiving evil tidings, writing bad letters or papers, foul-tongued, spend heavily, and incur royal displeasure (governmental penalty).

Sahaja: 3H:

Favourable: Good conduct, appreciation for good conduct, courage, happiness to siblings, increased help from others, good health, help and cooperation from siblings, hearing of agreeable news, exhibiting one's courage, enterprise or new business, leadership in an army, attainment of honour, receiving support from people and neighbours

Unfavourable: Misunderstanding with friends, supporters and well-wishers; misfortunes to siblings, ailments in respiration (asthma, etc.), neck, and right ear; mental affliction, bad conduct, or cowardice, the demise of his brother during evil counsel in undertakings, trouble through secret machinations of internal enemies, humiliation, shame, and loss of pride.

Sukha: 4H:

Favourable: Acquisition of vehicles, new land, new house, cattle, beds and house furniture, general prosperity, good health, help to relatives, success in agriculture, friendship with females, wealth, higher status, promotion in one's appointment.

Unfavourable: Distress to mother and maternal relatives, loss of cattle, beds, and house furniture, landed property and vehicles, heart trouble, general misery, sickness from impure water (cholera, typhoid, etc.), danger from water (drowning), sickness to dear friends and relatives.

Mantra: 5H:

Favourable: Birth of children, good health, peace of mind, expansion of influence, an increase of righteous conduct (Puṇya), merriment in the company of relatives, acquisition of a post of a councillor under the government, feeding others and enjoying plenty of good food and drinks, accomplishing meritorious acts, admired by the nobles and virtuous.

Unfavourable: Illness, danger (or death) to children, troubles caused by unrighteous deeds, mental unrest, irritable temperament, ill-health of the advisors, mind aberration, deception, wearisome wandering, stomach trouble, royal displeasure (governmental penalty, fines, or imprisonment) and bodily weakness.

Śatru: 6H:

Favourable: exhibition of courage, defeat of enemies, victory in litigations, conflicts and court cases, good health, recovery from ill-health, protection from ill-health, charity and generosity, immense power, living in all splendour and prosperity.

Unfavourable: occurrence of fresh wounds or ulcers in the organ ruled by the Rāśi (containing 6H or 6L), danger from thieves and enemies, trouble in waist and navel, obstacles in undertakings, afflicted by diseases signified by the afflicted Graha, suffering reversal, defeat in court cases, wicked acts, servile duties, being despised and scandalised.

Dārā: 7H:

Favourable: Marriage, recovery of lost wealth, enjoyment, happiness, safe return of relatives from foreign land, building of a good house, acquisition of new clothes, jewels, and beds, enjoying pleasures in the company of the life-partner, immensely powerful or virile, conducting marriages or other auspicious festivities in his family, undertaking pleasurable trips.

Unfavourable: Sickness or death or separation from the life-partner, disturbances in the journey, urinary troubles, fire hazard in spouse's house, distress to the person's son-in-law, affliction or suffering due to opposite sex, indulging with prostitutes, suffering from venereal diseases, wearisome wandering.

Randhra: 8H:

Favourable: Freedom from diseases, protection to longevity, courage, securing loans to acquire new houses, building mutts, discharge of debts, promotion or rise of status, cessation of quarrels, acquisition of buffaloes, cows, goats, and servants.

Unfavourable: Illness to servants, obstacles in undertakings, diseases in the anus, quarrels with all, financial losses due to thieves, rulers or enemies, loss of appetite, health troubles, a bad name, humiliation, excessive sorrow, nonsensical thoughts and attitude, increase of sexual appetite, jealousy, unconsciousness, poverty, fruitless rambling, defamation, and danger to life.

Dharma: 9H:

Favourable: Blessings from elders and parents, mental happiness, divine grace, an increase of fortune, meritorious acts, an increase of penance, philanthropy, happiness from grandchildren, endowed with the company of his wife, sons, grandchildren, and relations, enjoying continuous prosperity, happiness, and wealth, royal favour, reverence to Brāhmaṇas and Devatās.

Unfavourable: Illness to elders, father, and grandchildren; bad luck, divine wrath; dis-inclination to charitable acts, a decline of hard-earned merit, the ruin of one's power of penance, hard-heartedness, the wrath of the Devatā that had been worshipped formerly and suffer something untoward, trouble to his wife and children, wicked acts, one of his elders or his father may die, suffering from poverty.

Karma: 10H:

Favourable: Putting effort into public utilities, construction of wayside inns, new roads, council halls, and temples, success in all attempts, increase in reputation, increase in influence, rise in the profession, acquisition of subordinates, completing the undertaking commenced by him, leading a happy life, widely renowned, settling in a permanent position, being discreet and amicable, commanding great respect.

Unfavourable: Failures in efforts, loss of honour, ruin to subordinates, breaks in the profession, diseases in the ankle, exile, anything done by the person becomes fruitless, wicked in behaviour, fruitless travel to foreign lands, inauspicious happenings, leading a bad life and suffering troubles.

Lābha: 11H:

Favourable: Reduction of grief, accomplishment of desired objects, a gain of fresh sources of wealth and articles signified by the Graha, an interrupted influx of wealth, pleasant meeting with his kinsmen and friends, being served by servants, domestic happiness, and great prosperity.

Unfavourable: Illness to the elder brother and children, ailment in the left ear and legs, but the person gains articles of the Graha, evil tidings, suffering from misery, deception, and ear disease.

Vyāya: 12H:

Favourable: Heavy expenditure for good purposes, meritorious acts, gradual termination of previously committed sinful actions, recovery from illnesses, royal honours.

Unfavourable: Squandering of wealth, falling from a position, troubles in the feet and left eye, falling due to carelessness and sinful actions, suffering from various diseases, dishonour, and bondage, wealth disappears like the Kṛṣṇapakṣa Candra.

Āratī: Dhanyavād Guruji!

Jayanta: Guruji, kindly tell us about the application of this Daśā to the Varga Kuṇḍalī.

Ācārya: You "must not" compute this Daśā independently for Varga Kuṇḍalī. But you can still use this for the Varga Kuṇḍalīs. Here is how:

(1) Whichever Daśā is current, focus on that Daśā Rāśi in different Varga Kuṇḍalīs. If that Rāśi is fortified in a Varga, the matters of that Varga flourish. However, if the Rāśi is afflicted in a Varga, the matters of that Varga suffer.

(2) Find the Prāṇi Grahas in that Rāśi in the Varga from (a) Varga Lagna and (b) Daśālagna.

(3) Like in the case of Rāśikuṇḍalī, study the Graha placements from the Daśālagna.

(4) If you have the capacity, you can construct individual Aṣṭakavarga of the Varga Kuṇḍalīs and identify the Aṣṭakavarga scores in Sarvāṣṭakavarga and Bhinnāṣṭakavarga. Use the same principles as mentioned above.

(5) Always examine the Varga Gocaras. The Varga Gocaras are the Gocara of the Grahas through the relevant Vargas.

(6) Always restrict to the matters governed by the Varga. But you can use Ṣaṣṭhyāñśa Varga for all judging the entire life experiences.

Jayanta: Dhanyavād, Guruji. Should we also create Daśāpraveśa Cakra for this Daśā?

Ācārya: Yes, you must cast Daśāpraveśa Cakra for all Daśās, Antardaśās and other sub-Daśās. They bestow crucial insights on the workings of the Daśā.

Jayanta: For that, what year definition must we use?

Ācārya: Since it is a Rāśidaśā, use True Sauravarṣa, which is based on the true motion of Sūrya in the zodiac.

Jayanta: Kindly summarize the rules of reading Daśāpraveśa Cakra.

Ācārya: You can check my previous volumes, where I have extensively dealt with Daśāpraveśa Cakra. But let me give you the high-level rules.

(1) In Daśāpraveśa Cakra, the focus is mostly on the Daśālagna than the Daśāpraveśa Cakra Lagna. Daśālagna = 75%, Daśāpraveśa Cakra Lagna = 25%.

(2) Find the Rāśis that has Śubha Yogas and Aśubha Yogas. The Antardaśā of the Rāśis with Śubha Yogas will be favourable, and the Antardaśā of the Aśubha Yogas will be unfavourable.

(3) Find the Grahas in or aspecting the Daśālagna in Daśāpraveśa Cakra. Also, check the Bhāva from Daśālagna, the Daśeśa is placed. These will tell us about the significant events in the Daśā.

Jayanta: Should we cast Aṣṭakavarga of Daśāpraveśa Cakra?

Ācārya: If you have the means to do so, you can do that. That will give you additional insights. But that may be time-consuming.

Jayanta: What is next?

Ācārya: You must also examine the effects provided by Maharṣi Parāśara:

Effects of Grahas occupying or owning the Daśārāśi:

Sūrya: ill health due to blood or bile troubles.

Candra: gain of wealth and clothes, name and fame and birth of children.

Maṅgala: bilious fever, gout, and wounds.

Budha: acquisition of wealth and birth of children.

Guru: increase in the number of children, acquisition of wealth and enjoyment.

Śukra: acquisition of learning, marriage and gain of wealth.

Śani: all kinds of adverse happenings.

Effects of Navāñśa-Navanavāñśa pair: In assessing the net effects, the nature of the Graha occupying the Rāśi should also be considered.

(1) Meṣa Navāñśa: (Savya flow)

(1) Meṣa-Meṣa: distress due to troubles caused by the pollution of blood.

(2) Meṣa-Vṛṣabha: increase in wealth and agricultural product.

(3) Meṣa-Mithuna: advancement of knowledge.

(4) Meṣa-Karka: acquisition of wealth.

(5) Meṣa-Siṅha: danger from enemies.

(6) Meṣa-Kanyā: distress to wife.

(7) Meṣa-Tulā: kingship.

(8) Meṣa-Vṛścika: Vṛścika death.

(9) Meṣa-Dhanu: acquisition of wealth.

(2) Vṛṣabha Navāñśa: (Savya-Apasavya flow)

(1) Vṛṣabha-Makara: the tendency to perform undesirable deeds along with more adverse effects.

(2) Vṛṣabha-Kumbha: profits in business.

(3) Vṛṣabha-Mīna: success in all ventures. < *Siṅhavlokana*

(4) Vṛṣabha-Vṛścika^: danger from fire.

(5) Vṛṣabha-Tulā^: recognition from Government and reverence from all.

(6) Vṛṣabha-Kanyā^: danger from enemies.< *Maṇḍūka*

(7) Vṛṣabha-Karka^: distress to wife.<*Marakaṭa*

(8) Vṛṣabha-Siṅha^: diseases of eyes. < *Maṇḍūka*

(9) Vṛṣabha-Mithuna^: obstacles in earning a livelihood.

(3) Mithuna Navāñśa: (Apasavya-Savya flow)

(1) Mithuna-Vṛṣabha^: acquisition of wealth.

(2) Mithuna-Meṣa^: attacks of fever.

(3) Mithuna-Mīna^: affectionate relations with maternal uncle.

(4) Mithuna-Kumbha^: increase in the number of enemies.

(5) Mithuna-Makara^: danger from thieves.

(6) Mithuna-Dhanu^: increase in the stock of weapons. < *Siṅhavlokana*

(7) Mithuna-Meṣa: injury by some weapon.

(8) Mithuna-Vṛṣabha: quarrels or bickering.

(9) Mithuna-Mithuna: enjoyment.

(4) Karka Navāñśa: (Savya flow)

(1) Karka-Karka: distress.

(2) Karka-Siṅha: displeasure of the sovereign.

(3) Karka-Kanyā: reverence from kinsmen.

(4) Karka-Tulā: beneficence.

(5) Karka-Vṛścika: creation of obstacles by father.

(6) Karka-Dhanu: increase of learning and wealth.

(7) Karka-Makara: danger from water.

(8) Karka-Kumbha: increase in the production of agricultural products.

(9) Karka-Mīna: acquisition of more wealth and enjoyment.

(5) Siṅha Navāñśa: (Apasavya flow)

(1) Siṅha-Vṛścika^: distress and disputes.

(2) Siṅha-Tulā^: extraordinary gains.

(3) Siṅha-Kanyā^: gains of wealth. < *Maṇḍūka*

(4) Siṅha-Karka^: danger from wild animals. < *Marakaṭa*

(5) Siṅha-Siṅha^: birth of a son. < *Maṇḍūka*

(6) Siṅha-Mithuna^: increase of enemies.

(7) Siṅha-Vṛṣabha^: gains from the sale of cattle

(8) Siṅha-Meṣa^: danger from animals

(9) Siṅha-Mīna^: journeys to distant places.

(6) Kanyā Navāñśa: (Apasavya-Savya flow)

(1) Kanyā-Kumbha^: acquisition of wealth

(2) Kanyā-Makara^: financial gains

(3) Kanyā-Dhanu^: mingling with kinsmen. < *Siṅhavlokana*

(4) Kanyā-Meṣa: happiness from mother

(5) Kanyā-Vṛṣabha: the birth of children

(6) Kanyā-Mithuna: increase in enemies.

(7) Kanyā-Karka: love with some woman

(8) Kanyā-Siṅha: aggravation of diseases

(9) Kanyā-Kanyā: the birth of children.

(7) Tulā Navāṅśa: (Savya-Apasavya flow)

(1) Tulā-Tulā: financial gains

(2) Tulā-Vṛścika: good relations with kinsmen

(3) Tulā-Dhanu: happiness from father

(4) Tulā-Makara: disputes with mother

(5) Tulā-Kumbha: the birth of a son and financial gains

(6) Tulā-Mīna: entanglement with enemies < *Siṅhavlokana*

(7) Tulā-Vṛścika^: disputes with women

(8) Tulā-Tulā^: danger from water

(9) Tulā-Kanyā^: more financial gains.

(8) Vṛścika Navāṅśa: (Apasavya flow)

(1) Vṛścika-Karka^: financial gains< Marakaṭa

(2) Vṛścika-Siṅha^: opposition to the king< Maṇḍūka

(3) Vṛścika-Mithuna^: acquisition of land

(4) Vṛścika-Vṛṣabha^: financial gains

(5) Vṛścika-Meṣa^: danger from reptiles

(6) Vṛścika-Mīna^: danger from water

(7) Vṛścika-Kumbha^: profits in business

(8) Vṛścika-Makara^: suffering from diseases

(9) Vṛścika-Dhanu^: financial gains.

(9) Dhanu Navāṅśa: (Savya flow)

(1) Dhanu-Meṣa: financial gains

(2) Dhanu-Vṛṣabha: acquisition of more land

(3) Dhanu-Mithuna: success in ventures

(4) Dhanu-Karka: success all round

(5) Dhanu-Siṅha: increase in the accumulated wealth

(6) Dhanu-Kanyā: disputes

(7) Dhanu-Tulā: financial gains

(8) Dhanu-Vṛścika: affliction with diseases

(9) Dhanu-Dhanu: happiness from children.

(10) Makara Navāṅśa: (Savya-Apasavya flow)

(1) Makara-Makara: happiness from children

(2) Makara-Kumbha: gain of agricultural products

(3) Makara-Mīna: well-being < *Siṅhavlokana*

(4) Makara-Vṛścika^: danger from poison

(5) Makara-Tulā^: financial gains

(6) Makara-Kanyā^: increase in enemies. < *Maṇḍūka*

(7) Makara-Karka^: acquisition of property < *Marakaṭa*

(8) Makara-Siṅha^: danger from wild animals <*Maṇḍūka*

(9) Makara-Mithuna^ danger of falling from a tree

(11) Kumbha Navāñśa: (Apasavya-Savya flow)

(1) Kumbha-Vṛṣabha^: financial gains

(2) Kumbha-Meṣa^: diseases of the eyes

(3) Kumbha-Mīna^: journeys to distant places

(4) Kumbha-Kumbha^: increase in wealth.

(5) Kumbha-Makara^: success in all kinds of ventures

(6) Kumbha-Dhanu^: more enemies < *Siṅhavlokana*

(7) Kumbha-Meṣa: loss of happiness and enjoyment

(8) Kumbha-Vṛṣabha: death

(9) Kumbha-Mithuna: wellbeing.

(12) Mīna Navāñśa (Savya flow)

(1) Mīna-Karka: increase in wealth.

(2) Mīna-Siṅha: recognition by Government

(3) Mīna-Kanyā: financial gains

(4) Mīna-Tulā: gains from all sources

(5) Mīna-Vṛścika: fever

(6) Mīna-Dhanu: more enemies

(7) Mīna-Makara: conjugal disputes

(8) Mīna-Kumbha: danger from water

(9) Mīna-Mīna: good fortune all-round.

Kailāśa: What is the meaning of Savya, Savya-Apasavya, Apasavya-Savya and Apasavya flow?

Ācārya: They indicate the flow of Savya and Apasavya Navanavāñśas in a Navāñśa.

In the *Savya flow* (Meṣa-Karka-Dhanu-Mīna), all Navanavāñśas are Savya.

In the *Savya-Apasavya flow* (Vṛṣabha, Tulā, Makara), the Navanavāñśas move from Savya to Apasavya.

In the *Apasavya-Savya flow* (Mithuna, Kanyā, Kumbha), the Navanavāñśas move from Apasavya to Savya.

In the *Apasavya flow* (Siṅha, Vṛścika), all Navanavāñśas are Apasavya.

Kailāśa: Oh, I see!

Ācārya: In this manner, on the Kālacakra, prepared on the basis of Pāda of the Janma Nakṣatra, the Daśās of the Navāñśa Rāśis and their duration can be assessed, and prediction can be made for the *whole life* of the native.

Appropriate *remedial measures* (recitation of Mantras, oblations, etc.) should be taken to alleviate the adverse effects caused by Aśubha Daśās.

Jayanta: That makes sense, Guruji!

Ācārya: Maharṣi Parāśara concludes the Daśā by stating that the effects of Daśā in Rājayoga, etc. (as stated earlier) should be applied judiciously in Kālacakra Daśā. What he mentions here are the brief effects of Kālacakra. For detailed effects, all aspects of the Kuṇḍalī must be examined.

Jayanta: Noted, Guruji. Let us apply this in a Kuṇḍalī and see if it works.

Ācārya: Alright. Let us apply this in my Kuṇḍalī. In the Kuṇḍalī, Candra's sphuṭa is Vṛścika 16:30:58.43, Anurādhā4. Jayanta, which Navāñśa it is associated with?

Jayanta: According to the table above, Anurādhā4 is mapped to Meṣa^ Navāñśa. But we can apply the simple formula you mentioned before. Anurādhā is Apasavya, and in regular Navāñśa, Candra is in Vṛścika Navāñśa. Since it is Apasavya, we must flip it to Meṣa. Therefore, in Kālacakra Navāñśa, Candra is in Meṣa^ Navāñśa. "^" symbolizes Apasavya Navāñśa.

Ācārya: Very well, Jayanta. What is Candra's Navāñśa sphuṭa?

Jayanta: How to determine, Candra's Navāñśa sphuṭa?

Ācārya: Follow the simple formula "mod (sphuṭa * 9, 30)".

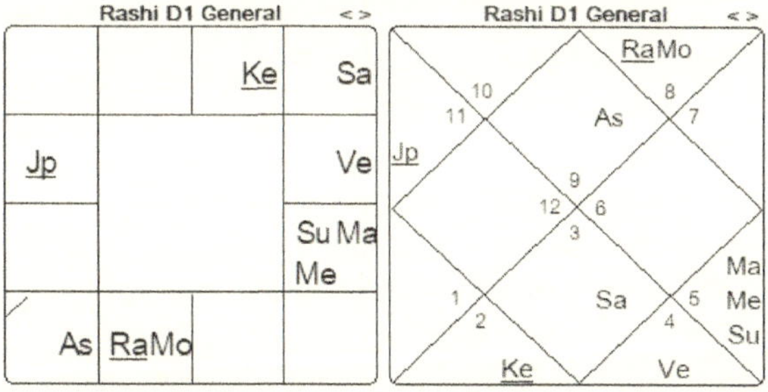

Jayanta: Alright, let me try. Candra is in Vṛścika. Candra's sphuṭa = (8-1) * 30 + 16 + 30/60 + 58.43/3600 = 226.512. Candra's Navāñśa sphuṭa is mod (226.512^ 9, 30) = 28.608.

Ācārya: That is right. Now find the Daśā elapsed. It is 28.608 / 30 * Rāśi Āyuṣa. Find how much has elapsed.

Jayanta: Candra is in Agni Navāñśa (Meṣa), whose Āyuṣa is 100y. So Daśā elapsed is 28.608 / 30 * 100 = 95.36. Daśā balance is 100 - 95.36 = 4.64.

Ācārya: Now find the Daśā at birth and how much is remaining.

Jayanta: The Daśā sequence for Savya-Meṣa is Meṣ-Vṛṣ-Mit-Kar-Siṅ-Kan-Tul-Vṛś-Dha. This is reversed for Apasavya Meṣa. So, the sequence for Apasavya-Meṣa is *Dha-Vṛś-Tul-Kan-Siṅ-Kar-Mit-Vṛṣ-Meṣ*. The duration of the Daśā and their cumulative duration is as follows.

Table 101

1	2	3	4	5	6	7	8	9
Dha	**Vṛś**	**Tul**	**Kan**	**Siṅ**	**Kar**	**Mit**	**Vṛṣ**	**Meṣ**
10	7	16	9	5	21	9	16	7
10	17	33	42	47	68	77	93	100

The person must be born in the last Daśā, which is Meṣa. Therefore, the person's birth occurred in Meṣa-Meṣa. The results are "distress due to troubles caused by the pollution of blood."

Ācārya: This is true as the person suffered from Bālāriṣṭa immediately after the birth. What is the next Daśā?

Jayanta: The person is born in the last Daśā of Meṣa Navāñśa. So, we must go to the Navanavāñśa Daśā of the next Navāñśa.

Ācārya: What is the next set of Navanavāñśa?

Jayanta: It should be Jyeṣṭhā1. Isn't it?

Ācārya: Yes, since Jyeṣṭhā is also Apasavya, we must move to that.

Jayanta: Jyeṣṭhā1 is mapped to Mīna^, and its Navanavāñśas are Mīn-Kum-Mak-Dha-Vṛś-Tul-Kan-Siṅ-Kar. The Daśā durations are:

Table 102

1	2	3	4	5	6	7	8	9
Mīn	**Kum**	**Mak**	**Dha**	**Vṛś**	**Tul**	**Kan**	**Siṅ**	**Kar**
10	4	4	10	7	16	9	5	21
10	14	18	28	35	51	60	65	86

So, the next Daśā is Mīna-Mīna. The results are: "good fortune all-round."

Ācārya: This was the saving grace, as the person was saved from Bālāriṣṭa. Also, Deha and Jīva are Kar and Mīn. The Rāśis are not afflicted, so the Daśā was not fatal.

Jayanta: The Daśā continued for 10 years, after which Mīna-Kumbha started.

Ācārya: Can you tell me why the native got married in his 31st year?

Jayanta: The Daśās and their dates are as follows:

Table 103

Navāñśa	Dasa	Duration	Start	End
Aries_9	Aries	4.634	25-Aug-74	13-Apr-79
Pisces_1	Pisces	10	13-Apr-79	13-Apr-89
Pisces_2	Aquarius	4	13-Apr-89	13-Apr-93
Pisces_3	Capricorn	4	13-Apr-93	13-Apr-97
Pisces_4	*Sagittarius*	*10*	*13-Apr-97*	*13-Apr-07*
Pisces_5	Scorpio	7	13-Apr-07	13-Apr-14
Pisces_6	Libra	16	13-Apr-14	13-Apr-30

Navāñśa	Dasa	Duration	Start	End
Pisces_7	Virgo	9	13-Apr-30	14-Apr-39
Pisces_8	Leo	5	14-Apr-39	13-Apr-44

Ācārya: Very good. You can go ahead with your analysis.

Jayanta: It occurred in *Mīna-Dhanu*. The Deha-Jīva for Dhanu is Meṣa and Dhanu. Both are not afflicted, so the period was not fatal. But Maharṣi Parāśara states that the person suffers from an increase of enemies.

Āratī: Kindly tell us the Deha and Jīva of the different Navāñśas.

Jayanta: Here you go. This is the same for both Savya and Apasavya Navāñśas and Navanavāñśas.

Table 104

Savya	Deha	Jīva
Meṣa	Meṣa	Dha
Vṛṣabha	Mak	Mit
Mithuna	Vṛṣ	Mit
Karka	Kar	Mīn
Siṅha	Vṛś	Mīn
Kanyā	Kum	Kan
Tulā	Tul	Kan
Vṛścika	Kar	Dha
Dhanu	Meṣ	Dha
Makara	Mak	Mit
Kumbha	Vṛṣ	Mit
Mīna	Kar	Mīn

Ācārya: The person suffered from several challenges as he had to undergo severe hardship and health troubles (fatigue) due to working in a non-governmental agency, travelling long distances to distant villages, and working under hot and sporadic climates of Jharkhand.

Jayanta: Let me focus on marriage.

From Daśārāśi (Dhanu), 7L Budha is in 9H. The Daśeśa dṛṣṭies 7H Mithuna and 7L Budha from Kumbha. This shows why marriage occurred in the Daśā.

Ācārya: That makes sense. Now, why did the person lose his father in that Feb 1994?

Jayanta: During that time, the person was running Mīna-Makara. This is not a good Daśā as per Maharṣi Parāśara, as the person suffers from conflicts and disputes. From Daśālagna Makara 9L Budha is in 8H, a Dusthāna. That indicates the danger to the father's life. Isn't it?

Ācārya: That is right as well. This shows that we must examine all Yogas from the Daśālagna. Now, tell me why there was childbirth in Sep 2006 and Sep 2007.

Jayanta: First child is born in Mīna-Dhanu, and the second child is born in Mīna-Vṛścika. 5H/5L from the Daśārāśi or Guru must get involved with this event.

The first child: From Dhanu, 5H is Meṣa, and 5L is Maṅgala. 5L is in 9H (Koṇa), promising children, and it is dṛṣṭied by Daśeśa and Putrakāraka Guru. This promises childbirth.

The second child: From Vṛścika, 5L is Guru in a Kendra. 5L and Putrakāraka Guru dṛṣṭies the Daśeśa Maṅgala. Daśeśa also dṛṣṭies 5H. This promises childbirth.

Ācārya: Now examine the Varga Kuṇḍalīs for marriage and childbirth.

Jayanta: The marriage should be seen from Navāñśa. The marriage occurred in Dhanu Daśā.

In the Navāñśa, Dhanu is 7H from Navāñśa Lagna, and it contains Dārākāraka Śukra. This promises marriage. From Daśālagna Dhanu, 7L Budha is in 9H promising marriage. Grahas in Trikoṇa promises the blessing of that Bhāva.

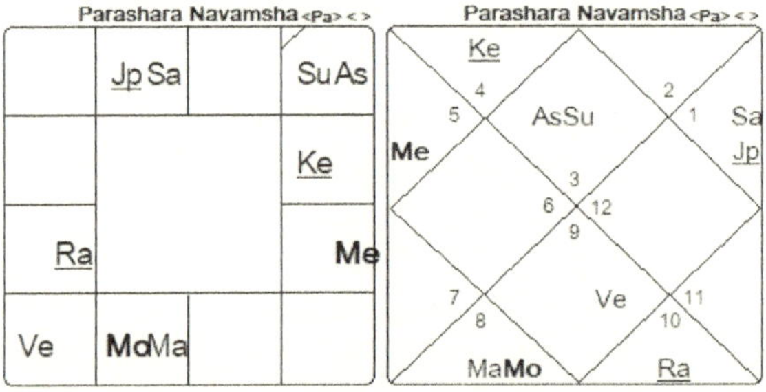

Ācārya: Very well! How about children?

Jayanta: Children should be examined from Saptāñśa.

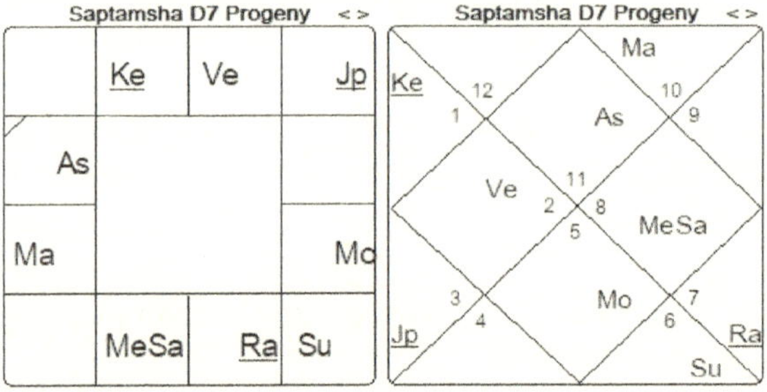

The first child is born in Dhanu. In Saptāñśa Dhanu is vacant. From Saptāñśa Lagna, the first child is denoted by 5H Mithuna. Mithuna has a Guru, and the first child is born in Guru's Rāśi.

The second child is born in Vṛścika. From Saptāñśa Lagna, the second child is denoted by 7H Siṅha. In Saptāñśa, Vṛścika has Budha and Śani. Śani is Saptāñśa Lagna in Vṛścika, promising children. In a Varga Kuṇḍalī, the Varga

Lagna and the Rāśi holding the Varga Lagneśa promise the indications of the Varga. The second child is seen from 7H, and 7L Śukra occupies that. Śukra aspects the Daśārāśi Vṛścika. This promises the second child.

Kailāśa: Guruji. What if the person was born Jyeṣṭhā last Pāda? What would have happened after the last Navanavāñśa of Jyeṣṭhā?

Jayanta: The Nakṣatra, Viśākhā Anurādhā and Jyeṣṭhā belong to Apasavya Tritārā. The Navāñśa mapping is as follows:

Dha* **Jye4**	Vṛś* **Viś1**	Tul* **Viś2**	Kan* **Viś3**
Mak* **Jye3**			Siṅ* **Viś4**
Kum* **Jye2**			Kar* **Anu1**
Mīn* **Jye1**	Meṣ* **Anu4**	Vṛṣ* **Anu3**	Mit* **Anu2**

Jyeṣṭhā4 ends with Dhanu. After which the Navāñśa will move to Vṛścika and its Navanavāñśa sequence. Jyestha4 (Dhanu^) is Dha-Vṛś-Tul-Kan-Siṅ-Kar-Mit-Vṛṣ-Meṣ. This will be followed by Vṛścika^, which is Dha^-Mak^-Kum^-Mīn^-Meṣ^-Vṛṣ^-Mit^-Siṅ^-Kar^. So, the Meṣa Daśā will be followed by Dhanu, which is a Siṅhavlokana jump.

Kailāśa: Oh, I see! Will it not be followed by Mūla1?

Ācārya: The Apasavya Triad is a self-contained whole, and the Antardaśā would continue with that. For a moment, let us suppose after Jyeṣṭha4, it moved to Mūla1. Mūla is a Savya Tārā. So, it's Kālacakra is:

Mīn **UĀṣ4**	Meṣ **Mūl1**	Vṛṣ **Mūl2**	Mit **Mūl3**
Kum **UĀṣ3**			Kar **Mūl4**
Mak **UĀṣ2**			Siṅ **PĀṣ1**
Dha **UĀṣ1**	Vṛś **PĀṣ4**	Tul **PĀṣ3**	Kan **PĀṣ2**

Mūla1 is mapped to Savya Meṣa, whose Navanavāñśa sequence is Meṣ-Vṛṣ-Mit-Kar-Siṅ-Kan-Tul-Vṛś-Dha. Jyeṣṭhā4 Navanavāñśa sequence is Dha-Vṛś-Tul-Kan-Siṅ-Kar-Mit-Vṛṣ-Meṣ. So, the end of Jyeṣṭhā is Meṣa, and the beginning of Mūla is also Meṣa. Do you think two Daśās can be of the same Rāśis?

Kailāśa: I can see where you are coming from. Meṣa Daśā followed by Meṣa Daśā does not make sense. I now understand why Apasavya Dhanu Navāñśa must move to Apasavya Vṛścika (instead of Savya Meṣa).

Ācārya: Glad that you can see the pattern and understand the rationale of keeping a Nakṣatra Triad as a self-contained whole.

Jayanta: Guruji! This makes sense.

Sunidhi: Guruji, the computations which you have shown above. Is this available in Jagannātha Horā?

Ācārya: Śrī PVR Nṛsiṅha Rao provided several options, but none of my computations. In my computations, the Daśā sequence and Dates are:

Table 105

Navāñśa	Daśā	Duration	Start	End
Meṣa^	Meṣa	4.634	25-Aug-74	13-Apr-79
Mīna^	Mīna	10	13-Apr-79	13-Apr-89
Mīna^	Kumbha	4	13-Apr-89	13-Apr-93
Mīna^	Makara	4	13-Apr-93	13-Apr-97
Mīna^	Dhanu	10	13-Apr-97	13-Apr-07
Mīna^	Vṛścika	7	13-Apr-07	13-Apr-14
Mīna^	Tulā	16	13-Apr-14	13-Apr-30
Mīna^	Kanyā	9	13-Apr-30	14-Apr-39
Mīna^	Siṅha	5	14-Apr-39	13-Apr-44
Mīna^	Karka	21	13-Apr-44	13-Apr-65

"^" represents Apasavya Navāñśa.

Jayanta, can you list down the Daśās given by the different options of Jagannātha Horā?

Option 1:

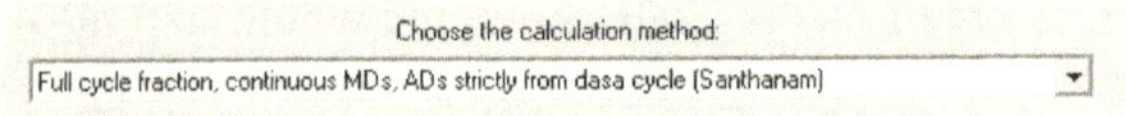

Kalachakra Dasa (From Moon of D-1, Apasavya, Paramayush: 83 yr, Deha: Ar, Jiva: Sg):

Maha Dasas:

Ta (Aswi2): 1969-07-11 - 1985-07-11

Ar (Aswi1): 1985-07-11 - 1992-07-11

Pi (Reva4): 1992-07-11 - 2002-07-12

Aq (Reva3): 2002-07-12 - 2006-07-12

Cp (Reva2): 2006-07-12 - 2010-07-12

Sg (Reva1): 2010-07-12 - 2020-07-11

Sc (UBha4): 2020-07-11 - 2027-07-12

Li (UBha3): 2027-07-12 - 2043-07-12

Vi (UBha2): 2043-07-12 - 2052-07-11

Option 2:

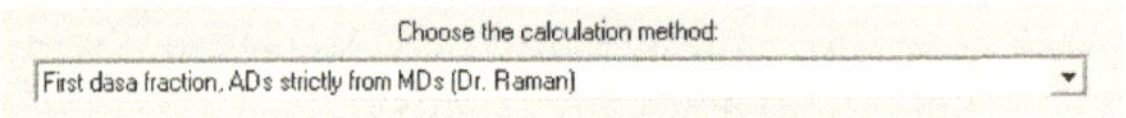

Kalachakra Dasa (From Moon of D-1, Apasavya, Paramayush: 100 yr, Deha: Ar, Jiva: Sg):

Maha Dasas:

Sg (Krit1): 1965-02-03 — 1975-02-03

Sc (Bhar4): 1975-02-03 — 1982-02-03

Li (Bhar3): 1982-02-03 — 1998-02-03

Vi (Bhar2): 1998-02-03 — 2007-02-04

Le (Bhar1): 2007-02-04 — 2012-02-04

Cn (Aswi4): 2012-02-04 — 2033-02-03

Ge (Aswi3): 2033-02-03 — 2042-02-04

Ta (Aswi2): 2042-02-04 — 2058-02-04

Ar (Aswi1): 2058-02-04 — 2065-02-04

Option 3:

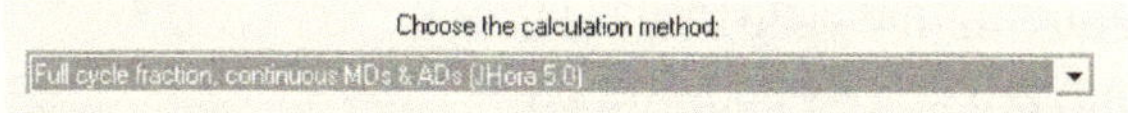

Kalachakra Dasa (From Moon of D-1, Apasavya, Paramayush: 83 yr, Deha: Ar, Jiva: Sg):

Maha Dasas:

Ta (Aswi2): 1969-07-11 — 1985-07-11

Ar (Aswi1): 1985-07-11 — 1992-07-11

Pi (Reva4): 1992-07-11 — 2002-07-12

Aq (Reva3): 2002-07-12 — 2006-07-12

Cp (Reva2): 2006-07-12 — 2010-07-12

Sg (Reva1): 2010-07-12 — 2020-07-11

Sc (UBha4): 2020-07-11 — 2027-07-12

Li (UBha3): 2027-07-12 — 2043-07-12

Vi (UBha2): 2043-07-12 — 2052-07-11

Option 4:

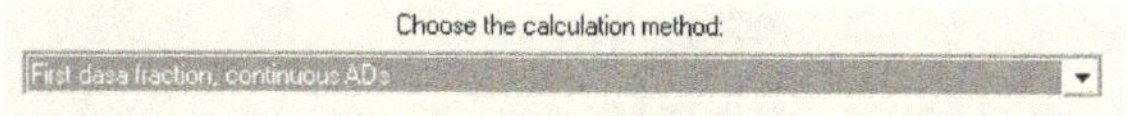

Kalachakra Dasa (From Moon of D-1, Apasavya, Paramayush: 100 yr, Deha: Ar, Jiva: Sg):

Maha Dasas:

Sg (Krit1): 1965-02-03 — 1975-02-03

Sc (Bhar4): 1975-02-03 — 1982-02-03

Li (Bhar3): 1982-02-03 — 1998-02-03

Vi (Bhar2): 1998-02-03 — 2007-02-04

Le (Bhar1): 2007-02-04 — 2012-02-04

Cn (Aswi4): 2012-02-04 — 2033-02-03

Ge (Aswi3): 2033-02-03 — 2042-02-04

Ta (Aswi2): 2042-02-04 — 2058-02-04

Ar (Aswi1): 2058-02-04 — 2065-02-04

Option 5:

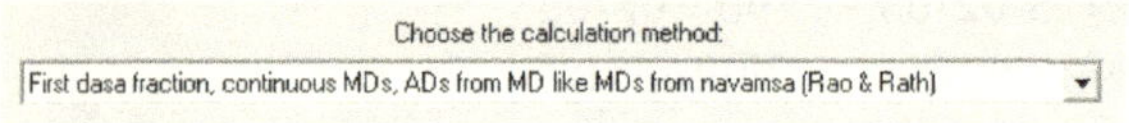

Kalachakra Dasa (From Moon of D-1, Apasavya, Paramayush: 100 yr, Deha: Ar, Jiva: Sg):

Maha Dasas:

Sg (Krit1): 1965-02-03 — 1975-02-03

Sc (Bhar4): 1975-02-03 — 1982-02-03

Li (Bhar3): 1982-02-03 — 1998-02-03

Vi (Bhar2): 1998-02-03 — 2007-02-04

Le (Bhar1): 2007-02-04 — 2012-02-04

Cn (Aswi4): 2012-02-04 — 2033-02-03

Ge (Aswi3): 2033-02-03 — 2042-02-04

Ta (Aswi2): 2042-02-04 — 2058-02-04

Ar (Aswi1): 2058-02-04 — 2065-02-04

Option 6:

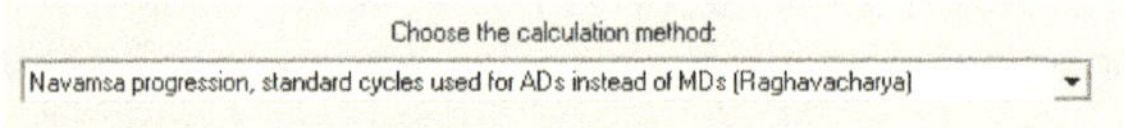

Kalachakra Dasa (From Moon of D-1, Apasavya, Paramayush: 88 yr, Deha: Ar, Jiva: Sg):

Maha Dasas:

Ar (Anu4): 1967-12-18 — 1974-12-18

Pi (Jye1): 1974-12-18 — 1984-12-17

Aq (Jye2): 1984-12-17 — 1988-12-17

Cp (Jye3): 1988-12-17 — 1992-12-17

Sg (Jye4): 1992-12-17 — 2002-12-18

Ar (Mool1): 2002-12-18 — 2009-12-18

Ta (Mool2): 2009-12-18 — 2025-12-18

Ge (Mool3): 2025-12-18 — 2034-12-18

Cn (Mool4): 2034-12-18 — 2055-12-18

Option 7:

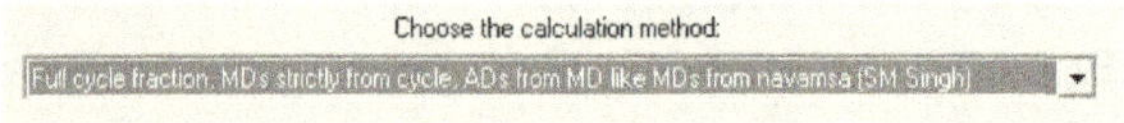

Kalachakra Dasa (From Moon of D-1, Apasavya, Paramayush: 100 yr, Deha: Ar, Jiva: Sg):

Maha Dasas:

Ar (Aswi1): 1972-02-26 — 1979-02-25

Sg (Krit1): 1979-02-25 — 1989-02-25

Sc (Bhar4): 1989-02-25 — 1996-02-26

Li (Bhar3): 1996-02-26 — 2012-02-26

Vi (Bhar2): 2012-02-26 — 2021-02-25

Le (Bhar1): 2021-02-25 — 2026-02-26

Cn (Aswi4): 2026-02-26 — 2047-02-26

Ge (Aswi3): 2047-02-26 — 2056-02-26

Ta (Aswi2): 2056-02-26 — 2072-02-26

Jayanta: Guruji, how is it that none of the options match your computations?

Ācārya: Different scholars have different interpretations of the Daśā. I was not satisfied with any of them, which is why, I have delineated the option which I found consistent. I have presented them here for the seekers to review, accept or reject it.

Jayanta: But can you tell us what are the crucial points of differences among the Jyotiṣa scholars?

Ācārya: Yes, I will point out some of them. But you must study their works on your own to see their interpretations. There is no point repeating everything they said at this place.

Jayanta: That will be a good start. Kindly elaborate on the key differences in opinions.

Ācārya: Here are the contentions.

Contention 1: How to prorate the first Daśā?

Option 1: Find Nakṣatra Pāda elapsed by Candra and apply this to the entire duration of the Navanavāñśa. This is called the full cycle fraction method. This is *recommended.*

Option 2: Find the Nakṣatra Pāda elapsed by Candra and apply this to the first Navanavāñśa of the Nakṣatra Pāda. This is called the first Daśā fraction method. This is *not* recommended.

Contention 2: What is the first Daśā?

Option 1: The first Daśā is of the Navanavāñśa occupied by Candra. This is based on the full cycle fraction method. This is *recommended.*

Option 2: The first Daśā is of the first Navanavāñśa of Candra's Nakṣatra Pāda. This is *not* recommended.

Contention 3: What Navāñśa is associated with Rohiṇī4? Rohiṇī is a Apasavya Nakṣatra.

Option1: Rohini4 is mapped to Siṅha Navāñśa. Rohiṇī1 is mapped to Vṛścika, Rohiṇī2 - Tulā, Rohiṇī3 - Kanyā and Rohiṇī4 - Siṅha. This is *recommended.* In the Kālacakra Navāñśa, Rohiṇī4 is mapped to Siṅha. But when we find the Navanavāñśa sequence, Rohiṇī4 is mapped to Karka. Many scholars miss this point and get erroneous results.

Option2: Rohiṇī4 is mapped to Karka Navāñśa. This is *not* recommended. The mapping of Rohiṇī4 to Karka is applicable to Navanavāñśa and not Navāñśa. This subtle distinction must be realized.

Jayanta: Guruji, regarding contention 3, how can you be so confident? Isn't it supposed to be consistent whether Rohini4 is mapped to Navāñśa or Navanavāñśa? I am not convinced about the need for the distinction.

Ācārya: You have asked a pertinent question. Let us examine this topic in detail. Maharṣi Parāśara states:

46.76. In the 4th Pāda of Rohiṇī, Vṛścika will be Deha and Mīna Jiva and the Lords of the Rāśis Mīna-Meṣa-Vṛṣabha-Mithuna-Siṅha-Karka-Kanyā-Tulā-Vṛścika will be the Lords.

Jayanta, can you tell me the Navanavāñśa sequence is related to which Navāñśa?

Jayanta: The Navāñśa sequence for Savya Siṅha is Vṛś^-Tul^-Kan^-Kar^-Siṅ^-Mit^-Vṛṣ^-Meṣ^-Mīn^. Therefore, the sequence for Apasavya Siṅha is Mīn^-Meṣ^-Vṛṣ^-Mit^-Siṅ^-Kar^-Kan^-Tul^-Vṛś^. Maharṣi Parāśara maps Rohiṇī4 to Apasavya Siṅha.

Ācārya: Now you see why I said that Rohiṇī4 is mapped to Siṅha instead of Karka.

Jayanta: I can see that, Guruji. Also, Apasavya Karka is Mīn-Kum-Mak-Dha-Vṛś-Tul-Kan-Siṅ-Kar. This is not what Maharṣi Parāśara mentions.

Ācārya: Now, also note what Maharṣi Parāśara has to say about Mṛgaśirā1 Nakṣatra-Pāda.

46.78. In the 1st Pad of Mṛgaśirā, Karka is Deha and Mīna is Jiva, and the Lords of the Rāśis Mīna-Kumbha-Makara-Dhanu-Vṛścika-Tulā-Kanyā-Siṅha-Karka will be the Dasha Lords in this order.

Can you check Jayanta? This Navanavāñśa sequence is mapped to which Nakṣatra-Pāda?

Jayanta: Guruji, this is mapped to Apasavya Karka.

Kailāśa: Gurubhrāta, how can you say that this Navanavāñśa sequence is mapped to Karka Navāñśa?

Jayanta: That is straightforward. This is the Utkrama (reverse) order of Savya Karka Navāñśa.

Kailāśa: Oh, I see. That makes sense.

Ācārya: Now you see, Jayanta, why Rohiṇī4 is mapped to Siṅha and Mṛgaśirā1 is mapped to Karka. Does this clear your doubt now that no *Karka-Siṅha flipping* is in the Apasavya Navāñśa?

Jayanta: It does. But how do we know that there is a flipping of the Navanavāñśa?

Ācārya: That is straightforward. Check the Mṛgaśirā4 Nakṣatra-Pāda, mapped to Apasavya Meṣa^ Navāñśa. Regarding this, Maharṣi Parāśara states:

46.81: In the 4th Pāda of Mṛgaśirā, Meṣa will be Deha and Dhanu Jiva and the Lords of the Rāśis Dhanu-Vṛścika-Tulā-Kanyā-Siṅha-Karka-Mithuna-Vṛṣabha-Meṣa will be the Daśā Lords.

Can you see the sequence of Kanyā-Siṅha-Karka-Mithuna? This is because of the Karka-Siṅha flip in the Apasavya Navanavāñśa. *You should see the subtle difference between Apasavya Navāñśa and Apasavya Navanavāñśa.*

Jayanta: This is unambiguously clear, Guruji. Dhanyavād for the detailed elaboration. I have another question. Guruji! Can you explain the "Rath and Rao" method of Jagannath Hora?

Ācārya: The following is from Śrī PVR Nṛsiṅha Rao's response to a question on an internet forum.

> Some Background on the "Rao & Rath" Method
>
> This "Rao & Rath" method of Kālacakra Daśā was discovered by me in a 1930 book authored in Telugu language by Sri Raghavacharya. I shared it with Pt Rath when he stayed at my house several years ago. Though I said I had not yet fully figured it out and wanted to work more on it, Pt Rath asked me to urgently write a paper on it for the upcoming SJC conference. I obliged and sent it to him. It was published under our two names and presented by Pt Rath at the conference.
>
> I worked further on this and later figured out Raghavacharya's actual teachings. I found them to be more logical than what I had [mis]understood before (and had mentioned to Sanjay and had written down for the SJC conference).
>
> I added it to JHora as "Raghavacharya method". Just as Viñśottarī Daśā is a Nakṣatra progression, the Raghavacharya method is a Navāñśa progression. All other methods of Kalachakra Daśā confuse Antardaśā tables taught by Parāśara for Mahādaśā tables. Raghavacharya method given in JHora uses those tables for Antardaśās and takes Mahādaśās simply by counting 9 Navāñśa from janma Navāñśa (just as you take 9 Nakṣatras for Viñśottarī Daśā)!
>
> This is the most logical interpretation of Kālacakra Daśā that I have ever seen. Sadly, there was a lot of confusion before I discovered this, and there continues to be a lot of confusion even after the simple and beautiful philosophy is discovered, understood, and shared on the internet. :-(
>
> I will soon write about my understanding of Kalachakra Daśā in Jyotish writings. I personally do not recommend the "Rao & Rath" method. It was half-baked research that was hastily presented. I disown it and wish people did (and do) not have to waste their time on it. Nevertheless, I will support it in JHora and fix the error in Apasavya Nakṣatras soon.
>
> Best regards,
>
> Narasimha

Jayanta: So, what is Raghavacharya's method?

Kailāśa: As per the options mentioned above, Option 6 is this method.

Ar (Anu4): 1967-09-11 — 1974-09-11

Pi (Jye1): 1974-09-11 — 1984-09-10

Aq (Jye2): 1984-09-10 — 1988-09-10

Cp (Jye3): 1988-09-10 — 1992-09-10

Sg (Jye4): 1992-09-10 — 2002-09-11

Ar (Mool1): 2002-09-11 — 2009-09-11

Ta (Mool2): 2009-09-11 — 2025-09-11

Ge (Mool3): 2025-09-11 — 2034-09-11

Cn (Mool4): 2034-09-11 — 2055-09-11

Ācārya: In this method, you can see that Anurādhā4 is mapped to Meṣa Apasavya Navāñśa. After that, the Daśā moves through Mīna, Kumbha, Makara, and Dhanu, and the Apasavya Cakra ends. After that, the Daśā moves to Savya Cakra, starting from Meṣa and continuing through Vṛṣabha, Mithuna and Karka.

Jayanta: So, there is no concept of Navanavāñśas contained in a Nakṣatra Pāda?

Ācārya: No, that principle is not followed, which makes this approach flawed. Maharṣi clearly states the results of the Navanavāñśas (nine Daśās) for every Navāñśa (Nakṣatra Pāda).

Kailāśa: What did Śrī Nṛsiṅha Rao respond to?

Ācārya: He responded to this email to the Sohamsa group.

om gurave namah

Dear Jyotishi

I was studying the Kālacakra Daśā for one chart today and found, to my amazement, that ALL the SIX methods of Kālacakra Daśā calculation given in Jagannath Hora, including the one called *Rao and Rath*, are WRONG.

Please do not use them and if you do so, it's your risk and don't ask me questions or help. The correct one is in Shri Jyoti Star. I have checked Jyeṣṭhā 4th Pada for this and need to check all others. Get your copy from www.vedicsoftware.com.

The correct order for this pada should be Pi-Ar-... and if we use full cycle iteration, then in the particular case I was studying, we get Cn-Vi...

For more details, please get hold of the Kalachakra paper/slides I used in London.

Best wishes

Sanjay Rath

Kailāśa: Noted, Guruji. Can you tell us about the calculations of Śrī Jyoti Star?

Ācārya: Here you go.

KalaCakra Ji:Sg/De:Ar

Start Date	Age	Dashas
12/ 4/ 1972	-2.4	Ari
13/ 4/ 1979	4.6	Pis
12/ 4/ 1989	14.6	Aqu
12/ 4/ 1993	18.6	Cap
12/ 4/ 1997	22.6	Sag
13/ 4/ 2007	32.6	Sco
13/ 4/ 2014 no	39.6	Libr
13/ 4/ 2030	55.6	Virg
13/ 4/ 2039	64.6	Leo
13/ 4/ 2044	69.6	Can
13/ 4/ 2065	90.6	Gem
13/ 4/ 2074	99.6	Tau
13/ 4/ 2090	115.6	Ari

In this Daśā, the first Daśā is of Meṣa, after which it is Mīna, Kumbha, Makara, Dhanu, Vṛścika, Tulā, Kanyā... Meṣa, in the Apasavya order.

The matches my calculation, but you must test with other cases to see if the computations are accurate. You may see some differences based on what Ayanāñśa you use. *I use "Sṛṣṭi Ayanāñśa", which is approximately Traditional Lahiri + 0°6'50".*

Kailāśa: How are the Antardaśās?

Ācārya: It is different from my calculation.

This is from Śrī Jyoti Star

KalaCakra Ji:Sg/De:Ar

Start Date	Age	Dashas	
17/ 12/ 1973	-0.7	Ari	Libr
30/ 1/ 1975	0.4	Ari	Virg
17/ 9/ 1975	1.1	Ari	Leo
23/ 1/ 1976	1.4	Ari	Can
13/ 7/ 1977	2.9	Ari	Gem
28/ 2/ 1978	3.5	Ari	Tau
13/ 4/ 1979	**4.6**	**Pis**	**Pis**
11/ 6/ 1980	5.8	Pis	Aqu
27/ 11/ 1980	6.3	Pis	Cap
16/ 5/ 1981	6.7	Pis	Sag
15/ 7/ 1982	7.9	Pis	Sco
8/ 5/ 1983	8.7	Pis	Libr
18/ 3/ 1985	10.6	Pis	Virg

As per my calculation, it is the following Antardaśā of Mīna Daśā.

Table 106

Daśā	Antardaśā	Start	End
Mīna	Karka	13-Apr-79	21-Sep-81
Mīna	Siṅha	21-Sep-81	22-Apr-82
Mīna	Kanyā	22-Apr-82	9-May-83
Mīna	Tulā	9-May-83	18-Mar-85
Mīna	Vṛścika	18-Mar-85	10-Jan-86
Mīna	Dhanu	10-Jan-86	10-Mar-87
Mīna	Makara	10-Mar-87	27-Aug-87

Daśā	Antardaśā	Start	End
Mīna	Kumbha	27-Aug-87	13-Feb-88
Mīna	Mīna	13-Feb-88	13-Apr-89

The Antardaśā given for Mīna Daśā by Śrī Jyoti Star is incorrect since as per Kālacakra, Mīna is subdivided into Kar-Siṅ-Kan-Tul-Vṛś-Dha-Mak-Kum-Mīn in Savya Kālacakra. If Mīna is in Apasavya Kālacakra, the subdivision is Mīn-Kum-Mak-Dha-Vṛś-Tul-Kan-Siṅ-Kar. In this case, Mīna Daśā is Savya, therefore, its subdivision is Kar-Siṅ-Kan-Tul-Vṛś-Dha-Mak-Kum-Mīn.

Āratī: The calculations are complex. So, if someone wishes to calculate it following your recommendations, is there a tool in which it can done?

Ācārya: I have saved an Excel calculator at the following location.

https://docs.google.com/spreadsheets/d/1vfXP3pKPudlEk27ltkoemxUcIRhFNZ44?rtpof=true&usp=drive_fs

You can use this to calculate this effortlessly. You can also learn about the computations by following the spreadsheet.

Sunidhi: Guruji, kindly demonstrate the Daśā through more examples.

Ācārya: Indeed. Let us do that. But ensure that the Candrasphuṭa is precise since a small difference in the sphuṭa can cause a big difference in the Daśā dates.

Sunidhi: Noted, Guruji.

Kailāśa: Can we investigate the assassination of political leaders?

Ācārya: Why not? Let us start with Śmt Indira Gandhi. Her Candra is in Makara 5:29:45.13. This maps to Kumbha Navāñśa. Her Daśās are:

Table 107

Navāñśa	Dasa	Duration	Start	End
Kumbha7	Meṣa	4.153	19-Nov-17	13-Jan-22
Kumbha8	Vṛṣabha	16	13-Jan-22	13-Jan-38
Kumbha9	Mithuna	9	13-Jan-38	14-Jan-47
Mīna1	Karka	21	14-Jan-47	14-Jan-68
Mīna2	Siṅha	5	14-Jan-68	13-Jan-73
Mīna3	Kanyā	9	13-Jan-73	14-Jan-82
Mīna4	Tulā	16	14-Jan-82	14-Jan-98
Mīna5	Vṛścika	7	14-Jan-98	14-Jan-05
Mīna6	Dhanu	10	14-Jan-05	14-Jan-15

She was assassinated in Mīna-Tulā (31 October 1984). Kailāśa, can you check her Deha and Jīva?

Kailāśa: The Deha and Jīva of the Rāśis are as follows:

Meṣa: Meṣa-Dhanu; Vṛṣabha: Makara-Mithuna; Mithuna: Vṛṣ-Mit; Karka: Kar-Mīn; Siṅha: Vṛś-Mīn; Kanyā: Kum-Kan; Tulā: Tul-Kan; Vṛścika: Kar-Dha; Dhanu: Meṣ-Dha; Makara: Mak-Mit; Kumbha: Vṛṣ-Mit; Mīna: Kar-Mīn.

She was born in Mīna Navāñśa, for which Deha and Jīva are Karka and Mīna. She has Śani in Deha, indicating bodily problems. She was assassinated in Tulā, for which the Deha is Tulā and Kanyā. In her Kuṇḍalī, both Rāśis are unoccupied.

If it were Mīna-Vṛścika, it would have made better sense. Deha for Vṛścika is Karka and Jīva is Dhanu. Karka has Śani and Dhanu has Rāhu.

Jayanta: Could it be possible that her birth time requires some adjustment?

Ācārya: Vṛścika starts in 98, and the event occurred in 84, a difference of 14y. In Kālacakra, at a high level, every year requires an adjustment of Candra's sphuṭa by 2.2'. This is equivalent to ~4 minutes in birth time per year. So, a 14-year change would need adjustment in the birth time by 14 * 4 = 56 min. This can't be the case.

Āratī: So, can we use this thumb rule that an adjustment of Daśā by 1 year would need adjustment to Candra's sphuṭa by 2.2' or the birth time by 4 min?

Ācārya: Yes, you can use this thumb rule for checking any possibility of birth time rectification.

Jayanta: So, let's assume that there is no scope for birth time rectification. In that case, she died in Mīna-Tulā. Let us examine Tulā.

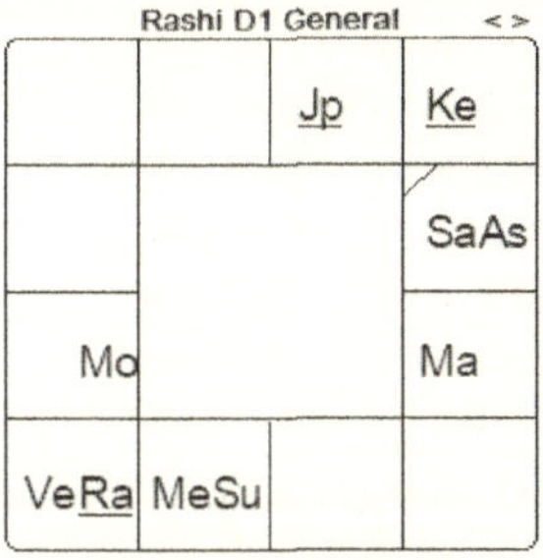

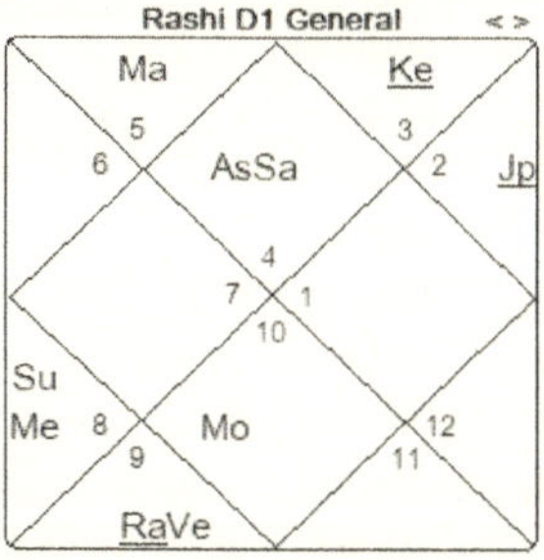

(1) From Janmalagna, Tulā is 4H, which is not a Dusthāna or a Mārakasthāna. But it is afflicted because its Lord Śukra is in 6H afflicted by Rāhu. The affliction to 4H can be painful. Her bodyguard shot her in her chest (4H).

(2) From Daśālagna, Tulā, Lagneśa is afflicted in 3H (death) by Rāhu, indicating death due to machinations. Involvement of Rāhu indicates duṣṭamaraṇa Yoga.

(3) From Daśālagna, Tulā, 8H has 6L Guru, and 8L Śukra is afflicted in 3H by Rāhu, in Guru's Rāśi.

These Yogas point towards her assassination.

Kailāśa: Dhanyavād, Guruji and Gurubhrāta.

Jayanta: Let us examine the Antardaśā of Tulā Daśā also.

Table 108

Antardaśā	Dur	Antar	Start	End
Tulā	16	3.084	14-Jan-82	13-Feb-85

Antardaśā	Dur	Antar	Start	End
Vṛścika	7	1.349	13-Feb-85	21-Jun-86
Dhanu	10	1.928	21-Jun-86	25-May-88
Makara	4	0.771	25-May-88	3-Mar-89
Kumbha	4	0.771	3-Mar-89	10-Dec-89
Mīna	10	1.928	10-Dec-89	14-Nov-91
Vṛścika^	7	1.349	14-Nov-91	21-Mar-93
Tulā^	16	3.084	21-Mar-93	20-Apr-96
Kanyā^	9	1.735	20-Apr-96	14-Jan-98

This occurred in Tulā Antardaśā. The same reason applies to Antardaśā also, as we have seen before. But the Deha-Jīva for Tulā is Tulā-Kanyā, which are not afflicted. It appears that some birthtime rectification may be needed.

Sunidhi: What if we used the year definition of Sāvana year?

Jayanta: Let us examine that. If we use the Sāvana year definition, the Daśā-Antardaśā will be as follows:

Table 109

Navāñśa	Daśā	Duration	Start	End
Kumbha7	Meṣa	4.153	19-Nov-17	23-Dec-21
Kumbha8	Vṛṣabha	16	23-Dec-21	30-Sep-37
Kumbha9	Mithuna	9	30-Sep-37	14-Aug-46
Mīna1	Karka	21	14-Aug-46	26-Apr-67
Mīna2	Siṅha	5	26-Apr-67	30-Mar-72
Mīna3	Kanyā	9	30-Mar-72	11-Feb-81
Mīna4	Tulā	16	11-Feb-81	19-Nov-96
Mīna5	Vṛścika	7	19-Nov-96	14-Oct-03
Mīna6	Dhanu	10	14-Oct-03	22-Aug-13

There is no change in Daśā, as the assassination occurred in Mīna-Tulā. But let me check the Antardaśā.

Table 110

Antardaśā	Dur	Antar	Start	End
Tulā	16	3.084	11-Feb-81	26-Feb-84
Vṛścika	7	1.349	26-Feb-84	26-Jun-85
Dhanu	10	1.928	26-Jun-85	21-May-87
Makara	4	0.771	21-May-87	22-Feb-88
Kumbha	4	0.771	22-Feb-88	26-Nov-88
Mīna	10	1.928	26-Nov-88	21-Oct-90
Vṛścika^	7	1.349	21-Oct-90	19-Feb-92
Tulā^	16	3.084	19-Feb-92	5-Mar-95
Kanyā^	9	1.735	5-Mar-95	19-Nov-96

We know the reason why she died in Mīna-Tulā. But the assassination occurred in Vṛścika.

Now, Deha-Jīva for Vṛścika is Karka-Dhanu, which Śani and Rāhu afflict. This actually makes better sense. Also, from Tulā Daśālagna, Vṛścika is the Māraka (2H) and has 12L Budha (loss). Sūrya is also Māraka from Janmalagna. She died due to a conspiracy, which Vṛścika rightfully denotes. It appears that the Sāvana year definition is giving good results.

Ācārya: Do not conclude the year definition as there could also be some impurities in the birth time and Ayanāñśa. But you can continue experimenting with the Daśā with Sāvana year, as I have done in the case studies section above.

Jayanta: Noted, Guruji!

Ācārya: Why not investigate the assassination of Śrī Rajiv Gandhi?

Jayanta: He was born on 20-Aug-44 with Candra in 4s 17:7:36.16 (Siṅha). This is mapped to Uttarāphālgunī2 and Gemini^ Navāñśa. His Daśās are:

Table 111

Navāñśa	Daśā	Dur	Start	End
Mithuna^2	Vṛṣabha	13.545	20-Aug-44	7-Mar-58
Mithuna^3	Meṣa	7	7-Mar-58	7-Mar-65
Mithuna^4	Dhanu^	10	7-Mar-65	7-Mar-75
Mithuna^5	Makara^	4	7-Mar-75	7-Mar-79
Mithuna^6	Kumbha^	4	7-Mar-79	7-Mar-83
Mithuna^7	Mīna^	10	7-Mar-83	7-Mar-93
Mithuna^8	Meṣa^	7	7-Mar-93	7-Mar-00
Mithuna^9	Vṛṣabha^	16	7-Mar-00	7-Mar-16
Vṛṣabha^1	Mithuna^	9	7-Mar-16	7-Mar-25

He was assassinated on 21 May 1991 in Mithuna-Mīna. The Deha-Jīva of Mithuna is Vṛṣ-Mit and Mīna is Kar-Mīn.

His Navāñśa Deha is vacant and Jīva has Śani. His Daśā Deha has Rāhu and Jīva is vacant. The Daśā can be fatal to his body because of Rāhu's effect. Let us examine why he was killed in Mīna Daśā. Mīna is vacant, but let us investigate the other factors. Here is my assessment:

(1) From Janmalagna, Mīna is 8H. 8L Guru is in Lagna and afflicted by Sūrya-Candra Yuti (an indicator of Amāvasyā).

(2) From Janmalagna, 8H, Mīna is dṛṣṭied by Śani and Maṅgala by both Graha and Rāśi Dṛṣṭi, indicating fatality.

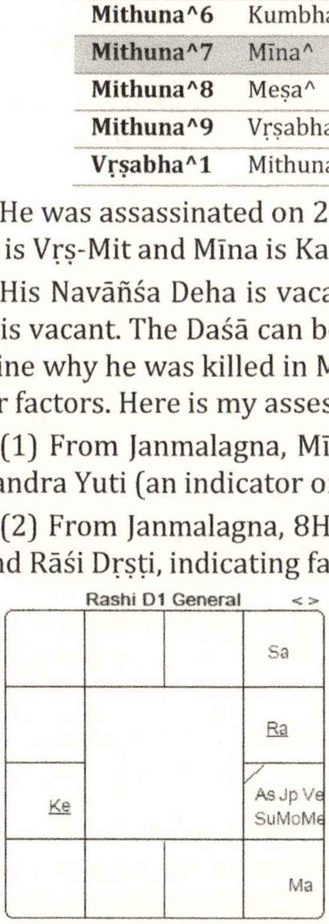

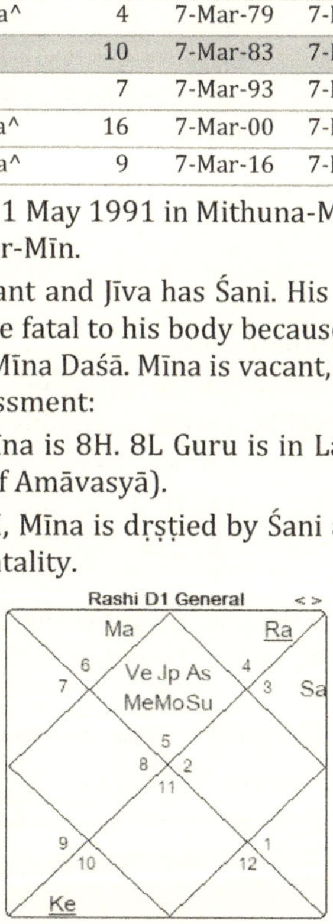

(3) From Daśālagna, Mīna, Lagneśa Guru is in a Dusthāna (6H, Siṅha) conjunct, Dusthāna Lords, 6L Sūrya and 8L Śukra.

(4) From Daśālagna, 8H is Tulā, and its lord Śukra is afflicted in a Dusthāna (6H, Siṅha) conjunct with 6L Sūrya, subject to Pāpakartari by Rāhu and Maṅgala, and also subject Śani dṛṣṭi.

(5) From Daśālagna, 3H has Rāśidṛṣṭi of Rāhu, indicating Duṣṭamaraṇa Yoga.

Kailāśa: Can we zoom into the Antardaśā of his death?

Jayanta: So, let us try.

Table 112: Antardaśā of Mīna^ Daśā

Mīna^	10y	Antar	Dur	Antar Dur	Start	End
Mīna^1	1	Mīna	10	1.163	7-Mar-83	5-May-84
Mīna^2	2	Kumbha	4	0.465	5-May-84	22-Oct-84
Mīna^3	3	Makara	4	0.465	22-Oct-84	10-Apr-85
Mīna^4	4	Dhanu	10	1.163	10-Apr-85	8-Jun-86
Mīna^5	5	Vṛścika	7	0.814	8-Jun-86	2-Apr-87
Mīna^6	6	Tulā	16	1.860	2-Apr-87	9-Feb-89
Mīna^7	7	Kanyā	9	1.047	9-Feb-89	27-Feb-90
Mīna^8	8	Siṅha	5	0.581	27-Feb-90	27-Sep-90
Mīna^9	9	Karka	21	2.442	27-Sep-90	7-Mar-93

He passed away in Mīna-Karka Daśābhukti. The Deha-Jīva for Karka is Kar-Mīn. Karka Deha has Rāhu, which is fatal. Here is my assessment:

(1) Bhuktirāśi Karka is in 12H from Janmalagna, afflicted by Rāhu. This is fatal.

(2) From Daśārāśi, Mīna, Karka is in 5H with Rāhu subject to Pāpakartari. This is fatal.

(3) From Bhuktilagna, 1H is subject to Pāpakartari, which is troublesome. It has Rāhu in 1H, which is fatal.

(4) From Bhuktilagna, 8H is Kumbha and 8L Śani is in 12H indicating danger to life. 8L in 12H indicates loss of life.

(5) From Bhuktilagna, Lagneśa Candra is in 2H, a Mārakasthāna and conjunct with Mārakeśa, subject to Pāpakartari by Rāhu and Maṅgala. This is fatal.

(6) From Bhuktilagna, 3H has Maṅgala indicating a Duṣṭamaraṇa Yoga. He was assassinated by blasting a bomb indicated by Rāhu in Bhuktilagna and Maṅgala in 3H.

There are all indications of fatality in Mīna-Karka Daśābhukti.

Kailāśa: Dhanyavād Gurubhrāta.

Ācārya: Well done Jayanta. I hope this puts all doubts to rest.

Sunidhi: Dhanyavād Guruji. This is clear now.

Jayanta: Can we apply Kālacakra Daśā in Varga Kuṇḍalī?

Ācārya: I have explained that before. Haven't I?

Jayanta: Yes, what I wish to know is whether we can create a separate Kālacakra Daśā for a Vargakuṇḍalī.

Ācārya: No, we should not.

Jayanta: Why not?

Ācārya: The definition of Kālacakra Daśā hinges upon the Navāñśa of Candra. This is a super sensitive Daśā. One Nakṣatra of Candra is equivalent to 354 years. The duration of nine Nakṣatras is 3186 years. In Viñśottarī, the duration of 9 Nakṣatras is 120 years. Therefore, Kālacakra is 26.55 (3186/120) times faster than Viñśottarī.

In this, 120° of Candra equals 3186 years, i.e., 2.26' per year.

This means if you create a Kālacakra Daśā for Navāñśa Varga, it is 0.25' per year. It takes 27.3 days for Candra to revolve around Pṛthvī, i.e., 360°. 1° is 27.3/360 = 4.55 hour. 1' is equivalent to 4.55/60 = 4.55 min. Therefore, a change of birth time by 1.138 min (0.25' * 4.55 min) can affect Kālacakra Daśā by 1 year.

With so many debates on Ayanāñśa and the difficulties in ascertaining the preciseness of birth time, thinking about creating an independent Kālacakra Daśā of a Vargakuṇḍalī is futile.

Jayanta: I understand now. What would you advise those who wish to use Kālacakra Daśā in Vargakuṇḍalī?

Ācārya: You compute Kālacakra Daśā only for Rāśi Kuṇḍalī and then check the disposition of Kālacakra Daśārāśi in different Vargakuṇḍalīs. I have already shown it before.

Jayanta: Noted, Guruji!

Kailāśa: Guruji, can you tell me if we can create independent Kālacakra Daśā for different Kārakas?

Ācārya: Yes, we should. Candra is the Kāraka for the person for whose Kuṇḍalī we are judging. If we wish to create an independent Kālacakra Daśā for the person's father, we "can" create an independent Kālacakra Daśā for Sūrya and so on. But it is not necessary.

Āratī: Why are you saying that Candra is the Kāraka for the Jātaka whose Kuṇḍalī we are assessing? Isn't Candra the Kāraka for Candra?

Ācārya: Āratī, look at it in this manner. A Bhāva is assessed from three factors: (1) The Bhāva, (2) The Bhāveśa and (3) Kāraka. For father, we must assess the Kuṇḍalī through factors (1) 9H, (2) 9L and (3) Sūrya. You can assess one's father's life from the twelve houses from 9H and Sūrya.

Now, we must use the same principle for the Jātaka. We should assess a Jātaka's life from the twelve houses from Lagna and Candra.

Āratī: Oh, I see now why we cast two Kuṇḍalīs, Lagna and Candra Kuṇḍalī. Dhanyavād, Guruji!

Kailāśa: Can you give an example of this?

Ācārya: In my Kuṇḍalī, Sūrya's sphuṭa is Siṅha 8:10:28.71. Feeding this information in the Excel file I created, the Daśā is as follows:

Table 113

Navāṅśa	Dasa	Dur	Start	End
Kanyā^4	Mithuna	5.547	25-Aug-74	11-Mar-80
Kanyā^5	Vṛṣabha	16	11-Mar-80	12-Mar-96
Kanyā^6	Meṣa	7	12-Mar-96	12-Mar-03
Kanyā^7	Dhanu^	10	12-Mar-03	12-Mar-13
Kanyā^8	Makara^	4	12-Mar-13	12-Mar-17
Kanyā^9	Kumbha^	4	12-Mar-17	12-Mar-21
Siṅha^1	Mīna^	10	12-Mar-21	13-Mar-31
Siṅha^2	Meṣa^	7	13-Mar-31	12-Mar-38
Siṅha^3	Vṛṣabha^	16	12-Mar-38	12-Mar-54

He passed away on 17 February 1994, which occurred in Vṛṣabha Daśā. In the Kuṇḍalī, Pitṛ Lagna is Siṅha (9H from Dhanu Lagna). From Pitṛ Lagna, Vṛṣabha is 10H with Ketu. A Krūra in Kendra is troublesome.

Let's examine the Antardaśā of Vṛṣabha Daśā.

Table 114

Antardaśā	Dur	Antar	Start	End
Makara	4	0.753	11-Mar-80	11-Dec-80
Kumbha	4	0.753	11-Dec-80	12-Sep-81
Mīna	10	1.882	12-Sep-81	1-Aug-83
Vṛścika^	7	1.318	1-Aug-83	24-Nov-84
Tulā^	16	3.012	24-Nov-84	29-Nov-87
Kanyā^	9	1.694	29-Nov-87	9-Aug-89
Karka^	21	3.953	9-Aug-89	23-Jul-93
Siṅha^	5	0.941	23-Jul-93	2-Jul-94
Mithuna^	9	1.694	2-Jul-94	12-Mar-96

The Antardaśā was of Siṅha in Vṛṣabha Daśā when he passed away. Karka to Siṅha is *Marakaṭa Gati*, which is also fatal.

The Deha-Jīva of Rāśis are as follows: *Meṣa*: Meṣ-Dha; *Vṛṣabha*: Mak-Mit; *Mithuna*: Vṛṣ-Mit; *Karka*: Kar-Mīn; *Siṅha*: Vṛś-Mīn; *Kanyā*: Kum-Kan; *Tulā*: Tul-Kan; *Vṛścika*: Kar-Dha; *Dhanu*: Meṣ-Dha; *Makara*: Mak-Mit; *Kumbha*: Vṛṣ-Mit; *Mīna*: Kar-Mīn.

We notice that Vṛṣabha Daśā, Deha-Jīva is Mak-Mit, and for Siṅha Antardaśā, it is Vṛś-Mīn. For the Daśā, the Jīva is afflicted, and for the Antardaśā, Deha is afflicted.

You can validate this principle: if the Deha of the Daśā and the Jīva of the Antardaśā are afflicted, then it can be fatal. Similarly, if the Jīva of the Daśā and the Deha of the Antardaśā are afflicted, then it can be fatal.

Kailāśa: Dhanyavād Guruji! Can we also investigate what the Daśās are if we consider 360 days a year definition?

Ācārya: Why would you do that?

Kailāśa: I wish to see the effect. Also, since it would require considerable research to establish which year definition is more effective, I would like to explore other possibilities.

Ācārya: Well, noted. Even if we used 360 days a year definition, the father passed away in Vṛṣabha-Siṅha. Here is the updated Antardaśā table.

Table 115

Antardaśā	Dur	Antar	Start	End
Makara	4	0.753	11-Feb-80	8-Nov-80
Kumbha	4	0.753	8-Nov-80	6-Aug-81
Mīna	10	1.882	6-Aug-81	15-Jun-83
Vṛścika^	7	1.318	15-Jun-83	1-Oct-84
Tulā^	16	3.012	1-Oct-84	21-Sep-87
Kanyā^	9	1.694	21-Sep-87	23-May-89
Karka^	21	3.953	23-May-89	15-Apr-93
Siṅha^	5	0.941	15-Apr-93	19-Mar-94
Mithuna^	9	1.694	19-Mar-94	19-Nov-95

Kailāśa: Oh, I see... In both cases, your father passed away in Vṛṣabha-Siṅha. So, we can't see the effect of different year definitions.

Ācārya: Yes, but you can test out different definitions. I suggest you also test the 354 days a year definition, even though there is not much Śāstraic evidence for that.

Kailāśa: Why?

Ācārya: Because the total duration of one Nakṣatra Pāda is 354 days, which equals the mean duration of a Candravarṣa.

Kailāśa: Oh, I see!

Ācārya: The mean duration of a lunation (Cāndramāsa) is 29d 12h 44m 3s (29.530589d). Therefore, it is common for a Cāndramāsa to alternate between 29 and 30 days. The mean period of 12 such lunations, which comprises a lunar year, is 354d 8h 48m 34s (354.36707d). Therefore, a Candravarṣa is 11 to 12 days shorter than a Sauravarṣa. To account for this difference, an Adhikamāsa is added to the Candravarṣa so that the two Calendars, Saura and Candra, are aligned.

Kailāśa: So, a Candravarṣa is about 354 days long. I see your point now. Can we investigate the effect of 354 days a year definition in this case?

Ācārya: Even then, the death occurred in Vṛṣabha Daśā, but the Antardaśā changes to Mithuna. Here is the revised Antardaśā table.

Table 116

Antardaśā	Dur	Antar	Start	End
Makara	4	0.753	9-Jan-80	2-Oct-80
Kumbha	4	0.753	2-Oct-80	25-Jun-81
Mīna	10	1.882	25-Jun-81	22-Apr-83

Antardaśā	Dur	Antar	Start	End
Vṛścika^	7	1.318	22-Apr-83	1-Aug-84
Tulā^	16	3.012	1-Aug-84	3-Jul-87
Kanyā^	9	1.694	3-Jul-87	22-Feb-89
Karka^	21	3.953	22-Feb-89	22-Dec-92
Siṅha^	5	0.941	22-Dec-92	20-Nov-93
Mithuna^	9	1.694	20-Nov-93	13-Jul-95

Siṅha to Mithuna is a Maṇḍūka jump, indicating danger. Also, Deha-Jīva of Mithuna is Vṛṣ-Mit. Vṛṣabha has Ketu and Mithuna has Śani. Therefore, both Deha and Jīva of Antardaśā are afflicted.

Kailāśa: Besides, Mithuna has Śani. Śani is 6L from Pitṛlagna, indicating a serious disease. In Mithuna, it can be in the respiratory apparatus of the body. So, death because of lung cancer is seen. Isn't it?

Ācārya: Yes, that is true. Compared to Siṅha, Mithuna explains it better. Siṅha also has some afflictions since Maṅgala Yuti and Śani Dṛṣṭi afflict its lord, Sūrya. Also, 2L from Pitṛ Lagna, a Māraka, is afflicted in the Pitṛ Lagna by Maṅgala and Śani.

Jayanta: So, the year can be one of the following:

(1) Mean solar year 365.2563.

(2) True solar year that depends on Sūrya's movement in the zodiac.

(3) 360 days Sāvana year.

(4) 354 days Candravarṣa (that is not aligned to Sauravarṣa).

Which one to use?

Ācārya: Let us use True Solar Year if you have Jyotiṣa software or Mean Solar Year if you don't. This is because Kālacakra is a Rāśidaśā, where I suggest using Sauravarṣa. On the other hand, in Viṅśottarī and other Udu Daśās, we should use 360 days a year definition. If future research on Kālacakra Daśā establishes that the Sāvanavarṣa or Candravarṣa is more effective, you can use them.

—|||—

30.3 THE PRELIMINARIES

TERMINOLOGIES

(1) Rāśis means Zodiac Signs. Grahas means Planets. Dṛṣṭi means aspect. Yuti means conjunction, and Pratiyuti means opposition. Yutidṛṣṭi means conjunction or aspect. Yutadṛṣṭa means being conjunct or dṛṣṭied by. Yuta means being conjunct by. Dṛṣṭa means being dṛṣṭied by. Krūrayutidṛṣṭi means malefic aspect or conjunction. Saumyayutidṛṣṭi means benefic aspect or conjunction. Krūras are malefics, Sūrya, Maṅgala, Śani, Rāhu and Ketu. Saumyas are benefics, Bṛhaspati and Śukra. Saumyayuta Budha is Saumya, Krūrayuta Budha is Krūra. Śuklapakṣi (waxing) Candra is Saumya, Kṛṣṇapakṣi (waning) Candra is Krūra. Budha with Saumya Candra is Saumya and Krūra Candra is Krūra. Budha alone is Saumya. Saumyayuti means conjunction with a benefic, and Krūrayuti means conjunction with a malefic. Saumyadṛṣṭi means aspect of a benefic, and Krūradṛṣṭi means aspect of a malefic. Saumyayuta means being conjunct with a benefic, and Krūrayuta means conjunct with a malefic. Saumyadṛṣṭa means being aspected by a benefic, and Krūradṛṣṭa means being aspected by a malefic. Saumyayutadṛṣṭa means being conjoined or aspected by a benefic. Krūrayutadṛṣṭa means being conjoined or aspected by a malefic.

(2) Dṛśyārdha means visible half. Adṛśyārdha means invisible half. Parivartana or Rāśi Parivartana means an exchange of Signs. Añśa Parivartana means exchange of Navāñśas (D9). Rāśyeśa (Rāśipati) means Rāśi dispositor and Añśeśa, Navāñśeśa or Añśapati means Navāñśa dispositor. Bhāvaphala means results arising from Bhāvas. Rāśiphala means results arising from Rāśis. Chayagrahas are the shadowy planets Rāhu and Ketu. Prakāśagraha means the Luminaries, Sūrya and Candra. Dreṣkāṇa is the Decanate and the 3rd division of a Rāśi. Navāñśa is the 9th division, and Dvādaśāñśa is the 12th division.

(3) Grahadṛṣṭi means planetary aspect, and Rāśidṛṣṭi means the aspect of the zodiac signs. Kuṇḍalī is the Sanskrit term for Kuṇḍalī. Asterisms or constellations are called Nakṣatras. Ucca is exalted; Uccatva is exaltation. Nīca is debilitated; Nīcatva is debilitation. Uccāñśa is the highest exaltation point, whereas Nīcāñśa is the deepest debilitation point. Mitra is the friend, and Śatru is the enemy. Mitratā means friendship, and Śatrutā means hostility. Daivajña means a seer or the knower of destiny (Daiva), another name for Jyotiṣī or Jyotiṣaśastri. Ojarāśi means odd sign, and Yugmarāśi means even sign. Puruṣa means male, and Strī means female. Puruṣajātaka means the horoscope of a male, and Strījātaka means the horoscope of a female.

ABOUT THE GRAHAS

(4) The Grahas are nine in number, called the Navagrahas. They are called planets in English. However, not all Grahas are planets; for instance, Sūrya is not a planet but a star. Similarly, Rāhu and Ketu are not planets but mathematical points of intersection between Candra's orbit around Pṛthvī and Pṛthvī's orbit around Sūrya (the ecliptic). The Grahas are Sūrya ☉ (the Sun), Candra ☽ (the Moon), Maṅgala ♂ (Mars), Budha ☿ (Mercury), Bṛhaspati ♃ (Jupiter), Śukra ♀ (Venus), Śani ♄ (Śani), Rāhu ☊ (Northern node) and Ketu ☋ (Southern node). Among them, Sūrya to Śani is called Vāra (weekday) Grahas because each of them governs a Vāra. The stated order is called the Vāra order. The results of Rāhu are experienced in Śani's Vāra and Ketu in Maṅgala's Vāra. This is according to the dictum Śanivat Rāhu, Kujavat Ketu.

(5) The Vāra order is derived from the Horā order, the order of Graha's speed. The Horā order is Śani, Bṛhaspati, Maṅgala, Sūrya, Śukra, Budha and Candra. Śani is the slowest, and Candra is the fastest. The concept of hour used in the modern reckoning of time has an uncanny resemblance with Horā, which is also hourly and of 2.5 Ghaṭi duration. The Horās have a powerful say on matters concerning a specific time. The Horeśa is the Hour lord, and Vāreśa is the Weekday lord.

(6) Besides the Navagrahas, three other Grahas are used in Western astrology: Prajāpati ♅, Varuṇa ♆ and Yama ♇. They are called Uranus, Neptune, and Pluto. They are not used in Jyotiṣa because several of their parameters, such as Rāśi ownership, exaltation, and Ṣaḍbala computation, are not delineated in the Śāstras. Besides that, they are not included in Viṁśottarī or other Daśā systems. They may be used in Gocara analysis as some modern scholars have done.

(7) Uranus is Prajāpati and stands for creative impulses (like Prajāpati Brahmā). Neptune is Varuṇa and signifies preservation (like Viṣṇu). Pluto is Yama and signifies annihilation (like Maheśvara). They represent the Guṇas, Rajas, Sattva, and Tamas. Prajāpati stands for creativity, reactivity, initiative, selfishness, and goal-orientedness. He creates shocks, surprises, and volatility. Varuṇa creates illusion and makes distinguishing between the real and the unreal difficult. He creates a transcendental (dreamy/reflective/meditative) state through which one moves from reality to surreality. He is Sattvaguṇi and is responsible for sustenance, harmony, radiance, spirituality, cooperation, and preservation. Yama seems to represent the impulse to transform, change and transcend. Yama is Tamoguṇi and is chaotic, like Ketu or meteors. He has the highest eccentric orbit (eccentricity of 0.2444), and its characteristics are elusive. He is responsible for mass destruction, pandemics, natural disasters, landslides, forest fires, pest infestation and everything that disrupts social order.

MEASURES OF TIME

(8) There are four kinds of measures in a day: **(1)** Horā based, **(2)** Yama based, **(3)** Muhūrta based, and **(4)** Ghaṭi based. According to Pt Rath, Budha governs the Horā system, Śani, Yama system, Bṛhaspati, Muhurta system, and Śukra, Ghaṭi system. In the Horā system, a day has 24 Horās, and each Horā is divided into 24 Kṣaṇa-Horās (momentary Horās). In the Yāma system, a day has 8 Yāmas and 16 Yamārdhas (or Kālas). The commencement of the Yamārdhas is aligned with the Sūryodaya and Sūryāsta. In the Muhūrta system, a day has 30 Muhūrtas. In the Ghaṭi system, a day has 60 Ghaṭikās, and a Ghaṭi has 60 Vighaṭikās. The Ghaṭi-Vighaṭi pairs are also called Nāḍīkā-Vināḍīkā and Daṇḍa-Pala.

(9) A day or Ahorātra is divided into 24 Horās (called Hours) that commence with the Sūryodaya. The 1st Horā is always lorded by the Vāreśa (weekday lord), followed by the next Graha in the ascending order of their speeds, which is Śani ♄ → Bṛhaspati ♃ → Maṅgala ♂ → Sūrya ☉ → Śukra ♀ → Budha ☿ → Candra ☽. The next day is always owned by the 4th Horā lord from the previous Vāra. In descending order, the Grahas' mean orbital speed in arc-min/day are ☽ 790.582', ☿ 245.540', ♀ 96.128', ☉ 59.136', ♂ 31.442', ♃ 4.983', ♄ 2.007', ♅ 0.704', ♆ 0.359', ♇ 0.239'. The speed of Rāhu/Ketu is ☊/☋ -3.179'. The -ve sign indicates that they move reversely compared to the rest.

(10) A day or Ahorātra is divided into 16 Kālas, 8 for the day and 8 for the night. The Dina Kālas commence at Sūryodaya (Sunrise), and the Rātri Kālas commence at Sūryāsta (Sunset). The Rātri Kalās commence from the 5th Graha in the Kāla order from the Vāreśa. For instance, on a Ravivāra, the Rātri Kāla commence with Śukra, Somavāra - Bṛhaspati and so on. The Grahas lord the Kalās in order Sūrya ☉ → Maṅgala ♂ → Bṛhaspati ♃ → Budha ☿ → Śukra ♀ → Śani ♄ → Candra ☽ → Rāhu ☊. This gives rise to Rāhukālam. Like Rāhukāla, the remaining seven Grahas also have their Kalās. During the day, the Rāhukālam for Ravivāra onwards is the 8th, 2nd, 7th, 5th, 6th, 4th and 3rd Kālas. During the night, the Rāhukālam is counted from the 5th Graha of Vāreśa.

AṄKA ŚĀSTRA

(11) The numeric correspondence of Grahas and numerals are 1-Sūrya, 2-Candra, 3-Bṛhaspati, 4-Rāhu, 5-Budha, 6-Śukra, 7-Ketu, 8-Śani, 9-Maṅgala. This is used in Aṅka Śāstra or Numerology.

GRAHA KĀRAKATVAS

(12) Each Graha governs matters called the significations or the Kārakatvas. A detailed understanding of the Kārakatvas is essential in Jyotiṣa. When a Graha is powerful in Ṣaḍbala and is subject to Śubhayutidṛṣṭi or Śubhakartari, the matters concerning the Graha are favourable, and it is not so if the Graha is weak or afflicted. This must be judged along with the Bhāva Kārakatvas.

(13) Sūrya denotes Ātmā, self, father, influence, health, vitality, wealth, and courage. *Affliction to the Graha causes high fever, eye troubles, diarrhoea, indigestion, head disease, epilepsy, heart diseases, and bile complaints.*

(14) Candra denotes mānas, mind, intellect, favour from Kings, mother, affluence, fame, imagination, romance, clothes, left eye, milk, and umbrella. *Affliction to the Graha causes leukoderma, cold, catarrh, jaundice, phlegmatic afflictions, diarrhoea, carbuncle, danger from horned and aquatic animals, indigestion, mental afflictions, impurity of blood, anaemia, diseases through women, i.e., sexual diseases etc.*

(15) Maṅgala denotes parākrama, courage, diseases, brothers, lands, enemies, paternal relations, army, heroic deeds, power contentions, strife, cuts, wounds, and fire. *Affliction to the Graha causes hydrocele, injuries from weapons, fire accidents, danger from dogs and wild animals, troubles from Lord Śiva Gaṇa and Bhairava, smallpox, ulcers, burns, acute fevers, haemorrhage, lameness caused by fire and injuries etc.*

(16) Budha denotes bodhana Śakti, learning, relatives, discrimination, maternal uncle, friends, speech, intelligence, education, analytical ability, power of judgement, mathematics, wisdom, commerce, wit, humour, art, writing, mimicry and acting. *Affliction to the Graha causes mental ailments, nervous disorders, skin ailments, leukoderma, leprosy, stomach or intestine ailments, indigestion, piles, speech impediments, curses of the devotees of Lord Viṣṇu and wisemen.*

(17) Bṛhaspati denotes happiness, children, intellect, knowledge, wealth, physical growth, philosophical nature, good conduct, morals, respect, peace, prosperity, health, corpulence, the performance of sacrifices and other religious rites, devotion to Guru and Devatās, royal favour, the blessings of Brāhmaṇas and preceptors, happiness through the blessing of Brāhmaṇas, and serpents, Veda, legal affairs, religious instructions. *Affliction to the Graha causes appendicitis, spleen enlargement, hernia, fever due to intestinal troubles, phlegmatic disorders, ear trouble, giddiness, troubles arising from the curses of Brāhmaṇas, serpents and Devatās, etc.*

(18) Śukra denotes passion, wife, vehicles, ornaments, love affairs, pleasures, conveyance, gems, sexual intercourse, marriage cows, dress, fine arts, pearls, garlands of flowers, jewels, palanquin dancing, and music. *Affliction to the Graha causes venereal diseases, diabetes, urinary diseases, eye troubles, Pāṁḍurogaḥ, anaemia, etc.*

(19) Śani denotes grief, misery, sorrow, longevity, death, poverty, servants, profession, dangers, imprisonment, agriculture, mental trouble, worry, falsehood, difficulties, melancholy, sins, misfortunes, imprisonment, captivity, reproach, blame, humiliation, fear. Affliction to the Graha causes paralysis, injuries from woods or stones, liver enlargement, rheumatism, diseases of the joints, danger from thieves and goblins, mental aberrations, asthma, constipation diseases due to retention of waste, etc.

(20) Rāhu denotes greed, paternal grandfather, imprisonment, friendship with lowly people, crawling insects, authority, theft, witchcraft, courage and Mohammedans. *Affliction to the Graha causes epilepsy, smallpox,* *death by hanging, starvation, troubles through departed souls, goblins, indigestion, leprosy, want of appetite, vomiting, tuberculosis, poison, hiccough, snakebite, insanity, fear, punishment from the king, etc.*

(21) Ketu denotes detachment, wisdom (jñāna), maternal grandfather, witchcraft, gossip, absence of religious faith, cheating, sinful acts, imprisonment, backbiting, and scandalmongering. *Affliction to the Graha causes itches, measles, smallpox, troubles through enemies possession by Preta or Piśāca, troubles through lowly people, diseases caused by past sins, troubles from rats and cats, fire accidents, leprosy, etc.*

APRAKĀŚA GRAHAS AND UPAGRAHAS

(22) Aprakāśa Grahas are those who do not have the light on their own, and they are derived from Meṣādi Sūryasphuṭa. Dhūma = Sūrya + 133°20'. Vyatipāta = 360 - Dhūma. Pariveṣa = Vyatipāta + 180. Indracāpa = 360 - Pariveṣa. Upaketu = Indracāpa + 16°40'. Sūrya = Upaketu + 30.

(23) According to Ācāryas Mantreśvara and other Ācāryas, when the day and night are divided into 30 parts, the Upagrahas rise in this manner. ☉ **Dina Kāla** 2, 26, 22, 18, 14, 10, 6. ☉ **Rātri Kāla** 14, 10, 6, 2, 26, 22, 18. ☽ **Dina Pariveṣa** 6, 2, 26, 22, 18, 14, 10. ☽ **Rātri Pariveṣa** 18, 14, 10, 6, 2, 26, 22. ♂ **Dina Mṛtyu** 10, 6, 2, 26, 22, 18, 14. ♂ **Rātri Mṛtyu** 22, 18, 14, 10, 6, 2, 26. ☿ **Dina Ardhaprahara** 14, 10, 6, 2, 26, 22, 18. ☿ **Rātri Ardhaprahara** 26, 22, 18, 14, 10, 6, 2. ♃ **Dina Yamaghaṅṭa** 18, 14, 10, 6, 2, 26, 22. ♃ **Rātri Yamaghaṅṭa** 2, 26, 22, 18, 14, 10, 6. ♀ **Dina Yamaśukra** 22, 18, 14, 10, 6, 2, 26. ♀ **Rātri Yamaśukra** 6, 2, 26, 22, 18, 14, 10. ♄ **Dina Māndi** 26, 22, 18, 14, 10, 6, 2. ♄ **Rātri Māndi** 10, 6, 2, 26, 22, 18, 14. The figure denotes the rising part for Ravivāra to Śanivāra. Dina Upagraha rising time = Sūryodaya + Dinamāna / 30 * rising part. Rātri Upagraha rising time = Sūryāsta + Rātrimāna / 30 * rising part.

(24) According to Maharṣi Parāśara when the day and night are divided into 8 parts, the Upagrahas rise in this manner. ☉ **Dina Kāla** 0, 6, 5, 4, 3, 2, 1. ☉ **Rātri Kāla** 3, 2, 1, 0, 6, 5, 4. ☽ **Dina Pariveṣa** 1, 0, 6, 5, 4, 3, 2. ☽ **Rātri Pariveṣa** 4, 3, 2, 1, 0, 6, 5. ♂ **Dina Mṛtyu** 2, 1, 0, 6, 5, 4, 3. ♂ **Rātri Mṛtyu** 5, 4, 3, 2, 1, 0, 6. ☿ **Dina Ardhaprahara** 3, 2, 1, 0, 6, 5, 4. ☿ **Rātri Ardhaprahara** 6, 5, 4, 3, 2, 1, 0. ♃ Dina Yamaghaṅṭa 4, 3, 2, 1, 0, 6, 5. ♃ **Rātri Yamaghaṅṭa** 0, 6, 5, 4, 3, 2, 1. ♀ Dina Yamaśukra 5, 4, 3, 2, 1, 0, 6. ♀ **Rātri Yamaśukra** 1, 0, 6, 5, 4, 3, 2. ♄ **Dina Guḻika** 6, 5, 4, 3, 2, 1, 0. ♄ **Rātri Guḻika** 2, 1, 0, 6, 5, 4, 3. The figure denotes the rising part for Ravivāra to Śanivāra. Dina Upagraha rising time = Sūryodaya + Dinamāna / 8 * rising part. Rātri Upagraha rising time = Sūryāsta + Rātrimāna / 8 * rising part.

ABOUT THE RĀŚIS

(25) The Rāśis are 12, which is Meṣa (Aries) [♈], Vṛṣabha (Taurus) [♉], Mithuna (Gemini) [♊], Karka (Cancer) [♋], Siṅha (Leo) [♌], Kanyā (Virgo) [♍], Tulā (Libra) [♎], Vṛścika (Scorpio) [♏], Dhanu (Sagittarius) [♐], Makara

(Capricorn) ♑, Kumbha (Aquarius) ♒ and Mīna (Pisces) ♓. They are classified into **(1)** Cara (Moveable), Sthira (Fixed), Ubhaya (Dual), **(2)** Oja (Odd), Yugma (Even), **(3)** Agni (Fire), Pṛthvī (Earth), Vāyu (Air) and Jala (Water), **(4)** East, South, West, and North in the order.

(26) The Rāśi ownerships are: Meṣa Maṅgala, Vṛṣabha Śukra, Mithuna Budha, Karka Candra, Siṅha Sūrya, Kanyā Budha, Tulā Śukra, Vṛścika Maṅgala, Dhanu Bṛhaspati, Makara Śani, Kumbha Śani, Mīna Bṛhaspati. Rāhu and Ketu are given co-lordship over Kumbha and Vṛścika as Rāhu is like Śani and Ketu is like Maṅgala.

JANMA RĀŚIPHALA

(27) Janmarāśi Phala: ♈ lustful, heroic, grateful, impulsive, fickle-minded, inflexible, haughty, easily calmed, passionate, fluctuating wealth, courageous, ambitious, daring, egoistic, enterprising, high status, self-respect; ♉ attractive, charitable, forgiving, phlegmatic, wealthy, popular, patient, passionate, indolent, happy, fortunate, fickle-minded, intelligent, respectable, commanding, influential, sound judgement; ♊ fond of gambling, gambling, adept in Śāstras expert in pleasing women, scientific outlook, a messenger, clever, witty, eloquent, refined tastes, fond of music, creative, capable, dexterous, persuasive, a thought reader; ♋ effeminate, short, wise, influential, charming, sensitive, impulsive, kind, compassionate, meditative, scientific outlook, prudent, frugal, conventional, friendly, fluctuating wealth; ♌ hate opposite sex, short-tempered, arrogant, courageous, happy, steady, belligerent, bold, fond of jungle and mountains, anxious, charitable, generous, stubborn, egoistic, arrogant, aristocratic; ♍ pious, tender, wise, modest, calm, sweet spoken, talkative, truthful, intelligent, insightful, principled, honest, virtuous, charitable, affluent, passionate, pensive, conventional; ♎ learned, tall, wealthy, honours Devatās, scholars and preceptors, intelligent, principled, just, clean, fond of travelling, business-minded, fond of arts, far-sighted, idealistic, clever, changeable, amicable, not ambitious; ♏ sickly, respectable, bodily injuries, separated from parents and preceptor, straightforward, open-minded, cruel, malicious intent, agitated, unhappy, wealthy, impulsive, stubborn, secretive; ♐ poetic, artistic, wealthy, upright, deep inventive intellect, charitable, articulate, eloquent, active, adept in Śāstras, proficient in fine arts, patron of arts and literature, author, hate relatives, fond of adulation, ceremonious, showy, pensive, not moved by threats; ♑ lazy, wanderer, beautiful eyes, grasping intellect, perceptive, active, strategic, fond of truth, pompous, showy, charity only for show, clever, crafty, popular, learned, miserly, dishonest, lack kindness, selfish, unpredictable, wretched, mean, pessimistic; ♒ covet others' wealth and women, pure, artistic, intuitive, esoteric, mystical, grateful, healer, energetic, emotional, stubborn, lonely, petulant, diplomatic, lustful, sinful, fluctuations in life; ♓ polite, virtuous, charitable, steady, good-reputation, proficient in fine arts and music, adept in the Śāstras, religious, adventurous.

GRAHA RĀŚIPHALA

(28) Brief Rāśiphala: Sūrya: ♈ fame ♉ hatred for women ♊ wealth ♋ cruelty, sharpness ♌ wisdom, learning ♍ poetry ♎ a liquor seller; ♏ wealth ♐ respectability ♑ avarice ♒ poverty ♓ without friends. **Maṅgala:** In the Rāśi of ☉ poor; ☽ wealthy; ♂ gluttonous; ☿ grateful; ♃ famous; ♀ illicit affairs; ♄ (♑) many sons, affluence, (♒) grief-stricken, wicked, liar. **Budha:** ☉ hated by women ☽ hate relatives; ♂ observing vows; ☿ intelligence, wealth ♃ honour, wealth ♀ beget sons ♄ gold from women; **Bṛhaspati:** ☉ army commander; ☽ wealth, wife, children; ♂ good friends; ☿ wide following, good clothes; ♃ governor of a province; ♀ wealth, happiness, gold; ♄ (♑) tactless, effeminate, jealous, disgraceful, short-tempered, mean, poor, unhappy, (♒) learned, philosophical, controversial, popular, compassionate, sympathetic, agreeable, prudent, humanitarian, melancholic, meditative; **Śukra:** ☉ wealth through women; ☽ wealth, freedom from grief; ♂ hate relatives; ☿ wealth, sin; ♃ wealth, intelligence; ♀ wide fame; ♄ subdued by women; **Śani:** ☉ deformed limbs, poverty, ☽ motherless; ♂ many friends; ☿ three-fold calamities; ♃ wealth, wife, children; ♀ a king; ♄ governor of a province.

(29) Rāśiphala: Sūrya: ♈ famous, clever, traveller, little wealth, bearer of arms. ♉ seller of perfumes and clothes, hates females, clever in drumming and music. ♊ educated, astrologer, wealthy. ♋ short-tempered, poor, doing other's work, exhausted from travelling and labour. ♌ fondness for forests, mountains and cattle, courageous, lack suaveness. ♍ skilful in writing, painting, poetry, philosophy, mathematics, and effeminate body. ♎ toddy-seller, drunkard, traveller, goldsmith, mean. ♏ cruel, adventurous, rash, seller of poisonous substances, loses wealth by robbers, skilled in military weapons, a destroyer. ♐ respected, wealthy, short-tempered, a doctor, an artisan. ♑ narrow-minded, ignorant, a seller of lowly articles, little wealth, covetous, enjoying at other's cost. ♒ mean, separated from children, poor. ♓ seller of water products, fond of women's company.

(30) Rāśiphala: Maṅgala: ♈ ♏ honoured by kings, commanders, travellers, merchants, wealthy, scarred body, thief, enjoying pleasures. ♉ ♎ subservient to women, an ungrateful friend, coveting other's wives, cheating, timid, unsocial. ♊ ♍ jealous, beget sons, friendless, grateful, clever in music and martial art, miserly, undaunted, mendicant. ♋ wealthy, gain from ships or travelling, intelligent, disabled, cruel. ♌ poor, enduring, travel to forests, few children and wife. ♐ ♓ many enemies, a minister, renowned, courageous and few children. ♑ much wealth, many children, a king or his equal. ♒ sorrowful, poor, traveller, untruthful, short-tempered.

(31) Rāśiphala: Budha: ♈ ♏ fond of gambling, borrowing, drinking, an atheist, thief, poor, bad wife, cheating, untruthful. ♉ ♎ follow orders, children, wife, wealth, charitable, respect elders. ♊ a liar, skilled in arts and sciences, polite, fond of pleasures. ♍ charitable, learned, noble qualities, happy, patient, pragmatic, resourceful, and fearless. ♋ wealth through water, hate his relations. ♌ Hate women, no wealth, happiness and children, traveller, stupid, fond of women, disgraced by his community. ♑ ♒ serve others, follow orders, poor, not fond of arts, debtor. ♐ respected by the king, learned, articulate, and presence of mind. ♓ respected by servants, a mean artist.

(32) Rāśiphala: Bṛhaspati: ♈ ♏ a commander, large family, children, wealth, charitable, good servants, forgiving, handsome, good wife, famous. ♉ ♎ healthy, happy, friends, wealthy, beget children, charitable, popular. ♊ ♍ surrounded by paraphernalia or titles, children, friends, a minister, an ambassador, happy. ♋ great wealth, gems, children, wife, enjoyment, intelligence, happiness. ♌ a commander, results of Karka. ♐ ♓ a king, minister or a commander, wealthy. ♑ mean, poor, unhappy. ♒ same results as Karka.

(33) Rāśiphala: Śukra: ♈ ♏ covet other women, lose money through flattery, hate his community. ♉ ♎ self-acquired wealth, respected by the king, chief of his men, renowned, courageous. ♊ serve the king, wealthy, learned. ♍ mean acts. ♑ ♒ popular, subservient to women, affairs with lowly women; ♋ two wives, mendicant, timid, lustful and beget sorrow through it. ♌ gain from a woman, a good-looking wife, and few children. ♐ many good qualities, wealthy. ♓ learned, wealthy, respected by the king, and very popular.

(34) Rāśiphala: Śani: ♈ ignorant, wanderer, cheat, friendless. ♏ imprisoned, getting whipped, capricious, merciless. ♊ ♍ childless, poor, shameless, unhappy, skilled in painting, protecting others, chief of man. ♉ affairs with lowly women, moderate wealth, many wives. ♎ famous, leader of his community/town/army/village, wealthy. ♋ poor, loose teeth, motherless, childless, ignorant. ♌ bad, childless, unhappy, carrying loads. ♐ ♓ good death, happy in the end, confident with the prince and the king, good children, wife and wealth, chief of village/town/army. ♑ ♒ covet other's women, wealth and other's houses, chief of town/village/army, short-sighted, dirty, permanent wealth, general prosperity, enjoying.

(35) Rāśiphala: Rāhu: ♈ Lazy, lack discernment, bravery, cowardice, dullness. ♉ Fickle-minded, lack trust, contented, ugly appearance. ♊ Long-lived, loving music, singer, practising Vedas and yoga, physically strong. ♋ Generous, charitable, victorious over enemies, cheated by relatives and friends, suffer poverty, diseased, shrewd, sometimes defeated. ♌ Clever, amicable, adept in policies and judgement, noble person, virtuous, visionary, working after due thoughts, danger from snakes. ♍ Popular, famous, sweet speech, poetic, writer, lover of dance and music, singer, simpleton. ♎ Short-lived, adept in getting things done (kāryakuśala), inheritance from diseased members, tooth diseases. ♏ Cunning, wicked, financially distressed, sickly, wealth destruction due to expenditure on diseases and vices; physically weak. ♐ Easily contented, adopted by others, hateful towards friends and relatives and cheating them, suffering from childhood, gaining unearned wealth (legacy, insurance, lottery, etc.), miserable married life. ♑ Promote quarrels, get fortunate after marriage, poet and virtuous. ♒ Visionary, wise, writer, reserved, frugal, bereft of family and relatives, tooth diseases, lack fortune ♓ Adept in music and art, devout, noble, virtuous, calm, and composed, peace-loving.

(36) Rāśiphala: Ketu: ♈ Extreme short-temper, arthritis and rheumatism, learned in many languages, fickle-minded, comfortable. ♉ miseries, poverty, lacking moral support from others, lacking energy and resolve, lazy, talkative. ♊ Arthritis and rheumatism, easily contented, arrogant, wrathful, hostility with others due to boastful nature, short-lived, simpleton, an ordinary person. ♋ Arthritis and rheumatism, troubled by ghosts and goblins, miserable. ♌ Extreme short-temper, timid, adept in various art forms, knowledgeable in many languages, intolerant, snake bite. ♍ Sickly, low digestive power, dull-witted, talk unnecessarily. ♎ Leprosy, excessive sensuality, short-tempered, sorrowful. ♏ Wrathful, cunning, talkative, anxiety due to lack of fortune, leprosy due to wrong lifestyle, addicted to vices. ♐ Untruthful, fickle-minded, cunning, enjoy others' wealth. ♑ Live overseas, hardworking, splendorous, valorous. ♒ Wandering, ear troubles, sorrowful, spendthrift, ordinary wealth. ♓ Ear troubles, live overseas, fickle-minded, unlucky, coward, diseased, devoted to work.

EFFECTS ON CANDRA

(37) Candra in Rāśi/Añśa dṛṣṭied by the Grahas: ♈ ♂ kingship, ☿ learning, ♃ virtues, ♀ mayorship, ♄ poverty, ☉ poverty; ♉ ♂ poverty, ☿ thievishness, ♃ kingship, ♀ learning, ♄ messenger, ☉ sickness; ♊ ♂ metallurgist, ☿ kingship, ♃ scholarship, ♀ fearlessness, ♄ weaver, ☉ penniless; ♋ ♂ warrior, ☿ poet, ♃ learned, ♀ respected teacher or a king, ♄ metallurgist, ☉ eye-disease; ♌ ♂ Jyotiṣī, ☿ wealthy, ♃ respected teacher or a king, ♀ king, ♄ barber, ☉ a great king; ♍ ♂ pure and virtuous, ☿ a king, ♃ an army commander, ♀ skilful, ♄ landlord, ☉ a king; ♎ ♂ a king, ☿ a goldsmith, ♃ a merchant, ♀ a king, ♄ a goldsmith, ☉ merchant; ♏ ♂ father of twins, ☿ fond of water, ♃ a king, ♀ defective limbs, ♄ wealthy, ☉ a king; ♐ ♂ protector of relatives, ☿ a king, ♃ leader of men, ♀ leader of men, ♄ showy, ☉ a cheat; ♑ ♂ a king, ☿ a scholar, ornamented, ♃ friendly, ♀ sacrificer or teacher, ♄ a king, ☉ adopting a boy; ♒ ♓ ♂ humorous, ☿ learned, ♃ a king, ♀ learned, ♄ virtuous, ☉ intelligent. Candra is beneficial when in yutidṛṣṭi from Grahas in the Rāśi/Añśa of the Lagneśa. Similarly, yutidṛṣṭi from a Graha in a Rāśi owned by a friend of the Lagneśa's Dreṣkāṇeśa is beneficial. When Sūrya is dṛṣṭied by Candra and other Grahas, the results are the same as for Candra being dṛṣṭied by others. Candra in Vargottamāñśa, Svāñśa, or another Graha's Añśa results in full-fledged, middling or meagre effects. As stated above, Candra's results are excellent when the Añśeśa is powerful.

(38) Candra's Añśaphala: In the Navāñśa of ♂ policeman or security personnel, interested in killing, single combat, quarrels, wealthy; ♀ foolish, jealous of others' spouses; ☿ poetic, happy, dancer, actor, thief, learned, artist, artisan; ☽ short stature, wealthy, ascetic, greedy; ☉ short-tempered, owner of treasure, a minister, a king, cruel, childless; ♃ expert in comedy, strong physique, a minister, righteous; ♄ fewer children, wretched, distressed, poor, affairs with a lowly woman.

GRAHA BHĀVAPHALA

(39) Sūrya Bhāvaphala: 1H a hero, stubborn, defective eyes, ruthless, not calm, fewer sons, unkind, warring, weak-sighted, speak less, live abroad, happy, ♈ cataract, wealthy, famous, strong, semi-blind, wealthy, learned, ♋ mean, poor, blear-eyed intelligent, firm, ♌ night-bind, head of the community; ♍ devoted to his wife, ungrateful. ♎ no courage, poor, immoral, ♓ subservient to women; **2H** wealthy, royal punishment and penalty, robbery, facial disease; **3H** learning, prowess, short-tempered, strong, surrounded by relatives at death, famous; **4H** depressed, discouraged, melancholic, afflicted, lack self-earned wealth, dependent, distressed, wise, courageous; **5H** no wealth and children, speak fast, sharp memory, fewer sons, not wealthy; **6H** powerful, subdue enemies, a king's minister, a leader, learned, famous.; **7H** subservient to women, not attached to wife, playful, agitated; **8H** fewer children, poor eyesight, fewer children, sickness, fame; **9H** wealth, happiness, virtuous, talented, wife and sons, discord with father, loss or separation from him; **10H** heroic, learning, royal service, brave, warring, widely famous; **11H** wealth, honour, very wealthy, obedient servants, dear to the ruler; **12H** fall from a position, poverty, disability, afflicted, live overseas.

(40) Candra Bhāvaphala: 1H dumb, deaf, blind, a servant, lack good speech, wisdom, wealth and strength; ♈ ♉ ♋ wealthy, happy, equal to a king; **2H** religious student, wealthy, courageous, wealthy, dear to women, easily contented; **3H** cruel slanderer, quarrelsome, cunning; **4H** virtuous, fond of sweet food, women's company and romance, modest, happy; **5H** beget daughters, lazy, a wife, wisdom, strength, self-earned wealth; **6H** poor digestion, poor sexual urge, cruel, envious, lazy, many enemies, overpower siblings; **7H** an administrator, learned, a prominent government servant, attached to wife, charitable; **8H** afflicted by diseases, wealthy, enjoy luxuries, wise, highly courageous; **9H** endowed with friends and wealth, virtuous, talkative, fond of company of women,

Pakṣabala: significantly wealthy; **10H** virtuous, righteousness, intelligence, wealth, acquire wealth through legitimate means, crafty, a clever wife; **11H** fame, intelligence, wealth, scholarly, possess cattle, favoured by the sovereign, modest; **12H** mean, defective limb, afflicted eyes, sufferings from women, fickle-minded. Sva/Ucca/Śuklapakṣi: happiness and wealth.

(41) Maṅgala Bhāvaphala: 1H bodily injuries and scars, brave, strong, mighty, respected, fickle-minded, short-lived, wild, idle, bilious diseases; **2H** eat forbidden food, heavy expenditure, defective limb, harsh speech; **3H** virtuous deeds, hate siblings, wealth through difficulties, become wealthy and lucky; **4H** sinful, fond of living in others' house, dependent, sickly, wealthy; **5H** grieving, spiteful, vicious, intelligent; **6H** sinful, lazy, idle; **7H** submissive women and wife, live abroad; **8H** difficult existence, forsaken by his wife and sons; **9H** violent, cruel, murderous; **10H** dear to people, highly intelligent; **11H** excellent qualities, extraordinarily talented; **12H** sinful, disabled.

(42) Budha Bhāvaphala: 1H learned, scholarly, wealthy, kind; **2H** wealthy, lucky; **3H** leader of men, become wealthy because of his talent; **4H** scholarly, learned; **5H** a minister, very intelligent, gracious speech, wise, honoured by the scholars; **6H** having enemies, argumentative, hate people, live abroad; **7H** appreciator of virtues, reconcile contradictions, discerning, charitable, widely famous; **8H** highly virtuous, famous, exceedingly wealthy, a king, wise; **9H** scholarly, learned, wealthy, kind, fearless, wealth and grains, enthusiastic; **10H** exceedingly wealthy, charitable, intelligent, famous; **11H** earn through fair means, wealthy, dear to women, exceedingly talented; **12H** cruel, unkind, spendthrift.

(43) Bṛhaspati Bhāvaphala: 1H learned, wise, long-lived, happy; **2H** pleasant speech, eloquent, wealthy, kind, devout; **3H** miserly, bad disposition, no wealth, ominous to siblings and relatives; **4H** happy, good wife, good food, residence, conveyances; **5H** wise, a good wife and sons, fortunate, scholarly, articulate speaker; **6H** subdue enemies, no enemies, a minister, prudent; **7H** intelligent, good wife and sons, a great scholar; **8H** mean, long-lived, a king, learned, subdue enemies; **9H** ascetic, much happiness, learned, radiant, virtuous, wealthy; **10H** blessed, wealthy, wide fame, meritorious deeds, exceedingly wealthy; **11H** greedy, several sources of gain, head of a treasury, principal member of his clan, well-versed in Śāstras, **12H** wicked, defective-limbed, spend on charity and entertainment.

(44) Śukra Bhāvaphala: 1H passionate, happy, exceedingly beautiful, seductive, submissive to women, wealthy, well versed in the Śāstras; **2H** quarrelsome, conscientious, cheerful face, kind; **3H** anxious for sexual pleasure, affairs with immoral women, not have wealth and luxuries; **4H** happy, forgiving, kind, wife and sons; **5H** many daughters, a minister or a leader, learned; **6H** no enemies, cunning, sickly, lose wealth and sons; **7H** tormented by passion, hate friends, befriend the influential; **8H** wavering, sick, wife, children, delighted; **9H** wisdom, virtues, luxuries, wife, sons; **10H** dear to women, a minister, public welfare; **11H** superior knowledge, wealth, kindness, financial gains, satisfaction;

12H righteous, fond of women's company, undutiful. Sva/Ucca: wealthy, marry a noblewoman.

(45) Śani Bhāvaphala: 1H sickly childhood, unclean, shabby, a wanderer, wicked, subservient to women, windy, disabled. Sva/Ucca: chief of his clan, wise, wealthy, kingly; **2H** no inheritance (or financial support) from the father, self-respect, courage, wealth, learned; **3H** witty, brave, unkind, disrespected; **4H** troubled by relatives, fewer sons, unhappy; **5H** dull-witted, fewer sons, eye diseases, a wanderer; **6H** helpful, subdue enemies, free from diseases (dignified Śani), famous; **7H** mean, fickle-minded, grieving, fond of wife despite non-cordial relationship; **8H** wealthy, sick, fewer sons, weak sighted, fickle-minded; **9H** devout, religious, righteous, protect dharma, expert of the Śāstras, wise, just, blessed with sons; **10H** optimistic, wealthy, chief of his caste, happy; **11H** lordly, famous, a scientist, expert in weapons and surgery; **12H** blame others, heavy expenditure, unhappy.

BIRTHTIME VERIFICATION

(46) Lagna rectification pointers: **1_ Meṣa Lagna:** Short-tempered, frequently travels, miserly, not have much happiness, emaciated body, faltering speech, bilious and windy complaints, clever in grasping, charitable and righteous, inclined to obstruct others' work, not have well-grown nails, indulge in mean trades, wife with questionable character, she has a defective organ, friendship with others, keep eyeballs rolling, prone to risk from water, a liar, wounded body.

46.1. Meṣa Navāñśa: Birth in an east-west street, south-facing house, a lane adjacent to the house, a lane near the third house, a temple of Lord Gaṇeśa or Lord Kṛṣṇa in the street, an array of trees can be viewed from the house, a dilapidated house behind the house, the village chief has no child; if the Lagneśa is in a Saumya Nakṣatra, the person is born in Śudra family; if it is aspected by Krūras, he is a Vaiśya. Lagneśa in Krūra Nakṣatra and receiving Saumyadṛṣṭi indicates that he is a Saivite.

46.2. Vṛṣabha Navāñśa: Birth in a south-north street, east-facing house, forest in the southwest direction. He has a dark complexion, a narrow forehead, a long face, and a long nose and talks slowly.

46.3. Mithuna Navāñśa: Normally a male birth, birth in the east-west street, north-facing house, Lord Śiva's temple in the east, Lord Gaṇeśa's temple in the western end, Vaiśya in caste, wheatish complexion, very famous, birth in the 2nd half Navāñśa - the birth is in a cart, baldish, uneven hands, arms are of uneven length.

46.4. Karka Navāñśa: Birth in a north-south street, east-facing house, a tamarind tree can be seen by the side of the house, pressed nose, prominent hair on toes, no brothers, no child, a neighbour has some physical deficiency, normally a male birth in the first half and female birth in the 2nd half, the female is with a mole on the left breast, curly and long hair.

46.5. Siṅha Navāñśa: Birth in a north-south street, the first half is normally a male birth, a temple in the corner, the neighbour is childless, with moles on the right side, kṣatriya Varṇa. The second half indicates short stature, birth in the southwest street, and a big tree in the south.

46.6. Kanyā Navāñśa: Lean thighs, uneven hands and back, talkative, softer body. In the first half, the person is initially lean and grows stout. In the second half, normally, females are born.

46.7. Tulā Navāñśa: The wife is of questionable character; the second half indicates Brāhmaṇa Varṇa, a tank near the house.

46.8. Vṛścika Navāñśa: Birth in a north-south street, east-facing house, several tamarind trees in the southwest, highly articulate, monkey-like face, serious venereal diseases, kill animals.

46.9. Dhanu Navāñśa: Birth in a north-south street, west-facing house, lean and tall, uneven forehead and ears.

(47) Lagna rectification pointers: **2_ Vṛṣabha Lagna:** Stout thighs, broad face, a farmer, owns a herd of cows, comfortable in the middle and the end of life, attached to other women, moles on the face and back, fond of quarrelling, can bearing adversities, respectful to parents, more female children, very particular in eating, fond of expensive robes and ornaments, early loss of father.

47.1. Makara Navāñśa: Birth in a north-south street, east-facing house, birth in the third house in the street, a lane opposite the house, moderate statured, unnatural habits, the neighbour is childless, a dilapidated well in the opposite direction.

47.2. Kumbha Navāñśa: Birth in an east-west street, north-facing house, tanks and trees in the vicinity, lazy, the third neighbour is childless, pleasing others, talking without sense, with a round head.

47.3. Mīna Navāñśa: A river in the east, a temple in the west, softer body, bright limbs, petals-like eyes, charitable.

47.4. Meṣa Navāñśa: Birth in a north-south street, defective limb, the neighbour in the east belongs to the person's caste, goat-like eyes, suffers from poverty, steals others' money, contracts venereal diseases.

47.5. Vṛṣabha Navāñśa: Birth in a north-south street, Lord Śiva's temple on the left, east of a Śudra colony, bull-like face, raised nose, black hair, broad thighs.

47.6. Mithuna Navāñśa: Birth in an east-west street, south-facing house, a water resort in the southwest, a neighbour is a prostitute, another neighbour has two wives, good-looking eyes, bright and black hair, bright body, clever, pleasant speech, jocular.

47.7. Karka Navāñśa: Birth in a south-west street, east-facing house, affectionate to the wife and the last son, soft-haired, hurtful to relatives.

47.8. Siṅha Navāñśa: Birth in an east-west street, north-facing house, river or stream behind the house, the third neighbour is childless, temples at both the entries of the street, tiger-like eyes, fierce nails.

47.9. Kanyā Navāñśa: Birth in a south-west street, east-facing house, a prostitute lives in the third house, timid, a gambler, weak lower limbs.

(48) Lagna rectification pointers: **3_ Mithuna Lagna:** Highly respected, eloquent, two mothers, marries a girl of choice, troubled by enemies, musical knowledge, interested in dance, music, etc., proficient in handiwork, jocular, particular in dressing, liked by learned people, disturbed at the slightest difficulty, not have good terms with the children, has landed property, can know others' mind, like to confine to the home, a sharp nose, black eyes, curly hair, very intelligent, prestigious, high education.

48.1. Tulā Navāñśa: Birth in an east-west street, south-facing house, tank in the southwest, hair on shoulders, sharp nose, lean legs, addicted to prostitutes.

48.2. Vṛścika Navāñśa: Birth in a north-south street, east-facing house, river in the south, fair body, round eyes, long face, highly intelligent.

48.3. Dhanu Navāñśa: Birth in a north-south street, east-facing house, onion warehouse in the east, mosque in the southeast, public clock in the northeast, hospital in the northwest, bluish body, beautiful forehead, interested in hunting, horseracing.

48.4. Makara Navāñśa: Birth in an east-west street, north-facing house, a temple in the west, dilapidated house in the vicinity, passionate.

48.5. Kumbha Navāñśa: Birth in a north-south street, west-facing house, temple facing the house, water supply between the street, a disabled person in the third house, honey-coloured eyes, ups and downs on the forehead, bad teeth, a gambler, red lips.

48.6. Mīna Navāñśa: Birth in an east-west street, north-facing house, broad face, big head.

48.7. Meṣa Navāñśa: Birth in a north-south street, east-facing house, hills in the surrounding area, protruding and copper-coloured eyes, broad chest.

48.8. Vṛṣabha Navāñśa: Birth in an east-west street, south-facing house, river in the east, a temple in the west, royal place in the northwest, strong intellect, knowledge of sexology, poetry.

48.9. Mithuna Navāñśa: Round, dark-coloured eyes, charming body, successful, very intelligent, fond of having sex, interested in poetry and worldly knowledge.

(49) Lagna rectification pointers: **4_ Karka Lagna:** Well-grown neck and hip, normally of short stature, walking fast, fond of water, more female children, cannot stay permanently in one place, susceptible to venereal diseases, inwardly mischievous, subservient to females, favours mean women, highly courageous, passionate, devoted, regular in pujā, immediately followed by a sister, may lose the spouse, the partner is taller.

49.1. Karka Navāñśa: East-west street, north-facing house, a temple of Amba in the street, lustrous face, beautiful body, black and long hair, smaller organs, and long hands.

49.2. Siṅha Navāñśa: Birth in a north-south street, east-facing house, a tree in the house, a lane adjacent to the house, blood-red complexion, high academic achievements, the spirit of renunciation, small joints, slender ankles.

49.3. Kanyā Navāñśa: Birth in an east-west street, south-facing house, a lane adjacent to the opposite house, temple in the east, fair body, beautiful eyes, lazy, clever.

49.4. Tulā Navāñśa: Birth in a north-south street, south-facing house, those living in the house earlier were childless, some relatives have adopted children, dark-complexioned, stout, tall stature, good looking eyes and nose, hospitable, energetic.

49.5. Vṛścika Navāñśa: Birth in an east-west street, north-facing house, lanes on either side, a temple in the southeast, head like a temple bell, long hands, broad eyebrows.

49.6. Dhanu Navāñśa: Birth in a north-south street, east-facing house, water resort in the vicinity, a gathering place in the northwest, stout, tall stature, influential, beautiful teeth, green in complexioned, i.e., wheatish and dark.

49.7. Makara Navāñśa: Birth in an east-west street, north-facing house, one of the family members has defective eyes, Lord Subrahmaṇya temple in the west, the hair fall frequently, visible blood veins, particularly on legs, rough in speech, looks like a crow.

49.8. Kumbha Navāñśa: Birth in a north-south street, east-facing house, walks like a tortoise, beautiful but pressed nose, dark complexion, engaged in mean handiwork.

49.9. Mīna Navāñśa: Birth in an east-west street, north-facing house, a tank in the northwest, prominent forehead, square body, stout nose.

(50) Lagna rectification pointers: **5_ Siṅha Lagna:** More taste for meat, governmental favours, a good politician, reach a high status in life, not very religious, lion-like face, short-tempered, prone to get into complications, lustrous, no marital harmony, the wife may be of questionable character, slender waist, accumulate landed property.

50.1. Meṣa Navāñśa: Even belly like a lion, fierce, sharp and blood-red nose, a big head, fearless, a prominent and fleshy chest.

50.2. Vṛṣabha Navāñśa: Prominent and broad face, a square body, wide eyes, broad chest, long arms, a big nose.

50.3. Mithuna Navāñśa: Birth in a north-south street, west-facing house, a gathering of sadhus in the house, hair grown on the arms, kind-hearted, round-necked, bright-bodied.

50.4. Karka Navāñśa: Birth in an east-west street, north-facing house, lane opposite the house, long hands, hair grown on the arms, black petal-like eyes, good hair on the head, multi-voiced, strong legs, ghee-like complexion.

50.5. Siṅha Navāñśa: Birth in a south-west street, east-facing house, bald head, bright eyes, loose stomach, long teeth, cruel.

50.6. Kanyā Navāñśa: Birth in an east-west street, south-facing house, a disabled son in the house, a temple in the northwest, rough hair on the head, tall stature, dark body, impressive speaker.

50.7. Tulā Navāñśa: Birth in a north-south street, east-facing house, a dis-reputed member in the family, conspicuous veins, long face, not harmonious, too much hair on the head, deceiving, cruel.

50.8. Vṛścika Navāñśa: Birth in an east-west street, south-facing house, a gathering of sadhus in the house, polite speech, depressed eyes, strong physique, low financial status, tricky.

50.9. Dhanu Navāñśa: Birth in a north-south street, east-facing house, a temple in the vicinity, adopted daughter in the neighbour's family, donkey-like face, shaky, longer eyes, lung disorders.

(51) Lagna rectification pointers: **6_ Kanyā Lagna:** Polite, proficient in ancient Śāstras, equally proficient in painting, poetry, very beautiful handwriting, a good friend, very kind, feminine features, interested in gardening, plantation, not like the brothers, liked by highly placed people, more female children, drooping shoulders, truthful, a great person in the field of justice.

51.1. Makara Navāñśa: Birth in a north-south street, west-facing house, a disabled person in the house, deer-like eyes, dark complexion, tall stature, sensual, clever.

51.2. Kumbha Navāñśa: Birth in an east-west street, north-facing house, a temple in the street, face comparable to Pūrṇacandra, bright body and eyes, loose stomach, plump thighs.

51.3. Mīna Navāñśa: Birth in a south-west street, east-facing house, light red complexion, the lower half of body is lean, large body, well versed in literature, steady, good looking.

51.4. Meṣa Navāñśa: Birth in an east-west street, west-facing house, Lord Gaṇeśa temple in the street, lotus-like feet, unclear in speech.

51.5. Vṛṣabha Navāñśa: Birth in a north-south street, east-facing house, a neighbour has a disabled child, fleshy lips and nose, large body, heavy growth of hair, strong ankles.

51.6. Mithuna Navāñśa: Birth in an east-west street, south-facing house, lustrous, noble, playful, proficient.

51.7. Karka Navāñśa: Birth in a north-south street, west-facing house, small face, raised back, grey hair with ageing, danger from water, stout legs, big stomach.

51.8. Siṅha Navāñśa: Birth in an east-west street, north-facing house, hills surrounding the place, smooth, yellow hair, beautiful eyes, fair complexion, tall stature, stout legs.

51.9. Kanyā Navāñśa: Birth in a north-south street, east-facing house, the third neighbour is childless, reputed, lustrous, worldly enjoyments, proficient in drawing and writing.

(52) Lagna rectification pointers: **7_ Tulā Lagna:** A long face, curly hair, lean physique, uneven limbs, waste money on women, devoted to learned people, highly learned, truthful, liked by brothers, good financial status, suffering from venereal diseases, generally artistic, dependent on others, fate largely depends on others, cannot alter the circumstances but faces them as they come.

52.1. Tulā Navāñśa: Birth in an east-west street, north-facing house, tamarind trees behind the house, fair complexion, wide eyes, long face, accumulate money, business in new articles.

52.2. Vṛścika Navāñśa: Birth in a north-south street, east-facing house, house separated from others, Lord Śiva's temple in the northeast, long teeth, round eyes, depressed chest, weak body, sparse hair on eyebrows, forgetful.

52.3. Dhanu Navāñśa: Birth in an east-west street, south-facing house, two temples in the street, third house dilapidated, fair complexion, horse-like face, protruding nose and nails, lean physique, prominent eyes.

52.4. Makara Navāñśa: Birth in a north-south street, west-facing house, a slight depression in the centre of the nasal bridge, fierce-looking, steady-minded, want of self-respect, affection to relatives.

52.5. Kumbha Navāñśa: Birth in an east-west street, north-facing house, a neighbour is childless, fair, stout, broad and good-looking eyes, hips, bright nails, well versed in Śāstras and worldly affairs.

52.6. Mīna Navāñśa: Birth in a north-south street, east-facing house, good intelligence, light red complexion, heavy body with short stature, short forehead, stingy.

52.7. Meṣa Navāñśa: Birth in an east-west street, south-facing house, a temple in the street, short stature, short-tempered, roaming, marries a bad woman, fewer children.

52.8. Vṛṣabha Navāñśa: Birth in a north-south street, east-facing house, a royal palace in the west, raised shoulders, cheeks, enjoys life, divided skull, reputed.

52.9. Mithuna Navāñśa: Birth in an east-west street, north-facing house, pleasing eyes, reputed, fair, intelligent, humorous, hospitable.

(53) Lagna rectification pointers: **8_ Vṛścika Lagna:** Stout, tall stature, mischievous, more attached to mother than father, fearful eyes, short nose, round belly, long fingers, vengeful, hurt his teachers, tactfully attract many girlfriends, encircled by enemies, a good wife, some are ignorant, and others are mystical, the ignorant ones are jealous, betraying, deceitful, whereas, the mystical ones are prudent and self-respected, both kinds are egoistic.

53.1. Karka Navāñśa: Birth in an east-west street, south-facing house, Lord Gaṇeśa's temple in the west, raised lips, attractive forehead, fair complexion, firm joints, prominent belly, the neighbour is childless.

53.2. Siṅha Navāñśa: Birth in a north-south street, east-facing house, large trees in the house, stout hands, red eyes, sadistic mind, hiding the money.

53.3. Kanyā Navāñśa: Birth in an east-west street, north-facing house, one neighbour has a disabled son, the other neighbour is childless, has good academic achievements, works hard, earns money, beautiful lips, decent speech, fair complexion, conceived before mothers' marriage.

53.4. Tulā Navāñśa: Birth in a north-south street, west-facing house, a portion of the house broken, fierce red eyes, sunken nose, contentment in food, drinks, uneven organs.

53.5. Vṛścika Navāñśa: Birth in an east-west street, south-facing house, poultry in the east, shameless, weak.

53.6. Dhanu Navāñśa: Birth in a north-south street, west-facing house, an undeveloped road in the opposite direction, an unknown temple in the northwest, broad mind, even temperament, prominent nose, very kind.

53.7. Makara Navāñśa: Birth in an east-west street, north-facing house, an area full of trees in the northeast, open mouth, teeth bent inwardly, visible veins, weak body.

53.8. Kumbha Navāñśa: Birth in a north-south street, west-facing street, river in the east, hills in the surrounding, open nostrils, not-so-good habits, coarse hair, dull-headed.

53.9. Mīna Navāñśa: Birth in an east-west street, north-facing house, a royal residence in the southeast, poultry in the northeast, animal-like appearance, blonde hair, fair complexion, very calm, stout body, dear to the preceptor.

(54) Lagna rectification pointers: **9_ Dhanu Lagna:** An open mind, honest, sympathetic, generous, two kinds of people, fortunate kind and unfortunate kind, fortunate is when Bṛhaspati is stronger than Śukra, the unfortunate kind that Śukra predominant; a Dhanu person is extravagant, reckless, erratic unless Bṛhaspati is powerful; he is philosophical and peace-loving; has long teeth, thick, long hair, irregular nails, stout body, big belly, diseased face; a chief member in the family; earns through the Government, the wife is cunning; he is well versed in politics, aptitude for the legal profession and medical pursuits; unhappy married life.

54.1. Meṣa Navāñśa: Birth in an east-west street; south-facing bouse, the landlord is childless, big nose, sheep-like eyes, beautiful teeth, soft and lustrous hair, large testicles, and fair complexion.

54.2. Vṛṣabha Navāñśa: Birth in a north-south street, east-facing house, big head, peculiar eyes, big nose, big cheeks.

54.3. Mithuna Navāñśa: Birth in an east-west street, north-facing house, a temple with a tank in the west, well versed in grammar, literature, proud, fierce appearance, hospitable to women, satisfaction from them, visible veins, humorous.

54.4. Karka Navāñśa: Birth in a north-south street, west-facing house, the person living in the opposite house has two wives, the neighbour is a quarrelling type of woman, the person intelligent, honey-coloured eyes, hand-to-mouth existence, fair complexion, abundant hair on the head, beautiful and stout body.

54.5. Siṅha Navāñśa: Birth in an east-west street, south-facing house, Lord Viṣṇu's temple in the street, stout neck, big face, wide eyes, broad forehead, superior life, steady mind.

54.6. Kanyā Navāñśa: Birth in a north-south street, east-facing house, a temple in the southwest, water storage in the northwest, bright eyes, interest in reading, academic achievements, good living.

54.7. Tulā Navāñśa: Birth in an east-west street, north-facing house, temples on either side, many people reside in the same block, dark complexion, kind-hearted, adjustable, calm, interested in accumulating money.

54.8. Vṛścika Navāñśa: Birth in a north-south street, east-facing house, a temple in the west, a royal residence in the northwest, low flat nose, broad head, revengeful, fearful eyes, respect to teachers.

54.9. Dhanu Navāñśa: Birth in an east-west street, south-facing house, fair complexion, face resembling a horse's face, medical achievements, a gentleman.

(55) Lagna rectification pointers: **10_ Makara Lagna:** Timid, stingy, irreligious, cruel, negative indications are lesser with a well-placed Śani, strong, prominent nose, much hair on the head, long hands, long legs, knowledge of music, Śāstras etc., not in good terms with relatives, bad odour from the body, generally ambitious, plodding, prudent, can organize events, cannot last long in service, many children, good in bringing them up, lacking marital harmony.

55.1. Makara Navāñśa: Birth in an east-west street, north-facing house, small white teeth, space between teeth, dark complexion, talks out of context, famous, pains in the neck, head, weak body, unsteady income, interest in songs and music.

55.2. Kumbha Navāñśa: Birth in a south-west street, east-facing house, lazy, angry, crooked tongue, interested in music, broad body, dear to many women, talkative, expert.

55.3. Mīna Navāñśa: Birth in an east-west street, south-facing house, Lord Gaṇeśa's temple in the street, trees on either side of the house, expert in music, famous, perfect eyes, fair complexion, beautiful nose, many friends, can achieve success in all undertakings.

55.4. Meṣa Navāñśa: Birth in a north-south street, west-facing house, red, round eyes, big forehead, weak limbs, messy hair, talks less, weak teeth.

55.5. Vṛṣabha Navāñśa: Birth in an east-west street, north-facing house, the house was acquired by an adopted son, prominent cheeks, nose, stomach, happy, fond of young ladies, can achieve success in all undertakings.

55.6. Mithuna Navāñśa: Birth in a north-south street, east-facing house, a temple in the street, bright body, beautiful, sensual, small and even teeth, pleasant speech, bread forehead.

55.7. Karka Navāñśa: Birth in an east-west street, south-facing house, Lord Viṣṇu's temple in the west, dark complexion, lazy, good speech, curly hair, broad physique, hard-hearted, softer hands and legs, intelligent, virtuous.

55.8. Siṅha Navāñśa: Birth in a south-west street, west-facing house, a disabled child in the opposite house, fierce looks, grotesque body, forehead swelled like a pot.

55.9. Kanyā Navāñśa: Birth in an east-west street, north-facing house, wide eyes, broad-hearted, highly intelligent, beautiful face, wise in politics.

(56) Lagna rectification pointers: **11_ Kumbha Lagna:** The most controversial figure in the circle, broad nostrils, get tired soon, lack marital harmony, early loss of wife, unsteady income, a liar, talebearer, the fate depends on the friends as he is easily affected by them, only a few are highly refined, secretly indulges in sinful acts, can walk longer and to longer distances, fluctuate between poverty and affluence.

56.1. Tulā Navāñśa: Birth in a north-south street, east-facing house, dark complexion, soft and weak body, prominent cheeks, adept in the Śāstras and literature, sensual, beautiful.

56.2. Vṛścika Navāñśa: Birth in an east-west street, south-facing house, the main road in the southeast, rough skin and nails, sparse hair, helpful to those in trouble, tall stature, dull-headed, virtuous, has a peculiar kind of head.

56.3. Dhanu Navāñśa: Birth in a south-west street, west-facing house, the village head is childless, has a strong and bright body, is liked by women, acquiring great knowledge of Śāstras and acts according to it.

56.4. Makara Navāñśa: Birth in an east-west street, north-facing house, a family member with a disabled child, controlled by the wife, fair complexion, broad-faced, subdue enemies, strong, courageous, enjoying worldly comforts and sex.

56.5. Kumbha Navāñśa: Birth in a south-west street or house, knowledge of the Śāstras, rough hair, dark complexion.

56.6. Mīna Navāñśa: Birth in an east-west street, south-facing house, a meeting place under a tree, tiger-like face, curly hair, firm, kills deer and snakes, dear to the king.

56.7. Meṣa Navāñśa: Birth in a north-south street, west-facing house, a neighbour with a disabled child, goat-like eyes and face, seeks sexual enjoyment in villages, subservient to the wife, suffers bilious diseases.

56.8. Vṛṣabha Navāñśa: Birth in an east-west street, north-facing house, a canal opposite to the house, the army chief, a king, strong teeth, wide eyes.

56.9. Mithuna Navāñśa: Birth in a north-south street, east-facing house, a family member with a disabled child, brown teeth, famous, good wife, son and wealth.

(57) Lagna rectification pointers: **12_ Mīna Lagna:** Depressed eyes, broad belly, prominent lips, teeth, literary attainments, like animals and agriculture, great knowledge in traditional studies, law, politics etc., many daughters, earning through brothers, consuming more water, good understanding with the wife, trading in fish, ship, pearls etc.

57.1. Karka Navāñśa: Bright body, soft-hearted, loved by the wife, fickle-minded, big nose, fond of eating meat.

57.2. Siṅha Navāñśa: Birth in a north-south street, east-facing house, beautiful, wanders in hills and forests.

57.3. Kanyā Navāñśa: Birth in an east-west street, west-facing house, beautiful eyes, virtuous, learned, liberal.

57.4. Tulā Navāñśa: Birth in a north-south street, west-facing house, virtuous, prominent nose, an expert in politics.

57.5. Vṛścika Navāñśa: Birth in an east-west street, north-facing street, a disabled child in the family, tall stature, impatient, beautiful eyes, small nose, a tendency to torture.

57.6. Dhanu Navāñśa: Birth in a south-west street, east-facing house, good looking, praiseworthy, ministerial position, small face, a gentleman.

57.7. Makara Navāñśa: Birth in an east-west street, south-facing house, self-respected, devoted to other religions, minister, suffers grief.

57.8. Kumbha Navāñśa: Birth in a north-south street, west-facing house, tall stature, big head, weak body, fewer sons, warrior.

57.9. Mīna Navāñśa: Birth in an east-west street, north-facing house, Lord Viṣṇu's temple in the street, short stature, softer disposition, courageous, broad chest, bright, virtuous, famous.

THE NAKṢATRAS

(58) The sky is divided into 27 Nakṣatras. They are 1 Aśvinī, 2 Bharaṇī, 3 Kṛttikā, 4 Rohiṇī, 5 Mṛgaśirā, 6 Ārdrā, 7 Punarvasu, 8 Puṣya, 9 Aśleṣā, 10 Maghā, 11 Pūrvāphālgunī, 12 Uttarāphālgunī, 13 Hastā, 14 Citrā, 15 Svāti, 16 Viśākhā, 17 Anurādhā, 18 Jyeṣṭhā, 19 Mūla, 20 Pūrvāṣāṛhā, 21 Uttarāṣāṛhā, 22 Śravaṇa, 23 Dhaniṣṭhā, 24 Śatabhiṣā, 25 Pūrvābhādra, 26 Uttarābhādra, and 27 Revatī. Each Nakṣatra has four subdivisions called the Pādas, Caraṇas or feet. Each Nakṣatra is of 13°20' duration and has 4 Caraṇas or feet, of which the duration is 3°20'.

(59) Starting from the Janmatārā, the Nakṣatras are grouped into three groups of 9 Tārās, called the Navatārā. The designations of the 9 Tārās are Janma, Sampat, Vipat, Kṣema, Pratyak, Sādhaka, Naidhana, Mitra, and Paramamitra.

(60) There is a 28th Nakṣatra, which is used in some special esoteric Cakras (diagrams) in Jyotiṣa, called the Abhijit Nakṣatra, which is known to be ruled by Lord Viṣṇu. **Abhijit Nakṣatra starts from the last Caraṇa of**

Uttarāṣāṛhā, and it extends till the 1/15th part of Śravaṇa. It lies between 276°40' to 280°53'20" in the Bhacakra (zodiac), which is Makara 6°40' to 10°53'20".

(61) The 27 Nakṣatras from Aśvinī onwards are governed by Ketu, Śukra, Sūrya, Candra, Maṅgala, Rāhu, Bṛhaspati, Śani, and Budha. Their **Viñśottarī periods** are 7, 20, 6, 10, 7, 18, 16, 19 and 17. The total of the periods is 120 years, the maximum longevity granted to a Manuṣya in Kaliyuga. Each year of this Viñśottarī Daśā is of 360 days duration, giving rise to 43200 days as the maximum longevity.

NAKṢATRA PHALA

(62) Nakṣatras Phala 1: Aśvinī to Aśleṣā: Aśvinī: fond of decoration, handsome, popular, skilful, intelligent. **Bharaṇī:** determined, truthful, healthy, skilful, happy. **Kṛttikā:** voracious eater, fond of other's wives, attractive and renowned. **Rohiṇī:** truthful, clean, following religious and moral principles, sweet in speech, fixed mind and handsome. **Mṛgaśirā:** capricious, skilful, cowardly, good speaker, hopeful, rich and enjoying. **Ārdrā:** conceited, pride, ungrateful, cruel, sinful. **Punarvasu:** religious endurance, happy, good, dull, sickly, thirsty and pleased with small gifts. **Puṣya:** control over passion, popular, learned, rich and charitable. **Aśleṣā:** pretending, clever, selfish, sinful, ungrateful, a cheat.

(63) Nakṣatras Phala 2: Maghā to Jyeṣṭha: Maghā: many servants, great wealth, enjoys pleasures, honours elders and Devatās and is very enterprising. **Pūrvāphālgunī:** sweet-spoken, liberal, handsome, fond of travelling and royal servant. **Uttarāphālgunī:** popular, self-acquired property, enjoying and happy. **Hastā:** enterprising, intelligent, shameless, drunkard, cruel, thievish. **Citrā:** fond of various clothes and garlands, good looks and limbs. **Svāti:** polite, merchant, kind-hearted, unable to endure thirst, sweet-tongued and generous. **Viśākhā:** jealous, greedy, handsome, clever speaker, quarrelsome, money maker. **Anurādhā:** chief of people, lives overseas, cannot bear hunger, is fond of travelling. **Jyeṣṭhā:** few friends, contented, charitable, wrathful.

(64) Nakṣatras Phala 3: Mūla to Revatī: Mūla: proud, wealthy, happy, good, steady, enjoying. **Pūrvāṣāṛhā:** good and pleasant wife, proud, a steady friend. **Uttarāṣāṛhā:** polite, knowing, virtuous, many friends, grateful, popular. **Śravaṇa:** rich surrounding, learned, good, charitable, attached to wife, wealthy, renowned. **Dhaniṣṭhā:** charitable, wealthy, courageous, fond of music. **Śatabhiṣā:** simple, truthful, sorrow through females, subdue enemies, adventurous, conflicting. **Pūrvābhādra:** sorrowful, loss of money through females, skilful, miserly. **Uttarābhādra:** eloquent and witty speaker, happy, many children and grandchildren, subdues enemies, charitable. **Revatī:** proportional physique, popular, courageous, clean and wealthy.

SĀYANA VS NIRĀYANA CAKRA

(65) The difference in the starting point of the Tropical and Sidereal zodiac is called the Ayanāñśa. The Tropical zodiac slowly moves backwards about the Sidereal Zodiac, used in Jyotiṣa. As the name suggests, the Sidereal Zodiac is based on fixed stars, whereas the Tropical Zodiac is based on a moving reference point called the Vernal Equinox (Vasanta Sampāta). The rate with which the Vernal equinox is receding is 50.28805" per year. The difference between the Nirāyana Meṣa 0° and the vernal equinox makes one full cycle in 25771.53 years of 365.25 days (9,413,051 days). The Ayanāñśa is 23°58'16" on J2000, i.e., 01.01.2000 12:00 GMT. It is called the Sṛṣṭyādi Ayanāñśa or Sṛṣṭi Ayanāñśa. The nearest zero Ayanāñśa epoch is 05 Dec 0283.

MEASURES OF TIME

(66) The Sunrise is called Sūryodaya; the Sunset is called Sūryāsta. The twilight is called Sandhyā. Morning is called Prātaḥ. Noon is called Madhyānha. The afternoon is called Aparānha. Midnight is called Madhyarātri. The Sūryodaya is when the first light of Sūrya appears on the eastern horizon.

(67) A whole day, including a day and night, is called an Ahorātra. The term Horā, used to describe the predictive aspect of Jyotiṣa, is derived from this term. The day is called Dina or Divā, and the night is called Rātri. The day and night are also called Divārātri. The day's duration is called Dinamāna, and the night's duration is called Rātrimāna. The day-birth is called Dinajanma, and the night-birth is called Ratrijanma.

(68) According to Nāradapurāṇa 56.109. there are 9 measures of time: **(1)** Brahma, **(2)** Daiva, **(3)** Manu, **(4)** Pitṛya, **(5)** Saura, **(6)** Savana, **(7)** Candra, **(8)** Nakṣatra and **(9)** Bṛhaspati. The practical reckoning is done only through five of these nine measures. The motion of the planets is reckoned through Sauramāna. In this measure, Sūrya's entry into Meṣa commences a year, and in a Rāśi – a month. The reckoning of the rainy season and pregnancy of women are reckoned through the Sāvanamāna. In this measure, a day is the period of two successive Sūryodayas, and a year is 360 such days. Within a year, the duration of a Ghaṭis, etc., needs to be seen from the Nākṣatramāna. In this measure, a day (sidereal day) is two successive rising of the same Nakṣatra. Times for Yajñopavīta, Muṇḍana, determination of the lords of the Tithi and the Year, the timing of fasting, etc., are done using the Cāndramāna. In this measure, each day (Tithi) is a 12° displacement of Candra from Sūrya, and a year commences with the yuti of Sūrya and Candra in Mīna. The Bārhaspatya mana is used in mundane analysis and is based on Bṛhaspati's mean motion. Bṛhaspati's mean motion through a Rāśi constitutes a Bārhaspatya Varṣa. There are 60 such years.

STRENGTH OF THE RĀŚIS

(69) In Dinajanma, the Śīrṣodaya Rāśis and the Dinabalī (day strong) Grahas, Sūrya and the two Gurus, Bṛhaspati, and Śukra are powerful. In Ratrijanma, the Pṛṣṭodaya Rāśis and the Rātribalī (night strong) Grahas, Candra, Maṅgala and Śani are powerful. In Sandhyā Janma, the Ubhayodaya Rāśi, and

Ubhayodaya Graha, Budha are powerful. Mithuna, Siṅha Kanyā, Tulā, Vṛścika and Kumbha are Śīrṣodaya Rāśis. Meṣa, Vṛṣabha, Karka, Dhanu and Makara are Pṛṣṭodaya Rāśis. Mīna is the only Ubhayodaya Rāśi. The Śīrṣodaya Rāśis rise with their head, Pṛṣṭodaya Rāśis rise with their legs or hind part, and the Ubhayodaya Rāśi rise sideward.

ABOUT THE DṚṢṬIS

(70) The aspects are called Dṛṣṭi, and there are two kinds of them, the Grahadṛṣṭi and the Rāśidṛṣṭi. The Grahadṛṣṭi is the dṛṣṭi of the Grahas, and the Rāśidṛṣṭi is the dṛṣṭi of the Rāśis. The Rāśidṛṣṭis are important in the Rāśidaśās, and the Grahadṛṣṭis are important in the Grahadaśās.

(71) The dṛṣṭis are classified as Koṇadṛṣṭi **(5/9)**, Caturasradṛṣṭi **(4/8)** and Upacayadṛṣṭi **(3/10)**. As per Grahadṛṣṭi, all Grahas aspect their 7th with Pūrṇadṛṣṭi **(100%)**. They have 75% (Tripāda) Caturasradṛṣṭi, 50% (Dvipāda) Koṇadṛṣṭi and 25% (Ekpāda) Upacayadṛṣṭi. When the dṛṣṭi is less than 100%, it is called Padadṛṣṭi, and they are Tripāda, Dvipāda and Ekpāda dṛṣṭi based on three quarter, two quarters and one-quarter aspect. Maṅgala, Bṛhaspati and Śani have special sight called Viśeśa dṛṣṭi. Maṅgala has Pūrṇadṛṣṭi on the Caturasra **(4/8)**, Bṛhaspati in the Koṇa **(5/9)** and Śani in the Upacaya **(3/10)**. No Graha aspect their 2-12, 6-11. These are the blind spots of the Grahas.

(72) Graha aspecting its Uccarāśi is called Uccadṛṣṭi, Svarāśi, Svadṛṣṭi, Mūlatrikoṇa, Mūladṛṣṭi, Mitrarāśi, Mitradṛṣṭi, Śatrurāśi, Śatrudṛṣṭi, and Nīcarāśi, Nīcadṛṣṭi. When a Bhāva receives Uccadṛṣṭi, Svadṛṣṭi, Mūladṛṣṭi and Mitradṛṣṭi the Bhāva prospers. When it receives a Śatrudṛṣṭi or Nīcadṛṣṭi, it suffers.

(73) As per Rāśidṛṣṭi, a Cararāśi dṛṣṭies the Sthirarāśis, except the one adjacent to it. A Sthirarāśi dṛṣṭies the Cararāśis, except the one adjacent to it. A Ubhayarāśi dṛṣṭies other Ubhayarāśis.

(74) The Vṛddhayavanas say that Candra is of medium strength for ten days commencing from Śukla Pratipada, i.e., S1 to S10. He is exceedingly strong during the following ten days, i.e., from S11 to K5. He has very little strength during the third ten-day period, i.e., K6 to K15. Candra, with brilliant rays at birth, circled by a bright halo and full, makes the native an unconquerable king.

GRAHA SAMBANDHA

(75) The relationship between two Grahas is called Graha Sambandha. There are two kinds of Sambandha: Naisargika (natural) and Tatkālika (temporal). The two Sambandhas combine to give rise to the Pañcadhā Sambandha, a fivefold relationship.

(76) Regarding the Naisargika Sambandha, note the Rāśis, which are the 2nd, 4th, 5th, 8th, 9th and 12th from the Mūlatrikoṇa of a Graha. The Graha "A" is friendly towards such Rāśis and their owners. Besides this, a Graha is friendly towards the Rāśi, where he attains Ucca. If Graha "A" is both friendly and hostile towards two Rāśis owned by a Graha "B", the said Graha "A" is neutral towards that Graha "B". A Graha is hostile towards the Rāśis and the Lord of the Rāśis that are in Upacaya and Saptama from its Mūlatrikoṇa.

(77) In Tatkālika Sambandha, a Graha is friendly towards a Graha who is in the 2nd, 3rd, 4th, 10th, 11th, or 12th from him. For Naisargika Sambandha, Rāhu's Mūlatrikoṇa should be taken as Kanyā and Ketu's Mīna.

(78) When a Graha (A) is both Naisargika and Tatkālika Mitra of another Graha (B), the Graha A becomes Graha B's Adhimitra. Similarly, Mitra and Sama become Mitra, Mitra and Śatru become Sama, Śatru and Sama become Śatru, and Śatru and Śatru become Adhiśatru. This gives rise to a fivefold relationship called Pañcadhā Sambandha. The Daivajña should consider these and declare the results accordingly.

(79) Naisargika Sambandha: **(1)** Sūrya is friendly to Candra, Maṅgala and Bṛhaspati; neutral to Budha; hostile to Śukra and Śani. **(2)** Candra is friendly to Sūrya and Budha; neutral to Maṅgala, Bṛhaspati, Śukra and Śani; hostile to none. **(3)** Maṅgala is friendly to Sūrya, Candra and Bṛhaspati; neutral to Śani and Śukra; hostile to Budha. **(4)** Budha is friendly to Sūrya and Śukra, neutral to Maṅgala, Bṛhaspati and Śani, and hostile to Candra. **(5)** Bṛhaspati is friendly to Sūrya, Candra and Maṅgala; neutral to Śani; hostile to Budha and Śukra; **(6)** Śukra is friendly to Budha and Śani; neutral to Maṅgala and Bṛhaspati; hostile to Sūrya and Candra. **(7)** Śani is friendly to Budha and Śukra, neutral to Bṛhaspati, and hostile to Sūrya, Candra and Maṅgala.

GRAHA DIGNITY

(80) The Uccarāśi and Uccāñśa of the Grahas are Sūrya Meṣa 10°, Candra Vṛṣabha 3°, Maṅgala Makara 28°, Budha Kanyā 15°, Bṛhaspati Karka 5°, Śukra Mīna 27° and Śani Tulā 20°. The seventh Rāśi/Añśa from the said Uccarāśi the Grahas have their Nīca Rāśi/Añśa.

(81) In Siṅha, the first 20° is Sūrya's Mūlatrikoṇa, and the remaining is his Svakṣetra. In Vṛṣabha, the first 3° is Candra's Ucca, and the rest is his Mūlatrikoṇa. In Meṣa Maṅgala, the first 12° is Mūlatrikoṇa, and the remaining is his Svakṣetra. In Kanyā, the first 15° is Budha's Ucca; the next 5° is his Mūlatrikoṇa and the last 10° his Svakṣetra. In Dhanu, the first 10° is Bṛhaspati's Mūlatrikoṇa, while the remaining 20° is his Svakṣetra. In Tulā, the first 15° is Śukra's Mūlatrikoṇa, and the next 15° is his Svakṣetra. The same is the case of Śani in Kumbha and Sūrya in Siṅha. Mūlatrikoṇa is connected to the Graha's root impulse, Svakṣetra is his home, the Uccakṣetra is the Graha's place of achievement and honour, whereas the Nīcakṣetra is the place of deprivation.

(82) A Graha in Ucca gives 100% Śubha results, while in Mūlatrikoṇa, it is 75% Śubha. In Svakṣetra, the Graha is 50% Śubha, while in Mitrarāśi, the Graha is 25% Śubha. In a Samarāśi, the Graha is only 12.5% Śubha. In Nīca/Śatru Rāśi, it is 0% Śubha. The Aśubha effects of such disposition are 100% - Śubha effects.

THE AVASTHĀS

(83) There are nine psychological states or Avasthās. Depending on such a state of the Graha, the Bhāva, occupied by it, obtain corresponding results. In a

Uccarāśi, a Graha is Dipta (radiant), Svarāśi Svastha (healthy), Adhimitrarāśi Pramudita or Mudita (happy), Mitrarāśi Śānta (peaceful), Samarāśi Dīna (unhappy), in Krūrayuti Vikala (restless), in Śatrurāśi Duḥkhita (grieving), in an Adhiśatru Rāśi Khala (mischievous), Asta Kopa (short-tempered).

RETROGRESSION AND COMBUSTION

(84) When a Graha is very close to Sūrya, it undergoes Astāṅgata or combustion. An Astāṅgata Graha is powerless and fails to protect its signification. Sūryasiddhānta gives the following orbs of combustion: Maṅgala 17°, Budha 12° (vakrī) 14° (mārgī), Bṛhaspati 11°, Śukra 8° (vakrī) and 10° (mārgī), Śani 15°.

(85) The opposite of combustion is retrogression or Vakragati. At retrogression, a Graha is very powerful as its disc is visible from Pṛthvī, and it is closest to Pṛthvī. Such a Graha is granted high Ceṣṭābala or Motional strength. The effects of a Vakrīgraha are unpredictable because it appears to move in a reverse direction. Normally, a Vakrī Graha in a Kuṇḍalī gives exceeding desire and determination to carry out its mandate based on its natural significations, ownership, and occupation. However, the effects are realised after great effort. The effects are also significantly high, as it is the result of arduous effort. Vakrī Śubhagrahas are greatly benevolent (Mahāśubha), and Vakrī Krūragrahas are greatly malevolent (Mahākrūra).

(86) However, It is prohibitive to have Vakrī Saumyagraha in a Dusthāna subject to Krūrayutidṛṣṭi or Pāpakartari, as that causes great suffering in life and even death. Vakrī Graha also causes one to make repeated efforts. Also, it shows things that arise time and again. Therefore, there must not be a Vakrīgraha in a Dusthāna; else, enemies may arise if, in the 6th, repeated expenditure may rise in the 12th, and there is a danger to life if a Vakrī Krūragraha is in the 8th.

THE VARGAS

(87) There are 16 kinds of subdivisions of a Rāśi called the Vargas or the Divisional charts. They are Rāśi D1, Horā D2, Dreṣkāṇa D3, Caturthāñśa D4, Saptāñśa D7, Navāñśa D9, Daśāñśa D10, Dvādaśāñśa D12, Kālāñśa D16, Viñśāñśa D20, Caturviṁśāñśa D24, Saptaviṁśāñśa D27, Triñśāñśa D30, Khavedāñśa D40, Akṣavedāñśa D45 and Ṣaṣṭhyāñśa D60.

(88) We should judge one's physique from Lagna, wealth from Horā, happiness through co-born from Dreṣkāṇa, fortunes from Caturthāñśa, children and grandchildren from Saptāñśa, spouse from Navāṅś, power (and influence) from Daśāñśa, parents from Dvādaśāñśa, benefits and adversities through conveyances from Kālāñśa, worship from Viṁśāñśa, learning from Caturviṁśāñśa, strength and weakness from Bhāñśa, evil effects from Triñśāñśa, auspicious and inauspicious effects from Khavedāñśa and all indications from both Akṣavedāñśa and Ṣaṣṭhyāñśa.

(89) There are four kinds of Vargas, viz. Ṣadvarga, Saptavarga, Daśavarga and Ṣoḍaśavarga. The Ṣadvargas consist of D1, D2, D3, D9, D12 and

D30. Adding the D7 to the Ṣadvargas, we get Saptavarga. Adding D10, D16 and D60 to the Saptavarga, we get the Dasavarga scheme. The Ṣoḍaśavarga contains all 16 Vargas.

(90) The Rāśi (D1), Dreṣkāṇa (D3), Navāñśa (D9) and Dvādaśāñśa (D12) are the most used Vargas for regular day-to-day predictions. Among them, Navāñśa is the most significant. When a Graha is in the same Rāśi and Navāñśa, it is called Vargottama, which is conducive to favourable results. A Vargottama Graha bestows favourable results, even if it is Nīca Vargottama. A Graha in the 1st Dreṣkāṇa of Cararāśi, 2nd of Sthirarāśi and the 3rd of Ubhayarāśi are in Vargottama Dreṣkāṇa in a special Dreṣkāṇa called Somanātha Dreṣkāṇa. A Graha in Vargottama Navāñśa is invariably in Vargottama Dreṣkāṇa.

THE 12 BHĀVAS

(91) 12 Bhāvas govern different areas of life. By judging each of these individual Bhāvas, we can judge one's entire Kuṇḍalī. The lord of a Bhāva is called Bhāvanātha, Bhāveśa, Bhāvādhipati or Bhāvapati. The lords of the 12 Bhāvas are respectively called 1 Lagneśa LL, 2 Dhaneśa 2L, 3 Sahajeśa 3L, 4 Sukheśa 4L, 5 Mantreśa/Suteśa 5L, 6 Ṣaṣṭheśa 6L, 7 Dāreśa 7L, 8 Randhreśa 8L, 9 Bhagyeśa/Dharmeśa 9L, 10 Karmeśa 10L, 11 Lābheśa 11L and 12 Vyāyeśa 12L.

(92) The 1st Bhāva is called the Tanubhāva. It denotes the body, its form, colour, caste, stay in foreign lands, strength, weakness, good and bad acts, place of residence, Bālāriṣṭa (infantile death), happiness and unhappiness.

(93) The 2nd Bhāva is called the Dhanabhāva. It denotes finance, money, wealth, eye, face, speech, family, food, tongue, teeth, death, begging, timidity, nose, and welfare of family members.

(94) The 3rd Bhāva is called the Sahajabhāva. It denotes younger siblings and cousins, courage, bravery, fear, voice, ear, fruits, father's death, strength, dress, mental stability, and firmness.

(95) The 4th Bhāva is called the Sukhabhāva. It denotes comfort, education, conveyance, heart, landed property, house, mother, friends, relatives, cattle, and buildings.

(96) The 5th Bhāva is called the Mantrabhāva. It denotes children, intelligence, meritorious deeds, charity, kingship, duty, respect for parents and success in attempts.

(97) The 6th Bhāva is called the Aribhāva. It denotes diseases, troubles from enemies, worries, injuries, litigation, sorrows, maternal uncle, injuries, armies, mental worries, and legal involvements.

(98) The 7th Bhāva is called the Dārābhāva. It denotes marriage, wife, travel, death journeys, change of residence and foreign travel.

(99) The 8th Bhāva is called the Randhrabhāva. It denotes longevity, misfortunes, sins, debts, hostility, death, difficulties, impediments, grief and unhappiness resulting from sins committed in previous births, sudden and untimely death and enemies.

(100) The 9th Bhāva is called the Bhāgyabhāva. It denotes the father, preceptor, devatā, Brāhmaṇa, guests, fortunes, meritorious deeds, righteousness, charities, and merits accrued from past births.

(101) The 10th Bhāva is called the Karmabhāva. It denotes livelihood, profession, occupations, commerce, trade, honour, rank, fame, authority, command, superior, boss, king, sovereign, government, dress, pilgrimage, and occupations of one's Varṇa (inherited from the father).

(102) The 11th Bhāva is called the Lābhabhāva. It denotes income, gains, profits, elder brother, ornaments, fulfilment of desires, acquisition of wealth and profits through commerce.

(103) The 12th Bhāva is called the Vyāyabhāva. It denotes losses, expenditures, misery, mokṣa (salvation), poverty, expenses, donations, charities, hostile activity, loss by theft, incarceration, bondage, encounters with thieves, the left eye, physical weakness, sin, sleeping comfort, feet, etc.

THE EFFECTS OF BHĀVA LORDS

(104) Effects of 1L: 1H: Physical happiness, prowess, intelligence, fickle-minded, two wives, affairs with other females. **2H**: Gainful, scholarly, happy, good qualities, religious, honourable, many wives. **3H**: Equal a lion in fearlessness, all kinds of wealth, honourable, two wives, intelligent, happy. **4H**: Paternal and maternal happiness, many brothers, lustful, virtuous, charming. **5H**: Mediocre happiness from children, lose the first child, honourable, wrathful, dear to king. **6H**: Krūrayuti and devoid of Saumyadṛṣṭi- lack physical happiness, troubled by enemies. **7H**: Krūra Lagneśa- the wife, does not live long. Saumya Lagneśa- wanders, faces poverty, and is dejected. Powerful Lagneśa- a king. **8H**: An accomplished scholar, sickly, thievish, wrathful, a gambler, affairs with others' wives. **9H**: Fortunate, dear to people, be a devotee of Śrī Viṣṇu, be skilful, eloquent in speech and be endowed with wife, sons, and wealth. **10H**: Endowed with paternal happiness, royal honour, famous, and self-earned wealth. **11H**: Always gainful, good qualities, virtues, fame, many wives. **12H**: Devoid of Saumyayutidṛṣṭi- bereft of physical happiness, wasteful expenditure, wrathful.

(105) Effects of 2L: 1H: Endowed with sons and wealth, inimical to his family, lustful, hard-hearted, do others' jobs. **2H**: Wealthy, proud, two or more wives, lack children. **3H**: Saumya Sahajeśa- Fearless, wise, virtuous, lustful, miserly. Krūra Sahajeśa- a heterodox. **4H**: Acquire all kinds of wealth. Ucca Dhaneśa or with Bṛhaspati- equal to a king. **5H**: Wealthy, the person and his children are adept in financial management and building wealth. **6H**: Saumyayuti- gains wealth through his enemies. Krūrayuti- loss through enemies, mutilation of shanks. **7H**: Affairs with others' wives, a doctor. Krūrayutidṛṣṭi- wife is of questionable character. **8H**: Abundant land and wealth, little marital felicity, lacking happiness from his elder brother. **9H**: Wealthy, diligent, skilful, sickly childhood, and happy later, visit shrines, observe religious yoga, etc. **10H**: Lustful, honourable, learned, many wives, much wealth, lack familial happiness. **11H**: All kinds of wealth, ever diligent, honourable, famous. **12H**: Adventurous, devoid of wealth, coveting others' wealth, lacking happiness from the eldest child.

(106) Effects of 3L: 1H: Self-made wealth, worshipping, fearless, intelligent but devoid of learning. **2H**: Corpulent, lacking courage, effort and enterprise, unhappy, covets others' wives and wealth. **3H**: Happiness through siblings, endowed with wealth and sons, cheerful, extremely happy. **4H**: Happy, wealthy, intelligent, wicked spouse. **5H**: Endowed with sons and virtues. Krūrayutidṛṣṭi- a formidable wife. **6H**: Hostile to his sibling, affluent, hostile to maternal uncle but dear to maternal aunt. **7H**: Serve the king, unhappy childhood, happiness at the end of life. **8H**: Thievish, lives by serving others and dies at the gate of the royal palace (royal punishment). **9H**: Lacking paternal bliss, fortunes through wife, happiness from children and other avenues. **10H**: All kinds of happiness, self-made wealth and nurture wicked females. **11H**: Gainful in trading, intelligent but devoid of learning, adventurous, serves others. **12H**: Spend on evil deeds, a wicked father, fortunate through a female.

(107) Effects of 4L: 1H: Endowed with learning, virtues, ornaments, lands, conveyances and maternal happiness. **2H**: Enjoy pleasures, abundant wealth, family life and honour, adventurous, cunning. **3H**: Fearless, endowed with servants, charitable, virtuous, self-earned wealth, and disease-free. **4H**: A minister, all kinds of wealth, skilful, virtuous, honourable, learned, happy, cordial, his spouse. **5H**: Happy, liked by all, devoted to Lord Viṣṇu, virtuous, honourable, self-earned wealth. **6H**: Lack maternal happiness, wrathful, a thief, a conjurer, independent in action, hostile. **7H**: Highly educated, sacrifices his patrimony, mute in an assembly of scholars. **8H**: Devoid of domestic and other comforts, not much parental happiness, neuter-like. **9H**: Dear to all, devoted to Devatās, virtuous, honourable, all kinds of happiness. **10H**: Royal honours, an alchemist, contented, endowed with comforts, conquer the five senses. **11H**: Secret diseases, virtuous, charitable, helpful to others. **12H**: Lack of domestic and other comforts, with vices, foolish, lazy.

(108) Effects of 5L: 1H: Scholarly, happiness from children, miserly, crooked, stealing others' wealth. **2H**: Many sons, wealthy, support his family, honourable, attached to his spouse, worldwide fame. **3H**: Attached to his sibling, a talebearer, miserly, always mind his work. **4H**: Happy, happiness from the mother, endowed with wealth and intelligence, a king, a minister, or a preceptor. **5H**: Virtuous and dear to friends. Saumyayuti- beget children. Krūrayuti- lack children. **6H**: Sons are his enemies; he may lose them and acquire an adopted or purchased son. **7H**: Honourable, devout, happiness from children, helpful to others. **8H**: Lacking happiness from children, cough and pulmonary disorders, wrathful, no happiness. **9H**: A prince or equivalent, author treatises, famous, shine in his race (Kuladīpaka). **10H**: Rājayoga, various pleasures, widely famous. **11H**: Learned, dear to people, an author of treatises, very skilful and endowed with many sons and wealth. **12H**: Lacking happiness from his sons, an adopted or purchased son.

(109) Effects of 6L: 1H: Sickly, famous, inimical to his relatives, wealthy, honourable, adventurous, virtuous. **2H**: Adventurous, famous in his community, live overseas, happy, eloquent, mind his work. **3H**: Wrathful, lacks courage, hostile to his siblings, disobedient servants. **4H**: Lacking happiness from the mother, intelligent, a talebearer, jealous, evil-minded, very wealthy. **5H**: Fluctuating finances, selfish, enmity with his sons and friends, happy, kind. **6H**: Enmity with his relatives, friendly to others, mediocre happiness in wealth matters. **7H**: Lack marital happiness, famous, virtuous, honourable, adventurous, wealthy. **8H**: Sickly, inimical, covet others' wealth and wives, impure. **9H**: Trade in wood and stones, fluctuations in trade and wealth. **10H**: Well known among his men, hostile to his father, happy in a foreign land, an orator. **11H**: Financial gains from enemies or competitors, virtuous, adventurous, lacking happiness from children. Krūra Ṣaṣtheśa- losses caused by enemies and robbers, danger to life caused by enemies and dacoits. **12H**: Spend on vices, hostile to learned people, torture living beings.

(110) Effects of 7L: 1H: Affairs with others' wives, wicked, skilful, devoid of courage, Vāta disorders. **2H**: Many wives, fortune through wife, procrastinating. **3H**: Loss of children, rarely a son survives, may beget a daughter. **4H**: Disobedient or non-committed wife, fond of truth, intelligent, religious, dental diseases. **5H**: honourable, endowed with all virtues, delighted, and with all kinds of wealth. **6H**: Sickly wife, hostile to her, wrathful, lacking happiness. **7H**: Happiness from wife, courageous, skilful, intelligent, Vāta disorder. **8H**: Lacking marital happiness, diseases afflicting the wife, arrogant and not devoted to the person, losses in trade, sickly, wrathful, lustful, and wasting money on unchaste women. **9H**: Affairs or the company of many women, cordial to his wife, many undertakings. Krūra Dāreśa- difficulties in begetting children. **10H**: Disobedient wife, religious, endowed with wealth and sons. **11H**: Gain of fortune through wife, less happiness from sons, beget daughters. **12H**: Penury, miserly, earning from clothes, wife is a spendthrift.

(111) Effects of 8L: 1H: Lack of physical felicity, wounds and injuries, hostility to Devatās and Brāhmaṇas. **2H**: Lack bodily vigour, little wealth, not regain lost wealth. **3H**: Lacking fraternal happiness and strength, lazy, devoid of servants. **4H**: Deprived of his mother, no house, lands and happiness, he betrays his friends. **5H**: Dull-witted, fewer children, long-lived, wealthy. **6H**: Subdue enemies, sickly childhood, and danger from snakes and water. **7H**: Two wives. Krūrayuti- downfall in business. **8H**: Long-lived. Weakness- medium lifespan, a thief, blameworthy, blames others. **9H**: Betray his religion, a heterodox, wicked wife, and steal others' wealth. **10H**: Lacking happiness from the father, a talebearer, lacking a good source of earning. Saumyadṛṣṭi- the evils are nullified. **11H**: Lack of wealth, miserable childhood, happiness later. Saumyayuti- long-lived. **12H**: Spend on evil deeds, short lifespan, more so if subject to Krūrayuti.

(112) Effects of 9L: 1H: Fortunate, honoured by the king, virtuous, charming, learned, honoured by the public. **2H**: A scholar, dear to all, wealthy, sensuous, happiness from wife and sons. **3H**: Fraternal happiness, wealthy, virtuous, charming. **4H**: Endowed with houses, conveyances and happiness, all kinds of wealth, devoted to his mother. **5H**: Endowed with sons and prosperity, devoted to elders, bold, charitable, and learned. **6H**: Meagre prosperity, lacking happiness from maternal relatives, ever troubled by enemies. **7H**: Happiness after marriage, virtuous and famous. **8H**: Not prosperous, lacking happiness from his elder brother. **9H**: Abundant fortunes, virtues, beauty, and much happiness from siblings. **10H**: A king or equivalent, a minister, an Army chief, virtuous, dear to all. **11H**: Wealth increases daily, devoted to elders, virtuous, meritorious deeds. **12H**: Loss of fortunes, expenditure on auspicious acts, becomes poor on account of entertaining guests.

(113) Effects of 10L: 1H: Scholarly, famous, a poet, sickly childhood and happiness later, wealth increases daily. **2H**: Wealthy, virtuous, honoured by the king, charitable, happiness from father and others. **3H**: Happiness from siblings and servants, fearless, virtuous, eloquent, truthful. **4H**: Happy, look after mother's welfare, lord over conveyances, lands and houses, virtuous, wealthy. **5H**: All kinds of learning, always delighted, wealthy, happiness from sons. **6H**: Lacking happiness from the father, skilful but lacking wealth, troubled by enemies. **7H**: Happiness from wife, intelligent, virtuous, eloquent, truthful, religious. **8H**: Devoid of meritorious acts, long-lived, blame others. **9H**: One born into a royal family becomes a king. A normal person becomes equal to a king, wealthy, happiness from children. **10H**: Skilful in all jobs, fearless, truthful, and devoted to elders. **11H**: Endowed with wealth, happiness and sons, virtuous, truthful, ever delighted. **12H**: Spend through royal abodes, fear from enemies, worried despite being skilful.

(114) Effects of 11L: 1H: Sincere, wealthy, happy, even-sighted, a poet, eloquent, ever gainful. **2H**: All kinds of wealth and accomplishments, charitable, religious, ever happy. **3H**: Skilful in all jobs, wealthy, happiness from siblings, sometimes gout pains. **4H**: Gain from maternal relatives, visit shrines, undertake pilgrimages, and happiness through houses and lands. **5H**: Happy, educated, virtuous, religious, happy. **6H**: Sickly, cruel, living overseas, troubled by enemies. **7H**: Gain through the wife's relatives, charitable, virtuous, sensual, and obedient to the spouse. **8H**: Reversals in undertakings, Dīrghāyu, wife predeceases him. **9H**: Fortunate, skilful, truthful, honoured by the king, affluent. **10H**: Honoured by the king, virtuous, faithful to his religion, intelligent, truthful, and controlling his senses. **11H**: Gain in all his undertakings, learning, and happiness increase daily. **12H**: Depend on good deeds, sensuous, many wives, and befriending barbarians (Mlecchas, or people of a different culture/religion).

(115) Effects of 12L: 1H: Spendthrift, frail constitution, Kapha disorder, lacking wealth and learning. **2H**: Spend on evil deeds, religious, speaking sweetly, righteousness, and happiness. **3H**: Lack of happiness from siblings, hostile to others, focused on self-nourishment. **4H**: Lack of happiness from the mother, financial losses, lands, conveyances and houses. **5H**: Devoid of sons and learning, spend wealth and visit shrines to beget a son. **6H**: Hostility with own men, wrathful, sinful, miserable, affairs with others' wives. **7H**: Expenditure through wife, lack conjugal bliss, bereft of learning and strength. **8H**: Ever gainful, affable speaker, medium lifespan, all good qualities. **9H**: Dishonour his elders, hostile even to friends, selfish, ever intent on achieving his ends. **10H**: Expenditure through royal people, moderate happiness from the father. **11H**: Financial losses brought up by others, sometimes gaining from others. **12H**: Heavy expenditure, lacking physical felicity, irritable, wrathful.

THE RULES OF BHĀVA ASSESSMENT

(116) Bhava analysis from Jātakapārijāta: **Rule 1-5: (1)** When a Saumya or the Bhāvanātha occupies/dṛṣṭies a Bhāva, the Bhāva prospers. If the Bhāva is subject to Krūrayutidṛṣṭi, the auspicious results are proportionally diminished. **(2)** If both Saumyas and Krūras influence a Bhāva, the results should be judged based on their relative strength. **(3)** When a Graha (Kāraka/Bhāvanātha) is in a Nīca/Śatru Rāśi, the Bhāva (owned/occupied) is spoilt. In contrast, when a Graha is in its Mūlatrikoṇa/Svakṣetra/Ucca/ Mitra Rāśi, the Bhāva prospers. **(4)** When a Bhāvanātha is in a dusthāna, its Bhāva is ruined. Similarly, when a Trikeśa occupies a Bhāva, the results of that Bhāva is ruined. Some redemption is expected when the Bhāva is subject to Saumyadṛṣṭi. **(5)** When a Bhāvanātha is in a Kendrakoṇa from the Lagna, subject to Saumyadṛṣṭi, in Ucca Varga (Dreṣkāṇa/Navāñśa) or powerful in Ṣaḍbala, the Bhāva prospers.

(117) Bhava analysis from Jātakapārijāta: **Rule 6-10: (6)** If Saumyas occupy the Kendrakoṇas from a Bhāva without Krūrayutidṛṣṭi, the Bhāva prospers. The results are mixed if both Saumyas and Krūras influence those places. If the Krūra so placed is the Bhāvanātha, it does not ruin the Bhāva. The effects are experienced in the Daśābhuktis of the Grahas. **(7)** A Bhāva is ruined if the Bhāvanātha is weak/afflicted in the following ways: (a) placed in the 8th house from the Bhāva, (b) Astaṅgata, (c) in a Nīca/Śatru Rāśi (d) without Saumyayutidṛṣṭi. **(8)** A Bhāva does not prosper if the Bhāvanātha's Rāśyeśa is in a Dusthāna, Śatrurāśi or Asta. **(9)** If a Graha is in a Dusthāna or Krūra/Nīca/Śatru Navāñśa, it is afflicted or powerless. Suppose the Graha is dṛṣṭied by a fortified Saumya who is in Ucca/Mitra Navāñśa. In that case, the weakness of the "weak/afflicted" Graha is curtailed, and some auspicious results of the Bhāva (owned/occupied) are experienced. **(10)** If the Bhāvanātha's Rāśyeśa is in a Duḥstha, then Bhāva becomes weak (in bestowing auspicious results). Similarly, if the Rāśyeśa is in a Svakṣetra, Ucca, Mitra or Sva Rāśi, the specific Bhāva becomes strong in bestowing auspicious results.

(118) Bhava analysis from Jātakapārijāta: **Rule 11-12: (11)** If from a Bhāva, the Bhāvanātha, Bhāvanātha's Mitra or the Bhāvanātha's Uccanātha are in the 2nd, 3rd, or 11th from the Bhāva, the Bhāva prospers, provided the Grahas are not in their Nīca/Śatru Rāśi or Asta. **(12)** A Graha produces its full Bhāva effects near the Bhāvamadhya. In other places, the effects are proportionally reduced.

BASICS OF SIDDHĀNTA

(119) There are 4320000 sidereal years in a Mahāyuga. In this, there are 1577917828 Sāvanadinas. In a Kalpa, there are 1000 Mahāyugas, and 1577917828000 Sāvanadinas. Sāvanadina is a civil day and is the duration between two sunrises.

(120) The J2000 (JD 2451545 01.01.2000 12:00 GMT) Mean Longitudes (Madhyasphuṭa) of the Grahas are Sūrya 256.482, Candra 195.631, Maṅgala 331.485, Budha 227.988, Bṛhaspati 10.405, Śukra 158.016, Śani 26.048, Rāhu 99.987, Ketu 279.987, Prajāpati (Uranus) 289.503, Varuṇa (Neptune) 281.231 and Yama (Pluto) 215.883.

(121) The Mean Revolutions (Bhagaṇa) of Grahas in Mahāyugas according to Sūryasiddhānta are Sūrya 4320000, Candra 57753336, Maṅgala 2296832, Budha Ucca 17937060, Bṛhaspati 364220, Śukra Ucca 7022376, Śani 146568, Rāhu/Ketu -232238. Their modern values of Bhagaṇa are Sūrya 4320028, Candra 57753364, Maṅgala 2296892, Budha Ucca 17937184, Bṛhaspati 364196, Śukra Ucca 7022300, Śani 146656, Rāhu/Ketu -232270, Prajāpati 51416, Varuṇa 26220 and Yama 17424.

(122) The Mean Daily Speed of the Grahas in degrees are Sūrya 0.985607, Candra 13.17636, Maṅgala 0.524033, Budha Ucca 4.092338, Bṛhaspati 0.083052, Śukra Ucca 1.602128, Śani 0.033455, Rāhu/Ketu -0.052992, Prajāpati 0.011731, Varuṇa 0.005981 and Yama 0.003975. Daily speed = Bhagaṇa * 360 / 1577917828, where 1577917828 is the Sāvanadina in a Mahāyuga.

(123) The Longitudes of Perihelion (w1) of the Grahas at J2000 are Candra 59.382, Budha 53.487, Śukra 107.796, Pṛthvī 78.959, Maṅgala 312.111, Bṛhaspati 350.304, Śani 68.89, Prajapati 148.463, Varuṇa 22.71, Yama 200.126. Their Kalpa Bhagaṇa, the Mean revolutions in a Kalpa are Candra 488125677.043, Budha 19128.474, Śukra 6815.741, Pṛthvī 38155.227, Maṅgala 54269.651, Bṛhaspati 21839.559, Śani 65016.932, Prajapati 11120.649, Varuṇa 1211.955, Yama -1162.62. Mean daily speed = Kalpa Bhagaṇa * 360 / 1577917828000.

(124) The Longitudes of the Ascending Node (N) of the Grahas at J2000 are Candra 101.072, Budha 24.368, Śukra 52.701, Pṛthvī 0.0, Maṅgala 25.742, Bṛhaspati 76.322, Śani 89.669, Prajapati 49.991, Varuṇa 107.815, Yama 86.331. Their Kalpa Bhagaṇa are Candra -232269736.9, Budha -14657.37, Śukra -32729.793, Pṛthvī 0.0, Maṅgala -32223.69, Bṛhaspati 15629.918, Śani -30018.722, Prajapati 6887.804, Varuṇa -727.58, Yama -972.001. Mean daily speed = Kalpa Bhagaṇa * 360 / 1577917828000.

(125) The Eccentricity (e) of their orbits are Candra 0.054900, Budha 0.205637, Śukra 0.006764, Pṛthvī 0.016732, Maṅgala 0.093365, Bṛhaspati 0.048536, Śani 0.055508, Prajapati 0.046857, Varuṇa 0.008954, Yama 0.248852.

(126) The Inclination (i) of the Grahas are Candra 5.1454, Budha 7.006, Śukra - 3.398, Pṛthvī 0.0, Maṅgala 1.852, Bṛhaspati 1.299, Śani 2.494, Prajapati 0.773, Varuṇa 1.77, Yama 0.249.

(127) The Mean Distance (a) of the Grahas from Sūrya in AU (Astronomical Unit) are Budha 0.387; Śukra 0.723, Pṛthvī 1.0, Maṅgala 1.524, Bṛhaspati 5.202, Śani 9.541, Prajāpati 19.188, Varuṇa 30.07, Yama 39.487. Candra's mean distance from Pṛthvī is 0.00257. 1 AU = 1.495978707E11 m.

(128) Modified JD or MJD values from 1950 to 2050 at 1 Jan 00:00 Hrs (Epoch = J2000): 50: -18262.5, 51: -17897.5, 52: -17532.5, 53: -17166.5, 54: -16801.5, 55: -16436.5, 56: -16071.5, 57: -15705.5, 58: -15340.5, 59: -14975.5, 60: -14610.5, 61: -14244.5, 62: -13879.5, 63: -13514.5, 64: -13149.5, 65: -12783.5, 66: -12418.5, 67: -12053.5, 68: -11688.5, 69: -11322.5, 70: -10957.5, 71: -10592.5, 72: -10227.5, 73: -9861.5, 74: -9496.5, 75: -9131.5, 76: -8766.5, 77: -8400.5, 78: -8035.5, 79: -7670.5, 80: -7305.5, 81: -6939.5, 82: -6574.5, 83: -6209.5, 84: -5844.5, 85: -5478.5, 86: -5113.5, 87: -4748.5, 88: -4383.5, 89: -4017.5, 90: -3652.5, 91: -3287.5, 92: -2922.5, 93: -2556.5, 94: -2191.5, 95: -1826.5, 96: -1461.5, 97: -1095.5, 98: -730.5, 99: -365.5, 00: -0.5, 01: 365.5, 02: 730.5, 03: 1095.5, 04: 1460.5, 05: 1826.5, 06: 2191.5, 07: 2556.5, 08: 2921.5, 09: 3287.5, 10: 3652.5, 11: 4017.5, 12: 4382.5, 13: 4748.5, 14: 5113.5, 15: 5478.5, 16: 5843.5, 17: 6209.5, 18: 6574.5, 19: 6939.5, 20: 7304.5, 21: 7670.5, 22: 8035.5, 23: 8400.5, 24: 8765.5, 25: 9131.5, 26: 9496.5, 27: 9861.5, 28: 10226.5, 29: 10592.5, 30: 10957.5, 31: 11322.5, 32: 11687.5, 33: 12053.5, 34: 12418.5, 35: 12783.5, 36: 13148.5, 37: 13514.5, 38: 13879.5, 39: 14244.5, 40: 14609.5, 41: 14975.5, 42: 15340.5, 43: 15705.5, 44: 16070.5, 45: 16436.5, 46: 16801.5, 47: 17166.5, 48: 17531.5, 49: 17897.5, 50: 18262.5.

(129) Julian Date JD = MJD + 2451545. Sṛṣṭi Ahargaṇa = JD + 714401708162.4604. Kali Ahargaṇa = JD - 588465.5395. The Sṛṣṭi and Kali Ahargaṇas are the continuous day count from Sṛṣṭi and Kali. The J2000 Sṛṣṭi Ayanāñśa is 23.971177. Sṛṣṭi Ayanāñśa = 23.971177 + MJD * 3.824477E-5.

(130) Day elapsed from Jan1 = date + month index – 1. For a non-leap year, the month indices are Jan- 0, Feb- 31, Mar- 59, Apr- 90, May- 120, Jun- 151, Jul- 181, Aug- 212, Sep- 243, Oct- 273, Nov- 304, Dec- 334. For a leap year, the month indices are Jan- 0, Feb- 31, Mar- 60, Apr- 91, May- 121, Jun- 152, Jul- 182, Aug- 213, Sep- 244, Oct- 274, Nov- 305, Dec- 335. We need to convert the local time to GMT using the following formula: GMT = Local time - Time zone. The time zone is +ve for East and -ve for West. For instance, for Singapore, the time zone is +8. If the local standard meridian (longitude) is known, we can also use GMT = Local time - Local standard longitude / 15. Precise Days Elapsed = Days elapsed + GMT / 24. MJD = MJD for the year + Precise Days Elapsed.

(131) Let us find the MJD (modified JD) on 22 July 2021 at 4:45 pm SGT, Singapore. The time zone for Singapore is GMT+8. First and foremost, let us find the time elapsed from midnight of the beginning of the year GMT, i.e., 01.01.2021 00:00 GMT. The time in GMT is 22.07.2021 16.75 - 8.0, which is 22.07.2021 8.75 hrs. For July, the month index is 181 for a non-leap year. Day elapsed from Jan1 = 22 + 181 - 1 = 202. Precise Days Elapsed = 202 + 8.75 / 24 = 202.364583. The

MJD for 2021 is 7670.5, as per the data stated above. The MJD = 7670.5 + 202.364583 = 7872.864583.

(132) Analytical model of computing Approximate Graha coordinates: **Step1:** Ascertain the MJD (days elapsed from J2000). **Step2:** Ascertain the Mean Longitude (l) of the Graha (lp) and Pṛthvī (le). **Step3:** Ascertain the Longitude of Perihelion (w1) of the Graha (w1p) and Pṛthvī (w1e). **Step4:** Determine the Mean Anomaly (M). M = l - w1. Mr = M in radians = M * π/180. This must be found for both the Graha (Mp) and Pṛthvī (Me). **Step5:** Determine the Eccentric Anomaly (E). E = Mr + e * sin(Mr) * (1 + e * cos(Mr)). Here, 'e' is the eccentricity of the Graha. Convert E2 to degrees by multiplying 180/π. This must be found for both the Graha (Ep) and Pṛthvī (Ee). **Step6:** Compute the Distance from Sūrya (r) and True Anomaly (v). y = a sqrt(1 - e^2) sin E; x = a (cos E - e); r = sqrt(x^2 + y^2). True Anomaly v = atan2 (y, x). Here, 'a' is the mean distance of the Graha. **Step7:** Find True Helio Longitude (l'). l' = longitude of perihelion + true anomaly = w1 + v. **Step8:** Find the Rectangular Helio Ecliptic Coordinate (x', y', z'). x' = r cos l'; y' = r sin l', z'=0. Compute this for the Graha (x'g, y'g) and the Pṛthvī (x'e, y'e). True helio longitude = atan2(y', x'). **Step9:** Find the rectangular Geo Ecliptic Coordinate xg = x'g – x'e, and yg = y'g – y'e. **Step10:** Find the distance of the Graha from Pṛthvī (r) and the True Longitude (l). The distance of the Graha from Pṛthvī r = sqrt(xg^2 + yg^2) and Geo longitude l = atan2(yg, xg). **Additional Notes:** For Sūrya and Candra, only Step1 to Step7 are needed. Sūryasphuṭa = Pṛthvī Sphuṭa + 180. Candrasphuṭa is derived from Pṛthvī instead of Sūrya. For Rāhu/Ketu, only Step1 and Step2 are needed.

(133) Sāyana Sphuṭa = Nirāyana Sphuṭa + Ayanāñśa, or Nirāyana Sphuṭa = Sāyana Sphuṭa - Ayanāñśa.

MṚTYUBHĀGA

(134) The Mṛtyubhāga of Grahas are as follows – **(1)** Sūrya: ♈ 20°, ♉ 9°, ♊ 12°, ♋ 6°, ♌ 8°, ♍ 24°, ♎ 16°, ♏ 17°, ♐ 22°, ♑ 2°, ♒ 3°, ♓ 23; **(2)** Candra: ♈ 8°, ♉ 25°, ♊ 22°, ♋ 22°, ♌ 21°, ♍ 1°, ♎ 4°, ♏ 23°, ♐ 18°, ♑ 20°, ♒ 20°, ♓ 10; **(3)** Maṅgala: ♈ 19°, ♉ 28°, ♊ 25°, ♋ 23°, ♌ 29°, ♍ 28°, ♎ 14°, ♏ 21°, ♐ 2°, ♑ 15°, ♒ 11°, ♓ 6; **(4)** Budha: ♈ 15°, ♉ 14°, ♊ 13°, ♋ 12°, ♌ 8°, ♍ 18°, ♎ 20°, ♏ 10°, ♐ 21°, ♑ 22°, ♒ 7°, ♓ 5; **(5)** Bṛhaspati: ♈ 19°, ♉ 29°, ♊ 12°, ♋ 27°, ♌ 6°, ♍ 4°, ♎ 13°, ♏ 10°, ♐ 17°, ♑ 11°, ♒ 15°, ♓ 28; **(6)** Śukra: ♈ 28°, ♉ 15°, ♊ 11°, ♋ 17°, ♌ 10°, ♍ 13°, ♎ 4°, ♏ 6°, ♐ 27°, ♑ 12°, ♒ 29°, ♓ 19°; **(7)** Śani: ♈ 10°, ♉ 4°, ♊ 7°, ♋ 9°, ♌ 12°, ♍ 16°, ♎ 3°, ♏ 18°, ♐ 28°, ♑ 14°, ♒ 13°, ♓ 15; **(8)** Rāhu: ♈ 14°, ♉ 13°, ♊ 12°, ♋ 11°, ♌ 24°, ♍ 23°, ♎ 22°, ♏ 21°, ♐ 10°, ♑ 20°, ♒ 18°, ♓ 8; **(9)** Ketu: ♈ 8°, ♉ 18°, ♊ 20°, ♋ 10°, ♌ 21°, ♍ 22°, ♎ 23°, ♏ 24°, ♐ 11°, ♑ 12°, ♒ 13°, ♓ 14; **(10)** Lagna: ♈ 1°, ♉ 9°, ♊ 22°, ♋ 22°, ♌ 25°, ♍ 2°, ♎ 4°, ♏ 23°, ♐ 18°, ♑ 20°, ♒ 24°, ♓ 10; **(11)** Māndi: ♈ 23°, ♉ 24°, ♊ 11°, ♋ 12°, ♌ 13°, ♍ 14°, ♎ 8°, ♏ 18°, ♐ 20°, ♑ 10°, ♒ 21°, ♓ 22. The glyphs of the Rāśis are ♈ Meṣa°, ♉ Vṛṣabha°, ♊

Mithuna°, ♋ Karka°, ♌ Siṅha°, ♍ Kanyā°, ♎ Tulā°, ♏ Vṛścika°, ♐ Dhanu°, ♑ Makara°, ♒ Kumbha°, ♓ Mīna. Grahas in Mṛtyubhāga suffer the danger of great peril and death. To find whether a Graha is in Mṛtyubhāga, "round up" the Graha's Sphuṭa and check it in the above list. Let us say Śukra is in Mīna 18°27'12". It is rounded up to 19°. We notice that 19° of Mīna is Śukra's Mṛtyubhāga; therefore, we conclude that Śukra is in Mṛtyubhāga.

AMṚTA, VIṢA AND UṢṆA GHAṬIKĀS

(135) Amṛta, Viṣa and Uṣṇa Ghaṭikās: When a Nakṣatra is divided into 60 parts called Nakṣatra Ghaṭikās, some of them are designated as Amṛta, Viṣa and Uṣṇa Ghaṭikās. In a Rāśi, there are 2.25 Nakṣatras and, therefore, 135 Nakṣatra Ghaṭikās. Given below are these special Nakṣatra Ghaṭikās mapped to the 12 Rāśis. To find whether a Graha is in any of these special Ghaṭikās, we use the formula Nakṣatra Ghaṭi = Sphuṭa / 30 * 135. Let us say, in a Kuṇḍalī, the Lagna is in Dhanu 9:46:41. Its Sphuṭa is 9 + 46/60 + 41/3600 = 9.778. The Nakṣatra Ghaṭi = 9.778 / 30 * 135 = 44.001 = 45th. We notice that Dhanu 44-48 is Amṛtaghaṭikā. Therefore, the Lagna is in Amṛtaghaṭikā. Again, suppose Candra is in Dhanu 24.222°. This equals 24.222° / 30 * 135 = 108.99 = 109th. Even Candra is in Amṛtaghaṭikā in Dhanu Rāśi. Lagna's Sphuṭa is 9.778° of Dhanu, which is **(9 - 1)** * 30 + 9.778° = 249.778° Meṣādi Sphuṭa. This is in 249.778°/13.333° = 18.73 = 19th Nakṣatra, which is Mūla. Similarly, Candra is in **(9 - 1)** * 30 + 24.222° = 264.222° Meṣādi Sphuṭa and his Nakṣatra is 264.222° / 13.333° = 19.82 = 20th Nakṣatra, which is Pūrvāṣāṛhā. Therefore, the Lagna is in Amṛitaghaṭikā of Mūla, and Candra is in Amṛtaghaṭikā of Pūrvāṣāṛhā. Grahas, Āruṛhas etc., in the Amṛitaghaṭikā, indicate prosperity; the Viṣaghaṭikā, destruction; and the Uṣṇaghaṭikā, pain and suffering.

(136) Amṛtaghaṭikā: Meṣa: 42-46, 108-112; Vṛṣabha: 39-43, 97-101; Mithuna: 8-12, 65-69; Karka: 9-13, 59-63, 131-135; Siṅha: 54-58, 104-108; Kanyā: 28-31, 90-94; Tulā: 14-18, 68-72, 128-132; Vṛścika: 49-53, 113-117; Dhanu: 44-48, 108-112; Makara: 29-33, 79-83; Kumbha: 4-8, 73-76, 130-134; Mīna: 63-67, 129-133.

(137) Viṣaghaṭikā: Meṣa: 50-54, 84-88; Vṛṣabha: 15-19, 85-89, 119-123; Mithuna: 41-45, 120-124; Karka: 35-39, 107-111; Siṅha: 30-34, 80-84; Kanyā: 3-7, 67-71, 125-129; Tulā: 44-48, 104-108; Vṛścika: 25-29, 89-93; Dhanu: 20-24, 84-88; Makara: 5-9, 55-59, 115-119; Kumbha: 48-52, 106-110; Mīna: 39-43, 105-109.

(138) Uṣṇaghaṭikā: Meṣa: 8-15, 115-120; Vṛṣabha: 6-15, 53-60; Mithuna: 25-30, 51-60, 98-105; Karka: 70-75, 96-105; Siṅha: 7-15, 115-120; Kanyā: 6-15, 53-60; Tulā: 25-30, 51-60, 90-98; Vṛścika: 67-75, 95-105; Dhanu: 1-8, 112-120; Makara: 5-15, 45-53; Kumbha: 22-30, 50-60, 90-98; Mīna: 67-75, 95-105.

AṢṬAKAVARGA

(139) In Sūrya's Aṣṭakavarga, Sūrya/Maṅgala/Śani is favourable in 1, 2, 4, 7, 8, 9, 10 and 11 from self. Śukra in 6, 7 and 12. Bṛhaspati in 5, 6, 9 and 11. Candra in 3, 6, 10 and 11. Budha in 3, 5, 6, 9, 10, 11 and 12. Lagna in 2, 3, 4, 6, 10 and 11.

(140) In Candra's Aṣṭakavarga, he is favourable in 1, 3, 6, 7, 10 and 11 from self. Śukra in 3, 4, 5, 7, 9, 10 and 11. Bṛhaspati in 1, 4, 7, 8, 10, 11 and 12. Sūrya in 3, 6, 7, 8, 10 and 11. Budha in 1, 3, 4, 5, 7, 8 and 10. From Maṅgala in 2, 3, 5, 6, 9, 10 and 11. Śani in 3, 5, 6 and 11. Lagna in 3, 6, 10 and 11.

(141) In Maṅgala's Aṣṭakavarga, he is favourable in 1, 2, 4, 7, 8, 10 and 11 from self. From Śukra, he's good in 6, 8, 11 and 12. Bṛhaspati in 6, 10, 11 and 12. Sūrya in 3, 5, 6, 10 and 11. From in 3, 5, 6 and 11. From Candra in 3, 6 and 11. Śani in 1, 4, 7, 8, 9, 10 and 11. Lagna in 1, 3, 6, 10 and 11.

(142) In Budha's Aṣṭakavarga, he is favourable in 1, 3, 5, 6, 9, 10 and 11 from self. Śukra in 1, 2, 3, 4, 5, 8, 9 and 11. Bṛhaspati in 6, 8, 11 and 12. Sūrya in 5, 6, 9, 11 and 12. Maṅgala/Śani in 1, 2, 4, 7, 8, 9, 10 and 11. Candra in 2, 4, 6, 8, 10 and 11. Lagna in 1, 2, 4, 6, 8, 10 and 11.

(143) In Bṛhaspati's Aṣṭakavarga, he is favourable in 1, 2, 3, 4, 7, 8, 10 and 11 from self. Śukra in 2, 5, 6, 9, 10 and 11. Budha in 1, 2, 4, 5, 6, 9, 10 and 11. Sūrya in 1, 2, 3, 4, 7, 8, 9, 10 and 11. Maṅgala in 1, 2, 4, 7, 8, 10 and 11. Śani in 3, 5, 6 and 12. Candra in 2, 5, 7, 9 and 11. Lagna in 1, 2, 4, 5, 6, 7, 9, 10 and 11.

(144) In Śukra's Aṣṭakavarga, he is favourable in 1, 2, 3, 4, 5, 8, 9 and 11 from self. Bṛhaspati in 5, 8, 9, 10 and 11. Budha in 3, 5, 6, 9 and 11. Sūrya in 8, 11 and 12. Maṅgala in 3, 5, 6, 9, 11 and 12. Śani in 3, 4, 5, 8, 9, 10 and 11. Candra in 1, 2, 3, 4, 5, 8, 9, 11 and 12. Lagna in 1, 2, 3, 4, 5, 8, 9 and 11.

(145) In Śani's Aṣṭakavarga, he is favourable in 3, 5, 6 and 11 from self. Bṛhaspati in 5, 6, 11 and 12. Budha in 6, 8, 9, 10, 11 and 12. Sūrya in 1, 2, 4, 7, 8, 10 and 11. Maṅgala in 3, 5, 6, 10, 11 and 12. Śukra in 6, 11 and 12. Candra in 3, 6 and 11. Lagna in 1, 3, 4, 6, 10 and 11.

(146) Trikoṇa Śodhana: (a) If in a Trikoṇa, all the three Rāśis have an equal number of Rekhās, remove all. (b) If one Rāśi has Zero Rekhā, no change in the other two Rāśis shall be made. (c) If all Rāśis have Rekhās, the least among them should be reduced from all the Rāśis of the group. (d) If two Rāśis of the group have Zero Rekhās, the third one is zeroised.

(147) Ekādhipatya Śodhana: This Śodhana is done only for Grahas owning two Rāśis. This Śodhana is applied when at least one of the Rāśi in the pair is unoccupied. When Grahas occupy both Rāśis, this Śodhana is not applied. This is also not applied when one of the Rāśis has zero Trikoṇa Śodhita Rekhās. There are two essential rules. Principle1: If one of the Rāśis is occupied: The Rekhās of the occupied Rāśi are subtracted from the unoccupied one. If the result is less than zero, it is limited to zero. Principle2: If both Rāśis are unoccupied: The least Rekhās among the Rāśis are subtracted from the Rekhās of both the Rāśis.

TRANSIT TIME

(148) The **average Transit Periods of Grahas** through a Rāśi **"in days"** are Sūrya/Budha/Śukra 30.438, Candra 2.277, Maṅgala 57.248, Bṛhaspati 361.221, Śani 896.732, Rāhu/Ketu -566.127, Prajāpati 2557.238, Varuṇa 5015.76 and Yama 7546.669. The period **"in months/years"**: It is 1.88 months for Maṅgala, 11.867 months for Bṛhaspati, 29.461 months for Śani, 18.599 months for Rāhu/Ketu, 7.001 years for Prajāpati, 13.732 years for Varuṇa and 20.662 years for Yama. The heliocentric transit period in days for Budha is 7.331, and Śukra is 18.725.

(149) The **Synodic Periods of Grahas "in days"** are Candra 29.531, Maṅgala 779.94, Bṛhaspati 398.867, Śani 378.091, Prajāpati 369.657, Varuṇa 367.487 and Yama 366.736, Rāhu/Ketu 346.623. The synodic period of Budha is 115.877, and Śukra 583.922. *The synodic period is the time taken for two consecutive conjunctions, a Graha with Sūrya.*

GOCARA OF GRAHAS

(150) Favourable Gocara: Gocara Sūrya is favourable in the 6th, 3rd and 10th from the Janmarāśi, Candra in the 3rd, 10th, 6th, 7th and 1st; Bṛhaspati in the 7th, 9th, 2nd and 5th; Maṅgala and Śani in the 6th and 3rd; Budha in the 6th, 2nd, 4th, 10th and 8th; all Grahas are favourable in the 11th; Śukra is favourable in all places besides the 10th, 7th and 6th, Rāhu and Ketu are similar to Sūrya.

(151) Gocara Vedha: Sūrya's favourable Gocara through 3rd, 6th, 10th or 11th is blocked by a Graha in 9th, 12th, 4th or 5th. Candra's favourable Gocara through 1st, 7th, 3rd, 6th, 10th or 11th is blocked by a Graha in the 5th, 2nd, 9th, 12th, 4th or 8th. Maṅgala's or Śani's favourable Gocara through 3rd, 6th or 11th is blocked by a Graha in 12th, 9th or 5th. Budha's favourable Gocara through 2nd, 4th, 6th, 8th, 10th or 11th is blocked by a Graha in 5th, 3rd, 9th, 1st, 7th or 12th. Bṛhaspati's favourable Gocara through 2nd, 11th, 9th, 5th or 7th is blocked by Graha in 12th, 8th, 10th, 4th or 3rd. Śukra's favourable Gocara through 1st, 2nd, 3rd, 4th, 5th, 8th, 9th, 11th or 12th is blocked by a Graha in 8th, 7th, 1st, 10th, 9th, 5th, 11th, 3rd or 6th. Sūrya and Śani do not block each other's favourable Gocara. Similarly, Candra and Budha do not block each other. This is because Sūrya - Śani and Candra - Budha are father and son pairs.

(152) Gocara Sūrya, from 1st onwards, indicates **(1)** fatigue, loss of wealth, irritation, suffering from diseases, wearisome journey; **(2)** loss of wealth, unhappiness, duped by others, obstinacy; **(3)** acquisition of a new position, financial gains, happiness, freedom from sickness, destruction of enemies; **(4)** diseases, impediments in sexual enjoyments; **(5)** mental agitation, ill-health, embarrassment; **(6)** recovery from diseases, destruction of enemies, alleviation of sorrows and mental anxieties; **(7)** tedious travelling, a disorder in the stomach and the anus, suffering of humiliation; **(8)** suffering from fear and diseases, invite quarrel, incur royal displeasure, suffer from excessive heat; **(9)** danger, humiliation, separation from his kith and kin, mental depression; **(10)** mighty undertaking is completed, a new position; **(11)** honour, wealth and freedom from diseases; **(12)** sorrow, loss of wealth, quarrel with friends and fever.

(153) Gocara Candra, from 1st onwards, indicates **(1)** dawning of fortune; **(2)** loss of wealth; **(3)** success; **(4)** fear; **(5)** sorrow; **(6)** freedom from disease; **(7)** happiness; **(8)** untoward events; **(9)** sickness; **(10)** attainment of one's cherished wishes; **(11)** joy and **(12)** expenditure.

(154) Gocara Maṅgala, from 1st onwards, indicates **(1)** melancholy of the mind, separation from one's relations, diseases caused by blood, bile or heat; **(2)** fear, hot words, loss of wealth; **(3)** success, happiness, gain of golden ornaments; **(4)** loss of position, stomach disorders such as dysentery, diarrhoea, etc., sorrow through relations; **(5)** fever, unnecessary desires, mental anguish caused through one's son, or quarrel with one's relations; **(6)** termination of strife and the withdrawal of enemies, alleviation of disease victory, financial gain and success; **(7)** misunderstanding with one's wife, eye-disease, stomach-ache etc.; **(8)** fever, anaemia, loss of wealth and honour; **(9)** humiliation, loss of wealth, retardation due to bodily weakness and wastage of several constituent elements of the body; **(10)** misbehave, suffer from exhaustion; **(11)** In financial gain, freedom from sickness, gain of landed property; **(12)** loss of wealth, suffer from diseases caused by excessive heat.

(155) Gocara Budha, from 1st onwards, indicates **(1)** loss of wealth; **(2)** financial gain; **(3)** fear from enemies; **(4)** influx of money; **(5)** quarrel with one's wife and children; **(6)** success; **(7)** misunderstandings; **(8)** acquisition of children, wealth etc.; **(9)** impediments; **(10)** all-round happiness; **(11)** prosperity; **(12)** fear of humiliation.

(156) Gocara Bṛhaspati, from 1st onwards, indicates **(1)** leaving the home country, heavy expenditure, ill will towards others; **(2)** acquiring money, having domestic happiness, words having weight; **(3)** loss of position, separation from one's friends, obstacle to business, disease; **(4)** sorrow through relations, humiliation, danger from Quadrupeds; **(5)** birth of children, friendship with the good, royal favour; **(6)** trouble from enemies and cousins, suffer from diseases; **(7)** travel on the auspicious undertaking, happiness from wife, blessed with children; **(8)** tedious journeys, unlucky, loss of money, feel miserable; **(9)** successful, enjoying prosperity; **(10)** danger to one's prosperity, position and children; **(11)** birth of children, new position, honour; **(12)** grief and fear due to properties.

(157) Gocara Śukra, from 1st onwards, indicates **(1)** all kinds of enjoyments, **(2)** financial gain; **(3)** prosperity; **(4)** increase of happiness and friends; **(5)** birth of children, **(6)** mishaps; **(7)** trouble to wife; **(8)** wealth; **(9)** happiness; **(10)** quarrel; **(11)** safety; and **(12)** financial gains.

(158) Gocara Śani, from 1st onwards, indicates **(1)** suffering from disease, the performance of funeral rites; **(2)** loss of wealth and children; **(3)** acquisition of position or employment, servants and money; **(4)** loss of wife, relation and wealth; **(5)** decline of wealth, loss of children, mental confusion; **(6)**

all-round happiness; **(7)** suffering to wife, danger during travel; **(8)** loss of children, cattle, friends and wealth, diseases; **(9)** financial losses, many obstacles in good actions, death of a relative who is like the father, perpetual sorrow; **(10)** sinful deed, loss of honour, suffer from a disease; **(11)** all kinds of happiness and wealth, unique honour; **(12)** wearied by fruitless business, robbed of money by enemies, wife and sons suffer from sickness.

(159) Gocara Rāhu, from 1st onwards indicates **(1)** sickness, death, squander money, financial loss, health issues, mental disturbance, restlessness; **(2)** financial losses, increased expenses, marital discord, disturbance from people, food related ailments, eyes ailments, troubles from arguments; **(3)** happiness, positivity, optimism, strong determination and zest, promotion, rise of status, financial gains, prosperity, victory in legal disputes, cordial relations with siblings; **(4)** sorrow, real estate dispute, lack of mental peace, trouble to mother's health, proneness to accidents, relocation; **(5)** financial losses, mental tension, grief, confusion, children issues, issues in love life, growth in business; **(6)** happiness, financial growth, profit from business, gain of property, respect and recognition, victory in legal disputes, gain from maternal uncle; **(7)** losses, financial challenges, loss of wealth too, marital discord, sickness to spouse, discord with co-workers, health issues, association of people from other caste/religion; **(8)** danger to life, physical ailments, sexual disease, mental tension, unnecessary fears, humiliation, subject to conspiracies, unexpected gain; **(9)** financial losses, shady financial dealings, sickness to parents, disputes with co-workers, travel abroad, progress in higher education, spiritual inclination; **(10)** financial gains, growth in career, promotion, rise in status, cordial relationship with seniors and co-workers, mentally distressed, sleeplessness, sickness to mother. **(11)** happiness, financial gains, rise in social status, income growth, travel abroad, peace at home, auspicious events at home, spiritual inclination; **(12)** increased expenses, financial challenges, business losses, travelling abroad, over-confidence, hurdles in career, mental tension, sickness to the spouse.

(160) Gocara Ketu, from 1st onwards indicates **(1)** mental tensions, health issues, increased expenses, troubles with debts, mental tension and confusion, misunderstanding in married life, troubles to social reputation; **(2)** financial vulnerability, increased expenses, theft, mental ailments, eye ailments, useless chatter, conflict with spouse; **(3)** financial gains, progress at work, rise of fame, travels, progress in education, good job prospects; **(4)** proneness to accidents, sickness to mother, financial fluctuations, mental tension, caution with travelling, property disputes; **(5)** increased expenses, issues with children, mental tension, troubled finances, frequent ups and downs; **(6)** progress at work, success in competitions, victory over opponents, financial improvement, business growth, spiritual pursuits, health issues; **(7)** health issues, distressed, anxiety, marital discord, troubled finances; **(8)** severe health issues, frequent fever and body aches, lack of mental peace, loss of fame, spiritual inclination, wealth loss; **(9)** travel abroad, pilgrimage, troubled finances, mental and physical distress, misunderstanding with children/siblings; **(10)** mental distress, financial challenges, halted business progress but satisfactory employment, societal challenges; **(11)** profits, gain from real estate, commencement of business, good income, marriage of children or other auspicious events, meditation, **(12)** marital disharmony, increased expenses, debt issues, spiritual progress, loss of name, travelling abroad.

DAŚĀ SYSTEMS

(161) Daśā Systems: There are several Daśā systems of which Viṁśottarī is generally applicable to all. In Adhyāya 46, Maharṣi Parāśara states that Daśās are of many kinds. Amongst them, Viṁśottarī is the most appropriate for the general populace. But the other Daśās, followed in special cases, are Aṣṭottarī, Ṣoḍaśottarī, Dvādaśottarī, Pañcottarī, Śatābdika, Caturaśītikā, Dvisaptatisama, Ṣaṣṭihāyanī, Ṣaṭtriṁśatsama. In Kaliyuga, the natural lifespan of a human being is generally taken as 120 years. Therefore, Viṁśottarī Daśā is considered to be the most appropriate and the best of all Daśās.

(162) Aṣṭottarī Daśā: According to Maharṣi Parāśara, this is recommended when Rāhu is not in the Lagna but in a Kendrakoṇa from the Lagneśa. Mānasāgarī 5.22 states that Viṁśottarī is applicable when born in Kṛṣṇapakṣa while Aṣṭottarī is applicable when born in Śuklapakṣa. Particularly when Rāhu is in a Kendra from the Lagneśa Ārdrādi Aṣṭottarī Daśā is applicable. But, when Rāhu is in a Koṇa from the Lagneśa, Kṛttikādi Aṣṭottarī Daśā is applicable (Bṛhatparāśara Harihara 35.21-22.).

(163) Ṣoḍaśottarī Daśā: This is recommended when **(1)** birth occurs during the daytime in Kṛṣṇapakṣa or at nighttime in Śuklapakṣa, or **(2)** when Lagna rises in Candra Horā in Kṛṣṇapakṣa, or, Sūrya Horā in Śuklapakṣa. **Notes:** In an Ojarāśi, the 1st Horā is owned by Sūrya and the 2nd Horā by Candra. In a Yugmarāśi, it is reversed, i.e., 1st is owned by Candra, and the 2nd is by Sūrya. This Daśā is applicable when there is alignment between Pakṣa and Horā.

(164) Ṣaṭtriṁśatsama Daśā: This is recommended when birth occurs during daytime, and Lagna rises in Sūrya's Horā, or the birth occurs during nighttime, and Lagna rises in Candra's Horā. **Notes:** There is an alignment between the birthtime and Horā.

(165) Dvādaśottarī Daśā is recommended when Lagna occupies a Navāṁśa of Śukra. **Notes:** This is also applicable when Śukra is in the Lagnāṁśa or he is in the Rāśi Tulya Aṁśa of the Lagna. For instance, if one is born in Dhanu Navāṁśa and Śukra is in the Dhanu Navāṁśa, this Daśā is applicable.

(166) Pañcottarī Daśā is recommended when Lagna rises in Karka Dvādaśāṁśa of Karka Rāśi. Śatābdika Daśā is recommended when Lagna is Vargottama. Caturaśītikā Daśā is recommended when the Karmeśa is in the Karma Bhāva. Dvisaptatisama Daśā is recommended when the Lagneśa is in either the Lagna or the Dārābhāva. Ṣaṣṭihāyanī Daśā is recommended when Sūrya is in the Lagna.

(167) Sudarśana Cakra Daśā: This is a straightforward and general-purpose Daśā. Using this Daśā, one can make annual, monthly and daily predictions. In this, each Rāśi is allotted a Daśā of 1 year. In the first year, the Daśā is of the Lagna; in the 2nd year, the 2nd Bhāva and so on. Each Daśā is divided into 12 Antardaśās, each of 1-month duration. Each Antardaśā is divided into Pratyantardaśās of 2.5 days duration, which is further sub-divided into 5 hours Vidaśās. The sub-period always commences from the Bhāva of the major period. Each Daśā is of 360 days duration, Antar is 30 days, Pratyantar 2.5 days, Vidaśā of 12.5 Ghaṭikās. This is based on the 360 Sāvanadina/year principle.

(168) In Sudarśana Cakra, Sūrya is considered Śubha in the first Bhāva and Krūra in the other Bhāvas. The Krūras do not produce evil effects if they are in their Uccarāśi. The effect of a Bhāva is as per the Graha occupying it. If a Bhāva is devoid of a Graha, then the dṛṣṭi of a Graha gives the results. If there is no occupation/dṛṣṭi, the lord is instrumental in giving the results. The effect of a Bhāva being occupied by a Saumya (or its lord or a Uccagraha) is auspicious, and a Krūra (or a Nīcagraha) is Aśubha. A Saumya loses its benevolence if it is in more Krūra Saptavargas. Similarly, a Krūra loses its malevolence if he is in more Saumya Vargas. A Graha's Svarāśi, Uccarāśi and Saumya Vargas are considered auspicious. The Vargas of Krūra, Nīca and Śatru are considered inauspicious.

(169) In Sudarśana Cakra Daśā, at the time of commencement of a Daśā, if there are Saumyas in the Kendrakoṇa, Randhra from the Daśā Rāśi, favourable effects are experienced in the concerned year, month etc. From the Daśārāśi, the Bhāva, which is occupied exclusively by Rāhu, or Ketu, is subject to danger. The same is the result of a Bhāva occupied mostly by Krūras. Saumyas in Bhāvas other than 12th/6th produces good results in the year/month. Krūras in the Triṣaḍāyas **(3/6/11)** from the Daśārāśi indicate prosperity in the year/month. What is seen at the commencement of a Daśā (Antar, etc.) should also be seen from the Janmakuṇḍalī. This means Saumyas in Kendrakoṇa/Randhra and Krūras in Triṣaḍāya bring prosperity, whereas Saumya in 12/6 is detrimental. The effects are determined only after assessing the Aṣṭakavarga.

(170) Every 12 years, the Sudarśana Cakra Daśā Bhāva (Rāśi) repeats. However, the results are still different. Different entry (commencement) charts cause the difference for the Bhāva. Therefore, the Daśā should be judged only after considering the commencement and natal charts.

—|||—

30.4
ABOUT "IN SEARCH OF JYOTISH"

The Book *"In Search of Jyotiṣa"* is a collection of 33 volumes containing several topics of Jyotiṣa, from beginning to advanced stages. This book focuses on retaining the authenticity of the subject as taught by the Maharṣis and the Ācāryas. I have retained the classical texts' originality while providing my thoughts, reflections, and interpretations. Jyotiṣa is vast, like a boundless ocean; therefore, mastering it in one's lifetime appears impossible. It is arduous to even go through each principle of Jyotiṣa, let alone master it. There are, however, a few who could attain a great deal of knowledge on this subject.

In my journey into the world of Jyotiṣa, which started in 1988, I studied numerous texts of the Maharṣis, Ācāryas and modern-day authors. However, I encountered challenges; firstly, not many authors have written copiously, sharing their experiences. Secondly, there are numerous contradictions, but few have explained how to reconcile or resolve them. **I have seen an attitude that "this is what my tradition and teacher teaches; therefore, the other teaching or interpretation must be incorrect".** Hardly many tried to reconcile the differences objectively. Among all authors, I hold Dr BV Raman at the highest pedestal for his yeoman service to the field of Jyotiṣa by writing several books on different topics explaining things in an easily understandable language.

Besides that, most books in the market are like an instruction manual or a coursebook, which instructs how to do this and do that. Several books are merely a narration of Jyotiṣa yogas. **I always hoped that there were books that explained the "why" behind the yogas.** For example, the classical texts state that when Candra is in Meṣa Rāśi, the native shall have such and such characteristics, but hardly anyone explains why that should be.

Hardly anyone explains the "Why" part of the equation, even among modern-day authors. **It always makes me curious about the "Why"; I reflected upon them and penned my thoughts.** I undoubtedly faced numerous challenges, but as time passed, the yogas revealed themselves like a beam of sunshine in a dark cloud. I believe the blessings of my Guru, my Iṣṭadevatā, my parents, and countless others manifested in the form of this knowledge flowing through me.

Perhaps I am open-minded because I am not indoctrinated into any specific tradition from a young age. While receiving knowledge from a tradition is a fantastic way of learning it fast and furthering it, it makes one too attached to it and not question it. It is a blessing in disguise that I have to work hard to get something that one gets merely because one is born into a family or under some circumstances. It must be my Karma that I had to be born in a situation where I had to uncover the secrets on my own. It is also a blessing that I am not overly attached to a preconceived notion and am always ready to question myself, my understanding, and my assumptions. **I do not outrightly reject a view and look for the truth behind it. The lack of preconceived notions helps me examine the thoughts and opinions of contradicting practitioners with an objective eye.**

The book "In Search of Jyotiṣa" is the outcome of the search for the divine principles that govern human lives and the lives of everything else, animate or inanimate. The idea that the same principles govern everything in the universe has always motivated me. This motivation pushed me to continue the journey without giving up. **I started penning down my thoughts on Jyotiṣa in 2004, and from 2012 onwards, it started taking the form of a Book.** I wrote two books before, which I never published, called the "Principles of Divination", a collection of principles from several classical texts. I didn't publish it because I did not want to publish another book of principles, yogas and Sūtras.

"In Search of Jyotiṣa" took at least eight years, if not more, but it contained the gist of experiences of my studies spanning 33 years. I kept writing on several topics without realizing that it had become humongous. There are 33 volumes of the book containing a range of topics, if not all. **I have also taken an unconventional approach to writing my thoughts on Lālkitāb. The focus has been to elucidate the principles.**

This book may not be a favourite among the exponents of Jyotiṣa, but my approach to Jyotiṣa is different. **I do not wish to decide what the readers should read or not.** I narrated my understanding and reflections, hoping someone would find it useful. **I do not belong to any specific tradition; therefore, I have no compulsion to follow any dictates. My Guru is Lord Śiva, and my tradition is that of a "Seeker".** I write on this subject with an open heart and mind, letting people choose what they wish to accept and what they do not.

I always believe that in my Kuṇḍalī, **Bṛhaspati's dṛṣṭi** on Dharmeśa Sūrya, Karmeśa Budha and Pañcameśa Maṅgala would keep in on the right track. I also believe that Ketu in the Trikoṇa to my Kārakāñśa and 2nd from Lagnāñśa would shower me with profound knowledge of this discipline. I do not wish to sound boastful, but I am a born Jyotiṣī and doing what I do best - sharing my reflections with the world! **I hope you find the journey into the world of Jyotiṣa equally engaging and enlightening. The list of 33 volumes of the book is as follows:**

Table 117: The 33 volumes

Book	Name	Content
Book 1	Introduction to Jyotiṣa	• The book introduces the discipline of Jyotiṣa. It covers the purpose of Jyotiṣa, its brief history, notable Jyotiṣīs, the current state, reflections on whether Jyotiṣa is a science, demonstrating how Jyotiṣa is a universal language. It

Book	Name	Content
		covers thoughts and reflections on why Jyotiṣa work must, i.e., the philosophical basis of this subject, the scope of Jyotiṣa. There are important yogas that make one a Jyotiṣī and the fundamental building blocks of this subject. It covers the scope of the books in the series "In Search of Jyotish" and a brief introduction about me.
Book 2	The Kārakatvas	• This book covers in detail the entire domain of Graha Kārakatvas, Rāśi Kārakatvas and Bhāva Kārakatvas. There is a detailed deliberation on several topics of Kārakatvas, including the Dhātus, Doṣas, Grahas and avocations, Aprakāśa Grahas and Upagrahas and several others. • This book aims to provide a thorough grounding on the Kārakatvas of the Grahas, Rāśis and Bhāvas. This is a crucial step for those wishing to enter the Jyotiṣa world. • For a Seasoned Jyotiṣī, it should serve as a good reference book, and I believe they would benefit from the detailed deliberation of topics such as Dhātus and Doṣas, classification of matter into Dhātu Mūla Jīva.
Book 3	Rāśi and Bhāva Phala	• This book covers the results of Graha's placement in Rāśis and Bhāvas. When Grahas move through Rāśis, they give rise to specific results. The aura of the Graha intermingles with the Rāśis, and the Graha takes different forms. Even though every Graha has its innate nature, they undergo significant modifications depending on the Rāśis they occupy. • Like Lord Viṣṇu has 10 Avatāras, and in each of the Avatāras, Lord Viṣṇu appears significantly different; the Grahas also take 12 different forms when they occupy the 12 Rāśis. Analysing the results of a Graha in a Bhāva without considering its specific form is misleading. In this book, I have assigned a name to each of these forms of the Grahas, which could help readily understand the form. Besides this, the forms are also affected by the dṛṣṭi of the Grahas, which are also specified. Also, given why a Graha manifests certain kinds of results in a Rāśi, based on my years of reflections. I hoped to find it when I started my Jyotiṣa studies, but not much literature is available. • The book also covers the Bhāva effects of the Grahas, and the results are excerpted from several classical texts, including Bṛhajjātaka, Sārāvalī and Phaladīpikā; also, given the results of Graha placement in different Bhāvas for the 12 different Lagnas, a total of 108 combinations. These are not exhaustive but can explain how Graha's Bhāvaphala changes for different Lagnas.
Book 4	Strength and Bhāva Analysis	• This chapter contains a detailed account of the computation of the strengths of Grahas, Rāśis and Bhāvas. A step-by-step computation of Ṣaḍbala is included in this chapter. Several topics, such as Ceṣṭā Bala, Yuddha Bala, etc., are clarified with examples. In the Abdamāsadinahorā Bala, it is demonstrated how to find the Sṛṣṭi and Kali Ahargaṇa, based on which the Sāvana Varṣa Lord must be found. It is also explained what the basis of the Lordship is for Horā, Vāra, Māsa and Varṣa.

Book	Name	Content
		• A detailed account of Rāśi and Bhāva Balas is also covered with worked-out examples. This dispels several doubts on the computation of the strength of various elements, viz., Graha, Rāśi and Bhāva. A detailed account of Graha yuddha is given, dispelling the doubts on when two Grahas must be considered in Grahayuddha and who is considered victorious. The ślokas support the arguments from Maharṣi Parāśara, Sūryasiddhānta, and Bṛhatsaṅhitā. • The second portion of the book contains a detailed account of how to judge a Bhāva methodically. The principles are adopted from Phaladīpikā Adhyāya 15 and are explained in great detail. This is followed by a detailed account of Bhāvanātha Bhāva Phala, covering the results of 12 Bhāveśas in 12 Bhāvas, a total of 144 combinations. I have given my thoughts and reflections on each of these topics, which I believe will dispel doubts in the mind of a seeker. A seasoned Jyotiṣī, I believe, will have a different perspective, which they find useful.
Book 5	Janma	• Janma means birth; therefore, this book covers almost everything that one must know on the subject of birth. It starts with the topic of deciphering birth circumstances from a Kuṇḍalī and an examination of yogas contained in several classical texts, including Bṛhatparāśara, Bṛhajjātaka, Sārāvalī, Jātakatattva and others. There are several illustrations of the effects of Grahas on birth circumstances. • This contains the yogas from Nāradapurāṇa regarding Śubha and Aśubha Janma, conditions of illegitimate birth, what is called Jāraja yoga, and their annulation. The Niṣeka and Ādhāna Kuṇḍalī deal with the construction and interpretation of the conception chart, which is also called the pre-natal epoch. The Viyoni Janma chapter details non-human birth, such as animals, plants, birds, etc., and how to decipher them. The principles of the naming chapter deal with naming a newborn child that is harmonious with the Kuṇḍalī. • The birth time rectification section provides a step-by-step method of rectifying a Kuṇḍalī with principles derived from several classical texts, including the Prāṇapada, Kunda, Janma Vighaṭika, Tattva and Antartattva method. A few more principles and guidance are given to verify one's Lagna. A section is dedicated to the casting of a Kuṇḍalī from Praśna when the Kuṇḍalī is lost, and the birth time is completely unknown. Yet another section is dedicated to the effects due to birth in several time elements such as Bārhaspatya Varṣa, several Tithis, Vāras etc. These effects help in fine-tuning the results in a Kuṇḍalī. • The Lost Horoscopy section provides several methods of constructing a Kuṇḍalī from Praśna. This is called Naṣṭajātaka and is useful if the birth time is unknown or inaccurate.

Book	Name	Content
Book 6	Ariṣṭa	• Ariṣṭas are the evil yogas in a Kuṇḍalī. This starts with examining the 21 flaws in time in which birth, Muhūrta or Praśna yields troublesome results. Then, the Nakṣatra Ariṣṭa section covers the danger caused by being born in a certain Nakṣatra. Next, the Gaṇḍānta birth covers the different Gaṇḍāntas. Then, it covers the topic such as Abhukta Mūla, Mūla Nivāsa, Mūlavṛkṣa and several other topics. Finally, the topic of Bālāriṣṭa is dealt with in great detail in a structured manner, starting with a robust foundation of the building blocks of such yogas. These involve assessment of Kṣīṇacandra, afflictions to Candra Lagna, Udaya Lagna and several others. • There is a careful analysis of several yogas that indicate danger to both the child, the mother, and, in some cases, the father. The Ariṣṭabhaṅga yogas indicate the protection one has from the evils in a Kuṇḍalī. These protections work throughout one's lifetime; therefore, identifying them is vital. The Yogas, such as Bṛhaspati in dignity in a Kendra, work throughout life and protect the native from several evils. Similarly, Śubhagrahas should be in Kendrakoṇas, and Krūragrahas in Triṣaḍāyas is a great protective force.
Book 7	Health and Longevity	• This book is divided into four sections: (1) Bodily characteristics, (2) Examination of longevity, (3) Cause and timing of death, and (4) Analysing diseases. Each of them covers significant areas. For instance, the bodily characteristics cover physical features, the predominant Guṇa of a person, the Varṇas or natural propensities, and the personality traits. The section on diseases thoroughly treats several diseases, including the brain, respiratory, eye, speech, etc.
Book 8	The 12 Bhāvas	• This book serves as an introduction to the 12 Bhāvas. Jyotiṣa is a vast subject, and each Bhāva comprises myriads of yoga. It is nearly impossible to do an exhaustive treatment of each Bhāva in a book like this because each Bhāva deserves to be covered in a separate volume dedicated to the Bhāva. However, this book aims to cover the width of Jyotiṣa at the expense of depth. This book includes a high-level assessment of a few crucial yogas of each Bhāva, those culled from Jyotiṣa classics Phaladīpikā and Sārāvalī. However, this is a compendium of yogas contained in several classical texts, including Bṛhatparāśara, Jātakatattva, Saṅketa Nidhi, Suka Jātaka, and a few other important texts.
Book 9	Nakṣatra	• This book covers in detail what one should know about the Nakṣatras. This includes the Nakṣatra Devatās, their classification into seven classes, the Purāṇic lore, the Hoḍā or Avakahada Cakra, details of each Nakṣatra, including their symbol, Devatās, etc. Tārās in the Nakṣatras, Nakṣatra and avocations, effects of Grahas and Bhāvanātha in the Nakṣatras, the Nakṣatra Puruṣa, Nakṣatra in the delineation of diseases, the blessing of Nakṣatras, usage of Nakṣatras in marital compatibility and a detailed delineation of birth in each Nakṣatra.

Book	Name	Content
Book 10	Crucial Building Blocks	• This book covers several topics that are not yet covered, including how to write a Kuṇḍalī the traditional way, detailed deliberation on the construction of Bhāva Kuṇḍalī, including the opinions of several scholars, Maharṣis and Ācāryas, the Graha Avasthās, including Bālādi, Jāgṛtādi, Dīptādi, Lajjitādi, Sayanādi and the Graha Samayas. • The section on the Aprakāśa Grahas and Upagrahas covers their computation and delineation in a Kuṇḍalī, the computation and usage of Prāṇapada, and deliberation on the Tattvas and Guṇas. • The section on Yogakārakas states the distinction between Auspicious vs Favourable, results due to ownership of a Bhāva, Yoga between Kendra-Koṇa Lords, Treatment of Rāhu and Ketu, The Kārakatvas of individual Bhāvanātha, and delineation of Yogakārakas for different Lagnas, that includes my reflections on the principles/ yogas presented by Ācārya Ramanuja, in Bhāvārtha Ratnākara.
Book 11	Yogas	• The book on Yoga covers the Yoga fundamentals, the Lagna yogas, Candra yogas, Sūrya yogas, the Nābhasa yogas, delineation of Paraspara Kārakas, Rājayogas of Maharṣi Parāśara and Ācārya Kalyāṇavarmā, and Rāja Sambandha yoga, Rājabhaṅga yoga, Adverse yogas from classical texts such as Jātakapārijāta, Bṛhajjātaka and Horāsāra. It covers the controversial yoga, the Kālasarpa yoga and its several variations. There is an exhaustive treatment of the Pravrājya yoga, and several other yogas are excerpted from classical texts of Maharṣi Garga, Maharṣi Suka, Ācārya Mahādeva, and Ācārya Ramanuja. There is also coverage of the Dvigraha, Trigraha, etc., yogas.
Book 12	Pañcāṅga and Muhurta	• It covers the five elements of Pañcāṅga, including the Nakṣatra, the Vāra, the Tithi, the Karṇa and the Nityayogas. The section on Muhūrta elements covers the concept of 30 Muhūrtas, Sūrya's Saṅkrānti, the effects of Lagna, delineation of the portfolio owner of a year, such as the King of the year, minister of the year, lord of vegetation, lord of grains etc. There is a detailed treatment of the principles of Muhūrta, the Pañcāṅga yogas, i.e., the special yogas that are formed due to Vāra-Nakṣatra, Vāra-Tithi, Nakṣatra-Tithi etc. The special Nakṣatra Ghaṭikās covers, the Viṣa, Uṣṇa, Amṛta Ghaṭikās. There is a delineation of Ānandādi yogas, the Samvatsara and Yugas, based on Bṛhaspati's mean motion, and the formation of adverse yogas such as Ekārgala, Vaidhṛti, Krūrasaṅyuta etc. • The Muhūrta section deals with the principles of choosing important Muhūrtas, including the 16 Saṅskāras, travel, education, treatment of diseases, coronation, installing a Devatā etc.
Book 13	Jyotish Siddhānta 1	• This contains two sections: Modern Astronomy and Siddhāntika Astronomy. The Modern Astronomy section

Book	Name	Content
		covers the measurement of time, the coordinate system, including equatorial and ecliptic coordinate systems, the transformation of coordinates, the computation of the mean and true position of Grahas as per the modern computation methods, coordinates of fixed stars, and examination of the concepts of obliquity and nutation. By studying this, one can determine the coordinates of Nakṣatras and Grahas per modern methods. • The Siddhāntika Astronomy section starts with a deliberation of the classical and medieval astronomers, the Hindu Astronomy vis-à-vis others, the time and place of Sūryasiddhānta, the fundamentals, the mean places of Grahas, the true places of Grahas, the nine measures of times, notes on Indian calendars, and the 60 Jovian years. By studying this, one can compute the true places of Grahas using the Siddhāntika methods. I have also proposed some adjustments (Bīja corrections) of Sūryasiddhānta values to tally with the modern values.
Book 14	Jyotish Siddhānta 2	• This book has three sections: the Astronomical events, the Computation of Lagna, and Ayanāñśa. The Astronomical events section covers Grahayuti, Astāṅgata, Vakragati, Grahayuddha, and Grahaṇa. Each topic contains the astronomical computations and astrological delineation of these events. • The Computation of Lagna section deals with the method of determining the Lagna on a date and time based on the traditional Śaṅku Chāyā method as well as the modern method of using sidereal time. • The Ayanāñśa section covers the history of Ayanāñśa, the difference between the two zodiacs, Nirāyana and Sāyana, seven different methods of determining Ayanāñśas, including the method of Sūryasiddhānta libration, the IAU's method, from the length of a Tropical and Sidereal day, Nakṣatra Method and others. After that, I captured the important Ayanāñśas in vogue in today's world before delving into Ācārya Varāhamihira's Ayanāñśa and Sṛṣṭi Ayanāñśa.
Book 15	Lagna Bhāva	• This book dives deep into the topic of the Lagna Bhāva. This contains six sections, viz., What is Lagnabhāva, The nature of Lagna Rāśi, Birth in different Lagnas, Graha Lagna Phala, and Lagneśa Bhāvaphala. This is perhaps the most detailed treatment of this Bhāvas ever done by an astrological writer.
Book 16	Special Lagnas	• There are five sections of this book, viz., The Viśeṣa Lagna, Candralagna, The Āruṛhalagna, The Svāṃśa Lagna, and the Kāraka Lagna. This does an exhaustive treatment of various things delineated from these several Lagnas. The Viśeṣa Lagna section covers the Bhāva Lagna, the Horālagna, the Vighaṭika Lagna, the Varṇada Lagna, and the Prāṇapada Lagna.
Book 17	Lagna yogas	• This is perhaps the most detailed delineation of the Lagna yogas from several classical texts. There are twelve sections of this book: Lagna fundamentals, success in the homeland or abroad, judging three portions of life, dṛṣṭi

Book	Name	Content
		yogas, facial features, personality traits, health and diseases, madness, speech-related yogas, fame, and fame renown, miscellaneous yogas, and yogas from other sources. Each of these sections has a detailed deliberation of the topic covered. For instance, the Lagna fundamentals contain Lagna Kārakatvas, strengths and weaknesses, body structure and complexion, physical felicity, and physical appearance. Similarly, success in the homeland or abroad, the characteristics of the foreign land, etc. This contains almost everything one needs to know about the Lagna Bhāva.
Book 18	Aṣṭakavarga	• This comprehensively covers the method of Aṣṭakavarga. There are eight sections viz., construction, the fundamentals, Rekhās and Karaṇas, Bhinnāṣṭakavarga, Samudāyāṣṭakavarga, Daśā application, Aṣṭakavarga Gocara, Kakṣyā, and Longevity estimation. This book is written after consulting several classical texts on this subject, including Bṛhatparāśara, Bṛhajjātaka, Sārāvalī, Phaladīpikā, Aṣṭakavarga Mahānibandha, Jātakapārijāta, Jātaka Deśamārga, and Praśnamārga. This book should be able to denounce several doubts, including whether Rāśi or Bhāva should be used for the construction of the Aṣṭakavarga, the Śodhanas, etc. This book does an exhaustive treatment of almost all the topics of Aṣṭakavarga.
Book 19	Important Methods and Tools	• This book covers several topics, including Pācakādi Sambandha, Śrī Kālidāsa's Principles, Special chakras, Pataki Riṣta, Tripāpa Cakra, Bhṛgu's Paddhati, Pañcaka, Candra's special avasthās such as Candrakriyā etc., Miscellaneous tools such as Mṛtyubhāga, Bhṛgubindu etc., the Bādhaka and Strī Jātaka. • The special Cakra section contains esoteric diagrams, including Navatārā Cakra, Ghātaka Cakra, Dimbha Cakra, Nara Cakra, Graha Puruṣa Cakras, The Śatapada Cakra, the Kālānala Cakras, Yamadaṁṣṭrā Cakra, Trināḍī Cakra, Gaja and Aśva Cakras, Pañcasvara Cakra, Sannāḍī Cakra, Koṭa Cakra and Sanghatta Cakra. • The Bhṛgu Paddhati contains the translation of Bhṛgu Sūtra, Bhṛgu Saṅhitā, and Bhṛgu Saral Paddhati (BSP).
Book 20	The Vargas	• This covers several topics of Vargas or Subdivisions of a Rāśi. This includes delineation of the 16 Vargas of Maharṣi Parāśara, the principles of analysing Vargas, the Varga dignities, the variations of Vargas, such as Parivṛtti Vargas etc., the different kinds of Horās, Navāñśas, Dreṣkāṇas etc. This also contains the usage of individual Vargas for delineating a Kuṇḍalī. • It contains an examination of whether the Vargas can be used as Kuṇḍalīs and what the Śāstras say about it. Several dictums from the classical texts are given to clarify the views of the classical authors. • There are staunch believers of both schools of thought, those who do not accept the concept of Bhāva and dṛṣṭi in

Book	Name	Content
		the Vargas, whereas there are those who support the view that Vargas should also be treated as Kuṇḍalīs. I do not wish to force anyone with what I believe; I only wish to present before the seekers what the different classical texts say on this topic to arrive at their conclusions.
Book 21	Nakṣatra and Nāḍī Jyotiṣa	• This book covers several facets of Nakṣatra and Nāḍī Jyotiṣa. The Nakṣatra Jyotiṣa delineates the core principles of the Mīna 1 Nāḍī, Mīna 2 Nāḍī, Kṛṣṇamūrti Paddhati (KP) and Iyer's Paddhati. Iyer's Paddhati is based on the legendary Jyotiṣī Śrī HR Sheshadri Iyer, whose book, the New Techniques of Prediction 3 volumes are cornerstones of Jyotiṣa. • Śrī Iyer did not exclusively deal with the Nakṣatras. Still, his determination and usage of Yogī and Avayogi and the usage of Nakṣatra is pathbreaking, which is why it is included in this book dedicated to Nakṣatra and Nāḍī Jyotiṣa. I have covered in detail some abstruse concepts with worked-out examples, such as the Starter and Ruler for assessment of Viñśottarī Daśā. • The Nāḍī Jyotiṣa section covers the essential principles from Saptaṛṣi Nāḍī and Bhṛgu Nandi Nāḍī. Besides providing a synopsis of the genre of Nāḍī Jyotiṣa, there is a detailed exploration of topics such as the blending of Kārakatvas and how the blending is affected by the sequence of Grahas having Yuti in a Rāśi. I am hoping that this book will provide wide coverage of topics from both Nakṣatra and Nāḍī Jyotiṣa that both beginners and advanced practitioners would find useful.
Book 22	Jaimini Sūtra	• This book introduces the subject of Jaimini Sūtra concisely to beginners. One who wishes to grasp the Sūtras quickly can find a systematic way of dealing with the subject. Jaimini Sūtra is complex and terse and requires years of Tapasyā to understand. I have given several examples to make the concept clearer. • It isn't easy to decipher and understand the profound meaning of a Sūtra without the guidance of a Guru. Therefore, this book does not intend to teach this complex subject; however, it presents a robust framework with apt translations to introduce this subject to an earnest seeker. One who wishes to pursue it further must study under a bonafide Guru.
Book 23	Praśnaśāstra	• This book covers, in great detail, the subject of Horary Astrology, also called Praśna Śāstra. This is built upon the foundation of several classical texts, including Praśnamārga, Praśnatantra, Daivajña Vallabha, Kṛṣṇīyam, Ṣaṭpañcāśikā and others. The concepts are explained in great detail and with examples. This covers topics such as Nimittas, Aṣṭamaṅgala Praśna, Manomuṣṭi Praśna, Kāryasiddhi Praśna, Devapraśna, analysis of dreams, and some esoteric Cakras like Candragupti Cakra which is used to locate water underground. • There is an exhaustive treatment of Praśnas relating to the 12 Bhāvas. For instance, the 2nd house Praśna deals with financial gains; the 4th house Praśna deals with

Book	Name	Content
		Agriculture, cultivation, and leasing agreements. The 6th house deals with matters concerning diseases, employee-employer relationships, etc. The treatment of each of these topics is detailed with copious notes and explanations.
Book 24	Jinendramāla	• Jinendramāla is an important Praśna text written by a Jain Monk, Upendrācārya. It has methods scantily found in other Praśna works, such as Praśnamārga. Concepts such as Chatra Rāśi, also called Kavippu, are explained in this work. Besides that, the book explains the concept of Yamagraha, also called Jāmakkol or Sāmakkol. These are the special position of Grahas in a Kuṇḍalī, which is determined by dividing a day into Yamas or Jāmams. The text gives the method of locating a treasure underground using Candragupti Cakra, explained in Praśnamārga in locating water underground. This method of Praśna is also called Jāmakkol Āruṛham and Sāmakkol Āruṛham and is widely used in southern India.
Book 25	Svara Śāstra	• Svaraśāstra is about breathing or Svara for regulating one's life or answering Praśna. The content of this book is based on the foundation laid by texts such as Praśnamārga, Svara Cintāmaṇi and Lord Śiva Svarodaya. The ślokas from these texts are examined in great detail and explained so that anyone with little or no knowledge of this subject can understand them. The Svara Śāstra has great usage in Horary; therefore, this is highly recommended for those who wish to master Praśna.
Book 26	Śrāpa and Puṇya Cakra	• Śrāpas are curses that manifest as great evil in one's life. Maharṣi Parāśara details several kinds of Śrāpas that cause denial or loss of children and are called Sutakṣaya Śrāpa. This book explains all about such Śrāpas and the remedial measures that can be undertaken to reduce the effects of such Śrāpas. • The Puṇya Cakra is cast at the moment of death of an individual. From this Kuṇḍalī, the whereabouts of the person who has left his mortal frame can be deciphered. How long the person is wandering on the early plane, whether the person has attained peace after death, which spirit worlds, the person is guided to, etc., can be known from this Kuṇḍalī.
Book 27	Lālkitāb	• Even though the Lālkitāb is not part of Vedic Astrology, it contains principles based on the same building blocks. The Kārakatvas for the Grahas, Bhāvas, etc., are the same, but their application differs. Even though several practitioners of this text use this for prescribing several remedies that can be done relatively easily, there is more to this text than remedies. • This book is a storehouse of principles that are hardly found elsewhere. For instance, the text claims that when Rāhu is in the Lagna, Sūrya becomes negative, and the house occupied by such Sūrya is ruined. Before delineating the results, the text juxtaposes the Grahas in the Bhāvas to the Rāśis. Several unique delineations, such

Book	Name	Content
		as Pucca Ghar, Andhe Graha, Sāthī Graha, etc., are explained to anyone who wishes to learn this text. Besides that, common remedies specified by the book are also stated. • Explained in the book, the concept of house Kuṇḍalī, i.e., the Kuṇḍalī of the house as well as Sāmudrika Śāstra, which includes corroborating the planetary positions in a Kuṇḍalī to the marks and Rāśis in one's Palm. This is an excellent text for those who wish to learn Astro palmistry.
Book 28	The Viñśottarī Daśā	• Daśās are crucial for timing events in Jyotiṣaśāstra. However, there are numerous Daśās besides the commonly used Viñśottarī Daśā. This book explains the 42 Daśā systems of Maharṣi Parāśara before delving deeper into Viñśottarī Daśā. A composite assessment of Daśā and Gocara follows this.
Book 29	The Special Daśās	• After covering the foundation of the Daśās and Viñśottarī Daśā in the Daśā System 1, this book covers several other Daśās. This includes Cara Daśā, Āyuṣa Daśās, Mūla Daśā, Yogini Daśā, Sudarśana Cakra Daśā, and other Daśās such as Kendrādi Rāśi Daśā and Dṛgdaśā. The Kendrādi Rāśi Daśā covers Lagna Kendrādi Rāśidaśā, Kāraka Kendrādi Rāśidaśā, and Sudaśā. The Sudaśā is used for timing wealth, and it commences from the Śrīlagna. • The Āyuṣa Daśās contain several Daśās related to longevity and death, and it covers the Daśās such as Niryāṇa Daśā, Brahmā Daśā, Śūladaśā, Niryāṇa Śūladaśā, Sthira Daśā, Navāñśa Daśā, and Maṇḍūka Daśā. The Maṇḍūka Daśā is specifically used along with a special Varga called the Rudrāñśa (D11). Some of these Daśās are also covered in the book on Jaiminīsūtra.
Book 30	Kālacakra Daśā	• The Kālacakra Daśā is a special Daśā that is based on both Rāśi and Nakṣatra. It is complex, and there are several opinions on the computation of this Daśā. I have explained the computation with detailed explanation and illustration, which would dispel doubts among the seekers. This Daśā uses a Varga called Navanavāñśa, which is a further subdivision of a Navāñśa into nine parts. Besides the Kālacakra Daśā, which is the most complex among all, also covered are the Kāla Daśā and Cakra Daśā.
Book 31	Other timing methods	• There are several other timing methods besides the Daśās and Gocaras. Covered in this book are the methods of Progression, Annual Horoscopy, and several other methods. The Progression section covers Rāśi Progression, Varga Progression, Daśā Progression, and Madhyagraha Progression. The Madhyagraha Progression is a special topic that cannot be found elsewhere because the concept of Madhyagraha or the mean Graha is not dealt with in a Jyotiṣa text. I have proposed this method based on my experience with Sūryasiddhānta. • The Annual Kuṇḍalī covers Varṣaphala, which is a Tājika Technique, and the Tithi Praveśa Cakra. The other timing method contains the Bhāgyodaya Varṣa, which is used for timing the rise of fortune. Also covered are the techniques

Book	Name	Content
		of Candra's Nakṣatra method, Hillaja's years, and Varṣa, Māsa and Dina Daśā.
Book 32	Gocara	• Gocara is the continuous movement of Grahas in the zodiac. This book covers several topics ranging from the common technique of Gocara of Grahas from Janmarāśi to Sarvatobhadra Cakra. • There are several other topics covered in this book, including the Gocara of Grahas over the Grahas and Bhaveśas in the Janmakuṇḍalī. Besides this, the Nakṣatra Caraṇa Gocara is used for the precise timing of events. • The Niryāṇa Prakaraṇa covers the Gocara, which indicates life threat or death. The Gocara of Śani indicates the 2.5-year period in which death can occur. That of Bṛhaspati indicates the year of death, that of Sūrya, the month, and Candra, the day of death. These principles must be applied in conjunction with the Daśā, such as Chidra Daśā, for accurately timing death.
Book 33	Remedies	• Remedies are an integral part of Jyotiṣa. Even though we are bound to face problems due to past-life karma, some remedies help us manage the pain and suffering. We have diseases, but we also have medicines and Āyurveda to cure them. Or at least make it more manageable. Like health troubles are caused by past life Karmas, other evils such as delay in marriage, frequent failures, etc., are also caused by past life Karmas. • The presence of problems in one's life does not mean that one must suffer unconditionally. If that were so, why would Maharṣi Parāśara suggest remedies for Gaṇḍānta birth, Māraka Daśās, etc.? Remedies do work, provided the right remedy is given, and the native is sincere in carrying out the remedy. If evil Karmas in the past gives us problems in this life, the good Karmas also allow us to overcome them. • This book details several topics, including specific Parihāra Sthalams, temples and shrines meant for overcoming the evils of Grahas. This includes Mantras, Vratas, Gemstones, Donations, and Charity. Also included is the usage of music or Rāgas for therapy.

ॐ

Om Tat Sat

Made in the USA
Coppell, TX
06 July 2025

51529498R00236